A HISTORY

OF THE

CORRUPTIONS OF CHRISTIANITY

BY

JOSEPH PRIESTLEY, LL.D., F.R.S.,

ETC. ETC.

REPRINTED FROM RUTT'S EDITION, WITH NOTES.

TO WHICH ARE APPENDED

CONSIDERATIONS IN EVIDENCE THAT THE APOSTOLIC AND
PRIMITIVE CHURCH WAS UNITARIAN,

EXTRACTED FROM PRIESTLEY'S REPLIES TO BISHOP HORSLEY, THE BENCH OF
BISHOPS, AND OTHERS.

SEVENTH THOUSAND.

LONDON:
THE BRITISH AND FOREIGN UNITARIAN ASSOCIATION,
178, STRAND.
1871.

Price 2s. 6d.

CONTENTS.

PART I.

THE HISTORY OF OPINIONS RELATING TO JESUS CHRIST.

The Introduction, page 1—Sect. I. Of the Opinion of the ancient Jewish and Gentile Churches, 3—Sect. II. Of the first Step that was made towards the Deification of Christ, by the Personification of the Logos, 8—Sect. III. The Supremacy was always ascribed to the Father before the Council of Nice, 16—Sect. IV. Of the Difficulty with which the Doctrine of the Divinity of Christ was established, 19—Sect. V. An Account of the Unitarians before the Council of Nice, 24—Sect. VI. Of the Arian Controversy, 26—Sect. VII. Of the Doctrine concerning the Holy Spirit, 29—Sect. VIII. The History of the Doctrine of the Trinity, from the Councils of Nice and Constantinople, till after the Eutychian Controversy, 34—Sect. IX. The State of the Doctrine of the Trinity in the Latin Church, 38—Sect. X. The History of the Doctrine of the Trinity after the Eutychian Controversy, 42—Sect. XI. A general View of the Recovery of the genuine Doctrine of Christianity concerning the Nature of Christ, 45.

PART II.

THE HISTORY OF OPINIONS RELATING TO THE DOCTRINE OF ATONEMENT.

The Introduction, page 51—Sect. I. That Christ did not die to make Satisfaction for the Sins of Men, 52—Sect. II. Of the true End and Design of the Death of Christ, 57—Sect. III. Of the Sense in which the Death of Christ is represented as a Sacrifice, and other figurative Representations of it, 60—Sect. IV. Of the Opinions of the Apostolical Fathers, 71—Sect. V. Of the Opinions of the Fathers till after the Time of Austin, 73—Sect. VI. Of the State of Opinions concerning the Doctrine of Atonement, from the Time of Austin to the Reformation, 82—Sect. VII. Of the Doctrine of the Reformers on the Subject of Atonement, 85.

PART III.

THE HISTORY OF OPINIONS CONCERNING GRACE, ORIGINAL SIN, AND PREDESTINATION.

The Introduction, page 93—Sect. I. Of the Doctrines of Grace, &c., before the Pelagian Controversy, 95—Sect. II. Of the Pelagian Controversy and the State of Opinions in consequence of it, 97—Sect. III. Of the Doctrine of Grace, &c., in the Middle Ages, and till the Reformation, 101—Sect. IV. Of the Doctrines of Grace, Original Sin, and Predestination, since the Reformation, 103.

PART IV.

THE HISTORY OF OPINIONS RELATING TO SAINTS AND ANGELS.

The Introduction, page 108—Sect. I. Part 1. Of the Respect paid to Saints in general, till the Fall of the Western Empire, 108—Part 2. Of Pictures and Images in

PART X.

THE HISTORY OF MINISTERS IN THE CHRISTIAN CHURCH, AND ESPECIALLY OF BISHOPS.

PART XI.

THE HISTORY OF THE PAPAL POWER.

APPENDICES TO PARTS X. AND XI.

PART XII.

THE HISTORY OF THE MONASTIC LIFE.

PART XIII.

THE HISTORY OF CHURCH REVENUES.

THE GENERAL CONCLUSION.

NEW APPENDIX.

The following List of the principal Ecclesiastical Writers, &c., after the Apostolic Age, with the Time when they flourished, chiefly from CAVE's HISTORIA LITERARIA, may be useful to the general reader :—

	A.D.		A.D.
Ignatius	101	Lactantius	303
Polycarp	108	Arius	315
Papias	110	Eusebius Pamphilus the historian	315
Basilides	120	Athanasius	326
Valentinus	125	Marcellus of Ancyra	330
Marcion	130	Photinus	344
Justin Martyr	140	Cyril of Jerusalem	350
Irenæus	167	Hilary	354
Theophilus	168	Eunomius	360
Hegesippus	170	Apollinarius (sen.)	362
Montanus	172	Epiphanius	368
Tatian	172	Optatus	368
Athenagoras	177	Basil	370
Artemon	187	Gregory (Nyssen)	370
Theodotus of Byzantium	192	Gregory (Nazianzen)	370
Clemens Alexandrinus	192	Apollinarius (jun.)	370
Tertullian	192	Ambrose	374
Symmachus	201	Jerom	378
Caius	210	Austin	396
Hippolytus	220	Chrysostom	398
Origen	230	Sulpicius Severus	401
Beryllus	230	Pelagius	405
Dionysius (of Alexandria)	247	Theodorus of Mopsuestia	407
Cyprian	248	Cyril of Alexandria	412
Noetus	250	Theodoret	425
Novatian	251	Nestorius	428
Gregory of Neocesarea	252	Eutyches	448
Paul of Samosata	260	Claudianus Mamertus	462
Sabellius	260	Facundus	540
Manes	277	Gregory the Great	590
Arnobius	303		

PREFACE TO THE NEW EDITION OF 1871.

BELIEVING, as all Christians do, in the divine origin of Christianity, and seeing at the present time the Church of Christ divided and distracted on a great number of questions, we may properly deem valuable whatever in any measure contributes to lead mankind to a better knowledge of the opinions and practices of the first Christians. The statement of Tertullian, "That is the true faith which is the most ancient, and that a corruption which is modern," is generally admitted; and so the New Testament, above all other books, is chiefly studied and prized. And next in importance, as helping to settle some questions about the true faith, is the knowledge of the opinions of the Christians immediately following the Apostolic age. Dr. Priestley, in an eminent degree, by the careful study of all the writings *extant* of the first five hundred years of the Christian era, has done a service for the reformation of religion. The present volume he spoke of as "the most valuable of all my writings." Many of its statements were severely canvassed by Bishop Horsley and others, and the author made a few corrections. "You have set me right," he said, "with respect to the exactness of *two* of my quotations, not one mistake having been discovered in it that at all affects my general design."—Many are not a little surprised and disappointed that Dr. Priestley should have excluded the Arians from his list of Unitarians, and thus weakened his argument by never calling into court some of the principal witnesses, simply because they believed in the *pre-existence* of Christ; for otherwise the Arians were essentially Unitarians. Dr. Priestley was a strict Humanitarian, regarding none as Unitarians but those who believed in Jesus Christ, "as *only* and properly a man;"—for this is the meaning of his phrase "a *mere man*," which has given much offence. Nevertheless, he was a firm believer in the supernatural power and divine mission of Christ. Dr. Priestley also unnecessarily, in one or two places of this volume, introduces his materialistic philosophy, with which not a few of his friends, in his own day, had no sympathy; and the same may be said of many Unitarians now.

The New Appendix aims but to give a few additional thoughts and quotations on an important controversy, and affords the reader some idea of his larger work, "A History of the Early Opinions concerning Jesus Christ," in two volumes. This work, which is out of print, and may possibly never be reprinted, contains some eighteen hundred quotations from the writings of the so-called orthodox fathers. The paragraphs in this Appendix are mere summaries, to convey to the reader some idea of that invaluable and scarce work. Dr. Priestley says, speaking of this history, "I find myself, in a great measure, upon new ground. At least I see reason to think that it has never been sufficiently examined by any person who has had the same general view of things that I have." Since his time other authors have gone over the ground, and with some additional results.

We are indebted to several gentlemen for services connected with this volume who have verified the numerous quotations and afforded useful hints. At the close of the last century this History stirred up much controversy, and may yet in some degree aid the religious inquirer to the solution of questions of polity and doctrine which still agitate the Christian world.

PREFACE TO RUTT'S EDITION.

DR. PRIESTLEY, as he has mentioned in his own Preface, designed to have added this *History*, as a fourth Volume to the *Institutes*, on their first publication in 1771. But other occupations intervened, till his materials became sufficient for a larger Work, and he had an increasing conviction of its utility and importance. His metaphysical discussions had led him still farther to consider the questions concerning the nature of Christ; nor during his excursion to the Continent in 1774, could he have failed to perceive the corrupt forms of religion under papal establishments, and their influence to foster the prejudices, and to increase the number of unbelievers.

Yet Dr. Priestley was not one of those credulous Protestants who satisfy themselves that the Reformers in the sixteenth century had left no corruptions of Christianity unreformed, in churches which, under their influence, were established by the civil power. Such establishments themselves, he justly regarded as no trifling corruptions; and as to some of the most censured representations in this Volume, their Author is justified by the published opinions of not a few dignified Churchmen. For what are the *special pleadings* of Bishop Burnet in his *Exposition*—Bishop Hoadley's *Plain Account* and his *Kingdom of Christ not of this World*—Dr. Clarke's *Scripture Doctrine*—Bishop Law's *Theory* "purged of ancient prejudices"—Dr. Jortin's *Remarks*, where he explodes "metaphysical and scholastic divinity from the Christian system;"—what are all these but forcible though indirect attacks on the Creeds and Ritual of their own Church?

It was not, however, to the consideration of a Churchman, formed in the liberal, though inconsistent, school of Hoadley, that Dr. Priestley recommended the following pages. Bishop Hurd was of another school. A highly accomplished classical scholar, and, in his earlier writings, no illiberal politician, he appears to have been content as a Theologian to *dwell in decencies*. Thus, as a Warburtonian Lecturer, in 1772, he could only discover a *papal* Man of Sin, though Mr. Evanson, whose inquiries were more extended, could assure the bishop that there were *many Antichrists*. Indeed, by a prelate who had congratulated the English Reformation because it advanced or was retarded as the superior judgment of the Civil Magistrate determined, Dr. Priestley's appeal would not be much regarded. It is to be regretted that it was received with a discourtesy too nearly bordering on *Warburtonian* arrogance.

The appeal to Mr. Gibbon was equally unsuccessful, had Dr. Priestley expected his approbation. But the spirit which the celebrated Historian discovered, on this occasion, I may find another opportunity to describe. Yet I form expectations, at this moment, with peculiar diffidence; from the impression of a very recent event of which the painful information has reached me, while concluding this Preface. I refer to the lamented death of Dr. Thomson, an encourager of this undertaking, on whose approbation of its progress I should have set no common value. May his family receive all the consolation which religion can bestow, when a Christian is called from the labours of life to the recompense of eternity, and may those who survive, especially in the same religious connexion, be taught and encouraged by his fair example.

J. T. RUTT.

Clapton, May 26, 1818.

DR. PRIESTLEY'S PREFACE.

AFTER examining the foundation of our Christian faith, and having seen how much valuable information we receive from it, in my *Institutes of Natural and Revealed Religion*, it is with a kind of reluctance, that, according to my proposal, I must now proceed to exhibit a view of the dreadful corruptions which have debased its spirit, and almost annihilated all the happy effects which it was eminently calculated to produce. It is some satisfaction to us, however, and is more than sufficient to answer any objection that may be made to Christianity itself from the consideration of these corruptions, that they appear to have been clearly foreseen by Christ, and by several of the apostles. And we have at this day the still greater satisfaction to perceive that, according to the predictions contained in the books of Scripture, Christianity has begun to recover itself from this corrupted state, and that the reformation advances apace. And though some of the most shocking abuses still continue in many places, their virulence is very generally abated; and the number is greatly increased of those who are most zealous in the profession of Christianity, whose lives are the greatest ornament to it, and who hold it in so much purity, that, if it was fairly exhibited, and universally understood, it could hardly fail to recommend itself to the acceptance of the whole world of Jews and Gentiles.

The clear and full exhibition of truly *reformed Christianity* seems now to be almost the only thing that is wanting to the universal prevalence of it. But so long as all the Christianity that is known to Heathens, Mahometans, and Jews, is of a corrupted and debased kind; and particularly while the profession of it is so much connected with *worldly interest*, it is no wonder that mankind in general refuse to admit it, and that they can even hardly be prevailed upon to give any attention to the evidence that is alleged in its favour. Whereas, when the system itself shall appear to be less liable to objection, it is to be hoped, that they may be brought to give proper attention to it, and to the evidence on which it rests.

Disagreeable as must be the view of these corruptions of Christianity to those who love and value it, it may not be without its use, even with respect to themselves. For the more their abhorrence and indignation are excited by the consideration of what has so long passed for Christianity, the more highly will they esteem what is truly so, the contrast will be so striking, and so greatly in its favour. Both these valuable ends, I hope, will be, in some measure, answered by this attempt to exhibit, what appear to me to have been the great deviations from the genuine system and spirit of Christianity, and the causes that produced them.

The following work has been so long promised to the public, that I cannot help being apprehensive lest my friends, and others, should not find their expectations from it fully answered. But they should recollect, that it was originally promised on a much smaller scale, viz. as the concluding part of my *Institutes of Natural and Revealed Religion*, which were drawn up for the use of young persons only.

I have since seen reason to extend my views, and to make this a separate work, larger than the whole of the *Institutes;* and perhaps I may not have succeeded sufficiently well in the uniform extension of the whole design. If, therefore, in any respect, either the composition, or the citation of authorities, should appear to be more adapted to my first design, I hope the candid reader will make proper allowance for it.

If my proper and ultimate object be considered, I flatter myself it will be thought that I have given reasonable satisfaction with respect to it; having shown that everything which I deem to be a *corruption of Christianity* has been a departure from the original scheme, or an *innovation.* It will also be seen, that I have generally been able to trace every such corruption to its proper source, and to show what circumstances in the state of things, and especially of other prevailing opinions and prejudices, made the alteration, in doctrine or practice, sufficiently natural, and the introduction and establishment of it easy. And if I have succeeded in this investigation, this *historical method* will be found to be one of the most satisfactory modes of argumentation, in order to prove that what I object to is really a corruption of genuine Christianity, and no part of the original scheme. For after the clearest refutation of any particular doctrine, that has been long established in Christian churches, it will still be asked, how, if it be no part of the scheme, it ever came to be thought so, and to be so generally acquiesced in; and in many cases the mind will not be perfectly satisfied till such questions be answered.

Besides this, I have generally given a short account of the recovery of the genuine doctrines of Christianity in the last age, though this was not my professed object; and a full *history of the reformation,* in all its articles, might be the subject of another large and very instructive work, though I apprehend not quite so useful as I flatter myself this will be.

I have not, however, taken notice of every departure from the original standard of Christian faith or practice, but only, or at least chiefly, such as subsists at this day, in some considerable part of the Christian world; or such as, though they may not properly subsist themselves, have left considerable vestiges in some Christian churches. I have not omitted, at the same time, to recite, as far as I was able, both the several steps by which each corruption has advanced, and also whatever has been urged with the greatest plausibility in favour of it; though I have made a point of being as succinct as possible in the detail of *arguments,* for or against any particular article of faith or practice.

In one article, however, I have considerably extended the argumentative part, viz. in my account of the doctrine of *atonement.* To this subject I had given particular attention many years ago; and Dr. Lardner and Dr. Fleming having seen what I then wrote, prevailed upon me to allow them to publish what they thought proper of it. This they did, under the title of *The Scripture Doctrine of Remission,* in the year 1761. When I published the *Theological Repository,* I corrected and enlarged that tract, and intended to write a still larger treatise on the subject, with the *history* of the doctrine annexed to it. I shall now, however, drop that design, contenting myself with giving the substance of the arguments in this work.

In the *Conclusion* of this work, I have taken the liberty, which I hope will not be thought improper, to endeavour to call the attention of *unbelievers* to the subject of the corruptions of Christianity (being sensible that this is one of the principal causes of infidelity), and also that of those who have influence with respect to the present *establishments* of Christianity, the reformation of many of the abuses I have described being very much in their power.

There is nothing, I hope, in the

manner of these addresses that will give offence, as none was intended. I trust, that from a sense of its infinite importance, I am deeply concerned for the honour of the religion I profess. I would, therefore, willingly do anything that may be in my power (and I hope with a temper not unbecoming the gospel) to make it both properly *understood*, and also completely *reformed*, in order to its more general propagation, and to its producing its proper effects on the hearts and lives of men; and, consequently, to its more speedily becoming, what it is destined to be, the greatest blessing to all the nations of the world.

As this work was originally intended to be nothing more than a Fourth Part of my *Institutes*, as mentioned above, I had contented myself with taking authorities from respectable modern writers, such as Dr. Clarke, Lardner, Jortin, Basnage, Beausobre, Le Clerc, Grotius, Du Pin, Fleury, Mosheim, Le Sueur, Giannone, &c. As my views extended, and I was led to imagine my work might be of some use to a higher class of readers, I found it necessary to have recourse to the original authorities in everything of consequence, especially for such articles as might be liable to be controverted in this country.   .

Accordingly, I have taken a good deal of pains to read, or at least look carefully through, many of the most capital works of the ancient Christian writers, in order to form a just idea of their general principles and turn of thinking, and to collect such passages as might occur for my purpose. Still, however, some things remain as I first wrote them, and sometimes from not having been able to purchase or conveniently procure the original writers.

But my object is not to give my readers a high idea of the extent of my reading, but simply a *credible account* of such facts as I shall lay before them; and I doubt not they will be as well satisfied of the fidelity of such writers as I have quoted, as they would have

been of my own. I can truly say that I have omitted nothing, the authority for which I think to be at all suspicious; and it will be seen that I have generally made use of such as, from the nature of the subject, are the least liable to exception. Where no writer is quoted, I suppose the fact to be well known to all who are conversant in these inquiries, and for which the common ecclesiastical historians are a sufficient authority.

To have compiled such a work as this from original authorities only, without making use of any modern writers, would have been more than any one man could have executed in the course of a long life. And what advantage do we derive from the labours of others, if we can never confide in them, and occasionally save ourselves some trouble by their means?

It will also be proper to observe, that I have sometimes made use of my own former publications, especially those in the *Theological Repository*, which, indeed, were originally intended for farther use. Thus I have partly copied, and partly abridged, what I had there written on the subject of *Atonement*, as mentioned before, and also on that of *Baptism*. Some things, too, will be found in this work copied, or abridged, from other works that bear my name, as the *Essay on the Lord's Supper*, on *Church Discipline*, and the *Disquisitions relating to Matter and Spirit*. But the whole of such extracts will not much exceed a single sheet; and I did not think it right to leave any of the pieces imperfect, merely to avoid a repetition of so small a magnitude, especially considering that the several publications may fall into different hands.

Since, however, I have written so largely on the subject of the *soul*, and the history of opinions relating to it, in the *Disquisitions*, I have omitted it altogether in this work, though it would have been a very proper part of it. I have only taken from that work a few particulars relating to the *state of the dead,* and a few other articles, without which this work would have been strikingly defective.

The whole of what I have called the *Sequel to the Disquisitions* (or *The History of the Philosophical Doctrine concerning the Origin of the Soul, and the Nature of Matter, with its influence on Christianity, especially with respect to the doctrine of the Pre-existence of Christ,* Vol. III. pp. 384-446) I wish to have considered as coming properly within the plan of this work, and essential to the principal object of it. Indeed, when I published the *Disquisitions,* I hesitated whether I should publish that part then, or reserve it for this *History.* But the rest of this work was not then ready, and it was of too much use for the purpose of the other not to go along with it. I wish the *general arguments against the pre-existence of Christ,* contained in Sect. VI. of that Sequel (pp. 421-439) to be particularly attended to.

In a subject so copious as this, I am far from supposing it probable that I have made no mistakes, notwithstanding I have used all the care and precaution that I could. If any such be pointed out to me, whether it be by a friend or an enemy, I shall be glad to avail myself of the intimation, in case there should be a demand for a second edition.[1] As some of my materials bear an equal relation to several of the subjects into which the work is divided, the reader will find a repetition of some things, but they are so few, and so useful in their respective places, that it hardly requires an apology. As to the repetition in the Appendix, the importance of the subject must apologize for it.

Though I have made no formal division of this work, except into separate *Parts* and *Sections,* the reader will perceive that I have, in the first place, considered the most important articles of Christian *doctrine,* and then those that relate to *discipline* and the *government of the church.*

[1] At the end of the *Reply,* which will follow this *History,* is a page containing a few corrections, &c. of which I have availed myself for this edition. The author says, "Having given the best attention that I can to the several remarks which have been made on this work, I have not yet seen any reason to make more than the following *corrections* and *additions.* It will be easily perceived that they are rather favourable than unfavourable to my principal object. Had I been convinced of any other oversight, I should with the same readiness have made the necessary alterations.' [Rutt.]

Dedication by Dr. Priestley.

TO THE REVEREND THEOPHILUS LINDSEY,[1] A.M.

DEAR FRIEND,

WISHING, as I do, that my name may ever be connected as closely with yours after death, as we have been connected by friendship in life, it is with peculiar satisfaction that I dedicate this work (which I am willing to hope will be one of the most useful of my publications) to you.

To your example, of a pure love of truth, and of the most fearless integrity in asserting it, evidenced by the sacrifices you have made to it, I owe much of my own wishes to imbibe the same spirit; though a more favourable education and situation in life, by not giving me an opportunity of distinguishing myself as you have done, has, likewise, not exposed me to the temptation of acting otherwise; and for this I wish to be truly thankful. For, since so very few of those who profess the same sentiments with you, have had the courage to act consistently with them, no person, whatever he may *imagine* he might have been

equal to, can have a right to presume that he would have been one of so small a number.

No person can see in a stronger light than you do the mischievous consequences of the corruptions of that religion, which you justly prize, as the most valuable of the gifts of God to man; and, therefore, I flatter myself, it will give you some pleasure to accompany me in my researches into the origin and progress of them, as this will tend to give all the friends of pure Christianity the fullest satisfaction that they reflect no discredit on the revelation itself; since it will be seen that they all came in from a foreign and hostile quarter. It will likewise afford a pleasing presage, that our religion will, in due time, purge itself of everything that debases it, and that for the present prevents its reception by those who are ignorant of its nature, whether living in Christian countries, or among Mahometans and Heathens.

The gross darkness of that *night* which has for many centuries obscured our holy religion, we may clearly see, is past; the *morning* is opening upon us; and we cannot doubt but that the light will increase, and extend itself more and more unto *the perfect day*. Happy are they who contribute to diffuse the pure light of this *everlasting gospel*. The time is coming when the detection of one error or prejudice, relating to this most important subject, and the success we have in opening and enlarging the minds of men with respect to it, will be far more honourable than any discovery we can make

[1] This excellent man died Nov. 3, 1808, in the 86th year of his age, having exemplified, both in active and declining life, the benign and cheering influence of Christian truth, while he laboured with the purest zeal to expose the corruptions by which it has been obscured. Dr. Priestley's first interview with Mr. Lindsey was in 1769, "at the house of Archdeacon Blackburne, at Richmond, where," says Mr. Belsham, "they passed some days together in that unreserved and delightful interchange of sentiments, and in those free and amicable discussions which would naturally take place among persons of high intellectual attainments, in whose estimation the discoveries of divine revelation held the most honourable place, and who were all equally animated with the same ardent love of truth, and with the same generous zeal for civil and religious liberty." *Mem. of Lindsey*, p. 34. See also Dr. Priestley's own *Memoirs*.

in other branches of knowledge, or our success in propagating them.

In looking back upon the dismal scene which the shocking corruptions of Christianity exhibit, we may well exclaim with the prophet, *How is the gold become dim! how is the most fine gold changed!* But the thorough examination of everything relating to Christianity, which has been produced by the corrupt state of it, and which nothing else would probably have led to, has been as *the refiner's fire* with respect to it; and when it shall have stood this test, it may be presumed that the truth and excellency of it will never more be called in question.

This corrupt state of Christianity has, no doubt, been permitted by the Supreme Governor of the world for the best of purposes, and it is the same great Being who is also now, in the course of his providence, employing these means to *purge his floor.* The civil powers of this world, which were formerly the chief supports of the anti-christian systems, who had given "their power and strength unto the beast," Rev. xvii. 13, now begin to *hate her*, and are ready to "make her desolate and naked," ver. 16. To answer their own political purposes, they are now promoting various reformations in the church;[1] and it can hardly be doubted, but that the difficulties in which many of the European nations are now involving themselves, will make other measures of reformation highly expedient and necessary.

Also, while the attention of men in power is engrossed by the difficulties that more immediately press upon them, the endeavours of the friends of reformation in points of *doctrine* pass with less notice, and operate without obstruction. Let us rejoice in the *good* that results from this *evil*, and omit

no opportunity that is furnished us, voluntarily to co-operate with the gracious intention of Divine Providence; and let us make that our primary object, which others are doing to promote their own sinister ends. All those who labour in the discovery and communication of truth, if they be actuated by a pure love of it, and a sense of its importance to the happiness of mankind, may consider themselves *as workers together with God*, and may proceed with confidence, assured that *their labour* in this cause *shall not be in vain*, whether they themselves see the fruit of it or not.

The more opposition we meet with in these labours, the more honourable it will be to us, provided we meet that opposition with the true spirit of Christianity. And to assist us in this, we should frequently reflect that many of our opponents are probably men who wish as well to the gospel as we do ourselves, and really think *they do God service* by opposing us. Even prejudice and bigotry, arising from such a principle, are respectable things, and entitled to the greatest candour. If our religion teaches us to *love our enemies*, certainly we should love, and, from a principle of love, should endeavour to convince those who, if they were only better informed, would embrace us as friends.

The time will come when the cloud, which for the present prevents our distinguishing our friends and our foes, will be dispersed, even that day in which *the secrets of all hearts will be disclosed* to the view of all. In the meantime, let us think as favourably as possible of all men, our particular opponents not excepted; and therefore be careful to conduct all *hostility*, with the pleasing prospect that one day it will give place to the most perfect *amity*.

You, my friend, peculiarly happy in a most placid, as well as a most determined mind, have nothing to blame yourself for in this respect. If, on any occasion, I have indulged too much asperity, I hope I shall, by your example,

---

[1] *Joseph*, Emperor of Germany, had suppressed the religious orders, in his dominions, and otherwise controlled the power of the church. Pope Pius VI. paid a visit to Vienna, in March 1782, from "a desire to put some stop to the heretical innovations of the Emperor." See N. Ann. Reg. III. pp. 64–66.

learn to correct myself, and without abating my zeal in the common cause.

As we are now both of us past the meridian of life, I hope we shall be looking more and more beyond it, and be preparing for that world, where we shall have no errors to combat, and, consequently, where *a talent for disputation* will be of no use; but where the *spirit of love* will find abundant exercise; where all our labours will be of the most friendly and benevolent nature, and where our employment will be its own reward.

Let these views brighten the evening of our lives, that *evening*, which will be enjoyed with more satisfaction, in proportion as the *day* shall have been laboriously and well spent. Let us, then, without reluctance, submit to that temporary rest in the grave, which our wise Creator has thought proper to appoint for all the human race, our Saviour himself not wholly excepted; anticipating with joy the glorious *morning of the resurrection*, when we shall meet that Saviour, whose precepts we have obeyed, whose spirit we have breathed, whose religion we have defended, whose *cup* also we may, in some measure, have drank of, and whose honours we have asserted, without making them to interfere with those of *his Father and our Father, of his God and our God*, that supreme, that great and awful Being, to whose will he was always most perfectly submissive, and for whose unrivalled prerogative he always showed the most ardent zeal.

With the truest affection,

I am, dear friend,

Your brother,

In the faith and hope of the gospel,

J. PRIESTLEY.

Birmingham, Nov. 1782.

A HISTORY

OF THE

CORRUPTIONS OF CHRISTIANITY.

PART I.

THE HISTORY OF OPINIONS RELATING TO JESUS CHRIST.

THE INTRODUCTION.

THE *unity of God* is a doctrine on which the greatest stress is laid in the whole system of revelation. To guard this most important article was the principal object of the Jewish religion; and, notwithstanding the proneness of the Jews to idolatry, at length it fully answered its purpose in reclaiming them, and in impressing the minds of many persons of other nations in favour of the same fundamental truth.

The Jews were taught by their prophets to expect a Messiah, who was to be descended from the tribe of Judah, and the family of David,—a person in whom themselves and all the nations of the earth should be blessed; but none of their prophets gave them an idea of any other than a man like themselves in that illustrious character, and no other did they ever expect, or do they expect to this day.

Jesus Christ, whose history answers to the description given of the Messiah by the prophets, made no other pretensions; referring all his extraordinary power to God, his Father, who, he expressly says, spake and acted by him, and who raised him from the dead: and it is most evident that the apostles, and all those who conversed with our Lord before and after his resurrection, considered him in no other light than simply as "a man approved of God, by wonders and signs which God did by him." Acts ii. 22.

Not only do we find no trace of so prodigious a change in the ideas which the apostles entertained concerning Christ, as from that of *a man like themselves,* (which it must be acknowledged were the first that they entertained,) to that of *the most high God,* or one who was in any sense their *maker* or *preserver,* that when their minds were most fully enlightened, after the descent of the Holy Spirit, and to the latest period of their ministry, they continued to speak of him in the same style; even when it is evident they must have intended to speak of him in a manner suited to his state of greatest exaltation and glory. Peter uses the simple language above quoted, of *a man approved of God,* immediately after the descent of the Spirit: and the apostle Paul, giving what may be called the Christian creed, says, 1 Tim. ii. 5, "There is one God, and one mediator between God and men, the man Christ Jesus." He does not say the *God,* the *God-man,* or the *super-*

angelic being, but simply *the man* Christ Jesus; and nothing can be alleged from the New Testament in favour of any higher nature of Christ, except a few passages interpreted without any regard to the context, or the modes of speech and opinions of the times in which the books were written, and in such a manner, in other respects, as would authorize our proving any doctrine whatever from them.

From this plain doctrine of the Scriptures, a doctrine so consonant to reason and the ancient prophecies, Christians have at length come to believe what they do not pretend to have any conception of, and than which it is not possible to frame a more express contradiction. For, while they consider Christ as the supreme, eternal God, the maker of heaven and earth, and of all things visible and invisible, they moreover acknowledge the Father and the Holy Spirit to be equally *God* in the same exalted sense, all three equal in power and glory, and yet all three constituting no more than one God.

To a person the least interested in the inquiry, it must appear an object of curiosity to trace by what means, and by what steps, so great a change has taken place, and what circumstances in the history of other opinions, and of the world, proved favourable to the successive changes. An opinion, and especially an opinion adopted by great numbers of mankind, is to be considered as any other *fact in history*, for it cannot be produced without an *adequate cause*, and is therefore a proper object of philosophical inquiry. In this case I think it not difficult to find causes abundantly adequate to the purpose, and it is happily in our power to trace almost every step by which the changes have been successively brought about.

If the interest that mankind have generally taken in anything, will at all contribute to interest us in the inquiry concerning it, this history cannot fail to be highly interesting, For, perhaps, in no business whatever have the minds of men been more agitated, and,

speculative as the nature of the thing is, in few cases has the peace of society been so much disturbed. To this very day, of such importance is the subject considered by thousands and tens of thousands, that they cannot write or speak of it without the greatest zeal, and without treating their opponents with the greatest rancour. If good sense and humanity did not interpose to mitigate the rigour of law, thousands would be sacrificed to the cause of orthodoxy in this single article; and the greatest number of sufferers would probably be in this very country, on account of the greater freedom of inquiry which prevails here, in consequence of which we entertain and profess the greatest diversity of opinions.

The various steps in this interesting history it is now my business to point out, and I wish that all my readers may attend me with as much coolness and impartiality as I trust I shall myself preserve through the whole of this investigation.[1]

---

[1] The following anecdote respecting the *History*, will show that the *spirit* of the *Synod of Dort*, had survived two centuries. "This book was burnt by the hands of the common hangman in the city of Dort, province of Holland, anno 1785:—a piece of intelligence communicated by me to Dr. Priestley in the hotel where I lodged in Birmingham, in a conversation I had the pleasure of having with that extraordinary man, a few weeks after that event. Having asked me with much earnestness, how he would be received in Holland, were he to appear there, I told him I did not exactly know how they might treat the original, but that he himself might be able to determine that point when I had told him that he had been burnt in effigy at Dort, a few weeks before I left Holland—a person's writings being often viewed as a picture of his mind, the burning of his *Corruptions* might be easily considered as burning *himself* in *effigy*. He deplored our ignorance and blindness. A greater philanthropist I never met with." *Note* by the Rev. Thomas Peirson, D.D. senior minister of the established English church in the city of Amsterdam. *Bibliotheca Peirsoniana*, p. 211.

This was not the first attempt to confute the author's opinions by the argument of *fire*. "In 1782, previous to the sale by auction of the Abbé Needham's library at *Bruxelles*, the licensers, as usual, went to burn the prohibited books. They destroyed 'Cudworth's Intellectual System,' *Priestley's Hartley*, a New Testament, and many others; but 'Christianity as old as the Creation,' escaped the flames." Mon. Mag. xxxiv. p. 521.

SECTION I.

OF THE OPINION OF THE ANCIENT JEWISH
AND GENTILE CHURCHES.

THAT the ancient Jewish church must have held the opinion that Christ was simply a *man*, and not either *God Almighty*, or a *super-angelic being*, may be concluded from its being the clear doctrine of the Scripture, and from the apostles having taught no other; but there is sufficient evidence of the same thing from ecclesiastical history. It is unfortunate, indeed, that there are now extant so few remains of any of the writers who immediately succeeded the apostles, and especially that we have only a few inconsiderable fragments of Hegesippus, a Jewish Christian, who wrote the history of the church in continuation of the *Acts of the Apostles*, and who travelled to Rome about the year 160; but it is not difficult to collect evidence enough in support of my assertion.

The members of the Jewish church were, in general, in very low circumstances, which may account for their having few persons of learning among them; on which account they were much despised by the richer and more learned gentile Christians, especially after the destruction of Jerusalem, before which event all the Christians in Judea, (warned by our Saviour's prophecies concerning the desolation of that country,) had retired to the northeast of the sea of Galilee. They were likewise despised by the Gentiles for their bigoted adherence to the law of Moses, to the rite of circumcision, and other ceremonies of their ancient religion. And on all these accounts they probably got the name of *Ebionites*, which signifies *poor* and *mean*, in the same manner as many of the early reformers from Popery got the name of *Beghards*, and other appellations of a similar nature. The fate of these ancient Jewish Christians was, indeed, peculiarly hard. For, besides the neglect of the gentile Christians, they were, as Epiphanius informs us, held in the greatest abhorrence by the Jews from whom they had separated, and who cursed them in a solemn manner three times, whenever they met for public worship.[1]

In general these ancient Jewish Christians retained the appellation of Nazarenes, and it may be inferred from Origen, Epiphanius and Eusebius, that the Nazarenes and Ebionites were the same people, and held the same tenets, though some of them supposed that Christ was the son of Joseph as well as of Mary, while others of them held that he had no natural father, but had a miraculous birth.[2] Epiphanius, in his account of the Nazarenes, (and the Jewish Christians never went by any other name,) makes no mention of any of them believing the divinity of Christ, in any sense of the word.

It is particularly remarkable that Hegesippus, in giving an account of the heresies of his time, though he mentions the Carpocratians, Valentinians, and others who were generally termed Gnostics, (and who held that Christ had a pre-existence, and was man only in appearance,) not only makes no mention of this supposed heresy of the Nazarenes or Ebionites, but says that, in his travels to Rome, where he spent some time with Anicetus, and visited the bishops of other sees, he found that they all held the same doctrine that was taught in the law, by the prophets, and by our Lord.[3] What could this be but the proper Unitarian doctrine held by the Jews, and which he himself had been taught?

That Eusebius doth not expressly say what this faith was, is no wonder, considering his prejudice against the Unitarians of his own time. He speaks of the Ebionites, as persons whom a malignant demon had brought into his power;[4] and though he speaks of them as holding that Jesus was the son of

[1] Epiphanii Opera, 1682. (Hær. 29.) I. p. 124. (P.)
[2] Ibid. pp. 123, 125. (P.)
[3] Eusebii Hist. 1720, L. iv. C. xxii. pp. 181, 182. (P.)
[4] Ibid. L. iii. C. xxvii. p. 121. (P.)

B 2

Joseph as well as of Mary, he speaks with no less virulence of the opinion of those of his time, who believed the miraculous conception, calling their heresy *madness*. Valesius, the translator of Eusebius, was of opinion that the history of Hegesippus was neglected and lost by the ancients, on account of the errors it contained, and these errors could be no other than the Unitarian doctrine. It is possible also, that it might be less esteemed on account of the very plain, unadorned style in which all the ancients say it was written.

Almost all the ancient writers who speak of what they call the heresies of the two first centuries, say, that they were of *two kinds;* the first were those that thought that Christ "was man in appearance only," and the other that he was "no more than a man."[1] Tertullian calls the former *Docetæ*, and the latter *Ebionites*. Austin, speaking of the same two sects, says, that the former believed Christ to be God, but denied that he was man, whereas the latter believed him to be man, but denied that he was God. Of this latter opinion Austin owns that he himself was, till he became acquainted with the writings of Plato, which in his time were translated into Latin, and in which he learned the doctrine of the *Logos*.

Now that this second heresy, as the later writers called it, was really no heresy at all, but the plain simple truth of the gospel, may be clearly inferred from the apostle John taking no notice at all of it, though he censures the former, who believed Christ to be man only in appearance, in the severest manner. And that this was the only heresy that gave him any alarm, is evident from his first epistle, chap. iv. ver. 2, 3, where he says that "every spirit that confesseth that Jesus Christ is come in the flesh (by which he must have meant *is truly a man*), is of God." On the other hand, he says, "every spirit that confesseth not that Jesus

Christ is come in the flesh is not of God, and this is that spirit of Antichrist, whereof you have heard that it should come, and even now already is it in the world." For this was the first corruption of the Christian religion by the maxims of Heathen philosophy, and which proceeded afterwards, till Christianity was brought to a state little better than Paganism.

That Christian writers afterwards should imagine that this apostle alluded to the Unitarian heresy, or that of the Ebionites, in the introduction to his gospel, is not to be wondered at; as nothing is more common than for men to interpret the writings of others according to their own previous ideas and conceptions of things. On the contrary, it seems very evident that, in that introduction, the apostle alludes to the very same system of opinions, which he had censured in his epistle, the fundamental principle of which was that, not the Supreme Being himself, but an emanation from him, to which they gave the name of *Logos*, and which they supposed to be the Christ, inhabited the body of Jesus, and was the maker of all things; whereas he there affirms, that the *Logos* by which all things were made, was not a being distinct from God, but God himself, that is, an attribute of God, or the divine power and wisdom. We shall see that the Unitarians of the third century, charged the orthodox with introducing a new and strange interpretation of the word *logos*.[2]

That very system, indeed, which made Christ to have been the *eternal reason*, or *Logos* of the Father, did not, probably, exist in the time of the apostle John, but was introduced from the principles of Platonism afterwards. But the Valentinians, who were only a branch of the Gnostics, made great use of the same term, not only denominating by it one of the æons in the

[1] Lardner's Hist. of Heretics, p. 17. (P.) Works, IX. pp. 234, 235.

[2] See *Beausobre* "Histoire Critique de Manichée et du Manichéisme," I. p. 540. (P.) "Les Nosticiens reprochoient aux Orthodoxes, d'introduire un langage étrange et nouveau, en appellant le Verbe, Fils de Dieu." L. iii. Ch. vi. Sect. xi.

system described by Irenæus, but also one of them that was endowed by all the other æons with some extraordinary gift, to which person they gave the name of *Jesus, Saviour, Christ* and *Logos*.[1]

The word *logos* was also frequently used by them as synonymous to *æon*, in general, or an intelligence that sprung, mediately or immediately, from the divine essence.[2] It is, therefore, almost certain, that the apostle John had frequently heard this term made use of, in some erroneous representations of the system of Christianity that were current in his time, and therefore he might choose to introduce the same term in its proper sense, as an *attribute of the Deity*, or *God himself*, and not a distinct being that sprung from him. And this writer is not to be blamed if, afterwards, that very attribute was personified in a different manner, and not as a figure of speech, and consequently his language was made to convey a very different meaning from that which he affixed to it.

Athanasius himself was so far from denying that the primitive Jewish church was properly Unitarian, maintaining the simple humanity and not the divinity of Christ, that he endeavours to account for it by saying, that "all the Jews were so firmly persuaded that their Messiah was to be nothing more than a man like themselves, that the apostles were obliged to use great caution in divulging the doctrine of the proper divinity of Christ."[3] But what the apostles did not teach, I think we should be cautious how we believe. The apostles were never backward to combat other Jewish prejudices, and certainly would have opposed this opinion of theirs, if it had been an error. For if it had been an error at all, it must be allowed to have been an error of the greatest consequence.

Could it rouse the indignation of the apostle John so much as to call those

Antichrist, who held that *Christ was not come in the flesh*, or was not truly man; and would he have passed uncensured those who denied the divinity of his Lord and Master, if he himself had thought him to be true and very God, his Maker as well as his Redeemer? We may therefore safely conclude that an opinion allowed to have prevailed in his time, and maintained by all the Jewish Christians afterwards, was what he himself and the other apostles had taught them, and therefore that it is the very truth; and consequently that the doctrine of the divinity of Christ, or of his being any more than a man, is an innovation, in whatever manner it may have been introduced.

Had the apostles explained themselves distinctly and fully, as its importance, if it had been true, required, on the subject of the *proper divinity of Christ*, as a person equal to the Father, it can never be imagined that the whole Jewish church, or any considerable part of it, should so very soon have adopted the opinion of his being a *mere man*.[4] To add to the dignity of their Master, was natural, but to take from it, and especially to degrade him from being *God*, to being *man*, must have been very unnatural. To make the Jews abandon the opinion of the divinity of Christ in the most qualified sense of the word, must at least have been as difficult as we find it to be to induce others to give up the same opinion at this day; and there can be no question of their having, for some time, believed what the apostles taught on that, as well as on other subjects.

Of the same opinion with the Nazarenes, or Ebionites among the Jews, were those among the Gentiles whom Epiphanius called *Alogi*, from their not receiving, as he says, the account that John gives of the *Logos*, and the writings of that apostle in general. But Lardner, with great probability,

---

[1] Irenæi Opera, 1702. L. i. Sect. iv. p. 14. (*P.*)
[2] *Beausobre*, I. p. 571. (*P.*) L. iii. Ch. ix. Sect. iii.
[3] *De Sententia Dionysii*, Athanasii Opera. 1630. I. pp. 553-4. (*P.*)

[4] By "mere man," Priestley always means a man approved of God, inspired and miraculously endowed by God, yet nothing more than a man.]

supposes, "there never was any such heresy"[1] as that of the *Alogi*, or rather that those to whom Epiphanius gave that name, were unjustly charged by him with rejecting the writings of the apostle John, since no other person before him makes any mention of such a thing, and he produces nothing but mere hearsay in support of it. It is very possible, however, that he might give such an account of them, in consequence of their explaining the *Logos* in the introduction of John's gospel in a manner different from him and others, who in that age had appropriated to themselves the name of orthodox.

Equally absurd is the conjecture of Epiphanius, that those persons and others like them, were those that the apostle John meant by *Antichrist*.[2] It is a much more natural inference that, since this writer allows these Unitarians to have been contemporary with the apostles, and that they had no peculiar appellation till he himself gave them this of *Alogi* (and which he is very desirous that other writers would adopt after him[3]), that they had not been deemed heretical in early times, but held the opinion of the ancient Gentile church, as the Nazarenes did that of the Jewish church; and that, notwithstanding the introduction, and gradual prevalence of the opposite doctrine, they were suffered to pass uncensured and consequently without a name, till the smallness of their numbers made them particularly noticed.

It is remarkable, however, that those who held the simple doctrine of the humanity of Christ, without asserting that Joseph was his natural father, were not reckoned heretics by Irenæus, who wrote a large work on the subject of heresies; and even those who held *that* opinion are mentioned with respect

by Justin Martyr, who wrote some years before him, and who, indeed, is the first writer extant, of the gentile Christians, after the age of the apostles. And it cannot be supposed that he would have treated them with so much respect, if their doctrine had not been very generally received, and on that account less obnoxious than it grew to be afterwards. He expresses their opinion concerning Christ, by saying that they made him to be a *mere man*, (ψιλος ανθρωπος,) and by this term Irenæus, and all the ancients, even later than Eusebius, meant *a man descended from man*, and this phraseology is frequently opposed to the doctrine of the miraculous conception of Jesus, and not to that of his divinity. It is not therefore to be inferred that, because some of the ancient writers condemn the one, they meant to pass any censure upon the other.

The manner in which Justin Martyr speaks of those Unitarians who believed Christ to be the son of Joseph, is very remarkable, and shows that though they even denied the miraculous conception, they were far from being reckoned heretics in his time, as they were by Irenæus afterwards. He says, "there are some of our profession who acknowledge him" (Jesus) "to be the Christ, yet maintain that he was a man born of man. I do not agree with them, nor should I be prevailed upon by ever so many who hold that opinion; because we are taught by Christ himself not to receive our doctrine from men, but from what was taught by the holy prophets and by himself."[4]

This language has all the appearance of an *apology* for an opinion contrary to the general and prevailing one, as that of the humanity of Christ (at least with the belief of the miraculous conception) probably was in his time. This writer even speaks of his own opinion of the pre-existence of Christ, (and he is the first that we certainly

<hr>

[1] Hist. of Heretics, p. 446. (*P.*) Works, IX. p. 516. Lardner's words are ". . . My own opinion . . . . . . is that this is a *fictitious heresy*, and that *there never were any Christians* who rejected St. John's Gospel and First Epistle, and yet received . . . the other books of the New Testament."

[2] *Hær.* 51, Sect. iii. Opera, I. p. 424. (*P.*)

[3] Ibid. p. 423. (*P.*)

[4] *Dial.* Edit. Thirlby, pp. 234-5. (*P.*)

know to have maintained it, on the principles on which it was generally received afterwards,) as a doubtful one, and by no means a necessary article of Christian faith. "Jesus," says he, "may still be the Christ of God, though I should not be able to prove his pre-existence, as the Son of God who made all things. For though I should not prove that he had pre-existed, it will be right to say that, in this respect only, I have been deceived, and not to deny that he is the Christ, if he appears to be a man born of men, and to have become Christ by election."[1] This is not the language of a man very confident of his opinion, and who had the sanction of the majority along with him.

The reply of Trypho the Jew, with whom the dialogue he is writing is supposed to be held, is also remarkable, showing in what light the Jews will always consider any doctrine which makes Christ to be more than a man. He says, "They who think that Jesus was a man, and, being chosen of God, was anointed Christ, appear to me to advance a more probable opinion than yours. For all of us expect that Christ will be born a man from men, (ανθρωπος εξ ανθρωπων,) and that Elias will come to anoint him. If he therefore be Christ, he must by all means be a man born of man."[2]

It is well known, and mentioned by Eusebius, that the Unitarians in the primitive church, always pretended to be the oldest Christians, that the apostles themselves had taught their doctrine, and that it generally prevailed till the time of Zephyrinus, bishop of Rome, but that from that time it was corrupted;[3] and as these Unitarians are called *Idiotæ* (common and ignorant people) by Tertullian, it is more natural to look for ancient opinions among them, than among the learned who are more apt to innovate. With such manifest unfairness does Eusebius, or a more ancient writer, whose sentiments he adopts, treat the Unitarians, as to say that Theodotus, who appeared about the year 190, and who was condemned by Victor the predecessor of Zephyrinus, was the first who held that our Saviour was a mere man;[4] when in refuting their pretensions to antiquity, he goes no farther than to Irenæus, Justin Martyr and Clemens; in whose second and spurious epistle only it is to be found, and the *ancient hymns*, not now extant, but in which, being poetical compositions, divinity was probably ascribed to him, in some figurative and qualified sense; though Eusebius in his own writings alone might have found a refutation of his assertion. Epiphanius, speaking of the same Theodotus, says, that his heresy was a branch (αποσπασμα) of that of the *Alogi*, which sufficiently implies that they existed before him.[5]

The *Alogi*, therefore, appear to have been the earliest gentile Christians, and Dr. Berriman supposes them to have been a branch of the Ebionites.[6] In fact, they must have been the same among the Gentiles, that the Ebionites were among the Jews. And it is remarkable that, as the children of Israel retained the worship of the one true God all the time of Joshua, and of those of his contemporaries who outlived him; so the generality of Christians retained the same faith, believing the strict unity of God, and the proper humanity of Christ, all the time of the apostles and of those who conversed with them, but began to depart from that doctrine presently afterwards; and the defection advanced so fast, that in about one century more, the original doctrine was generally reprobated and deemed heretical. The manner in which this corruption of the ancient doctrine was introduced, I must now proceed to explain.

[1] *Dial.* Edit. Thirlby, pp. 233-4. (*P.*)
[2] Ibid. p. 235. (*P.*)
[3] Hist. L. v. C. xxviii. p. 252. (*P.*)
[4] Ibid.
[5] *Hær.* 54, Opera, I. p. 462. (*P.*)
[6] "An Historical Account of the Trinitarian Controversy," 1725, p. 82. (*P.*)

SECTION II.

As the greatest things often take their rise from the smallest beginnings, so the worst things sometimes proceed from good intentions. This was certainly the case with respect to the origin of Christian Idolatry. All the early heresies arose from men who wished well to the gospel, and who meant to recommend it to the Heathens, and especially to philosophers among them, whose prejudices they found great difficulty in conquering. Now we learn from the writings of the apostles themselves, as well as from the testimony of later writers, that the circumstance at which mankind in general, and especially the more philosophical part of them, stumbled the most, was the doctrine of a *crucified Saviour*. They could not submit to become the disciples of a man who had been exposed upon a cross, like the vilest malefactor. Of this objection to Christianity we find traces in all the early writers, who wrote in defence of the gospel against the unbelievers of their age, to the time of Lactantius; and probably it may be found much later. He says, "I know that many fly from the truth out of their abhorrence of the cross."[1] We, who only learn from *history* that crucifixion was a kind of death to which slaves and the vilest of malefactors were exposed, can but very imperfectly enter into their prejudices, so as to feel what they must have done with respect to it. The idea of a man executed at Tyburn, without anything to distinguish him from other malefactors, is but an approach to the case of our Saviour.

The apostle Paul speaks of the crucifixion of Christ as the great obstacle to the reception of the gospel in his

[1] Lactantii *Epitome* (Divinarum Institutionum), 1718. C. II. p. 143. (*P.*) "Scio equidem multos, dum abhorrent nomen crucis, refugere a veritate." Opera, 1748, II. p. 38.

time; and yet, with true magnanimity, he does not go about to palliate the matter, but says to the Corinthians (some of the politest people among the Greeks, and fond of their philosophy), that *he was determined to know nothing among them* but "Jesus Christ and him crucified:" for though this circumstance was "unto the Jews a stumbling-block, and unto the Greeks foolishness," it was to others "the power of God and the wisdom of God." 1 Cor. i. 23, 24. For this circumstance at which they cavilled, was that in which the wisdom of God was most conspicuous; the death and resurrection of a man, in all respects like themselves, being better calculated to give other men an assurance of their own resurrection, than that of any super-angelic being, the laws of whose nature they might think to be very different from those of their own. But, "since by man *came* death, so by man *came* also the resurrection of the dead." 1 Cor. xv. 21.

Later Christians, however, and especially those who were themselves attached to the principles of either the Oriental or the Greek philosophy, unhappily took another method of removing this obstacle; and instead of explaining the wisdom of the divine dispensations in the appointment of a man, a person *in all respects like unto his brethren*, for the redemption of *men*, and of his dying in the most public and indisputable manner, as a foundation for the clearest proof of a real resurrection, and also of a painful and ignominious death, as an example to his followers who might be exposed to the same, &c., &c., they began to raise the dignity of the *person* of Christ, that it might appear less disgraceful to be ranked amongst his disciples. To make this the easier to them, two things chiefly contributed; the first was the received method of interpreting the Scriptures among the learned Jews, and the second was the philosophical opinions of the heathen world, which had then begun to infect the Jews themselves.

It has been observed that after the translation of the Old Testament into Greek, which was done probably in the time of Ptolemy Philadelphus, King of Egypt, in consequence of which the Jewish religion became better known to the Greeks, and especially to the philosophers of Alexandria, the more learned of the Jews had recourse to an allegorical method of interpreting what they found to be most objected to in their sacred writings; and by this means pretended to find in the books of Moses, and the prophets, all the great principles of the Greek philosophy, and especially that of Plato, which at that time was most in vogue. In this method of interpreting Scripture, Philo, a learned Jew of Alexandria, far excelled all who had gone before him; but the Christians of that city, who were themselves deeply tinctured with the principles of the same philosophy, especially Clemens Alexandrinus and Origen, who both believed the pre-existence of souls, and the other distinguishing tenets of Platonism, soon followed his steps in the interpretation of both the Old and the New Testament.[1]

One method of allegorizing, which took its rise in the East, was the personification of things without life, of which we have many beautiful examples in the books of Scripture, as of *wisdom* by Solomon, of *the dead* by Ezekiel, and of *sin* and *death* by the apostle Paul. Another mode of allegorizing was finding out resemblances in things that bore some relation to each other, and then representing them as *types* and *antitypes* to each other. The apostle Paul, especially if he be the author of the Epistle to the Hebrews, has strained very much, by the force of imagination, to reconcile the Jews to the Christian religion, by pointing out the *analogies* which he imagined the rites and ceremonies of the Jewish religion bore to something in Christianity. Clemens Romanus, but more especially Barnabas, pushed this

method of allegorizing still farther. But the fathers who followed them, by employing both the methods, and mixing their own philosophy with Christianity, at length converted an innocent allegory into what was little better than Pagan idolatry.

It had long been the received doctrine of the East, and had gradually spread into the western parts of the world, that besides the supreme divine mind, which had existed without cause from all eternity, there were other intelligences, of a less perfect nature, which had been produced by way of *emanation* from the great original mind, and that other intelligences, less and less perfect, had, in like manner, proceeded from them: in short, that all spirits, whether demons, or the souls of men, were of this divine origin. It was supposed by some of them that even *matter* itself, which they considered as the source of all evil, had, in this intermediate manner, derived its existence from the Deity, though others supposed matter to have been eternal and self-existent. For it was a maxim with them all, that "nothing could be created out of nothing." In this manner they thought they could best account for the origin of evil, without supposing it to be the immediate production of a good being, which the original divine mind was always supposed by them to be.

In order to exalt their idea of Jesus Christ, it being then a received opinion among the philosophers that all souls had pre-existed, they conceived his soul not to have been that of a common man (which was generally supposed to have been the production of inferior beings), but a principal *emanation* from the divine mind itself, and that an intelligence of so high a rank either animated the body of Jesus from the beginning, or entered into him at his baptism. There was, however, a great diversity of opinion on this subject; and, indeed, there was room enough for it, in a system which was not founded on any observation but was

[1] " Le Platonisme devoilé, ou Essai touchant le verbe Platonicien." 1700, p. 145. (*P.*)

the mere creature of fancy. But all these philosophizing Christians had the same general object, which was to make the religion of Christ more reputable, by adding to the dignity of our Lord's person.

Thus, according to Lardner, *Cerinthus*, one of the first of these philosophizing Christians, "taught one Supreme God, but that the world was not made by him, but by angels;" that Jesus "was a man born of Joseph and Mary, and that at his baptism, the Holy Ghost, or the Christ, descended upon him;" that Jesus "died and rose again, but that the Christ was impassible." [1] On the other hand, Marcion held that Christ was not born at all, but that "the son of God took the exterior form of a man, and appeared as a man; and without being born, or gradually growing up to the full stature of a man, he showed himself at once in Galilee, as a man grown." [2] All the heretics, however, of this class, whose philosophy was more properly that of the East, thought it was unworthy of so exalted a person as the proper *Christ* to be truly a man, and most of them thought he had no real flesh, but only the appearance of it, and what was incapable of feeling pain, &c.

These opinions the apostles, and especially John, had heard of, and he rejected them, as we have seen, with the greatest indignation. However, this did not put a stop to the evil, those philosophizing Christians either having ingenuity enough to evade those censures, by pretending these were not their opinions, but others somewhat different from theirs, that properly fell under them, or new opinions really different from them, (but derived in fact from the same source, and having the same evil tendency,) rising up in the place of them; for they were all calculated to give more dignity, as they imagined, to the person of their master. The most remarkable change in these opinions

was that, whereas the earliest of these philosophizing Christians supposed, in general, that the world was made by some superior intelligence of no benevolent nature, and that the Jewish religion was prescribed by the same being, or one very much resembling him, and that Christ was sent to rectify the imperfections of both systems; those who succeeded them, and whose success at length gave them the title of orthodox, corrupted the genuine Christian principle no less, by supposing that Christ was the being who, under God, was himself the maker of the world, and the medium of all the divine communications to man, and therefore the author of the Jewish religion.

As Plato had travelled into the East, it is probable that he there learned the doctrine of divine emanations, and got his ideas of the origin of this visible system. But he sometimes expresses himself so temperately on the subject, that he seems to have only allegorized what is true with respect to it; speaking of the divine mind as having existed from eternity, but having within itself *ideas* or *archetypes* of whatever was to exist without it, and saying that the immediate seat of these ideas, or the intelligence which he styled *Logos*, was that from which the visible creation immediately sprung. However, it was to this principle in the divine mind, or this being, derived from it, that Plato, according to Lactantius, gave the name of *a second God*, saying, "the Lord and maker of the universe, whom we justly call God, made a second God, visible and sensible." [3]

By this means, however, it was, that this *Logos*, originally an *attribute* of the divine mind itself, came to be represented, first by the philosophers, and then by philosophizing Christians, as an *intelligent principle* or *being*, distinct from God, though an emanation from him. This doctrine was but too convenient for those who wished to re-

---

[1] Hist. of Heretics, p. 150. (*P.*) Works, IX. p. 325.
[2] Ibid. p. 227. (*P.*) Works, IX. pp. 378–9.

[3] *Epitome*, C. xlii. p. 106. (*P.*) "Dominus et factor universorum, quem Deum vocari existimavimus, secundum fecit Deum, visibilem et sensibilem." Opera, II. p. 30.

commend the religion of Christ. Accordingly, they immediately fixed upon this *Logos* as the intelligence which either animated the body of Christ, or which was in some inexplicable manner united to his soul; and by the help of the allegorical method of interpreting the Scriptures, to which they had been sufficiently accustomed, they easily found authorities there for their opinions.

Thus, since we read in the book of Psalms, that *by the word of the Lord* (which, in the translation of the Seventy, is the *Logos*) *the heavens were made, &c.* they concluded that this *Logos* was Christ, and therefore, that, under God, he was the maker of the world. They also applied to him what Solomon says of *wisdom*, as having been *in the beginning with God*, and employed by him in making the world, in the book of Proverbs. But there is one particular passage in the book of Psalms in which they imagined that the origin of the *Logos*, by way of emanation from the divine mind, is most clearly expressed, which is what we render, *My heart is inditing a good matter*, Psalm xlv. 1, this *matter* being *Logos* in the Seventy, and the verb ερευγομενος *throwing out.* Nothing can appear to us more ungrounded than this supposition, and yet we find it in all the writers who treat of the divinity of Christ for several centuries, in ecclesiastical history. After this we cannot wonder at their being at no loss for proofs of their doctrine in any part of Scripture.

But Philo, tho the Jew, went before the Christians in the personification of the *Logos*, and in this mode of interpreting what is said of it in the Old Testament. For he calls this divine word *a second God*, and sometimes attributes the creation of the world to this second God, thinking it below the majesty of the great God himself. He also calls this personified attribute of God his πρωτογονος, or his *first-born*, and the *image of God.* He also says, that he is neither unbegotten, like God, nor begotten, as we are, but the middle

between the two extremes.[1] We also find that the Chaldee paraphrasts of the Old Testament, often render *the word of God*, as if it was a being, distinct from God, or some angel who bore the name of God, and acted by deputation from him. So, however, it has been interpreted, though with them it might be no more than an idiom of speech.

The Christian philosophers having once got the idea that the *Logos* might be interpreted of Christ, proceeded to explain what John says of the *Logos*, in the introduction of his gospel, to mean the same person, in direct opposition to what he really meant, which was that the *Logos*, by which all things were made, was not a being, distinct from God, but God himself, being his attribute, his wisdom and power, dwelling in Christ, speaking and acting by him. Accordingly we find some of the earlier Unitarians charging those who were called orthodox with an innovation in their interpretation of the term *Logos.* "But thou wilt tell me something strange, in saying that the *Logos* is the Son." *Hippolytus contra Noetum*, quoted by Beausobre.[2]

We find nothing like *divinity* ascribed to Christ before Justin Martyr, who, from being a philosopher, became a Christian, but always retained the peculiar habit of his former profession. As to Clemens Romanus, who was contemporary with the apostles, when he is speaking in the highest terms concerning Christ, he only calls him *the sceptre of the majesty of God.*[3] Whether Justin Martyr was the very first who started the notion of the pre-existence of Christ, and of his super-angelic or divine nature, is not certain, but we are not able to trace it any higher. We find it, indeed, briefly mentioned in the *Shepherd of Hermas*, but though this is supposed by some to be the Hermas mentioned by Paul, and to have written

---

[1] See "Le Platonisme devoilé," Ch. x. pp. 98–107; and Le Clerc's Comment on the Introduction to the First Chapter of John. (*P.*)
[2] *Histoire*, I. p. 540. (*P.*) L. iii. Ch. vi. Sect. xL [Note 2.]
[3] *Epistle*, Sect. xvi. (*P.*)

towards the end of the first century, others suppose this to be the work of one Hermes, brother of Pius, Bishop of Rome, and to have been written about the year 141, or perhaps later; and as this work contains such a pretension to visions and revelations, as I cannot but think unworthy of the Hermas mentioned by Paul, I cannot help being of this opinion. He says, "having seen an old rock and a new gate, they represent the son of God, who was more ancient than any creature, so as to be present with the Father at the creation, *ad condendam creaturam*."[1] The book was written in Greek, but we have only a Latin version of it.

Justin Martyr being a philosopher, and writing an apology for Christianity to a philosophical Roman emperor, would naturally wish to represent it in what would appear to him and other philosophers, the most favourable light; and this disposition appears by several circumstances. Thus he represents virtuous men, in all preceding ages, as being in a certain sense, *Christians ;* and apologizing for calling Christ the *son of God*, he says, that "this cannot be new to them who speak of Jupiter as having sons, and especially of Mercury, as his interpreter, and the instructor of all men, (λογον τον ἑρμηνευτικον και παντων διδασκαλον)."[2] On the same subject he says, "If Christ be a mere man, yet he deserves to be called the Son of God, on account of his wisdom, and the Heathens called God (i.e. Jupiter), the father of gods and men ; and if, in an extraordinary manner, he be the *Logos* of God, this is common with those who call Mercury the *Logos* that declares the will of God, (λογον τον παρα Θεου αγγελτικον)."[3]

With this disposition to make his religion appear in the most respectable light to the Heathens, and having himself professed the doctrine of Plato, can it be thought extraordinary, that he eagerly caught at the doctrine of the *Logos*, which he found ready formed to his hands in the works of Philo, and that he introduced it into the Christian system; that Irenæus, who was also educated among the philosophers, about the same time, did the same thing; or that others, who were themselves sufficiently pre-disposed to act the same part, should follow their example?

That the doctrine of the separate divinity of Christ was at first nothing more than a personification of a divine attribute, or of that wisdom and power by which God made the world, is evident from the manner in which the earliest writers who treat of the subject mention it. Justin Martyr, who was the first who undertook to prove that Christ was the medium of the divine dispensations in the Old Testament, as that "he was the person sometimes called an *Angel*, and sometimes *God* and *Lord*, and that he was the *man* who sometimes appeared to Abraham and Jacob, and he that spake to Moses from the fiery bush,"[4] does it, as we have seen above, with a considerable degree of diffidence; saying, that "if he should not be able to prove his pre-existence, it would not therefore follow that he was not the Christ." And as new opinions do not readily lay firm hold on the mind, forms of expression adapted to preceding opinions, will now and then occur; and as good sense will, in all cases, often get the better of imagination, we sometimes find these early writers drop the personification of the *Logos*, and speak of it as the mere attribute of God.

Thus Theophilus, who was contemporary with Justin, though a later writer, says, that when God said *let us make man*, he spake to nothing but his own *logos*, or wisdom ;[5] and, according to Origen, Christ was the eternal reason, or wisdom of God. He says, that, " by the second God, we mean only a virtue " (or perhaps power) " which comprehends all other virtues, or a reason which comprehends all

---

[1] *Hermæ* Pastor, L. iii. Sim. ix. Sect. xii. p. 115. (*P.*) Wake's *Gen. Epist.* Ed. 4, p. 320.
[2] *Apol.* I. Ed. Thirlby, p. 31. (*P.*)
[3] Ibid. p. 33. (*P.*)

[4] *Dial.* Edit. Thirlby, p. 264. (*P.*)
[5] Ad *Antolycum*, 1684, L. ii. p. 114. (*P.*)

other reasons, and that this reason (λογος) is particularly attached to the soul of Christ." [1] Also, explaining John i. 3, he says, " God can do nothing without reason (παρα λογον), i.e. without himself" (παρ᾽ ἑαυτον). [2]

Athenagoras, who wrote in the second century, calls Christ the first production (γεννημα) of the Father; but says he was not always actually produced (γενομενον), for that from the beginning, God, being an eternal mind, had reason (λογος) in himself, being from eternity rational (λογικος). [3]

Tatian, who was also his contemporary, gives us a fuller account of this matter. He says, " when he (that is, God) pleased, the word (*logos*) flowed from his simple essence; and this word not being produced in vain, became the first-begotten work of his spirit. This we know to be the origin of the word: but it was produced by *division*, not by *separation*, for that which is divided (μερισθεν) does not diminish that from which it derives its power. For, as many torches may be lighted from one, and yet the light of the first torch is not diminished, so the word (*logos*) proceeding from the power of the Father, does not leave the Father void of *logos*. Also, if I speak and you hear me, I am not void of speech (*logos*) on account of my speech (*logos*) going to you." [4]

If Irenæus had this idea of the generation of the *Logos*, as no doubt he had, it is no wonder that he speaks of it as a thing of so wonderful a nature. " If any one," says he, " asks us, how is the Son produced from the Father, we tell him that whether it be called *generation*, *nuncupation*, or *adapertion*, or by whatever other name this ineffable generation be called, no one knows it; neither Valentinus, nor Marcion, nor Saturninus, nor Basilides, nor Angels, nor Archangels, nor Principalities, nor Powers; but only the Father who begat, and the Son who is begotten." [5]

Tertullian, whose orthodoxy in this respect was never questioned, does not seem, however, to have any difficulty in conceiving how this business was, but writes in such a manner, as if he had been let into the whole secret; and we see in him the wretched expedients to which the orthodox of that age had recourse, in order to convert a mere *attribute* into a *real person*. For it must be understood that when the doctrine of the divinity of Christ was first started, it was not pretended, except by Irenæus in the passage above quoted (who was writing against persons who pretended to more knowledge of this mysterious business than himself), that there was anything *unintelligible* in it, or that could not be explained. Everything, indeed, in that age, was called a *mystery* that was reputed *sacred*, and the knowledge of which was confined to a few; but the idea of *unintelligible*, or *inexplicable*, was not then affixed to the word mystery. The heathen mysteries, from which the Christians borrowed the term, were things perfectly well known and understood by those who were *initiated*, though concealed from the vulgar.

" Before all things," says this writer, " God was alone; but not absolutely alone, for he had with him his own *reason*, since God is a rational being. This reason the Greeks called *Logos*, which word we now render *Sermo*. And that you may more easily understand this from yourself, consider that you, who are made in the image of God, and are a reasonable being, have reason within yourself. When you silently consider with yourself, it is by means of reason that you do it." [6]

---

[1] Origen contra Celsum. 1677, L. v. p. 259. (*P.*)
[2] Ibid. p. 247. (*P.*)
[3] Athenagoræ Opera, 1685, Apol. p. 83. (*P.*)
[4] Oratio contra Græcos, at the end of Justin's Works, 1686, p. 145. (*P.*)

[5] L. ii. C. xxviii. p. 176. (*P.*)
[6] " Ante omnia, Deus erat solus . . . Ceterum ne tunc quidem solus ; habebat, enim, secum, rationem suam . . . Rationalis etiam Deus . . . Hanc Græci Λογον dicunt, quo vocabulo etiam *Sermonem* appellamus. Idque, quo facilius intelligas ex teipso ante recognosce ut ex imagine et similitudine Dei, quam habeas et tu in temetipso rationem, qui es animal rationale . . . Vide

Upon this stating of the case, it was natural to object, that the reason of a man can never be converted into a *substance*, so as to constitute a thinking being, distinct from the man himself. But, he says, that though this is the case with respect to man, yet nothing can proceed from God but what is substantial. "You will say," says he, "but what is *speech* besides a *word* or *sound*, something unsubstantial and incorporeal? But I say that nothing unsubstantial and incorporeal can proceed from God, because it does not proceed from what is itself unsubstantial; nor can that want substance, which proceeds from so great a substance."[1]

Having in this manner (lame enough to be sure) got over the great difficulty of the conversion of a mere *attribute* into a *substance*, and a thinking substance too, this writer proceeds to ascertain the time when this conversion took place; and he, together with all the early Fathers, says that it was at the very instant of the creation. "Then," says he, "did this speech assume its *form* and *dress*, its *sound* and *voice*, when God said, *Let there be light*. This is the perfect nativity of the *word*, when it *proceeded from God*. From this time making him equal to himself" (by which phrase, however, we are only to understand *like* himself) "from which procession he became his son, his first-born, and only begotten, before all things."[2]

This method of explaining the origin of the personality of the *Logos* con-

tinued to the council of Nice, and even afterwards. For Lactantius, who was tutor to the son of Constantine, gives us the same account of this business, with some little variation, teaching us to distinguish the Son of God from the angels, whom he likewise conceived to be emanations from the divine mind. "How," says he, "did he beget him? (that is Christ). The Sacred Scriptures inform us that the Son of God is the *sermo* or *ratio* (the speech or reason) of God, also that the other angels are the breath of God, *spiritus Dei*. But *sermo* (speech) is breath emitted, together with a *voice*, expressive of something; and because *speech* and *breathing* proceed from different parts, there is a great difference between the Son of God and the other angels. For they are mere *silent breathings* (spiritus taciti), because they were created not to teach the knowledge of God, but for *service* (ad ministrandum). But he being also a *breathing* (spiritus), yet proceeding from the mouth of God with a voice and sound, is the *word;* for this reason, because he was to be a teacher of the knowledge of God," &c.[3] He therefore calls him *spiritus vocalis*. Then, in order to account for our breathings not producing similar spirits, he says that "our breathings are *dissoluble*, because we are mortal, but the breathings of God are permanent; they

---

quum tacitus tecum ipse congrederis, ratione hoc ipsum agi intra te, &c. *Adv. Praxeam*, C. v. pp. 502–3. Tertulliani Opera, 1675. (*P*.)
[1] Quid est enim, dices, *sermo* nisi *vox*, et *sonus oris* . . . vacuum nescio quid, et inane, et incorporale? At ego nihil dico de Deo inane et vacuum prodire potuisse, ut non de inani et vacuo prolatum, nec carere substantia, quod de tanta substantia processit, &c. Ibid. C. vii. pp. 503–4. (*P*.)
[2] Tunc . . . ipse sermo speciem et ornatum suum sumit, sonum et vocem, quum dicit Deus *fiat lux*. Hæc est nativitas perfecta sermonis, dum ex Deo procedit . . . Exinde cum parem sibi faciens, de quo procedendo filius factus est *primogenitus*, ut ante omnia genitus, et unigenitus, ut solus Deo genitus. Ibid. p. 503. (*P*.)

[3] Lactantii Opera, 1560. Inst. L. iv. Sect. viii. pp. 370–1. (*P*.) "Primum nec sciri a quoquam possunt, nec enarrari, opera divina: sed tamen sanctæ litteræ docent, in quibus cautum est, illum Dei filium, Dei esse sermonem, sive etiam rationem; itemque cæteros angelos Dei spiritus esse. Nam sermo est spiritus cum voce aliquid significante prolatus. Sed tamen quoniam spiritus et sermo diversis partibus feruntur, siquidem spiritus naribus, ore sermo procedit, magna inter hunc Dei filium et cæteros angelos differentia est. Illi enim ex Deo taciti spiritus exierunt; quia non ad doctrinam Dei tradendam, sed ad ministerium creabantur. Ille vero cum sit et ipse spiritus, tamen cum voce ac sono ex Dei ore processit, sicut verbum, ea scilicet ratione, quia voce ejus ad populum fuerat usurus; id est, quod ille magister futurus esset doctrinæ Dei et cœlestis arcani ad homines perferendi: quod ipsum primo locutus est, ut per eum ad nos loqueretur, et ille vocem Dei ac voluntatem nobis revelaret." Opera, I. p. 289.

live and feel, because he is immortal, the giver of sense and life." [1]

All the early Fathers speak of Christ as not having existed always, except as reason exists in man, viz. an attribute of the Deity; and for this reason they speak of the Father as not having been a Father always, but only from the time that he made the world. " Before anything was made," says Theophilus, "God had the *logos* for his council; being his *νους* or *φρονησις* (reason or understanding); but when he proceeded to produce what he had determined upon, he then emitted the *logos*, the first-born of every creature, not emptying himself of *logos* (reason), but *λογον γεννησας* (begetting reason), and always conversing with his own *logos*" [2] (reason).

Justin Martyr also gives the same explanation of the emission of the *logos* from God, without depriving himself of reason, and he illustrates it by what we observe in ourselves. For, "in uttering any word," he says, "we beget a word (*logos*), not taking anything from ourselves, so as to be lessened by it, but as we see one fire produced from another." [3]

Clemens Alexandrinus calls the Father alone *without beginning* (*αναρχος*) and immediately after he characterizes the Son, as the *beginning*, and the *first-fruits* of things (*αρχην και απαρχην των οντων*) from whom we must learn the Father of all, the most ancient and beneficent of beings. [4] Tertullian expressly says that God was not always a father or a judge, since he could not be a father before he had a son, nor a judge before sin; and there was a time when both *sin* and the *son* (which made God to be a *judge* and a *father*) were not." [5]

This language was held at the time of the council of Nice, for Lactantius says, "God, before he undertook the making of the world, produced a holy and incorruptible spirit, which he might call his *Son;* and afterwards he by him created innumerable other spirits, whom he calls *angels.*" [6] The church, says Hilary, "knows one unbegotten God, and one only begotten Son of God. It acknowledges the Father to be [eternal and] without origin, and it acknowledges the origin of the Son from eternity, not himself without beginning, but from him who is without beginning (*ab initiabili*)." [7] It is not impossible that Hilary might have an idea of the eternal generation of the Son, though the fathers before the council of Nice had no such idea. For the Platonists in general thought that the creation was from eternity, there never having been any time in which the Divine Being did not act. But, in general, by the phrase *from eternity,* and *before all time,* &c., the ancient Christian writers seem to have meant any period before the creation of the world.

Consistently with this representation, but very inconsistently with the modern doctrine of the Trinity, the fathers supposed the Son of God to have been begotten *voluntarily,* so that it depended upon the Father himself whether he would have a son or not. " I will produce you another testimony from the Scriptures," says Justin Martyr, " that in the beginning, before all the creatures, God begat from himself a certain reasonable power (*δυναμιν λογικην*) who by the spirit is sometimes called *the glory of God,* sometimes *God,* sometimes the *Lord* and *Logos,* because he is subservient to his Father's will, and was begotten at his Father's pleasure." [8]

Novatian says, " God the Father is

---

[1] Lactantii Opera, 1660. Inst. L. iv. Sect. viii. pp. 370–1. (*P.*) "Nostri spiritus dissolubiles sunt, quia mortales sumus. Dei autem spiritus et vivunt et manent et sentiunt; quia ipse immortalis est et sensus et vitæ dator. Opera, I. p. 290.
[2] Ad Autolycum, L. ii. p. 129. (*P.*)
[3] *Dial.* Edit. Thirlby, pp. 266–7. (*P.*)
[4] Strom. L. vii. Opera, p. 700. (*P.*)
[5] Ad Hermogenem, C. iii. p. 234. *Paris,* 1675. (*P.*)

[6] Inst. L. iv. C. vi. p. 364. (*P.*) "Deus igitur machinator constitutorque rerum,...antequam præclarum hoc opus mundi adoriretur, sanctum et incorruptibilem spiritum genuit, quem Filium nuncuparet. Et quamvis alios postea innumerabiles per ipsum creavisset, quos angelos dicimus," &c. Opera, I. p. 284.
[7] De Trinitate, L. iv. (*P.*)
[8] *Dial.* Ed. Thirlby, p. 266. (*P.*)

calls him the only God (*solus et verus Deus*);[1] and according to several of the most considerable of the early Christian writers, a common epithet by which the Father is distinguished from the Son, is, that he alone is (αυτοθεος) or *God of himself.*

Origen, quoted by Dr. Clarke, says, "Hence we may solve the scruple of many pious persons, who, through fear lest they should make two Gods, fall into false and wicked notions....We must tell them that he who is of himself God, (αυτοθεος) is *that God* (ὁ Θεος) (as our Saviour, in his prayer to his Father says, *that they may know thee, the only true God;*) but that whatever is God besides that self-existent person, being so only by communication of his divinity, cannot so properly be styled (ὁ Θεος) *that God*, but rather (Θεος) a divine person."[2]

the form of a man, speaking by the order of the principal God." Again, "then, at length, did God Almighty, the only God, send Christ."[7]

Such language as this was held till the time of the council of Nice. Alexander, who is very severe on Eusebius, bishop of Nicomedia, who was an Arian, says, in his circular letter to the bishops, "the Son is of a middle nature between the first cause of all things, and the creatures, which were created out of nothing."[8] Athanasius himself, as quoted by Dr. Clarke, says, "the nature of God is the cause both of the Son and of the Holy Spirit, and of all creatures."[9] He also says, "There is but one God, because the Father is but one, yet is the Son also God, having such a sameness as that of a son to a father."[10]

Lactantius says, "Christ taught that there is one God, and that he alone ought to be worshipped; neither did he ever call himself God, because he would not have been true to his trust, if, being sent to take away gods (that is, a multiplicity of gods) and to assert one, he had introduced another besides that One...Because he assumed nothing at all to himself, he received the dignity of perpetual priest, the honour of sovereign king, the power of a judge, and the name of God."[11]

Hilary, who wrote twelve books on the doctrine of the Trinity, after the council of Nice, to prove that the Father himself is the only self-existing God, and in a proper sense the only true God (*quod solus innascibilis et quod solus verus sit*) after alleging a passage from the prophet Isaiah, quotes

Arnobius says, "Christ, a God, under

[7] Arnobius adversus *Gentes*, 1610. L. ii. pp. 50, 57. (*P.*)
[8] Theodorit. Eccles. Hist. L. i. C. iv. pp. 16. 17. (*P.*)
[9] P. 276. (*P.*)
[10] P. 222. (*P.*)
[11] *Institut.*, L. iv. C. xiv. (*P.*) "Decuit enim quod unus Deus sit, eumque solum coli oportere; nec unquam se ipse Deum dixit, quia non servasset fidem, si missus ut deos tolleret, et unum assereret, induceret alium, præter Unum. ...Propterea quia tam fidelis extitit, quia sibi nihil prorsus assumpsit, ut mandata mittentis impleret, et sacerdotis perpetui dignitatem, et regis summi honorem, et judicis potestatem, et Dei nomen accepit." Opera, I. p. 309.

[1] L. iii. C. vi. p. 209. (*P.*)
[2] Scrip. Doc. p. 338.
[3] Sandii Nucleus Hist. Eccl. p. 94. (*P.*)
[4] Contra *Celsum*, L. vi. p. 323. (*P.*)
[5] Novatiani Opera, 1724. C. xxiii. (*P.*)
[6] Ibid. C. xxxi. (*P.*)

in support of it the saying of our Saviour, "This is life eternal, that they might know thee the only true God, and Jesus Christ whom thou hast sent."[1] Much more might be alleged from this writer, to the same purpose.

Lastly, Epiphanius says, "Who is there that does not assert that there is only one God, the Father Almighty, from whom his only begotten Son truly proceeded?"[2]

Indeed, that the Fathers of the council of Nice could not mean the Son was strictly speaking equal to the Father, is evident from their calling him *God of God*, which in that age was always opposed *to God of himself* (αυτοθεος) that is, *self-existent* or *independent;* which was always understood to be the prerogative of the Father. It is remarkable that when the writers of that age speak of Christ as *existing from eternity*, they did not therefore suppose that he was properly *self-existent*. Thus Alexander, bishop of Alexandria, says, "We believe that the Son was always from the Father; but let no one by the word *always* be led to imagine him *self-existent* (αγεννητος) for neither the term *was*, nor *always*, nor *before all ages*, mean the same thing as *self-existent* (αγεννητος)."[3]

On these principles the primitive fathers had no difficulty in the interpretation of that saying of our Lord, "my Father is greater than I." They never thought of saying, that he was *equal to the Father with respect to his divinity, though inferior with respect to his humanity;* which is the only sense of the passage that the doctrine of the Trinity in its present state admits of. For they thought that the Son was in all respects, and in his whole person, inferior to his Father, as having derived his being from him.

Tertullian had this idea of the passage when he says, "the Father is all substance, but the Son is a derivation from him, and a part, as he himself

declares, 'the Father is greater than I.'"[4] It is also remarkable, as Mr. Whiston observes, that the ancient fathers, both Greek and Latin, never interpret Phil. ii. 7, to mean an equality of the Son to the Father.[5] Novatian says, "He, therefore, though he was in the form of God, did not make himself equal to God (*non est rapinam arbitratus equalem se Deo esse*), for though he remembered he was *God of God* the Father, he never compared himself to God the Father, being mindful that he was of his Father, and that he had this, because his Father gave it him."[6]

It also deserves to be noticed, that notwithstanding the supposed derivation of the Son from the Father, and therefore their being of *the same substance*, most of the early Christian writers thought the text "I and my Father are one," was to be understood of an unity or harmony of *disposition* only. Thus Tertullian observes, that the expression is *unum, one thing*, not *one person;* and he explains it to mean *unity, likeness, conjunction*, and of the *love that the Father bore to the Son.*[7] Origen says, "let him consider that text, 'all that believed were of one heart and of one soul,' and then he will understand this, 'I and my Father are one.'"[8] Novatian says, one *thing* (*unum*) being in the neuter gender, signifies an agreement of society, not an unity of person, and he explains it by this passage in Paul, "he that planteth and he that watereth are both one."[9] But the fathers of the council of Sardica, held A.D. 347, reprobated the opinion that the union of the Father and Son consists in consent and concord only, apprehending it to be a *strict unity of substance;*[10] so much farther was the doctrine of the Trinity advanced at that time.

---

[5] Collections, p. 109. (*P.*)
[6] Opera, C. xvii. p. 84. (*P.*)
[7] Adv. *Praxeam*, C. xxii. p. 513. (*P.*)
[8] Contra *Celsum*, L. viii. p. 386. (*P.*)
[9] C. xxvii. p. 99. (*P.*)
[10] Theodorit. L. ii. C. viii, p. 82. (*P.*)

SECTION IV.

OF THE DIFFICULTY WITH WHICH THE
DOCTRINE OF THE DIVINITY OF CHRIST
WAS ESTABLISHED.

It is sufficiently evident from many circumstances, that the doctrine of the divinity of Christ did not establish itself without much opposition, especially from the *unlearned* among the Christians, who thought that it savoured of *Polytheism*, that it was introduced by those who had had a philosophical education, and was by degrees adopted by others, on account of its covering the great *offence of the cross*, by exalting the personal dignity of our Saviour.

To make the new doctrine less exceptionable, the advocates for it invented a new term, viz. *economy* or *distribution*, as it may be rendered; saying they were far from denying the *unity of God*, but that there was a certain economy, or distribution respecting the divine nature and attributes, which did not interfere with it; for that, according to this economy the Son might be God, without detracting from the supreme divinity of the Father. But this new term, it appears, was not well understood or easily relished, by those who called themselves the advocates for the *monarchy of the Father*, a term much used in those days, to denote the supremacy and sole divinity of the Father, in opposition to that of the Son. All this is very clear from the following passage in Tertullian:

"The simple, the ignorant, and the unlearned, who are always the greater part[1] of the body of Christians, since the rule of faith itself," (meaning perhaps the *apostles' creed*, or as much of it as was in use in his time,) "transfers their worship of many gods to the one true God, not understanding that the unity of God is to be maintained, but with the *economy,*

dread this economy, imagining that this number and disposition of a trinity is a division of the unity. They therefore will have it, that we are worshippers of the two, and even of three Gods; but that they are the worshippers of one God only. We, they say, hold the *monarchy*. Even the Latins have learned to bawl out for monarchy, and the Greeks themselves will not understand the economy;"[2] monarchy being a Greek term and yet adopted by the Latins, and economy, though a Greek term, not being relished even by the Greek Christians.

Upon another occasion we see by this writer how offensive the word *Trinity* was to the generality of Christians. "If the number of the Trinity still shocks you," &c., says he.[3] For this reason, no doubt, Origen says, "that to the carnal they taught the gospel in a literal way, preaching Jesus Christ, and him crucified, but to persons farther advanced, and burning with love for divine celestial wisdom," (by which he must mean the philosophical part of their audience) "they communicated the *Logos*."[4]

Origen candidly calls these adherents to the doctrine of the strict unity of God, pious persons (φιλοθεους). "Hence," says he, "we may solve the scruple of many pious persons, who, through fear lest they should make two gods, fall into false and wicked notions." He endeavours to relieve them in this manner. "This scruple of many pious persons may thus be

[1] This shows that the greater part of Christians, in the time of Tertullian, were Unitarians, and exceedingly averse to the doctrine of the Trinity. (*P.*)

[2] "Simplices enim quippe ne dixerim imprudentes et idiotæ, quæ major semper credentium pars est, quoniam et ipsa regula fidei a pluribus diis seculi ad unicum et Deum verum transfert, non intelligentes unicum quidem, sed cum suâ economiâ esse, credendum, expavescunt ad economiam. Numerum et dispositionem trinitatis divisionem præsumunt unitatis . . . Itaque duos et tres jam jactitant, a nobis prædicari, se vero unius Dei cultores præsumunt . . . Monarchiam inquiunt tonemus . . . Monarchiam sonare student Latini, economiam intelligere nolunt etiam Græci." Adv. *Praxeam*, Sect. iii. p. 502. (*P.*)

[3] "Si te adhuc numerus scandalizat trinitatis," &c. Adv. *Praxeam*, Sect. xii. p. 506.

[4] Preface to his Comment on John, Opera, II. p. 255. (*P.*)

solved. "We must tell them, that he who is of himself God, (αυτοθεος) is that God, (God with the article) (ὁ Θεος),—but that whatsoever besides that self-existent person," is "rather a divine person, is God without the article, (Θεος)" as was observed before.[1] How far this solution of the difficulty was satisfactory to these pious, unlearned Christians does not appear. It does not seem calculated to remove a difficulty of any great magnitude.

That these ancient Unitarians, under all the names by which their adversaries thought proper to distinguish them, have been greatly misrepresented, is acknowledged by all who are candid among the moderns. The learned Beausobre, himself a Trinitarian, is satisfied that it was a zeal for the unity of God that actuated the Sabellians[2] (who were no more than Unitarians under a particular denomination). Epiphanius says, that when a Sabellian met the orthodox, they would say, "My friends, do we believe one God or three?"[3]

Eusebius speaking with great wrath against Marcellus of Ancyra, allows that he did not deny the personality of the Son, but for fear of establishing two Gods.[4] This also appears from the manner in which Eusebius expresses himself when he answers to the charge of introducing two Gods. "But you are afraid, (φοβῃ) perhaps, lest acknowledging two distinct subsistences, you should introduce two original principles, and so destroy the monarchy of God."[5]

Basil complains of the popularity of the followers of Marcellus, whose disciple Photinus is said to have been, at the same time that the name of Arius

was execrated. "Unto this very time," says he, in his letter to Athanasius, "in all their letters they fail not to anathematize the hated name of Arius; but with Marcellus, who has profanely taken away the very existence of the divinity of the only begotten Son, and abused the signification of the word *Logos*, with this man they seem to find no fault at all."[6]

It was impossible not to perceive that this *economy*, and the style and rank of *God*, given to Christ, made a system, entirely different from that of the Jews, as laid down in the Old Testament. For Christians either had not at that time laid much stress on any argument for the doctrine of the Trinity drawn from the books of Moses, or at least had not been able to satisfy the Jews, or the Jewish Christians, with any representations of that kind. Tertullian, therefore, makes another, and, indeed, a very bold attempt for the same purpose, saying, that it was peculiar to the Jewish faith so to maintain the unity of God, as not to admit the Son or Spirit to any participation of the divinity with him; but that it was the characteristic of the gospel, to introduce the Son and Spirit, as making one God with the Father. He says, that God was determined to renew his covenant in this *new form*. I shall give his own words, which are much more copious on the subject, in a note.[7]

When the philosophizing Christians went beyond the mere personification of a divine attribute, and proceeded to speak of the *real substance*, as I may say, of the divine *Logos*, they were evidently in danger of making a diversity, or a separation in the divine nature.

---

[1] Clarke's *Scrip. Doc.* p. 338. See *supra*, p. 17.

[2] "Lorsque j'en recherche la source 〈L'Heresie Sabellienne〉, je n'en trouve point d'autre que la crainte de multiplier la Divinité, en multipliant les Personnes Divines, et de ramener dans l'Eglise le Polythéisme, qui renverse le premier principe de la Religion. C'est ce que témoignent assez unanimément les anciens Pères." L. iii. Ch. vi. Sect. viii. l. p. 535.

[3] *Hær.* 62, Opera, I. p. 514. (*P.*)

[4] Ibid. p. 536. (*P.*)

[5] Clarke's *Scrip. Doc.* p. 345. (*P.*)

[6] Opera, III. p. 80. (*P.*)

[7] "Judaicæ fidei ista res sic unum Deum credere, ut Filium adnumerare ei nolis, et post Filium, Spiritum. Quid ⬛n erit inter nos et illos, nisi differentia ista. Quod opus evangelii . . . . si non exinde Pater et Filius et Spiritus . . . . unum deum *sistunt.* Sic Deus voluit novare sacramentum, ut nove unus crederetur per Filium et Spiritum, et coram jam Deus in suis propriis nominibus et personis cognosceretur, qui et retro per Filium et Spiritum predicatus non intelligebatur." Adv. *Praxeam*, Sect. xxx. p. 518. (*P.*)

That the common people did make this very objection to the new doctrine is clearly intimated by Tertullian. "When I say that the Father is one, the Son another, and the Spirit a third, an unlearned or perverse person understands me as if I meant a *diversity*, and in this diversity he pretends that there must be a separation of the Father, Son and Spirit." [1]

The objection is certainly not ill stated. Let us now consider how this writer answers it: for at this time it was not pretended that the subject was above human comprehension, or that it could not be explained by proper comparisons. In order, therefore, to show that the Son and Spirit might be produced from the Father, and yet not be separated from him, he says that God produced the *Logos* (*Sermonem*) as the root of a tree produces the branch, as a fountain produces the river, or the sun a beam of light. [2] The last of these comparisons is also adopted by Athenagoras, in his Apology, in which he describes a beam of light as a thing not detached from the sun, but as flowing out of it, and back to it again. [3] For one Hierarchas had been censured for comparing the production of the Son from the Father to the lighting of one candle at another, because the second candle was a thing subsisting of itself, and entirely separated from the former, so as to be incompatible with unity. [4]

Justin Martyr, however, as we have seen, made use of the same comparison, and as far as appears, without censure. But after his time, the ideas of philosophizing Christians had undergone a change. He and his contemporaries were only solicitous to make out something like divinity in the Son, without considering him as united in one substance with the Father, the unity of God being then defended on no other principle than that of the supremacy of the Father; so that, though Christ might be called God in a lower sense of the word, the Father was God in a sense so much higher than that, that strictly speaking, it was still true that there was but one God, and the Father only was that God. But, by the time of Hilary, the philosophizing Christians, finding perhaps that this account of the unity of God did not give entire satisfaction, were willing to represent the Son, not only as deriving his being and his divinity from the Father, but as still inseparably united to him, and never properly detached from him; and, therefore, the former comparison of one torch lighted by another would no longer answer the purpose. But this could not be objected to the comparison of the root and the branch, the fountain and the stream, or the sun and the beam of light, according to the philosophy of those times. For, in all these cases, things were produced from the substance of their respective origins, and yet were not separated from them.

These explanations suited very well with the doctrine of the Trinity as held by the council of Nice; when it was not pretended, as it is now, that each person in the Trinity is equally eternal and uncaused. But they certainly did not sufficiently provide for the distinct personality of the Father, Son and Spirit; which, however, especially with respect to the two former, they asserted. With respect to the latter, it is not easy to collect their opinions; for, in general, they expressed themselves as if the Spirit was only a divine power.

In order to satisfy the advocates of the proper unity of God, those who then maintained the divinity of Christ make, upon all occasions, the most solemn protestations against the introduction of two Gods, for the deification of the Spirit was then not much objected to by them. But they thought

---

[1] "Ecce enim dico alium esse Patrem, et alium Filium, et alium Spiritum. Male accipit idiotes quisque aut perversus hoc dictum, quasi diversitatem sonet, et ex diversitate separationem protendat Patris, Filii et Spiritus. Adv. *Praxeam*, Sect. ix. p. 504. (*P.*)

[2] Adv. *Praxeam*, C. viii. p. 504. (*P.*)

[3] P. 86. (*P.*)

[4] See Hilary de Trinitate, L. iv. [Sect. xii.] Opera, p. 59. (*P.*)

that they guarded sufficiently against the worship of two Gods, by strongly asserting the inferiority and subordination of the Son to the Father; some of them alleging one circumstance of this inferiority, and others another.

Tertullian cautions us not to destroy the monarchy when we admit a Trinity, since it is to be restored from the Son to the Father.[1] Novatian lays the stress on Christ's being begotten and the Father not begotten. "If," says he, "the Son had not been begotten, he and the Father being upon a level, they would both be unbegotten, and, therefore, there would be two Gods," &c.[2] Again, he says, "when it is said that Moses was appointed a God to Pharaoh, shall it be denied to Christ, who is a God, not to Pharaoh, but to the whole universe?"[3] But this kind of divinity would not satisfy the moderns.

Eusebius's apology for this qualified divinity of Christ (for the manner in which he writes is that of an *apology*, and shows that this new doctrine was very offensive to many in his time) turns upon the same hinge with the former of these illustrations of Novatian. "If," says he, "this makes them apprehensive lest we should seem to introduce two Gods, let them know that, though we do indeed acknowledge the Son to be God, yet there is [absolutely] but one God, even he who alone is without original and unbegotten, who has his divinity properly of himself, and is the cause even to the Son himself, both of his being, and of his being such as he is; by whom the Son himself confesses that he lives (declaring expressly, *I live by the Father*) ..... and declares to be greater than himself," and "to be even his God."[4] This, indeed, is written by an Arian, but it is the language of all the Trinitarians of his time: for then it had not occurred to any person to say that the *one God* was the Trinity, or the Father,

Son and Spirit in conjunction, but always the Father only. The distinction between *person* and *being*, which is the salvo at present, was not then known. Some persons in opposing Sabellius, having made three *hypostases*, which we now render *persons*, separate from each other, Dionysius, Bishop of Rome, quoted with approbation by Athanasius himself, said that it was making three Gods.[5]

I have observed before, and may have occasion to repeat the observation hereafter, that, in many cases, the phraseology remains when the ideas which originally suggested it have disappeared; but that the phraseology is an argument for the pre-existence of the corresponding ideas. Thus it has been the constant language of the church, from the time of the apostles, and is found upon all occasions in their writings, that *Christ suffered;* meaning, no doubt, in his *whole person*, in everything which really entered into his constitution. This, however, was not easily reconcilable with the opinion of any portion of the divinity being a proper part of Christ; and therefore the Docetæ, who first asserted the divine origin of the Son of God, made no scruple to deny, in express words, that Christ suffered. For they said, that *Jesus* was one thing, and the *Christ*, or the heavenly inhabitant of Jesus, another; and that when Jesus was going to be crucified, Christ left him.

Irenæus, writing against this heresy, quotes the uniform language of the Scriptures as a sufficient refutation of it; maintaining that *Christ himself*, in his whole nature, suffered. "It was no *impassible Christ*," he says, "but Jesus Christ himself, who suffered for us."[6] It is evident, however, that this writer, who was one of the first that adopted the idea of the divinity of Christ (but on a principle different from that of the Docetæ, viz. the personification of the *Logos* of the Father),

[1] Adv. *Praxeam*, C. iv. p. 502. (*P.*)
[2] C. xxxi. p. 122. (*P.*)
[3] C. xx. p. 77. (*P.*)
[4] Clarke's *Scrip. Doc.* p. 343. (*P.*)

[5] De *Synodo Nicœna*, Opera, p. 275. (*P.*)
[6] L. iii. C. xx. p. 246. (*P.*)

could not himself strictly maintain the passibility of his whole nature; for then he must have held that something, which was a proper part of the Deity himself, was capable of suffering. He, therefore, but in a very awkward and ineffectual manner, endeavours to make a case different from that of the Docetæ, by supposing a *mixture* of the two natures in Christ.

"For this reason," he says, "The word of God became man, and the Son of God became the Son of man, being mixed with the word of God, that receiving the adoption, he might become the Son of God. For we could not receive immortality, unless we were united to immortality," &c.[1] Origen also, in his third book against Celsus, speaks of the mixture of the humanity with the divinity of Christ. He even speaks of the mortal quality of the very body of Christ, as changed into a divine quality.[2]

This confusion of ideas and inconsistency appears to have been soon perceived. For we presently find that all those who are called *orthodox*, ran into the very error of the Docetæ, maintaining that it only was the *human nature* of Christ that suffered, while another part of his nature, which was no less essential to his being *Christ*, was incapable of suffering; and to this day all who maintain the proper divinity of Christ, are in the same dilemma. They must either flatly contradict the Scriptures, and say, with the Docetæ, that Christ did not suffer, or that the divine nature itself may feel pain. This being deemed manifest impiety, they generally adopted the former opinion, viz. that the human nature of Christ only suffered, and contented themselves with asserting some inexplicable mixture of the two natures; notwithstanding the idea of one part of the *same person* (and of the intellectual part too) not feeling pain, while the other did, is evidently inconsistent with **any idea** of proper *union* or *mixture*.

The very next writer we meet with, after Irenæus, viz. Tertullian, asserts, contrary to him, that it was not Christ, but only the human nature of Christ, that suffered. "This voice," says he, "'My God, my God, why hast thou forsaken me?' was from the *flesh* and *soul*, that is, the *man*, and not the *word* or *spirit*, that is, it was not of *the God*, who is impassible, and who left the Son while he gave up his man to death."[3] What could any of the Docetæ have said more?

Arnobius expresses himself to the same purpose. Speaking of the death of Christ, with which the Christians were continually reproached, "That death," says he, "which you speak of, was the death of *the man* that he had put on, not of himself, of the burden, not of the bearer."[4]

Hilary, who wrote after the council of Nice, went even farther than this, and maintained at large that the body of Christ was at all times incapable of feeling pain, that it had no need of refreshment by meat and drink, and that he ate and drank only to show that he had a body. "Could that hand," says he, "which gave an ear to the man that Peter smote, feel the nail that was driven through it? And could that flesh feel a wound which removed the pain of a wound from another?"[5]

Later writers, indeed, did not follow Hilary in this extravagance, but Epiphanius says, that Christ in his death upon the cross, suffered nothing in his divinity.[6] This, too, is the language of those who are called orthodox at this day, but how this is consistent with their doctrine of *atonement*, which

---

[3] "Hæc vox carnis et animæ, id est hominis, non sermonis, non spiritus, id est non dei, propterea emissa est, ut impassibilem deum ostenderet qui sic filium dereliquit dum hominem ejus tradidit in mortem." Adv. *Praxeam*, C. xxx. p. 518. (*P.*)
[4] "Mors illa quam dicitis assumpti hominis fuit, non ipsius, gestaminis, non gestantis." Adversus *Gentes*, L. i. p. 22. (*P.*)
[5] L. x. p. 244. (*P.*)
[6] *Hær.* 20, Opera, I. p. 49. (*P.*)

[1] L. iii. C. xxi. Opera, p. 249. (*P.*)
[2] Ibid. p. 186. (*P.*)

supposes an *infinite satisfaction to have been made* to the justice of God by the death of Christ, does not easily appear.

SECTION V.

AN ACCOUNT OF THE UNITARIANS BEFORE THE COUNCIL OF NICE.

BEFORE I proceed to the Arian controversy, I must take notice of those who distinguished themselves by maintaining the proper humanity of Christ in this early period. That the Christian church in general held this doctrine till the time of Victor, was the constant assertion of those who professed it about this time, and I think I have shown that this was true.

One of the first who distinguished himself by asserting the simple humanity of Christ, was Theodotus of Byzantium, who, though a tanner, is acknowledged to have been a man of ability, and even of learning. He is said to have been well received at Rome, and at first even by Victor, the bishop of that city, who afterwards excommunicated him.

About the same time appeared Artemon, from whom those who maintained this opinion were by some called *Artemonites;* but it appears from the writings of Tertullian, that they were more generally called *Monarchists,* from their asserting the proper unity of the divine nature, and the supremacy of God the Father with respect to Christ. By their enemies they were called *Patripassians,* because they were charged with asserting that the Father was so united to the person of Christ, as even to have suffered with him. But Lardner treats this as a calumny.[1] It should seem, however, that some of them went so far (since Tertullian so particularly quotes it as their own language) as to say that the Father felt compassion for his suffering Son.[2] But

this language might be used by them in a figurative sense, in which sense various passions are in the Scriptures ascribed to God.

Beausobre[3] thinks them to have been entirely free from this imputation, and imagines it to have arisen from their adversaries, designedly or undesignedly, mixing their own ideas with theirs, and especially confounding the two terms *Logos* and *Son of God.* In consequence of this, when the Unitarians asserted that the Father and the *Logos* were one person, they would of course charge them with maintaining that the Father suffered in the Son. Indeed Tertullian, as Beausobre observes, contradicts himself when he charges the Unitarians with this opinion, because in other parts of his writings, he expressly says that they believed the Father to be *impassible.*[4]

Praxeas the Montanist, and a man of genius and learning, against whom Tertullian writes, was an Unitarian, and so probably were many others of that sect.[5] For their peculiar opinions and practices, as Montanists, had no relation to any particular opinion concerning the nature of Christ.

It is very evident, that about this time the Unitarians were very numerous in all parts of the Christian world; and as they were not distinguished by having assemblies separate from those of other Christians, which Mosheim allows,[6] their opinion certainly could not be deemed *heretical.* It is even acknowledged that many of these Unitarians (though none of their writings are now come down to us) were men of science. They are particularly said to have been addicted to geometry, and are also said to have treated questions in theology in a geometrical method; but no particulars of this kind are known to us. It is very possible that this circumstance (which is mentioned

---

[1] Hist. of Heretics, p. 413. (*P.*) Works, IX. p. 497.
[2] Adv. Praxeam, Sect. xxix. p. 518. (*P.*)

[3] Vol. I. p. 538. (*P.*) L. iii. C. vi. Sect. x.
[4] Vol. I. p. 534. (*P.*) L. iii. C. vi. Sect. vii.
[5] Lardner's Hist. of Heretics, pp. 398, 411. (*P.*) Works, IX. pp. 488, 496.
[6] Ecclesiastical History, 2nd edit. 1758, I. p. 191. (*P.*) Cent. ii. Pt. ii. Ch. v. Sect. xx.

by their adversaries by way of reproach) might have arisen from their endeavouring to show, that if the Father, the Son, and the Holy Spirit, (if this last was then considered as a distinct person,) were each of them God, in any proper sense of the word, there must be more gods than one. Such geometry as this, I doubt not, gave great offence.

In the following century, viz. the third, we find Noetus, Sabellius, and Paul, bishop of Samosata, the most distinguished among the Unitarians. Noetus was of Smyrna, and is said to have been a disciple of Artemon. Sabellius was bishop or priest of Cyrene, in Africa, in which country the Unitarian opinion, as taught by Noetus, is said to have been generally adopted. It is, indeed, said by ecclesiastical historians, that many bishops in this country were brought over to this opinion by Sabellius. But it is much more probable that they held the same opinion before. In that age the prevailing bias was to magnify the personal dignity of Christ, and not to lessen it; so that we find few or no clear instances of any who, having once maintained that Christ was either God or a super-angelic being, and the maker of this world under God, came afterwards to believe that he was merely a man. Both Noetus and Sabellius were charged by their adversaries with being Patripassians: but the Unitarians of that age asserting, as the Socinians now do, that all the divinity of the Son, was that of the Father residing in him, and acting by him, was sufficient to give a handle for that injurious representation of their opinion.

There was nothing peculiar in the doctrine of Sabellius, though he is generally charged with maintaining that there were three persons in the Trinity, but that these three *persons* or rather *characters*, (προσωπα) were only different names or attributes of the same person or being. If this was a fair representation, Sabellius and his followers must have meant to disguise their Unitarian sentiments in terms appropriated to the orthodoxy of their age. But though many persons are said to do this at present, Sabellius himself is not charged with it by any of his opponents. On the contrary, he is generally said to have been a disciple of Noetus. It is therefore probable, as Beausobre conjectures, that this representation arose from his adversaries misapprehending what he said concerning the Father and the Son being *one*, and concerning the *Father being in him*, and *doing the works*, as our Saviour expresses himself. At the same time Sabellius might mean nothing more than the most avowed Socinians mean by such language at this day.

Paul, bishop of Samosata, a man of genius and learning, but said to have been of a profligate life, and charged with the arrogance and ambition of other bishops of great sees in those times, made himself obnoxious by maintaining the Unitarian principles, and was condemned for them in several councils held at Antioch, as well as on other accounts. His opinions are acknowledged to have spread much, and to have alarmed the orthodox greatly.[1] But when we read of such persons as this bishop making many converts to the doctrine of the humanity of Christ, I cannot help suspecting, for the reason mentioned above, that it is to be understood of the numbers who were before of that opinion, being encouraged by men of their learning, ability and influence, to declare themselves more openly than they had done before; having been overborne by the philosophizing Christians of that age, the current of men's opinions having for some time set that way. This Paul of Samosata is represented by Epiphanius as alleging, in defence of his doctrine, the words of Moses, *the Lord thy God is one Lord;* and he is not charged by him, as others were, with maintaining that the Father suf-

---

[1] Sueur, A.D. [264,] 265. *(P.)*

fered;[1] and indeed from this time we hear no more of that accusation, though the tenets of the Unitarians most probably continued the same.

To these we might add, as falling within the same century, Beryllus, bishop of Bostra, in Arabia, said to have been a man of learning and modesty, and to have maintained that Christ had no being before he was born of the Virgin Mary, and had no divinity besides that of the Father residing in him.[2] But he is said to have been converted to the orthodox faith by Origen. It is to be regretted that we have no further information concerning this bishop and other Christians in Arabia. Many of them, we are told, maintained, contrary to the philosophy of their times, that the soul died with the body, and that all men would be in a state of insensibility from the time of their death to that of the general resurrection.[3]

I shall close this account of the ancient Unitarians with just mentioning Photinus, bishop of Sirmium, though he flourished after the council of Nice; because he is the last of the Unitarians we read of till the revival of the doctrine in the last age. For though it can hardly be supposed that the opinion of the simple humanity of Christ was wholly extinct, those who maintained it were overborne and silenced by the Trinitarians on the one hand, and the Arians on the other. And of the two, the latter were full as hostile to them as the former. This Photinus is said to have been a man of great eloquence. He continued in his bishopric, notwithstanding his being condemned in three several synods or councils, especially in one held at Milan, A.D. 345, being extremely popular in his see; but at length he was expelled by a council held at Sirmium itself, in 351. This last council was called by order of the emperor Constantius, and consisted chiefly of Arian bishops.

Here I reluctantly bid adieu to what I apprehend to be the genuine doctrine of the Scriptures concerning the nature of Christ, but we shall see it reappear with growing lustre in a later period.

SECTION VI.
OF THE ARIAN CONTROVERSY.

THERE were several things relating to the divinity of Christ, which had not been determined by the Christian fathers, before the time of Constantine. Thus, though the term *begotten* had been generally used in speaking of the origin of the Son, by way of emanation from the Father, the term *created*, and others of a similar meaning, had been used occasionally, and as far as appears without giving offence; nor indeed could it well have done so in an age in which all creation was considered as of the same kind, every substance (at least all intelligent substances or spirits) being supposed to have been derived ultimately from the same divine essence. This language we find used by Lactantius and Hilary, after it had begun to be disliked and reprobated, and therefore it was probably used by them through inadvertence.

Lactantius, however, speaking of the origin of the Son, says, " As when he was created in his first spiritual birth, he was, from God alone, made a holy spirit; so in his second carnal birth, from his mother alone, he became holy flesh."[4] Hilary says, "God the Father is the cause of all, without beginning, and solitary; but the Son was produced by the Father without time, and was created and founded before the ages. He was not before he was born, but he was born without time. Before all time he alone subsists from the Father alone." As it is not easy to give an exact translation of this passage, on

[1] *Hær.* 65, Opera, I. p. 608. (*P.*)
[2] Eusebii Hist. L. vi. C. xxxiii. p. 297. (*P.*)
[3] Ibid. C. xxxvii. p. 299. (*P.*)

[4] *Epitome*, C. xliii. p. 114. (*P.*) "Quemadmodum in prima nativitate spirituali creatus, et ex solo Deo sanctus spiritus factus est, sic in secunda carnali ex sola matre genitus, caro sancta fieret." Opera, II. p. 32.

account of its extreme obscurity, I shall give it at length in the note.[1] This writer seems to have thought, as the generality of the Ante-Nicene Fathers did, that there was a time when Christ was not: but we shall find that after the Arian controversy this opinion was condemned.

It was in consequence of the controversy occasioned by Sabellius, in Africa, that the peculiar opinions of Arius were started. Sabellius having asserted that there was no difference between the divinity of the Father and that of the Son, Dionysius, bishop of Alexandria, was thought to have advanced, in opposition to him, something derogatory to our Saviour, as that his divinity was so far different from that of the Father, that he was not even of the *same substance* with the Father; which, as we have seen, was contrary to the opinion of those who were deemed orthodox in that age. However, he justified himself in such a manner as gave satisfaction.

But not long after this, Alexander, another bishop of Alexandria, being led by the same controversy to discourse concerning Christ, in the presence of Arius, a presbyter of the same church (with whom he seems to have had some previous difference), among other things, in favour of the dignity of Christ, advanced that the Father did not precede the Son a single moment, and that he had issued from all eternity out of the substance of the Father himself. This, being in some respects an advance upon the generally received doctrine, provoked Arius to reply. He allowed that Christ existed before all time, and before the ages, as the only begotten Son of God, but he said that he had no being before he was begotten. He also asserted, in the course of the debate, that Christ was neither of the substance of the Father,

nor formed out of pre-existing matter, but, like other things, was created out of nothing, It seems also to have been the opinion of Arius and his followers, but was not perhaps advanced at that time, that this pre-existent spirit was the only intelligent principle belonging to Christ, being in him what the *soul* was supposed to be in other men.

The prejudices of the Christians of that age against the doctrine of the proper divinity of Christ must have been very general, and very strong, to have made this doctrine of Arius so popular as we find it presently was. It was a doctrine that does not appear to have been publicly maintained before. But, possibly, the difficulty of conceiving how a mere *attribute* of the divine nature could become a *real person*, which had been the orthodox opinion, might have gradually led men to think that Christ had been produced by way of simple *emanation* from God, like other intelligences or spirits. And when the Scripture doctrine of the creation of all things out of nothing began to take place of the doctrine of the philosophers, who asserted the impossibility of any such creation, the opinion of Arius that Christ was made out of nothing would naturally succeed to that of his emanation from the Father; so that it is possible that the minds of the more learned Christians might have been fully prepared to receive that doctrine before it was openly published by him.

Indeed, the appeal of Arius to Eusebius of Nicomedia, and other learned and eminent bishops of that age, proves that he did not imagine that he had advanced an opinion that was altogether peculiar to himself; and their ready reception of his doctrine, and the countenance which they gave him, who was only a presbyter, and had nothing extraordinary to recommend him, is a stronger proof of the same thing. The Arian doctrine, however, was a kind of medium between that of the *simple humanity* of Christ, which was far

---

[1] "Deus Pater est causa omnium, omnino sine initio, solitarius; Filius autem sine tempore editus est a Patre, et ante secula creatus et fundatus. Non erat antequam nasceretur, sed sine tempore ante omnia natus, solus a solo Patre subsistit." L. iv. p. 59. (*P.*)

from being entirely extinguished, though it was less and less relished, and that of his *proper divinity*, which made him to be of the same substance with the Father, and a kind of rival of his dignity, at which it is no wonder that the minds of many revolted. This circumstance, therefore, of the Arian doctrine being the medium between two great extremes, was alone sufficient to recommend it to many.

It is acknowledged that Arius, in the course of the controversy, had many abettors in Egypt, where the difference first arose; and among them were many persons distinguished by their genius and learning, as well as by their rank and station in the world. Notwithstanding those advantages on the side of Arius, Alexander prevailed so far, that, in two councils, which he summoned on the occasion, Arius was deprived of his office, and excommunicated. Upon this he retired into Palestine, where he was countenanced by a great number of bishops, but more especially by Eusebius, bishop of Nicomedia, one of the most distinguished of any in that age, both for his learning and moderation.

The emperor Constantine, having endeavoured in vain to compose these differences in the religion which he had lately professed, and especially to reconcile Arius and Alexander, at length called a general council of bishops at Nice, the first which had obtained that appellation, and in this council, after much indecent wrangling and violent debate, Arius was condemned, and banished to Illyricum, a part of the Roman empire very remote from Alexandria, where the controversy originated. But, notwithstanding this condemnation, so far were the Christians of that age from having any opinion of the infallibility of councils, that the doctrine of Arius triumphed both over the decrees of this celebrated assembly, and the authority of the emperor, who was afterwards induced to think better of Arius. He, therefore, recalled him from banishment, and ordered Alexander, his bishop, to admit him to communion. But Arius died before the order could be executed.

Constantius, the successor of Constantine, and also some others of the emperors, favoured the Arians, and in those reigns their doctrine was by far the most generally received throughout the Roman empire. The bishops of that profession held many councils, and they are acknowledged to have been very full. But at length Arianism was in a great measure banished from the Roman empire by the persecutions of the emperor Theodosius, who interested himself greatly in favour of the Trinitarian doctrine. The Arians took refuge in great numbers among the Burgundians, Goths, Vandals, and other unconquered barbarous nations, whom they were a great means of bringing over to the Christian faith; and all of them, without exception, professed the Arian doctrine, till it was overpowered by the influence and authority of the bishops of Rome. The Vandals were long the support of Arianism in Africa, but it never recovered its credit after their extirpation from that province by the arms of the emperor Justinian.

So far was the council of Nice from giving general satisfaction, that Hilary, presently afterwards, complains of the Arians as being in all the provinces of the Roman empire;[1] and, in the next reign, Arianism was very near becoming the universal doctrine of the Christian church, and of course would have been deemed orthodox.

The debates occasioned by this famous council made a great revolution both in the language and in the opinions of those who were deemed orthodox. It is the natural effect of controversy to push men as far as possible from that extreme which they wish to avoid, so as often to drive them into the opposite extreme. This was remarkably the case on this occasion; and no controversy ever interested so many persons, and those so deeply, as this

---

[1] *De Trinitate*, L. vi. p. 99. (*P.*)

did, and indeed continues to do to this day.

In order to keep quite clear of Arianism, which made Christ to be a *mere creature*, those who approved of the decrees of the council began to express themselves, as Mosheim acknowledges, in such a manner as that they appeared to "substitute three gods in the place of one."[1] And many of them seemed to imagine that they sufficiently maintained the unity of the Godhead by asserting that the Father, Son and Holy Spirit were each of them of the same divine nature, as three or more men have each of them the same human nature.

This was certainly giving up the unity of the divine nature; and yet, being obliged by the whole tenor of revelation to maintain the doctrine of only *one God*, in conjunction with this new doctrine of three separate Gods, such a manifest inconsistency was introduced, as nothing could cover but the pretence that this doctrine of the Trinity was inexplicable by human reason. And then the word *mystery*, which had before been applied to the doctrine of the Trinity, in common with other things which were simply deemed *sacred*, began to be used in a new sense, and to signify, not as before, a thing that was *secret*, and required to be explained, but something absolutely *incapable of being explained*, something that must be believed, though it could not be understood. But the whole doctrine, as it was afterwards generally professed, and as it now stands in every established Christian church, was not finally settled before the composition of what is called the *Athanasian Creed*, and its reception into the offices of public worship.

When this creed was made, and by whom, is uncertain. It appeared about the end of the fifth century, and is by some ascribed to Vigilius Tapsensis.[2]

Though this creed contains a number of as direct contradictions as any person, the most skilled in logic, can draw up, it still keeps its ground, guarded from all human inspection, like the doctrine of transubstantiation, by this new but thin veil of *mystery*.[3] But before I proceed to give a more particular account of this farther change in the doctrine, I must note by what steps the *Holy Spirit* came to be reckoned a distinct person in this Trinity.

SECTION VII.

OF THE DOCTRINE CONCERNING THE HOLY SPIRIT.

THERE is very little in the Scriptures that could give any idea of the distinct personality of the Holy Spirit, besides the figurative language in which our Lord speaks of the *advocate*, or *comforter*, as we render it (παρακλητος), that was to succeed him with the apostles after his ascension. But our Lord's language is, upon many occasions, highly figurative; and it is the less extraordinary that the figure called *personification* should be made use of by him here, as the peculiar presence of the Spirit of God, which was to be evidenced by the power of working miracles, was to succeed in the place of a real person, viz. himself, and to be to them what he himself had been, viz. their advocate, comforter and guide.

That the apostles did not understand our Lord as speaking of a real person, at least afterwards, when they reflected upon his meaning, and saw the fulfilment of his promise, is evident from

---

[1] Vol. I. p. 296. (*P*.) Cent. iv. Pt. ii. Ch. iii. Sect. i.

[2] Jortin's Remarks, IV. p. 313. (*P*.) "A. 481. Vigilius Tapsensis hath been supposed, by many, to have been the maker of the Athanasian Creed, about this time. Others are of a different opinion. But it matters little by whom, or where, or when it was composed." Jortin, Eccles. Hist. 1805, III. p. 131.

[3] This Creed, of which scarcely anything is intelligible but the damnatory clauses, has very lately been *worthily*, though unsuccessfully, employed to serve the purposes of political retaliation, under the *thin veil* of zeal for the established religion and the public morals. See the Trial of W. Hone, for a *Parody of the Creed of St. Athanasius*, 1818.

their never adopting the same language, but speaking of the spirit as of a *divine power* only. The apostle Paul expressly speaks of the spirit of God as bearing the same relation to God that the spirit of a man bears to man, 1 Cor. ii. 11 : "What man knoweth the things of a man, save the spirit of man, which is in him ? Even so the things of God knoweth no man, but the spirit of God."

Besides, the writers of the New Testament always speak of the Holy Spirit as the same spirit by which the ancient prophets were inspired, which was certainly never understood by them to be any other than the Divine Being himself, enabling them, by his supernatural communications, to foretell future events.

Also, the figurative language in which the Holy Spirit and his operations are sometimes described by them, is inconsistent with the idea of his being a separate person; as being *baptized* with the spirit, being *filled* with the spirit, *quenching* the spirit, &c., in all which the idea is evidently that of a *power*, and not that of a *person*.

For these reasons I think it possible, that we should never have heard of the opinion of the real distinct personality of the Holy Spirit, if it had not been for the form of baptism supposed, but without reason, to be given in the gospel of Matthew, where the apostles are directed to baptize *in the name of the Father, the Son and the Holy Spirit.* For though the meaning of these words, as explained by pretty early writers in the primitive church, is nothing more than "baptizing into that religion which was given by the Father, by means of the Son, and confirmed by miraculous power," and this particular form of words does not appear to have been used in the age of the apostles, who seem to have baptized *in the name of Jesus* only; yet since this form did come into universal use, after forms began to be thought of importance, and in it the Father and Son were known to be real persons, it

was not unnatural to suppose that the *Spirit*, being mentioned along with them, was a real person also.

It was a long time, however, before this came to be a fixed opinion, and especially an article of faith, the Christian writers before and after the council of Nice generally speaking of the Holy Spirit in a manner that may be interpreted either of a *person* or of a *power*. But it is evident, that when they seem to speak of the Holy Spirit as of a person, they suppose that person to be much inferior to God, and even to Christ. Some of them might possibly suppose that the Holy Spirit was an emanation from the Divine Essence, and similar to the *Logos* itself; but others of them speak of the Holy Spirit as a *creature* made by Christ, by whom they supposed all other creatures to have been made.

With respect to the apostolical fathers, their language on this subject is so much that of the Scriptures, that we are not able to collect from it any peculiar or precise ideas. It is probable, therefore, that they considered the Holy Spirit as a power, and not a person.

Justin Martyr, who was one of the first that supposed the *Logos* to be Christ, never says, in express words, that the Spirit is God, in any sense; and when he mentions worship as due to the Spirit, it is in the same sentence in which he speaks of it as due to angels. "Him," says he, meaning God, "and the Son that came from him, and the host of other good Angels, who accompany and resemble him, together with the prophetic Spirit, we adore and venerate; in word and truth honouring them."[1] In another place he says, "we place the Son in the second place, and the prophetic Spirit in the third."[2] Again, he places "the *Logos* in the second place, and the Spirit which moved on the water, in the third."[3] It is not improbable but that this writer might consider

[1] Apol. I. 27. (*P.*)
[2] Ibid. p. 19. (*P.*)
[3] Ibid. pp. 87, 88. (*P.*)

the Holy Spirit as a person, but as much inferior to the Son, as he made the Son inferior to the Father.

Tertullian in one place evidently confounds the *Holy Spirit* with the *Logos*, and therefore it is plain that he had no idea of a proper third person in the Trinity. Speaking of the Spirit of God which overshadowed the Virgin Mary, he said, " It is that Spirit which we call the *word*. For the Spirit is the substance of the word, and the word the operation of the spirit, and those two are one."[1] But in another place he says, " the Spirit is a third after God and the Son; as the fruit, proceeding from the branch, is the third from the root."[2]

Origen speaks of it as a doubt whether the Holy Spirit be not a creature of the Son, since all things are said to have been made by him.[3]

Novatian says, "that Christ is greater than the Paraclete; for the Paraclete would not receive from Christ, unless he was less than Christ."[4]

The author of the *Recognitions*, a spurious but an ancient work, and never charged with heresy, says, " that the Holy Spirit, the Paraclete, is neither God, nor the Son, but was made by him that was made, or begotten, (*factus per factum*) viz. by the Son, the Father only being not begotten nor made."[5]

One reason why those fathers who had modified their theological tenets by the principles of the heathen philosophy did not readily fall into the notion of the personality, or at least the divinity, of the Holy Spirit, might be that there was nothing like it in the philosophy of Plato, which had assisted them so much in the deification of Christ. A *third principle* was indeed sometimes mentioned by the Platonists, but this was either the soul of the world, or the material creation itself; for there are different representations of the Platonic doctrine on this subject.

At length, however, the constant usage of the form of baptism mentioned by Matthew, together with the literal interpretation of our Saviour's description of the Holy Spirit, probably, gave most of the primitive Christians an idea of its being a *person*; and the rest of the language of Scripture would naturally enough lead them to conclude that he must be a divine person. But it was a long time before these things coalesced into a regular system.

The fathers of the council of Nice said nothing about the divinity, or the personality of the Holy Spirit; nor was it customary in the time of Basil to call the Holy Spirit God. Hilary interprets baptizing in the name of the Father, the Son and the Holy Spirit, by the equivalent expressions of the *author, the only begotten,* and *the gift.*[6]

That little is said concerning the separate divinity of the Spirit of God in the Scripture is evident to every body; but the reason that Epiphanius gives for it will not be easily imagined. In order to account for the apostles saying so little concerning the divinity of the Holy Spirit, and omitting the mention of him after that of the Father and the Son; (as when Paul says, " there is one God and Father of all, of whom are all things, and one Lord Jesus Christ, by whom are all things,") he says, that " the apostles writing by the inspiration of the Spirit, he did not choose to introduce much commendation of himself, lest it should give us an example of commending ourselves."[7]

What is most particularly remarkable is, that the fathers of the council of Sardica, held in 347, a council called by the authority of the emperors Constance and Constantius, a hundred and sixty bishops being present, of whom Athanasius himself was one, and two

---

[1] Adv. *Praxeam*, C. xxvi. p. 515. (*P.*)
[2] Ibid. C. viii. Opera, p. 504. (*P.*)
[3] In *Joannem*, Opera, II. p. 276. (*P.*)
[4] C. xxiv. (*P.*)
[5] L. iii. C. viii (*P.*)

[6] De Trinitate, L. ii. Opera, p. 22. (*P.*)
[7] *Hær*. 57, Opera, I. p. 485. (*P.*)

hundred more approving of the decrees after they had been sent to them, (a council in which it was decreed that the Father, Son and Spirit, was *one hypostasis*, which they say the heretics call ουσια, and that the Father never was without the Son, nor the Son without the Father,) did not distinguish between the *Holy Spirit* and the *Logos*, any more than Tertullian did in the passage quoted above. They say, " We believe in the Paraclete, the Holy Spirit, whom the Lord himself promised and sent. He did not suffer, but the man which he put on, and which Christ took from the Virgin Mary, which could suffer: for man is liable to death, but God is immortal."[1]

Basil says that "the Spirit is superior to a created being, but the title unbegotten (αγεννητος) is what no man can be so absurd as to presume to give to any other than to the supreme God." Then speaking of his not being begotten, like the Son, but proceeding from the Father, he says, "neither let any man think that our refusing to call the Spirit a creature is denying his personality" (ὑποστασις).[2]

The subject might have longer remained in this unsettled state, if Macedonius, an eminent Semi-Arian, who had been expelled from the church of Constantinople, had not expressly denied the divinity of the Holy Spirit; maintaining, as some say, that it was only the Spirit or power of God; or, according to others, that he was a creature like the angels, but superior to them. This opinion being much talked of, had many abettors, especially in Egypt. But Athanasius, who was then concealed in the deserts of that country, hearing of it, wrote against it, and he is said to have been the first who applied the word *consubstantial* to the Spirit, it having before been applied to the Son only.

It was some time, however, before any public notice was taken of this opinion of Macedonius; and in a council held at Lampsacum, in 365, a council demanded by the Catholic bishops, though the greater number of those who actually met were Arians, the opinion of Macedonius, as Socrates the historian observes, appeared to have gained more ground than ever, and would probably have been the received opinion, had it not been for the interference of an orthodox emperor in the business.

At length, in what is called the second general council, which was held at Constantinople in 381, under Theodosius the Great, the opinion of Macedonius was condemned, though thirty-six of the bishops present were in favour of it. In the creed drawn up by this council, it is said, " We believe in the Holy Spirit, the Lord and Giver of life, who proceeded from the Father, and who ought to be adored and glorified with the Father and the Son, and who spake by the prophets." This clause is now generally annexed to the Nicene Creed, though no such thing had been determined at the time of that council.

Thus, at length, the great outline of the present doctrine of the Trinity was completed, though many points of less consequence still remain to be adjusted, as we shall see in the prosecution of this subject; and the doctrine of the *consubstantiality* of the Spirit with the Father and the Son, though implied, is not directly expressed in the decrees of this council.

As the doctrine of the divinity of Christ was very unpopular at first, so that of the divinity of the Holy Spirit appears to have been so too, as we may clearly infer from the writings of Basil. He speaks[3] of all people being interested in the debate on the subject, and even of his own disciples, as presuming to act the part of judges in the case; asking questions not to learn, but to puzzle and confound their teachers. The argument by which he represents himself and his orthodox brethren as

[1] Theodorit. L. ii. C. viii. p. 82. *(P.)*
[2] Adv. Eunomium, L. iii. Opera, I. p. 758. *(P.)*
[3] Hom. xxvii. Contra *Sabellianos*, I. p 523. *(P.)*

most frequently urged was the following:—Everything must necessarily be either *unbegotten, begotten* or *created.* If the Holy Spirit be unbegotten, he must be the same with the Father, and if he be begotten, he must be the Son: if therefore, he be a *person* distinct from both, he must be a creature. For the good father's answer to this objection, I must refer my reader to his twenty-seventh homily which is against the Sabellians.

I shall close this article with a short account of the word *Trinity,* and of the advantage which this doctrine gave the Heathens. The first appearance of the word *Trinity* is in the writings of Theophilus, bishop of Antioch, but it is not clear that by it he meant a Trinity consisting of the same persons that it was afterwards made to consist of, and certainly not a Trinity of persons in the Godhead. He says,[1] that the three days which preceded the creation of the heavenly bodies on the fourth day, in the first chapter of Genesis, represent the sacred mystery of the Trinity, viz. " *God,* the *word* and *wisdom.*" He adds, " the fourth day is the type of man, who needs light, that there may be God, the word, wisdom, man." This passage is certainly obscure enough, and it could hardly have been imagined from it that by *wisdom* he meant the *Holy Spirit,* the third person in the modern Trinity, had not the same term been used by other writers, and especially by Tatian, who was contemporary with Theophilus. For he also makes a Trinity, of *God, his word,* and *his wisdom.* About the same time Irenæus mentions the same three members, though he has not the word Trinity. " There is always," says he, " with God, his word and wisdom, his Son and Spirit, by whom and in whom he made everything freely."[2] After this we find the word *Trinity* in common use, but long before it was imagined that the three persons which constituted it, were con-

substantial, coeternal, and equal in power and glory.

Both the *term* and the *doctrine* of the Trinity occur in a piece entitled *Expositio Fidei,* ascribed to Justin Martyr; but this is evidently spurious, and of a date much later than the time of Justin. It is remarkable too, that Clemens Alexandrinus, who was in the very centre of the Platonism of those days, and who did not write till after Theophilus, never uses the term but once, and then it is to denote the bond of Christian graces, *faith, hope* and *charity.*[3]

We cannot wonder that this introduction of new objects of worship by Christians, should not pass unnoticed by the Heathens; and as it was chiefly a wish to recommend their religion to others, that gave them their original bias towards exalting the person of Christ, they were very properly punished by the advantage which the Heathens took of this very circumstance.

The *incarnation of the eternal word,* appears to have been a subject of ridicule to Celsus, who compares it to the fable of the transformations of Jupiter, in the history of Danaë, &c. He also justifies the Polytheism of the Heathens by the example of the Christians in this respect. " If Christians," says he, " worshipped only one God, they might have some pretence for despising all others; whereas they render these immense honours to a mere upstart."[4] To this, Origen answers, by alleging the text, " I and my Father are one," explaining it by *all the disciples being of one heart and one mind.* But so might the heathen gods have been one.

The emperor Julian did not overlook this obvious topic of reproach to Christians. He particularly upbraided them with calling Mary the *mother of God,* and charges them with contradicting Moses, who taught that there is but one God.

[1] Ad Autolycum, L. ii. p.
[2] Ibid. L. iv. C. xxxvii. p. 330, (P.)

[3] *Strom.* L. iv. p. 495. (P.)
[4] Contra *Celsum,* L. viii. p. 385.

SECTION VIII.

THE HISTORY OF THE DOCTRINE OF THE
TRINITY FROM THE COUNCILS OF NICE
AND CONSTANTINOPLE, TILL AFTER THE
EUTYCHIAN CONTROVERSY.

BEFORE I relate what was peculiar to those who obtained the name of *ortho-dox* in this controversy, I shall just mention the divisions of the Arians, which contributed much to the prejudice of their cause, as they often proceeded to great violence against each other.

The original and proper Arians held simply, that the Son was *created out of nothing,* some time before the creation of the world, which they said was made by him. But presently after, there arose among them a sect that were called *Semi-Arians,* the chief of whom were George, of Laodicea, and Basilius, of Ancyra, who held that, though Christ was a creature, yet he was, by special privilege, made of the *same nature* with the Father, whereas the proper Arians maintained that he was wholly of a different nature.

In 391 we find mention of another division among the Arians, viz. whether the Father could be properly so called from all eternity, before he had a Son. On this frivolous question, of mere words, the Arians are said to have divided with great bitterness, so as to have formed separate assemblies. But it must be considered that the history of these divisions is only given by their enemies. Before I give any account of more modern Arianism, I shall proceed with the state of Trinitarianism after the council of Nice.

No sooner was the general outline of the doctrine of *three persons in one God* settled, but the orthodox began to divide upon questions of great nicety; and human passions and interests always mixing with these debates, the different parties anathematized each other with great violence.

The first dispute was about the use of the word *hypostasis,* which we now render *person,* but which had generally been considered as very nearly synonymous with *essence,* (ουσια). In general, the Greeks understood it in a different sense; and having in view the Sabellians, who were said to assert the identity of the Father, Son and Spirit, said that there were *three hypostases* in the divine nature. On the other hand, the Latins, willing to oppose the Arians, who made the Son to be of a different nature from the Father, usually said that there was but *one hypostasis* in the Trinity; and we have seen that the fathers of the council of Sardica had decided in the same manner.

This dispute terminated more happily than almost any other in the whole compass of church history. For a council being held on the subject, at Alexandria, in 372, the fathers found that they had been disputing about words, and therefore they exhorted Christians not to quarrel upon the subject. Ever after, however, the phraseology of the Greeks prevailed, and the orthodox always say that there are *three* hypostases, or persons, in the unity of the divine essence.[1]

By this happy device, and that of declaring the doctrine to be *incomprehensible,* the Trinitarians imagine that they sufficiently screen themselves from the charge of *Polytheism* and *Idolatry.* Whereas, if they did but pretend to affix any ideas to their words, they must see that the device can avail them nothing. If by *person,* or any other term which they apply to each of the three members of the Trinity, they mean *an intelligent principle,* having a real consciousness, they must, to all intents and purposes, admit *three Gods.* This was thought to be unavoidable by the council of Sardica, which therefore asserted *one* hypostasis, in agreement with the original idea of the Son being an emanation from the Father, but not separated from his essence. Whereas, now, the original idea, on which the doctrine of the divinity of Christ was formed, is entirely abandoned, and in reality

[1] See Suicer's Thesaurus, under the word *hypostasis.* (P.)

another doctrine is received; a doctrine which all the Ante-Nicene fathers, who had no idea of any distinction between *hypostasis* and *essence*, would have reprobated, as downright Polytheism. The Arians, in a council held at Constantinople in 360, rejected the use of the word *hypostasis*, as applied to the Divine Being.

There seems to have been no reason why Christ should have been supposed to have had any more than one intelligent principle, and yet we have seen that some of the Ante-Nicene fathers thought there was in Christ a proper *human soul*, besides the *logos*, which constituted his divinity. But perhaps they might have been reconciled to this opinion by the popular notion of demons possessing men, who yet had souls of their own. Or by *anima*, which is the word that Tertullian uses, they might mean the *sensitive principle* in man, as distinct from the *animus*, or *rational principle*, a distinction which we find made by Cicero and others.

However, after the council of Nice, and about the year 370, Apollinaris the younger, bishop of Laodicea, who had distinguished himself by taking an active part against the Arians, being attached to the principles of the Platonic philosophy, (according to which there are *three principles* in man, viz. his *body*, together with the *rational* and *sensitive soul*, but not more than these three,) thought that the *body*, the *sensitive principle*, and the *logos*, were sufficient to constitute Christ, and therefore he asserted that Christ had no proper human soul. In consequence of this, he was charged with maintaining that the Deity suffered on the cross, but whether he himself avowed this opinion, does not appear. This doctrine, which was so far analogous to that of the Arians, that it supposed only one intelligent principle in Christ, was well received by great numbers of Christians in all the eastern provinces of the Roman empire; but it was condemned in a synod at Rome, and being likewise borne down by im-perial authority, at length it became extinct.

Whiston, who was certainly well read in Christian antiquity, asserts, that Athanasius seems never to have heard of the opinion of Christ having any other soul than his divinity, and that the idea of a human and rational soul in Christ was one of the last branches of this heresy.[1] This writer also asserts, that there does not appear in Athanasius's Treatise on the Incarnation the least sign of the *hypostatical union*, or communication of properties, which he says the orthodox have been since forced to devise in support of their notions.[2]

This business, however, was finally settled on the occasion of what is called the heresy of Nestorius, bishop of Constantinople, which, though small in its origin, has had great consequences, the effects of it remaining to this day.

This being an age in which great compliments were paid to the Virgin Mary, among other appellations, it became customary to call her the *mother of God*, and this was a favourite term with the followers of Apollinaris. This phraseology Nestorius, who had distinguished himself by his opposition to the Apollinarians, declared to be improper, and said it was sufficient to call her the *mother of Christ*. To justify this, he was led to assert that there are *two distinct natures in Christ*, the divine and the human, and that Mary was the mother of the latter only.

This doctrine had many followers, and even the monks of Egypt were induced, in consequence of it, to discontinue their custom of calling Mary the mother of God. Cyril, then bishop of Alexandria, a man of a haughty and imperious temper, was highly offended at this; and having engaged in his interest Celestine, bishop of Rome, he assembled a council at Alexandria, in 430, and in this council the opinion of Nestorius was condemned, and a severe anathema was pronounced against him.

Nestorius, not being moved by this, excommunicated Cyril in his turn. But at length Theodosius the younger called a general council at Ephesus, in 431, in which Cyril, though a party concerned, presided; and without hearing Nestorius, and during the absence of many bishops who had a right to sit in that council, he was condemned, and sent into banishment, where he ended his days.

In this factious manner was the great doctrine of the *hypostatical union* of the two natures in Christ (which has ever since been the doctrine of what is called the catholic church) established. The opinion of Nestorius, however, was zealously maintained by Barsumas, bishop of Nisibis; and from this place it was spread over the East, where it continues to be the prevailing doctrine to this day. The opinion of Nestorius was also received in the famous school of Edessa, which contributed greatly to the same event.

This controversy was, in fact, of considerable consequence, there being some analogy between the doctrine of Nestorius and that of the ancient Unitarians, or modern Socinians; as they both maintained that Christ was a mere man. But, whereas the Socinians say that the divinity of the Father resided in Christ, the Nestorians say that it was the *Logos*, or the second person of the Trinity, that resided in him.

But "the union between the *Son of God* and the *son of man*," they said, "... was not an union of *nature*, or of *person*, but only of *will and affection;* that Christ was therefore to be carefully distinguished from God, who dwelt in him, as in his temple." In this manner did the Nestorians, who had had several disputes among themselves, settle the matter, "in several councils, held at Seleucia."[1]

The opposition that was made to the heresy of Nestorius produced another, formed by Eutyches, abbot of a convent of monks at Constantinople, who had had a great hand in the condemnation of Nestorius. Eutyches was so far from being of the opinion of Nestorius, that he asserted that there was but *one nature* in Christ, and that was the *divine*, or the *incarnate word*. Hence he was thought to deny the human nature of Christ; but he was generally supposed to mean that the human nature was *absorbed* in the divine, as a drop of honey would be absorbed, and no more distinguished, if it should fall into the sea. There were other explanations and distinctions occasioned by this doctrine, which I think it not worth while to recite.

It may be proper, however, to observe, that the minds of many persons, especially in Egypt, were prepared for this opinion by another which had obtained there, and which I have observed to have been maintained by Hilary, viz. that the body of Christ was incorruptible, and not subject to any natural infirmity. Theodosius the Great[2] fell into this opinion in his old age. According to this doctrine, the human nature of Christ, being of so exalted a kind, might easily be supposed to have become so in consequence of its being absorbed, as it were, in the divine, so as to partake of its properties. It was, therefore, no wonder that they should express themselves as if they considered Christ to have, in fact, but one nature.[3]

Eutyches was condemned by a council held at Constantinople, probably in 448, and in consequence of it was excommunicated and deposed. But he was acquitted by another council held at Ephesus, in 449. However, in a general council, called *the fourth*, held at Chalcedon, in 451, he was condemned finally, and from that time it has been the doctrine of what is called the *catholic church*, that, "in Christ there are *two distinct natures*, united *in one person*, but without any change, mixture, or confusion."

---

[1] Mosheim, I. pp. 411, 412. (*P.*) Cent. v. Pt. ii. Ch. v. Sect. xii.

[2] This is evidently an error. The author means the emperor *Justinian.*]

[3] Sueur, A.D. 568. (*P.*)

The doctrine of Eutyches continued to be professed by many, notwithstanding the decrees of the council. It was almost universally received in the patriarchates of Antioch and Alexandria, and it is found in the East to this day. In 535 the Eutychians divided, some of them maintaining that there were some things which Christ did not know, while others asserted that he knew everything, even the time of the day of judgment.[1]

By the decision of the council of Chalcedon, the modern doctrine of the *Trinity* was nearly completed, the union of the *two natures* in Christ corresponding to that of the *three persons* in the Deity; and it was thought to answer many objections to the divinity of Christ from the language of the Scriptures, in a better manner than the Ante-Nicene fathers had been able to do. These frankly acknowledged a real superiority in the Father with respect to the whole nature of Christ; but the later Trinitarians, by means of this convenient distinction of *two natures in one person*, could suppose Christ to be fully equal to the Father as *God*, at the same time that he was inferior to him as *man;* to know the day of judgment as God, no less than the Father himself, though, at the same time, he was entirely ignorant of it considered as man.

It might seem, however, to be some objection to this scheme, that, according to it, the evangelists must have intended to speak of one *part* of Christ only, and to affirm concerning that, what was by no means true of his whole person, at the same time that their language cannot be interpreted but so as to include his whole pesson. For, certainly, it is not natural to suppose that by the word *Christ* they meant anything less than his whole person: much less can we suppose that our Saviour, speaking concerning *himself*, could mean only a *part of himself.* By means of this distinction, modern Trinitarians are able to say that the

[1] See *Rutt's Priestley*, Vol. II. p. 307. *Note.*

human nature of Christ only suffered; and yet its union with the divine nature (though it was so imperfect an union as to communicate no sensation to it) was sufficient to give it the same merit and efficacy as if it had been divine. To such wretched expedients, which do not deserve a serious consideration, are the advocates for this Christian polytheism reduced.

Thus, to bring the whole into a short compass, the first general council gave the Son the same nature with the Father, the second admitted the Holy Spirit into the Trinity, the third assigned to Christ a human soul in conjunction with the eternal *Logos*, the fourth settled the hypostatical union of the divine and human nature of Christ, and the fifth affirmed, that, in consequence of this union, the two natures constituted only one person. It requires a pretty good memory to retain these distinctions, it being a business of *words* only, and *ideas* not concerned in it.

Before I proceed any farther, it may not be amiss to give a brief account of some other particulars relating to the Eutychian doctrine, though they were hardly heard of in this part of the world; and the opinions that were then entertained in the East are not worth reciting, except to show into what absurdities men may fall, when they get out of the road of plain truth and common sense.

The decisions of the council of Chalcedon were condemned by those who called themselves *Monophysites*, a sect which sprung from the Eutychians. They maintained that the divinity and humanity of Christ were so united, as to constitute only *one nature*, yet, without any change, confusion, or mixture of the two natures; saying, that in Christ there is one nature, but that nature is twofold and compounded.

In the sixth century, the Monophysites acquired new vigour by the labours of a monk, whose name was Jacob, surnamed Baradeus, or Zanzales, and who died bishop of Edessa. From him the sect of Monophysites now go by the name of Jacobites in the East. Monophysites were afterwards divided into a variety of other sects; and the Armenians, who are of that denomination, are governed by a bishop of their own, and are distinguished by various rites and opinions from the other Monophysites.

It was long debated among the Monophysites whether the body of Christ was created or uncreated, and whether it was corruptible or not; and some of them maintained that though it was corruptible, it was never actually corrupted, but was preserved from corruption by the energy of the divine nature. The Monophysites had also many controversies concerning the sufferings of Christ; and among them Xenias of Hierapolis maintained that Christ suffered pain not in his nature, but by a submissive act of his will. Some of them also affirmed, that all things were known to the divine nature of Christ, but not to his human nature.

"From the controversies with the Monophysites, arose the sect of the Tritheists, whose chief was John Ascusnage, a Syrian philosopher," who, "imagined in the Deity three natures or substances, joined together by no common essence." The great defender of this opinion was "John Philoponus, an Alexandrian philosopher." A third sect was "that of the Damianists, who were so called from Damian, bishop of Alexandria..... They distinguished the *divine essence* from the *three persons*," and "denied that each person was God, when considered in itself, and abstractedly from the other two. But they affirmed, ... that there was a *common divinity*, by the joint participation of which each person was God."[1]

Had these subtle distinctions occurred while the Roman empire was united under one head, councils would probably have been called to decide concerning them, solemn decrees, with the usual tremendous anathemas annexed to them, would have been made, and the Athanasian Creed would not then, perhaps, have been the most perplexed and absurd thing imposed upon the consciences of Christians.

SECTION IX.

THE STATE OF THE DOCTRINE OF THE TRINITY IN THE LATIN CHURCH.

FROM the time of the complete separation of the eastern and western empires, the Greek and Latin churches had but little connexion, and their writings being in different languages, were very little known to each other; few of the Latins being able to read Greek, or the Greeks Latin. Though, therefore, the members of both churches were much addicted to theological discussions, they took a quite different turn, and except upon very particular occasions, did not interfere with each other.

With respect to the doctrine of the *Trinity*, there was this difference between the eastern and western churches, that as the eastern empire was under one head, and the emperor resided at Constantinople, which was the centre of all the Grecian literature, he frequently interfered with the disputes of the ecclesiastics; in consequence of which councils were called, decrees were made, and the orthodox articles of faith immediately enforced by imperial authority. Whereas the western empire being broken into many parts, and the studious theologians dispersed in different convents all over Europe, their speculations were more free; and though the authority of the Pope preserved a kind of union among them, yet the popes of the middle ages being sovereign princes, seldom interfered with religious tenets, unless they had some apparent influence with respect to their spiritual or temporal power. This was perhaps the reason why no new councils were called, and no new decrees were made respecting the doctrine of the Trinity.

[1] Mosheim, I. pp. 473, 474. (P.) Cent. vi. Pt. ii. Ch. v. Sect. v.

Since, however, what had been determined by the first general councils was received in the West, as well as in the East, the liberty of speculating on this subject was very much confined; so that instead of inventing doctrines materially new, divines rather confined themselves to devising new modifications, and new modes of explaining the old ones. In this field the human faculties have, perhaps, appeared to as great advantage as in any other, within the whole compass of speculation. We are only apt to regret that such wonderful abilities, and so much time, should have been employed on no better objects. But when, in some future period, all the labours of the mind of man shall be compared, it will, I doubt not, appear, that the studies of the *schoolmen*, to whom I am now alluding, were not without their use.

Frivolous, however, as I think the objects of their inquiries were, I do not think that the world could ever boast of greater men, with respect to acuteness of speculation, than Peter Lombard[1] and Thomas Aquinas, especially the latter. When I only look over the contents of his *Summa*, and see the manner in which a few articles are executed, (for no Protestant, I imagine, will ever think it worth his while to read many sections in that work,) and consider the time in which he lived, how much he wrote besides, and the age at which he died, viz. forty-seven, I am filled with astonishment.[2] He seems to have exhausted every subject that his own wonderful ingenuity could start, and among the rest the doctrine of the Trinity has by no means been overlooked by him.

[1] *Master of the Sentences*, named from his native country of *Lombardy*. He was bishop of Paris in 1159, and died in 1164.—Nouv. Dict. Hist. IV. p. 1052.

[2] He died in 1274. His *Summa* is thus described by a writer of his own church: "Solide dans l'établissement des principes, exact dans les raisonnemens, clair dans l'expression, il pourroit être le meilleur modèle des Théologiens, s'il avoit traité moins de questions inutiles, s'il avoit eu plus de soin d'écarter quelques preuves peu solides." Ibid. V. p. 552.

But the first who seems to have led the way, though in a remote preceding period, to the refinements of the schoolmen in later ages, and whose authority established the principal articles of orthodoxy, so that his opinions were generally received as the standard of faith, was Austin, who flourished after the great outline of the doctrine of the Trinity was drawn in the general councils of Nice and Constantinople.

In this writer we find the doctrine of the Trinity treated in a manner considerably different from that of preceding writers. For, in his time the doctrine established by the general councils had affected the *language* commonly used in treating the subject; so that words had begun to be used in senses unknown to the ancients. Thus, before the council of Nice, whenever the word *God* occurred in the Scriptures, and the Supreme God was meant by it, it had always been understood as referring to the Father only; and in this manner all the ancient fathers explained every passage in which the word God, as distinguished from Christ, occurred; and they had recourse to such expedients as have been mentioned in the early period of this history, to account for the divinity of Christ, without supposing that he had any title to be comprehended under that general expression.

But in the writings of Austin we often find the words *God* and *Trinity* to be synonymous. For he maintained that all the three persons are to be understood, though they are not expressly mentioned, and he allowed no real prerogative whatever to the Father; an idea which would have staggered all the Nicene fathers. So far was he from supposing that the Father was truly greater than the Son, that he says, "two or three of the persons are not greater than any one of them." This, says he, "the carnal mind does not comprehend, because it can perceive nothing to be true, but with respect to things that are *created*, and cannot perceive the *truth itself*, by which they are created."[1] He condemns those who had said that the Father alone is immortal and invisible,[2] and he blames Hilary for ascribing eternity to the Father only.[3] He so far, however, adheres to the *language* of his predecessors, as to say that the Father alone is *God of God* (*ex Deo*).[4] But by this he could not mean what the Nicene fathers meant by it.

Austin is also bolder, and more copious in his illustrations of the doctrine of the Trinity, by comparisons with other things; though the doctrine being farther removed from human comprehension, it was then become much less capable of being explained in that way. Among other things, he finds a resemblance of the Trinity in the *memory, understanding.* and *will* of man.[5] But then none of these powers, separately taken, constitute a man; and his other comparisons are, by his own confession, still more lame and inadequate than this.

As my readers will probably wish to see in what manner some of those texts of Scripture, which are usually alleged in support of the doctrine of the Trinity, were understood by this writer, I shall recite his interpretation of a few on which they have seen the comments of the earlier fathers, that they may see how the doctrine itself had changed in his time. He explains John xiv. 28, *My Father is greater than I,* by saying, that "Christ having emptied himself of his former glory, and being in the form of a servant, was then less, not only than his Father, but even than himself, even at the very time in which he was speaking; for he did not so take the form of a servant, as to lose the form of God."[6] He explains *Christ giving up the kingdom to God, even the Father,* by saying that the whole Trinity is intended in that expression,

himself and the Holy Spirit not excluded.[7] His manner of explaining Mark xiii. 32, in which it is said that the *Son knows not the time of the day of judgment,* is still more extraordinary. For he says, that by *not knowing* is to be understood his *not making others to know.*[8] He seems to understand Philip ii. 6, of a perfect equality with God. And, lastly, he says, that by the Father and Son being *one,* we are to understand the *consubstantial unity* of the Son with the Father.[9] Most of these interpretations were then quite new; but now these, or such as these, are in the mouths of all Trinitarians.

After Austin, we find a long period of great darkness in the western church, and in this period his credit was firmly established; so that we find him quoted as an authority, almost equal to that of the councils, and even the Scriptures themselves. But the age of great refinement in speculation began about the time of Berenger and Anselm, two of the greatest scholars of their time; and had not the former of them been unfortunately heterodox in the doctrine of the eucharist,[10] he would have been the most celebrated for his learning and abilities of all his contemporaries.

Anselm, though he writes with wonderful acuteness, is not systematical. He does not professedly treat of the Trinity, and indeed we find little in him that is particularly remarkable on this subject, besides an obscure intimation that the doctrine might have been known by natural reason.[11] In proving

[7] Ibid. L. i. C. x. p. 250. (*P.*)
[8] Ibid. C. xii. p. 253. (*P.*)
[9] Ibid. L. iv. C. ix. p. 303. (*P.*)
[10] *Berengarius,* archdeacon of Angers, was condemned in a council at Rome, in 1059, for maintaining the *errors* of John Scotus Erigena, which were afterwards revived by the *Sacramentarians.* See Nouv. Dict. Hist. I. p. 382. "Berengarius was for almost thirty years together baited in one council after another, and died about the year 1088." See "Bertram, concerning the Body and Blood of the Lord," 1688, p. 37. From *Bertram,* Ridley and his brethren learned their *qualified* notion of Christ's *presence* in the Sacrament, of which rite scarcely any *churchman* before Hoadley ventured to give *a plain account.*
[11] Ad *Romanos,* C. i. Anselmi Opera, 1612, II. p. 11. (*P.*) Anselm, archbishop of Canterbury,

[1] De *Trinitate,* L. viii. C. i. *Augustini* Opera, 1569, III. p. 346. (*P.*)
[2] Ibid. L. ii. C. viii. p. 267. (*P.*)
[3] Ibid. L. vi. C. x. p. 332. (*P.*)
[4] Ibid. L. xv. C. xvii. p. 463. (*P.*)
[5] Ibid. L. x. C. xi. p. 376. (*P.*)
[6] Ibid. L. i. C. vii. pp. 246, 260. (*P.*)

the eternity of Christ, he says, "*Christ is the wisdom of God, and the power of God;* if, therefore, God had ever been without Christ, he must have been without wisdom and without power."[1] And he says, that "Christ by his own power rose from the dead."[2] Lastly, in answer to the question why we may not as well say that there are *two persons* in Christ, as *two natures,* he says, "as in God, the Father, Son, and Spirit, are three persons, and but one God; so in Christ, the Godhead is one person, and the manhood another person; and yet these are not two persons, but one person."[3] My reader, I hope, will not be disappointed in finding no great light on this subject from this learned archbishop; nor must he form much higher expectations either from Peter Lombard or Thomas Aquinas.

Peter Lombard has many new distinctions on the subject of the Trinity; and, as an article of some curiosity, I shall recite a few things from him, as well as from Thomas Aquinas, who wrote in the century following, and who is abundantly more copious, as well as more systematical.

Peter Lombard illustrates Austin's comparison of the three persons in the Trinity, by the *memory, understanding* and *will* of man, observing, that they all comprehend one another. "Thus we can say, I remember that I remember, that I understand, and that I will; I can also say I understand that I understand, that I remember, and that I will; and, lastly, I can say I will that I will, understand, and remember."[4] He decides the question whether the Father begat the Son willingly or unwillingly, by saying that he begat him *by nature,* and not by *will* (natura non voluntate[5]), so that he retained the idea without adopting the offensive expression *nolens.* It is something extraor-

dinary that he owns that he cannot distinguish between the generation of the Son and the procession of the Spirit.[6]

After asserting, after Austin, that no one person in the Trinity is less than the other two, or than all the three, he says, "he that can receive this, let him receive it; he that cannot, let him, however, believe it; and let him pray that what he believes he may understand."[7] In this, which is certainly not a little curious, this subtle writer seems to have been followed by some moderns; and the last article I shall quote from him is not less curious, though I believe none of the moderns will choose to adopt his language; which, however, is very honest. After asking why, as we say that the Father is God, the Son God, and the Holy Spirit God, we may not say there are *three Gods;* "Is it," says he, "because the Scripture does not say so? But neither does the Scripture say that there are three persons in the Trinity. But this does not *contradict* the Scripture, which says nothing about it; whereas it would be a contradiction to the Scripture to say there are *three Gods,* because Moses says, Hear, O Israel, the Lord thy God is one Lord."[8] As to a contradiction with respect to *reason* and *common sense,* this writer seems to have made no difficulty of it, not having thought it worth his while to take it into consideration.

I must mention another peculiarity of Peter Lombard, because it was the occasion of some controversy. He, like the Damianists in the East, made some distinction "between the *divine essence* and the *three persons in the Godhead.*" But on this he was attacked in a large work by Joachim, abbot of Flora, who "denied that there was anything, or any *essence,* that belonged in common to the three persons...by which doctrine the *substantial* union between the three persons was taken away," and nothing but a *numerical* or *moral* union was left.

died in 1109, aged 75. See Biog. Brit. I. pp. 205–215. There is a list of his works, p. 213, *note.*
[1] Ad *Cor.* C. i. II. p. 102. (*P.*)
[2] Ad *Rom.* C. x. II. p. 67. (*P.*
[3] De *Incarnatione,* C. v. III. p. 89. (*P.*)
[4] Petri Lombardi *Sententiæ,* L. i. Dist. iii. p. 21. (*P.*)
[5] Ibid. L. i. Dist. vi. p. 42. (*P.*)

[6] Ibid. Dist. xiii. p. 73. (*P.*)
[7] Ibid. L. i. Dist. xix. p. 115. · (*P.*)
[8] Ibid. Dist. xxiii. p. 130. (*P.*)

This explication was, therefore, condemned by Innocent the Third, in 1215.[1]

Though Thomas Aquinas writes very largely on the subject of the Trinity, he has not much that is peculiar to himself. He defines a *person* to "be an individual substance of a rational nature,"[2] and pretends to demonstrate, *à priori*, that there must be more persons than one in the divine essence,[3] but not more than three.[4] And, lastly, after asserting that the Holy Spirit proceeds from the Son as well as from the Father, he says, that the Father and Son are but one origin (unum principium) of the Holy Spirit.[5]

SECTION X.

THE HISTORY OF THE DOCTRINE OF THE TRINITY AFTER THE EUTYCHIAN CONTROVERSY.

THE doctrine of the Trinity, as it was ever held in the western part of the world, had now received its last improvements; and indeed continued with little alteration from the time of Austin. A few more subtleties, however, were started upon the subject, especially in the East, which require to be noticed.

In 519, some monks of Scythia, at the head of whom was P. Fullo, having a dispute with one Victor, a deacon in Constantinople, whom they accused of being a Nestorian, insisted upon his saying that *one of the persons in the Trinity was crucified for us*, an expression which no Nestorian would use. They both appealed to the Pope's legates, who were then at Constantinople. But though these thought the words capable of a good sense, yet, since they might be suspected of the Eutychian

heresy, they thought it was better not to use them. The monks, not satisfied with this decision, appealed to Pope Hormisdas, who condemned the expression, but his successor, John, approved of it. Then, finding that the expression was not generally relished, they proposed to change it, and to say that the *Logos*, or the *Word*, had *suffered for us*; but this was also thought to savour too much of Entychianism.[6] Happily this controversy ended without any serious consequences.

It has been observed, that all the ancient, orthodox fathers supposed that there was a time when the Son of God was not, and that the *Logos* became a *person* immediately before the creation, having been originally nothing but an *attribute of the divine nature*. This opinion, it seems, was not quite extinct in the year 529. For we then find a decree of a synod of Vaison, in France, condemning it, and the preamble shows that the opinion was pretty general: "Because," say they, "not only in the apostolic see, but also in all the East, and in all Africa and Italy, heretics blasphemed, saying that the Son of God was not always with the Father, but had a beginning in time, they ordered it to be chanted in the common service, Glory to the Father, and to the Son, and to the Holy Spirit, *as it was in the beginning.*" A form which has continued to be in use ever since.[7]

The next controversy of which I shall give an account, shows, at the same time, the subtlety of the mind of man in devising distinctions, and the impotence of power to restrain or guide it. In the seventh century, the emperor Heraclius, considering the detriment which his empire received from the migration of the persecuted Nestorians, and their settlement in Persia, was very desirous of uniting the Monophysites, and thought to prevent the diversity of opinions among them by inducing them to accede to the following proposition (suggested to him, it is said, by Anastasius,

---

[1] Mosheim, III. p. 134. (*P.*) The "sentence, however," adds Mosheim, "did not extend to the person or fame of the abbot himself. . . . . *Joachim* has at this day a considerable number of adherents and defenders, more especially among those of the Franciscans, who are called *Observants.*" Eccl. Hist. Cent. xiii. Pt. ii. Ch. v. Sect. xv.

[2] Thomæ Aquinatis *Summa*, 1631, Pt. i. Qu. xxix. Art. i. p. 70. (*P.*)

[3] Ibid. Qu. xxx. p. 72. (*P.*)

[4] Ibid. Qu. xxxiii. p. 80. (*P.*)

[5] Ibid. Qu. xxxvi. p. 85. (*P.*)

[6] Sueur, A.D. 519. (*P.*)

[7] Ibid. A.D. 529. (*P.*)

the chief of the Jacobites, and who pretended to renounce Eutychianism, in order to be made bishop of Antioch), "There was in Jesus Christ, after the union of the two natures, but *one will* and one operation." Accordingly he published an edict in favour of this doctrine, which was called that of the *Monothelites*, in 630.

It was afterwards confirmed in a council, and for some time seemed to have the intended effect. But soon after it was the occasion of new and violent animosities, in consequence of the opposition made to it by Sophronius, a monk of Palestine. He, being raised to the see of Jerusalem, was the occasion of a council being held at Constantinople in 680, which was called the *sixth general council*, in which the doctrine of the Monothelites was condemned. Notwithstanding this condemnation, this doctrine was embraced by the Mardiates, a people who inhabited Mount Libanus, and were afterwards called Maronites, from Maro, their first bishop; but in the twelfth century they joined the church of Rome.[1]

In the condemnation of this doctrine, it is remarkable that it was not stated, nor anything opposite to it asserted; the writings only which contained it being condemned, as containing propositions "impious and hurtful to the soul;" and they were therefore ordered to be exterminated and burned. It is, indeed, no wonder that those who are called orthodox with respect to the doctrine of the Trinity, should be embarrassed with *two intelligent principles* in one person, in what manner soever they may imagine them to be united. If there be but one intelligent principle, or nature, there can be but one *will*, but if there be *two* intelligent principles, it is natural to expect two *wills*. But then what certainty can there be that these two wills will always coincide, and what inconvenience would there not arise from their difference?

The Christian fathers who first imagined that Christ was the *Logos* of the Father, had no dispute about the sense in which he was *the Son of God*. That he was so by adoption, and not in his own nature, as immediately derived from God, had been peculiar to those who held his proper humanity. But in the eighth century, Felix, bishop of Urgella, in Spain, would have introduced a distinction in this case, in fact uniting the two opinions. For he held "that Christ, considered in his divine nature, was *truly* and *essentially* the Son of God, but that considered as a man, he was only so, *nominally* and by *adoption.*" But this opinion was condemned by several councils, and especially in one held by Charlemagne, at Ratisbon, in 792.[2]

But the most ridiculous of all opinions that was, perhaps, ever seriously maintained, and which yet proceeded from an unfeigned respect to Christ, (and which I mention only to relieve my readers from their attention to things that were either of a more serious nature, or that had more serious consequences,) was one that was started in the ninth century, about the manner in which Christ was born of the Virgin. For, Paschasius Radbert, the same who was so much concerned in establishing the doctrine of transubstantiation, composed in this century "an elaborate treatise, to prove that Christ was born without his mother's womb being opened, in the same manner as he came into the chamber where his disciples were assembled, after his resurrection, though the door was shut."[3]

A controversy much more serious in its consequences, as it ended in the final separation of the Greek and Latin churches, was started in the same century, about the *procession of the Holy Spirit.* In the Nicene Creed, with the addition which was afterwards made to it, it is said, *I believe in the Holy Spirit, which proceeds from the Father;* and by this it was probably meant that the

---

[1] Sueur, A.D. 629 and 680. Mosheim, [Vol. II.] p. 37. (*P.*) Eccl. Hist. Cent. vii. Pt. ii. Ch. v. Sect. xi.

[2] Mosheim, II. p. 100. (*P.*) Eccl. Hist. Cent. viii. Pt. ii. Ch. v. Sect. iii.

[3] Ibid. p. 162. (*P.*) Cent. ix. Pt. ii. Ch. iii. Sect. xxvi.

Holy Spirit, as a distinct person, bore a similar relation to the Father, as the source of divinity, to that which the Son, or the *Logos* bore to him. But the Scriptures expressly asserting that the Spirit was sent by the Son, or proceeded from the Son, it probably came by degrees to be imagined, that his *nature* was derived from that of the Son, as well as from that of the Father; but we hear no consequence of this, till the year 447, when the words *Filioque*, were added to the creed, by the order of a synod in Spain, whence it passed into Gaul. In this state things continued till the eighth century, when the question was a good deal agitated, as appears by a council of Gentilli held in 766; and in 809 Charlemagne ordered a council to be held at Aix-la-Chapelle, in which the question concerning the Holy Spirit was discussed.

In consequence of this, the Latins, in general at least, held that the Spirit proceeded from the Father and the Son, and in the churches of France and Spain, the creed was usually read in this manner: " I believe in the Holy Spirit, which from all eternity proceeded from the Father and the Son." This, however, was not the practice at Rome, and Leo the Third, at least for some time, ordered the creed to be read as formerly. At length the Greeks took offence at this addition, and Photius, bishop of Constantinople, wrote against it, as an innovation; and after much debating on the subject, in the year 1054, the two churches finally separated, and excommunicated one another on account of this difference.

When an attempt was made to reunite the two churches, at the council of Ferrara, in 1439, this procession of the Holy Spirit was thus explained, viz. " The Holy Spirit is eternally from the Father and the Son, and he proceeds from them both eternally, as from a single principle, and by one single procession." [1] If my readers have any ideas from these words, it is more than I can pretend to.

[1] " Histoire des Papes," IV. p. 124 (*P.*)

No people in the world were so much addicted to religious controversy as the Greeks. In the later period of that empire, notwithstanding the declining state of their affairs, and the perpetual inroads first of the Saracens and then of the Turks, it continued to be one of their most serious occupations; and some of the emperors themselves entered into these debates with as much eagerness as any mere divines. One of the most extraordinary instances of this occurs in the twelfth century, when a warm contest arose at Constantinople about the sense of these words of Christ, " My Father is greater than I." The emperor Emanuel Comnenus held a council upon it, in which he obtruded his own sense of them, which was, that they " related to *the flesh that was hid in Christ, and that was passible*, i.e. subject to suffering; and not only ordered this decision to be engraved on tables of stone, in the principal church of Constantinople, but also published an edict in which capital punishments were denounced against all such as should presume to oppose this explication, or teach any doctrine repugnant to it." [2] However, the following emperor, Andronicus, cancelled the edict, and did everything in his power to put an end to the contest. But whether the severe penalties which he enacted against those who engaged in them had the effect he intended, we are not told. His measures do not seem to have been better adapted to gain his end than those of his predecessor.

I shall close the account of these idle disputes, with mentioning one that was started in Barcelona, in 1351, " concerning the kind of worship that was to be paid to the *blood of Christ*," and which was revived " at Brixen in 1462," when " *Jacobus a Marchia*, a celebrated Franciscan, maintained publicly in one of his sermons, that the *blood* which Christ shed upon the cross did not belong to the *divine nature*, and, of con-

[2] Mosheim, II. 435, 436. (*P.*) This Emperor "from an indifferent Prince was become a wretched Divine." Eccles. Hist. Cent. xii. Pt. ii. Ch. iii. Sect. xvi.

sequence, was not to be considered as the object of *divine* and immediate worship." But the Dominicans opposed this doctrine, and appealed to Pius II., who contrived to put off the decision, so that the question remained undetermined in the church of Rome to this day.[1]

Lastly, to conclude this Section, I must observe, that about the tenth century, a festival began to be held in honour of the *Holy Trinity*, in some cathedrals, and in monasteries, and that John XXII., who distinguished himself so much by his opinion concerning the beatific vision, fixed the office for it in 1334, and appointed the celebration of it to be on the first Sunday after Pentecost; and accordingly on this day it has been kept by the church of Rome, and the church of England, ever since.

SECTION XI.

A GENERAL VIEW OF THE RECOVERY OF THE GENUINE DOCTRINE OF CHRISTIANITY CONCERNING THE NATURE OF CHRIST.

WE are not able to trace the doctrine of the proper *humanity of Christ* much later than the council of Nice; the Arian doctrine having been much more prevalent for a considerable time afterwards, especially by the influence of the emperors Constantius and Valens; and the Arians were no less hostile to this primitive doctrine than the Trinitarians themselves. At length, though all the northern nations that embraced Christianity were at first of the Arian persuasion, yet, chiefly by the influence of the Popes, they became gradually Trinitarians, and continued so till near the reformation.

The first traces that we perceive of the revival of the ancient doctrine, are among the Albigenses. For I cannot say that I perceive any among the proper Waldenses, and the Albigenses were

probably rather Arians than what we now call Socinians. It would seem, however, that if the Waldenses (the first reformers from Popery, and who may be traced as far as the time of Claudius, bishop of Turin) were Trinitarians, they did not originally lay much stress on that doctrine. For, in their confession of faith, composed in 1120, which was sixty or seventy years before Valdo of Lyons, there is nothing under the article of *Jesus* concerning his divinity, nor yet in that of 1544, which was presented to the king of France.[2] In the first of these it was only said, that "Christ was promised to the fathers, and was to make satisfaction for sin." But after the time of the reformation by Luther, the Waldenses, in a confession of faith, presented to the king of Bohemia, in 1535, acknowledge expressly, "one essence of divinity in three persons, according to the Nicene Creed and that of Athanasius," both of which they mention.[3]

But no sooner were the minds of men at full liberty to speculate concerning the doctrines of Christianity, and circumstances excited them to it, but, while Luther and Calvin retained the commonly received opinion with respect to Christ, there were many others of that age who revived the primitve doctrine, though there were Arians among them. The greater number, however, were of those who were afterwards called Socinians, from Faustus Socinus,

---

[1] Ibid. II. pp. 269, 270. (P.) The Pope decreed "that both sides of the question might be lawfully held, until Christ's Vicar upon earth should find leisure and opportunity for examining the matter, and determining on what side the truth lay." Cent. xv. Pt. ii. Ch. iii. Sect. xiv.

[2] Francis I. The first article, on the object of worship, is strictly *Unitarian* and as different from the first article of the *Church of England* as possible. The second article describes *Jesus Christ* entirely in scripture language. Jortin quotes the *Confession* at length, in the Latin version of *Sandius*, (Hist. Eccl. p. 425,) and thinks that Erasmus "would probably have approved it." *Life of Erasmus*, A.D. 1586. 4to. p. 611.

[3] Jean Leger's "Histoire des Eglises Evangéliques des Vallées du Piemont, ou Vaudoises," 1669, pp. 94, 97 and 109. (P.) In the *Confession*, 1120, Art. II. is in these words, "We believe that there is one God, Father, Son and Holy Spirit." Through the whole fourteen articles there is no other reference to a *Trinity*. Of *Christ*, it is said, Art. VI., that "he was born at the time appointed by God his Father." See "A True Copy of an Ancient Confession," &c., from Moreland's *History*, p. 57, in "the History of Popery," 1735, I. pp. 423, 424.

who distinguished himself by his writings among those of them who settled in Poland, where they had many churches, and continued in a flourishing state till the year 1658, when they were, with great cruelty and injustice, banished from that country.[1] This event, however, like others of a similar nature, contributed to the spreading of their doctrine in other countries.

In England this doctrine appears to have had many advocates about the time of the civil war,[2] the most dis-

tinguished of whom were the truly learned and pious Mr. Biddle,[3] and his patron the most excellent Mr. Firmin; and it does not appear that there were many, if any, Arians among them, the term *Unitarian* being then synonymous to what is now called *Socinian*. Afterwards, however, chiefly by the influence of Mr. Whiston and Dr. Clarke in the Established Church, and of Mr. Emlyn and Mr. Peirce among the Dissenters, the Arians became so much the more numerous body, that the old Unitarians

[1] See Toulmin's Socinus, p. 274. The king, who banished them, was John Cazimir, a cardinal, who had been a Jesuit. In 1668 he abdicated, and became abbot of *St. Germain des Prez*, at Paris, where he died in 1672. In a chapel dedicated to this *St. Casimir*, is a tomb with a long inscription, *Eternæ Memoriæ Regis Orthodoxi*. Among his exploits are "Sociniani regno pulsi, ne Casimirum, haberent regem, qui Christum, Deum non haberent." See "A New Description of Paris," 1687, Pt. ii. p. 97.

[2] One of these was *Paul Best*, of whose life and writings I know nothing, but whose sufferings, from the Long Parliament, will sufficiently appear by the following passages in Whitelocke's *Memorials:*—

"1646, January 28. The day of the monthly fast. In the evening the House met, and heard a report from the *Committee of Plundered Ministers*, of the blasphemies of one Paul Best, who denied the *Trinity of the Godhead*, and the *Deity of Christ*, and the *Holy Ghost*. The House ordered him to be kept close prisoner, and an *ordinance* to be brought in to punish him with death." This committee was named from the design of its first appointment in 1642, to reimburse ministers who had suffered from the Royalists.

"February 16. The *Committee of Plundered Ministers* ordered to draw up an *Ordinance* for punishing Paul Best for his blasphemies.

"March 28. Debate of the blasphemies of Paul Best. Divines ordered to confer with him to convince him of his sin, and that a charge be prepared against him.

"April 3. Paul Best brought to the bar, heard his charge, and by his answer confessed the Trinity, and that he hoped to be saved thereby; but denied the *three persons*, as a jesuitical tenet."

It is well known what Unitarians of that age understood, when they *confessed the Trinity*, though it was too much like an unworthy subterfuge, to employ the term. What became of Paul Best I cannot find. Whitelocke records, "April 29, An ordinance to be brought in, for punishment of heresies and such as divulge them," and "1647, July 24, Order to burn a pamphlet of *Paul Best's*, and the printers to be punished."

That virulent foe of *Toleration*, Thomas Edwards, the *shallow Edwards* in Milton's Sonnet, speaks of "*Paul Best's* damnable doctrines against the Trinity," and denounces two *Independent Ministers* in the city. One of them had declared that Paul Best's "imprisonment

would do no good;" that he should be made "to sweat with arguments," but that the magistrate had "no authoritative power under the gospel to remedy it." The other said, "that the magistrate might not punish such," and "had nothing to do in matters of ·religion, but in civil things only." Edwards adds, on the authority of "a common councilman of good worth,—that an Independent Minister, within a few miles of London, one Mr. L., had said to him, 'that men ought not to be troubled for their consciences, but Papists should be suffered; and for his part, if he knew any Papists, who were at their devotions of beads, images, &c., he would not have them hindered or disturbed.'" It is to be regretted that we have not the names of these three ministers who were *lights shining in a dark place*. See *Gangrœna*, Ed. 3rd, 1646, p. 46.

Another Anti-Trinitarian of this period, whose name has been preserved, was *John Frye*, a member of the Long Parliament, to which he was chosen for Shaftesbury, first in 1640, when his election on some account was made void, and again in 1646. He was "suspended for writing a book against the Trinity; but upon declaring that he abominated the opinions charged upon him, restored February 3, 1648-9, but disabled February 24, 1650-1, for the same kind of offence." Mr. F. was one "of the commissioners appointed for the trial of the king, who occasionally attended, but did not sign the warrant for beheading him." *Parl. Hist.* Ed. 2nd, IX. p. 27. Of these transactions, Whitelocke has the following account:—

"1650-1, February 24. *Mr. Fry*, a Member of Parliament, being accused by *C. Downes*, another Member in Parliament, for a book written by *Mr. Fry*, and *Mr. Fry* having printed another book with all this matter in it; the House voted this to be a breach of the *privilege of Parliament*. They voted other matters in the book to be *erroneous, profane and highly scandalous*. That the book be burnt, and *Mr. Fry* disabled to sit in Parliament as a member thereof."

The accuser was "Colonel John Downes, one of the Regicides, and a Member of the Council of State." One of Mr. Fry's pieces was entitled "A Brief Ventilation of that Chaffie and Absurd Opinion of Three Persons, or Substances in the Godhead." On this the Parliament sat "from morning to night in debate." See Wood, Art. *Cheynell*, in *Athen. Oxon.* 1692, II. pp. 246, 247.

[3] See Toulmin's Socinus, p. 278, and his *Review* of Biddle's Life, 1791, *passim*. Also Dr. *Towers*, in Brit. Biog. 1770, VI. p. 79. Mr. John Farington, of the Inner Temple, appears to have been

were in a manner extinct. But of late years, Dr. Lardner[1] and others having written in favour of the simple humanity of Christ, this doctrine has spread very much, and seems now to be the prevailing opinion among those who have distinguished themselves by their freedom of thinking in matters of religion. This has been more especially the case since the application made to parliament by some members of the church of England for relief in the business of subscription,[2] and more particularly so since the erection of the *Unitarian Chapel* by Mr. Lindsey, (who, from a principle of conscience, on this ground only, voluntarily resigned his preferment in the church of England,) and the publication of his *Apology*, with its *Sequel*, and other excellent works, in vindication of his conduct and opinion.[3]

It is something extraordinary, that the Socinians in Poland thought it their duty, as Christians, and indeed essential to Christianity, to pray to Jesus Christ, notwithstanding they believed him to be a mere man, whose presence with them, and whose knowledge of their situation, they could not therefore be assured of; and though they had no authority whatever in the Scriptures for so doing, nor indeed in the practice of the primitive church till near the time of the council of Nice. Socinus himself was of this opinion, and is thought to have given too much

Biddle's earliest biographer. Wood has given a full and remarkably fair account of him, perhaps recollecting that Biddle's bitterest persecutors were also the foes of the crown and the mitre. He thus writes at the conclusion of his article:—

"By the filth of a prison, in hot weather, contracting a disease, he died thereof, in the month of September (one tells me the 2nd, and another the 22nd day), about five of the clock in the morning, to the great grief of his disciples, in 1662. Whereupon his body being conveyed to the burial-place joining to *Old Bedlam*, in Moorfields, near London, was there deposited by the brethren, who soon after took care that an altar monument of stone should be erected over his grave, with an inscription thereon, showing that *he was Master of Arts of the University of Oxon, and that he had given to the world great specimens of his learning and piety.* He had in him a sharp and quick judgment, and a prodigious memory; and being very industrious withal, was in a capacity of devouring all he read. He was wonderfully well versed in the Scriptures, and could not only repeat all St. Paul's Epistles in English, but also in the Greek tongue, which made him a ready disputant. He was accounted, by those of his persuasion, a sober man in his discourse, and to have nothing of impiety, folly or scurrility to proceed from him. Also, so devout, that he seldom or never prayed without being prostrate or flat on the ground."

Wood thus mentions that extraordinary youth who translated Biddle's Catechism into Latin: "Nathanael Stuckey, who had been partly bred up in grammar and logic by Biddle, or, at least, by his care, died 27th Sept. 1665, aged 16 years, and was buried close to the grave of Biddle, as it appears by an inscription engraven for him on one side at the bottom of Biddle's monument." *Athen. Oxon.* II. p. 202.

The "burial place" of Biddle was "the New Churchyard in *Petit France*, given by the City, and consecrated June 4, 1617," for the burial of strangers, especially of the French, who were numerous there. That ground is now part of the site of New Broad Street, and it is, probably, vain to inquire after Biddle's tomb.

Yet, though his tomb cannot be discovered, his scriptural doctrine of the divine unity, for which he *endured a great fight of afflictions*, has not been lost; but taught, in the very neighbourhood which contains his ashes, with a zeal, ability, and the recommendation of an exemplary life like his own, and in connexion with those ideas of the divine influence, and the divine character, to which Biddle had but partially attained. I refer to the exertions of my valued friend, the late Mr. Vidler, lost to his family and his Christian associates, too near the age at which Biddle *rested from his labours;* but whose enlightened views of truth, with his energy and success in recommending them, happily survive, in the same connexion. *Primo avulso non deficit alter.*

[1] "In 1759, Dr. Lardner published, but without his name, 'A Letter written in the year

1730, concerning the Question whether the Logos supplied the Place of a human Soul in the Person of Jesus Christ.' To this letter, which is supposed to have been originally addressed to Lord Barrington, were now added 'Two Postscripts.' It is observable, that Dr. Lardner did not derive his opinions from the study of the Socinian authors." Dr. L. also, about the same time, revised for publication Mr. Cardale's "True Doctrine of the New Testament concerning Jesus Christ." *Dr. Kippis,* Life of Dr. Lardner, 1788, pp. lviii. lix. lxvii.

[2] See "List of the Petitioning Clergy, 1772," Mon. Repos. XIII. pp. 15–17. There are interesting particulars on this subject in Mr. Belsham's Mem. of Lindsey, pp. 46–62.

[3] Mr. Lindsey's temporary chapel was opened by him on Sunday, April 17, 1774, and the present chapel, March 29, 1778. See *Mem.* of L. pp. 110 and 138. The *Apology* was published in Jan. 1774, a 4th Ed. 1782, and this year (1818) it has been reprinted by the Unitarian Society. The *Sequel* was published in 1776. Dr. Priestley published a pamphlet, entitled, "A Letter to a Layman, on the Subject of Mr. Lindsey's Proposal for a Reformed English Church, on the Plan of Dr. Clarke. 1774."

of his countenance to the imprisonment and other hardships which Francis Davides suffered for opposing it.[1] However, the famous Simon Budnæus was also of those who denied that any kind of worship ought to be paid to Jesus Christ, contrary to the opinion of Socinus."[2]

Many of those who went by the name of Anabaptists at the beginning of the Reformation, held the doctrine of the simple humanity of Christ; insomuch that, before the time of Sociuus, they generally went by that name. Among these one of the first was Lewis Hetzer, who appeared in 1524, and who "about three years afterwards was put to death at Constance."[3]

Several of the Socinians of that age held the doctrine of the personality of the Holy Spirit, considering him as a being of a super-angelic order. Of this opinion was Mr. Biddle.[4]

The first Arians in England were of the opinion of the original Arians, viz. that Christ was the first of all creatures, and even existed from eternity, by an eternal derivation from his eternal Father, that he was the immediate maker of the world, and of all things, visible and invisible, and appeared in a divine

character to the patriarchs and prophets before he was born of the Virgin Mary. But, besides that this doctrine savours of that of the pre-existence of all human souls, a doctrine which has no countenance in reason or revelation (though it was generally held by philosophers at the time that the Trinitarian and Arian doctrines were broached, and indeed served as a necessary foundation for them), it has staggered many, when they reflect coolly upon the subject, to think that so exalted a being as this, an *unique* in the creation, a being next in dignity and intelligence to God himself, possessed of powers absolutely incomprehensible by us, should inhabit this particular spot in the universe, in preference to any other in the whole extent of perhaps a boundless creation.

It cannot, also, but be thought a little extraordinary, that there should be no trace of the apostles having ever regarded their Master in this high light. For, being Jews, they would certainly consider him *at first* as a man like themselves, since no Jew ever expected any other for their Messiah. Indeed, it can never be thought that Peter and others would have made so free with our Lord, as they sometimes did, if they had considered him as their *maker*, and the being who supported the whole universe; and therefore must have been present in every part of the creation, giving his attention to everything, and exerting his power upon everything, at the same time as he was familiarly conversing with them. Moreover, the history of the *temptation*, whether it be supposed to be a reality, or a vision, must be altogether improbable on such a supposition. For what could be the offer of the kingdoms of this world, supposing *all* of them, without exception, to have been intended, to him who made the world, and was already in possession of it? And there is no trace of the apostles, after their supernatural illumination, discovering the great mistake they had been under with respect to this subject. On the contrary, they continued to speak as if their former

---

[1] See this question examined by Dr. Toulmin. *Socinus*, pp. 82-95.

[2] Mosheim, IV. p. 199. (*P.*) Cent. xvi. Pt. ii. Sect. iii. Ch. iv. xxii. xxiii. According to *Sandius*, Budnæus recanted. "Delapsus est in opinionem de Christo Domino, divino cultu non honorando,.....postea tamen opiniones suas retractasse, atque cum fratribus in gratiam rediisse perhibetur." *Bibl. Anti-Trin.* 1684, p. 54.

[3] Ibid. IV. p. 169. (*P.*) Ibid. III. Mosheim describes *Hetzer* as "one of the wandering and fanatical *Anabaptists*," but this name seems generally to provoke that historian's ill-will: and Hetzer, according to *Sandius*, to whom Mosheim refers, must have deserved more respectable epithets. Sandius attributes to him, among other pieces, one against the deity of Christ, which Zuinglius suppressed. Hetzer was beheaded, Feb. 4, 1529. *Bibl. Anti-Trin.* p. 17.

[4] He believed that "there is one principal minister of God and Christ, peculiarly sent from heaven to sanctify the church, who, by reason of his eminency and intimacy with God, is singled out of the number of the other heavenly ministers or angels....and that this minister of God and Christ is the Holy Spirit." See Biddle's *Confession*, Art. vi. p. 18, and his *Twelve Arguments*. Unit. Tracts, 4to. 1691, Vol. I. See also Toulmin's *Review*, p. 90.

ideas of him had been just, never giving him any higher title than that of *a man approved of God*, &c.

If it be supposed that while Christ was on earth he ceased to discharge the high office he held before, viz. *supporting all things by the word of his power*, there will be some difficulty in supposing *how*, and *by whom*, it was performed in that interval. For certainly it would not have been delegated to Christ, or any other created being, if there had not been some impropriety in its being done immediately by God himself. That our Lord had a knowledge of the rank he held before he came into the world, must, I think, be allowed by all Arians, if they give any attention to many circumstances in the gospel history, especially to our Lord's praying for the *glory which he had with the Father before the foundation of the world*, which all Arians suppose to refer to his preexistent state.

For these, I suppose, and other reasons which might be alleged, a middle opinion has been adopted by some Arians. For they consider Christ merely as a preexistent Spirit, but one who never had any business out of this world, and had no concern in making it; nor do all of them suppose that Christ was even the medium of divine communications to the patriarchs, &c. But then they do not seem to consider that many of the texts which, when interpreted literally, refer to the pre-existence of Christ, refer also, by the same mode of interpretation, to his being the maker of the world, &c., &c., so that if these texts do not prove both these particulars, they prove neither of them. If those texts which seem to speak of *both* these circumstances, viz. the pre-existence of Christ, and his making of the world, will admit of some *other* construction, much more may those which seem to refer to his pre-existence only.

Besides, if we once give up the idea of Christ having been the maker of the world, and content ourselves with supposing him to have been a being of a much more limited capacity, why may

we not be satisfied with supposing him to have been a *mere man?* The purposes of his mission certainly could not require more. For it cannot be said that anything is ascribed to him that a mere man (aided, as he himself says he was, by the power of God, his Father) was not equal to. And in other respects there seems to be a peculiar propriety in a man like ourselves being employed on such a commission as that of Christ, with respect to *man;* as his being an example to us, and especially in his resurrection being the resurrection of a man like ourselves, and therefore a more proper pattern of our own, and consequently a greater encouragement to us to look for the same. So that all the advantages of the Socinian hypothesis (and it cannot be denied to have some) are abandoned, and yet the peculiar ones of the original Arian hypothesis are not preserved, in the more qualified one, while no new advantage can be claimed by it.

With respect to the Trinitarians of the present age, and especially with us in England, those who have written on the subject are far from being agreed in their opinions, and therefore ought to be classed very differently from one another. But as they can agree in using the same phraseology, and mankind in general look no farther, they pass uncensured, and the emoluments of the establishment are equally accessible to them all. They are all, however, reducible to two classes, viz. that of those who, if they were ingenuous, would rank with Socinians, believing that there is no proper divinity in Christ, besides that of the Father; or else with Tritheists, holding three equal and distinct Gods. For, it cannot be pretended that the words *being* and *persons*, have any definable difference in their corresponding ideas, when applied to this subject.

Dr. Waterland, and the generality of the more strict Trinitarians, make three proper distinct persons in the Trinity, independent of each other, which is nothing less than making three distinct Gods. Mr. Howe would have helped out this hypothesis by supposing a mutual *self-consciousness* among them. But this is equally arbitrary and ineffectual; since three perfectly distinct intelligent beings still remain. For, supposing a proper self-consciousness to be communicated to *three men*, this circumstance could never be imagined to make them *one man*.

Bishops Pearson and Bull were of opinion, "that though God the Father is the *fountain* of the Deity, the whole divine nature is communicated from the Father to the Son, and from both to the Spirit; yet, so as that the Father and Son are not separate, nor separable from the divinity, but do still exist in it."[1] But this *union* is a mere hypothetical thing, of which we can neither have *evidence* nor *ideas*. If the Father be the sole fountain of Deity, he only is *God*, in the proper sense of the word, and the two others can be nothing but *creatures*, whether they exist *in* the Deity (of which also we have no idea) or *out* of him.

"Dr. Wallis," says Dr. Doddridge, "thought the distinction between the three persons was only *modal;* which seems also to have been Archbishop Tillotson's opinion." If so, they were both of them nothing more than Sabellians, whom all the ancients classed with Unitarians. In the same class also, ought to be ranked Dr. Thomas Burnet, who "maintains one self-existent and two dependent beings; but asserts, that the two latter are so united to, and inhabited by the former, that, by virtue of that union, divine perfections may be ascribed, and divine worship paid to them."[2] This too was evidently the opinion of Dr. Doddridge himself, and probably that of a great number of those who were educated under him, and perhaps also that of

Dr. Watts.[3] But, in fact, this scheme only enables persons to use the language, and to enjoy the reputation of orthodoxy, when they have no just title to either. For the divinity of the Father *dwelling in*, or ever so intimately *united to*, what is confessed to be a *creature*, is still no other than the divinity of the Father in that creature, and by no means any proper divinity of its own.

Besides, whatever we may fancy we can do by *words*, which are arbitrary things, and which we can twist and vary as we please, the properties and prerogatives of divinity *cannot* be communicated. The Divine Being cannot give his own supremacy; and whatever he can *give*, he must have a power of *withdrawing*, so that if he should communicate any extraordinary powers to *Christ* or to the *Holy Spirit*, (supposing this to have been a distinct being,) he can, whenever he pleases, withdraw those powers; and for the same reason, as he voluntarily gave them their *being*, he must have a power of taking away *that* also. How then can they make two parts of a proper *Trinity in the divine nature*, and be said to be *equal in power and glory* with the Father?

Christians should be ashamed of such unworthy subterfuges as these. The most fearless integrity, and the truest simplicity of language, become Christians, who wish to know, and to propagate truth. Certainly, if men be *deceived*, they are not *instructed*. All that we can gain by ambiguous language is, to make our readers or

[1] Doddridge's Lectures, p. 403. (*P.*) Prop. cxxvii.

[2] Ibid. p. 402. (*P.*

[3] He was certainly suspected by the strict Trinitarians, as appears by a pamphlet entitled "The Scripture Doctrine of the Trinity vindicated, in opposition to Mr. Watts's Scheme of one divine Person and two divine Powers, by Abraham Taylor. Ed. 2nd, 1728." The author was Tutor of an *Independent* Academy at Deptford. It would, I believe, be found, on examination of Watts's later publications, that his faith in a *Trinity* never recovered the shock it must have received from Mr. Tomkins's "*Appeal* — concerning the plain Sense of Scripture," 1722, in answer to his "Christian Doctrine of the Trinity, or Father, Son and Spirit, Three Persons and One God."

hearers imagine that we think as they do. But this is so far from disposing them to change their opinions, or to lay aside their prejudices, that it can only tend to confirm them. As to any inconveniences we may bring upon ourselves by an undisguised avowal of whatever we apprehend to be *the truth,* we may assure ourselves, that the *God of truth,* whom we honour by our conduct, will reward us, at least, with that *inward peace of mind,* which can never be enjoyed by those who so miserably prevaricate in a business of such moment as this. And what are all the honours and emoluments of this world, without that satisfaction of mind?

Light having thus, at length, sprung up in the Christian world, after so long a season of darkness, it will, I doubt not, increase to *the perfect day.* The great article of the *unity of God* will, in time, be uniformly professed by all that bear the Christian name; and then, but not before, may we hope and expect, that, being also freed from other corruptions and embarrassments, Christianity will recommend itself to the acceptance of Jews and Mahometans, and become the religion of the whole world. But so long as Christians in general are chargeable with this fundamental error of worshipping more Gods than one, Jews and Mahometans will always hold their religion in abhorrence. As, therefore, we wish to see the general spread of the gospel, we should exert ourselves to restore it to its pristine purity in this respect.

PART II.

THE HISTORY OF OPINIONS RELATING TO THE DOCTRINE OF ATONEMENT.

THE INTRODUCTION.

As the doctrine of the *divine unity* was infringed by the introduction of that of the divinity of Christ, and of the Holy Spirit (as a person distinct from the Father), so the doctrine of the *natural placability of the Divine Being,* and our ideas of the equity of his government, have been greatly debased by the gradual introduction of the modern doctrine of *atonement,* which represents the Divine Being as withholding his mercy from the truly penitent, till a full satisfaction be made to his justice; and for that purpose, as substituting his own innocent Son in the place of sinful men.

This corruption of the genuine doctrine of revelation is connected with the doctrine of the divinity of Christ; because it is said that sin, as an offence against an *infinite Being,* requires an *infinite satisfaction,* which can only be made by an *infinite person,* that is, one who is no less than God himself. Christ, therefore, in order to make this infinite satisfaction for the sins of men, must himself be God, equal to the Father. The justice of God being now fully satisfied by the death of Christ, the sinner is acquitted. Moreover, as the sins of men have been thus imputed to Christ, his righteousness is, on the other hand, imputed to them; and thus they are accepted of God, not on account of what they have done themselves, but for what Christ had done for them.

As I conceive this doctrine to be a gross misrepresentation of the character and moral government of God,

E 2

and to affect many other articles in the scheme of Christianity, greatly disfiguring and depraving it; I shall show, in a fuller manner than I mean to do with respect to any other corruption of Christianity, that it has no countenance whatever in reason, or the Scriptures; and, therefore, that the whole doctrine of *atonement*, with every modification of it, has been a departure from the primitive and genuine doctrine of Christianity.

SECTION I.

THAT CHRIST DID NOT DIE TO MAKE
SATISFACTION FOR THE SINS OF MEN.

IT is hardly possible not to suspect the truth of this doctrine of *atonement*, when we consider that the general *maxims* to which it may be reduced, are nowhere laid down, or asserted, in the Scriptures, but others quite contrary to them.

It is usual with the sacred writers, both of the Old and New Testament, to assign the reasons of such of the divine proceedings respecting the human race, as are more difficult to be comprehended, and the necessity and propriety of which are not very obvious, and might be liable to be called in question. Such is the divine condescension to the weakness, short-sightedness, and even the perverseness of men. He is willing that we should be satisfied that *all his ways are equal*, that they are all just, reasonable and expedient, even in cases where our concern in them is not very apparent. Much more, then, might we expect an explanation of the divine measures, when the very end which is answered by them is lost if we do not enter into the reasons of them, as is evidently the case with respect to the doctrine of atonement; since the proper end of the measures which this opinion represents the Divine Being to have taken was the *display of his justice*, and of his *abhorrence of sin* to the subjects of his government.

Is it not surprising, then, that, in all the books of scripture, we nowhere find the *principle* on which the doctrine of atonement is founded? For though the sacred writers often speak of the malignant nature of sin, they never go a single step farther, and assert that, "it is of so heinous a nature, that God cannot pardon it without an adequate satisfaction being made to his justice, and the honour of his laws and government." Nay, the contrary sentiment occurs everywhere, viz. that repentance and a good life are, *of themselves*, sufficient to recommend us to the divine favour. Notwithstanding so many notorious sinners, particular persons, and whole nations, are addressed by inspired persons, and their conduct strongly remonstrated against in the course of the sacred history, none of them are ever directed to anything farther than their own hearts and lives. *Return unto me, and I will return unto you*, is the substance of all they say on these occasions.

Certainly, then, we ought to suspend our assent to a doctrine of this important nature, which no person can pretend to deduce except by way of *inference* from particular expressions, which have much the air of figure and allusion. On the other hand, it seems natural to explain a few obscure expressions and passages, by other numerous, plain and striking texts, relating to the same subject; and these uniformly represent God as our universal parent, pardoning sinners *freely*, that is, from his natural goodness and mercy, whenever they truly repent and reform their lives.

All the declarations of divine mercy are made without reserve or limitation to the truly penitent, through all the books of scripture, without the most distant hint of any regard being had to the sufferings or merit of any being whatever. It is needless to quote many examples of this. One only, and that almost the first that occurs, may suffice.

It is the declaration that God made of his character to Moses, presently after the Israelites had sinned in making the golden calf. Exod. xxxiv. 6, 7: " And the Lord passed by before him, and proclaimed, the Lord, the Lord God, merciful and gracious, long-suffering, and abundant in goodness and truth, keeping mercy for thousands, forgiving iniquity, and transgression and sin." In the New Testament also we are said to be "justified freely by the grace of God." Rom. iii. 24. Tit. iii. 7. Now, certainly, if the favour had been procured by the suffering of another person, it could not have been said to be bestowed *freely*.

Agreeably to this, David, and other pious persons in the Old Testament, in their penitential addresses to the Divine Being, never plead anything more than their own repentance, and the free mercy of God. Thus David, Ps. xxv. 6, 7: " Remember, O Lord, thy tender mercies, and thy loving-kindnesses, for they have been ever of old. Remember not the sins of my youth nor my transgressions; according to thy mercy remember thou me, for thy goodness' sake, O Lord."

If the doctrine of atonement be true, it cannot, however, be pretended that David, or any other pious person in the Old Testament, was at all acquainted with it; and therefore the *belief* of it cannot be necessary to salvation, or indeed of much consequence. Had this doctrine, on which so much stress is now laid, been true, we should have expected that Job, David, Hezekiah, Nehemiah and Daniel should have been reproved whenever they presumed to mention their integrity before God, and took refuge in his mercy only, without interposing the sufferings or merits of the Messiah to mediate for them. Also, some strong clauses should have been annexed to the absolute and unlimited declarations of the divine mercy that are so frequent in the Old Testament, which would have restrained and fixed their meaning, in order to prevent the dangerous constructions to which they are now too much open.

Indeed, admitting the popular doctrine of atonement, the whole of the Old Testament is, throughout, a most unaccountable book, and the religion it exhibits is defective in the most essential article. Also the Jews in our Saviour's time had certainly no idea of this doctrine. If they had, they would have expected a suffering, and not a triumphant Messiah.

With respect to forgiveness of injuries, the Divine Being always proposes his own conduct to our imitation; and in the Lord's Prayer we are required " to forgive others, as we hope to be forgiven ourselves." Now it is certainly required of us, that if our brother only *repent*, we should forgive him, even though he should repeat his offence seven times a day. Luke xvii, 4. Upon the same generous maxim, therefore, we cannot but conclude that the Divine Being acts towards us.

The parables, by which our Lord represents the forgiving mercy of God, are the farthest possible from being calculated to give us an idea of his requiring anything more than merely repentance on the part of the offender. What else can we infer from the parable of the prodigal son, or the master whose servant owed him a thousand talents, &c.?

If our Lord had considered the Jews as having lost sight of the fundamental principle of their religion, he would certainly have pointed it out to them, and have drawn their attention to it. If, therefore, the proper end of his coming into the world had been to make satisfaction to the justice of God by his death, (which certainly they who did not expect a suffering Messiah could have no idea of,) he would have taken some opportunity of explaining it to them. But nothing of this kind occurs in the whole course of his preaching; and though he frequently speaks of his death, it is never as having had such an end.

Our Lord speaks of repentance, of

good works, and of the mercy of God, in the very same strain with that of Moses and the prophets, and without giving any intimation that their doctrine was defective on those heads. In his account of the proceedings of the day of judgment, the righteous are represented as thinking humbly of themselves, but they never refer themselves to the sufferings or merit of their judge, as the ground of their hopes; though nothing can be conceived to have been more natural and pertinent on the occasion.

Whenever our Lord speaks of the *object of his mission* and death, as he often does, it is either in a more general way, as for the salvation of the world, to do the will of God, to fulfil the scripture prophecies, &c., or more particularly, to give the fullest proof of his mission by his resurrection from the dead, and an assurance of a similar resurrection of all his followers. He also compares his being raised upon the cross to the elevation of the serpent in the wilderness, and to seed buried in the ground, as necessary to its future increase. But all these representations are quite foreign to anything in the doctrine of atonement.

When our Lord takes so much pains to reconcile the apostles to his death, in several discourses, of which we have a particular account in the gospel of John, he never tells them that he must die in order to procure the pardon of their sins; nor do we find the least hint of it in his solemn intercessory prayer before his death. On the contrary, he speaks of their sufferings and death in the same light as his own. To James and John he says, Mark x. 39, "Ye shall, indeed, drink of the cup which I drink of, and with the baptism that I am baptized with, shall ye be baptized." And he recommends his own example to them, in laying down his life for them, John xv. 12, 13.

After he is risen from the dead, he keeps the same profound silence on the subject of the supposed true and only great cause of his death; and as little do we find of it in the history of the book of Acts, after the minds of the apostles were fully illuminated with the knowledge of the gospel. They only *call upon all men everywhere to repent and believe the gospel, for the remission of their sins.*

The apostle Peter, in his discourse to the Jews, immediately after the descent of the Holy Spirit, and again in the temple, upon the cure of the impotent man, paints in the blackest colours the sin of the Jews in crucifying our Lord; but though he exhorts them to repentance, he says not one word of *satisfaction, expiation,* or *atonement,* to allay any apprehension they might have of the divine justice. And a fairer opportunity he could not have wished to introduce the subject. How fine a turn might he have then given to the popular cry of the same nation, at the time of our Lord's crucifixion, *His blood be on us, and on our children!* Instead of this, he only exhorts them to repent, and to believe that Jesus was the Messiah, for the remission of their sins. What he says concerning the death of Christ is only that "he was delivered to them by the determinate council and foreknowledge of God, and that with wicked hands they had put him to death." Acts ii. 23, iii. 17, 18.

Stephen, in his long speech at his trial, makes frequent mention of the death of Christ, but he says not one word of his being a propitiation for sin, to lead his hearers to consider it in that light.

What could have been a fairer opportunity for introducing the doctrine of satisfaction for sin by the death of Christ than the evangelist Philip had, when he was explaining to the Eunuch the only prophecy in the Old Testament which can be construed to represent it in that light? And yet in the whole story, which is not a very concise one, there is no mention of it. And when the Eunuch declares his faith, which gave him a right to

Christian baptism, it is simply this, that *Jesus is the Son of God.*

The apostle Peter, preaching to Cornelius, the first of the proper Gentile converts, is still silent about this fundamental article of the Christian faith. Much he says of Jesus Christ, that *God anointed him with the Holy Spirit, and with power,* that *he went about doing good,* &c. He also speaks of his death and resurrection, but nothing at all of our good works being accepted through his sufferings or merit. On the contrary, what he says upon the occasion may, without any forced construction, be turned against this favourite opinion. Acts x. 34: "Of a truth I perceive that God is no respecter of persons, but, in every nation, he that feareth him, and worketh righteousness, is accepted with him."

The apostle Paul before the Jews at Antioch, Acts xii. 28; at Thessalonica, ch. xvii.; before Agrippa, ch. xxvi.; and at Rome, ch. xxviii., on all these occasions treats, and sometimes pretty largely, concerning the death of Christ, but never with any other view than as an event that was foretold by the prophets. He shows the Jews the aggravation of their sins, and exhorts them to repentance and to faith in Christ, but nothing farther. In his preaching to Heathens at Lystra, Acts xiv., and at Athens, ch. xvii., he discourses concerning the supremacy and goodness of the one living and true God, and exhorts them to turn from their lying vanities; for (xvii. 30, 31), "the times of this ignorance God winked at; but now commandeth all men everywhere to repent, because he hath appointed a day in the which he will judge the world in righteousness, by that man whom he hath ordained, whereof he hath given assurance unto all men in that he hath raised him from the dead." Now, in all this there is not one word of the true gospel scheme of salvation by Jesus Christ, according to some. There is nothing evangelical; all is legal and carnal.

When we find the apostles to be absolutely silent, where we cannot but think there was the greatest occasion to open themselves freely concerning the doctrine of atonement; when, in their most serious discourses, they make use of language that really sets it aside; when they never once directly assert the necessity of any satisfaction for sin, or the insufficiency of our good works alone to entitle us to the favour of God and future happiness, must we build so important an article of faith on mere *hints* and *inferences* from their writings? The doctrine is of too much importance to stand on such a foundation.

It has been pretended, that the apprehension of some farther satisfaction being made to divine justice, besides repentance and reformation, is necessary to allay the fears of sincere penitents. They would else, it is said, be subject to perpetual alarms, lest all they could do would be ineffectual to restore them to the divine favour. But till clear instances be produced of persons actually distressed with these fears and doubts, I can treat this case as no other than an imaginary one.

In fact, there is no reason to believe that any of the human race, if they be left to their own natural unperverted apprehension of things, will ever fall into such doubts and uncertainties as all mankind are sometimes represented to be involved in. On the contrary, that God is a merciful being seems to have been a favourite opinion of all mankind in all ages; except in some religious systems in which the object of worship was not the true God, but some being of a low and revengeful nature, like the most capricious and depraved of mankind.

We have seen in the Old Testament, that the Jews had never any other idea than that God was placable on repentance. We find no other sentiment in Job or his friends, and certainly no other among the Ninevites, or among the Jews of later ages, as the books of Apocrypha, Philo, Josephus, and all their later writings, testify. We also see nothing of any other opinion in the doctrine of the Hindoos, or other oriental nations.

It is remarkable that Dr. Clarke, when, like others before him, he represents all mankind as absolutely at a loss on what terms God would receive offenders into his favour, produces not so much as a single *fact* or *quotation*, in support of what he asserts, though he is known to be peculiarly happy in his choice of the most pertinent ones on all other occasions. He gives us, indeed, a general reference to *Plato's Alcibiades the Second*,[1] but I do not find, in all the conversation between Socrates and Alcibiades in that dialogue, that either of them drops the least hint of their uncertainty about the divine favour in case of sincerity, or the least doubt that human virtue is not, *of itself*, a sufficient recommendation to his acceptance. All that they appear to be at a loss about is for some one to teach them what to pray for, lest, through their ignorance, they should ask of the gods things hurtful to themselves. They express no want of any person to intercede with God for them, or one whose sufferings or merit might avail with God for their acceptance.

Besides, if men should have any doubt concerning the divine placability, I do not see that they must therefore imagine that he would accept the sufferings of *another* instead of *theirs*; but rather, that he would be absolutely inexorable and rigorous in exacting *of themselves* the punishment of their crimes. Fears of this kind it is very possible that men may have entertained, but then there is nothing in the doctrine of atonement that is calculated to allay such fears. But the divine declarations concerning his own placability, which abound in the Scriptures, must be sufficient to answer every purpose of that kind.

It is urged, however, in favour of the doctrine of atonement, that the scheme is absolutely necessary in the moral government of God, because that, upon different principles, no satisfaction is made to his offended justice. But I answer, it becomes us ever to bear in mind that the divine justice is not a blind principle, which, upon provocation, craves satisfaction indiscriminately, of all that come within its reach, or that throw themselves in its way. In the Deity, *justice* can be nothing more than a modification of *goodness*, or *benevolence*, which is his sole governing principle, the object and end of which is the supreme happiness of his creatures and subjects. This happiness being of a moral nature, must be chiefly promoted by such a constitution of the moral government we are under, as shall afford the most effectual motives to induce men to regulate their lives well. Every degree of severity, therefore, that is so circumstanced as not to have this tendency, viz. to promote repentance and the practice of virtue, must be inconsistent with the fundamental principle of the moral government of God, and even with justice itself, if it have the same end with divine goodness, the happiness of God's creatures.

Now, that any severity is necessary to be exercised on such offenders as are truly penitent, even in human governments, is owing to the imperfection of government when administered by men. For were magistrates judges of the hearts of men, there would result no manner of inconvenience from pardoning all offenders who were become truly penitent and reformed; since hereby the offenders themselves would become useful members of society, and the penetration of the magistrates would effectually prevent any persons from taking advantage of such lenity.

This is exactly the case in the moral government of an all-seeing God. Here, therefore, measures formed upon the justest principles of equity may be taken, without hazarding the ends of government, measures which might be

---

[1] See Clarke's *Discourse*, Pt ii. Prop. vi. Ed. 8, pp. 291-296. See also a passage from *Second Alcibiades*, Rutt's Priestley. II. p. 105, Note *.

pernicious in any human administration. In the all-perfect government of God, therefore, there is no occasion to exercise any severity, even on penitents themselves. How absurd, then, it would be to exercise it on *others*, which yet the doctrine of atonement requires! Certainly, then, it must give the mind unfavourable impressions of the divine government, which, if not corrected by something else, must have an unfriendly aspect upon their virtue. Yet, notwithstanding this, the influence which the doctrine of atonement has upon *practice*, is strongly urged in its favour.

Admitting, however, that the popular doctrine of atonement should raise our ideas of the *justice*, or rather the severity of God, it must, in the same proportion, sink our ideas of his *mercy;* so that what the doctrine may have seemed to gain on the one hand, it loses on the other. And, moreover, though in order to the forgiveness of sin, some farther severity on the part of God be supposed necessary, yet, according to the doctrine of atonement, this severity is so circumstanced, as entirely to lose its effect. For, if the severity be to work upon men, the offenders themselves should feel it. It will be the same thing with the bulk of mankind, who are the persons to be wrought upon, whether the Divine Being animadvert upon the vices that are repented of, or not, if the offenders know that they themselves shall never feel it. This disinterested generosity might, indeed, induce some offenders to spare the lives of their substitutes; but if the sufferings had been endured already by some person of sufficient dignity, on the behalf of all future transgressors, it is impossible to conceive how the consideration of it should be any restraint at all; since nothing that any man could then do would expose any other to farther suffering.

SECTION II.

OF THE TRUE END AND DESIGN, OF THE DEATH OF CHRIST.

HAVING shown that the death of Christ is not to be considered as having made atonement, or satisfaction, to God for the sins of men, I shall now endeavour to show what the end and use of it really were. Now, the principal design of the life, as well as the death of Christ, seems to be not so much what we may expect to find in any particular texts, or single passages of the evangelists, or other writers of the New Testament, as what is suggested by a view of the history itself, what may be called the *language of the naked facts*, and what cannot but be understood wherever they are known. What has been written by Christians may assist us to conceive more accurately concerning some particulars relating to Christianity, but that must be of more importance, which does not require to be written, what the facts themselves necessarily speak, without any interpretation. Let us, therefore, examine what it is that may be clearly deduced from the history, and how much of Christianity could not but have been known, if nothing had been written, provided a general idea of the life and death of Christ could have been transmitted to us in any other way.

If, then, we attend to the general facts recorded by the evangelists, we cannot but find that they afford the most satisfactory evidence of a resurrection and a future life. The history of Jesus contains (what cannot be said of any other history in the world) an authentic account of a man like ourselves, invested by Almighty God with most extraordinary powers, not only teaching, without the least ambiguity or hesitation, the doctrine of a future life of retribution for all mankind, and directing the views of his disciples to it, in preference to anything in this world; but passing his own life in a voluntary exclusion from all that men call great, and that others pursue with so much assiduity; and, in obedience to the will of God, calmly giving up his life, in circumstances of public ignominy and torture, in the fullest persuasion, that he should receive it again with advantage. And in the accomplishment of his own prediction, he actually arose from the dead the third day. After this, he was seen by all those persons who had the most intimate knowledge of him before, and he did not leave them till after having conversed with them, at intervals, for a considerable time, in order to give them the most satisfactory evidence of the identity of his person.

Since, then, the great object of our Lord's mission was to teach the doctrine of a resurrection to a future immortal life, we see the necessity of his own death and resurrection as *a proof of his doctrine.* For whatever he might have *said* or *done* while he lived, he could not have given the most satisfactory proof even of his own belief of a resurrection, unless he had actually died in the full expectation of it. Hence it is that the apostles glory in the consideration both of the death and of the resurrection of Christ; as, 1 Cor. i. 22-24, "The Jews require a sign, and the Greeks seek after wisdom; but we preach Christ crucified, unto the Jews a stumbling-block, and unto the Greeks foolishness; but unto them which are called, both Jews and Greeks, Christ the power of God, and the wisdom of God;" also 1 Cor. xv. 14 and 20, "If Christ be not risen, then is our preaching vain, and your faith is also vain. —But now is Christ risen from the dead, and become the first-fruits of them that slept."

There is another manner in which we may be assisted in forming an idea of what is most essential to Christianity. Suppose a number of persons, educated in the Christian faith, to be cast upon a remote island without any Bible. It is probable they would first of all lose all distinct remembrance of the apostolical epistles, which may show that these are a part of the New Testament

the least necessary to be attended to. After this, they would be apt to forget the particular discourses of our Lord; but the last thing they would retain would be the idea of a man, who had the most extraordinary power, spending his time in performing benevolent miracles, voluntarily submitting to many inconveniences, and last of all to a painful death, in a certain expectation of being presently raised to an immortal life, and to great happiness, honour, and power after death; and that these his expectations were actually fulfilled. They would also remember that this person always recommended the practice of virtue, and assured his followers that they would also be raised again to immortal life and happiness, if they persevered in well-doing, as he had done.

Now, allowing that those persons, thus cut off from all communication with other Christians, should retain only these general ideas of Christianity, (and it is hardly to be conceived that they could retain less,) yet, would anybody say they were not Christians, or that they were not possessed of the most important and practical truths of Christianity, those truths which are most instrumental in purifying the heart and reforming the life?

Though there is no occasion to cite *particular texts* for what is clearly suggested by the *history* itself, and what could not but be known of it, if all that has been written concerning it were lost, yet express texts are by no means wanting to show that the true and proper design of the gospel, and consequently of the preaching and of the death of Christ, was to ascertain and exemplify the great doctrines of a resurrection and of a future state. I shall content myself with reciting only a few of them. John vi. 40: "This is the will of him that sent me, that every one which seeth the Son, and believeth on him, may have everlasting life, and I will raise him up at the last day." xi. 25, 26: "I am the resurrection and the life. He that believeth in me, though he were dead, yet shall he live; and whosoever liveth and believeth in me shall never die." x. 10: "I am come that they might have life, and that they might have it more abundantly." Rev. i. 18: "I am he that liveth and was dead, and behold I am alive for evermore; and have the keys of *the grave*, and of death."

The apostles, in all their writings, seem clearly to have understood this to have been the principal object of the mission of Christ. Thus Paul says concerning Christ, 2 Tim. i. 10, he "hath abolished death, and hath brought life and immortality to light through the gospel."

This doctrine of a resurrection to immortal life, and the making an express regard to it the principal sanction of the laws of virtue, is not only essential in the Christian scheme, but is an advantage peculiar to Christianity. The discourses of our Saviour relating to this subject appear, at first sight, to be in a strain quite different from that of any other teacher of virtue before him, inspired or uninspired. And what is above all, the *example* of a man, either living or dying, in the certain prospect of a speedy resurrection to an immortal life, was never before exhibited on the face of the earth. The object of the missions of other prophets was always something inferior and introductory to this.

It is allowed that the argument for our having an interest in a future life, drawn from the consideration of the resurrection of Christ, is weakened by any opinion that represents him as of a nature superior to our own. But if, with the author of the epistle to the Hebrews, we conceive him to be *in all respects as we are*, his resurrection cannot but be considered as a pattern and a pledge of ours. Hence the peculiar propriety of the divine appointment, explained by Paul, 1 Cor. xv. 21, that since by man came death, by man should also come the resurrection of the dead; and that, as in consequence of our relation to Adam *all should die*,

so in consequence of our relation to Christ, who is called *the second Adam*, we should *all be made alive*. The same argument is also more fully illustrated by the same apostle, in the 5th chapter of his epistle to the Romans, in which, what we suffer by one man is contrasted by what we gain by another man.

The great object of the mission and death of Christ being to give the fullest proof of a future life of retribution, in order to supply the strongest motives to virtue, we see the greatest propriety in those texts, in which this ultimate end of his sufferings is immediately connected with them; as Titus ii. 14, "Who gave himself for us, that he might redeem us from all iniquity, and purify unto himself a peculiar people, zealous of good works;" Eph. v. 25, 26, "Christ loved the church and gave himself for it, that he might sanctify and cleanse it," &c.; Rev. i. 5, "Unto him that loved us, and washed us from our sins in his own blood," &c.

Also, true religion being by means of Christianity extended to the Gentile world as well as the Jews, this ultimate end, viz. the abolition of the Jewish ritual, at least with respect to the Gentiles, is sometimes immediately connected with the mention of his death; as Eph. ii. 13, "But now in Christ Jesus, ye who sometimes were far off are made nigh, by the blood of Christ;" Col. ii. 14, "Blotting out the handwriting of ordinances, that was against us, which was contrary to us, and took it out of the way, nailing it to the cross."

Besides the principal object of the death of Christ, other uses of it are occasionally mentioned, but they are such as are perfectly consistent with this. For instance, Christ having submitted to all these sufferings for so great and benevolent a purpose, it was highly proper that he should be *rewarded* for it; and the Divine Being has, therefore, in this case, exhibited an illustrious example of the manner in which he will always crown obedience to his will. Moreover, Christ, being a man like ourselves, and therefore influenced by hopes and fears, it was reasonable that he should have a view to this glorious reward, in order to support him under his sufferings, as is particularly expressed in the following passages. Rom. xiv. 9: "For, to this end, Christ both died and rose, and revived, that he might be Lord both of the dead and living." Heb. xii. 2: "Who for the joy that was set before him, endured the cross, despising the shame, and is set down at the right hand of the throne of God."

As Christ was intended to be our *example* and pattern, in his life, death, and resurrection from the dead, his sufferings were absolutely necessary to qualify him for the work on which he was sent. This is expressed in the following passages, which also clearly show the necessity of his being a man like ourselves, in order to undergo sufferings like ours. Heb. ii. 10, 11: "For it became him for whom are all things, and by whom are all things, in bringing many sons unto glory, to make the captain of their salvation perfect, through sufferings; for, both he that sanctifieth, and they who are sanctified, are all of one (that is, of one nature and rank), for which cause he is not ashamed to call them brethren." Ver. 14: "Forasmuch then as the children are partakers of flesh and blood, (that is, are men,) he also himself likewise took part of the same," (that is, was a man also.) Ver. 17, 18: "Wherefore, in all things, it behoved him to be made like unto his brethren.—For in that he himself has suffered, being tempted, he is able to succour them that are tempted." Ver. 8: "Though he were a Son, yet learned he obedience by the things which he suffered, and being made perfect, he became the author of eternal salvation unto all them that obey him."

As Christ was the person foretold by the ancient Jewish prophets, and he carried the proper and ultimate object of the law of Moses into execution, in a more extensive manner than it had ever been done before, giving a proper extent and force to its moral precepts, Christ is properly said to have come to *fulfil the law*, and for the accomplishment of ancient prophecies. Matt. v. 17: "Think not that I am come to destroy the law, or the prophets; I am not come to destroy but to fulfil." Acts iii. 18: "But those things which God before had shewed by the mouth of all his prophets, that Christ should suffer, he hath so fulfilled."

Lastly, as the end of Christ's mission necessarily required him to undergo a great variety of sufferings, he is, with propriety, said to come in order to exhibit to mankind a most perfect *example* of voluntary obedience to the will of God, under the severest trial of it; and his example is justly proposed to us under our trials and sufferings. 1 Pet. ii. 21: "Christ also hath suffered for us, leaving us an example, that ye should follow his steps." 1 John iii. 16: "Hereby perceive we the love of God, because he (that is, Christ) laid down his life for us; and we ought to lay down our lives for the brethren."

SECTION III.

OF THE SENSE IN WHICH THE DEATH OF CHRIST IS REPRESENTED AS A SACRIFICE, AND OTHER FIGURATIVE REPRESENTIONS OF IT.

HAVING explained the one great and primary end of the life and death of Christ, and also pointed out the other secondary and subordinate ends which were likewise really answered by it, I shall now attempt to illustrate the *figurative representations* that are made of it by the sacred writers. These have unfortunately misled many Christians, and have been the occasion of their entertaining opinions concerning the end of Christ's coming into the world, quite different from those which appear upon the very face of the history; opinions which are contradicted by the whole tenor of revelation, and which are extremely injurious to the character of the ever-blessed God.

The most remarkable of these figurative representations of the death of Christ, is that in which he is compared to a *sacrifice;* and, as a figure, it is just and beautiful. In every sacrifice the victim is slain for the benefit of the person on whose account it is offered; so Christ, dying to procure the greatest possible benefit to the human race, is said to have given his life a sacrifice for us; and, moreover, as the end of the gospel is to promote the reformation of sinners, in order to procure the pardon of sin, the death of Christ is more expressly compared to a *sin-offering.*

These points of resemblance between the death of Christ and the Jewish sacrifices, sufficiently justify and explain the language of the Scriptures relating to it. From this circumstance, however, has arisen a notion, that the sacrifices prescribed in the Jewish law were *types* of this great, complete, and expiatory sacrifice of the death of Christ, which now supersedes and abrogates them. On account, therefore, of the great stress which has been laid on this view of the death of Christ, I shall consider it more fully than it would otherwise deserve.

All the texts in which Christ is indisputably represented as a sacrifice are the following. Eph. v. 2: "Christ also hath loved us, and hath given himself for us, an offering and a sacrifice to God, for a sweet-smelling savour." Heb. vii. 27: "Who needeth not daily, ...to offer up sacrifices, first for his own sins, and then for the people's; for this he did once when he offered up himself." The same allusion is also frequent in this epistle. We find it also, 1 Pet. i. 2, 19, Rev. v. 6, and 1 John ii. 2: "and he is the propitiation for our sins." The same *expression* occurs ch iv. 10. But these two are the only places in which the word *propitiation* (*ιλασμος*) occurs in the New Testament.

With respect to these texts, it is obvious to remark, that the far greater part of them are from one epistle of an unknown writer, (for it is not *certain*, at least, that the epistle to the Hebrews was written by Paul,) which is allowed,

in other respects, to abound with the strongest figures, metaphors and allegories; and the rest are too few to bear the very great stress that has been laid upon them. Besides, the *manner* in which this idea is introduced in these texts, which is only *indirectly*, intimates plainly enough, that a few circumstances of resemblance are sufficient to justify the allusion. Had the writers really considered the death of Christ as the *intended antitype* of the sacrifices under the law; had this been the great and principal end of his death, it would have been asserted in the fullest and plainest manner, and references to it would certainly have been much more *direct* and frequent than they are.

It is something similar to this view of the death of Christ, as a sacrifice, that he is also called a *priest*, and a *high priest*, especially by the author of the epistle to the Hebrews. But this very circumstance might have given us to understand, that both the representations are merely figurative, because both taken together are hardly consistent, at least they make a very harsh figure, and introduce confusion into our ideas.

That the death of Christ is no proper sacrifice for sin, or the intended antitype of the Jewish sacrifices, may be inferred from the following considerations.

1. Though the death of Christ is frequently mentioned, or alluded to, by the ancient prophets, it is never spoken of as a sin-offering. For the propriety of our translation of Isaiah liii. 10, may be doubted;[1] or if it be retained, it cannot be proved to exhibit anything more than a figurative allusion. Now, that this great event of the death of Christ should be foretold, with so many particular circumstances, and yet that the proper, the ultimate, and the great end

[1] Mr. Dodson thus translates the verse: "Yet it pleased Jehovah to crush him with affliction. Since he is made an offering for sin, he shall see a seed, and shall prolong his days, and the gracious purpose of Jehovah shall prosper in his hand." Mr. D. also proposes to transpose a passage from ch. lvii. See *Isaiah*, 1790, pp. 115-119, and 334-336.

of it should not be pointed out, is unaccountable.

2. Great weight is given to this observation by the converse of it, viz. that the Jewish sacrifices are nowhere said, in the Old Testament, to have any reference to another more perfect sacrifice, as might have been expected if they really had had any such reference. On the contrary, whenever the legal sacrifices are declared by the prophets to be insufficient to procure the favour of God, as they often are, the only thing that is ever opposed to them, as of more value in the sight of God, is *good works* or *moral virtue;* as Ps. li. 16, 17, " Thou desirest not sacrifice, else would I give it. Thou delightest not in burnt-offering. The sacrifices of God are a broken spirit; a broken and a contrite heart, O God, thou wilt not despise." To the same purpose see Isaiah i. 11, &c., Hos. vi. 6, Amos v. 22, Mic. vi. 6.

The wisest of the Jews in our Saviour's time speak exactly in the same strain, and in the presence of our Lord himself; who is so far from disapproving of it, that he gives his own sanction to the sentiment in the most open manner. A scribe says, Mark xii. 32-34, " There is one God, and there is none other but he; and to love him with all the heart, &c. is more than whole burnt-offerings and sacrifices. And when Jesus saw that he answered discreetly, he said unto him, Thou art not far from the kingdom of God." Having a perfect knowledge of the *law,* he was prepared for embracing the *gospel.*

The general strain of the passages, quoted and referred to above, cannot but appear very extraordinary, if the Jewish sacrifices had in reality any reference to the death of Christ, and were intended to prefigure it, as types to an antitype.

3. Many other things, besides the death of Christ, are expressly called *sacrifices* by the sacred writers; and if it be universally allowed to be in a figurative sense only, why may not this be the case with the death of Christ also? Isa. lxvi. 20: "They shall bring all your brethren for an offering unto the Lord." Rom. xii. 1: "That ye present your bodies a living sacrifice, holy, acceptable unto God, which is your reasonable service."

4. Christians in general are frequently called *priests,* as well as Christ himself. 1 Pet. ii. 5: "Ye are an holy priesthood, to offer up spiritual sacrifices."

5. The death of Christ cannot be considered as a proper sacrifice for sin, because many things essential to such a sacrifice were wanting in it, especially its not being provided and presented by the sinner.

6. We meet with many figures in the writings of the apostles no less bold than this. Thus the body of Christ is the *veil* through which we pass to the holy of holies. We are said to be *circumcised* in his circumcision, and to be *buried* with him by baptism. Our sins are *crucified* with him, and we *rise again* with him to *newness of life.* After meeting with figures like these (and many more might be mentioned quite as harsh as these), can we be surprised that Christ, who died to promote the reformation of the world, should be called *a sacrifice for the sins of men?*

Still less shall we wonder at this, if we consider how familiar all the rites of the Jewish religion were to the minds of the apostles, so that whatever they were writing about, if it bore any resemblance to that ritual, it was sure to obtrude itself. It must also be considered, that the death of Christ was the greatest objection to Christianity both with Jews and Gentiles; and what could tend more to remove this prejudice, with both of them, and especially the Jews, than taking every opportunity of describing it in language which to them was so familiar and respectable?

7. It has been said by some, that sacrifices were originally intended to prefigure the death of Christ; and that, in themselves considered, they were of such a nature, that they would never have been thought of by man, without an express command from God.

But whether sacrifices were originally appointed by God, or a method which men themselves thought of, (which I think not improbable,) of expressing their gratitude to God, for his favours to them, when we consider the circumstances in which they were used, they appear easily to fall under either the general notion of *gifts*, or the more particular one of *entertainments*, furnished at the expense of the person who was dependent and obliged. They were therefore always considered as *acknowledgments* for favours received from, or of *homage* due to, God or man. In like manner, they might be used to deprecate the anger of God or man, or to procure favours of any other kind, by begetting in the mind of our patron an opinion of our respect and esteem for him.

To all these purposes served sacrifices before and under the law of Moses. Without a sacrifice or some other gift, the Jews were not allowed to approach the tabernacle or the temple, that is, the house of God. They were expressly commanded *never to appear before God empty, lest wrath should be upon them*, which was agreeable to a custom that is still universal in the East, never to appear in the presence of any prince, or great man, without a present.

That the offering of an animal upon the altar was considered, in the law of Moses, in the same light as any other offering or gift, and a sacrifice for sin as any other sacrifice, is evident from several facts in the Jewish history, and from several circumstances in their ritual. In many cases, where a person was not able to provide an animal for a sacrifice, an offering of flour was accepted. The Philistines also, when they were convinced of their fault in taking captive the ark of God, returned it with a present of golden mice and emrods, to make atonement for them, evidently in the place of a sacrifice; and from the Grecian history it appears that (αναθηματα,) or presents of gold, silver, statues, &c., were considered by them as equivalent to expensive sacrifices for any purpose whatever.

In the Jewish ritual, the ceremonies attending a sacrifice for sin did not differ in anything material from those that were used in any other sacrifice. Whatever was the occasion of the sacrifice, the person who offered it laid his hand, in a solemn manner, on the head of the victim, which was the formal *presentation* of it, the animal was slain, and the blood sprinkled. Part of the victim was always burnt on the altar, a part was the portion of the priest, and in some cases the remainder was eaten by the offerer. When, therefore, the Jews sacrificed an animal as a sin-offering, the use and signification of the *sacrifice itself*, were the same as if it had been intended to procure any other favour; and there was no more *bearing of sin*, or anything properly *vicarious* in the offering of the animal that was made a sin-offering, than if it had been sacrificed on an occasion of thanksgiving, or on any other account.

From all that has been said concerning sacrifices under the law, and the history of their uses, they appear to have been considered as *circumstances attending an address to the Deity*, and not as things that were of any avail in themselves. It was not the sacrifice, but the priest that was said to *make atonement*; nor was a sacrifice universally necessary for that purpose. For, upon several occasions, we read of atonement being made when there was no sacrifice. Phineas is said to have made atonement for the children of Israel by slaying the transgressors, Num. xxv. 13. Moses made atonement by prayer only, Exod. xxxii. 30. And Aaron made atonement with incense.

Whenever the writers of the Old Testament treat largely concerning sacrifices, it is evident the idea they had of them was the same with that which they had concerning *gifts*, or presents of any other nature. Thus the Divine Being is represented as saying, Ps. l. 9, 14, " I will take no bullock out of thy house, nor he-goat out of thy folds. For every beast of the forest is mine, and the cattle upon a thousand hills. I know all the fowls of the mountains; and the wild beasts of the field are mine. If I were hungry, I would not tell thee; for the world is mine, and the fulness thereof. Will I eat the flesh of bulls, or drink the blood of goats? Offer unto God thanksgiving, and pay thy vows unto the Most High," &c.

Lastly, if the death of Christ had been a proper sacrifice, and the forgiveness of sins had depended upon it only, we should hardly have found the *resurrection of Christ* represented as having had the same use; as Rom. iv. 25, He "was raised again for our justification." As figures of speech, these things are consistent enough, but not otherwise.

8. Had the death of Christ been simply and properly a *sacrifice,* we should not expect to find it denominated in any manner that was inconsistent with this representation, which, however, is very common in the Scriptures. If there be a resemblance to the death of Christ in those things to which they compare it, the writers are sufficiently justified, as such *figures of speech* are adapted to give a strong view of what they wish to describe; but if no figure be intended, they are chargeable with real inconsistency, in calling the same thing by different names. If one of the representations be real, and the rest figurative, how are we to distinguish among them, when the writers themselves give us no intimation of any such difference? This circumstance alone seems to prove that they made use of all these representations in the same view, which, therefore, could be no other than as comparisons in certain respects.

Because the word *atonement* frequently occurs in the Old Testament, and in some cases atonements are said to have been made for sin by sacrifices, this whole business has, on this account more particularly, been thought to refer to the death of Christ, as the only atoning sacrifice. But this notion must be given up if we consider the meaning of *atonement* under the Jewish dispensation.

From comparing all the passages in which atonement is mentioned, it is evident that it signifies the making of anything *clean* or *holy,* so as to be fit to be used in the service of God, or, when applied to a person, fit to come into the presence of God; God being considered as, in a peculiar manner, the king and sovereign of the Israelitish nation, and, as it were, keeping a court among them. Thus atonement was said to be made for the *altar,* Exod. xxix. 36, and for a *house* after having been infected with leprosy, Lev. xiv. 53. Aaron made atonement for the *Levites,* Num. viii. 12, when they were dedicated to their office and ministry, when no sin, or offence, is said to have been done away by it. Atonement was also made at the purification of a leper, Lev. xiv. 18. Burnt-offerings that were wholly *voluntary* are said to be accepted to make atonement for the offerer, Lev. i. 3, 4. Atonements were also appointed after involuntary uncleanness and sins of ignorance, as well as in some cases of wilful transgression, upon repentance and restitution; but in this case it had no relation to the pardon of sin in the sight of God, but only to the decency and propriety of public worship, for which a man who had so offended was considered as disqualified. Guilt, in a moral sense, is never said to be atoned for by any sacrifice, but the contrary is strongly expressed by David and others.

The English word *atonement* occurs but once in the New Testament, and in other places the same word in the original (καταλλαγη) is rendered *reconciliation;* and this word is never used by the Seventy in any passage relating to legal atonements.

Had the death of Christ been the proper atoning sacrifice for the sins of men, and as such been prefigured by the atonements in the Jewish dispensation, we might have expected not only to have been expressly told so, (if not from the first, at least after the fulfilment of the prophetic type,) but also that the time, and other circumstances of the death of Christ, should have corresponded to those of the types of it. Christ being put to death at the feast of passover, might lead us to imagine that his death had some reference to that business; but if he had died as a proper *expiatory sacrifice*, it might have been expected that he would have died on the *day of expiation*, and at the time when the high priest was entering into the holy of holies. Had this been the case, I much doubt whether it would have been in the power of any *reasons*, though ever so solid, to have prevented men from considering the one as a proper type of the other. Now the want of this coincidence should lead our minds off from making such a comparison.

In one passage of the New Testament, Christ is said to have died as a *curse* for us. Gal. iii. 13: "Christ hath redeemed us from the curse of the law, being made a curse for us."[1]

Mention is made of several kinds of *things accursed* under the Jewish constitution, but in general they were things devoted to destruction. Christ, therefore, may, in a figurative way of speaking, be considered as a *curse* for us, in consequence of his devoting himself to death for us. But that this can be nothing more than a figure is evident, because this idea of a curse is inconsistent with that of a sacrifice, and therefore shows that both these representations are to be considered as mere figures of speech. Though in some of the Heathen sacrifices the victim was an animal abhorred by the god to which it was offered, as the goat sacrificed to Bacchus; yet in the Jewish sacrifices the victim was always a clean and useful animal, and perfect in its kind. And nothing *accursed* was

ever suffered to be brought to the altar of God. Cities and cattle accursed were in the law devoted to utter destruction. Not one sheep or ox of all the cattle of Jericho, or of the Amalekites, was permitted to be sacrificed.

Christ is also compared to the *paschal lamb* among the Jews. 1 Cor. v. 7: "Christ our passover is sacrificed for us." Also when the legs of Jesus were not broken upon the cross, it is said, John xix. 36, "These things were done, that the Scripture should be fulfilled, a bone of him shall not be broken," evidently referring to the same words in Exod. xii. 46, which relate to the *paschal lamb.*

There are, moreover, several other circumstances in the evangelical history which lead us to this view of the death of Christ, especially that of his being crucified at the feast of passover, and of his institution of the Lord's supper at that time, and seemingly in resemblance of it, as if it was to be considered in the same light. However, the *paschal lamb* was far from being a proper *sacrifice*. It is never so denominated in the Old Testament, except once, Exod. xii. 27, where it is called "the sacrifice of the Lord's passover." But this could be only in some secondary or partial sense, and not in the proper and primary sense of the word. For there was no priest employed upon the occasion, no part was burned or offered unto the Lord. And certainly no *propitiation* or *atonement* is said to have been made by it, and therefore it was very far from being a sin-offering.

Christ, with respect to his death, is by himself compared to the *serpent* which was exposed by Moses in the wilderness, that those of the people who looked upon it might be cured of the bite of such serpents. Here the analogy is obvious. The distempers of which they were cured were of the body, but those of which we are cured by the gospel are of the mind. John iii. 14: "And as Moses lifted up the serpent in the wilderness, even so must the Son of man be lifted up." Ch.

[1] See *Lardner* on this text. *Post. Serm.* Works, X. p. 506.

F

xii. 32: "And I, if I be lifted up, . . . will draw all men unto me." In this latter text the allusion is perhaps different from that above mentioned; for here Christ, being raised above the earth by means of the cross, is represented as drawing men from earth towards heaven.

I shall close this account of the figurative representations of the death of Christ that occur in the New Testament, with a view of the principal *uses* that the sacred writers make of it in illustrating other things. They show that the apostles were glad to take every opportunity of considering the death of Christ *in a moral view*, as affording the strongest motives to a holy life. They also show a fondness for very strong figures of speech. For the greater part of the metaphors in the following verses are much bolder, and more far-fetched than comparing the death of Christ to a sacrifice. Rom. vi. 3, 4: "Know ye not, that so many of you as were baptized into Jesus Christ, were baptized into his death? Therefore we are buried with him by baptism into death; that, like as Christ was raised up from the dead. by the glory of the Father, even so we also should walk in newness of life," &c. Gal. ii. 20: "I am crucified with Christ, nevertheless I live, yet not I, but Christ liveth in me." vi. 14: "God forbid that I should glory, save in the cross of our Lord Jesus Christ, by whom the world is crucified unto me, and I unto the world." See also Eph. ii. 5, 6.

Besides the death of Christ being expressly called a *sacrifice*, and various sacrificial expressions being applied to it, the language of Scripture is thought to favour the doctrine of atonement in various other respects, perfectly corresponding with the idea of its being a proper sacrifice, and irreconcilable with other views of it. I shall, therefore, briefly consider every representation which I can find of this nature.

1. Christ is frequently said to have *died for us*. But, in general, this may be interpreted of his dying *on our ac-* count, or *for our benefit*. Or if, when rigorously interpreted, it should be found that if Christ had not died, we must have died, it is still, however, only *consequentially so*, and by no means properly and *directly* so, as a *substitute* for us. For if, in consequence of Christ not having been sent to instruct and reform the world, mankind had continued unreformed, and the necessary consequence of Christ's coming was his death; by whatever means, and in whatever manner it was brought about, it is plain that there was, in fact, no other alternative, but his death or ours. How natural then was it, especially to writers accustomed to the strong figurative expression of the East, to say that he died *in our stead*, without meaning it in a strict and proper sense, as if God had absolutely required the death of Christ, in order to satisfy his justice for our sins, and as a necessary means of his forgiving us! Nothing but declarations much more definite and express, contained at least in some part of Scripture, could authorize us to interpret in this manner such general expressions as the following. John x. 11: "I am the good shepherd; the good shepherd giveth his life for the sheep." xv. 13: "Greater love hath no man than this, that a man lay down his life for his friends." 1 Pet. iii. 18: "Christ hath once suffered for sins, the just for the unjust, that he might bring us to God." John xi. 50: "It is expedient for us that one man should die for the people, and that the whole nation perish not."

A shepherd, in risking his life for his sheep, evidently gives his life for theirs, in a sufficiently proper sense; because if he had not thrown himself in the way of the wild beasts that were rushing upon his sheep, they must have died. But here was no compact between the beasts and the shepherd; the blood of the sheep was not due to them, nor did they accept of that of the shepherd in its stead. This case is, therefore, no proper parallel to the death of Christ, on the principle of the doctrine of atonement.

2. Christ is said to have given his life as a *ransom* (λυτρον) for us, but it is only in two passages that this view of it occurs, viz. Matt. xx. 28, and Mark x. 45, both of which contain the same expressions, as delivered by our Saviour on the same occasion : "The Son of man came not to be ministered unto, but to minister, and to give his life a ransom for many." 1 Tim. ii. 6 : "Who gave himself a ransom (αντι-λυτρον) for all." We meet, however, with other expressions similar to these, as Tit ii. 14: "Who gave himself for us, that he might redeem us from all iniquity, and purify unto himself a peculiar people, zealous of good works."

In all these cases, the price of redemption is said to have been given by Christ; but had we been authorized to interpret these expressions as if we had been doomed to die, and Christ had interposed, and offered his life to the Father in the place of ours, the representation might have been expected to be uniform; whereas, we find, in general, that the price of our redemption is given by God; as John iii. 16: "God so loved the world, that he gave his only begotten Son, that whosoever believeth on him should not perish, but have everlasting life." Rom. viii. 32: "He that spared not his own Son, but delivered him up for us all, how shall he not with him also freely give us all things?"

This language, on the part of God, or of Christ, is very proper, considered as figurative. For, if nothing but the mission of Christ could have saved the world, and his death was the necessary consequence of his undertaking it, God is very properly said to have given him up for us; or, since he undertook the work voluntarily, and from the love that he bore to man, he also may be said to have given his life as a ransom for ours; and thus these texts come under the same general idea with those explained above. In a figurative sense the gospel may be said to be the most *expensive provision* that God has made for recovering men from the power of sin, in order to purchase them, as it were, for himself.

3. Christ is said to *bear the sins of men* in the following texts. Isaiah liii. 11: "He shall bear their iniquities." Ver. 12: "He bare the sins of many." 1 Pet. ii. 24: "Who his own self bare our sins in his own body on the tree." Heb. ix. 28: "So Christ was once offered to bear the sins of many." But the idea we ought to annex to the term *bearing sin*, is that of *bearing it away*, or *removing it*, an effect which is produced by the power of the gospel. These texts are, therefore, similar to 1 John iii. 5: "And ye know that he was manifested to take away our sins; and in him is no sin." The phrase, *bearing sin*, is never applied, under the law, but to the *scape-goat*, on the day of expiation, which was not sacrificed, but, as the name expresses, was turned out into the wilderness.

We see clearly in what sense the evangelist Matthew understood the passage above quoted from Isaiah; when, speaking of some of our Saviour's miraculous cures, he says, ch. viii. 17, "That it might be fulfilled which was spoken by *Esaias* the prophet, saying, Himself took our infirmities, and bare our sicknesses." Now how did Christ bear the diseases of men? Not by taking them on himself, and becoming diseased as they had been, but by radically curing them. So also Christ *bears*, that is, *bears away*, or *removes*, the sins of men, by healing their distempered minds, and restoring them to a sound and virtuous state, by the power of his gospel.

4. Some who are willing to give up the idea of Christ dying as a proper sacrifice for us, or in our stead, say, nevertheless, that God forgives the sins of men *for the sake of the merits*, or at the *intercession*, of Christ, and that this appears to be analogous to the divine conduct in other respects; as

God is often said to show favour to some on the account of others, and especially to have favoured the Israelites on account of their relation to Abraham, Isaac and Jacob; and for this reason they say we are required to ask *in the name of Christ.* The texts, however, which bear this aspect are very few, perhaps none besides the following. 1 John ii. 1: "If any man sin, we have an advocate with the Father, Jesus Christ the righteous."

It is not denied, that it may be consistent with the maxims of divine government, to show favour to some persons on the account of others, to whom they bear a near relation. It is a wise maxim in human government, because we are, in many cases, as much concerned for others as for ourselves; and therefore a favour to a man's children, and posterity, may be the proper reward of his own merit, and also answer other ends of a *reward,* by being a motive to other persons to behave well. But, in general, favours distributed in this manner, are such as it is perfectly consistent with divine rectitude to grant to men without any regard to others, as giving the land of Canaan to the posterity of Abraham, &c. When the Jews incurred actual guilt, they were always punished like any other people, and by no means spared on account of their relation to Abraham. On the contrary, they are often said to have been more severely punished for not improving their privileges, as his descendants, &c.

Admitting, however, that God may be represented as forgiving sin, in particular cases, on this principle; if *all sin* be forgiven for the sake of Christ only, we ought, at least, to have been expressly told so. Our Saviour never says that forgiveness of sin was procured by him, but he always speaks of the free mercy of God in the same manner as the prophets who preceded him; and it is particularly remarkable that in his last prayer, which is properly *intercessory,* we find nothing on the subject.

If any stress be laid on Christ being said to be our *advocate,* the Holy Spirit is much more frequently and properly called so, and by our Lord himself; and he is represented by Paul as acting the part of an advocate and intercessor. Rom. viii. 26: "The Spirit itself maketh intercession for us."

"Repentance and remission of sins" are said to be "preached in the name of Christ," Luke xxiv. 47; and "through him," Acts xiii. 38; and all who believe in him are said to have "remission of sin,...through his name," ch. x. 43. But this phraseology is easily explained on the idea that the preaching of the gospel reforms the world, and that the remission of sin is consequent on reformation. In one passage, indeed, according to our translation, God is said to forgive sin *for the sake of Christ.* Eph. iv. 32: "Be ye kind one to another, tender-hearted, forgiving one another, even as God, for Christ's sake, hath forgiven you."[1] But in the original it is *in Christ,* and may be understood of *the gospel of Christ.* Had sin been forgiven, in a proper and strict sense, for the sake of Christ, the word *freely* would hardly have been used, as it often is, with relation to it, as in Rom. iii. 24; for this implies that forgiveness is the free gift of God, and proceeds from his essential goodness and mercy, without regard to any foreign consideration whatever.

The very great variety of manners in which the sacred writers speak of the method in which the pardon of sin is dispensed, is a proof that we are to allow something to the use of figures in their language upon this subject; for some of these phrases must be accommodated to the others. In general, the pardon of sin is represented as the act of God himself, but in some particular cases it is said to be the act of Christ. Matt. ix. 6: "But that ye may know that the Son

[1] On this mistranslation, see [Rutt's Priestley,] Vol. II. p. 296. *Note.*

of man hath power on earth to forgive sins." Col. iii., 13 : "Even as Christ forgave you, so also do ye." But upon a careful examination of such texts as these, and the comparison of them with those in which the pardon of sin seems to be represented as dispensed in consideration of the *sufferings*, the *merits*, the *resurrection*, the *life*, or the *obedience* of Christ, (for all these views of it occur,) we cannot but conclude that they are partial representations, which, at proper distances, are allowed to be inconsistent, without any charge of impropriety ; and that, according to the plain general tenor of Scripture, the pardon of sin is, in reality, always dispensed by the free mercy of God, on account of men's personal virtue, a penitent upright heart, and a reformed exemplary life, without regard to the sufferings, or merit, of any being whatever.

On this subject I would refer my readers to a very valuable essay on the doctrine of Atonement, in the *Theological Repository*,[1] in which the writer (who is the Rev. Mr. Turner of Wakefield) shows, that in the Old Testament, to make atonement for any *thing* or *person*, signifies, as I have mentioned above, making it, or him, *clean*, or *proper for the divine service ;* and that in the New Testament, similar expressions, which are there used by way of figure or allusion, " relate only to the establishment and confirmation of those advantages we at present enjoy by the gospel, and particularly of a free and uninterrupted liberty of worshipping God according to the institutions of Christ, granted to us *in the*

gospel ;[2] just as the legal atonements served (though far more imperfectly) similar purposes under that dispensation." But he says he doth not recollect any texts in which the death of Christ is represented as the *cause, reason,* or *motive,* why God has conferred these blessings on man.

The advocates for the doctrine of atonement must be embarrassed when they consider that, the godhead of Christ being incapable of suffering, his *manhood* alone was left to endure all the wrath of God that was due for every sin which he forgives; and surely one man (and that which actually suffered of Christ, on their own principles, was no more) could never make a sufficient atonement for the sins of the *whole world,* or even of the *elect* only, especially considering, as they do, that the sufferings of Christ were but temporary, and the punishment due to sin eternal.

There is a considerable difference in opinion, also, with respect to the *place* or *scene* of this expiatory suffering. In general it is thought to be been, in part, at the time of the agony in the garden, and in part on the cross. But to account for this extraordinary suffering, they are obliged to suppose something uncommon and undescribable in it, to which nothing in the common feelings of human nature ever corresponded, though at the same time it was only human nature that suffered.

Bishop Burnet was aware of this difficulty, and he expresses his ideas of it in a very natural manner, so as to show clearly how his scheme was pressed with it. In his *Exposition of the Thirty-nine Articles,* he says, " It is not easy for us to apprehend in what that agony consisted. For we understand only the agonies of pain or of conscience, which last arise out of the horror of guilt, or the apprehension of the wrath of God. It is, indeed, certain that he who had no sin could

---

[1] Vol. III. pp. 385–433. (*P.*) In his *Memoirs,* Dr. Priestley ascribes the origin of the Theol. Repos. to a sight of some critical notes by Mr. Turner, whose contributions to that publication were numerous and highly important. Mr. T. (in whose intercourse Dr. P. expresses himself particularly happy while he resided at Leeds) was of the party, at Richmond, mentioned in the Note, p. 3. He afterwards, in concert with Mr. Cappe, defended Mr. L. against a rude attack by a clergyman, and was his frequent correspondent. See *Mem. of Lindsey,* pp. 35, 91. *Notes.*

[2] " In consequence of his death." *Orig.* Theol. Repos. III. p. 431.

have no such horror in him; and yet it is as certain that he could not be put into such an agony only through the apprehension and fear of that violent death which he was to suffer the next day. Therefore we ought to conclude that there was an inward suffering in his mind, as well as an outward visible one in his body. We cannot distinctly apprehend what that was, since he was sure both of his own spotless innocence, and of his Father's unchangeable love to him. We can only imagine a vast sense of the heinousness of sin, and a deep indignation at the dishonour done to God by it, a melting apprehension of the corruption and miseries of mankind by reason of sin, together with a never-before-felt withdrawing of those consolations that had always filled his soul. But what might be farther in his agony and in his last dereliction, we cannot distinctly apprehend. Only this we perceive, that our minds are capable of great pain, as well as our bodies are. Deep horror, with an inconsolable sharpness of thought, is a very intolerable thing. Notwithstanding the bodily or substantial indwelling of the fulness of the godhead in him, yet he was capable of feeling vast pain in his body, so that he might become a complete sacrifice, and that we might have, from his sufferings, a very full and amazing apprehension of the guilt of sin. All those emanations of joy with which the indwelling of the eternal word had ever till then filled his soul, might then, when he needed them most, be quite withdrawn, and he be left merely to the firmness of his faith, to his patient resignation to the will of his heavenly Father, and to his willing readiness of drinking up that cup which his Father had put in his hand to drink." [1]

All this only shows how miserably men may involve themselves in systems unsupported by facts. Our Saviour, as an innocent man, could have no

terrors of a guilty conscience, and therefore he could feel nothing but the dread of his approaching painful and ignominious death. But having a clearer idea of this, as we perceive in the history, and consequently of the agony of it, than other men generally have of approaching sufferings, the apprehension which he was under, no doubt, affected his mind more than we can well conceive. Those who consider Christ as something more than a man, cannot imagine how he should be so much affected in those circumstances; but there is no difficulty in the case with those who consider him as a being made *exactly like themselves*, and perhaps of a delicate, tender habit.

As to the sins of others, it is natural to suppose that his mind would be less at leisure to attend to them then than at any other time, his mind being necessarily occupied with the sense of his own sufferings; and accordingly we find that all he says upon that occasion respects himself only. "Father, if it be possible, let this cup pass from me. Nevertheless, not as I will, but as thou wilt." That the presence of God forsook him, whatever he meant by it, is not at all supported by fact; and when he was much oppressed with sorrow, an angel was sent on purpose to comfort and strengthen him.

He went through the scene of his trial and crucifixion with wonderful composure, and without the least appearance of anything like agony of mind. His saying, "My God, my God, why hast thou forsaken me?" was probably nothing more than his reciting the first verse of the twenty-second Psalm, to which he might wish to direct the attention of those who were present, as it contained many things peculiarly applicable to his case. There is nothing in this scene, any more than in his agony in the garden, but what is easily explicable, on the supposition of Christ being a man; and to suppose that he was then under any agony of mind, impressed upon him, in any inexplicable manner, by

---

[1] Burnet's Expos. *Art.* II. *ad fin.* Ed. 4, pp. 54, 55. See Mon. Repos. II. p. 317, &c.

the immediate hand of God, in order to aggravate what he would naturally suffer, and thereby make his sufferings an adequate expiation for the sins of the world, is a mere arbitrary supposition, not countenanced by any one circumstance in the narration.

Calvin, as we shall see, supposed the great scene of our Saviour's sufferings to have been in *hell*, in the interval between his death and the resurrection.[1] But this is an hypothesis no less arbitrary and unsupported than any other.

Having now seen what the Scriptures contain concerning the doctrine of atonement, let us see what Christians in after ages have built upon it. The foundation we shall find very inadequate to the superstructure.

SECTION IV.

OF THE OPINIONS OF THE APOSTOLICAL FATHERS.

WHEN any mode of speech may be understood either in a *literal* or in a *figurative* sense, there must be some difficulty in ascertaining the real meaning of the person who makes use of it. For it is the same thing as if the word was properly ambiguous. Thus, a Papist and a Protestant equally make use of the words of our Saviour, *this is my body*, but it does not therefore follow that they think alike with respect to the Lord's supper. For one of them uses the expression as a mere figure of speech, meaning that the bread and wine are representations, or memorials, of the body and blood of Christ; whereas the other takes them to be the body and blood itself, without any figure.

In like manner, it cannot be determined from the primitive Christians calling the death of Christ *a sacrifice for sin*, a *ransom*, &c., or from their saying, in a general way, that Christ died in our stead, and that he *bore our*

---

[1] See *Institut.* L. ii. C. xvi. Sect. viii.–x.

sins, or even if they carried this figurative language a little farther, that they really held what is now called *the doctrine of atonement*, viz. that it would have been inconsistent with the maxims of God's moral government to pardon any sin whatever, unless Christ had died to make satisfaction to divine justice for it: because the language above mentioned may be made use of by persons who only believe that the death of Christ was a necessary circumstance in the scheme of the gospel, and that this scheme was necessary to reform the world.

According to the modern system, there is nothing in any of the good works of men that can at all recommend them to the favour of God; that their repentance and reformation is no *reason* or *motive* with him to forgive their sins, and that all the mercy which he ever shows them is on the account of the righteousness of Christ imputed to them. But it will appear that this language was altogether unknown in the early ages of Christianity; and, accordingly, Basnage ingenuously acknowledges that the ancients speak meagrely (*maigrement*) of the satisfaction of Christ, and give much to good works;[2] a sufficient indication, I should think, that they had no such ideas as he had concerning the satisfaction of Christ, and that they considered the good works of men as *in themselves* acceptable to God, in the same manner as the virtue or merit of Christ was acceptable to him. I shall, however, quote from the early Christian writers as much as may enable us to perceive how they thought with respect to this subject.

In the [first] epistle of Clemens Romanus are some expressions which, taken singly, might seem to favour the doctrine of atonement. But the general strain of his writings shows that he had no proper idea of it. Exhorting the Corinthians to repentance, and to virtue in general, he mentions the

---

[2] Histoire de la Religion des Eglises Reformées, 4to. 1725, I. p. 75. (*P.*)

example of Christ in the following manner: "Let us consider what is good and acceptable, and well pleasing in the sight of him that made us. Let us look steadfastly to the blood of Christ, and see how precious his blood is in the sight of God, which, being shed for our salvation, has obtained the grace of repentance for all the world."[1] This seems to be little more than a repetition of what is said in the book of Acts, of Christ being " exalted as a prince and a saviour, to give repentance and remission of sins."

He farther says, "Let us search into all the ages that have gone before, and let us learn that our Lord has, in every one of them, still given place for repentance to all such as would turn to him." He then mentions the preaching of Noah to the old world, and of Jonah to the Ninevites, of whom he says, "Howbeit, they, repenting of their sins, appeased God by their prayer, and were saved though they were strangers to the covenant of God." After this he recites what Isaiah, Ezekiel, and other prophets have said to this purpose; and in all his subsequent exhortations he seems to have no idea of anything but repentance and the mercy of God, and the immediate consequence of it, without the interposition of anything else. "Wherefore," says he, "let us obey his excellent and glorious will, and, imploring his mercy and goodness, let us fall down upon our faces before him, and cast ourselves upon his mercy."[2]

This writer also speaks of virtue alone as having immediately great power with God. "And especially, let them learn how great a power humility has with God, how much a pure and holy charity avails with him, how excellent and great his fear is, and how it will save all such as turn to him with holiness in a pure mind."[3] He speaks of the efficacy of faith in the same language with the apostle

Paul. The Jews, he says, "were all greatly glorified, not for their own sakes, or for their own works, or for the righteousness which they themselves had wrought, but through his will" (in consequence of the blessing promised to Abraham). "And we also, being called by the same will in Christ Jesus, are not justified by ourselves, either by our own wisdom, or knowledge, or piety, or the works which we have done, in the holiness of our hearts, but by that faith by which God Almighty has justified all men from the beginning."[4] But by *faith* this writer only means another virtue of the mind, viz. that regard to God, belief in his promises, and submission to his will, which supports the mind of man in great difficulties and trials. This was plainly his idea of the justification of Abraham himself. "For what was our Father Abraham blessed; was it not that through faith he wrought righteousness and truth?"[5]

It is possible that persons not acquainted with the writings of the apostolical fathers would imagine that, when they used such phrases as, being *justified by the blood of Christ*, they must mean, as some now do, that without the death of Christ our repentance would have been of no avail: but when we consider all that they have written, and the language of those who followed them, who treat more fully on the subject, and who appear not to have been sensible that they thought differently from them with respect to it, we shall be satisfied that those phrases conveyed no such ideas to them as they now do to us.

Barnabas, speaking of the Jewish sacrifices, says, "These things, therefore, has God abolished, that the new law of our Lord Jesus Christ, which is without the yoke of any such necessity, might have the spiritual offerings of men themselves. For so the Lord saith

[1] Sect. vii. *Cotilerii,* Ed. I. p. 150. (*P.*) Wake's Gen. Ep. p. 6.
[2] Sect. vii. and ix. (*P.*) Gen. Ep. pp. 7, 8.
[3] Sect. xxi. (*P.*) Gen. Ep. p. 19.

[4] Sect. xxxii. (*P.*) Gen. Ep. p. 25.
[5] Sect. xxxi. (*P.*) Gen. Ep. p. 24.

again, to those heretofore, Did I at all command your fathers, when they came out of the land of Egypt, concerning burnt-offerings or sacrifices? But this I commanded them, saying, Let none of you imagine evil in your hearts against his neighbour, and love no false oath. Forasmuch, then, as we are not without understanding, we ought to apprehend the design of our merciful Father. For he speaks to us, being willing that we, who have been in the same error about the sacrifices, should seek and find how to approach unto him; and therefore he thus bespeaks us: The sacrifice of God is a broken spirit. A broken and a contrite heart God will not despise."[1] This is not substituting the sacrifice of Christ in the place of the sacrifices under the law, but moral virtue only.

In the Shepherd of St. Hermas (if this should be thought to be the work of the Hermas mentioned by Paul) we find nothing of the doctrine of atonement, but strong expressions denoting the acceptableness of repentance and good works only. "Then," says he, "shall their sins be forgiven, which they have heretofore committed, and the sins of all the saints, who have sinned even unto this day, if they will repent with all their hearts, and remove all doubt out of their hearts."[2] He farther says, "Whosoever have suffered for the name of the Lord are esteemed honourable by the Lord, and all their offences are blotted out, because they have suffered death for the name of the Son of God."[3]

It seems pretty evident that *so far* we find no real change of opinion with respect to the efficacy of the death of Christ. These writers adopt the language of the apostles, using the term *sacrifice* in a figurative sense, and represent the value of good works, without the least hint or caution, lest we should thereby detract from the merits of Christ, and the doctrine of salvation by his imputed righteousness.

[1] Sect. ii. *Cotilerii*, Ed. p. 57. (*P.*) Gen. Ep. pp. 161, 162.
[2] Vis. ii. Sect. ii. (*P.*) Gen. Ep. p. 2(6.
[3] Sim. ix. Sect. xxviii. (*P.*) Gen. Ep. p. 186.

SECTION V.

OF THE OPINION OF THE FATHERS TILL AFTER THE TIME OF AUSTIN.

THAT it was not the received doctrine of the Christian church within this period, that Christ did, in any proper sense, make the Divine Being placable to men, but that the pardon of sin proceeded from the free mercy of God, independently of his sufferings and merit, may, I think, be clearly inferred from several considerations.

1. This doctrine, on which so much stress has been laid by some moderns, is never enumerated as an article of Christian faith, in any ancient *summary of Christian doctrine;* and the early Christian writers, especially those who made apologies for Christianity, had frequent occasion to do it; and we have several summaries of this kind.

To say nothing of the apologies of Justin Martyr, Athenagoras and Tertullian, who give accounts of the principal articles of Christian faith, but may be thought to do it too concisely for us to expect that they should take notice of such a doctrine as this, (though the great importance of it, in the opinion of those who hold this doctrine, is such, as ought to have given it the preference of any other,) I cannot help laying particular stress on the omission of it by Lactantius, who treats professedly of the system of Christianity, as it was generally received in his days. Yet, in his *Divine Institutions,* there is so far from being any mention of the necessity of the death of Christ to atone for the sins of men, that he treats of the nature of sin, of the mercy of God, and of the efficacy of repentance, as if he had never heard of any such doctrine.

We see his sentiments on these subjects very fully in his treatise De Ira Dei.[4] And when he professedly considers the reasons of the incarnation and death of Christ, he only says, that, "example was necessary to be exhibited to men as well as precepts, and therefore

[4] C. xix. xx. (*P.*) Lactant. Op. II. pp. 37. 38,

it was necessary that God should be clothed with a mortal body, be tempted, suffer and die."[1] He gives no other reason whatever. Again, he says, "Christ was made flesh, because he was not only to *teach*, but also to *do*, and to be an example, that none might allege in their excuse the weakness of the flesh."[2]

Cyprian, an early writer, often mentions the humiliation and sufferings of Christ, but always either as an example, or simply as foretold by the prophets.

Arnobius says, that "Christ permitted his man—that is, the man to whom he was united—to be killed, that, in consequence of it, (viz. his resurrection afterwards,) it might appear that what they had been taught concerning the safety of their souls was safe, or to be depended upon, and that death was not to be defeated any other way."[3]

Austin, in several places, speaks of the end of Christ's life and death, but never as designed to make satisfaction for the sins of men, but generally as an example. "In his passion he showed what we ought to endure; in his resurrection, what we are to hope for." Speaking of the incarnation in general, he says, "Christ assumed a human body, and lived among men, that he might set us an example of living and dying and rising again." When he speaks figuratively, it is plain he did not carry his ideas so far as the orthodox now do. "In his death," he says, "he made a gainful traffic; he purchased faithful men and martyrs. He bought us with his blood. He laid down the price of our redemption." But he likewise says, "Martyrs have returned

what was laid out for them, that is, have given what was purchased. even their lives."[4]

Some orthodox writers complain of the imperfect knowledge which the primitive Christian writers had of the Christian system in this respect. "Gallæus observes," according to Lardner, "that Lactantius says little or nothing of Christ's priestly office." Lardner himself adds, "I do not remember that Jerome has anywhere taken notice of this, but it is likely enough to be true; and that Lactantius did not consider Christ's death, in the modern way, as a propitiatory sacrifice for sin, or a satisfaction made to divine justice for the sins of the human race. This may be argued from his passages, before transcribed, concerning the value of repentance, and the ends of Christ's death." He adds that "many other ancient Christians will come in for their share in this charge. For," according to Matthias Flacius Illyricus, "the Christian writers who lived soon after Christ and his apostles discoursed, like philosophers, of the law and its moral precepts, and of the nature of virtue and vice: but they were totally ignorant of men's natural corruption, and the mysteries of the gospel, and Christ's benefits. His countryman, Jerome," he says, "was well skilled in the languages, and endeavoured to explain the Scriptures by versions and commentaries. But, after all, he was able to do very little, being ignorant of the human disease, and of Christ the physician, and wanting both the key of Scripture, and the Lamb of God, to open to him."[5]

The same Flacius, or some other learned writer of his time, observes concerning Eusebius, Bishop of Cæsarea, that "it is a very low and imperfect description which he gives of a Christian, making him only a man who, by the knowledge of Christ and his doctrine, is brought to the worship of the one true God, and the practice of

[1] Epitome, C. 1. p. 142. (*P.*) "Superest respondere etiam iis, qui putant inconveniens fuisse, nec habere rationem, ut Deus mortali corpore indueretur, ut hominibus subjectus esset, ut contumelias sustineret, cruciatus etiam mortemque pateretur. . . . Si non fecerit. præceptis suis fidem derogabit. Exemplis igitur opus est, ut ea, quæ præcipiuntur, habeant firmitatem, et si quis contumax extiterit, ac dixerit non posse fieri, præceptor illum præsenti opere convincat." Op. II. pp. 37, 38.

[2] Ibid. p. 143. (*P.*) Ergo ideo corporatus est, ut cum vincenda esse carnis desideria doceret, ipse faceret prior, ne quis excusationem de carnis fragilitate prætenderet." Op. II. p. 38.

[3] Adversus *Gentes*, L. i. p. 24. (*P.*)

[4] Lardner's Credib. X. pp. 299, 300. (*P.*) Works, V. pp. 121, 122.

[5] Ibid. VII. pp. 145, 146. (*P.*) Works, IV. p. 61.

sobriety, righteousness, patience, and other virtues. But he has not a word about regeneration, or imputed righteousness."[1]

I cannot forbear adding what Dr. Lardner very pertinently subjoins to this quotation: " Poor, ignorant, primitive Christians, I wonder how they could find the way to heaven! They lived near the times of Christ and his apostles. They highly valued, and diligently read, the Holy Scriptures, and some of them wrote commentaries upon them; but yet, it seems, they knew little or nothing of their religion, though they embraced and professed it with the manifest hazard of all earthly good things; and many of them laid down their lives rather than renounce it. Truly we of these times are very happy in our orthodoxy; but I wish that we did more excel in those virtues which they, and the Scriptures likewise, I think, recommend, as the distinguishing properties of a Christian. And I am not a little apprehensive, that many things which now make a fair show among us, and in which we mightily pride ourselves, will in the end prove *weeds* only, on which the owner of the ground sets no value."[2]

2. Some controversies were started in the primitive times which could not have failed to draw forth the sentiments of the orthodox defenders of the faith, on this subject, if they had really believed the death of Christ to be a proper sacrifice for sin; and that, without it, God either could not, or would not, pardon any sin.

All the Docetæ, and the Gnostics in general, who believed that Christ was man only in appearance, and did not really suffer, could have no idea of the meritorious nature of his death, as such; and yet this is never objected to any of them by Irenæus, or others, who write the most largely against them.

The Manicheans also did not believe that Christ died, and consequentially,

as Beausobre, who writes their history, observes, they must necessarily have ascribed the salvation of the soul to the doctrine and the example of Christ; and yet none of the primitive fathers who write against them observe, that the great end of Christ's coming into the world would then be defeated, in that the sins of men would not be satisfied for.[3] Austin, who writes against the Manicheans, and from whom, on account of his doctrine of *grace and original sin*, we might expect a complete system of atonement, never objects to them their want of such a doctrine, but combats them on other principles.

3. Had the ancient Christian writers had the ideas which some of the moderns have concerning the all-sufficient sacrifice of Christ, and the insufficiency of good works, they could not have expressed themselves as they generally do with respect to the value of repentance and *good works* in the sight of God.

Cyprian says, " What sinners ought to do, the divine precepts inform us, viz. that satisfaction is made to God by good works, and that sins are done away by the merit of compassion." (*Operationibus justis Deo satisfieri, misericordiæ meritis peccata purgari.*)[4]

Lactantius says, "Let no one who has been led into sin by the impulse of passion despair of himself, for he may be restored if he repent of his sins, and by good works make satisfaction to God (satisfaciat Deo): for if we think our children to be corrected when they repent of their faults, why should we despair of the clemency of God being pacified by repentance (penitendo posse placari?")[5] Again, " Whoever, there-

[1] Lardner's Credib. VII. pp. 145, 146. (P.) Works, IV. p. 61.

[2] Ibid. p. 62.

[3] Ibid. VI. p. 294. (P.) Works, pp. 488, 489.

[4] De Opere et Eleemosynis, Opera Ed. Caillau, p. 476.

[5] Inst. L. vi. C. xxiv. p. 631. (P.) "Nec tamen deficiat aliquis, aut de se ipse desperet, si aut cupiditate victus, aut libidine impulsus, aut errore deceptus; aut vi coactus, ad injustitiæ viam lapsus est. Potest enim reduci, ac liberari, si eum pœniteat actorum, et ad meliora conversus, satisfaciat Deo. . . . Nam si liberos nostros, cum delictorum suorum cernimus pœnitere, correctos esse arbitramur, et abdicatos, abjec-

fore, obeys the divine precepts, is a worshipper of the true God, whose sacrifices are gentleness of mind, an innocent life and good works."[1]

The manner in which Austin speaks of the merit of good works, shows that he could not have had any proper idea of the satisfaction of Christ. "By these alone," says he, "we secure happiness. In this way we recover ourselves. In this way we come to God, and are reconciled to him, whom we have greatly provoked. We shall be brought before his presence, let our good works there speak for us, and let them so speak that they may prevail over our offences. For whichsoever is most will prevail, either for punishment or for mercy."[2]

4. The merit of *martyrdom* was held in the highest esteem by all the primitive Christians. If, therefore, good works in general were thought by them to have merit with God, much more may we expect to find that they had this idea of what they considered as the most heroic act of virtue. And indeed the language of the primitive Christians on the subject of martyrdom is exceedingly inconsistent with any notion of atonement for sin by the death of Christ alone, without regard to anything that man can do for himself.

Ignatius, in a fragment of an epistle preserved by Chrysostom, speaking of certain crimes, says, that they could not be wiped out even by the blood of martyrdom. He also wishes that his own sufferings might be accepted as a *purification* and *price of redemption* for them (περιψημα και αντιψυχον).[3]

Origen says, "Christ has laid down his life for us. Let us also lay down

our lives, I will not say for him, but for ourselves, and for those who may be edified by our martyrdom. . . . . . And, perhaps, as we are redeemed by the blood of Christ, Jesus having received a name above every name, so some will be redeemed by the blood of martyrs."[4] And yet this writer says, "Christ offered his own life not unlike those who of their own accord devoted themselves to death, to deliver their country from some pestilence," &c.[5] As this language could only be figurative in this writer, we may conclude that it is no otherwise to be interpreted when we meet with it in other writers of those times.

5. The great virtue which the ancient fathers ascribed to *baptism*, and the *Lord's supper*, with respect to the forgiveness of sins, shows plainly that they did not consider the wrath of God as pacified by the death of Christ once for all. And though the Lord's supper was a commemoration of the death of Christ, it is plain that they did not consider the administration of it merely as an application of his merits or sufferings to themselves; but as having a virtue independent of that, a virtue originating from the time of the celebration. This will be abundantly evident when I come, in the course of this work, to show the abuses of those institutions. However, what they say concerning baptism will not admit of such an interpretation as some persons, not well acquainted with their writings, might be disposed to put on similar expressions relating to the eucharist.

Among others, Tertullian frequently speaks of baptism as washing away the guilt of sin. In several of the ancient liturgies, particularly that of Chrysostom, the priest prays that the eucharist may serve for the remission of sins and the communication of the Holy Spirit. It is well known, that at length the church of Rome, in pursuance of the same train of thinking,

---

[1] Inst. L. vi. C. xxiv. p. 686. (*P.*) "Quisquis igitur his omnibus præceptis cœlestibus obtemperaverit, hic cultor est verus Dei, cujus sacrificia sunt, mansuetudo animi, et vita innocens et actus boni." Op. I. p. 506.

[2] Lardner's Credib. X. p. 302. (*P.*) Works, IV. p. 123.

[3] Le Clerc's Historia Eccl. A.D. 116. (*P.*)

tosque rursus tamen suscipimus, fovemus amplectimur: cur desperemus clementiam Dei Patris pœnitendo posse placari?" Op. I. pp. 502, 503.

[4] Lardner's Credib. III. p. 226. (*P.*) Works, II. p. 462.

[5] Contra Celsum, L. i. pp. 24, 25. (*P.*) Αναλογον τοις αποθανουσιν ὑπερ πατριδων.

came to consider the eucharist to be as proper a *sacrifice* as the death of Christ itself, and as having the same original independent virtue.

6. Many of the ancient writers, in imitation of the author of the epistle to the Hebrews, call the death of Christ a *sacrifice*, and also say that it was prefigured by the sacrifices under the law. But that this was no fixed determinate view of the subject with them, is evident from their language upon other occasions; especially when, like the prophets of old, they oppose *good works*, and not *the death of Christ*, to the sacrifices under the law, as being of more value than they were.

Lactantius, in his Epitome of Divine Institutions, speaking of sacrifices, says, "the true sacrifice is that which is brought from the heart," meaning good works.[1] With respect to the same, he also says, "These are victims, this is a piacular sacrifice, which a man brings to the altar of God, as a pledge of the disposition of his mind."[2]

Though, therefore, in the Clementine liturgy, contained in the *Apostolical Constitutions*, Christ is called a *high priest*, and is said to be himself the *sacrifice*, the *shepherd*, and also the *sheep*, "to appease his God and Father, to reconcile him to the world, and to deliver all men from the impending wrath,"[3] we must not infer (notwithstanding, in these general terms, this writer seems to express even the proper principle of the doctrine of atonement) that, if he had dwelt longer on the subject, he would have been uniform in his representations. If this *was* the opinion of the author of that liturgy, and those who made use of it, it did not generally prevail. For the principles of that doctrine will very clearly appear to have been altogether unknown to the most eminent writers of that age.

One might have imagined that when Justin Martyr says that "Christ took (ειληφε) the sins of men,"[4] his idea had been that he made himself responsible for them. But the tenor of all his writings shows that he was very far from having any such idea. He will not even admit that, in any proper sense, Christ can be considered as having been made *a curse* for us. He says that, "when in the law they are said to be accursed who were crucified, we are not to suppose that the curse of God lies against Christ, by whom he saves those who have done things worthy of a curse." Again he says, "if the Father of all chose that his Christ should receive (αναλαβεσθαι) the curses of all men, (that is, be cursed or hated by all men,) knowing that he would raise him again after he was crucified and dead, will you consider him who endured these things, according to his Father's will, as accursed?"[5]

Austin says, "Christ took their punishment but not their guilt." And again, "by taking their punishment and not their guilt, he abolished both the guilt and the punishment."[6] But it is to be considered, as was observed above, that Austin was certainly ignorant of the *principle* of the doctrine of atonement; so that we can only suppose him to have meant that Christ suffered upon our account, and for our benefit; and though if he had not suffered, we must, it would have been not *directly*, but by *remote consequence*. His saying that Christ did not take the *guilt* of our sins, shows clearly that he had no idea of his bearing our sins in the common acceptation of the word, so as to make himself answerable for them; and therefore he could not, in a proper sense, be said to take the punishment of them.

---

[1] C. lviii. p. 173. (*P.*) "Hoc est sacrificium verum, non quod ex arca, sed quod ex corde profertur, non quod manu, sed quod mente libatur." Op. II. p. 47.

[2] C. lxvii. p. 215. (*P.*) "Hæc, sunt quæ debeat cultor Dei exhibere; hæ sunt victimæ, hoc sacrificium placabile: hic verus est cultus, quum homo mentis suæ pignora in aram Dei confert." Op. II. p. 60.

[3] *Apost. Con.* Brett's Ed. p. 8. (*P.*)

[4] *Apol.* I. Ed. Thirlby, p. 73. (*P.*) Αυτος αμαρτιας πολλων ειληφε, from Isaiah, liii. 12.

[5] *Dial.* Ed. Thirlby, pp. 345, 346. (*P.*)

[6] Grotius de *Satisfact.* Test. Vet. Op. IV. p. 345. (*P.*)

7. When the ancient Christian writers do speak of the mission and death of Christ, as reversing the effects of sin, and restoring things to the same state in which they were before the fall, so as to make them once more immortal, their idea was not that this was effected by procuring the pardon even of that sin of Adam, by which death was entailed upon his posterity; but by means of Christ doing (which indeed they did not clearly explain) what Adam was not able to do. "For this reason," says Irenæus, "was the word of God made man, and he who was the Son of God, became the son of man, that man, being mixed with the word of God, he might, by receiving the adoption, become the Son of God. For we could not otherwise receive incorruptibility and immortality, unless we were united to incorruptibility and immortality. But how could we be united to incorruptibility and immortality, unless that which we are had become incorruptible and immortal; that so, what was corruptible might be absorbed by what was incorruptible, and what was mortal by immortality, that we might receive the adoption of sons?"[1]

I am far from pretending to explain, and much less to defend this passage of Irenæus. But it is evident, that it is not capable of receiving any light from the principle of the doctrine of atonement. If this writer had had the same idea that many now have of it, he could not have been so embarrassed on the subject.

The same general object of the death of Christ is expressed by Lactantius, but without annexing to it any particular explanation, in the following passage of his Epitome: "Therefore the Supreme Father ordered him to descend upon earth, and put on a human body, that, being subject to the passions of the flesh, he might teach virtue and patience, not by words only, but also by actions. Wherefore he was born again of a virgin, without a

[1] *Hær.* L. iii. C. xxi. p. 249. (*P.*)

father, as a man, that, as when he was created by God alone, in his first spiritual nativity, he was made a holy spirit, so being born of his mother alone, in his second carnal nativity, he might become holy flesh; that by his means the flesh which had been subject to sin, might be delivered from death."[2]

Athanasius did plainly consider Christ as dying in the place of men who were subject to death. But he does not say that it was to satisfy the justice of God for their sins, but to procure the resurrection of mankind in general, the wicked as well as the righteous, to a future life; which is by no means the idea of those who now maintain the doctrine of atonement, though it may be said to be an approach towards it.

"It was," says he, "an instance of his love to mankind, that both instead of the death of all men before, the law which related to that mortality, might be disannulled, as having its power entirely satisfied in the Lord's body, and so had no more place against the rest of mankind; and also, that he might recover and revive those men that were returning to corruption from death, by making their bodies his own, and by the grace of the resurrection; and so might extinguish the power of death with respect to them, as stubble is plucked out of the fire. For the Word being conscious that the mortality of all men could not otherwise be put an end to than by the dying of all men, and it being impossible that the Word, which was immortal, and the Son of the Father, should die; for this cause he took to himself a body that could die, that the same

[2] C. xliii. p. 113. (*P.*) "Jussit igitur eum Summus Pater descendere in terram, et humanum corpus induere, ut subjectus passionibus carnis, virtutem ac patientiam non solum verbis, sed etiam factis doceret. Renatus est ergo ex virgine sine patre, tanquam homo; ut quemadmodum in prima nativitate spirituali creatus, et ex solo Deo sanctus spiritus factus est, sic in secunda carnali ex sola matre genitus, caro sancta fieret, ut per eum caro quæ subjecta peccato fuerat, ab interitu liberaretur." Op. II. p. 32.

body, by partaking of that Word, which was over all, might be an equivalent for the death of all, and yet might afterwards continue incorruptible, on account of the Word that was the inhabitant, and so corruption might afterwards cease from all men by the grace of the resurrection."[1] Also in the liturgy ascribed to Nestorius, Christ is said to have "undergone for men the punishment due to their sins, giving himself to die for all whom death had dominion over."[2]

It is evident, from all these passages, that these writers had no idea of Christ's so suffering for men, as to endure for them any part of the punishment that was to be inflicted in a future world, but only to procure the reversion of the sentence passed upon man in consequence of the fall of Adam; so far, that, though all men should actually die, they should not continue subject to death, but have the benefit of a resurrection.

8. It appears, that by some means or other, probably the too literal interpretation of the figurative language of Scripture, such an advance was made towards the doctrine of atonement, in the period of which I am now treating, that it was generally supposed that the death of Christ was a *price* paid for our redemption from the power of death, and that without it there would have been no resurrection from the dead. But this system was so far from being completed, that these writers could not determine to whom this price was paid; and in general it was agreed that it was paid to the *devil*, to whom mankind had been given over, in consequence of the sin of Adam.

Origen was clearly of this opinion. "If," says he, "we are bought with a price, as Paul affirms, we must have been bought from some person whose slaves we were, who also demanded what price he pleased, that he might dismiss from his power those which he

held. But it was the devil that held us. For to him we had been given over for our sins. Wherefore, he demanded the blood of Christ, as the price of our redemption." He goes on to observe, that "till the blood of Christ was given, which was so precious that it alone could suffice for the redemption of all, it was necessary for all those who were under the law to give each his own blood, in a kind of imitation of a future redemption; and therefore that we, for whom the price of Christ's blood is paid, have no occasion to offer a price for ourselves, that is, *the blood of circumcision*."[3] In this place, therefore, he supposes that the rite of circumcision, and not the sacrifice of animals, was intended to prefigure the death of Christ, and to serve as a kind of temporary substitute for it.

This writer also compares the death of Christ to that of those in the heathen world who devoted themselves to death, to avert public calamities from their country. "It is requisite, for some secret and incomprehensible reasons in nature, that the voluntary death of a righteous man should disarm the power of evil demons, who do mischief by means of plagues, dearths, tempests, &c. Is it not probable, therefore," he says, "that Christ died to break the power of the great demon, the prince of the other demons, who has in his power the souls of all the men that ever lived in the world?"[4]

This opinion, however, of the price of our redemption being paid to the devil, appears not to have been universally acquiesced in; and Gr. Nazianzen takes it up as a question that had not been discussed before; and after proposing several schemes, and not appearing to be satisfied with any of them, he gives his own opinion with considerable diffidence. "We may inquire," he says, "into a fact, and an opinion, which had been overlooked by many,

---

[1] *Athan.* Opera, I. p. 61. (*P.*)
[2] *Apost. Con.* Brett, p. 94. (*P.*)

[3] *Orig.* Opera, II. p. 486. (*P.*)
[4] *Orig.* Contra Celsum, L. i. p. 25. (*P.*) See the Quotation, p. 76. Note 5.

but which I have diligently considered, viz. to whom, and for what, was the blood of Christ shed. We were in the possession of the devil, being sold to him for sin, we having received the pleasures of sin in return. But if the price of redemption could only be received by him who had possession of us, I ask *to whom* was this blood paid, and for what cause? For if it was paid to that wicked one, it was shameful indeed; and if he not only received a price from God, but God himself was that price, for such a price it was certainly just that he should spare us. Was the price paid to the Father? But how, for we were not held by him, and how could the Father be delighted with the blood of his only begotten Son, when he would not receive Isaac, who was offered to him by Abraham? Or rather, did the Father receive the price, not because he desired, or wanted it, but because it was convenient that man should be sanctified by what was human in God, that he, by conquering the tyrant, might deliver us, and bring us to him?"[1]

The opinion which this writer mentions in the last place, and that to which we may, therefore, suppose he was most inclined, is, that the death of Christ is, in some manner, instrumental to our *sanctification*, that is, to our being made fit to be offered to God, and to be made his property, after having been in the power of the devil, but he does not say that it was for our *justification*. He, therefore, had no proper idea of what is now called the doctrine of atonement. Indeed, he expresses himself with so much uncertainty, that some may still think he was, upon the whole, of the opinion of Origen, viz. that the price of our redemption was paid to the devil, but that it was more than he was fairly entitled to.

That the devil was the person to whom the price of our redemption was due, seems to have been the general

opinion of speculative writers till the age of the schoolmen. Ambrose says, "we were pledged to a bad creditor, for sin....Christ came, and offered his blood for us."[2] This writer has a distinction with respect to our redemption by Christ, which is something curious. For he says, "the flesh of Christ was given for the salvation of the body, and his blood for the salvation of the soul." I do not know that any of the moderns follow him in this. Optatus Milevitanus also speaks of the devil being in possession of men's souls, before they were redeemed by the blood of Christ.[3]

Austin writes so fully on this subject, and his opinions in general acquired such an ascendency in the Western church, for many centuries after his death, that I shall give a larger extract from his writings. "What," says he, "is the power of that blood, in which, if we believe, we shall be saved; and what is the meaning of being reconciled by the death of his Son? Was God the Father so angry with us, that he could not be pacified without the death of his Son? By the justice of God the race of man was delivered to the devil; the sin of the first man being transferred to all his posterity, the debt of their first parents binding them: not that God did it, or ordered it, but he permitted them to be so delivered. But the goodness of God did not forsake them, though in the devil's power, nor even the devil himself, for he lives by him. If, therefore, the commission of sin, through the just anger of God, subjects man to the power of the devil, the remission of sins, by the gracious forgiveness of God, delivers man from the devil. But the devil was not to be overcome by the power, but by the justice of God; and it pleased God, that in order to deliver man from the power of the devil, the devil should be overcome not by power, but by justice. What then is the justice (or rather *righteousness*)

1 Greg. Nazian. Opera, 1630. *Orat.* xlii. p. 691. (P.)

2 Grotii Op. Test. Vet. IV. p. 344. (P.)
3 Opera, p. 80. (P.)

by which the devil was conquered; what but the righteousness of Jesus Christ? And how is he conquered? Because, though there was in him nothing worthy of death, he (that is, the devil) killed him. Was not, then, the devil to have been fairly conquered, though Christ had acted by power, and not by righteousness? But he postponed what he *could* do, in order to do what *ought to be done.* Wherefore it was necessary for him to be both God and man; man, that he might be capable of being killed; and God, to show that it was voluntary in him. What could show more power than to rise again, with the very flesh in which he had been killed? He, therefore, conquered the devil twice, first by righteousness, and then by power." He also says, "the blood of Christ is given as a price, and yet the devil having received it, is not enriched, but bound by it, that we might be delivered from his bonds."[1]

This last quotation contains an antithesis of which all the writers of that age were too fond, and to which they sometimes sacrificed more than they ought to have done. From the same fondness for antithesis, without perhaps intending to be understood in the manner in which his expressions will now be naturally understood by many, he says, "Christ alone suffered punishment without bad deserts, that by him we might obtain favour without good deserts."[2]

Proclus of Constantinople also, a writer of the same age, but somewhat later than Austin, considered the price of our redemption as paid to the devil. "The devil," he says, "held us in a state of servitude, boasting that he had bought us.....It was necessary, therefore, that all being condemned, either they should be dragged to death, or a sufficient price be paid; and because no angel had wherewithal to

pay it, it remained that God should die for us."[3]

9. Lastly, nothing, perhaps, can show more clearly how far the primitive Christians were from entertaining the idea that many now do concerning the efficacy of the death of Christ, as instrumental to the pardon of all sin, than their interpretation of some of those texts in which the doctrine of atonement is now supposed to be contained.

Clemens Alexandrinus explains Rom. iv. 25, *he was delivered for our offences,* by saying that Christ was the corrector and director of sinners, so that he alone can forgive sins, being appointed a pedagogue by the universal Father. He explains Matt. xxvi. 28, in which our Lord calls the wine, *his blood which is shed for many,* "by his word or doctrine, which was poured out for many, *for the remission of sins,*" and interprets what our Lord says in the 6th chapter of John's gospel, about eating his flesh and drinking his blood, of faith and hope, which supports the soul;[4] and to prove that blood may represent word or doctrine, he alleges Gen. iv. 10, in which it is said, the blood of Abel cried unto God.

Upon the whole, I think it must appear sufficiently evident, that the proper doctrine of atonement was far from being settled in the third or fourth centuries, though some little approach was made towards it, in consequence of supposing that what is called a *ransom* in a figurative sense, in the New Testament, was something more than a figure; and therefore that the death of Christ was truly a *price paid for our redemption,* not indeed directly from *sin,* but rather from *death,* though it was not settled *to whom* this price was paid. In general the writers of those times rather seem

---

[1] Augustin de *Trin.* L. xiii. C. ii. Op. III. pp. 414 and 417. (*P.*)
[2] *Contra duas Pelagianorum Epistolas,* L. iv. Op. VII. p. 915. (*P.*)

[3] Grotii Op. Test. Vet. IV. p. 346. (*P.*) Milton, the *orthodoxy* of whose *Paradise Lost* has, probably, been overrated, seems to have supposed that an angel might have made the *Atonement,* had any one of them possessed sufficient *charity* and resolution. See B. iii. line 213–221.
[4] *Pæd.* L. i. Opera, pp. 110, 158. (*P.*)

G

to have considered God as the person who paid the price, than he that received it. For, man being delivered into the power of the devil, they considered the price of redemption as paid to him. As to the forgiveness of sins, it was represented by all the fathers, and even by Austin himself, as proceeding from the free grace of God, from which free grace he was farther induced to give up his Son, as the price of our redemption from the power of the devil. We must, therefore, proceed farther, before we come to any regular system of atonement, founded on fixed principles, such as are now alleged in support of it.

SECTION VI.

OF THE STATE OF OPINIONS CONCERNING THE DOCTRINE OF ATONEMENT, FROM THE TIME OF AUSTIN TO THE REFORMATION.

AFTER Austin, we find but few writers of eminence for several centuries, owing to the great confusion of the times; so that he being the last very considerable writer in the Western church, his works went down to posterity with peculiar advantage, having no rival of any note. He was, therefore, considered as an authority, and his opinions were seldom disputed. But having himself formed no fixed opinion with respect to the doctrine of atonement, his doctrines of *grace, original sin* and *predestination,* were not connected with it, as they now are. We shall find, however, that though not immediately, yet by degrees, something more like the present doctrine of atonement got established before the æra of the Reformation.

About two centuries and a half after Austin, we find Gregory the Great, who was the most considerable writer in his time. But he also was far from having any consistent notions on this subject. For, at the same time that he insists upon the necessity of some expiation, he says, that our redemption might have been effected by Christ in some other way than by his death. He says, "The rust of sin could not be purged without the fire of torment; Christ therefore came without fault, that he might subject himself to voluntary torment, and that he might bear the punishment due to our sins." But he says, "Christ might have assisted us without suffering, for that he who made us could deliver us from suffering without his own death. But he chose this method, because by it he showed more love to us."[1]

In Theodorus Abucara, a Greek writer of the ninth century, we find something more like the doctrine of atonement, than in any writer in the Latin church. Indeed, as far as the extract given us by Grotius goes, it is very express to the purpose. But how he would have explained himself if he had written more largely on the subject, I cannot tell. He says, " God, by his just judgments, demanded of us all the things that are written in the law; which, when we could not pay, the Lord paid for us, taking upon himself the curse and condemnation to which we were obnoxious." Again, he says, " Christ, the mediator, reconciled us to God."[2]

In the Latin church, however, the doctrine of atonement does not appear to have been fixed in the eleventh century; at least if we may judge of it by the writings of Anselm, who was one of the greatest theologians of that age, and one of the first who distinguished himself by that peculiar kind of acuteness of speculation, which was carried much farther some time afterwards, in what is called the age of the *schoolmen.* This, however, we may say, that all the ideas of Anselm on this subject, would not be adopted by those who are advocates for the doctrine of atonement at present. He says, " that of innumerable other methods, by which God, being omnipotent, might have

[1] In Job ii. Cap. 12; xxx. Cap. 26. Op. fol. 13, 123. (*P.*)
[2] Grotii Op. Test. Vet. IV. pp. 347, 348. (*P.*)

saved men, he chose the death of Christ, that by it he might, at the same time, manifest his love to men." "Was the Father," says he, " so angry with men, that unless the Son had died for us, he would not be appeased? No: for the Father had love for us even when we were in our sins."[1] Yet he says, "Human nature could not be restored unless man paid what for sin he owed to God; and that which Christ ought not to pay but as man, he was not able to pay but as God; so that there was a necessity that God should be united to man."[2]

This seems, indeed, to be the proper language of the doctrine of atonement. But he afterwards expresses himself in a manner not quite so favourable to that scheme, for he says, "As Christ died without any sin of his own, a reward was due to him; and because he, being God, could not receive any addition of happiness, the reward was bestowed on those on whom he chose that it should be conferred; and on whom could he more justly choose to have it bestowed, than upon his relations and brethren, whom he saw in so miserable a state; that that might be remitted to them which they owed for their sins, and that might be given to them, which on account of their sins they wanted?"

Something more like the doctrine of atonement occurs in Theophilus, a Greek writer of the age of Anselm. But the quotation from him in Grotius, is so short, that, as in the case of Abucara, I cannot tell how he would have explained himself if he had written more largely upon the subject. It may be observed, however, that as Grotius was professedly collecting authorities in support of the doctrine of atonement, he would not have omitted anything that he had found more to his purpose. "The Father," says this writer, " was angry; wherefore Christ, being made a mediator, reconciled him

to us. How? By bearing what we ought to have borne, viz. death."[3] By this, however, he might not mean the *wrath of God in a future state*, but simply *death*, respecting the whole human race, which we have seen to be the opinion of the primitive fathers. And this, indeed, might be all that Abucara intended to express in the passage above quoted.

In the following century we meet with Peter Lombard, the greatest authority in the school of theology before the appearance of Thomas Aquinas; but in him we find nothing more settled about the doctrine of atonement than in the time of Austin. This writer, in his book of *Sentences*, in which he meant to comprise the sum of universal theology, treating of the manner in which we are delivered from sin and the devil by the death of Christ, says, that "in the death of Christ the love of God towards us is made conspicuous, and by means of it we are moved and excited to love God, who hath done so much for us, and thus we become justified, that is, being free from sin, we become righteous. The death of Christ, therefore, justifies us, because by means of it love is excited in our hearts."[4]

He adds, but more obscurely, that, " in another manner also, we are justified by the death of Christ, viz. because by faith in it we are freed from sin, looking to it as the children of Israel looked to the brazen serpent; so that though after the death of Christ the devil may tempt us, as he did before, he cannot conquer us as he did before. Thus Peter was overcome by temptation before the death of his Master, but afterwards behaved with the greatest boldness before the Jewish rulers." Again, treating of the manner in which we are delivered from punishment by the death of Christ, he says, that "the penance enjoined by the church would not suffice without the sufferings of Christ, co-operating

---

[1] Ad Rom. C. v. Op. II. p. 31. (*P.*)
[2] *Cur Deus Homo*, L. ii. C. xviii. Op. III. p. 68. (*P.*)

[3] Grotii Op. Test. Vet. IV. p. 348. (*P.*)
[4] L. iii. Dist. 19, 20, p. 596. (*P.*)

with it; so that the sins of good men before the death of Christ were borne with by God until that event." He says, however, "we are not to suppose that the death of Christ so reconciles us to God, as that he then begins to love those whom he before had hated: for, that God always loved men, and that he might have chosen any other method to redeem us from sin than by the death of Christ, if he had pleased; but that he chose this method because in this manner the devil is overcome not by *power*, of which he was a lover, but by *righteousness*, which he hated. For we being the captives of the devil, God might have released us by his authority only." This is the same view of this subject that was before given by Austin.

In this last quotation from Peter Lombard, we find some remains of the old doctrine of redemption from the power of the devil; but in Bernard, who was Lombard's contemporary, we find more of the proper doctrine of satisfaction, but not very fully stated, and mixed with some principles not very consonant to it. Upon the whole, however, his doctrine on this subject is nearer to that of the moderns than anything we meet with before the Reformation. He also speaks of *imputed sin* and *imputed righteousness* more expressly, I believe, than any who had gone before him. He says, that, "since man, by sin, became obnoxious to two kinds of death, the one spiritual and voluntary, the other corporeal and necessary, God by his corporeal and voluntary death obviated both. Had he not suffered corporeally, he had not paid our debts; had he not suffered voluntarily, there would not have been any merit in it." "God-man," says he, "taking the punishment, and being free from the guilt, dying of his own accord, merits life and righteousness for us." Death, he says, "is driven away by the death of Christ, and his righteousness is imputed to us. Shall the sin of Adam be imputed to me? And shall not the righteousness of

Christ belong to me also? We are much more truly born of God according to the spirit, than we are born of Adam according to the flesh."[1] "A foreign righteousness," says he, "is given to man who wanted his own. It was man that owed, and it was man that paid. The satisfaction of one is imputed to all."[2] But in all this he is speaking of *natural death* only, and therefore he did not in fact go beyond the ideas of Austin.

Notwithstanding this language, so exceedingly favourable to the doctrine of atonement, he speaks of the power that God and every person has, to forgive sins committed against himself. "Can I," says he, "forgive an offence against myself? The Omnipotent certainly can. We know, therefore, that Christ can forgive sin by the power of his divinity, and we cannot doubt of his willingness."[3]

The great oracle of the Latin church was Thomas Aquinas; and his doctrine, we may presume, was that which was most generally received in that church, and retained till the time of the Reformation. The following quotations from his *Summa* show that his doctrine of satisfaction was a mixed one. He says, that "in consequence of sin man was a debtor to God as a judge, and to the devil as a tormentor. And with respect to God, justice required that man should be redeemed, but not with respect to the devil; so that Christ paid his blood to God, and not to the devil. It was not naturally impossible for God," he says, "to be reconciled to man without the death of Christ, but this was more convenient, as by this means he obtained more and better gifts than by the mere will of God."[4] He says, that "God might have remitted the sins of men by his mere will, but that it is more convenient to do it by the death of Christ, on account of the various uses which it

[1] Bernardi. Op. Picard, 1009. *Ad Milites Templi,* C. xi. p. 837. (*P.*)
[2] Ibid. *Epist.* cxc. p. 1556. (*P.*)
[3] Ibid. *Ad Milit.* C. xi. p. 837. (*P.*)
[4] *Summa,* Pt. iii. Ques. xlviii. Art. vi. p. 120. (*P.*)

answered at the same time, especially moral ones;" and among others he mentions our being thereby the more excited to love God, and that Christ thereby gave an example of obedience, humility and fortitude. He says, that "the guilt of sin is taken away by the renovating power of grace, and the punishment by Christ, as a man, making satisfaction to God."[1] He illustrates the merits of Christ with respect to Christians, by the idea of his being the head, and they the body, as if, says he, a man by means of his hands should redeem himself from a punishment due for a sin committed by his feet. Lastly, he maintained that baptism, penance, and the other sacraments, derived their virtue from the death of Christ.[2]

It appears from these extracts, that the Latin church was far from having any consistent doctrine of atonement, though a great deal was ascribed to the death of Christ. We shall find, in another part of this work, that though the writers of this age admitted the doctrine of Austin concerning *grace*, they were not without expedients to make room for the doctrine of the *merit* of good works, and even to provide *a fund of merit*, transferable to those who had it not, of which the court of Rome made a most intemperate use. This doctrine of *merit*, would naturally check the tendency which the divines of that church might otherwise have had, to perfect their doctrine of satisfaction for sin by the death of Christ; and it was in opposition to this doctrine of human merit, that Luther, and some others of the reformers, laid the great stress which we find they did upon the doctrine of the merit of Christ, and the satisfaction made for our sins by his death. With them, therefore, and with them only, shall we find the doctrine of atonement completed in all its parts. How this business stood in the Greek church, I have had no opportunity of tracing; but, from the few specimens I

have given of it, it should seem, that their opinions were nearer to those of our reformers than those of the church of Rome.

It is very remarkable, that we find nothing like a *controversy* on the subject of this doctrine in all the Western church, quite down to the Reformation; nor do we find anything of this kind in the Greek church, except that, in the twelfth century, the emperor Emanuel Comnenus exercised himself and his divines with this question, "In what sense it was, or might be affirmed, that an incarnate God was at the same time the *offerer* and the *oblation?*"[3] But nothing of any consequence resulted from it.

SECTION VII.

OF THE DOCTRINE OF THE REFORMERS ON THE SUBJECT OF ATONEMENT.

THE first who separated from the church of Rome were the *Waldenses*, of Piedmont, in the Alps. They seem to have had their origin from the time of Claudius, bishop of Turin, who distinguished himself by his opposition to the worship of images, and other innovations of the church of Rome, in the tenth century. With them we find a general outline of the doctrine of atonement, in the confession of faith which they presented to the king of France in 1544; in which they say, that "the fathers, to whom Christ was promised, notwithstanding their sin, and their impotence by the law, desired the coming of Christ to satisfy for their sins, and to fulfil the law by himself."[4] But we find nothing of this subject in their older confessions. In general, however, it cannot but appear probable, that as the advocates of the church of Rome were inclined to explain away the doctrine of *grace*, and to introduce that of *merit*, those who

---

[1] *Summa*, Pt. iii. Ques. xlvi. Art. iii. p. 111. (*P.*)
[2] Ibid. Ques. xxii. xlviii. Art. vi. pp. 57, 120. (*P.*)
[3] Mosheim, II. p. 435. (*P.*) Cent. xii. Pt. ii. Ch. iii. Sect. xv.
[4] Leger, *Histoire*, p. 94. (*P.*)

wished for a reformation of the abuses of penance, purgatory and indulgences, which were founded on the doctrine of *merit*, would lean to the other extreme, and lay great stress on the satisfaction made for sin by the death of Christ alone.

Wickliffe seems to have been a firm believer of the doctrine of predestination, and also of the absolute necessity of the death of Christ, in order to the forgiveness of sin, if his sentiments be faithfully represented by Du Pin, who censures him for maintaining that God could not pardon sin without the satisfaction of Jesus Christ; that he can save none but those who are actually saved; and that he wills sin in order to bring good out of it.[1] And Mr. Gilpin represents him as maintaining that "all men, as far as the merit of another can avail, are partakers of the merits of Christ."[2] This, however, is not very consistent with the doctrine of predestination.[3]

But after the reformation by Luther, we find the doctrine of satisfaction, or atonement for sin by the death of Christ, reduced to a regular system, grounded on certain principles, and pursued to its proper extent. It cannot be said of the divines since that period, as it may perhaps be said of some before it, that what we meet with in them on this subject were only casual expressions or hasty and unsettled thoughts, and that if they had written more fully and professedly on the subject, they might, perhaps, have advanced what would have been inconsistent with it. There can be no doubt but that the principles of this doctrine were the real persuasion of many of the first reformers; that they considered it as an article of the utmost consequence, and that even the doctrine of the divinity of Christ was only a secondary consideration with respect to it. Since the reason of the incarnation of Christ, they say, was the giving merit to his sufferings and death, and to enable him to make an infinite satisfaction for sin, which was of infinite magnitude, and which required nothing less to expiate it at the hands of a righteous and just God.

That the first reformers should so eagerly catch at this doctrine, and lay the stress they did upon it, may be accounted for upon two considerations. The first is, that the controversy began on the subject of *indulgences*, which were built on the doctrine of *merit*, and this was most effectually opposed by disclaiming merit altogether, undervaluing all good works, and building all hopes of future happiness on the perfect satisfaction that Christ has made to the justice of God for us, and his righteousness imputed to us.

Another circumstance which contributed to give them this turn, was, that Luther had been a friar of the order which bore the name of Austin. He was much conversant in his writings, and therefore would have a leaning not only to his doctrines of grace, original sin, and predestination, but also to this of satisfaction, which, though it was not properly advanced by Austin himself, had been gradually established on his general principles.

The doctrine of Luther and his followers on this subject, we see in the Confession of Faith presented to the emperor Charles the Fifth, at Augsburg, in 1530, where we find it asserted, that "Christ died to reconcile the Father to us, and that he might be a true sacrifice for the guilt not only of original sin, but also for all the actual sins of men."[4]

This doctrine is more fully expressed in the Helvetic Confession of the year 1536, and which was approved by all the Protestant churches in Europe at that time. It is there declared, that "Christ took upon him, and bore the

---

[1] Hist. XIII. p. 117. (*P.*)
[2] Life of Wickliffe, p. 68. (*P.*)
[3] See Toplady's *Historic Proof*, I. pp. 191—196. Dr. Towers says of Wickliffe, that "in some part of his writings he speaks so strongly of fate, that he appears an absolute predestinarian. In other parts he expresses himself in so cautious a manner, that it seems as if his principles were not fixed upon the subject." Brit. Biog. I. p. 49.

[4] Syntagma Confessionum Fidei, 1654, p. 10. (*P.*)

sins of the world, and satisfied divine justice. God therefore, on account of the passion and resurrection of Christ only, is propitious to our sins, nor does he impute them to us, but he imputes the righteousness of Christ for ours; so that we are not only cleansed from our sins, but also presented with the righteousness of Christ, and being absolved from sin, we become righteous, and heirs of eternal life. Therefore, properly speaking, God alone justifies us, and only for the sake of Christ, not imputing to us our sins, but imputing to us his righteousness."[1]

But the proper principle of this doctrine, as providing an infinite satisfaction for offences of infinite magnitude, is most fully expressed in the synod of Dort, held in 1618. " God," say they, " is not only supremely merciful, but supremely just. But his justice requires that our sins, being committed against his infinite Majesty, must be punished not only with temporal, but with eternal pains, both of body and mind; which pains we cannot escape till the justice of God be satisfied. But when we could not make satisfaction, God gave his only-begotten Son to satisfy for us; and he was made sin and a curse upon the cross in our stead."[2]

Notwithstanding the satisfaction, thus supposed to be made to the justice of God, by the sufferings of Christ, it is evident that there must be some method of *appropriating* the benefit of these sufferings to individuals; for otherwise all mankind would have an equal claim to it. And since it would favour the doctrine of human merit too much, to suppose that the merit of Christ's suffering was always applied to persons of a certain character and conduct, advantage was taken of an expression of the apostle Paul, that we are *saved by faith alone;* interpreting it, as if it was something altogether independent of *good works,* or even of a good disposition of mind, which always precedes good works, and constitutes what-

ever merit they have. This application of the merits of Christ was, therefore, said to be made by something to which they gave the name of *faith,* but at the same time they disclaimed its being either of the nature of a *work,* or of *faith,* in the usual sense of the word, viz. the *belief of a truth.* They therefore contented themselves with defining it by its *effects;* and this has been done, as might be supposed, very differently, and generally in figurative language, which conveys no determinate ideas, and therefore leaves the mind in great uncertainty, whether it be possessed of it or not.

In the Saxon Confession, faith is defined to be " not the knowledge of any historical fact, but the embracing of all the articles of faith, and especially this, *I believe the remission of sins,* not to others only, but to myself also."[3] It is also there called, " an acquiescing confidence in the mediator." In the Synod of Dort, it is called " an instrument by which we lay hold of the righteousness of Christ;" and it is always supposed to be something that is imparted by God, and nothing which can be acquired by man himself. So, also, that *repentance* on which salvation is promised, is said, in the Augustan Confession, to be " the free gift of God, and to be given not on account of any works that we have done, or may do."[4]

It is evident, that the more careful divines have been to explain *faith,* as something that is neither of the nature of a *work,* nor yet the proper *belief* of anything, the more inexplicable and uncertain they have left it. In consequence of this, persons of a warm imagination more readily fancy that they have experienced this kind of *inward operation,* or *feeling;* while persons of more sober minds have often great doubts and distress on this account. This *act of faith,* as it is sometimes called, is also represented either as coincident, or the same thing with

---

[1] Syntagma Confessionum Fidei, 1654, p. 26. (*P.*)
[2] Canon i. ii. (*P.*)

[3] Syntagma, p. 57. (*P.*)
[4] Art. iv. (*P.*)

the *new birth*, without which no man can be called a child of God, or an heir of eternal life. But when the phraseology of Scripture, and the reason of the thing, are considered, we cannot but be satisfied, that *faith* is the belief of the gospel, or of those historical facts which are contained in the writings of the evangelists; and, that the *new birth* is that change of character and conduct which is produced by that belief.

This improved doctrine of satisfaction being held up by the reformers in opposition to the popish doctrine of merit, did not a little embarrass the divines of the Church of Rome, among whom that doctrine had never been brought to any certain standard, so that there has always been room for great diversity of opinion on the subject.

In the debate about *imputed righteousness* in the Council of Trent, it was agreed by all the divines, that Jesus Christ had merited for us, and that his merit is imputed to us; but Dominicus a Soto maintained that the term ought to be exploded, because neither the Fathers nor the Scriptures ever used it, and especially because the Lutherans had abused it, affirming that imputed righteousness is the sole justification of man. He added, that it cut off all the necessity of satisfaction, and equalled the meanest of all saints to the blessed virgin.[1]

At length the council condemned certain assertions of Luther, especially that God converts those whom he will, even though they resist; and some in the writings of Zuinglius, viz. that in predestination and reprobation men have no power, but only the will and pleasure of God; that the justified cannot fall from grace, &c.[2] After much debating on the subject, the decrees of this council were so framed, that it was hoped they might have satisfied all parties. But in consequence of this,

there was so much ambiguity in them, that they decided nothing;[3] and the controversy among the Catholics themselves went on just as before; persons of the most opposite sentiments appealing to the same decrees of this council.

Among other things it was determined by them, that the grace by which men are justified is merited by Christ.[4] And upon the whole, it is evident, that their decrees are in favour of that set of opinions which is termed *orthodox*, in all the established churches among the reformed.

We are not to conclude that because this doctrine of satisfaction for sin by the death of Christ, was held up by almost all the reformers as an article of so great magnitude and importance, that, therefore, it was soon so reduced to a system, as that there was no diversity of opinion about it. Nay, it appears that some very essential points belonging to it were then, and indeed still are, undetermined; and they are things of such a nature as, in fact, leave great doubts with respect to the very foundation of the doctrine itself.

Calvin makes it essential to the satisfaction of Christ, that his death should be both voluntary (which, indeed, others had said before him), and also that he should be condemned in a court of justice. "Had Christ been killed," said he, "by robbers, or in a sedition, his death would have been no kind of satisfaction; but by being condemned before a judge, it is plain that he assumed the character of a guilty person."[5] I should imagine, however, that many very orthodox persons of this day would think, that there might have been the same merit in the death of Christ, with

[1] Hist. of the Council of Trent, abridged by Jurieu, p. 122. (*P.*)
[2] Ibid. p. 130. (*P.*)

[3] See *Sessio Sexta*, 13 Jan. 1547, C. i-x.
[4] Du Pin's History of the 16th Century, p. 50. (*P.*)
[5] Institutiones, L. ii. C. xvi. Sect. v. (*P.*) "Si a latronibus jugulatus fuisset vel tumultuario casus per seditionem vulgi, in ejusmodi morte nulla satisfactionis species exstitisset. Verum ubi reus ad tribunal sistitur, testimoniis arguitur, et premitur, ipsius judicis ore, morti addicitur: his documentis intelligimus ipsum personam sontis et malefici sustinere." Ed. 1602, fol. 172.

respect to his making satisfaction for the sins of men, if the malice of his enemies had brought him to any kind of violent death, though there had been no sentence of an iniquitous court of justice for the purpose.

It is now generally thought that the scene of Christ's meritorious sufferings, when he actually bore the sins of men, and suffered the punishment due to them, was either in his agony in the garden, or in his death upon the cross; but Calvin says, "nothing would have been done by the mere death of Christ, if he had not also afterwards descended into hell, where he sustained that death which is inflicted by an angry God on the wicked."[1] To this he applies what the author of the epistle to the Hebrews says of Christ's *praying with strong cries and tears*, which he says was, lest he should be swallowed up by the wrath of God as a sinner.[2] In another place, however, he says, that in general Christ takes our sins and purchases righteousness for us by the whole course of his obedience.[3] But this is a thing about which those who now believe the doctrine of atonement are not agreed.[4]

It is evident, however, that Calvin believed the real descent of Christ into hell, not for the sake of *preaching to the spirits in prison*, or, as the primitive fathers understood it, to those who died under the old dispensation, but that he might there suffer the proper torments of the damned, and bear the wrath of God that had been merited by the sins of men. Yet he says, "God was not really angry with Christ, though he made him bear all the effects of his anger."[5] He would certainly, however, have been the proper object of God's anger, if, as he maintains, "the stain (that is the guilt) as well as the punishment of sin, was laid upon him, so that it ceased to be imputed to men."[6] If God was neither displeased with men because their guilt was transferred to Christ, nor with Christ to whom it was transferred, what was the object of his anger, and how was his justice really satisfied?

A more difficult question, and to which it is impossible that any satisfactory answer should be given, is, how the sufferings of Christ can be deemed *infinite*, so as to make atonement for sins of infinite magnitude, when the divine nature of Christ, to which alone infinity belongs, is impassible, and his human nature could bear no more than that of any other man? It must be exceedingly difficult to conceive how any supposed *union* of the two natures can be of any avail in this case, unless, in consequence of that union, the divine nature had borne some share of the sufferings, which the scheme requires to be infinite, and this idea is justly disclaimed as impious. Osiander the Lutheran maintained that Christ, as man, was obliged to obey the law of God himself, and therefore that he made expiation for sin as God; but Stancarus, another Lutheran divine, in opposition to him, maintained that the office of mediator belonged to Christ as man only. Both these opinions, this writer says, are dangerous.[7] This is not the only case in which we see men bewildering themselves, and puzzling others, by depart-

---

[1] Institutiones, L. ii. C. xvi. Sect. x. (*P.*) "Nihil actum erat si corporea tantum morte defunctus fuisset Christus : sed opera simul pretium erat ut divinæ ultionis severitatem sentiret : quo et iræ ipsius intercederet et satisfaceret justo judicio." Ed. 1602, fol. 174.

[2] Ibid. Sect. xi. (*P.*) "Christus ergo cum lacrymis et clamore valido orans, a metu suo exauditur: non ut a morte sit immunis, sed ne absorbeatur ut peccator. Ibid. fol. 175.

[3] Ibid. Sect. v. (*P.*) "Jam ubi quæritur quomodo abolitis peccatis dissidium Christus inter nos et Deum sustulerit, et justitiam acquisierit quæ eum nobis faventem ac benevolentem redderet : generaliter respondeo potest, toto obedientiæ suæ cursu hoc nobis præstitisse." Ibid. fol. 172.

[4] See Doddridge's Lectures, p. 421. (*P.*) Prop. clxx.

[5] Institutiones, L. ii. C. xvi. Sect. xi. (*P.*) "Neque tamen innuimus Deum fuisse unquam illi vel adversarium vel iratum." Ed. 1602, fol. 175.

[6] Ibid. Sect. vi. (*P.*) "Filius Dei, omni vitio purissimus, iniquitatum tamen nostrarum probrum ac ignominiam induit, ac sua vicissim puritate nos operuit." Ibid. fol. 173.

[7] Mosheim, IV. p. 47. (*P.*) Cent. xvi, Pt. ii Ch. i. Sect. xxxvi.

ing from the plain path of truth and common sense.

Such, however, is the constitution of things, that we are not authorized to expect any great good without a proportionable mixture of evil. The case of Luther, and of Calvin too, was such, that the reformation of the errors and abuses of Popery could not have been expected of them, or of their followers, but on principles equally erroneous. Happily, however, other persons, unconnected with them, were able, even at that time, to hit the happy medium between the popish doctrine of *merit*, as a foundation for the abuses of penance, indulgences, &c., and that of the total *insignificance of good works* to procure the favour of God. If by our good works we procure the favour of God to ourselves, which is the uniform language of the Scripture, and yet no portion of one person's merit be considered as capable of being transferred to another (which, indeed, is in the nature of things impossible), the very foundation of the popish doctrine of *supererogation*, and consequently of *indulgences*, is overturned; and yet no one false or dangerous principle is introduced in its place.

Faustus Socinus, who distinguished himself so much in recovering the original doctrine of the proper *humanity of Christ*, as to give occasion to all who now hold that doctrine to be called by his name, saw clearly the absurdity of what was advanced by the other reformers concerning satisfaction being made to the justice of God by the death of Christ. Indeed, it immediately follows from his principles, that Christ being only a man, though ever so innocent, his death could not, in any proper sense of the word, atone for the sins of other men. He was, however, far from abandoning the doctrine of *redemption* in the Scripture sense of the word, that is, of our deliverance from the guilt of sin by his gospel, as promoting repentance and reformation, and from the punishment due to sin, by his power of giving eternal life to all that obey

him. But, indeed, if God himself freely forgives the sins of men upon their repentance, there could be no occasion, properly speaking, for anything farther being done to avert the punishment with which they had been threatened. What he says on the subject is as follows:—

"We are thus saved from the punishment of our sins by Christ, because, by his great power in heaven and earth, he brings it about, that no proper punishment can reach us; and by the same power he will accomplish our entire and perpetual freedom from death, which is the wages of sin, and its principal and peculiar punishment. But this method of rescuing us from the punishment of our sins is very different from that which implies a satisfaction for them.... Nothing can be more repugnant to each other than a *free pardon* and *satisfaction*.... Indeed, no man of judgment and piety ought to entertain the idea of a satisfaction for sin; ... since it plainly does very much derogate from the power and authority, or goodness and mercy of God."[1]

He farther observes, that "although John the Baptist, when he ascribes to Christ the *taking away sin*, hath called him a *lamb*, and in that mode of expression, without doubt, alluded to the expiatory sacrifices" in the law, yet he apprehends that in this the Baptist alluded "to Christ in his *whole character*, who, in many ways, takes away the sins of the world." In support of this he alleges, "that in the expiatory

[1] Toulmin's Socinus, pp. 185, 186. (P.) "A pœnis siquidem peccatorum nostrorum ideo per Christum liberamur, quia Christus summa illa sua in cœlo et in terra potestate efficit, ne ullæ propriæ peccatorum pœnæ nos attingant, et tandem eadem potestate efficiet Phil. iii. 21, ut a morte quæ stipendium peccati est Rom. vi. 23, et ejus quam maxime propria pœna, prorsus atque in perpetuum liberi simus. Hæc certe ratio liberandi a pœnis peccatorum diversissima est ab ea, quæ satisfactione pro ipsis continetur... Nihil autem invicem magis pugnare potest, quam gratuita remissio seu condonatio, et satisfactio; quippe quod vel potentiæ et auctoritati, vel certe bonitati et misericordiæ ipsius Dei aperte ac plurimum deroget." *Christ. Relig. Instit.* F. Socini Opera, 1656, p. 665, Col. i. See also *The Racorian Catechism,* Sect. v. Ch. viii. in the Translation of the Rev. T. Rees, 1818, pp. 303-320.

sacrifices of the law, which were expressly offered for sin, no *lamb* was sacrificed."[1]

Grotius, having written a treatise in defence of the doctrine of satisfaction, against Socinus, gave occasion to a most excellent answer by Crellius, in defence of the Socinian doctrine on this subject; and to this, Grotius did not think proper to make any reply.

In England, this doctrine of atonement seems to have got as firm possession of the minds of men, as that of the divinity of Christ. It is the doctrine of the established churches of England and Scotland, and is retained, at least in some qualified sense, even by many who do not hold the divinity of Christ, at least, those who are styled Arians.[2] For, that a Socinian should hold this doctrine, in any sense, is hardly possible. We are not, however, to expect a sudden and effectual reformation in this or in any other capital article of the corruption of Christianity.

To establish this article was a work, as we have seen, of long time, and therefore we must be content if the overthrow of it be gradual also. Great buildings do not often fall at once, but some apartments will still be thought to be habitable, after the rest are seen to be in ruins. It is the same with great *systems of doctrine*, the parts of which have long gone together. The force of evidence obliges us at first to abandon some *one* part of them only, and we do not immediately see that, in consequence of this, we ought to abandon others, and at length the *whole*. And, indeed, could this have been seen from the beginning, it would have been with much more difficulty that we should have been prevailed upon to abandon any part. The very proposal might have staggered us; and any doubt with respect to the whole, might have been followed by universal scepticism. It hath pleased Divine Providence, therefore, to open the minds of men by easy degrees, and the detection of one falsehood prepares us for the detection of another, till, before we are aware of it, we find no trace left of the immense and seemingly well-compacted system. Thus, by degrees, we can reconcile ourselves to abandon all the parts, when we could never have thought of giving up the whole.

There are many who can by no means think that God has, in a proper sense, accepted of the death of Christ in lieu of that of all men, (having no idea of the possibility of *transferring guilt*, and consequently of transferring punishment,) who yet think that the death of Christ serves to show the divine displeasure at sin, in such a manner, as that it would not have been expedient to pardon any sin without it; and they think that the sacrifices under the law had a real reference to the death of Christ in the scheme of the gospel; while others think the death of Christ was necessary to the pardon of sin, and our restoration to eternal life, in some method of which we have no clear knowledge, being only obscurely intimated in the Scriptures, and therefore could not be intended to produce its effect by any operation on our minds.

In time, however, I make no doubt, but that an attention to what seems now to be ascertained with respect to the moral character and government

---

[1] Toulmin's Socinus, p. 194. (*P.*) Cujus rei etiam argumentum esse potest, quod in expiatoriis illis legis sacrificiis, quæ nominatim pro peccato offerebantur, nullus agnus immolabatur. Ex quo apparet, cum Baptista Christum agnum appellavit, alterius etiam cujuspiam rei, præter sacrificia illa, rationem habuisse, et ad puritatem, innocentiam ac mansuetudinem illius respexisse, totumque Christum ea translatione quodammodo exprimere voluisse; præsertim cum, ut dictum est, Christus non ipsa sui immolatione tantum, sed pluribus aliis modis peccata tollat." *Prælect. Theol.* Op. I. p. 591. Col. 2.

[2] Among these Mr. Martin Tomkins, of whom see p. 50, Note, and Dr. John Taylor were distinguished. The former published, in 1732, "Jesus Christ, the Mediator between God and Men; an Advocate for us with the Father; and a Propitiation for the Sins of the World." Dr. Priestley says in his *Memoirs*, that he "left the academy, with a qualified belief of the doctrine of Atonement, such as is found in that book." Dr. John Taylor published, in 1751, "The Scripture Doctrine of Atonement examined; first, in relation to Jewish Sacrifices; and then to the Sacrifice of our blessed Lord and Saviour Jesus Christ." Of this piece there was a second enlarged edition.

of God, viz. that he is a being purely *good*, that in him, justice is only a modification of benevolence, that he simply wishes the happiness of all his creatures, and that virtue is a necessary means of that happiness; that he is incapable of introducing any *unnecessary evil*, and that his displeasure at sin is sufficiently shewn by the methods which he takes to promote the reformation of sinners, and by the punishment of those who continue unreformed: these, I say, together with other considerations, suggested in the argumentative part of this division of my work, will in time eradicate whatever yet remains of the doctrine of atonement; a doctrine which has no foundation in reason, or in the Scriptures, and is indeed a modern thing.

In fact, the only hold it has on the minds of many Protestants, is by means of such a literal interpretation of single texts of Scripture, as gives the doctrine of transubstantiation a like hold on the minds of Papists. Besides, it must, I am persuaded, lead many persons to think rationally on this subject, and especially to abandon all *middle opinions* with respect to it, to observe, as they must do if they give due attention to the language of Scripture, that those particular texts on which they are disposed to lay so much stress, give no countenance to any middle doctrine. For they must either be interpreted literally, according to the plain and obvious sense of the words, which will enforce the belief of proper vicarious punishments, or they must be interpreted *figuratively*; and then they will not oblige us to believe the doctrine of atonement in any sense, or that Christ died a sacrifice in any other manner, than as any person might be said to be a sacrifice to the cause in which he dies.

It is now, certainly, time to lay stress on the interpretation of particular texts, and to allow more weight to general considerations, derived from the whole tenor of Scripture and the dictates of reason; and if there should be found any difficulty in accommodating the one to the other, (and I think there is even less of this than might have been expected,) the former, and not the latter, should remain unaccounted for. Time may clear up obscurities in particular texts, by discovering various readings, by the clearer knowledge of ancient customs and opinions, &c. But arguments drawn from such considerations as those of the moral government of God, the nature of things, and the general plan of revelation, will not be put off to a future time. The whole compass and force of them is within our present reach, and if the mind be unbiassed, they must, I think, determine our assent.

It is certainly a great satisfaction to entertain such an idea of the Author of the universe, and of his moral government, as is consonant to the dictates of reason and the tenor of revelation in general, and also to leave as little obscurity in the principles of it as possible; that the articles of our creed on this great subject may be few, clear and simple. Now it is certainly the doctrine of reason, as well as of the Old Testament, that God is merciful to the penitent, and that nothing is requisite to make men, in all situations, the objects of his favour, but such moral conduct as he has made them capable of. This is a simple and a pleasing view of God and his moral government, and the consideration of it cannot but have the best effect on the temper of our minds and conduct in life. The general tenor of the New Testament is likewise plainly agreeable to this view of things, and none of the *facts* recorded in it require to be illustrated by any other principles. In this, then, let us acquiesce, not doubting but that, though perhaps not at present, we shall in time be able, without any effort or straining, to explain all particular expressions in the apostolical epistles, &c. in a manner perfectly consistent with the general strain of their own writings, and the rest of the Scriptures.

PART III.

THE HISTORY OF OPINIONS CONCERNING GRACE, ORIGINAL SIN AND PREDESTINATION.

THE INTRODUCTION.

Next to the opinions concerning the *person of Christ*, none have agitated the minds of men more, or produced more serious consequences, than those relating to the doctrines of *grace, original sin* and *predestination*, which have so many connections, that I think it proper to treat of them all together.

That it must be naturally in the power of man to do the will of God, must be taken for granted, if we suppose the moral government of God to be at all an equitable one. He that made man, certainly knew what he was capable of, and would never command him to do what he had not enabled him to perform; so as to propose to him a *reward* which he knew he could never attain, and a punishment which he knew he had no power of avoiding. If it be worth our while to inquire at all into the government under which we live, we must begin with assuming these first principles. For, otherwise, we have nothing to do but to await whatever he who made us hath pleased to determine concerning us, nothing that we can do in the case being able to alter it.

Supposing, therefore, that God did not mean to tantalize his creatures, in the most cruel and insulting manner, every moral precept in the Scriptures is a proof that man has naturally a power of obeying it, and of insuring the reward annexed to the observance of it. Now moral precepts, with express sanctions of rewards and punishments, abound in the Scriptures; and men are even expostulated with, in the most earnest manner, and persuaded to the practice of their duty, by the most solemn assurances, that *God is not willing that any should perish*, and by repeated warnings, that their destruction will lie at their own door; the general tenor of the preaching of the old prophets being, *Turn ye, turn ye, from your evil way. Why will ye die, O house of Israel?* Also, everything that is of a moral nature in the New Testament is uniformly delivered in the same strain.

Notwithstanding this, it hath been imagined that all these representations are to be accommodated to a system, according to which, the whole race of mankind received so great an injury by the fall of Adam, that from that time none of his posterity have been capable even of forming a good thought, and much less of doing all that God requires of them; and, moreover, that they are all so far involved in the consequences of his fall, and his sin is considered as so much *their own*, (he being their representative, standing in their place, and acting for them,) that they are even properly punishable for it, and liable on that account to everlasting torment, though they had never sinned themselves. It is believed, however, that God hath been pleased to save certain individuals of mankind from this general ruin, but that it was not from any respect to the better character or conduct of such individuals, but of his mere *free and arbitrary grace*. It is also part of the same system, that every good thought and purpose, in the hearts even of those who are thus *elected*, is immediately inspired by God, and that without this continual assistance, to which they give the name of *grace*, no man has any choice but of evil, from the moment of his birth to his death.

It is not easy to imagine, *a priori*, what could have led men into such a train of thinking, so evidently contrary to the plain dictates of reason, and the most natural interpretation of Scripture. There is, indeed, an appearance of *humility* in ascribing everything that is good to God; but to ascribe to him, as all men must do, those *powers* by which we are enabled to perform good works, comes, in fact, to the same thing. *What have we,* as the apostle says, *that we have not received ?* How, then, are we the less indebted to God, whether *he works all our works in us and for us,* by his own immediate agency, or, he does it *mediately,* that is, by means of those powers which he has given us for that purpose? With respect to the character of the Divine Being, it certainly loses more by the idea of the predestination of the greatest part of mankind to inevitable destruction, than it can gain by the belief of an arbitrary interference in favour of a few. The whole scheme, therefore, certainly tends to make the divine character and government appear less respectable, indeed execrable.

In fact, it is probable that such a scheme as this would never have entered into the mind of any man, who had been left to his own speculations on the subject, or to his study of the Scriptures. Accordingly, we find that the principal parts of this system were first suggested in the heat of controversy; and when the mind was once prepossessed in favour of some of the maxims of it, the rest were gradually introduced to complete the scheme; and the Scriptures, as in all other cases, were afterwards easily imagined to favour the preconceived hypothesis.

Indeed, the more amiable part of the system, or that which ascribes everything that is good immediately to God, without respect to second causes, has considerable countenance from the piety of the sacred writers; but their language on this subject will appear to be as *just* as it is *pious,* when it is rightly interpreted. Many persons, no doubt, will be more easily reconciled to the doctrine of *election* by previously imagining that they themselves are in the number of the elect; and while they can thus fancy themselves to be the peculiar favourites of heaven, they can better bear to consider the rest of mankind as abandoned by the same Being to a severer fate. Also, in general, all men are sufficiently inclined to look off from the dark and most objectionable side of any scheme of principles which they adopt.

With respect to the fall of Adam, all that we can learn from the Scriptures, interpreted literally, is, that the laborious cultivation of the earth, and the mortality of his race, were the consequence of it. This is all that is said by Moses, and likewise all that is alluded to by the apostle Paul, who says, that *by one man sin entered into the world.* For what he adds, *all have sinned,* can only mean that all are involved in that *death* which was the consequence of his sin. If, indeed, this be interpreted literally, it will imply that all are involved in his *guilt* as well as in his sufferings. But this is so unnatural an interpretation, and so evidently contrary to sense and reason, (sin being in its own nature a personal thing, and not transferable,) that the text was never understood in this sense till the system, the history of which I am writing, was so far advanced as to require it, and to have prepared the minds of men for it. In like manner, the words of our Saviour, *this is my body,* was always understood to mean a *memorial* of his body, till the minds of men were gradually prepared to bear a literal interpretation of them; and then that interpretation was made use of to support the doctrine which suggested it.

In like manner, there is a *predestination* spoken of by the apostle Paul; but, in general, it means the good-will and pleasure of God, in giving certain people peculiar privileges, and especially the knowledge of the gospel, for the improvement of which they were answerable. If he does speak of *future glory*, as the consequence of this predestination, it was upon the presumption that they improved those advantages, and by that means made themselves the proper subjects of future happiness. Or, possibly, in some cases, the apostle, considering God as the ultimate and proper author of everything that is good, and of all happiness, might overlook the immediate means and steps, and with this sense of piety and comprehension of mind, might speak of future glory itself as the gift of God, and therefore might make no difference in his mind, at that time, between predestination and foreknowledge. But the tenor of all his writings shows, that it was far from being his intention to represent future glory as given by an *arbitrary decree* of God, without any respect to the good works which alone can fit men for it; which good works are as much in a man's power as any other action of which he is capable.

Having premised these general observations, I now proceed to show by what steps these principles of the utter inability of man to do the will of God, as derived from the fall of Adam, the imputation of his sin to all his posterity, and the arbitrary predestination of some to eternal life, and the consequent rejection, or reprobation, of the rest of mankind, by which they are devoted to certain and everlasting destruction, were first introduced, and at length got the firm establishment they now have in the creeds of almost all Christian churches.

SECTION I.

OF THE DOCTRINES OF GRACE, ETC. BEFORE THE PELAGIAN CONTROVERSY.

It is remarkable that we find hardly any trace of what are now called the doctrines of *grace, original sin,* or *pre-*

destination before the *Pelagian controversy,* which was near the end of the fourth century. I believe all the moderns are agreed, that it was clearly the opinion of all the ancient fathers, that God has left it entirely in the power of every man to act well or ill. Basnage, who was himself sufficiently orthodox in the modern sense of the word, acknowledges, that though the fathers in general thought that we are indebted to the grace of God for all our virtues, yet they say that the beginning of salvation is from man, and that it depends entirely upon himself.[1] It is not denied, however, but that they might believe an internal influence upon the mind on extraordinary occasions; but, as Vossius observes, none before Austin supposed that there was an immediate concurrence of divine grace, necessary to *every* good thought or action.[2]

"God," says Justin Martyr, "has not made man like trees and quadrupeds, (δενδρεα και τετραποδα,) who can do nothing from choice and judgment; for he would not be worthy of reward or praise, if he did not of himself choose what was good, but was *made* good; nor, if he was wicked, could he be justly punished, as not having been such of himself, but only what he had been made."[3] In support of this he quotes Isa. i. 16: "Wash ye, make ye clean," &c. Basnage says,[4] that the ancients maintained free-will with much warmth, granting men an entire power to be converted or not. Clemens Alexandrinus and Origen, he says, were at the head of this party.

It is remarkable that Austin himself, before he engaged in the controversy with Pelagius, held the same opinion concerning free-will with the rest of the fathers who had preceded him, and was far from denying this. In particular, he acknowledges, that before this time he had been of opinion, that faith, or at least the beginning of faith, and a desire of conversion, was in the

[1] Hist des Eglises Reform. I. p. 169. (*P.*)
[2] Historia Pelagianismi, p. 291. (*P.*)
[3] *Apol.* I. Ed. Thirlby, p. 65. (*P.*)
[4] Hist. des Eglises Reform. p. 76. (*P.*)

power of man.[1] It was a saying of his, "If there be not grace, how should God save the world, and if there be not free-will, how can he judge the world?"[2] No man," says he, "can be justly condemned for doing that which he was not able to resist."[3] Citing a passage in the son of Sirach, (Eccles. xv. 14, 17,) "God left man in the hands of his counsel, he placed life and death before him, that that which he pleased should be given him," he says, "Behold here is a very plain proof of the liberty of the human will; for how does God command, if man has not free-will, or power to obey."[4] He also proves, that it is in our power to change the will, from these words of our Saviour, "Make the tree good and the fruit good," &c.[5]

We have almost the same unanimous opinion of the ancients, concerning the effects of the *sin of Adam,* as concerning the natural capacity of man with respect to virtue and vice; and they had occasion to speak to this subject very early, in consequence of the opinion of the Gnostics in general, and the Manicheans in particular; who held that the souls of men were originally of different ranks, and sprang from different principles, good beings having produced some of them, and bad beings the rest; on which account they said some were naturally *carnal* and others *spiritual.* Accordingly, they had taught that sin arose not from the free-will of man, but from the substance of *matter,* which they held to be the only source of evil; so that some souls were wicked not by *choice,* but by *nature.*

In opposition to this, Origen maintained, that all souls were by nature equally capable of virtue or vice, and that the differences among men arose merely from the freedom of the will, and the various uses of that freedom; that God left man to his liberty, and rewarded or punished him according to the use he made of it.[6]

It is evident, however, that Origen must have maintained, according to his known philosophical principles, that perfect freedom with respect to virtue and vice was only enjoyed by man in his pre-existent state. For he, with other Platonists, maintained that the souls of men had sinned in heaven, and therefore were united to such bodies as were a clog and a prison to the soul, and that the *flesh* laid upon it a kind of necessity of sinning. Chrysostom also says, that with an infirm body we derive from Adam a proneness to inordinate affections.[7] But he was far from supposing that men were in any other manner sufferers by the fall of Adam; and least of all that they were personally responsible for his conduct of himself. Le Sueur laments that this writer was not quite orthodox with respect to original sin, grace and free-will; but he apologizes for him, as having written before the heresy of Pelagius broke out.[8]

The fathers who, in general, held that the punishment of Adam's sin "was only *mortality,*...declare, that God subjected *men* to this mortality not out of anger, but out of wisdom and clemency, to beget in them a hatred of sin, and that sin might not be eternal in them."[9] But Titus, bishop of Bostra, who was before Pelagius, taught that death was natural, and not the effect of sin.[10]

Vossius acknowledges, that Clemens Alexandrinus had no knowledge of original sin;[11] and "Epiphanius truly blames Origen, and John of Jerusalem, for saying that the image and similitude of God was lost in man after the expulsion of Adam out of paradise."[12]

Austin himself, in his controversy

---

1 *De Prædestinatione,* L. i. C. iii. Op. VII. p. 1235. (*P.*)
2 *Epist.* xlvi. Op. II. p. 160. (*P.*)
3 *De Duabus Animabus,* C. x. Op. VI. p. 153. (*P.*)
4 *De Gratia,* C. ii. Op. VII. p. 1299. (*P.*)
5 *Contra Adimantum,* C. xxvi. Op. V. p. 210. (*P.*)

6 See his *Philocalia,* p. 50, &c. (*P.*)
7 Opera, IX. p. 136. (*P.*)
8 A.D. 407. (*P.*)
9 Whitby on the *Five Points,* 1710. Preface, p. ix. (*P.*)
10 Basnage, Hist. des Eglises Reform. I. p. 167. (*P.*)
11 Hist. Pelag. p. 160. (*P.*)
12 Whitby, Ibid. p. 391. (*P.*)

with the Manicheans, declared that it is impossible that souls should be evil by nature.[1] So far was he from supposing that men were responsible for Adam's conduct, that he said, "no man is wise, valiant or temperate, with the wisdom, valour or temperance of another, or righteous with the righteousness of another."[2]

The testimony of the fathers in this period is no less clear against the doctrine of *predestination* to eternal life, without respect to good works. All the fathers before Austin, says Whitby, interpreted what the apostle Paul says of predestination, in the 8th and 9th chapters of his epistle to the Romans, of those whom God foreknew to have good purposes; and in a similar manner they explain all the other texts from which the doctrine of election and reprobation is now deduced : and Austin himself, in his controversy with the Manicheans, interpreted them in the same manner. Melancthon says, that all the ancients, except Austin, asserted that there was some cause of election in ourselves; and Prosper, who took the part of Austin, acknowledged that the Pelagians treated his doctrine as a novelty.[3]

Justin Martyr could have no knowledge of arbitrary predestination, when he said, " if everything come to pass by fate, it is plain that nothing will be in our power. If it be fate that this man shall be good, and the other bad, the one is not to be praised, nor the other blamed."[4]

Didymus, who taught theology at Alexandria, (afterwards condemned for his adherence to Origen, but on no other account,) says, that predestination depends upon God's foreknowledge of those who would believe the gospel, and live according to it;[5] and Jerome was so far from believing the modern doc-

trine of election and reprobation, that he thought that no Christian would finally perish.

It is sufficiently evident from these testimonies, that the doctrine of the utter inability of man to do the will of God, of the corruption of our nature by the fall of Adam, and of our responsibility for it, together with the doctrine of absolute, unconditional election of some to eternal life, and of the reprobation of the rest of mankind, were altogether unknown in the primitive church. We must now consider the Pelagian controversy, and the remarkable change which it occasioned with respect to these doctrines.

SECTION II.

OF THE PELAGIAN CONTROVERSY AND THE STATE OF OPINIONS IN CONSEQUENCE OF IT.

PELAGIUS was a British monk, allowed by Austin himself to have been a man of irreproachable morals, who travelled in company with Celestius, another monk and a native of Ireland, and with him resided some time at Rome, a little after the year 400. As far as appears, these two men had no opinions different from those which we have seen to have been generally held by the Christian writers of that age; but being men of sense and virtue, they opposed with warmth some growing abuses and superstitions, especially with respect to the efficacy of baptism.

This rite, we shall find, was very soon imagined to have a power of *washing away sin ;* and a notion of a similar nature had also prevailed respecting the Lord's supper. But it was the former of these superstitions that happened to come in the way of Pelagius to oppose. As an argument that baptism could not of itself be of any avail to the pardon of sins, he urged the application of it to infants, who had no sin : he maintained that nothing but good works are

[1] *De Duabus Animabus,* C. xii. Op. VI. p. 155, &c. (*P.*)
[2] *De Libero Arbitrio,* L. ii. C. xix. Op. I. p. 663. (*P.*)
[3] *Five Points,* pp. 101–108. (*P.*)
[4] *Apol.* I. Edit. Thirlby, p. 64. (*P.*)
[5] Basnage Hist. des Eglises Reform. I. p. 168. (*P.*)

H

of any avail in the sight of God; and that to these alone, which it is in every man's power to perform, the pardon of sin is annexed.

It does not appear that these doctrines, which were the outlines of what has since been called the *Pelagian heresy*, met with any opposition at Rome. But retiring from that city on the approach of the Goths, these monks went to Africa, and Celestius remaining there, Pelagius proceeded to Palestine, where he enjoyed the protection of John, bishop of Jerusalem, while his friend, and his opinions, met with a very different reception from Austin, bishop of Hippo, who, in his account of what followed, says he was first staggered at hearing it asserted, that "infants were not baptized for the remission of sins, but only that they might be sanctified in Christ;"[1] by which was probably meant, that they were dedicated to God, and destined to be instructed in the principles of the Christian religion.

Upon this, Celestius and his friend were gradually engaged in a warm contest, in the course of which (as was certainly the case with respect to Austin, their principal opponent) they were probably led to advance more than had originally occurred to them, in order to make their system more complete. Among other things, they are said to have asserted that mankind derives no injury whatever from the fall of Adam; that we are now as capable of obeying the will of God as he was; that otherwise it would have been absurd and cruel to propose laws to men, with the sanction of rewards and punishments; and that men are born as well without vice as without virtue. Pelagius is also said to have maintained that it is even possible for men, if they will use their best endeavours, to live entirely without sin. This, Jerome says, he borrowed from Origen, from whom it passed to Rufinus, Evagrius, Ponticus and Jovinian, whom he calls the patriarchs of the Pelagian heresy.

Pelagius did not deny what may be called *external grace*, or that the doctrines and motives of the gospel are necessary, but he admitted nothing of *internal grace*. He acknowledged, indeed, that the *power* we have to obey the will of God, is the gift of God to us; but he said that the *direction* of this power depends upon ourselves. He even said to have advanced, after Titus of Bostra above mentioned, that we do not die in consequence of the sin of Adam, but by the necessity of nature, and that Adam himself would have died if he had not sinned.[2] Much farther was he from supposing that the *second death*, or the punishment of the wicked in a future world, was any consequence of the sin of Adam.

In several of these positions, Pelagius appears to have gone farther than the generality of Christians in his time, even of those in the East, where he met with the most favourable reception. He was particularly censured by Chrysostom and Isidore, for asserting that man had no need of any inward assistance, which was generally believed to be afforded, especially on extraordinary occasions, and that man had received no injury whatever from the sin of Adam.

Austin, in his controversy with the Pelagians, made no difficulty of renouncing many of the things which he had advanced against the Manicheans. "Yet," says Whitby, "he hath been able to say nothing in answer to some of the arguments produced by him in *their* confutation;" and "the exceptions which he makes to some of his own rules, and the answers he attempts to make to some of his own arguments are vain, false and absurd." Thus he had before defined sin to be "the will to do that from which we have the power to abstain;" but afterwards he said, he had then "defined that which was only sin, and not that which is also, *pœna peccati*, the punishment of sin."[3]

In opposition to the doctrine of human

---

[1] *De Peccatis*, &c. L. iii. C. vi. Op. VII. p. 725. (P.)

[2] Austin *De Hœresibus*, Sect. lxxxviii. Op. VI. p. 33. (P.)

[3] *Five Points*, p. 392. (P.)

merit, he asserted that divine grace is necessary to bend the will, for, that without this we are free only to do evil, but have no power to do good.

As the Heathens could not be said to have had that grace of God, spoken of in the gospel, by the help of which alone Austin supposed that good works were performed; to be consistent with himself he maintained that none of the works of the Heathens were properly good, and that even the good works of Cornelius would have availed nothing without faith in Christ.[1] Sometimes, indeed, he would allow that the good works of the Heathens would entitle them to a temporary reward, and lessen their future torments.[2] But he likewise distinguished himself by saying that such good works were only a kind of *shining sins.* In support of this doctrine, he said that Christ would have died in vain, if, in any other manner than by faith in him, men could have attained to true faith, virtue, righteousness and wisdom.[3] But in this he did not attend to the doctrine of Paul, who says, that *they who have not the law are judged without law; they being a law to themselves; their own consciences accusing or else excusing them.*

With respect to *original sin,* Austin strenuously maintained that infants derive sin from Adam, and that his guilt was, in some way, entailed upon them, so that they are obnoxious to punishment on account of it; though he acknowledges it was no proper guilt of theirs, but only that of their ancestor, the *sin* being an act of his will only.[4] Afterwards, an improvement was made upon this doctrine by the disciples of Austin, who asserted, that a covenant was made with all mankind in Adam, as their first parent, and that he was made to represent them all; so that, had he obeyed, all his posterity would have been happy through his obedience; but that in his

disobedience they are all sinners, his act being imputed and transferred to them all.

Austin maintains that baptism is necessary to recover men from that state of perdition into which the fall of Adam had brought them, and therefore that all who were not baptized were in a state of damnation. To prove that infants had sinned in Adam, he urged, that otherwise Christ could not be their Saviour.[5] He appears, however, to have been shocked at the thoughts of exposing infants to the torments of hell on account of the sin of Adam only; and therefore he maintained that, though they were in hell, their punishment was so little, that they would rather choose to exist under it, than not to exist at all.[6] This was afterwards dressed up as a division, or partition in hell, and was called *Limbus Infantum.* Before the Pelagian controversy, Austin had said that the souls of infants, dying unbaptized, went neither to heaven nor to hell, but went to a place where they neither enjoyed the vision of God, nor suffered the pains of the damned.[7]

Since, according to the preceding doctrine, the very first motion towards any good work, such as faith and repentance, is immediately from God, and it is not in the power of man to contribute anything towards it, Austin was obliged, in pursuance of his doctrine, to maintain that God had, of his own arbitrary will, predestinated to eternal life all that were actually saved, while the rest of mankind were left exposed to a punishment which they had no power of avoiding. At the same time, however, maintaining, according to the universal opinion of that age, that baptism was the Christian *regeneration,* and washed away all sin, original and actual, he was under a necessity of distinguishing between *regeneration* and *salvation;* maintaining that justifying faith, and regenerating grace might be lost, or that the regenerate might have all grace, but not that of perseverance, since it depended upon the decree and good pleasure of God, whether they would persevere to the end or not.[1] In this respect those who now maintain the doctrine of predestination differ very considerably from Austin, maintaining that none are truly *regenerated* except the *elect,* and that all these will certainly persevere to the end, and be saved. In the Church of Rome, however, and also in that of England, *regeneration* and *baptism* are confounded, and the terms are used as expressing the same thing.[2]

Austin, whose influence in the churches of Africa was uncontrolled, procured the opinions of his adversary to be condemned in a synod held at Carthage in 412; but they prevailed notwithstanding. The Pelagian doctrine was received with great applause even at Rome. There the conduct of the bishops of Africa, who had stigmatized it as heretical, was condemned, and Pope Zozimus was at the head of those who favoured Pelagius. Austin's doctrine of predestination, in particular, was not confirmed by any council within a century after his death; and though it was defended by the most celebrated divines in the West, it was never generally received in the East, and was controverted by many in Gaul, and the favourers of it explained it with more or less latitude. This controversy, which began with the doctrine of grace, and was extended to original sin and predestination, rent the church into the most deplorable divisions in all succeeding ages, and they have been continued, with little intermission, to the present time.

This controversy was, however, almost wholly confined to the Western church, while the Greeks continued in the state in which the Christian church in general has been represented to have been before the Pelagian controversy; supposing that election or predestination was always made with a view to men's good works. Chrysostom, as well as John of Jerusalem, continued to hold opinions very different from those of Austin, though these were very soon generally received in the Western church; and just in the heat of this controversy, Cassian, a disciple of Chrysostom, coming to Marseilles, taught a *middle doctrine,* which was, that "the first conversion of the soul to God was the effect of its free choice," so that all *preventing,* as it was called, or *predisposing grace,* was denied by him; and this came to be the distinguishing doctrine of those who were afterwards called *Semi-Pelagians.* Prosper and Hilary, who were bishops in Gaul, gave an account of this doctrine to Austin, but it was so popular, that he did not venture to condemn it altogether, or to call it an impious and pernicious heresy.[3] This controversy also interested many persons, and much was written on both sides of the question.

The peculiar opinion of the Semi-Pelagians is expressed in a different manner by different writers, but all the accounts sufficiently agree. Thus some represent them as maintaining that inward grace is not necessary to the first beginning of repentance, but only to our progress in virtue. Others say that they acknowledged the power of grace, but said that faith depends upon ourselves, and good works upon God; and it is agreed upon all hands, that these Semi-Pelagians held that predestination is made upon the foresight of good works, which also continued to be the tenet of the Greek church.

The Semi-Pelagian doctrine is acknowledged by all writers to have been well received in the monasteries of Gaul, and especially in the neighbourhood of Marseilles; owing in a great measure to the popularity of Cassian, which

---

[1] Vossii Historia Pelagianismi, p. 565. (*P.*)

[2] The question whether *baptism* be *regeneration* has, very lately, been started, and is still warmly agitated among the clergy of the Church of England.

[3] Basnage, Hist. des Englises Reform. I. p.192. Mosheim, I. p. 427. (*P.*) Cent. v. Pt. ii. Ch. v. Sect. xxvii.

THE DOCTRINE OF GRACE.

counteracted the authority of Austin, and to the irreproachable lives of those who stood forth in defence of it. Prosper, writing to Austin about these Semi-Pelagians, says, "they surpass us in the merit of their lives," and are in high stations in the church.[1]

The assistance of Austin, though he was then far advanced in life, was called in to combat these Semi-Pelagians, and it was the occasion of his writing more treatises on these subjects. In these he still strenuously maintained, that the predestination of the elect was independent of any foresight of their good works, but was according to the good pleasure of God only, and that perseverance comes from God, and not from man.

Notwithstanding the popularity of the Semi-Pelagian doctrine, and its being patronized by some persons of considerable rank and influence, the majority of such persons must have been against it; for we find that it was generally condemned whenever any synod was called upon the subject. But there were some exceptious. Thus one which was assembled at Arles, about A.D. 475, pronounced an anathema against those who denied that God would have all men to be saved, or that Christ died for all, or that the Heathens might have been saved by the law of nature.[2] Upon the whole, it cannot be said that the doctrine of Austin was completely established for some centuries; nor indeed was it ever generally avowed in all its proper consequences, and without any qualifications, till after the Reformation, when the Protestants espoused it, in opposition to the Popish doctrine of merit.

SECTION III.

OF THE DOCTRINE OF GRACE, ETC. IN THE MIDDLE AGES, AND TILL THE REFORMATION.

It is pretty evident that, notwithstanding the great nominal authority of Aus-

tin, whom it was seldom reckoned safe expressly to contradict upon the whole, the Semi-Pelagian doctrine may be said to have been most prevalent in England and in France, especially during the sixth and seventh centuries. All the *grace* that was generally contended for in this period, was that which they supposed to be imparted at baptism, or a kind of supernatural influence which did not fail to accompany or to follow men's own endeavours. Consequently, the operation of it in practice did not materially differ from that of Semi-Pelagianism itself. All the difference in speculation was, that, whereas Pelagius supposed the power of man to do the will of God was given him in his formation, and was therefore properly inherent in him, as much as his bodily strength, that which was asserted by his opponents in these ages was something foreign indeed to a man's self, and imparted at another time, or occasionally, but still, in fact, at *his command*, and the doctrine of *reprobation* was never much relished.

In a council held at Orange, in 529, against the Pelagians and Semi-Pelagians, it was determined, that "all those who have been baptized, and have received grace by baptism, can and ought to accomplish the things which belong to their salvation; Jesus Christ enabling them...provided they will labour faithfully." And not only do the fathers assembled upon this occasion profess not to believe that there are men destined to evil or sin by the will of God, but they say that, "if there be any who will believe so great an evil, they denounce [a hundred] anathemas upon them with all detestation."[3]

In this state things continued, the Pelagian or Semi-Pelagian doctrine being generally received, till about the middle of the ninth century. For, notwithstanding the credit of Austin's name, and the authority of his writings, yet no books were more generally read in those ages than *Cassian's Col-*

---

[1] Sueur, A.D. 429. (P.)
[2] Vossius, p. 696. Basnage, Hist. des Eglises Reform. II. p. 699. (P.)

[3] Sueur, A.D. 529. (P.) See [Rutt's Priestley] Vol. III. p. 535. Note †.

lections, which was thought to be the best book of institutions for a monk to form his mind upon, and which gave a strong impression in favour of the doctrine of the Greek church. This was very apparent in the ninth century, when Godeschalchus was severely reproved by Hincmar for asserting some of Austin's doctrines, and laying particular stress upon them.

This Godeschalchus was a monk of Orbais, in the diocese of Rheims, who, being fond of Austin's doctrines, carried them rather farther than Austin himself had done; teaching, among other things, that baptism did not save men, that God had predestinated the greatest part of mankind to damnation, and that none would be saved but the elect, for whom only Christ had shed his blood. In this he was opposed by Rabanus Maurus; and a council being held on the subject, at Mayence, and also at Creci, he was condemned, and at length died in prison. Remi, archbishop of Lyons, wrote in his favour, and maintained that Godeschalchus had not said that God predestinated the reprobate to sin and wickedness, but only that he abandoned them to their own free-will, to be punished because they would not believe: and in a council held at Valence in Dauphiny, in which Remi himself presided, the decrees of the former council were annulled. But still the members of this council founded the doctrine of divine decrees on God's prescience that the wicked would destroy themselves. We find no other decisions of any synod or council after this, and different opinions continued to be held on the subject.[1]

When we come to the age of the proper *schoolmen,* it is somewhat difficult, notwithstanding they write professedly and at large on all these subjects, to state their opinions with precision, as they seem to confound themselves and their readers with such nice distinctions. In general, Austin

being the oracle of the schools, his doctrine was professed by them all, even by the Franciscans, as well as the Dominicans. They only pretended to dispute about the true sense of his writings. His general doctrine with respect to grace and predestination was so well established, that we only find some subtle distinctions upon the subject, and some evasions of his doctrine by those who did not altogether relish it.

It was agreed among the theologians of this age, that infants are properly chargeable with the sin of Adam, and liable to damnation on that account, because the will of Adam was in some sort the will of the infant. Thomas Aquinas endeavours to prove that it was only the first sin of Adam that could be transferred to his posterity, and that vitiated all his offspring, his subsequent offences affecting himself only. He farther maintains that original sin, being communicated in the act of generation, a person born miraculously cannot have it.[2]

According to some of the schoolmen, the power of man was but inconsiderable, even before the fall. Peter Lombard says, that "by the grace of God given to man, he could resist evil, but could not do good. Free choice," he says, "is the faculty of reason and will, by which, with the help of grace, we can choose good, or without it, evil."[3]

"Thomas Aquinas—not only asserted all St. Austin's doctrine (especially that of predestination), but added this to it, that, whereas formerly it was, in general, held that the providence of God did extend to all things whatsoever, he thought this was done by God's concurring immediately to the production of every thought, action, motion or mode." And, not to make "God the author of sin, a distinction was made between the *positive act* of sin, which was said not to be evil, and the want of its conformity to

[1] Vossii Historia Pelagianismi, p. 734. (*P.*)

[2] Summa, II. pp. 166, 168. (*P.*)
[3] Sententiæ, L. ii. Dist. iv. pp. 391, 392. (*P.*)

the law of God, which, being a nega-tion, was no positive being."[1]

There is no small difficulty in settling the opinion of Thomas Aquinas about grace, though he writes so largely on the subject. He says, that a man can-not even prepare himself for the grace of God without prior grace. Yet he says, in general, that a man must pre-pare himself for receiving grace, and that then the infusion of grace neces-sarily follows. He also says, that a man's free will is necessary to receive the grace by which he is justified. And yet he says, that it cannot be known to any person, except by reve-lation, whether he has grace.[2] No modern fanatic can say anything more favourable to the doctrine of instanta-neous conversion than this writer does. "The justification of a sinner," he says, "is in an instant;" and, again, that "it is the greatest work of God, and altogether miraculous."[3]

The manner in which this writer and other catholics make room for the doc-trine of *merit*, together with these high notions concerning grace, which they never professedly abandoned, is not a little curious. "A man may merit of God," says Thomas Aquinas, "not ab-solutely, indeed, but as receiving a re-ward for doing that which God enables him to do." Yet he still acknowledges, that a man cannot merit the *first grace*, either for himself or for another, and that Christ alone can do this.[4]

If Thomas Aquinas could find room for the doctrine of merit in his system, which was professedly built on that of Austin, it may well be presumed, that the disciples of Duns Scotus (the head of the Franciscan order, as Aquinas was the chief of the Dominicans), and who opposed the doctrine of Aquinas as much as he could, were not less favourable to the doctrine of merit. Burnet says, that "Scotus, who was a Franciscan, denied the pre-determina-tion and asserted the freedom of the will," and that Durandus denied that immediate concourse of God with the human will, which had been asserted by Aquinas, but that in this "he has not had many followers, except Adola and some few others."[5]

At length, the members of the Church of Rome not only attained to a firm persuasion concerning the doctrine of merit, notwithstanding the slender ground on which it was built, but ima-gined that not only Christ, but also some *men*, and especially martyrs, and those who lived a life of great austerity, had even more merit than themselves had occasion for; so that there re-mained some good works in the balance of their account more than they wanted for their own justification. These they termed *works of supererogation*, and imagined that they might be trans-ferred to the account of other persons. The whole accumulated stock of this merit was called the *treasure of the church*, and was thought to be at the disposal of the Popes. Clement VI., in his bull for the celebration of the jubilee in 1350, speaks of this treasure as composed of "the blood of Christ, the virtue of which is infinite, of the merit of the virgin mother of God, and of all the saints."[6] This doctrine was the foundation for those *indulgences*, of which an account will be given in another place, and the monstrous abuse of which brought about the Reforma-tion by Luther.

SECTION IV

OF THE DOCTRINES OF GRACE, ORIGINAL SIN, AND PREDESTINATION, SINCE THE REFORMATION.

As good generally comes out of evil, so sometimes, and for a season at least, evil arises out of good. This, however, was remarkably the case with respect to these doctrines, in consequence of

[1] Burnet on the Articles, p. 194. (*P.*) Art. xvii. Ed. 4. p. 147.
[2] Summa, II. pp. 243–252. (*P.*)
[3] Ibid. pp. 254, 255. (*P.*)
[4] Ibid. II. pp. 257, 258. (*P.*)

[5] Exposition, p. 194. (*P.*) Art. xvii. p. 147.
[6] Memoires pour la Vie de Petrarch, III. p. 75. (*P.*)

the reformation by Luther. For the zeal of this great man against the doctrine of *indulgences*, and that of *merit*, as the foundation of it, unhappily led him and others so far into the opposite extreme, that from his time the doctrines of grace, original sin, and predestination, have been generally termed the *doctrines of the Reformation*, and everything that does not agree with them has been termed *popish*, and branded with other opprobrious epithets.

These doctrines, I observed, originated with Austin, and though they never made much progress in the Greek church, they infected almost all the Latin churches. We see plain traces of them among the Waldenses, who were the earliest reformers from Popery. For, in the Confession of their Faith bearing the date of 1120, they say, "We are sinners in Adam and by Adam," and in another Confession, dated 1532, they say, that "all who are or shall be saved, God has elected from the foundation of the world; and that whoever maintains free-will, denies predestination, and the grace of God."[1] Wickliffe also "asserted the necessity of being assisted by divine grace. Without this, he saw not how a human being could make himself acceptable to God."[2]

But if we were sufficiently acquainted with all the opinions of the Waldenses, and other early reformers, we might, perhaps, meet with many things that would qualify the seeming rigour of these articles. It is certain, however, that neither among the ancient reformers, nor among the Dominicans, or any others who leaned the most to the doctrine of Austin in the Church of Rome, was the scheme so connected in all its parts, and rendered so systematical and uniform, as it was by Luther and the reformers who followed him. Besides that Luther was led to lay the stress that he did upon the doctrine of grace, in consequence of the

abuse of that of the doctrine of *merit* in the Church of Rome, he had himself been, as was observed before, a monk of the order of Austin, and had always been a great admirer of his writings. Also most of those of the Church of Rome who first opposed him were of a different persuasion; the doctrines of Austin having been either abandoned, or nearly explained away, by the generality of the divines of that age. Upon the whole, therefore, it was not to be expected, that such a person as Luther was, should begin a reformation upon any more liberal principles. The fact, however, is notorious.

"Luther," says the translator of Mosheim, "carried the doctrine of *justification by faith* to such an excessive length, as seemed, though perhaps contrary to his intention, to derogate not only from the necessity of good works, but even from their obligation and importance. He would not allow them to be considered either as the *conditions* or *means* of salvation, nor even as a preparation for receiving it." He adds, that "the doctrines of *absolute predestination, irresistible grace,* and *human impotence,* were never carried to a more excessive length.... by any divine than they were by Luther."[3] Amsdorf, a Lutheran divine, maintained, Mosheim says, "that good works were an impediment to salvation." Flacius, another Lutheran, held, that original sin was not an *accident,* but of "the very *substance* of human nature."[4]

In some of the first Confessions of Faith published by the Lutherans, and others of the first reformers, the doctrines of grace, original sin, and predestination,[5] are laid down with remarkable rigour, and a studied exactness of expression. The Augustan Confession says, "On the account of Adam's sin we are liable to the wrath of God, and eternal death, and the corruption of human nature is propagated

---

1 Leger, *Histoire*, pp. 87, 95. (*P.*)
2 Gilpin's Life of him, 1765, p. 75. (*P.*)

Eccl. Hist. IV. pp. 36 Note [q], 40 Note [b].
(*P.*) Cent. xvi. Sect. iii. Pt. ii. xvii. xxx. *Notes.*
4 Ibid. pp. 39, 43. (*P.*) Ibid. xxix, xxxiii.
5 Ibid. p. 40. Note [b].

from him. This vice of our origin (*vitium originis*) is truly a damning sin, and causing eternal death to all who are not born again by baptism and the spirit."[1] We find, however, some expressions rather stronger than even these in the Gallic Confession: "We believe that this vice," (*vitium*,) meaning original sin, "is truly a sin, which makes all and every man, not even excepting infants in the womb, liable, in the sight of God, to eternal death."[2] If any doctrine can make a man shudder, it must be this. Believing this, could any man (unless he had a firmer persuasion than most men can, by the force of any imagination, attain to, of himself being among the number of the elect) bless God that he is a descendant of Adam?

Calvin held these doctrines with no less rigour; and as the Lutherans afterwards abandoned them, they are now generally known by the name of *Calvinistic doctrines.* As to "the most ancient Helvetic Doctors," says Mosheim, "their sentiments seemed to differ but very little from those of the Pelagians; nor did they hesitate in declaring, after the example of *Zuingle*, that the kingdom of heaven was open to all who lived according to the dictates of right reason;" but *Calvin*, when he came among them, "maintained that the everlasting condition of mankind in a future world was determined, from all eternity, by the *unchangeable order* of the Deity," arising from "no other motive than his own *good pleasure* and *free will.*"[3]

Luther's rigid doctrine of election was opposed by Erasmus, who wished well to the Reformation, but was concerned as well for the violence with which it was carried on, as for the unjustifiable length to which Luther carried his opposition, especially with respect to the doctrine of predestination. Luther never answered the last piece of Erasmus on the subject of

free-will; and Melancthon, the great friend of Luther, and the support of his cause, being convinced by the reasoning of Erasmus, came over to his opinion on that subject. And it is very remarkable, that by degrees, and indeed pretty soon afterwards, the Lutherans in general changed also; and some time after the death of Luther and Melancthon, the divines who were deputed by the elector of Saxony, to compose the famous book entitled *The Concord*, abandoned the doctrine of their master, and taught that the decree of election was not absolute, that God saves all who will believe, that he gives all men sufficient means of salvation, and that grace may be resisted.[4]

The principles of all the other reformed churches are, however, still Calvinistic, and among them those of the Churches of England and of Scotland, notwithstanding the generality of divines of the former establishment are acknowledged to be no great admirers of that system.

In Holland, there was no obligation on the ministers to maintain what are called the Calvinistic doctrines, till the synod of Dort; when, by the help of faction in the state, the Calvinistic party in that country prevailed, and those who opposed them, and in consequence of *remonstrating* against their proceedings, got the name of *Remonstrants*, were cruelly persecuted and banished. It is remarkable, however, as Mosheim observes, that since the time of that synod, "the doctrine of absolute decrees lost ground from day to day."[5]

With respect to the Church of Rome, it cannot be denied, that the cause of sound morality had suffered much by means of many sophistical distinctions, introduced by their divines and casuists about the time of the Reformation, as by the distinction of sins into *venial* and *mortal;* the latter of which only, they say, deserve the pains of hell, whereas the former may be atoned for

---

[1] Eccl. Hist. IV. p. 9. (*P.*)
[2] Ibid. p. 80. (*P.*)
[3] Ibid. pp. 72, 73, 80. (*P.*) Cent. **xvi.** Sect. iii. Pt. ii. C, ii, vii, xii,

[4] Basnage, *Histoire*, II. p. 265. (*P.*) See Toplady, *Hist. Proof*, I. p. 318.
[5] Eccl. Hist. IV. p. 499. (*P.*) Cent. **xvii.** Sect. ii, Pt. ii. Ch, ii, xii,

by penances, liberality to the church, &c. It was another of their tenets, that if men do not put a bar to the efficacy of the sacraments, particularly that of penance; if there had been but "imperfect acts of sorrow accompanying them," (such as sorrow for the difficulties a man brings himself into by his vices,) "the use of the sacraments does so far complete those weak acts, as to *justify* us."[1] The Jesuits introduced several other exceedingly dangerous maxims with repect to morals; but they were never received by the Catholics in general, and were sufficiently exposed by their enemies the Jansenists, within the pale of that church.

The fathers of the Council of Trent found much difficulty in settling the doctrines of grace and predestination, many of the members, particularly the Dominicans, being attached to the doctrine of Austin. At length their sole object was to make such a decree as should give the least offence, though it should decide nothing. Among other things, it was determined that "good works are, of their own nature, meritorious of eternal life;" but it is added, by way of softening, that it is through the goodness of God "that he makes his own gifts to us to be merits in us."[2] It is, says Burnet, "the doctrine of a great many in the Church of Rome, and which seems to be that established at Trent, ...that the remission of sins is to be considered as a thing previous to justification, and ...freely given in Christ Jesus; and that in consequence of this there is such a grace infused, that thereupon the person becomes truly just, and is considered as such by God;" but this, he adds, "is but a question about words."[3]

At the Council of Trent, Catarin revived an opinion which was said to have been invented by Occam, and supported by some of the schoolmen, viz. that God has chosen a small number of persons, as the blessed virgin, and the apostles, &c. whom he was determined to save without any foresight of their good works, and that he also wills that all the rest should be saved, providing for them all necessary means for that purpose, but, that they are at liberty to use or refuse them.[4] This opinion was that of Mr. Baxter in England, from whom it is frequently with us, and especially the Dissenters, called the *Baxterian scheme*.[5] Upon the whole, the Council of Trent made a decree in favour of the Semi-Pelagian doctrine.[6]

At first, Bellarmine, Suarez, and the Jesuits in general, were predestinarians, but afterwards the fathers of that order abandoned that doctrine, and differed from the Semi-Pelagians only in this, that they allowed a *preventing grace*, but such as is subject to the freedom of the will.

The author of this, which is commonly called *the middle scheme*, or the doctrine of *sufficient grace for all men*, was Molina, a Jesuit;[7] from whom the favourers of that doctrine were called *Molinists*, and the controversy between them and the *Jansenists*, (so called from Jansenius,[8] a great advocate for the

[1] Basnage, *Histoire*, II. p. 612. (*P.*)
[5] Dr. Kippis says, that "Baxterianism strikes into a middle path between Calvinism and Arminianism, endeavouring in some degree, though perhaps not very consistently, to unite both schemes, and to avoid the supposed errors of each." Biog. Brit. II. p. 22. Milton has immortalized this *scheme*, P. L. III. line 183-202.
[6] See Canon xxxii. p. 40.
[7] A native of Spain, who entered the *Society* at the age of 18. He died at Madrid in 1600, aged 65. His work, which produced the sect of the *Molinists*, was printed at Lisbon in 1588, and entitled *De Concordia Gratiæ et Liberi Arbitrii*. See Nouv. Dict. Hist. IV. p. 551.
[8] He was born in Holland, in 1585, and in 1604 removed to Paris, where he took his degrees. He was afterwards deputed by the University of Louvain to the King of Spain, whom he gratified by writing a book against the French. Philip IV. made him bishop of *Ypres*, where he died in 1638, of the plague, in the midst of his charitable attentions to the people of his diocese. His book, which gave occasion to the sect of the *Jansenists*, is entitled "Augustinus *Cornelii Jansenii Episcopi*, seu Doctrina *Sancti Augustini*, de humanæ Naturæ Sanitate, Ægritudine, Medicina adversus

[1] Burnet on the Articles, p. 161. (*P.*) Art. xi. Ed. 4, p. 125.
[2] Ibid. p. 156. (*P.*) Art. xii. Ed. 4, p. 128. See *Sessio* vi. *De Justificatione*, "Concil. Trident. Canones et Decreta." *Rothomagi*, 1781, 18mo. pp. 35, 36, 40.
[3] Ibid. p. 160. (*P.*) Art. xi. Ed. 4, p. 124.

doctrines of Austin,) has been as vehement as any controversy among Protestants on the same subject. And though besides the Council of Trent, whose decrees are copious enough, appeals were frequently made to the Popes, and their decisious were also procured, the controversy still continues. Of so little effect is the authority of men to prevent different opinions in articles of faith. Different Popes have themselves been differently disposed with respect to these doctrines; and on some occasions a respect for the Jesuits, who were peculiarly devoted to the Popes, was the means of procuring more favour to the tenets which they espoused, than they would otherwise have met with.

Among Protestants, there are great numbers who still hold the doctrines which are termed *Calvinistic* in their greatest rigour; and some time ago they were usually distinguished into two kinds, viz. the *Supralapsarians*, who maintained that God had originally and expressly decreed the fall of Adam, as a foundation for the display of his justice and mercy; while those who maintained that God only *permitted* the fall of Adam, were called *Sublapsarians*, their system of decrees concerning election and reprobation being, as it were, subsequent to that event. But if we admit the divine prescience, there is not, in fact, any difference between the two schemes; and accordingly that distinction is now seldom mentioned.

It is evident that, at present, the advocates for the doctrine of absolute and unconditional election, with the rest that are called *Calvinistic*, consist chiefly of persons of little learning or education; and were the creeds of the established Protestant churches to be revised, the articles in favour of those doctrines would, no doubt, be omitted. But while they continue there, and while the spirit of them is diffused through all the public offices of religion, the belief of them will be kept up among the vulgar, and there will always be men enow ready to accept of church preferment on the condition of subscribing to what they do not believe, and of reciting day after day such offices as they totally disapprove.

Things have been so long in this situation, especially in England, where the minds of the clergy are more enlightened, and where few of them, in comparison, will even pretend that they really believe the articles of faith to which they have subscribed, according to the plain and obvious sense of them;[1] and the legislature has been so often applied to in vain to relieve them in this matter, by removing those subscriptions, that we cannot now reasonably expect any reformation of this great evil, till it shall please Divine Providence to overturn all these corrupt *establishments* of what is called Christianity, but which have long been the secure retreat of doctrines disgraceful to Christianity. For they only serve to make hypocrites of those who live by them, and infidels of those who, without looking farther, either mistake these corruptions of Christianity for the genuine doctrines of it, or, being apprized of the insincerity of the clergy in subscribing them, think that all religion is a farce, and has no hold on the consciences of those who make the greatest profession of it. With all this within ourselves, how unfavourable is the aspect that these doctrines exhibit to the world at large, and what an obstruction must they be to the general propagation of Christianity in the world!

I cannot help making this general

Pelagianos et Massilienses tribus tomis comprensa;" first printed at Louvain in 1640. On this work, which Leibnitz extolled as *un ouvrage profond*, the author was employed twenty years, during which he had read *Augustin* through nit, ten times, and thirty times, that father's treatise against the Pelagians. See *Nouv. Dict. Hist.* III. pp. 432, 433.

[1] Dr. Paley, who was generally better employed, has provided for these *unbelieving* subscribers some convenient excuses. See what Mr. Wakefield justly called "a *shuffling* chapter on subscription to articles of religion" in Paley's *Moral Philosophy*.

reflection at the close of these three parts of my works, which relate to those gross corruptions of Christianity, which exist in their full force in all established Protestant churches. In what follows, the *Catholics*, as they are called, are more particularly concerned; though, it will be seen, that, even with respect to them, many Protestant churches are far from being blameless.

PART IV.

THE HISTORY OF OPINIONS RELATING TO SAINTS AND ANGELS.

THE INTRODUCTION.

THE idolatry of the Christian church began with the deification and proper worship of Jesus Christ, but it was far from ending with it. For, from similar causes, Christians were soon led to pay an undue respect to men of eminent worth and sanctity, which at length terminated in as proper a worship of them, as that which the heathens had paid to their heroes and demigods, addressing prayer to them, in the same manner as to the Supreme Being himself. The same undue veneration led them also to a superstitious respect for their *relics*, the places where they had lived, their pictures and images, and indeed everything that had borne a near relation to them; so that at length, not only were those persons whom they termed *saints*, the objects of their worship, but also their relics and images; and neither with respect to the external forms, nor, as far as we can perceive, their internal sentiments, were Christians to be at all distinguished from those who bowed down to wood and stone, in the times of Paganism.

That this is a most horrid corruption of genuine Christianity I shall take for granted, there being no trace of any such practice, or of any *princi-* ple that could lead to it, in the Scriptures; but it may be useful to trace the causes and the progress of it, from the earliest ages of the Christian church to the present time. And in order to do it as distinctly as possible, I shall divide the history of all the time preceding the Reformation into two periods; the former extending to the fall of the Western empire, or a little beyond the time of Austin, and the latter to the Reformation itself; and I shall also consider separately what relates to *saints in general*, to the *Virgin Mary* in particular, to *relics*, and to *images*.

SECTION I.

PART I.

OF THE RESPECT PAID TO SAINTS IN GENERAL, TILL THE FALL OF THE WESTERN EMPIRE.

THE foundation of all the superstitious respect that was paid to dead men by Christians, is to be looked for in the principles of the heathen philosophy, and the customs of the pagan religion. It was from the principles of philosophy, and especially that of Plato, that Christians learned that the soul was a thing distinct from the body, and capable of existing in a separate conscious state when the body was laid in the grave.[1] They also thought that it frequently hovered about the place where the body had been interred, and was sensible of any attention that, was paid to it.

Christians, entertaining these notions, began to consider their dead as still present with them, and members of their society, and consequently the objects of their prayers, as they had been before. We therefore soon find that they prayed for the dead, as well as for the living, and that they made oblations in their name, as if they had been alive, and had been capable of doing it themselves. And afterwards, looking upon some of them, and especially their martyrs, as having no want of their prayers, but as being in a state of peculiarly high favour with God, and having more immediate access to him, it was natural for them to pass in time, from praying *for them*, to praying *to them*, first as intercessors to God for them, and at length as capable of doing them important services, without any application to the Divine Being at all. The idolatrous respect paid to their *remains*, and to their *images*, was a thing that followed of course.

The first step in this business was a custom which cannot be said to have been unnatural, but it shows how much attention ought to be given to the beginnings of things. It was to meet at the tombs of the martyrs, not by way of devotion to them, but because they thought that their devotion to God was more sensibly excited in those places; and few persons, perhaps, would have been aware of any ill consequence that could have followed from it. Indeed, had it not been for

the philosophical opinions above mentioned, which were brought into Christianity by those who before held them as philosophers, and which gradually insinuated themselves into the body of Christians in general, it might have continued not only a harmless, but an useful custom.

Christians meeting for the purpose of devotion at those places, they would naturally bless God for such examples of piety and fortitude as the martyrs had exhibited, and excite one another to follow their examples. Indeed, their very meeting together at those places for that purpose, was doing them so much honour, as could not fail, of itself, to make other persons ambitious of being distinguished in the same manner after their deaths.

It was also an early custom among Christians to make offerings annually in the name of the deceased, especially the martyrs, as an acknowledgment, that though they were dead, they considered them as still living, and members of their respective churches. These offerings were usually made on the anniversary of their death. Cyprian says, that "if any person appointed one of the clergy to be a tutor or curator of his will, these offerings should not be made for him."[2] So that, as they considered the dead as still belonging to their communion, they had, as we here find, a method of excommunicating them even after death.

The beginning of this superstitious respect for the martyrs seems to have been at the death of Polycarp, and in forty years afterwards it had degenerated into this gross superstition. For Tertullian says, "We make oblations for the dead, and for their martyrdom, on certain days yearly."[3]

Afterwards, this respect paid to martyrs and *confessors*, or those who, having been doomed to death, happened to be released, exceeded all bounds, and in many respects did unspeakable mischief to the church. Nothing was

[1] To give my readers full satisfaction on this subject, I must refer them to my *Disquisitions relating to Matter and Spirit*, in which the doctrine of a *soul* is traced from the Oriental to the Grecian philosophy, and is shown to have been a principle most hostile to the system of *revelation* in every stage of its progress. (*P.*) See [Rutt's Priestley,] Vol. III. pp. 384–431.

[2] Opera, *Epis.* p. 3. (*P.*)

[3] Pierce's *Vindication*, 1718, p. 515. (*P.*)

esteemed more glorious than what they called the *crown of martyrdom;* and on the anniversary festivals, instituted to the honour of each martyr, their memories were celebrated with panegyrical orations. In their prisons they were visited by Christians of all ranks, proud to minister to them in the very lowest offices, and to kiss their chains; and if they happened to escape with life from their torture, their authority was ever after most highly respected in the decision of all controversies, in absolving persons from the ordinary discipline of the church, and restoring them to communion on whatever terms they thought fit.

As it happened that some of these *confessors* were not men of the best moral character, at least became corrupted, in consequence, perhaps, of the superstitious respect with which they were everywhere received, Cyprian makes heavy complaints of the relaxation of church discipline by this means. They were often exceedingly dissolute themselves, and screened the vices of others.

The respect paid to martyrs was gradually extended, in some degree, to others, who also were considered after their deaths as those who had triumphed over the world, and were gone to receive the prize for which they had contended. In imitation of carrying in triumph those who won the prizes in the Grecian games, Christians interred their dead with singing of psalms and lighted tapers. "Tell me," says Chrysostom, "what mean the lamps lighted at funerals? Is it not because we accompany the dead, as so many magnanimous champions? What mean the hymns? Is it not because we glorify God, and render thanks to him, that he has already crowned the deceased, delivering him from all his toil and labour?"[1]

As these festivals on the anniversaries of the martyrs were not in general use till long after the death of the most eminent of them, and particularly of all the apostles and their contemporaries,

it was impossible to fix the dates of them except by conjecture; and we presently find that advantage was taken of this circumstance to appoint their celebration on those days which had been appropriated to pagan festivals. And as the Christians of that age introduced every mark of festivity on these occasions, that the Heathens had been accustomed to in their former worship, there was no change but in the object of it; so that the common people, finding the same entertainment at the usual times and places, they were more easily induced to forsake their old religion, and to adopt the new one, which so much resembled it, and especially in the very things which had kept them attached to the old one. This circumstance would have growing weight in the time of the Christian emperors, when the Christian festivals becoming more popular, would be attended by greater numbers, which would add considerably to the entertainment. This was, indeed, the avowed design of placing the festivals as they did; and Gregory Thaumaturgus, who lived in the third century, is particularly commended by Gregory Nyssenus for thus changing the Pagan festivals into Christian holidays, allowing the same carnal indulgences, with a view to draw the Heathens to the religion of Christ, that the new religion might appear the less strange to them.[2]

As the Christians had been used to meet, for the purpose of public worship, at the tombs of the martyrs; when the empire became Christian they sometimes erected magnificent buildings on those places, and such churches were said to be built *to their honour,* and were distinguished by their names, as they continue to be to this day; and when they had not the martyrs themselves to bury there, at least they got some of their *relics.* And when most of the churches were distinguished in this manner, it was the custom to give names to others merely in honour of particular saints, angels, &c. Thus we have churches dedicated to St. Michael, to Christ, and the Trinity. In this manner, by degrees, each remarkable saint had his proper temple, just as the Heathen gods and heroes had theirs. This practice was approved by the greatest men of that age. Eusebius, in effect, says, " Why should we Christians not shew the same regard to our saints and martyrs that the Pagans paid to their heroes ?"[1]

SECTION I.

Part II.

OF PICTURES AND IMAGES IN CHURCHES.

TEMPLES being now built in honour of particular saints, and especially the martyrs, it was natural to ornament them with paintings and sculptures, representing the great exploits of such saints and martyrs; and this was a circumstance that made the Christian churches still more like the Heathen temples, which were also adorned with statues and pictures; and this also would tend to draw the ignorant multitude to the new worship, making the transition the easier.

"Paulinus, a convert from Paganism, of senatorial rank, celebrated for his parts and learning, and who died afterwards bishop of Nola," in Italy, distinguished himself in this way. He " rebuilt, in a splendid manner, his episcopal church, dedicated to *Felix the Martyr;* on whose porticoes were painted the miracles of Moses and of Christ, together with the acts of Felix and the other martyrs, whose relics were there deposited." This, he says, " in one of his poems,...was done with a design to draw the rude multitude, habituated to the profane rites of Paganism, to a knowledge and good opinion of the Christian doctrine; by learning from these pictures what they were not capable of learning from books, the lives and acts of Christian saints."[2]

The custom of having pictures in churches being once begun, (which was about the end of the fourth or the beginning of the fifth century, and generally by converts from Paganism), the more wealthy among the Christians seem to have vied with each other, who should build and ornament their churches in the most expensive manner, and nothing perhaps contributed more to it than the example of this Paulinus.

It appears from Chrysostom, that pictures and images were to be seen in the principal churches of his time, but this was in the East. In Italy, they were but rare in the beginning of the fifth century; and a bishop of that country, who had got his church painted, thought proper to make an apology for it, by saying, that the people being amused with the pictures would have less time for regaling themselves.[3] The origin of this custom was probably in Cappadocia, where Gregory Nyssenus was bishop, the same who commended Gregory Thaumaturgus for contriving to make the Christian festivals resemble the Pagan ones.

Though many churches in this age were adorned with the images of saints and martyrs, there do not appear to have been many of Christ. These are said to have been introduced by the Cappadocians; and the first of these were only symbolical ones, being made in the form of a lamb. One of this kind Epiphanius found in the year 389, and he was so provoked at it, that he tore it. It was not till the council of Constantinople, called *In Trullo,* held so late as the year 707, that pictures of Christ were ordered to be drawn in the form of men.[4]

SECTION I.

Part III.

OF THE VENERATION FOR RELICS.

CONSIDERING the great veneration which Christians in very early ages enter-

[1] Jortin, III. p. 14. *(P.)*
[2] Middleton's *Letter from Rome,* p. 242. *(P.)* Works, 4to. III. pp. 128, 129.

[3] Sueur, A. D. 401. *(P.)*
[4] Ibid. A. D. 707. *(P.)*

tained for martyrs, we are not surprised that they should pay a superstitious respect to their *relics;* but we do not find any account of their collecting things of this kind in the first or second century. Neither Trypho, Celsus, nor any of those who wrote against Christianity at first, make this objection to it; but Julian and Eunapius reproached the Christians with it very severely. It was, indeed, about the time that the empire became Christian, that the respect for relics began to make much progress. When Palestine was purged from idols, many persons visited it, and especially the tomb of our Saviour, out of pious curiosity; and *holy earth,* as it was called, from Jerusalem, was much valued in the time of Austin.

This respect for relics was much forwarded by the eloquence of preachers, and by no person more than Chrysostom. "I esteem the city of Rome," says he, "not because of the pillars of marble, but because of the pillars of the church therein, the bodies of St. Peter and St. Paul. Who can now afford me the favour of being stretched out on the body of St. Paul, of being nailed to his sepulchre, of beholding the dust of that body which bore the marks of the Lord Jesus, and that mouth by which Christ himself spake? I long to see the sepulchre wherein is enclosed that armour of righteousness, that armour of light, those members which still live, and which were dead whilst living. I long to see those chains, those bonds," &c.[1]

It appears that about the year 386, the piety of many persons consisted chiefly in carrying and keeping bones and relics, and that many persons, who traded in them, abused the credulity of the people. A law was made by Theodosius to prevent this, but it had little effect. Among other methods by which they gained credit for their relics, it was usual in this age to pretend that revelations were made to persons, to inform them where they should discover the bones of particular martyrs.

The bodies of many of the martyrs having been buried in obscure places, and exposed, when the persecution ceased they were brought to light, and decently interred. Thus began the *translation of relics,* which was afterwards performed with great ceremony and devotion; the possession of them being esteemed the most valuable of treasures, not less than the bones of some of the heroes of antiquity, or particular images of some of their gods, which had likewise been carried from place to place with great solemnity, and probably afforded a pattern for this translation of Christian relics. In 359, Constantius caused the bodies of St. Andrew and St. Luke to be taken out of their sepulchres, and carried with great pomp to Constantinople, to the temple of the twelve apostles, which was a church that had been built to their honour by Constantine. This is the first example of the translation of the bodies of saints into churches; and the custom being once begun, was afterwards carried to the greatest excess.[2]

But the translation of the relics of the martyr Stephen, in the time of Austin, was one of the most remarkable things of this kind in that age, and the account of it is given by Austin himself. These bones of St. Stephen, after they had lain buried and unknown for near four centuries, were said to have been discovered by Gamaliel, under whom St. Paul had studied, to one Lucianus, a priest; and being found by his direction, they were removed with great solemnity, and, as was pretended, with many miracles, into Jerusalem. The fame of these relics was soon spread through the Christian world, and many little portions of them were brought away by pilgrims, to enrich the churches of their own countries. And wherever any relics were deposited, an oratory or chapel was always built over them, and this was called a memorial of that martyr whose relics it contained. Several relics of St.

---

[1] In Eph. *Hom.* viii. Opera, X. p. 1078. (*P.*)

[2] Sueur, A. D. 359. (*P.*)

Stephen having been brought by different persons into Africa, as many memorials of him were erected in different places, of which three were particularly famous, and one of them was at Hippo, where Austin himself was bishop. In all these places, illustrious miracles were said to be wrought continually. For, long before this time, miracles had been said to be wrought by saints, living and dead.

These abuses did not advance to this height without opposition, though the only person that distinguished himself greatly by his remonstrances on this subject, in this age, was Vigilantius, a priest of Barcelona. He saw that this superstitious respect for the saints, as they were called, their images and their relics, was introducing Paganism into the Christian church, and he wrote against it with great earnestness. " We see," says he, " in effect, a Pagan rite introduced into our churches under the pretext of religion, when heaps of wax candles are lighted up in clear sunshine, and people everywhere kissing and adoring, I know not what, contemptible dust, preserved in a little vessel, and wrapt up in precious linen. These men do great honour truly to the blessed martyrs, by lighting up paltry candles to those whom the Lamb, in the midst of the throne, illuminates with all the lustre of his majesty." St. Jerome, who answers him, does not deny the practice, nor its being borrowed from the Pagans, but defends it. " That," says he, " was once done to idols, and was then to be detested, but this is done to the martyrs, and is therefore to be received.' [1]

SECTION I.

PART IV.

OF WORSHIP PAID TO SAINTS AND ANGELS.

HAVING shown the general progress of the respect paid by Christians to their

[1] Middleton's *Letter from Rome*, p. 240. (*P.*) Works, pp. 127, 128.

saints and martyrs, and also to their images and relics, I shall show by what steps these saints and martyrs became the objects of their proper *devotion*. But before Christians prayed *to* their dead saints, they used to pray *for* them; and the foundation of both these practices was the doctrine of *a soul*, as a substance distinct from the body, and capable of thinking and acting without it, which was borrowed from Pagan philosophy.

Most of the fathers were particularly addicted to the doctrine of Plato, who taught that the souls of the dead, after quitting their bodies, have influence in the affairs of men, and take care of them. Eusebius approved of the opinion, and endeavoured to confirm it. Theodoret also, in his sermon on the martyrs, tells the Pagans that it was the opinion of Plato, in order to show that Christians have reason to think the same thing of their martyrs.[2]

Till the middle of the fourth century it was the general belief that the abode of the souls of the faithful was in subterraneous places, or at least here below, near the earth; but towards the end of this century they were supposed by some to be above, but not in the place where they could enjoy the beatific vision of God. From the former opinion came the custom of praying for the dead, which began so early as the beginning of the third century; the objects of these prayers being their quiet repose in their present situation, and a speedy and happy resurrection. They even prayed for the Virgin Mary; and there are also instances of their praying for the damned, in order to lessen their torments.

It was not very soon a general or fixed opinion, that the souls of the dead were in places where they could hear and attend to what was passing among the living. But thinking more highly of martyrs than of other persons, it was soon imagined that their state after death might be better than that

[2] Sueur, A. D. 407. (*P.*)

I

of others. For, while the rest of the dead were supposed to be confined in Hades, which was à subterraneous place, waiting for the resurrection of their bodies, they thought that the martyrs were admitted to the immediate presence of God, and to a state of favour and power with him. Indeed, so early as the middle of the third century, when many went to solicit the prayers of those who were prisoners doomed to death, they would request that, after their death, they would be mindful of the living; and some are even said to have agreed with one another, that whichever of them should die first, he should use his interest in favour of the survivor.[1]

So far, however, was it from being usual to pray to saints in the third century, that Origen says, they were not to pray to any *derived being* (ουδενι των γεννητων), not even to Christ himself, but to God the Father of all.[2]

Prayer *to* the dead began with the martyrs, as well as prayers *for* the dead, but not till near the end of the fourth century, when it was imagined that they might hear those who invoked them near the place of their interment. But it appears by the Constitutions, and several of the writings of that time, that the public offices were yet preserved pure. In the fifth century they prayed to God to hear the intercessions of the saints and martyrs in their behalf; but there is a great difference between this and praying to the saints themselves, as if they could hear and help the living; and when the custom of invoking them was introduced, many had doubts on the subject, and therefore to their invocations of them added, "if they were present, and had any influence in things below," &c.

Austin himself was much perplexed about this; and in one place says, "It is true the saints do not themselves hear what passes below, but they hear of it by others, who die and go to

them."[3] In another place he supposes that the martyrs may assist the living, because they attend where their monuments are. Basil, however, in his homily on the forty martyrs, supposes that they were present in the temples and joined in the prayers of the faithful, but he does not say that the faithful should pray to them.[4]

One of the first instances of direct invocation of the dead is that of Theodosius the Younger, who, casting his eyes upon the coffin of Chrysostom, asked pardon of him for Arcadius his father, and Eudoxia his mother, because he considered that saint as more particularly present there than elsewhere. But at that time they did not invoke the saints in general, as the apostles, &c., but only those at whose tombs they attended; and there are but few examples of invoking the Virgin Mary till far in the fifth century.

Austin is the first who takes notice that praying for the martyrs, which had long been the custom of Christians, did not agree with the invocation of them, which began to gain ground in his time. He says, that it injures the martyrs to pray to God for them, and that when the church mentions them in her prayers, it is not to pray for them, but to be helped by their prayers. Yet, in all the genuine writings of Austin, it does not appear that he ever directly invoked the saints, except by way of apostrophe, as an orator, or in a simple wish that the saint would pray for him. Also praying for the dead in general, and even for the apostles and martyrs, continued, and was not abolished but by the full establishment of the invocation of them. Gregory the First, who contributed most to it, in the beginning of the seventh century, supposed some of the saints to enjoy the beatific vision of God, though most persons still believed that not even the martyrs would be admitted to that vision before the

---

[1] History of Ancient Ceremonies, p. 26. (*P.*)
[2] Whitby on John xvii. 2. (*P.*)
[3] *De Cura pro Mortuis,* C. xiv. Opera, IV. p. 890. (*P.*)
[4] Opera, I. p. 959. (*P.*)

resurrection; and Hugh de Victor, so late as 1130, says, that many still doubt whether the saints hear the prayers of those who invoke them, and that it is a question difficult to decide.[1]

It appears that Austin was very sensible of the growing superstition of his time, and said, with apparent disapprobation, "I know there are some who adore sepulchres and paintings."[2] But this does not imply a direct invocation of them. Paulinus of Nola, his contemporary, went every year to Rome, to show his respect to the tombs of the martyrs, because, as he said, he had great confidence in their intercession; and about the year 337, Constantine built a magnificent church in honour of the twelve apostles, intending to be buried there, that after his death he might partake of the prayers that would be made there in their honour.[3] But neither does this imply a direct invocation of them. In the ancient litanies all the invocations of our Saviour ended with these words, *Lord have mercy upon us* (Κυριε ελεισον), repeated many times; but the litanies of the saints consisted of nothing more than an enumeration of their titles, to which, but in later times, they added the words *ora pro nobis.* Examples of the former may be seen in Basil and Chrysostom.[4]

In the fifth century no opposition was made to the invocation of saints. The common opinion then was, that their souls were not so entirely confined to the celestial mansions, but that they visited mortals, and travelled through various countries; though it was still thought that they more especially frequented the places where their bodies were interred. Also, the images of the saints were by this time honoured with particular worship in several places, and it was imagined by many, that this worship, or the forms of consecration, which were soon introduced, drew

into the image the propitious presence of the saint, or celestial being, whom it represented; the very notion which had prevailed with respect to the statues of Jupiter and Mercury, &c.

This excessive veneration for the dead, and for their relics, was greatly promoted by the eloquent preachers or declaimers of those times. Athanasius, Gregory Nazianzen, and Chrysostom, distinguished themselves in this way. The last of these writers, celebrating the acts of the martyr Babylas, bishop of Antioch, says, "The Gentiles will laugh to hear me talk of the acts of persons dead and buried, and consumed to dust; but they are not to imagine that the bodies of martyrs, like to those of common men, are left destitute of all active force and energy; since a greater power than that of the human soul is superadded to them, the power of the Holy Spirit; which, by working miracles in them, demonstrates the truth of the resurrection."[5]

To see to what excess this superstitious worship of the dead was carried, in the period of which I am now treating, I shall recite at length, from Dr. Middleton, a passage of Theodoret, one of the Greek fathers, which shows us, as he says, the state of Christianity in the fifth century: "The temples of our martyrs," says this father, "are shining and conspicuous, eminent for their grandeur and the variety of their ornaments, and displaying far and wide the splendour of their beauty. These we visit, not once, or twice, or five times in the year, but frequently offer up hymns, each day, to the Lord of them. In health we beg the continuance of it: in sickness the removal of it. The childless beg children;...and when these blessings are obtained, we beg the secure enjoyment of them. When we undertake any journey, we beg them to be our companions and guides in it; and when we return safe, we pay them our thanks. And that those who pray with faith and sincerity

---

[1] Sueur, A. D. 487. (*P.*)
[2] *De Moribus Ecclesiæ*, L. i. C. xxxiv. Opera, I. p. 774.(*P.*)
[3] Suenr, A. D. 337. (*P.*)
[4] Ibid. A. D. 463. (*P.*)

[5] Middleton's Inquiry, p. 152. (*P.*) Works, I. p. 123.

I 2

obtain what they ask, is manifestly testified by the number of offerings which are made to them, in consequence of the benefits received. For some offer the figures of eyes, some of feet, some of hands, made either of gold or of silver, which the Lord accepts, though but of little value, measuring the gift by the faculties of the giver. But all these are the evident proofs of the cures of as many distempers; being placed there as monuments of the fact, by those who have been made whole. The same monuments likewise proclaim the power of the dead; whose power also demonstrates their God to be the true God."[1]

But we shall perhaps form a still clearer idea of the firm possession that these superstitions had obtained in the minds of the generality of Christians, when we consider what little respect the manly sense of Vigilantius, who set himself to oppose the progress of these corrupt practices, procured him from Jerome, the most learned writer of his age. Unhappily we have nothing from Vigilantius, but what his opponent himself has given us from him, in his answer. But even this is abundantly sufficient to satisfy us with respect to the good sense of the one, and the bigoted violence of the other, together with the character of the age in which they lived.

Vigilantius maintained, as the articles are enumerated by Middleton, "that the honours paid to the rotten bones and dust of the saints and martyrs, by.... lodging them in their churches, and lighting up wax candles before them, after the manner of the Heathens, were the ensigns of idolatry. That the celibacy of the clergy was a heresy, and their vows of chastity the seminary of lewdness. That to pray for the dead, or to desire the prayers of the dead, was superstitious; and that the souls of the departed saints and martyrs were at rest in some particular place, whence they could not remove

themselves at pleasure, so as to be present everywhere to the prayers of their votaries. That the sepulchres of the martyrs ought not to be worshipped, nor their fasts and vigils to be observed." And lastly, "that the signs and wonders said to be wrought by their relics, and at their sepulchres, served to no good end or purpose of religion."

"These were the *sacrilegious* tenets, as Jerome calls them, which he could not hear with patience, or without the utmost grief, and for which he declared Vigilantius to be 'a most detestable heretic, venting his foul-mouthed blasphemies against the relics of the martyrs, which were daily working signs and wonders.' He bids him 'go into the churches of those martyrs, and he would be cleansed from the evil spirit which possessed him, and feel himself burnt, not by those wax candles, which so much offended him, but by invisible flames, which would force that demon who talked within him, to confess himself to be the same who had personated a Mercury, perhaps a Bacchus, or some other of their gods among the Heathens.' At which wild rate," says Dr. Middleton, "this good father raves on, through several pages, in a strain much more furious than the most bigoted Papist would use at this day in defence of the same rites."[2] All the modern ecclesiastical historians give the same account of this Vigilantius.[3]

I must not conclude the history of this period without observing that some undue respect was paid to *angels*, who were believed to transact much of the business of this world, by commission from God. This arose from the opinions of the Gnostics, and is alluded to by the apostle Paul, who says, that some through a *voluntary humility* worshipped angels, *being vainly puffed up in their fleshly minds.* Col. ii. 18.

It seems probable that some undue

---

[1] Introductory Discourse, p. 69. (*P.*) Works, I. pp. xlvii. xlviii.

[2] Ibid. p. 131, &c. (*P.*) Works, I. pp. lxxxix. xc.
[3] See Mosheim, I. pp. 392, 393. (*P.*) Cent. v, Pt. ii. Ch. iii. Sect. xiv.

respect was paid to angels, as well as to Christ and the Holy Spirit, in the time of Justin Martyr, for he says, "him (God) and the Son that came from him, and the host of other good angels, who accompany and resemble him, together with the prophetic spirit, we adore and worship, in word and truth honouring them."[1] With this writer, however, and the Christians of his time, it is not probable that this respect for angels amounted to praying to them. For we find that praying to angels, which had been practised in Phrygia and Pisidia, was forbidden as idolatrous by the Council of Laodicea. in 364.

SECTION I.

PART V.

OF THE RESPECT PAID TO THE VIRGIN MARY, IN THIS PERIOD.

As our Saviour became the object of worship before any other man, so his mother soon began to be considered with a singular respect, and at length she engrossed so much of the devotion of the Christian world, that I shall make a separate article of it, in each period of this part of my work.

It is remarkable that, excepting what was said to Mary by the angel, *henceforth all generations shall call thee blessed*, no particular compliment is paid to her in all the history of the evangelists. She is only mentioned as a pious woman, among several others, and was committed to the care of John by our Lord, as he hung upon the cross. Nay, several expressions of our Lord, though not really disrespectful, yet show that, in his character of a teacher sent from God, he considered her only as any other person or disciple.

When she applied to him about the failure of wine, at the marriage feast in Cana, he replied, *Woman, what hast thou to do with me?* and gave her no

satisfaction with respect to what he intended to do. And again, when she and some others of his relations were endeavouring to make their way through a crowd, in order to speak to him, and he was told of it, he replied, *Who is my mother, and who are my brethren? He that does the will of God, the same is my brother, and sister, and mother.* In the book of Acts her name is but once mentioned, as one of those who were assembled with the apostles after the ascension of Jesus, Acts i. 14, so that where or how she lived, or died, we have no knowledge at all. On how narrow a foundation does the excessive veneration that was afterwards paid to the *blessed Virgin*, as she is now called, rest!

The first mention that we find of any particular respect paid to the Virgin Mary, was in the time of Epiphanius, when some women used to offer to her cakes called *collyrides*, from which they got the name of Collyridians; and as men had no concern in it, except by permitting their wives to do it, it is called by this writer a *heresy of the women*. He himself greatly disapproved of it, and wrote against it. This may be thought extraordinary, since oblations at the tombs of the dead were very common in this age. But as it was not known where the Virgin Mary was interred, the offering of cakes to her was a new step in the worship of the dead, and was therefore more particularly noticed. It is plain, however, from his account of this affair, that prayers were then offered to the Virgin Mary, and by some of the orthodox, as they were called, though he himself rejected the thought of it with indignation.

In a piece of Athanasius, entitled *De Sanctissima Deipara*, we find a long address to the Virgin, but it seems to have been a piece of oratory, and we can hardly infer from it that it was his custom to address his devotions to her. In it he says, "Hear, O daughter of David, and of Abraham; incline thine ear to our prayers, and

[1] *Apol.* I. Edit. Thirlby, p. 11. (*P.*)

forget not thy people;" and again, "Intercede for us, lady, mistress, queen, and mother of God."[1]

The first who was particularly noticed, as introducing this worship of the Virgin, is Peter Gnapheus, bishop of Antioch, in the fifth century, who appointed her name to be called upon in the prayers of the church. This devotion, however, seems to have taken its rise towards the end of the fourth century, and in Arabia, where we read of a controversy respecting her; some maintaining, that, after she was delivered of Jesus, she lived with her husband Joseph as his wife. This was violently opposed by others, who, running into the other extreme, worshipped her " as a goddess, and judged it necessary to appease her anger, and seek her favour by libations, sacrifices, the oblations of cakes (*collyridæ*), and such like services," as Epiphanius censured.[2]

To persons much acquainted with ecclesiastical history, nothing of this kind will appear extraordinary. Otherwise we might be surprised how it should ever have been considered as a thing of any consequence, whether the mother of Christ had any commerce with her husband or not. The presumption is, that, as they lived together, at least after the birth of Jesus, she had. However, the respect paid to *virginity* in that age was so great, that it was thought to derogate from her virtue and honour, to suppose that she ever had any commerce with man; and therefore, without any proper evidence in the case, it was *presumed* that she must have continued a virgin; and to maintain the contrary was even deemed heretical. In the Council of Capua, in 389, Bonosus, a bishop in Macedonia, was condemned for maintaining that Mary, the mother of Jesus, was not always a virgin; following, it is said, the heresy of Paulinus.

When the doctrine of *original sin* was started, the veneration for the Virgin Mary was so great, that doubts were entertained whether she might not have been exempt from it, as well as her son. Austin maintained that no person ever lived without sin except the Virgin Mary, concerning whom he, however, only says he will not hold any controversy, for the honour that we owe to our Saviour.[3]

After the deification and worship of Christ, it was natural that the rank of his mother should rise in some proportion to it. Accordingly we find, that after Christ was considered as God, it became customary to give Mary the title of *mother of God* ($\theta\epsilon\sigma\tau\sigma\kappa\sigma\varsigma$). This, however, was not done, at least generally, till after the Council of Chalcedon in 451. This title of mother of God happened to be a favourite term with Apollinaris and his followers, and in consequence of this, perhaps, it was, that Nestorius violently opposed this innovation, thinking it sufficient that Mary should be called *the mother of Christ.*

This opposition, however, operated as in many other cases, viz. to increase the evil; and in the third council of Ephesus, in which Nestorius was condemned, it was decreed that Mary should be called the mother of God. From this time she was honoured more than ever; but still she had not the titles that were given her afterwards of *queen of heaven, mistress of the world, goddess, mediatrix, gate of paradise, &c.*

SECTION II.

PART I.

OF THE WORSHIP OF SAINTS, IN THE MIDDLE AGES, AND TILL THE REFORMATION.

TILL the beginning of the fifth century prayers to saints were only occasional, as at the place of their interment, or

[1] *Opera,* I. p. 1041. (*P.*)
[2] *Hæres.* lxxviii. lxxix. pp. 1003, 1057. Mosheim, I. p. 351. (*P.*) Cent. iv. Pt. ii. Ch. v. Sect. xxv.

[3] *De Natura et Gratia,* C. xxxvi. Op. VII. p. 747. (*P.*)

on the anniversary of their death, &c., because at that time it was generally supposed that their souls were hovering about that place, and there, also, was the scene of all the miracles that were originally ascribed to them. But when it came to be a general persuasion, that the souls of the martyrs, and other persons of eminent sanctity, were admitted to the immediate presence of God, and were capable of a general inspection of the affairs of the world, prayers to them were no longer confined to the place of their interment, or to the chapels and churches erected over them.

It was now imagined that the souls of these illustrious dead could hear the prayers that were addressed to them in all places and at all times. For, as for the great difficulty of a human being (whose faculties are of course limited) being capable of knowing what passes in more than one place at a time, they seem not to have considered it. Or they might suppose the power of an unembodied spirit, not now confined to any particular corporeal system, to be incapable of any limitation. Or they might suppose that God had endued them with faculties of which they were not naturally capable before. Certain, however, it is, that in the middle ages, the common people addressed their prayers to dead men with as little apprehension of their not being heard by them, as if they had been praying to the Divine Being himself.

In fact, the Christian saints succeeded, in all respects, to the honours which had been paid to the pagan deities; almost all of whom had been supposed to have been men whose extraordinary merit had exalted them to the rank and power of gods, after their death. This analogy between the two religions made the transition very easy to the bulk of the common people; and the leading men among the Christians perceiving this, and being themselves not averse to the ceremonies and pomp of the ancient idolatry, contrived to make the transition still easier, by preserving

everything that they possibly could in the ancient forms of worship, changing only the objects of them.

About the eleventh century this was done without disguise, and though *images* were not common, and we read of no *statues* in Christian churches at that time, yet, in other respects, the worship of the saints was modelled according to the religious services which had been paid to the heathen gods. Some time afterwards we find that Christians had the same temples, the same altars, and often the same images with the Pagans, only giving them new names. Dr. Middleton was shown " an antique statue of a young Bacchus," which was " worshipped under the title of a female saint." [1]

" The noblest heathen temple now remaining in the world is the Pantheon or Rotunda" at Rome, " which, as the inscription over the portico [2] informs us, *having been* impiously dedicated of old by Agrippa to Jove, and all the gods, was piously reconsecrated by Pope Boniface IV. (A.D. 607) to the blessed Virgin and all the saints. With this single alteration," says Dr. Middleton, " it serves as exactly for all the purposes of the *popish*, as it did for the *pagan* worship, for which it was built. For as in the old temple every one might find the god of his country, and address himself to that deity whose religion he was most devoted to, so it is the same thing now. Every one chooses the patron whom he likes best; and one may see here different services going on at the same time at different altars, with distinct congregations around them, just as the inclinations of the people lead them to the worship of this or that particular saint." [3]

As men are greatly influenced by *names*,

[1] Letter from Rome, p. 160. (*P.*) Works, III. p. 84.
[2] " Pantheon, &c. Ab Agrippa Augusti Genero Impie Jovi, Cæterisque Mendacibus Diis a Bonifacio IIII. Pontifice Deiparæ et S. S. Christi Martyribus Pie Dica'um," &c. Ibid. See also *Les Conformitez*, &c., 1667, p. 167.
[3] Middleton's Letter p. 161. (*P.*) Works, III. pp. 84, 85.

it was even contrived that the name of the new divinity should as much as possible resemble the old one. Thus the saint *Apollinaris* was made to succeed the god *Apollo*, and St. *Martina* the god *Mars*. It was farther contrived that, in some cases, the same *business* should continue to be done in the same place, by substituting for the heathen god a Christian saint of a similar character, and distinguished for the same virtues. Thus, there being a temple at Rome in which sickly infants had been usually presented for the cure of their disorders, they found a Christian saint who had been famous for the same attention to children; and consecrating the same temple to him, the very same practices are now continued as in the times of Heathenism.[1]

Farther, as it had been customary to hang up in the heathen temples, particularly those of Æsculapius, pictures of scenes in which persons had supposed they had been relieved by the interposition of their gods, and especially of limbs that had been diseased, and were afterwards cured, &c., the same custom, as I have hinted already, was very early introduced into the Christian churches; and in later ages, I doubt not, these exhibitions were more numerous than they had ever been in the times of Heathenism.

Dr. Middleton, who observed the present popish worship with this view, mentions other points of resemblance, so numerous, and so little varied, that he says he could have imagined himself present in the ancient heathen temples; and he is confident that a considerable knowledge of the ancient heathen ritual might be learned from them.[2] Candles are continually burn-

ing in the present churches as in the former temples, incense is always smoking, many of the images are daubed with red ochre, as those of the heathen gods often were, their faces are black with the smoke of candles and incense, people are continually on their knees, or prostrate before them; and, according to the accounts of all travellers, the prayers that are addressed to them are of the same nature, and urged with the same indecent importunity. They are also followed by the same marks of resentment, if their requests be not granted, as if they hoped to get by foul means what they could not obtain by fair. Mr. Byron informs us that, being in danger of shipwreck, a Jesuit who was on board brought out an image of some saint, which he desired might be hung up in the mizen shrouds; and this being done, he kept threatening it, that if they had not a breeze of wind soon he would throw it into the sea. A breeze springing up, he carried back the image with an air of great triumph.[3]

As the Heathens had gods of particular countries, so the Christians of these ages imagined that one saint gave particular attention to the affairs of one country, and another saint to those of another. Thus, St. George was considered as the patron of England, St. Denis of France, St. Januarius of Naples, &c.

In all countries different saints were supposed to attend to different things, each having his proper province. Thus, St. George is invoked in battle, St.

rupted succession, from the priests of *old*, to the priests of *new* Rome; whilst each of them readily explained and called to my mind some passage of a classic author, where the same ceremony was described, as transacted in the same form and manner, and in the same place, where I now saw it executed before my eyes: so that as oft as I was present at any religious exercise in their churches, it was more natural to fancy myself looking on, at some solemn act of idolatry in *old Rome*, than assisting at a worship instituted on the principles and formed upon the plan of Christianity." Middleton's *Letter*. Works, III. pp. 68, 69. See also the Strictures of Warburton, *Div. Leg.* Pt. i. (Works, 8vo. IV. p. 126), and Middleton's *Postscript*, Works, III. p. 120.

³ *Voyage*, p. 207. (*P.*)

---

[1] Middleton's Letter, p. 167. (*P.*) Works, III. pp. 88, 89.

[2] "Nothing, I found, concurred so much with my original intention of conversing with the ancients, or so much helped my imagination, to fancy myself wandering about in old *heathen* Rome, as to observe and attend to their religious worship; all whose ceremonies appeared plainly to have been copied from the rituals of primitive *Paganism*; as if handed down, by an unin-ter-

Margaret in childbearing, St. Genevieve for rain, and St. Nicholas, or St. Anthony, by seamen, &c.

Also, as with the Heathens, the same god was thought to be worshipped to more advantage in one place than another, this was imagined to be the case with respect to the new divinities. For, as there was a Jupiter Ammon, a Jupiter Olympius, and a Jupiter Capitolinus, so the Papists have one Virgin Mary of Loretto, another of Montserrat, &c. And though there be a church dedicated to the Virgin in a town where a person lives, yet he will often think it worth his while to make a pilgrimage of some hundreds of miles to worship the same virgin in some other place, which she is supposed to honour with more particular attention, and to have distinguished by more miracles, &c.

So many persons had acquired the reputation of *saints* in the ninth century, that the ecclesiastical councils found it necessary to decree that no person should be considered as a saint, till a bishop in the province had pronounced him worthy of that honour; and the consent of the Pope was likewise generally thought expedient, if not necessary. No saint, however, was created by the authority of any pope before Udalric, bishop of Augsburgh, received that honour from John XV. in the tenth century; though others say it was Savibert who was first canonized by Leo III. after his life and pretensions had been regularly examined.[1] At length, Alexander III., in the twelfth century, asserted the sole right of canonization, to the Pope.

This business of *canonization* was also copied from Paganism, the senate of Rome having taken upon it to pronounce what persons should be *deified*, and having decreed that honour to several of their emperors, to whom temples were consequently erected, and worship regularly paid. Also the title of *Divus*, which had been given by the

decree of the senate to deified men, was now adopted by the Christians, and given to their canonized saints. The consequence of a regular canonization was, that the name of the saint was inserted in the calendar in red letters; he might then be publicly invoked and prayed to, churches and altars might be dedicated to him, masses might be said in his honour, holidays might be kept in his name, his image also might be set up and prayed to, and his relics might be reverently laid up and worshipped.

Considering who they were that directed this business of canonization, and what kind of merit weighed most with them, it is no wonder that many of these canonized persons were such as had little title to the appellation of saints. They were generally miserable enthusiasts, some of them martyrs to their own austerities, and sometimes men who had distinguished themselves by nothing but their zeal for what was imagined to be the *rights of the church*, and their opposition to the temporal princes of their times; such as Thomas à Becket of this country.

As many of the persons to whom divine honours are paid in catholic countries began to be distinguished in this manner before there were any regular canonizations, and in times of great ignorance, we are not surprised, though we cannot help being amused, at the gross mistakes that were sometimes made in this serious business; several of the names, the most distinguished by the honours that are paid to them, being those of persons altogether *imaginary*, so that the object of their worship never had any existence. Such is *St. Ursula* and the eleven thousand virgins. This woman is said to have been a native of Cornwall, who with her virgins travelled to Rome, and in their return through Germany, accompanied by Pope Cyriacus, suffered martyrdom at Cologne. Baronius himself says, there never was any pope of that name.

In this class also we must put the

[1] Mosheim, II. p. 219. (*P.*) Cent. x. Pt. ii. Ch. iii. Sect. iv. Basnage, *Histoire*, II. p. 691.

seven sleepers, who are said to have slept in a cave from the time of Decius to that of Theodosius, or, as they reckon it, 162 years; and who, to the confutation of some who denied the resurrection, awakened after that interval, and looked as fresh as ever. No better claim has *St. George,* the patron of this country, or *St. Christopher,* who is said to have been twelve feet, or twelve cubits high, and to have carried our Saviour over an arm of the sea upon his back. From the words *Vera Icon,* or the *true image,* meaning that of our Saviour, impressed upon a handkerchief, they have made Saint *Veronica,* and supposed this handkerchief to have been given to her by our Saviour himself.

Several mistakes have been made by supposing that words beginning with an S were intended to express the name of some saint, and from the remainder of the word they have accordingly composed the name of an imaginary person. Thus, in all probability, from *Soracte,* the name of a mountain, they have got the name of *St. Oreste,* softening the sound after the Italian manner; and what is more extraordinary, from a fragment of an inscription, which, in all probability was originally *præfectus viarum,* the S only remaining of the word *præfectus,* and *viar* of the word following, they have made *St. Viar;* and the Spaniards, in whose country this inscription was found, fancying that this new saint had distinguished himself by many illustrious miracles, solicited Pope Urban to do something to his honour. In England particular honour was paid to *St. Amphibolus,* which appears to have been nothing but a *cloke* that had belonged to St. Alban.[1]

Besides particular festivals for particular saints, the Papists have a festival for the commemoration of *all saints* in general, lest, as we may suppose, any should have been omitted in their calendar. This was introduced by Gregory IV.

These new objects of worship presently engrossed almost all the devotion of the vulgar, who think they may make more free with these inferior divinities than they can with the Supreme Being; so that the name of the true God the Father is seldom made use of by them.[2] And those persons who have attached themselves to any particular saint have become most passionately fond of them, and have been led to magnify their power to a degree which excites both our pity and indignation.[3] There is a book entitled *The Conformity of St. Francis,* intended to show how nearly he approached to Christ, in his birth, miracles, and all the particulars of his life. But nothing was ever so extraordinary as the accounts of Ignatius, by his followers the Jesuits; and it is the more so, as he lived in modern times.

Some of the Jesuits have said, it was no wonder that Moses worked so many miracles, since he had the name of God written upon his rod; or that the apostles worked miracles, since they spake in the name of Christ: whereas, St. Ignatius had performed as many miracles as the apostles, and more than Moses, in his own name. Others of them have said that only Christ, the apostle Peter,

---

[1] Middleton's *Letter,* pp. 173, 174. (*P.*) On *Soracte,* Addison says, "In my way to Rome, seeing a high hill standing by itself in the Campania, I did not question but it had a classic name, and upon inquiry, found it to be Mount *Soracte.* (Hor. Carm. L. i. 9.) The Italians at present call it, because its name begins with an S, St. *Oreste.*" Remarks on Italy, 1705, p. 164. On St. *Viar,* see Mabill. *Iter. Ital.* p. 145, quoted in Middleton's Works, III. p. 91.

[2] Mr. Brydone says, he "remarked with how little respect the people of Sicily passed the chapels that were dedicated to God. They hardly deigned to give a little inclination of the head; but when they came near those of their favourite saints, they bowed down to the very ground." *Travels,* II. p 127. (*P.*)

[3] Mr. Swinburne says, that from what he saw, he is "apt to suspect, that the people in Spain trouble themselves with few serious thoughts on the subject of religion; and that, provided they can bring themselves to believe that their favourite saint looks upon them with an eye of attention, they take it for granted that, under his influence, they are freed from all apprehension of damnation in a future state, and indeed," he adds, "from any great concern about the moral duties of this life." *Travels,* p. 174. (*P.*)

the blessed Virgin and God, could even contemplate the sanctity of St. Ignatius. They also applied to him this passage of Scripture, *God has in these last times spoken unto us by his Son*[1].

Though the state of the Catholic church has been improved in several respects by means of the Reformation, in consequence of which several abuses were so fully exposed that little has since been said in defence of them; yet, it was a long time before anything was done by authority to remedy this shocking abuse. The Council of Trent connived at all these things. They did nothing to check the invocation of saints, and indeed, by their decrees, the applying to them directly for help and assistance is encouraged.[2] But not long ago a very considerable reformation of the calendar, in this respect, was made by Pope Benedict XIV.[3]

[1] Basnage, *Histoire*, II. p. 693. (*P.*)

[2] Et quamvis in honorem et memoriam sanctorum nonnullas interdum missas ecclesia celebrare consueverit; non tamen illis sacrificium offerri docet, sed Deo soli, qui illos coronavit. Unde nec sacerdos dicere solet, offero tibi sacrificium, Petre, vel Paule, sed Deo, de illorum victoria gratias agens, eorum patrocinia imploret; ut ipsi pro nobis intercedere digneutur in cœlis, quorum memoriam facimus in terris." Sess. xxii. C. iii. *De Messis in Honorem Sanctorum*, Con. Trid. Can. et Decret. pp. 151,152. The authorities adduced for thus honouring the saints are *Augustin* and *Cyril*.

[3] *Prosper Lambertini*, who was Pope from 1740 to his death in 1758, at the age of 83. His biographer thus records his merits as a reformer. "Chaque année de son Pontificat a été marquée par quelque Bulle, pour réformer des abus, ou pour introduire des usages utiles." Of his works, in twelve volumes folio, the eight first were on the beatification and canonization of saints. This Pope received an extraordinary compliment from Mr. Horace Walpole, (Lord Orford,) on his return from Italy, by an inscription in Italian, of which the following is the sense according to the French version:

Prosper Lambertini, bishop of Rome, surnamed Benedict XIV., who, though an absolute prince, reigns with as much equity as a Doge of Venice. To restore the lustre of the *Tiara*, he employs only his virtues; the means by which he acquired it. Loved by Papists, esteemed by Protestants; a priest, humble and disinterested; a prince without a favourite; a Pope without a *nephew*; (sans népotisme,) an author without vanity; in one word, a man whom neither power nor persuasion can draw aside. The son of a favourite minister, who never made his court to any prince, nor did homage to any ecclesiastic, presents, in a free Protestant country, this merited offering to the best of the Roman Pontiffs. See Nouv. Dict. Hist. I. p. 376. Dr. John de *Launoy*, in the

Together with the worship of saints, that of *angels* also gained much ground in this period. Pope Gregory IV. appointed a festival in honour of St. Michael, which, indeed, had long been observed both in the East and in Italy, and was then almost universal in the Latin church. So proper objects of worship are angels considered to be by the Papists, that they pray to them directly, for the pardon of sin and eternal life.[4] Of all the saints, it is only the Virgin Mary that is addressed in such a high style of devotion as this.

SECTION II.

PART II.

OF THE WORSHIP OF THE VIRGIN MARY.

WITH such an astonishing increase of the veneration of saints and martyrs, (Christians having first prayed *for* them, then hoped and prayed for their intercession with God, till at last they made direct addresses *to* them,) it will naturally be expected that their devotion to the Virgin Mary would advance no less rapidly. Accordingly we find such particular attention paid to her, that both the Son and the Father are with many persons almost entirely overlooked. In words, indeed, they pretend that the devotion addressed to her falls short of that which is paid to God, as it exceeds that which is paid to other saints, calling the devotion that is paid to God by the name of *Latria*, that to the saints *Dulia*, and that to the Blessed Virgin *Hyperdulia*; but these distinctions are only nominal, and, in fact, if there be any difference, it seems to be rather in favour of the Virgin, as appears by their using ten *Aves*, or salutations of

seventeenth century, attained, by his critical examination of their pretensions, the title of unrouster of saints, (*le Dénicheur des Saints.*) Ibid. IV. p. 58. See also Bayle, Art. *Launoy*, in Middleton's Works, III. p. 33.

[4] Basnage, I. p. 303. (*P.*)

the Virgin, for one *Pater*, or the Lord's Prayer, and by that humble prostration with which they continually pay their devotion to her.

The prayers that are constantly addressed to her are such as these: "Mary, the mother of grace, the mother of mercy, do thou defend us from our enemies and receive us in the hour of death: pardon the guilty: give light to the blind." Also "by the right of a mother command our Redeemer, is an allowed address to her."[1] The psalms which contain an address to God are applied to the Virgin Mary by Cardinal Bonaventure, in his *Psalter of the Blessed Virgin;*[2] and one of their greatest doctors declared, that "all things that are God's are the Virgin Mary's: because she is both the spouse and the mother of God."[3]

Let us now see by what steps this progress was made; for, strong as was the propensity to this kind of idolatry, times and proper circumstances were requisite to bring it to this height. It is said that Peter Fullo, a monk of Constantinople, introduced the name of the Virgin Mary into the public prayers about the year 480; but it is certain she was not generally invoked in public till a long time after that.[4] Justinian in giving thanks for his victories, and praying, only says, "we ask this also by the prayers of the holy and glorified Mary, mother of God, and always a virgin;" it being the custom

Burnet on the Articles, p. 308. (*P.*) "Maria, Mater gratiæ, Mater misericordiæ, tu nos ab hoste protege, et hora mortis suscipe. . . . Solve vincla reis, profer lumen cæcis . . . Jure matris impera Redemptori." Art. xxii. Ed. 4, pp. 226, 227.

[2] "Ps. vii. 'O thou my good Lady, in thee have I put my trust.' ix. 'I will praise thee, O Lady, with all my heart.' xvi. 'Preserve me, O Lady. Rejoice in our Lady, O ye righteous, I will always give thanks unto our Lady, her praise shall be in my mouth continually.' And so on, throughout the whole book." Hist. of Popery, 1735, I. p. 87.

[3] Hist. of Popery, I. p. 164. (*P.*) "Omnia quæ Dei sunt, *Mariæ* sunt, quia Mater et Sponsa Dei illa est. *Chrysost.* a Visit. I. De Verb. Dom. L. iv. C. viii. And *Bernard de Busti*, in *Mariali.* Pt. xii. avers, *Tot Creaturæ serviunt gloriosæ Mariæ Virgini, quot serviunt Trinitati.* As many creatures honour the Virgin, as do the Trinity." *Hist.* 1735, I. p. 87.

[4] Sueur, A. D. 483. (*P.*)

at that time to make use of the intercession of the Virgin, but not to invoke her directly.

When it was thought proper to keep up the festivals and ceremonies of the Pagan religion, and only to change the objects of them, the Virgin Mary was sure to come in for her share of these new honours, together with other saints. Accordingly we find that, whereas the Pagans had used, in the beginning of February, to celebrate the feast of Proserpine with burning tapers; to divert them from this impiety, Christians instituted, on the same day, the feast of *Purification*, in honour of the Virgin Mary, and called it *Candlemas*, from the lights that were used on the occasion.[5] This institution is ascribed to *Pope Vigilius*, about the year 536, though others fix it to the year 543. But before this time there had been a feast on that day called ὑπαπαντη, or *the meeting*, in commemoration of Simeon meeting Mary on the day of her purification, and taking Jesus in his arms, when he was presented in the temple. But there was not then any invoking of the Virgin, no crying *Ave Maria stella*, nor lighting wax candles in her honour.[6] The feast of the *immaculate conception* was also added about the same time.[7]

Though we know few particulars of the *life* of the Virgin Mary, and nothing at all concerning her *death*; yet, it was so much taken for granted, that she went immediately into heaven (though other saints were obliged to wait for the beatific vision, till the resurrection,) that about the ninth century a festival was instituted in commemoration of her *assumption*.

"The worship of the Virgin Mary" also "received new accessions of solemnity and superstition" in the tenth century. Towards the conclusion of it, "a custom was introduced . . . . of cele-

[5] "On a remedié par ce changement à l'obstination du Paganism que l'on eut plutôt irrité si on eut enterpris d'ôter entièrement la chose." *Rhenanus* on Tortullian, in "Les Conformitez des Cérémonies," 1667, p. 113.

[6] Sueur, A. D. 542. (*P.*)

[7] Mosheim, I. p. 466. (*P.*) Cent. vi. Pt. ii. Ch. iv. *ad fin.*

brating masses and abstaining from flesh in her honour every Sabbath-day;" and after this, what was called *the lesser office* of the Virgin was confirmed by Urban in the following century. In this tenth century also, the *rosary* and *crown* of the blessed Virgin were first used. "The *rosary* consists of fifteen repetitions of the Lord's Prayer, and a hundred and fifty salutations of the blessed Virgin; while the *crown*, according to the different opinions of the learned concerning the age of the Virgin, consists of six or seven repetitions of the Lord's Prayer, and six or seven times ten salutations or *Ave Marias.*"[1] Peter Damiani speaks of the *lesser office* of the Virgin as a new form of devotion, instituted in his time, as also of Saturday being consecrated to her honour; as Monday was to that of the angels.[2]

We have seen that some persons, in the former period, entertained a suspicion that the Virgin Mary might perhaps be born without original sin. In the progress of things, which I have been describing, these suspicions were not likely to lose ground. However, it was far from being the universal opinion, that she was born in any more favourable circumstances than other persons. The first controversy on this subject was about the year 1136, when the canons of Lyons started the opinion of the *immaculate conception*, as it now began to be called, and would have established an office for celebrating it, but Bernard opposed it. The Thomists, or the followers of Thomas Aquinas, opposed that opinion till the year 1300, when Scotus, a Dominican or Cordelier, first made it a *probable opinion*, and his followers afterwards made it an *article of faith*, whilst the Franciscans or Jacobines held a contrary opinion; and the controversy between them continued three hundred years, and indeed has not regularly been decided to this day.

The University of Paris declared for the immaculate conception, and there were several Popes on both sides of the question. John XXII. favoured the Jacobines on account of the hatred he bore to the Cordeliers, who took the part of the emperor Lewis, of Bavaria, whom he had excommunicated. Sixtus IV., who was a Cordelier, favoured the opinion which had always been maintained by his order; and in the year 1474, he published a bull, in which he prohibited any censure of the opinion of the immaculate conception as heretical, and confirmed the new service that had been made for the festival of that conception.

This controversy continued till the Council of Trent, which confirmed the constitution of Sixtus IV., but without condemning the opinions of the Jacobines.[3] This did not lessen the controversy; the Dominicans still maintaining the immaculate conception, and the Franciscans opposing it. Spain was perfectly in a flame about it, of which the very sign-posts of this day bear witness. For travellers say, that, in going from Barcelona to Granada, to the name of the Virgin Mary is always added "Sin peccado concebida," *conceived without sin.*[4] At length Alexander V., unable to settle the controversy in any other manner, in 1667 ordered that there should be no more preaching on the subject.[5]

The devotion paid to the Virgin is

[1] Mosheim, II. pp. 224, 225. (*P.*) Cent. x. Pt. ii. Ch. iv. *ad fin.*
[2] Fleury, A. D. 1062. (*P.*)

[3] Hist. of the Council of Trent, p. 103. (*P.*) "Declarat tamen hæc ipsa sancta Synodus, non esse suæ intentionis comprehendere in hoc decreto, ubi de peccato originali agitur, beatam et immaculatam Virginem Mariam Dei genetricem, sed observandas esse ii constitutiones felicis recordationis Sixti Papæ IV. sub pœnis in eis constitutionibus contentis, quas innovat." Sess. v. *Decretum de Peccato originali,* ad fin. Con. Trid. *Can. et Decret.* p. 14.
[4] Mr. Swinburne says, "I believe there is scarcely a house in Granada that has not over its door in large red characters, 'Ave Maria purissima, sin peccado concebida.' A military order in that country swear to defend by word and deed the doctrine of the immaculate conception. The peasants near Alicant, instead of saluting strangers in any other way, bawl out 'Ave Maria purissima,' to which they expect to be answered, 'Sin peccado concebida,' or 'Deo gratias.'" *Travels,* pp. 190, 199. (*P.*)
[5] Histoire des Papes, V. p. 342. (*P.*)

very little, if at all, lessened since the Reformation. At Einsilden, or *Notre Dame des Erémites*, in Switzerland, says Mr. Coxe, crowds of pilgrims from all quarters resort to adore the Virgin, and to present their offerings; and it is computed that, upon a moderate calculation, their number amounts yearly to a hundred thousand.[1]

The last circumstance that I shall relate, concerning the Virgin Mary, is, that in 1566, some Flemings began to wear medals in their hats in her honour, representing what was supposed to be a miraculous image of her at Hale, in Hainault, and which they wore, to distinguish them from the Protestants of that country. The Pope blessed and consecrated these medals, granting a remission of the punishment of sin to those that wore them; and this gave a beginning to the consecration of medals.[2]

SECTION II.

PART III.

OF THE WORSHIP OF IMAGES IN THIS PERIOD.

WE have seen how, in the preceding period, a fondness for pictures and images had made some progress among Christians, in consequence of an undue veneration for the *persons* whom they represented. In the natural progress of things, images were treated with more and more respect, till it was imagined that the homage paid to the saint required the same to be paid to his image. It was even imagined that he was so far present to the image, as to communicate to it the powers of which he himself was possessed; the image being a kind of *body* to the soul of the saint.

This was the very state of things

among the Heathens. For they imagined that, after the forms of consecration, the invisible power of the god, to whom any image was dedicated, was brought to reside in it, and to entitle it to the same respect as if it had been the god himself in person. At length, therefore, Christians came to be idolaters in the same gross sense in which the Heathens had ever been so; being equally worshippers both of dead men and of their images. But no great progress had been made in this business at the close of the last period.

At that time pictures and images in churches were chiefly used for the purpose of ornament, for the commemoration of the saints to which they were dedicated, and the instruction of the ignorant. Gregory the Great encouraged the use of them, so that the honour paid to them was much increased towards the end of the sixth century, and more in the following. And when Serenus, bishop of Marseilles, seeing the bad consequence of introducing these images, not only ordered that no person should fall down before them, or pay them any homage, but that they should be removed from the churches of his diocese, Gregory disapproved of his conduct, praising his zeal, but blaming him for breaking the images. He, therefore, only desired that they might not be worshipped, but would have them preserved in the churches, on the principle, that those who could not read might be instructed by them.[3] But in little more than a century the see of Rome changed its doctrine on the subject, Gregory II. being strenuous for the worship of images.

The first who openly espoused the doctrine of images in the West was Pope Constantine, the predecessor of Gregory II.; and there seems to have been as much of *policy* as of *religion* in the measures which he took with respect to it. The emperor Philippicus had taken an active part in opposition to images, and had ordered them to be

[1] Travels, p. 57. (*P.*)
[2] Histoire des Papes, V. p. 10.

[3] Sueur, A. D. 599. (*P.*) [Basnage, I. p. 307.]

removed from churches, in order to put a stop to the idolatrous veneration that was beginning to be paid to them. This the Pope, who wished for an occasion of quarrelling with the emperor, in order to make himself independent of him, resented so highly, that, in a synod held on the occasion, he not only condemned his conduct in that respect, but excommunicated him as a heretic, and pronounced him unworthy of the empire, authorizing and exhorting his subjects to revolt from him. This new heresy was called that of the Iconoclasts, or the *breakers of images.* By picking this quarrel with the emperor, this Pope and his successors asserted not only their independence of the emperors of Constantinople, but their superiority to them.

Gregory II., who succeeded Constantine, and the emperor Leo Isauricus, were at continual variance on this subject of images; the latter pulling them down from the churches, and the former excommunicating him for it, and also pronouncing his subjects absolved of their allegiance to him, and forbidding them to pay him tribute.

Something farther was done in favour of images by Stephen III., or rather IV., in opposition to Constantine II., whom he had deposed, and who had. called a synod in which the worship of images had been condemned. This Stephen called another synod, in which, another innovation in Christian worship was made, or at least authorized, viz. the worshipping of God himself by an image. For they condemn the execrable and pernicious decree of the former synod, by which the condition of the immortal God was made worse than that of men. "Is it lawful," say they, " to set up statues of mortal men, both that we may not be ungrateful, and that we may be excited to imitate their virtuous actions; and shall it not then be lawful to set up the image of God, whom we ought always, if it were possible, to have before our eyes?"[1]

[1] *Platina de Vita Stephani III.*

On this poor pretence was the authority of the second commandment, which expressly forbids the worshipping of the true God by images, entirely set aside. This is so palpable a contradiction of the doctrine of the Scriptures, that the second commandment is entirely left out in several of the copies of the ten commandments among the Papists, and one of the others is split into two, for the sake of preserving the number *ten,* and to hide this falsification from the common people.

The incensing of statues, which had been a constant heathen practice, is said to have been introduced into the Christian worship of images by Leo III.

The worship of images had many fluctuations in the East, some of the emperors favouring it and others discouraging it; but at length the proper adoration of them was fully established in the second Council of Nice, held in the year 787, under the emperor Constantine Porphyrogenita, or rather his mother Irene, a most ambitious and violent woman. This, which was denominated *the second Nicene Council,* decreed that images should be made according to the form of the venerable cross; meaning what we call *crucifixes,* or images of our Saviour upon the cross; that they might be made of any materials, that they should be dedicated, and put into churches, as well as upon walls, in private houses, and upon the public roads. It was appointed in this council, that, in the first place, images should be made of our Saviour, in the next place of the Virgin Mary (called by them the *immaculate mother of God*), then of the venerable angels, and lastly of all saints, that the honour of adoration may be rendered to them; not, however, that of *Latria,* which they say belongs only to the divine nature, but, " as we approach with reverence the type of the venerable and vivifying cross, and the holy evangelists, with oblations, perfumes and lights. For the honour that is done to the image is reflected upon the prototype, and he who adores the image, adores the subject of it." They add, as usual, "Let all who think otherwise be excommunicated." It is to be observed, that no *statues*, or even bas-reliefs, were permitted by this council. These were not yet admitted into churches, as they were afterwards.[1] So passionately fond were the Greeks of this species of worship, that they esteemed this second Council of Nice "as a most signal blessing derived to them from the immediate interposition of heaven; and accordingly instituted, in commemoration thereof, an anniversary festival, which was called *the feast of orthodoxy.*"[2]

The fathers of this council "expressed a detestation of an image made to represent the *Deity*. Though they had the sanction of Pope Stephen's synod in the Latin church, and though this practice was not soon general, even in the West, at length pictures and images, even of God the Father and of the Trinity, became common. The Council of Trent favours them, "provided that they be *decently made:* directions are also given concerning the use of the image of the Trinity in public offices; ...and such as have held it unlawful to make such images were especially condemned at Rome in 1690."[3]

In the West, notwithstanding the favour shown to images by the Popes, the worship of them did not go down so well as it did in the East, owing to the opposition that was made to it by Charlemagne. He called a council at Frankfort in 794, in which the second Council of Nice was condemned. Images, however, were allowed to be kept in churches, for the purpose of ornament and instruction, but *worship* was forbidden to be paid to them. The same disposition, so hostile to image worship, continued to influence the successors of Charlemagne. For we find that, in a synod held at Paris, by order of Lothaire, in 825, on the subject of images, it was ordered, as before, to keep them, but not to worship them. Another council was held at Paris by Louis the Meek, in 844, in which the same decrees were repeated.

But the greatest opposition to the worship of images in this age was made by Claudius, bishop of Turin, a man of distinguished abilities and zeal, and from whom the Waldenses, who continued to oppose this and almost every other corruption of the Church of Rome, seem to have had their origin. This eminent bishop not only wrote with great earnestness and force upon the subject, but perceiving how violently the common people went into the worship of images, and that he could not by any other means check the progress of it, he ordered all the images and crosses in his diocese to be demolished. For this conduct he was generally blamed, even in France and Germany, but not for opposing the worship which was then paid to images. About the same time, Agobard, bishop of Lyons, wrote excellently against the worship of images, and also against dedicating churches to any but God.[4]

The worship of images did not continue, without some interruption, after the second Council of Nice, even in the East. But as one woman, Irene, had procured their worship to be ordered at that time; so another woman, Theodora, governing her son Michael III., procured their final establishment in 842. But the Greeks never had any images besides those on plain surfaces, or pictures: they never approved of

[1] Sueur, A. D. 787. *(P.)*

[2] Mosheim, II. pp. 149, 150. *(P.)* Cent. ix. Pt. ii. Ch. iii. Sect. xv.

[3] Burnet on the Articles, p. 293. *(P.)* Art. xxii. Ed. 4, p. 216. On the authority of Roman Catholic writers, Burnet has described the Council of Trent as allowing images of "the Deity and the Trinity," but nothing appears of such allowance in the *decree* "De invocatione, veneratione, et reliquiis sanctorum, et sacris imaginibus." The images to be set up and retained in churches are three: "Christi, Deiparæ Virginis et aliorum Sanctorum." The use of them is thus described: "Per imagines, quas osculamur et coram quibus caput aperimus et procumbimus, Christum adoremus, et sanctos quorum illa similitudinem gerunt veneremur." This use of them is then described as sanctioned by the second Council of Nice. Sess. xxv. Con. Trid. *Can. et Decret.* p. 234.

[4] Sueur, A. D. 827. *(P.)*

statues.[1] Notwithstanding the opposition to the worship of images by the emperors of the West, yet at length, through the influence of the Roman pontiffs, even "the Gallican clergy began to pay a certain kind of religious homage to the saintly images," towards the end of the ninth century; and in this "their example was followed by the Germans and other nations." [2]

It has been asserted that, properly speaking, worship never was paid to images by Christians, but that when they bowed before them, they only addressed themselves to the saints whom they represent. But that their regards *do* terminate in the image itself, as much as they do in any living man, whom they should address, is evident, not only from a variety of considerations, suggested by the history of image worship, but from the acknowledgment of those who practise it; which puts it beyond all doubt, that they suppose a real power to reside in the image itself, just as they suppose the spirit of a man to be in a man.

In the eleventh century it was de-bated in the Greek church, whether there was an *inherent sanctity* "in the images of Jesus Christ and of the saints;" and though it was determined in a council, "that the images of Christ and of the saints . . . . did in no sense partake of the nature of the divine Saviour, or of these holy men," yet it was maintained that "they were enriched with a certain communication of divine grace."[3]

The Latin church has by no means been behind that of the Greeks in this respect. For, if we judge by the practice of the church of Rome, and even by some of their acknowledgments, it will be evident that a proper *Latria*, or such worship as they themselves think is due to God, is also to be given to images. Those who write in favour of it "frequently cite this hymn, *Crux ave, spes unica, auge piis justitiam, reisque dona veniam ;* that is, Hail cross, our only hope, increase righteousness in the godly, and pardon the guilty." "It is expressly said in the Pontifical, *Cruci debetur Latria,*" that *Latria* is due to the cross. This favours the opinions of those who say that *Latria* is " to be given to all those images, to the originals of which it is due," as to Christ; as the *Dulia* is to be given to the images of the saints, and the *Hyper-dulia* to those of the Virgin Mary.[4] The Council of Trent only decreed that *due worship* should be given to images, but did not define what that due worship is.

Among acts of worship, they reckon the oblation of incense and lights; and the reason given by them for all this is, because the honour of the image or type passes to the original or prototype; so that direct worship was to terminate in the image itself. And Durandus passed for little less than a heretic, because he thought that images were worshipped only improperly; because at their presence we call to mind

---

[1] The following relations are by an intelligent observer, who was Chaplain to the British Embassy at Constantinople in 1669 : " Before you enter the church, is a covered porch, usually arched, running out at each side the portal, with seats against the wall, upon which are *painted* several images, as of our blessed Saviour, the Virgin Mary, St. John, St. George and the like, and of that saint particularly to whose memory the church is consecrated ; but very wretchedly, and without beauty or proportion." *Account of the Greek Church,* by Tho. Smith, 1680, p. 63.
"The Greeks have so great prejudice to all engraven images, and especially if they are embossed and prominent, that they inveigh severely and fiercely against the Latins, as little less than idolaters, and symbolizing with the very heathen. . . . . But as for the pictures, whether in colours or painted, of our Saviour and of the saints, they account them sacred and venerable. These they reverence and honour by bowing, and kissing them, and saying their prayers before them. With these the partition that separates the *Bema,* or chancel, from the body of the church, is adorned. At set times, the priest, before he enters into it, makes three low reverences (προσκυνησεις, μετανοιας) before the image of Christ, and as many before that of the Virgin Mary : and he does the like in the time of celebration, and oftentimes perfumes them with his incense pot." Ibid. pp. 211, 212.
[2] Mosheim, II. p. 151. (*P.*) Cent. ix. Pt. ii. Ch. iii. Sect. xvi.

[3] Ibid. II. p. 329. (*P.*) Cent. xi. Pt. ii. Ch. iii. Sect. xii.
[4] Burnet on the Articles, p. 295. (*P.*) Art. xxii. Ed. 4, p. 217.

ɩ

the object represented by them, which we worship by means of the image, as if the object itself was before us.

Thomas Aquinas, and many others after him, expressly teach "that the same acts and degrees of worship which are due to the original, are also due to the image. They think an image has such a relation to the original, that both ought to be worshipped by the same act; and that to worship the image with any other sort of acts, is to worship it on its own account, which they think is idolatry." On the other hand, those who adhere "to the Nicene doctrine think that the image is to be worshipped with an inferior degree" of homage; and "that otherwise idolatry must follow; so that, whichever of the two schemes be adopted, idolatry must be the consequence, with some or other of the advocates for this worship." [1]

SECTION II.

PART IV.

OF THE RESPECT PAID TO RELICS IN THIS PERIOD.

IF so much respect was paid to the *images* of saints, we shall not wonder that even more account was made of their *relics*, which bear a still nearer relation to them; and if an invisible virtue, viz. all the power of the saint, could be supposed to accompany every separate image of any particular saint, they could not hesitate to ascribe the same to every relic of him, even the cloth or rags that had belonged to him, and the very earth on which he had trod.

A superstitious respect for relics, and especially for the true cross of Christ, is observed to have advanced much in the sixth century; and many persons then boasted of having in their possession the real wood of that cross. And

when image-worship began, that of relics followed, as an accessary. The enshrining of relics (in his zeal for which Julian IV., about the year 620, distinguished himself) made the most excellent sort of images, and they were thought to be the best preservative possible, both for soul and body. No presents were considered as of more value than relics; and it was an easy thing for the popes to furnish the world plentifully with them, especially after the discovery of the *catacombs*, which was a subterraneous place where many of the Romans deposited their dead.

It is observed by historians, that the demand for relics was exceedingly great in the ninth century, and that the clergy employed great dexterity in satisfying that demand. In general, some persons pretended to have been informed in a dream, where such and such relics were to be found, and the next day they never failed to find them. As the most valued relics came from the East, the Greeks made a gainful traffic with the Latins for legs, arms, skulls, jawbones, &c., many of them certainly of Pagans, and some of them not human; and recourse was sometimes had to violence and theft, in order to get possession of such valuable treasure.[2]

We may form some idea of the value that was put upon some relics in that superstitious and ignorant age, from the following circumstance, and this is only one instance of great numbers that might be collected from history. Boleslas, a king of Poland, willing to show his gratitude to Otho, the third emperor of Germany, who had erected his duchy into a kingdom, made him a present of an arm of St. Adalbert in a silver case. The emperor was far from slighting the present, but placed it in a new church which he had built at Rome in honour of this Adalbert. He also built a monument in honour of the same saint.[3]

---

[1] Burnet on the Articles, p. 294. (*P.*) Art. xxii. Ed. 4, p. 216.

[2] Mosheim, II. p. 141. (*P.*) Cent. ix. Pt. ii. Ch. iii. Sect. vi.

[3] Sueur, A. D. 1000. (*P.*)

The greatest traffic for relics was during the Crusades; and that many impositions were practised in this business, was evident from the very pretensions themselves; the same thing, for example, the skull of the same person, being to be seen in different places, and more wood of the true cross of Christ than, they say, would make a ship. In this the Greeks had the same advantage that the Romans had by means of the catacombs, which contained a sufficient quantity of bones, to which it was easy to give the names of celebrated Christian martyrs; and, at a distance from Rome, no inquiry could be made concerning them.

Besides all this, a happy method was thought of by Gregory I., or some other person of that age, to multiply the virtue of relics, without multiplying the relics themselves; for, instead of giving the relic of any saint, he contented himself with putting into a box a piece of cloth, which was called *brandeum*, which had only touched the relics. It is said, that, in the time of Pope Leo, some Greeks having doubted whether such relics as these were of any use, the Pope, in order to convince them, took a pair of scissors, and that on cutting one of these cloths, blood came out of it.[1]

We cannot wonder at the great demand for relics, when we consider the virtues that were ascribed to them by the priests and friars who were the vendors of them in that ignorant age. They pretended that they had power to fortify against temptations, to increase grace and merit, to fright away devils, to still winds and tempests, to secure from thunder, lightning, blasting, and all sudden casualties and misfortunes; to stop all infectious disorders, and to cure as many others as any mountebank ever pretended to do. Who that had money would choose to be without such powerful preservatives?

The fathers of the Council of Trent appointed relics to be venerated, but, with their usual caution, they did not determine the degree of it. This great abuse was effectually removed in all Protestant churches at the Reformation, though many other things equally near to the first principles of Christianity were left to the sagacity and zeal of a later period.

Among the Catholics the respect for relics still continues, though, with the general decrease of superstition, this must have abated in some measure. The Holy Land is still a great mart for these commodities. Haselqnist says, that the inhabitants of Bethlehem chiefly live by them, making models of the holy sepulchre, crosses, &c. Of these there was so large a stock in Jerusalem, that the procurator told him he had to the amount of fifteen thousand piastres in the magazine of the convent. An incredible quantity of them, he says, goes yearly to the Roman Catholic countries in Europe, but most to Spain and Portugal. Many are bought by the Turks, who come yearly for these commodities.[2]

[1] Basnage, *Histoire*, I. p. 305. (P.)

[2] Travels, p. 149.

PART V.

THE HISTORY OF OPINIONS CONCERNING THE STATE OF THE DEAD.

THE INTRODUCTION.

I THINK that I have sufficiently proved, in my *Disquisitions relating to Matter and Spirit*, that, in the Scriptures, the state of *death* is represented as a state of absolute insensibility, being opposed to *life*. The doctrine of the distinction between *soul* and *body*, as two different substances, the one material and the other immaterial, and so independent of one another, that the latter may even die and perish, and the former, instead of losing anything, be rather a gainer by the catastrophe, was originally a doctrine of the oriental philosophy, which afterwards spread into the Western part of the world. But it does not appear that it was ever adopted by the generality of the Jews, and perhaps not even by the more learned and philosophical of them, such as Josephus, till after the time of our Saviour; though Philo, and some others, who resided in Egypt, might have adopted that tenet in an earlier period.

Though a distinction is made in the Scriptures between the principle, or seat, of thought in man, and the parts which are destined to other functions; and in the New Testament that principle may sometimes be signified by the term *soul;* yet there is no instance, either in the Old or New Testament, of this soul· being supposed to be in one place and the body in another. They are always conceived to go together, so that the perceptive and thinking power could not, in fact, be considered by the sacred writers as any

other than a *property* of a living man, and therefore as what ceased of course when the man was dead, and could not be revived but with the revival of the body.

Accordingly, we have no promise of any reward, or any threatening of punishment, after death, but that which is represented as taking place at the general resurrection. And it is observable that this is never, in the Scriptures, called, as with us, the resurrection *of the body* (as if the soul, in the meantime, was in some other place), but always the resurrection *of the dead*, that is, of the man. If, therefore, there be any *intermediate state*, in which the soul alone exists, conscious of anything, there is an absolute silence concerning it in the Scriptures; death being always spoken of there as a state of rest, of silence, and of darkness, a place where *the wicked cease from troubling*, but where the righteous *cannot praise God*.[1]

This is the sum of the argument from the Scriptures, and comes in aid of the arguments from reason and the nature of things, which show the utter incapacity of any connection between substances so totally foreign to each other, as the *material* and *immaterial* principles are always described to be; things that have no common property whatever, and therefore must be incapable of all mutual action. I think I have shown that, let the immaterial principle be defined in whatever manner it is possible to define it, the supposition of it explains no one pheno-

---

[1] See [Rutt's Priestley] Vol. II. pp. 60, 354–364.

menon in nature; there being no more conceivable connection between the powers of thought, and this *imma-terial*, than between the same powers and a *material* principle; and for any-thing that appears, our ignorance concerning the nature of this principle should lead us to suppose that it *may*, just as well as that it *may not*, be compatible with matter.

All that can be said is, that we can see no *relation* between the principle of sensation and thought, and any system of matter; but neither do we perceive any relation which matter bears to *gravity*, and various other properties, with which we see that it is, in fact, endued. The same great Being, therefore, that has endued matter with a variety of powers, with which it seems to have no natural connection, may have endued the living human brain with this power of *sen-sation* and *thought*, though we are not able to perceive *how* this power should result from matter so modified. And since, judging by experience, these powers always *do* accompany a certain state of the brain, and are never found except accompanying that state, there is just the same reason why we should say that they necessarily *inhere in*, and *belong to*, the brain in that state, as that electricity is the necessary property of glass, and magnetism of the load-stone. It is *constant concomi-tancy*, and nothing else, that is the foundation of our conclusions in both cases, alike.

There is not, in fact, any one phe-nomenon in favour of the opinion of the soul being a separate substance from the body. During life and health, the sentient powers always accompany the body, and in a temporary cessation of thought, as in a swoon, apparent drowning, &c., there never was an in-stance in which it was pretended that the soul had been in another place, and came back again when the body was revived. In all these cases, the powers of *sensation* and *thought* are, to all appearance, as much suspended as

those of *breathing* and *moving;* and we might just as well inquire where the latter had been in the interval of apparent death, as where the former had been at the same time.

There is, indeed, an imperfect mental process going on during sleep; but this seems to be in proportion to the imperfection of the sleep; for when it is perfectly sound, and the brain pro-bably completely at rest, there is no more sensation or thought than during a swoon or apparent drowning. Or, if there had been sufficient evidence of uninterrupted thought during the soundest sleep, still it might be sup-posed to depend upon the *powers of life*, which were still in the body, and might keep up some motion in the brain.

The only proof of the power of thought not depending upon the body, in this case, would be the soul being afterwards conscious to itself, that it had been in one place, while the body had been in another. Whereas, in dreams we never have any idea but that of our whole-selves having been in some different place, and in some very different state, from that in which we really are. Upon the whole, there-fore, there can be no more reason to think that the *principle of thought* belongs to a substance distinct from the body, than that the *principle of breathing* and of *moving* belongs to another distinct substance, or than that the principle of sound in a bell belongs to a substance distinct from the bell itself, and that it is not a *power* or *property*, depending upon the state into which the parts of it are occasionally put.

How men came to imagine that the case was otherwise, is not easy to say, any more than how they came to im-agine that the sun, moon, and stars were animated, and the proper objects of adoration. But when once, in conse-quence of any train of thinking, they could suppose that the effects of the heavenly bodies, and of the other in-animate parts of nature, were owing to invisible powers residing in them, or to something that was not the object of their external senses, they might easily imagine man to have a principle of a similar kind; and then it was easy enough to advance one step farther, and to suppose that this invisible principle was a thing independent of the body, and might subsist when that was laid in the grave.

It was a long time, however, before men got quite clear of the idea of the necessary connection between the corporeal and the spiritual part of man. For it was long imagined that this invisible part of man accompanied the body in the place of its interment, whence came the idea of the *descent of the soul*, shade, or ghost, into some subterraneous place; though afterwards, by attending to the subject, and refining upon it, philosophers began to think that this invisible part of man, having nothing gross or heavy in its composition, might *ascend* rather than *descend*, and so hover in some higher region of the atmosphere. And Christians, having an idea of a *local heaven*, somewhere above the clouds, and of God and Christ residing there, they came in time to think that the souls of good men, and especially of martyrs, might be taken up thither, or into some place adjoining to it, and where they might remain till the resurrection.

SECTION I.

OF THE OPINIONS CONCERNING THE DEAD TILL THE TIME OF AUSTIN.

In the second and third centuries, those who believed that there was a soul distinct from the body, supposed that after death it went to some place under ground; but as this is not the doctrine of the Scriptures, it could not have been the general opinion of Christians at the first; and how long they kept to the genuine doctrine of revelation, and the dictates of reason and common sense, in this respect, cannot be determined. It appears, however, that there were some Christians who did so, and that in Arabia this doctrine was held by some so late as the third century. For we are informed that they maintained that the soul perishes with the body, but that it will be raised to life again, by the power of God, at the resurrection. It is said, however, that they were induced to abandon this opinion by the arguments and influence of Origen.[1]

It was in Arabia also that we find the opinion of Christ having no proper divinity of his own, but only that of the Father residing in him, and that he had no existence at all before his appearance in this world. This opinion is likewise said to have been confuted by Origen.[2] Du Pin says, that Tatian also held the opinion of the Arabians with respect to the soul.[3]

It is to be regretted that we have no farther accounts concerning these Christians. Ecclesiastical historians call them *philosophers*; but the system which they held was fundamentally different from that of any other philosophy in those times. It cannot, however, be supposed that this opinion was peculiar to these people. The Jewish Christians, at least, must have retained it, and probably as long as they continued to subsist. But we have no distinct account of their opinions, or of anything relating to them. They were not writers themselves, and those that were had little intercourse with them, or value for them.

Whenever the Jews received the opinion of the separate existence of the soul, it was in the imperfect state above mentioned. For they held that there was a place below the earth, which they called *paradise*, where the souls of good men remained; and they distinguished this from the *upper paradise*, where they were to be after the resurrection. The Christians borrowed

[1] Euseb. Hist. L. vi. C. xxxvii. I. p. 299. *(P.)* See [Rutt's Priestley] Vol. II. p. 375.
[2] Ibid. L. vi. C. xxxiii. p. 297. *(P.)*
[3] Bibliotheca Patrum, I. p. 55. *(P.)*

their opinion from the Jews, and supposed that *Hades*, or the place of souls, was "divided into two mansions, in one whereof the souls of the wicked remained in grief and torment, and in the other those of the godly, in joy and happiness; both of them expecting the general resurrection-day."[1]

Into this general receptacle of souls, it was the opinion of the early fathers, that Christ descended, to preach; they supposing these to be the *spirits in prison* mentioned by the apostle Peter, 1 Pet. iii. 19. And as it is said in the gospel that he came *not to call the righteous, but sinners to repentance*, some of them supposed either that he did not give much attention to the good, or that they did not attend to him; for they say that, whereas he brought away many of the wicked, he left those of the good where they were. But perhaps the original tradition was, that in consequence of converting them, he removed them from the place where the wicked were confined, to this subterraneous paradise, where the souls of the righteous remain, in joyful expectation of a happy resurrection. Others, however, thought that our Saviour preached so effectually, as to empty the whole of this *limbus patrum* (for so also they called the precincts within which these ancient patriarchs were confined) and carried all the souls with him into heaven.[2] But this must have been a late opinion, because it was not supposed in the time of the fathers, that the souls of good men in general would be with Christ, and enjoy what was then called *the beatific vision of God*, till the resurrection.

This opinion is clearly stated by Novatian, for he says, "Nor are the regions below the earth void of powers (*potestatibus*) regularly disposed and arranged; for there is a place whither the souls of the righteous and of the wicked are led, expecting the sentence of a future judgment."[3] This was evidently the uniform opinion of Christian writers for many centuries after this time.

The article concerning the *descent of Christ into hell*, in what we call the *Apostles' Creed*, is not mentioned by any writer before Rufinus, who found it in his own church at Aquileia; but it was not then known at Rome, or in the East. At first also, the expression was καταχθωνια, but "in the creed that carries Athanasius's name, though made in the sixth or seventh century, the word was changed into ᾁδης or *hell*. But yet it seems to have been understood to signify Christ's *burial*, there being no other word put for it in that creed."[4] But in the declension of the Greek, and chiefly in the Latin tongue, the term *hades*, or *hell*, began to be applied to the mansion of wicked souls; some of the fathers imagining *hades* to be in the centre of the earth, others under the earth, and some being uncertain about its situation.

The high opinion that soon began to be entertained of the heroism and merits of the martyrs, led Christians to suppose that a preference would be given to their souls after death. For while the souls of ordinary Christians were to wait their doom in some intermediate state, or to pass to their final bliss through a purgation of fire, it came to be the general belief that martyrs were admitted to the immediate presence of God and of Christ, the fire of martyrdom having purged away all their sins at once.

It was the opinion of most of the early fathers that the world was to be destroyed by fire, and also that all men were to pass through this fire, that the good would be purified by it, and the wicked consumed. The former part of this doctrine they might learn from the apostle Peter; but it does not clearly appear whence they derived the latter part of it. It is evident, how-

---

[1] History of the Apostles' Creed, p. 198, &c. (*P.*) Ed. 5, pp. 190–192.
[2] Burnet on the Articles, p. 71. (*P.*) Art. iii. Ed. 4, p. 57.

[3] *De Trinitate*, C. i. p. 5. (*P.*)
[4] Burnet on the Articles, p. 69. (*P.*) Art. iii. Ed. 4, p. 56.

ever, that they had no proper idea of the eternity of hell torments. And it was the opinion of Origen, and after him of Gregory Nazianzen, and probably of others of the fathers, that the wicked, after being thus punished according to their deserts, would come out purified, and obtain mercy.[1] Ambrose thought that the wicked would remain in this fire, which was to consume the world, but how long does not appear.[2] Hilary maintained, that after the day of judgment all must pass through the fire, even the Virgin Mary herself, in order to purify them from their sins. This opinion was the first idea of a doctrine of *Purgatory*, which was so great a source of gain to the monks and priests in after ages.

Austin speaks very doubtfully with respect to the dead. He sometimes seems very positive for *two states* only; but as he asserted the last probatory fire, so he seems to have thought that good souls might suffer some grief in their sequestered state, before the last day, on account of some of their past sins, and that they might rise to their proper consummation by degrees. See his sentiments on this subject pretty much at large in his *first question to Dulcidius;*[3] where he inclines to think that they who have faith in Christ, but love the world too much, will be saved, *but so as by fire;* whereas they who, though they profess faith in Christ, yet neglect good works, will suffer eternally. In his treatise De Civitate Dei,[4] he does not seem disposed to controvert the opinion of those who say that all will be saved at last, through the intercession of the saints.

The Gnostics are said to have maintained that the greatest part of mankind would be *annihilated* at the day of judgment, which was probably the same thing that was meant by those who said that they would be *con-sumed in* the fire that was to destroy the world.

SECTION II.

OF THE OPINIONS CONCERNING THE STATE OF THE DEAD, FROM THE TIME OF AUSTIN TILL THE REFORMATION.

IN the last period we have seen something like the doctrine of *Purgatory*, but it is so exceedingly unlike the present doctrine of the Church of Rome on that subject, that we can hardly imagine that it could even serve as a foundation for it. The ancient fathers only thought that when this world would be destroyed by fire, that fire would purify the good, and destroy the wicked. Whereas, this purgatory is something that is supposed to take place immediately after death, to affect the soul only, and to terminate sooner or later, according to circumstances, especially the pains that are taken in favour of the dead, by the masses and other good offices of the living, as well as by their own benefactions and bequests for religious uses before their death.

On the whole, therefore, it looks as if this doctrine of purgatory had been built upon some other ground; and nothing is so likely to furnish a groundwork for it, as the notions of the Heathens concerning the state of souls in the regions below, which were always supposed capable of being brought back again. Also the popular opinions of the Northern nations concerning the state of souls after death were, in many cases, similar to those of the Greeks and Romans; and such opinions as these would not easily quit their hold of the common people on their conversion to Christianity; and being held, together with the opinion of the fathers above mentioned, the present doctrine of purgatory might, in time, be the produce of both.

It is generally said that the foundation of the present doctrine was laid

---

[1] Sueur, A. D. 389. (P.)
[2] Ibid. A. D. 397. (P.)
[3] Op. IV. p. 658. (P.)
[4] Lib. xxi. C. xviii. (P.)

by Gregory the Great, who lived in the sixth century, about 160 years after Austin. But his opinions on the subject were very little different from those of Austin himself, and of others before him, of which an account has been given in the former period; Gregory, however, did suppose that there was a purgatory to expiate the slight offences of which very good men might be guilty; but he does not say that this punishment would always be by means of fire, nor did he suppose this expiation to be made in the same place, but sometimes in the air, and sometimes in sinks, &c., or places full of filth and nastiness. He also speaks of some good men whose souls went immediately to heaven. But in one way he certainly did greatly promote the doctrine, viz. by the many idle stories which he propagated about what happened to particular souls after they had left their bodies, as concerning the soul of King Theodoric, which was boiled in the pot of Vulcan.[1]

Narrow, however, as these foundations were, the monks were very industrious in building upon them, finding it the most profitable business they were ever engaged in; and about the tenth century the present system seems to have been pretty well completed. For, then, not even the best of men were supposed to be exempted from the fire of purgatory; and it was generally represented as not less severe than that of hell itself. But then souls might always be delivered from it by the prayers and masses of the living, which prayers and masses might always be had upon certain pecuniary considerations; and the fables and fictitious miracles that were propagated to secure the belief of this new kind of future state, were innumerable.

Thomas Aquinas says, that the place of purgatory is near to that in which the damned are punished; that the pains of purgatory exceed all the pains of this life; that souls are not pun-

ished by demons, but by divine justice only, though angels or demons might conduct them to the place. By the pains of purgatory, he says, venial sins are expiated even *quod culpam*, or from the guilt of them, and that some are delivered sooner than others.[2]

The present doctrine of the Church of Rome on the subject of purgatory, is, "that every man is liable both to temporal and eternal punishment for his sins; that God, upon the account of the death and intercession of Christ, does, indeed, pardon sin as to its eternal punishment; but the sinner is still liable to temporal punishment, which he must expiate by acts of penance and sorrow in this world, together with such other sufferings as God shall think fit to lay upon him.[3] But if he does not expiate these in this life, there is a state of suffering and misery in the next world, where the soul is to bear the temporal punishment of its sins, which may continue longer or shorter till the day of judgment; and in order to the shortening this, the prayers and supererogations of men, here on earth, or the intercessions of the saints in heaven, but above all things, the sacrifice of the mass, are of great efficacy. This is the doctrine of the Church of Rome, as asserted in the Councils of Florence and Trent."[4]

Before this time, the opinions concerning purgatory were exceedingly various, with respect to the place of purgatory, the nature of the pains of it, and indeed everything belonging to it. Eckius maintained that it was in the bottom of the sea. Others would have it to be in Mount Etna, Vesuvius, or some other burning mountain. Sir Thomas More says, that the punishment will be only by fire, but Fisher, his fellow-sufferer, by fire and by water. Lorichius says, neither by fire nor

[1] Sueur, A. D. 594. (P.)

[2] Summa, III. p. 446, &c. (P.)
[3] Petrarch says, "I pray God every day to make my purgatory in this world." Mémoires pour la Vie de Petrarch, III. p. 277. (P.)
[4] Burnet on the Articles, p. 269. (P.) Art. xxii. Ed. 4, p. 197. See *Sess.* xxv. *Decretum de Purgatorio.* Con. Trid. Can. et Decret. p. 233.

water, but by the violent convulsions of hope and fear. Fisher maintained that the executioners would be the holy angels, but Sir Thomas More thought they would be the devils. Some again thought that only *venial* sins are expiated in purgatory, but others that *mortal* sins are expiated there likewise. Dennis the Carthusian thought that the pains of purgatory would continue to the end of the world; but Dominicus a Soto limited it to ten years, and others made the time to depend on the number of masses, &c., that should be said on their behalf, or on the will of the Pope. Thomas Aquinas, as has been seen above, makes the pains of purgatory to be as violent as those of hell; whereas, the Rhemists say that souls are not in a bad condition there; and Durandus, holding a middle opinion, gives them some intermission from their pains on Sundays and holidays. Bede tells a long story of a Northumberland man, who, after he died, returned to life again, and said that he had passed through the middle of a long and large valley, which had two lakes in it, in one of which souls were tormented with heat, and in the other with cold; and that when a soul had been so long in the hot lake that it could endure no longer, it would leap into the cold one; and when that became intolerable, it would leap back again. This uncertainty was so great, that the whole doctrine must have been discredited, if it had not been for the profits which the popes, the priests, and the friars, made of it.[1]

The living, being, by means of this doctrine of purgatory, deeply interested in the fate of the dead, and having them very much at their mercy, the mistaken compassion and piety of many persons could not fail to be excited in their favour. Before the tenth century it had been customary, in many places, to put up prayers on certain days for the souls that were confined in purgatory, but these were made by each religious society for its own members and friends; but in this century a "yearly

festival . . . in remembrance of *all departed souls*, was instituted by...Odilo, abbot of Cluni, and added to the Latin calendar towards the conclusion of the century." [2]

The Greeks, though in most respects they had superstitions similar to those of the Latins, yet they never adopted their notions concerning purgatory. At the time that this opinion was formed in the West, the two churches had very little intercourse with each other; and besides, the Greeks were so alienated from the Latins, that the reception of it by the latter would have rendered the former more averse to it.

According to the doctrine of purgatory, the moment that any soul is released from that place, it is admitted into heaven, to the presence of God and of Christ, and made as happy as it can be in an unembodied state, which was contrary to the opinion of the early fathers, viz. that all souls continued in *hades* until the resurrection, or, at most, that an exception was made in favour of the martyrs. However, this doctrine of purgatory, and the opinion of the efficacy of prayers, and of masses, to procure complete happiness for those who were exposed to it, at length obliterated the ancient doctrine, as appeared when an attempt was made to revive something like it by Pope John XXII.

Towards the conclusion of his life, this pope incurred the disapprobation of the whole Catholic church, by asserting, "in some public discourses, that the souls of the faithful, in their intermediate state, were permitted to behold Christ, as man, but not the face of God or the divine nature. . . . This doctrine highly offended Philip VI., king of France," who caused it to be examined and "condemned by the divines of Paris, in 1333." The pope, being alarmed at this opposition, softened his opinion in the year following, by saying, "that the unembodied souls of the righteous beheld the divine es-

---

[1] Staveley's Romish Horseleach, p. 205. (*P.*)

[2] Mosheim, II. p. 223. (*P.*) Cent. x. Pt. ii. Ch. iv. Sect. ii.

sence as far as their separate state and condition would permit;" and for fear of any ill consequences, from dying under the imputation of heresy, when he "lay upon his death-bed, he submitted his opinion to the judgment of the church." His successor, Benedict XII., after much controversy, established the present doctrine, viz. "that the souls of the blessed, during their intermediate state, do fully and perfectly contemplate the divine nature."[1]

It may just deserve to be mentioned, at the close of this period, that the doctrine of the resurrection of the same body, was questioned by Conon, bishop of Tarsus, in the sixth century; who, in opposition to Philoponus, a philosopher of Alexandria, (who had asserted that both the form and the matter of the body would be restored at the resurrection,) maintained that the *form* would remain, but that the *matter* would be changed.[2]

SECTION III.

OF THE REVIVAL OF THE GENUINE DOCTRINE OF REVELATION CONCERNING THE STATE OF THE DEAD.

So general was the belief of a purgatory in this Western part of the world, that Wickliffe could not entirely shake it off. But though he believed in a purgatory, "he saw the absurdity of supposing that God intrusted any man with a power to release sinners from such a state: but whether the souls of the dead might be profited by the prayers of the living, he seems to have been in doubt."[3]

The ancient Waldenses, however, who separated from the Church of Rome before the doctrine of purgatory had got established, never admitted it; and presently after the Reformation by Luther, we find it abandoned by all who left the Church of Rome, without exception, so that this doctrine is now peculiar to that church.

The doctrine of *a soul*, however, and of its existence in a separate conscious state, from the time of death to that of the resurrection, which was the foundation of the doctrine of purgatory, and of many other abuses of Popery, was still retained by most. But Mosheim mentions some Anabaptists who held that the soul sleeps till the resurrection;[4] and the Helvetic confession condemns all those who believed the sleep of the soul,[5] which shows that a considerable number must have maintained it. Luther himself was of this opinion; though whether he died in it has been doubted.[6] It was, however, the firm belief of so many of the reformers of that age, that had it not been for the authority of Calvin, who wrote expressly against it, the doctrine of an *intermediate conscious state* would, in all probability, have been as effectually exploded as the doctrine of purgatory itself.

Several persons in this country have, in every period since the Reformation, appeared in favour of *the sleep of the soul*, and it always had a considerable number of followers. Of late this opinion has gained ground very much, especially since the writings of the present excellent bishop of Carlisle, and of archdeacon Blackburne on the subject. But I think the doctrine of an intermediate state can never be effectually extirpated, so long as the

---

[1] Mosheim, III. pp. 157, 158. (*P.*) Cent. xiv. Pt. ii. Ch. ii. Sect. ix. See [Rutt's Priestley] Vol. III. p. 376. Dr. Maclaine, the translator of Mosheim, remarks, that "all this Pope's heretical fancies, about the *beatific vision*, were nothing, in comparison with a vile and most enormous *practical heresy* that was found in his coffers after his death, viz. twenty-five millions of florins, of which there were eighteen in specie, and the rest in plate, &c., squeezed out of the people and the inferior clergy during his pontificate." Ibid. *Note*, p. 158.
[2] Ibid. I, p. 473. (*P.*) Cent. vi. Pt. ii. Ch. v. Sect. x.

[3] Gilpin's *Life of him*, p. 70. (*P.*) See also Brit. Biog. I. p. 48.
[4] Vol. IV. p. 163. (*P.*) Cent. xvi. Sect. iii. Pt. ii. C. iii. Sect. xxiii.
[5] Syntagma, p. 10. (*P.*)
[6] See Blackburne's *Hist. View*, Appendix, Ed. 2, p. 344.

belief of a separate soul is retained. For while that is supposed to exist independently of the body, it will not be easily imagined to sleep along with it, but will be thought to enjoy more or less of a consciousness of its existence.[1]

But when, agreeably to the dictates of reason, as well as the testimony of Scripture rightly understood, we shall acquiesce in the opinion that man is an *homogeneous being*, and that the powers of sensation and thought belong to the brain, as much as gravity and magnetism belong to other arrangements of matter, the whole fabric of superstition, which had been built upon the doctrine of a soul and of its separate conscious state, must fall at once. And this persuasion will give a value to the gospel, which it could not have before, as it will be found to supply the only satisfactory evidence of a future life. For though a future state of retribution might appear sufficiently consonant to some appearances in nature, yet when the means of it, or the only method by which it could be

brought about, (viz. that of the resurrection of the very body that had putrefied in the grave, or had been reduced to ashes,) were so little visible, (since, to all appearance, men die exactly like plants and brute animals, and no analogy drawn from *them* can lead us to expect a revival,) we must eagerly embrace that gospel, in which alone this important truth is clearly brought to light. It is in the gospel alone that we have an express assurance of a future life, by a person fully authorized to give it, exemplified also in his own person; he having been actually put to death, and raised to life again, for the purpose of giving us that assurance.

To give this value to revelation, by proving the proper and complete *mortality of man*, on the principles of reason and scripture, is the object of my *Disquisitions relating to Matter and Spirit*, to which, and also to what I have added in support of it, in my discussion of the subject with Dr. Price,[2] I beg leave to refer my readers.

---

[1] See *The State of the Dead*, in [Rutt's Priestley] Vol. III. pp. 374–379.

[2] See ibid.,Vol. IV. pp. 18–121; also Vol. II. pp. 354–364; and Vol. III. pp. 181, 182, 242–258.

PART VI.[*]

THE HISTORY OF OPINIONS RELATING TO THE LORD'S SUPPER.

THE INTRODUCTION.

THERE is nothing in the whole history that I have undertaken to write, so extraordinary as the abuses that have been introduced into the rite of the *Lord's Supper*. Nothing can be imagined more simple in its original institution, or less liable to misapprehension or abuse; and yet, in no instance

[*] Vol. II. Ed. 1782.

whatever, has the depravation of the original doctrine and custom proceeded to a greater height, or had more serious consequences.

In allusion, perhaps, to the festival of the passover, our Lord appointed his disciples to eat bread and drink wine in remembrance of him; informing them that the bread represented his body, which was going to be broken, and the wine his blood, which was about to be shed for them; and we are informed by the apostle Paul, that this rite is to continue in the Christian church till our Lord's second coming. Farther than this we are not informed in the New Testament. We only find that the custom was certainly kept up, and that the Christians of the primitive times probably concluded the public worship of every Lord's day with the celebration of it. As the rite was peculiar to Christians, the celebration of it was, of course, in common with joining habitually in the public worship of Christians, an open declaration of a man's being a Christian, and more so, indeed, than any other visible circumstance; because other persons might occasionally attend the public worship of Christians, without bearing any proper part in it themselves.

Let us now see what *additions* have been made to this simple institution, in several periods, from the primitive times to our own. And for this purpose it will be most convenient to divide the whole history into four parts; the first from the age of the apostles to that of Austin, including his time, and that of the great men who were his contemporaries; the second extending from that period to the time of Paschasius; the third, from him to the Reformation; and the fourth, from that time to the present. In writing the history of this subject, in each of the periods, I shall first note the changes of opinion with respect to the Lord's supper itself, together with the change of language which took place in consequence of it. I shall then give an account of the superstitious practices that were grounded on those opinions; and lastly, I shall relate what particulars I have met with relating to the manner of celebration.

SECTION I.

THE HISTORY OF THE EUCHARIST TILL AFTER THE TIME OF AUSTIN.

THE first new idea which was superadded to the original notion of the Lord's supper, was that of its being a *sacrament*, or an oath to be true to a leader. For the word *sacrament* is not to be found in the Scriptures, but was afterwards borrowed from the Latin tongue, in which it signified the oath which a Roman soldier took to his general. Thus, in the first century, Pliny reports, that the Christians were wont to meet together before it was light, and to bind themselves by a sacrament.[1] This, I would observe, is but a small deviation from the original idea of the Lord's supper; and though it be not the same with the true idea of it, as before explained, yet it cannot be said to be *contrary* to it. Afterwards the word sacrament came to be used by Christian writers in a very loose manner, for everything that was looked upon to be solemn or mysterious, and, indeed, as Bishop Hoadly observes, for almost everything relating to religion.[2]

The next idea which was added to the primitive notion of the Lord's supper was of a much more alarming nature, and had a long train of the worst consequences. This was the considering of this institution as a *mystery*. And, indeed, the Christians affected very early to call this rite one of the *mysteries of our holy religion*. By the term *mystery* was meant, originally, the more secret parts of the heathen worship, to which select persons only were admitted, and those under an oath of secrecy. Those mysteries were also called *initiations*: those who were initiated were supposed to be pure and holy, while those who were not initiated were considered as impure and profane; and by these

[1] "Essent soliti ante lucem convenire; seque sacramento abstringere." L. x. Ep. xcvii.
[2] "Cyprian speaks of the many and great sacraments of the Lord's Prayer." *Plain Account*, App. Ed. 6, p. 178.

mysteries the Heathens were more attached to their religion than by any other circumstance whatever. This made the first Christians (many of whom were first converted from Heathenism, and who could not all at once divest themselves of their fondness for pomp and mystery) wish to have something of this nature, which was so striking and captivating, in the Christian religion; and the rite of the Lord's supper soon struck them as what might easily answer this purpose.

When this new idea was introduced, they, in consequence of it, began to exclude all who did not partake of the ordinance from being present at the celebration of it. Those who did not communicate were not even allowed to know the method and manner in which it was administered. Tertullian, who wrote at the end of the second century, seems to allude to this practice. " Pious initiations," he says, "drive away the profane," and "it is of the very nature of mysteries to be concealed," as those of Ceres in Samothrace;[1] but as he is there defending the Christians from the charge of practising abominable rites in secret, he may only mean that, on the supposition of such practices, no person could reveal them, their enemies not being present, and they would hardly do it themselves. Indeed, it is most probable that this custom of concealing the mysteries did not take place till the middle of the third century.[2] After this time, the Council of Alexandria reproached the Arians with displaying the holy mysteries before the Catechumens, and even the Pagans; whereas "that which is holy," they say, "should not be cast to the dogs, nor pearls before swine."[3] In the fourth century it was usual to call the eucharist a most tremendous mystery, a dreadful solemnity, and terrible to angels.[4]

Another new idea annexed to the eucharist was that of its being a *sacrifice;* and this too was in compliance with the prejudices of the Jews and Heathens, who, in the early ages, used to reproach the Christians with having no sacrifices or oblations in their religion. We soon find, however, that this language was adopted by them, and applied to the Lord's supper. This language is particularly used by Cyprian, and in general the Lord's supper was called an *eucharistical sacrifice,* though, in fact, they only considered it as a *memorial* of the sacrifice of Christ, or of his death upon the cross.

It is evident, from the nature of the thing, that neither baptism nor the Lord's supper operates as a charm, or produces any immediate effect upon the mind, besides impressing it with proper sentiments and affections, such as become Christians, and such as are naturally excited by the use of these symbols. But we find, in very early ages, that both baptism and the Lord's supper were imagined to operate in a different and more direct method, so that the use of them was supposed to depend upon the mere act of administration. Both Justin Martyr and Irenæus thought that there was such a sanctification of the elements, that there was *a divine virtue* in them.

This idea of there being a real virtue in the elements of bread and wine, after they were consecrated, or set apart for this particular purpose, opened a door to endless superstitions, and some of a very dangerous kind; as Christians were led by it to put these merely external rites in the place of moral virtue, which alone has the power of sanctifying the heart, and making men acceptable in the sight of God. After this we are not surprised to find (and it appears as early as the second century) that both baptism and the Lord's supper were thought to be *necessary to salvation.*

It is too early to look for the notion of the transmutation of the bread and

---

[1] Apol. C. vii. Opera, p. 8. **(P.)**
[2] Larroche, p. 125. **(P.)**
[3] Sueur, A. D. 333. **(P.)**
[4] See Middleton, *Introd. Dis.* Works, I. p. xll.

wine into the real body and blood of Christ; but we find even in this early age language so highly figurative (calling the symbols by the name of the things represented by them) as very much contributed to produce this opinion in after ages. It was the custom with the early fathers to say that the bread and wine *passed* into the body and blood of Christ, and even that they are *transelemented* into them. They also use other expressions to the same purpose; meaning, however, by them, nothing more than that a divine virtue was communicated to them.[1]

"We do not consider," says Justin Martyr, "this bread and wine as common bread and wine. For, as Jesus Christ was made flesh, and had flesh and blood to procure our salvation, so we learn that this aliment, over which prayers have been made, is changed, and that by which our flesh and blood are nourished is the body and blood of Jesus Christ. For the evangelists teach us that Jesus Christ took bread, and said *this is my body:* he also took the wine, and said *this is my blood.*"[2] Tertullian, however, says, that by the words *this is my body,* we are to understand the *figure* of my body.[3]

The language of Cyril of Jerusalem, on this subject, is peculiarly strong, and might very well mislead his hearers, whatever ideas he himself might annex to it. He says to the young communicants, "Since Christ has said, *this is my body,* who can deny it? Since he has said, *this is my blood,* who can say it is not so? He formerly changed water into wine, and is he not worthy to be believed, when he says that he has changed the wine into his blood? Wherefore let us, with full assurance of faith, take the body and blood of Christ. For under the form of bread, the body is given to them, and under the form of wine, his blood." He then tells his pupils they

must not judge of this by their senses, but by faith.[4]

This writer carried his idea of the sanctity of the consecrated elements so far, as not to allow that they ever went into the *excrements* of the body; maintaining that they entered wholly into the substance of the communicants; and Chrysostom supported this opinion by the comparison of *wax,* which is consumed in the fire, without leaving ashes or soot.[5] This was going very far indeed for so early an age.

About two hundred years after Christ, Christians applied their thoughts very much to the giving of mystical significations to the sacraments, as they were also fond of mystical interpretations of scripture. Among other allusions, a happy one enough was this, that the sacramental bread, being composed of many grains of wheat, and the wine being made of many grapes, represented the body of the Christian church, which was composed of many believers, united into one society. Cyprian was the first who advanced that by the *wine* was meant the blood of Christ, and by the water (which they always at that time used to mix with the wine) the *Christian people;* and that by the *mixture* of them the union between Christ and his people was represented. This idea continued a long time in the church. But some supposed that this *water and wine* were a memorial of the *water and blood* which issued from the side of Christ, when he was pierced with the spear, as he hung on the cross.[6]

It was a natural consequence of this superstitious respect for the eucharistical elements, that many persons began to be afraid of communicating. Accordingly we find that, whereas originally, all Christians who were baptized, and not under sentence of excommunication, received the Lord's supper, yet in the time of Chrysostom, so many abstained from this part

---

[1] Larroche, p. 221. (*P.*)
[2] Edit. Thirlby, p. 96. (*P.*)
[3] Opera, p. 408. (*P.*)

[4] Cat. 4ta. Op. p. 392. (*P.*)
[5] Basnage, *Histoire,* I. p. 135. (*P.*)
[6] Larroche, p. 5. (*P.*)

of the service, that he was obliged to reprove them for it with great severity; and various methods were taken to engage them to attend it.

When the bread was called the body of Christ, the *cloth* which covered it was usually called *the cloth of the body*, and was considered as entitled to some particular respect. And we find that Optatus reproached the Donatists, that they had taken away these body-cloths, and that they had washed them as if they had been dirty. Also, Victor of Vita complained that Proculus (the executioner of the cruelties of Genseric, king of the Vandals, against the Catholics) had made shirts and drawers of them. This body-cloth was to be of very fine linen, and not of silk, or of purple, nor of any coloured stuff, agreeable to an order made by Pope Silvester, or, as some say, Pope Eusebius. In this age the table on which the eucharist was celebrated was called the "mystic table;" and Theophilus, to whom Jerome (if the epistle be genuine) writes, says, that the "very utensils and sacred coverings were not to be considered, like things inanimate, and void of sense, to have no sanctity, but to be worshipped with the same majesty as the body and blood of our Lord."[1]

In the fourth century, the Lord's supper was celebrated sometimes at the tombs of the martyrs, and at funerals, which custom gave rise to the masses which were afterwards performed in honour of the saints, and for the dead. Also, in many places, about the same time, the bread and wine were held up to the view of the people, before they were distributed, that they might be seen and contemplated with religious respect; from which the adoration of the symbols was afterwards derived.

Towards the end of the fourth century, it was thought wrong to commit the blood of Christ to so frail a thing as *glass*. Jerome reproaches a bishop of Toulouse with this, he being a rich man, and able to afford a better vessel, and more proper for the purpose.[2]

As the primitive Christians considered their joint-partaking of the Lord's supper as a bond of union among themselves, it was natural to send part of the elements to those persons whose infirm state of health, or necessary avocations, would not allow them to be present. For the same reason consecrated bread was also sent to the neighbouring, and often to distant parishes, as a token of brotherly communion. This they did, particularly at the feast of Easter; and, provided no superstitious use had been made of it, there seems to have been little to complain of in the custom. However, the Council of Laodicea thought proper to forbid this sending out of the elements, as a custom borrowed from the Jews and the heretics. But Pope Innocent, who lived a century after, still continued to send consecrated bread to the neighbouring parishes.[3]

But the greatest abuse that was made of this custom was in consequence of the consecrated elements being thought to be of use to the sick, in a medicinal way, and to be a means of preserving persons in journeys, and upon voyages; and as persons might not always have carried home with them enough for these uses, it was the custom for the priests to keep a quantity of the consecrated bread to distribute occasionally, as it might be wanted. Austin says, "If any one fall sick, let him receive the body and blood

[1] Middleton's *Introd. Dis.* p. 57. (*P.*) Dr. Priestley, in his edition of the *Corruptions*, had attributed this representation to *Jerome*, on the authority of the Latin original, given in a note by Dr. Middleton. But in his corrections, mentioned p. 12 (Rutt's Priestley, Vol. V.), he proposed the alteration of his text (which I have made) on the authority of "the writer of the *Critical Review*," who says that Dr. Middleton quoted the edition of Jerome's Works in 1706, while, in the Basil edition of 1563, which he describes as most authentic, the opinion is attributed by Jerome to Theophilus. The reviewer adds, that the whole passage is probably spurious. See Middleton's Works, I. p. xlii. Note, and *Crit. Rev.* IV. p. 193.

[2] Larroche, p. 53. (*P.*)
[3] Basnage, *Histoire*, I. p. 111. (*P.*)

of Christ, and let him keep a part of this little body, that he may find the accomplishment of what St. James says, *Let those who are sick go to the church to receive strength of body.*"[1] This same father also mentions a woman who had made a plaister of the sacramental bread for a sore eye.[2]

Some of the ancient Christians used to bury the sacramental bread together with the dead, thinking, no doubt, that it would be of as much use to them in that long journey as it had been in other shorter ones. However, in a council held at Carthage in 419, this practice was condemned; but it appears that the custom was not wholly laid aside at the end of the eighth century, though it had been prohibited again by the sixth general council in 691. The reason was, that to bury these sacred elements was now thought to be a profanation of them; so that a custom which took its rise from one degree of superstition, was abolished by a greater degree of it; and of this we shall have other instances in the course of this history.

Having thus noted the changes in the doctrine of the eucharist, and the superstitious practices which in these early times were derived from the erroneous opinions of Christians on the subject, I shall now relate what I have been able to collect concerning the manner in which it was administered.

In the first place, it cannot be denied that, in the primitive times, all those who were classed among the *faithful*, received the eucharist every Lord's day. After reading the Scriptures, and the exposition of them, or the sermon, at which others might attend, they proceeded to the public prayer, in which the audience bore their part, at least by saying occasionally *Amen*, and the service constantly closed with the celebration of the eucharist. We even find that young children, and indeed infants, communicated. This was clearly the case in the time of Cyprian.[3] The custom continued in the Western church till near the time of the Reformation, and it is still the practice of the Eastern churches, and of every other part of the Christian world that was never subject to the see of Rome.[4]

The different classes of Christians in the primitive times, as they respected the Lord's supper, were as follows. There were four orders of the Catechumens. The first were instructed at their own houses; the second heard the exposition in the church; the third attended the public prayer; and the fourth were those who were completely ready for baptism; for till that time they did not attend the celebration of the eucharist, but were formally dismissed at what is called *missa cate-chumenorum*, as the final dismission of the assembly was called *missa fide-lium*.[5]

The primitive Christians communicated after supper, but the custom of celebrating it in the morning was frequent in the church in the time of Tertullian, in consequence, no doubt, of a superstitious reverence for the elements, which led them to think that it was wrong to eat anything before they partook of them; but it was still usual to communicate in the evening, on Holy Thursday. Chrysostom being charged with giving the eucharist to some persons after a repast, said, "If I have done it, let my name be blotted from the catalogue of bishops, and let

---

[1] Basnage, *Histoire*, I. p. 161. (*P.*)
[2] Larroche, p. 6. (*P.*)

[3] On whose authority (*de lapsis*, p. 175) Middleton says, "this sacrament was administered, in all their public communions, to infants, even of the tenderest age, before they were able to speak." Works, I. p. xli.
[4] See [Rutt's Priestley] Vol. II. pp. 337, 338, and the *Notes*. I find on a farther examination of Smith's *Account*, that the *catechumeni* were only debarred from witnessing "the second or great procession," previous to the *consecration*. He says that "they give the eucharist, in both kinds, to little children of one or two years of age, sometimes to new-born infants, after they have been christened, in case of imminent danger of death; grounding their belief of an absolute necessity of this sacrament upon John vi. 53. Smith's *Greek Church* in 1669, p. 161.
[5] Sueur, A. D. 216. (*P.*)

L

me not be reckoned among the orthodox."[1]

It having been customary with the
Jews, whenever they made a solemn
appearance before God, to bring some
oblations, these Christians, whenever
they assembled for public worship,
(which they also considered as an appearing before God, and especially in
the more solemn part of the service,
the administration of the eucharist,)
brought with them a quantity of bread
and wine,[2] and especially the first-
fruits of their corn and grapes. Of
these *offerings*, or *oblations*, as they
then affected to call them, a part was
reserved for the eucharist, and part
also was eaten afterwards in common,
in what they called their *agapæ*, or
love-feasts, but the remainder was
appropriated to the maintenance of the
ministers and of the poor. Besides
bread and wine, it was the custom to
offer many things of value at the same
time. But at length they limited the
oblations which were made on this
particular occasion to bread and wine
only; and afterwards they usually
made for this purpose *one great loaf*,
or cake, which they said represented
the unity of the church, and which
was broken in public, and distributed
to as many as communicated. In the
fourth century some churches substituted what they called *eulogies*, or
holy bread, for the bread of the Lord's
supper.[3]

The ancients in general believed
that the water was mixed with the
wine, in our Saviour's own administration of the eucharist, and therefore
they did the same. This mixture of
water with the wine is mentioned by

Tertullian, and Cyprian pretends that
it was of singular use. We find that
some Christians communicated with
water only, from which they were
called Aquarians.[4] These were not
only Manicheans, who abhorred wine,
but also others who were in the scheme
of mortifying the flesh by abstaining
from marriage, and the use of flesh
meat, as well as of wine.

When the elements began to be considered in a superstitious light, as
something more than mere bread and
wine, there must have been a time
when they imagined that this change
took place; and in the early ages it
was supposed to be made by the
prayer which preceded the administration, and not by any particular
form of words; and this is the idea
that the Greek Church still retains
concerning consecration. But afterwards, though it is not easy to determine when, the change was supposed
to take place as the priest was
pronouncing the words, *This is my
body*, in Latin, *hoc est corpus meum*;
as if there had been some peculiar virtue in the sound of those words, when
pronounced by a person duly qualified
to use them. Thus also the Heathens
imagined that the presence of the invisible Divinity was made to dwell in
an image, by the priest pronouncing
some form of words, which was termed
consecrating them.

The eucharistical elements being now
considered as something *holy*, it was
natural to suppose that a degree of
holiness belonged also to the table on
which the service was performed, and
therefore that it ought to be prepared
by some ceremony, for this holy purpose. Gregory Nyssen, the same whose
eloquence on the subject of the eucharist has been recited already, is said to
have been the first who performed any
ceremony of this kind. It was about
the fourth century, as is generally
agreed, that places of worship began

---

[1] Basnage, *Histoire*, I. p. 132. (P.) "The
Greeks communicate fasting, looking upon it as
a thing very unlawful and scandalous to taste a
drop of wine, or eat the least bit of bread, for
several hours before they receive." Smith's
Account, p. 158.

[2] To prepare for "the sacrament of the holy
eucharist,...the priests and deacons...carry the
gifts of bread and wine, presented by the people,
to the altar of the *Prothesis*; by this oblation,
separating them from profane and common use."
Ibid. p. 125.

[3] Basnage, *Histoire*, I. p. 112. (P.)

[4] Also called *Encratites* [Hydroparastates].
See Mosheim. Vol. I. p. 180. Cent. ii. P. ii. Ch. v.
s. ix.

to be consecrated, though in some very simple manner, and it was then forbidden to celebrate the Lord's supper except in consecrated places. When churches were built with more magnificence, under Constantine, there was a particular place called the *sanctuary*, where the table or altar stood.

Lights in the day-time were usual in many ceremonies in the heathen religion, whence an idea of *cheerfulness*, and of *sacredness* also, was annexed to them; and the Christians of those ages were but too ready to adopt the religious customs of the Heathens, partly from their own attachment to them, and also with a view to make their religion more inviting to the Pagans. The custom of using wax-lights at the eucharist, in particular, probably began in the time of Austin, in the fifth century. For, in the time of Gregory I. they were used at baptism; and Isidore of Seville, who was contemporary with Gregory, speaks of it as a thing established. "Those," says he, "who in Greek are called *Acolytes*, are in Latin called *link-bearers*, because they carry lights when the gospel is read; or, when the sacrifice is offered, not to dissipate darkness, but to express joy, to declare, under the type of corporeal light, the light spoken of in the gospel." In blessing these torches and flambeaux, they said, "O Jesus Christ, bless this wax, we beseech thee, that it may receive of thee such a power and benediction, that, in all places where it shall be lighted and set, the devil may tremble and fly for fear, and may no more attempt to molest or seduce those who serve thee."[1] It must be observed that this custom of using lights at the celebration of the eucharist began in the East, a little after the time of Gregory Nazianzen.

The blessing of the bread and wine used by our Saviour himself was probably nothing more than a very short prayer, such as we commonly use before meat. But when the administration of the eucharist came to be a principal part of solemn religious worship, it is probable that the prayer which preceded it, and from which the whole service got the name of *eucharist*, was of some length, especially as we do not find that prayer was used in any other part of the service. In the third century it is particularly observed, that the prayers which preceded the celebration of the eucharist were considerably lengthened, as well as that the solemnity and pomp with which it was administered were increased; and that at this time persons in a state of penitence, and others, were excluded from it, in imitation of the heathen mysteries.

It was the custom within this period to ask forgiveness of one another, as well as to give the *kiss of peace*, or charity, before communion, the men kissing the men, and the women the women. They also used to kiss the hand of the priest. This custom of asking pardon before communicating, was used in France in the eleventh century.[2]

At first the deacons generally administered the elements, but in the fourth Council of Carthage, they were only suffered to administer in cases of necessity. Afterwards they administered the cup only, while the priest who celebrated gave the bread. Sometimes women served on this occasion, and though it was forbidden by Pope Gelasius, the practice continued in many places till the tenth century.[3]

Cyril, of Jerusalem, at the end of the fourth century, exhorted his communicants to receive the bread by supporting the right hand with the left, also to receive it in the hollow of the hand, and to take care that no crumb of it fell to the ground; and that in receiving the wine, they should approach it with the body a little bowed, in token of veneration. The sixth general council ordered that the hands should be held in the form of a cross. It was the custom in the time of Jerome, to kiss

---

[1] Larroche, p. 537. *(P.)*

[2] Ibid. p. 120. *(P.)*
[3] Ibid. p. 123. *(P.)*

L 2

the bread; and in the liturgy of Chrysostom, used by the Greeks, it is directed that he who receives the elements should kiss the hand of the deacon from whom he receives them.[1] It is needless to note the progress of superstition in all these observances.

When the service was ended, the congregation was dismissed by the priest, saying *Ite, Missa est;* which Polidore Virgil acknowledges was also the form of dismissing the idolatrous services of the Pagans.[2] There was, likewise, as was observed before, a formal dismission of the catechumens, before they proceeded to the celebration of the eucharist, in the same words, and from this term *missa,* the whole service came afterwards to be called by that name, which by corruption is in the English language *mass.*

The primitive Christians did frequently eat in common, before the celebration of the Lord's supper. To this kind of entertainment, to which every person brought what he thought proper, they gave the name of *agapé* or *lovefeast;* and it is thought to be alluded to in the epistles of Peter and Jude, 2 Pet. ii. 13; Jude 12. This custom, however, of eating in common having been abused, it was forbidden by the Council of Laodicea in 360. But before this time, when it began to be thought improper to eat anything before the eucharist, this feast was omitted till after the celebration.[3]

Such was the progress of superstition in this age of the church, which abounded with men of learning, and writers. We are not to expect a reformation of these abuses, in the next period of gross darkness, and while the same causes of corruption, and especially a fondness for pagan customs, and a willingness to gain over the Pagans by adopting them, continued and increased. We have now seen how the pagan notion of *mysteries,* together with that of a *sanctifying power* in the elements themselves, contributed to introduce a train of superstitious practices into the Christian church; but we must go much deeper into this superstition in the two following periods, with less pleasing prospects than in the last. We have seen the shades of the evening close upon us; we must now prepare to pass through the darkness of the night, but with the hope that, as we come nearer to our own times, the daylight will visit us again.

SECTION II.

THE HISTORY OF THE EUCHARIST FROM
THE TIME OF AUSTIN TO THAT OF
PASCHASIUS.

In this period we find a very considerable advance towards the doctrine of *transubstantiation,* which was afterwards established in the Western church; but the first great step towards it, as well as almost all the abuses of which an account is given in the last Section, was made in the East, where Anastasius, a monk of Mount Sinai, (in a treatise against some heretics who asserted that the body of Christ was impassible,) said, that the elements of the Lord's supper were the true body and blood of Christ; for that when Christ instituted the eucharist, he did not say, this is the *type* or *antitype* of my body, but *my body.* This is evidently a language unknown to all the ancients, when they spoke not rhetorically but gravely on the subject; and yet, on the whole, it is certain that he did not mean so much as was afterwards understood by that mode of speaking.[4]

But John Damascenus, another monk, and a celebrated writer in the East, not only followed Anastasius in his language, but made a real change in the *ideas* annexed to it; saying that,

[1] Larroche, p. 119. (*P.*)
[2] Sueur, A. D. 398. (*P.*)
[3] Mosheim, I. p. 104. (*P.*) Cent. 1. Pt. ii. Ch.
iv. Sect. vii.

[4] Sueur, A. D. 687. (*P.*)

" when some have called the bread and wine *figures* or *signs* of the body and blood of Christ, as Basil, they spake of them not after consecration, but before the oblation was consecrated." " Jesus," he says, " has joined to the bread and wine his own divinity, and made them to be his body and blood." He illustrates this in the following manner :—" Isaiah saw a *lighted coal ;* now a lighted coal is not mere wood, but wood joined to fire ; so the bread of the sacrament is not mere bread, but bread joined to the divinity ; and the body united to the divinity is not one and the same nature, but the nature of the body· is one, and that of the divinity united to it, another."[1] In the second Council of Nice, when it was urged on one side that Christ had no other image than the sacrament, it was argued by the council, that the sacrament after consecration was no image, but properly his body and blood.[2] This has been the faith of the Greek Church ever since the time of this Damascenus, who wrote in the beginning of the eighth century ; and his name is as great an authority in the Eastern church, as that of Thomas Aquinas was afterwards in the Western.

In reality, the Greeks must consider the eucharistical elements as *another body of Christ*, to which his soul, or his divinity, bears the same relation that it did to the body which he had when on earth, and with which he ascended to heaven. They must suppose that there is, as it were, a multiplication of bodies to the same soul. No real change, however, is by them supposed to be made in the substance of the bread and wine ; only from being mere bread and wine, it becomes a new body and blood to Christ.

Whether this new opinion spread into the West, does not distinctly appear, and the two churches had not, at that time, much communication with each other. But from the same general causes the idea of something mystical

and sacred in the eucharistical elements kept .advancing in the West, as well as in the East ; and they were considered as bearing some peculiar relation to Christ ; who was, therefore, thought to be, in some extraordinary manner, *present* with them, but in *what manner*, they had not perhaps any distinct idea.

When the eucharistical elements were considered as so peculiarly sacred, we are not surprised to find that many methods were used to prevent the loss or waste of them. Among other methods, they began, pretty early in this period, to take the bread dipped in the consecrated wine. This was particularly noticed in the eleventh Council of Toledo, in 675, and in another at Braga in Gallicia, in which a decree was made to put a stop to this practice ; but still it was allowed that the eucharist might be administered to sick persons and young children in this manner. The Armenians still receive the eucharist in this way, and the Moscovites take the bread and wine together in a spoon.[3]

I have observed that, in the former period, it was usual for the communicants to carry some of the consecrated bread home with them, and to take it with them when they went on a journey ; but in the Council of Saragossa, within the present period, they who did not eat the bread at the time of communicating were anathematized. Thus a greater degree of superstition put an end to a practice which had been introduced by a less degree of it. However, the practice of consecrating a great quantity of bread was kept up ; and in the time of Charlemagne, express directions were given for keeping it, in order

---

[1] Larroche, p. 367. (*P.*)
[2] Taylor, *Grand Apostacy*, p. 160. (*P.*)

[3] Larroche, p. 146. (*P.*) "The priest takes a spoon, fills it full of red wine, puts into it a small piece of bread, and tempereth them both together, so delivers the spoon to the communicants....After this, he delivereth them bread by itself, and then wine mixed with a little warm water, to represent the blood and water which flowed from our Saviour's side." The *Russian Catechism—Ceremonies of the Muscovites*, 1725, Ed.2, pp. 65, 66.

to communicate the sick.[1] This consecrated bread, it had been the custom to keep in a close chest in the church; but at the Council of Tours, in 567, it was ordered that the *host* (as it was then called) should be kept not in a chest, but under the title of the cross, to excite the devotion of the people.[2]

Among other superstitious customs within this period, we find that sometimes the consecrated wine was mixed with ink, in order to sign writings of a peculiarly solemn nature. Thus Pope Theodore, in the seventh century, signed the condemnation and deposition of Pyrrhus, the Monothelite; it was used at the condemnation of Photius by the fathers of the Council of Constantinople, in 869; and Charles the Bald, and Bernard, count of Barcelona, also signed a treaty with the sacramental wine, in 844. It is evident, however, from this very abuse of the eucharistical elements, that they were not at that time supposed to be the real body and blood of Christ; for, since they have been thought to be so, it would be deemed a great profanation to make any such use of them.

It is not denied that, originally, the celebration of the Lord's supper was a part of the public worship in which all the congregation of the faithful joined; but in the Church of Rome at present the priest alone communicates in general, while the congregation are mere spectators of what he is doing, and only join in the prayers. This was occasioned by the superstitious veneration for the elements, from which was naturally derived an idea of some particular preparation being necessary for the receiving of them. The first notice that we find of this kind of *mass* was about the year 700; but we have seen that, even in the time of Chrysostom, the people in general began to decline communion; but in the time of Charlemagne, the priests were forbidden to celebrate mass alone; and Pope Soter

ordained that no person should celebrate mass, unless the priest made a third.[3] Among other accusations of John XII., he was charged with celebrating mass without communion.[4]

No laws, however, could long check the torrent of this abuse. It being imagined that the celebration of the mass was offering the most acceptable sacrifice to God, which would avail for the pardon of sin, and for redeeming souls out of purgatory, large sums of money were given and bequeathed to the priests for this purpose, which proved a source of immense wealth to them. But this abuse was much increased when monks were allowed, by Pope Gregory, to do the office of priests. This order of men had much leisure for the purpose, and an idea of peculiar sanctity was annexed to their character in the minds of the common people.

To the monks may be attributed the origin of *private chapels*, and the multiplication of altars in churches for celebrating several masses at the same time. For, according to ancient custom, it was not lawful to say more than one mass, at which all assisted; and it was a thing unheard of that any person should celebrate mass on the same day, upon the same altar, a custom which is still observed in the Eastern churches. For the Greeks have but one altar in one church, nor do we find the mention of any more in the Western church till the eighth century. But in the time of Adrian I., who lived towards the end of the eighth century, there is mention made of the *great altar*, to distinguish it from others in the same church. Whenever the phrase occurs in any period prior to this, by *altars* we are to understand the *tombs of the martyrs*, which are often so called.[5] The first mention that we have of the eucharist being celebrated more than once in the course of the same day in any church, is in the fifth century, when Leo I. ordered it on great

[1] Larroche, p. 167. (*P.*) Smith found this custom in the Greek Church at Constantinople, in 1669. See his *Account*, p. 162.
[2] Sueur, A. D. 567. (*P.*)

[3] Larroche, p. 126. (*P.*)
[4] Sueur, A. D. 963. (*P.*)
[5] Larroche, p. 47. (*P.*)

festival days, when the crowds were so great that the churches could not contain those that resorted to them.

To induce the common people to continue their offerings after they ceased to communicate, they were given to understand, that provided they kept up that custom, the service would still be useful to them; and instead of a real communion with bread and wine duly consecrated, the priests gave them a kind of substitute for it, and a thing of a much less awful nature, viz. bread, over which they prayed, and to which they gave the name of *hallowed bread.* This was about the year 700.[1]

It was in consequence of few persons offering themselves to communion, that the priests got a habit of speaking in a very low voice, a custom which was afterwards continued through superstition. This is said to have begun about the end of the tenth century; and some say that it proceeded from a report that God had punished with sudden death some shepherds who sang the words of consecration in the fields.[2]

Having noted these general abuses respecting the eucharist, I shall now consider the method in which it was administered, going over the different parts of the service for that purpose; and we shall find traces enow of superstition, every step that we take.

As there is nothing prescribed in the New Testament concerning the order of public worship, or the mode of celebrating the Lord's supper, different churches fell naturally into different methods with respect to them, as we see in what remains of several of the ancient liturgies. That of most churches had probably been gradually altered, especially as men's ideas with respect to the nature of the service itself had changed. The present *canon of the mass,* as it is now used in the Church of Rome, was, for the most part, composed by Gregory the Great,

who made more alterations in it than any of his predecessors. He introduced into it many pompous ceremonies, but it was several centuries before this canon was adopted by all the members of the Latin church. In 699, Pope Sergius added to the canon of the mass, that while the priest is breaking the bread, he should sing three times, *Lamb of God who taketh away the sin of the world, have mercy upon us;* but that the third time, instead of the words *have mercy upon us,* he should say, *grant us peace.*[3]

Since the celebration of the eucharist was now considered as a *proper sacrifice,* the table on which it was offered came of course to be an *altar;* and as altars in the Jewish church, and among the Pagans, were consecrated, the Christian altars must be so too. The first mention that is made of the consecration of altars, (more than was observed to have been done by Gregory Nyssenus,) is in the Council of Agde, in 506, when they were ordered to be consecrated both by chrism and by the benediction of the priest. In the ninth century they added water to the chrism, and incense, and other things. They also consecrated *three table-cloths* of several fashions, and a kind of *veil* of several colours, according to the different days, &c.[4]

In order to be better entitled to the name of *altars,* and to correspond to the altars in the Jewish and Pagan religions, all the wooden tables were removed, and all altars were ordered to be made of stone. And it was farther alleged in favour of this custom, that Jesus Christ is called *the corner-stone* and foundation of the church. This institution is ascribed to Silvester; but the decree is not found. It was a council of Epaone, in 517, that forbade the consecration of altars, unless they were made of stone.[5]

To the due consecration of altars it is now requisite that there should be

---

[1] Hist. of Ancient Ceremonies, p. 88. (*P.*)
[2] Larroche, p. 79. (*P.*)

[3] Sueur, A. D. 699. (*P.*)
[4] Larroche, p. 49. (*P.*)
[5] Basnage, I. pp. 46, 47. (*P.*)

relics in them; but this was far from being the case originally. For a council in the seventh century ordered, that altars should not be consecrated in any place where a body had been interred.[1] The last thing which I shall observe in respect to altars is, that Bede is the first who makes any mention of *portable* ones.

It was the custom in all this period not only to make use of *lights*, though in the day-time, during the celebration of the eucharist, but of *incense* also; and both these appendages were borrowed from the heathen sacrifices, and were first adopted by the Greeks, and so early as the middle of the fifth century; mention being then made of assembling the church by flambeaux and perfumes. But it is not said that this was for the celebration of the eucharist in particular.[2]

Originally, the *bread* that was used for the celebration of the Lord's supper was such as was presented among other offerings on the occasion. Afterwards it was the custom to make one great loaf or cake, to supply all the communicants; and this was broken at the time of the celebration, and distributed in small pieces to the communicants. But this custom being attended with some loss, some priests in Spain began, about the seventh century, to prepare the eucharistical bread in a different manner, baking small round pieces on purpose, that there might not be occasion to break it at all. But this innovation was not generally approved, and it was expressly forbidden by the Council of Toledo, in 693.[3] In time, however, the increasing superstition of the age got the better of this regulation, and the custom of making small round *wafers* for the purpose of communion, at length became universal in the church.

It was the custom in the primitive church, as I have already observed, to give what is called the *kiss of peace*,

or of charity, immediately before communion. This, in time, was thought to be an indecent practice, and therefore ought to have been laid aside altogether. However, Leo III., at the end of the ninth century, changed this custom for that of kissing a plate of silver or copper, with the figure of a cross upon it, or the relic of some saint after the consecration of the elements.[4]

In the fifth century it was the custom for men to receive the bread with their naked hands, and the women (who perhaps did not expose their hands naked) in a clean cloth, which obtained the name of *dominica*. Afterwards, in the farther progress of superstition, it came to be the custom to receive it in vessels of gold, &c.; but this was forbidden in the sixth general council in 680, and they were again ordered to receive it with the hand.[5] It has been already observed, that *glass* was thought to be too brittle a thing to receive the holy elements. Glass vessels, however, continued to be made use of, so that it was thought necessary to forbid the use of them in a council held at Rheims under Charlemagne; and in another council, held in the year 895, wooden vessels were forbidden to be used for that purpose; and at present the Latin church does not suffer the consecration to be made in anything but in a chalice of gold or silver, or at least of pewter; and a council held at Albi, in 1254, commands all churches, the yearly rent of which amounts to fifteen French livres, to have a silver chalice.[6]

In the primitive times we find no mention of any particular *position of the body*, as more proper than any other for receiving the Lord's supper; but as superstition kept gaining ground, the *East* began to be held peculiarly sacred, as it always had been held by the Heathens, who worshipped with their faces turned that way; and about the year 536, Pope Vigilius ordered that

---

1 Basnage, I. p. 48. *(P.)*
2 Larroche, p. 526. *(P.)*
3 Ibid. p. 36. *(P.)*

4 Ancient Ceremonies, p. 90. *(P.)*
5 Larroche, p. 555. *(P.)*
6 Ibid. p. 53. *(P.)*

those who celebrated mass should always direct their faces towards the East.[1]

We see the effects of superstition as well in the method of disposing of what remained of the consecrated elements, as in the use of them. Some churches used to burn all that remained after communion. This was the custom at Jerusalem, and it is so with the Greeks at present; at least, says Fleury,[2] they are reproached with it. At Constantinople it was formerly eaten by young scholars, sent from the school for that purpose, as is related by Evagrius, who wrote at the end of the sixth century. The Council of Toledo, in 693, left it to the liberty of each particular church, either to keep what remained of the consecrated elements, or to eat it; but, in the latter case, it was ordained that the quantity consecrated should be moderate, that it might not oppress the stomachs of those who were appointed to take it. But, in whatever manner they disposed of these sacred elements, it was the custom not to leave any of them till the next day.[3]

One would imagine that we had seen superstition enough in this one article of Christian faith and practice within this period; but we shall find much greater abuses in the next: and notwithstanding the greater light of the present age, they continue unreformed in the Church of Rome to this day.

SECTION III.

THE HISTORY OF THE EUCHARIST, FROM THE TIME OF PASCHASIUS TO THE REFORMATION.

WE are now arrived at the most distinguished æra in the history of the eucharist; after having seen how much

1 Ancient Ceremonies, p. 76. (*P.*)
2 A. D. 1054. (*P.*)
3 Larroche, p. 171. (*P.*)

the eucharistical elements in this age of darkness had gained in point of *sacredness* and *solemnity*, and how awful a thing the act of communicating was generally apprehended to be; so that commonly the priest alone communicated, and the people very seldom, except at the time of the greater festivals, and especially at Easter.

This was in consequence of the people in general being impressed with a confused notion that the eucharistical elements were, in some sense or other, *the body and blood of Christ*, and therefore that Christ himself was *present* in them. But in what manner he was present they seem to have had no clear idea. This general notion, however, paved the way for the capital addition that was made to the doctrine of the eucharist by Paschasius Radbert, a monk of Corbie, in France, who undertook to explain the manner in which the body of Christ is present in the eucharist.

This he did in a treatise[4] published in the year 818, in which he maintained that not only the bread and wine were changed, by consecration, into the real body and blood of Christ; but that it was the same body that had been born of the Virgin Mary, and that had been crucified and raised from the dead. It was in support of this opinion that he wrote the two books *On the Delivery of the Virgin Mary*, which I had occasion to mention before; in which he maintained, that it was performed in a miraculous manner, without any opening of the womb.[5]

This opinion Paschasius himself seems to have been sensible was bold and *novel*. For the first time that he mentions it, after calling the eucharistical elements the body of Christ in general, he adds, "and to say something more surprising and wonderful, (*ut mirabilius loquar*,) it is no other flesh than that which was born of the Virgin

4 "Of the Body and Blood of Jesus Christ in the Eucharist." Radbert became abbot of Corbie, where he died in 865. *Nouv. Dict. Hist.* IV. pp. 879, 880.
5 Sueur, A. D. 818. (*P.* See p. 43, *supra.*

Mary, which suffered upon the cross, and which was raised from the grave."[1]

Not depending entirely upon the *reasons* which he was able to allege in favour of so extraordinary an opinion, he likewise produced in support of it, what was no uncommon thing with the monks, and what had no small weight with the common people, in that ignorant age, namely, an *apparition*, which for its singular curiosity, and as a specimen of the impositions of those times, I shall relate.

A priest, whose name was Plecgills, officiating at the tomb of St. Ninus, wished, out of love, and not infidelity, to see the body of Jesus Christ; and falling upon his knees, he asked of God the favour to see the nature of the body of Jesus Christ, in this mystery, and to hold in his hand the form of that little child which the Virgin had borne in her lap; when an angel cried to him, "Get up, quickly, and look at the infant, which that holy woman hath carried, for he is clothed in his corporeal habit." The priest declared, that being quite terrified he looked up, and saw upon the altar the child that Simeon had held in his arms, that the angel told him he might not only see but *touch* the child, and that accordingly he took him and pressed the breast of the child to his own, and after embracing him frequently, he kissed the God, joining his lips to the lips of Jesus Christ. After this he replaced the beautiful limbs of the god upon the altar, praying to God that he might resume his former figure, and that he had scarcely finished his prayer, when rising from the ground, he found that the body of Jesus Christ was restored to its former figure, as he had requested.[2]

Notwithstanding this miracle, and everything else that Paschasius could allege in favour of his doctrine, it excited great astonishment, and was opposed by many persons of learning and eminence. Among others, the em-

peror Charles the Bald was much offended at it, and by his particular order the famous Bertram, or Rattram, wrote against the new opinion of Paschasius,[3] and at the same time against his peculiar notion concerning the delivery of the Virgin.

In consequence of this, the doctrine of Paschasius, though published in the ninth century, does not appear to have gained many advocates till the eleventh, when it was opposed by Berenger, archdeacon of the church of Angers, in France, (whom I mentioned before as one of the most eminent scholars of his age,) and his writings on this subject made a great impression on the minds of many; so that no less than ten or twelve councils were held on this subject, in all of which the doctrine of Berenger was condemned. Matthew of Westminster says, that it had infected almost all France, Italy, and England; and though, when he was threatened, he was weak enough to sign a recantation of his opinion, he certainly died in the belief of it. Berenger was followed by Peter and Henry de Bruis, whose disciples were called *Petrobrussians*, and by the Albigenses in general; who in the twelfth century separated from the church of Rome. Arnold of Brescia also taught the same doctrine in Italy, and for this and his declaiming against the Church of Rome in general, he was burned at Rome, in 1155.[4]

It is remarkable that for two centuries the popes did not interfere in the controversy about Paschasius. Most probably they thought with his adversaries; and as very few joined him at

[1] Sueur, A. D. 818. (*P.*)
[2] Ibid. A. D. 818. (*P.*)

[3] See p. 40, Note [10], *supra*. Bertram's book was first translated into English in 1548, by Wm. Hugh, under this title, "A Boke of Bertram the Priest intreating of the Body and Blood of Christ, written to Charles the Great [Bald] 700 years ago." It was translated again by Sir H. Lynde, in 1686. Of this there was a 2nd Edition in 1688. See Wood, *Athen. Oxon.* I. pp. 62, 513.
[4] Larroche, p. 473. (*P.*) *Arnold*, a disciple of Abelard, was *crucified*, burnt, and his ashes thrown into the Tiber, lest his followers should convert them into relics, says a French biographer. See *Nouv. Dict. Hist.* I. p. 212. Arnold suffered under Adrian IV., the only Pope who was an Englishman.

first, and he was openly opposed by the learned men of the age, it seemed as if his opinion would have died away of itself. As soon, however, as it was perceived that the doctrine went down with the common people, and that it promised to give a high idea of the dignity and power of the priesthood, the popes were ready enough to enforce it by their decrees, as we have seen in the case of Berenger. It was not, however, till the beginning of the thirteenth century that this doctrine was made an article of faith, viz. by a decree of Innocent III. at the Council of Lateran, in 1215, the term *transubstantiation* having been first used by Stephen, bishop of Autun, in the beginning of the twelfth century.

Even notwithstanding this decree, several divines openly maintained a different opinion, thinking it sufficient to acknowledge the *real presence*, though they explained the manner of it differently from Innocent and the followers of Paschasius; and "John, surnamed *Pungens Asinus*, a subtile doctor of the university of Paris, ... substituted consubstantiation in the place of *transubstantiation* towards the conclusion of this century." [1] Others say that he maintained the *assumption* of the consecrated bread by the divinity. However, he did not deny that the substance of the bread and wine remained in the elements; and yet the faculty at Paris did not condemn his opinion, but declared that both this, and the common doctrine of transubstantiation, were probable ways of making the body of Christ exist in the sacrament.

As the monks had contributed greatly to the establishment of almost every other corruption of Christianity, they were no less active in promoting this. Among others, the name of Odo, bishop of Clugni, in France, in the tenth century, is mentioned as having been of eminent use on this occasion. Indeed, another Odo, archbishop of Canterbury,

of that age, is likewise said to have been a great promoter of it. But there does not appear to have been any public act in favour of the doctrine of transubstantiation in England, before the Council of Oxford which condemned Wickliffe.[2]

We cannot be surprised, that the circumstance of all the known properties of bread and wine remaining in the eucharistical elements after consecration, should not a little embarrass the advocates for the change of them into real flesh and blood. On this account, Innocent III. acknowledged that, after consecration, there did remain in the elements a certain *paneity* and *vineity*, as he called them, which satisfied hunger and thirst. But afterwards, they who maintained that the consecrated host retained the nature of bread, and nourished the body, and especially that any part of it was turned into *excrement*, were, in derision, called *Stercorarists*. This term of reproach shows in what abhorrence all those who did not assent to this new doctrine were then held. If ridicule and contempt were a proper *test of truth*, I doubt not but that those who defended the absurd doctrine of transubstantiation would have had the advantage of the argument. Protestants would now only laugh at being called Stercorarists, but at that time the laugh would probably not have been with us, but against us. That was not an age of experiment, or it might have been easily decided, viz. by giving a man nothing but consecrated bread, whether it turned to nourishment and excrement or not; but the very proposal would have been deemed impious, and might have been very hazardous to the proposer.

Considering the great difficulty of forming any conception concerning this conversion of the bread and wine into real flesh and blood, it is no wonder that many doubts should have been started, and different opinions should have been held concerning it; and, that they should even continue to be held,

---

[1] Mosheim, III. p. 106. (*P.*) Cent. xiii. Pt. ii. Ch. iii. Sect. xiv.

[2] In 1385. See Brit. Biog. I. pp. 38–41.

notwithstanding the most authoritative decisions respecting it. Peter Lombard, contemporary with Stephen of Autun above mentioned, approved of this doctrine of transubstantiation, but could not determine of what *kind* the change was; whether it was only *formal*, or *substantial*, that is, whether it affected the sensible properties of the elements, or the real substance of them.[1]

It was also a question whether the *water* (which it was always the custom to mix with the wine before consecration) was changed immediately into the blood of Christ, or whether it was changed into wine first. Paschasius himself had asserted the former, but after long debates it was determined by Innocent III., and the schoolmen supported him in it, that the water is changed into wine before it is changed into the blood of Christ.[2]

In this, and several other respects, a considerable latitude of opinion was formerly allowed in the Church of Rome; and indeed the doctrine of *transubstantiation* did not properly become an article of faith before it was made to be so by the Council of Trent. The cardinal D'Ailli, at the Council of Constance, spoke of the doctrine of transubstantiation as an *opinion* only, and said that it could not be clearly inferred from the Scriptures, that the substance of bread did not remain in the sacrament.[3]

At the Council of Trent, the Franciscans maintained that the body of Christ descended from heaven, in order to be changed into the form of bread and wine, though it did not quit its former place; whereas, the Dominicans said, that Jesus Christ did not come from any other place, but that he was formed in the host, the substance of the bread being changed into that of his body. The council did not decide

this question, but in their decrees made use of such terms as both parties might adopt.[4]

When the great difficulty of one single conversion of any particular quantity of bread and wine into the body and blood of Christ was got over, one would imagine that another difficulty, no less insuperable, would have occurred, with respect to the multitude of consecrations performed in different places at the same time. But Guimond, who wrote against Berenger, in 1075, made nothing of these, or of still greater difficulties. Every separate part," says he, " of the eucharist is the whole body of Christ. It is given entire to all the faithful. They all receive it equally. Though it should be celebrated a thousand times at once, it is the same indivisible body of Christ. It is only to *sense* that a single part of the host appears less than the whole, but our senses often deceive us." It is acknowledged that there is a difficulty in *comprehending* this, but there is no difficulty in *believing* it. The only question is, whether God has been willing to make this change? " It is like the voice of a single man, which all the audience hears entire." He exhorts heretics to yield to the truth, because, says he, " we are not now contending for victory, as in the schools, or for any temporal interest, as in the secular courts. In this dispute nothing less is depending than eternal life."[5]

When it was objected to Guimond, that the rats sometimes eat the consecrated bread, he replied, that either the senses were deceived, or the body of Christ did not suffer any more in the rat, than in the sepulchre, or that the devil put real bread into it, on which men and rats might feed.[6]

---

[1] Larroche, p. 183. (*P.*)

[2] See Basnage's *Histoire des Eglises Réformées*, II. p. 681, where this and other difficulties on the same subject are particularly considered. It is sufficient for my purpose to give a specimen of them. (*P.*)

[3] Larroche, p. 492. (*P.*)

[4] Basnage, II. p. 669. (*P.*) Canon I. is in these words: " Si quis negaverit, in sanctissimæ eucharistiæ sacramento contineri vere, realiter et substantialiter corpus et sanguinem una cum anima et divinitate Domini nostri Jesu Christi, ac proinde totum Christum, sed dixerit tantummodo esse in eo ut in signo, vel figura, aut virtute; anathema sit." Sess. xiii. C. viii. 8, Con. Trid. *Can. et Decret.* p. 75.

[5] Fleury. (*P.*) [A. D. 1075.]

[6] Basnage, I (b). p. 120. (*P.*)

The language in which some of the Popish priests have boasted of the power which this doctrine of transubstantiation gives them, would excite the greatest ridicule, if there was not a mixture of impiety with the absurdity of it. "On our altars," say some of them, "Jesus Christ obeys all the world. He obeys the priest, let him be where he will, at every hour, at his simple word. They carry him whither they please. He goes into the mouth of the wicked as well as of the righteous. He makes no resistance, he does not hesitate one moment."[1] Some priests boasted that they had even more power than the Blessed Virgin, because they could create their Creator whenever they pleased; whereas she had conceived him but once.[2]

So much is made to depend on the power and *will* of the priest, with respect to the eucharist, and the sacraments in general, in the Church of Rome, as, I should think, must occasion a good deal of anxiety on the part of those who receive them. For they believe that the efficacy of all the sacraments depends upon the *intention* of him that administers them. This is expressly determined in a decree of Pope Eugenius; and at the Council of Trent an anathema was pronounced on those who denied it. This is even "carried so far, that, in one of the rubrics of the Missal, it is given as a rule, that if a priest who goes to consecrate twelve *hosties*, should have a general intention to leave out one of them," it will affect them all.[3] Luther mentions some priests at Rome, who acknowledged that, instead of pronouncing the proper words of consecration, only said to themselves, *Bread thou art, and bread thou shalt remain.*[4]

All the disputes about the nature of the eucharistical elements were not confined to the Western church, in this period; for at the beginning of the thirteenth century the Greeks were much agitated about this subject; some affirming that the *mysteries*, as they called them, were incorruptible, while others maintained that they were not: when Zonaras, a Greek friar, happily found out a middle way, which showed no less ingenuity than had been displayed on the same subject by many of the monks or schoolmen in the West. The consecrated bread, he said, was the flesh of Christ, as dead, and therefore corruptible; but that after it was eaten, and thereby gone, as it were, into the sepulchre, it became incorruptible; because the body of our Lord did not remain long dead and buried, but rose again.[5]

The doctrine of transubstantiation was the cause of a great variety of new ceremonies and institutions in the Church of Rome. Hence, among other things, those rich and splendid receptacles which were formed for the residence of God, under this new shape, and the lamps and other precious ornaments that were designed to beautify this habitation of the Deity; and hence the custom of carrying about this divine bread in solemn pomp, through the public streets, when it is to be administered to sick and dying persons, with many other ceremonies of a like nature. But what crowns the whole was the *festival of the holy sacrament.*

This was an institution of Urban IV., in 1264, on the pretended revelation of one Juliana, a woman of Liege, who said that it was showed her from heaven, that this particular festival day of the holy eucharist had always been in the councils of the sovereign Trinity; but that now the time of revealing it to men was come. In the decree of Urban it is said, "this festival day properly belongs to the sacrament, because there is no saint but what has his proper festival; that this is intended to confound the unbelief and extravagance of heretics, and to repair all the faults that men might

---

[1] Basnage, I. p. 26. (*P.*)
[2] Ibid. I (b). p. 423. (*P.*)
[3] Burnet on the Articles, p. 370. (*P.*) Art. xxvi. Ed. 4, p. 272.
[4] Basnage, II. p. 687. (*P.*)

[5] Larroche, p. 494. (*P.*)

be guilty of in other masses."[1] This festival is attended with a procession, in which the host is carried in great pomp and magnificence. No less a person than Thomas Aquinas composed the office for this great solemnity.

Notwithstanding all this pomp and splendour, which seldom fail to have charms for the bulk of mankind, this decree of Urban was not universally observed; and therefore it was confirmed by another bull of Clement V. But when the minds of men were a little enlightened after the Reformation by Luther, this solemnity became the topic of much ridicule. On this account Catharine of Medicis wrote to the Pope in 1561, as Thuanus informs us, to request the abolition of this festival, because it was the occasion of much scandal, and was not at all necessary. It may not be amiss to give a more particular account of some of the other new superstitions mentioned above.

It was towards the end of the sixth century that the *elevation of the host* was first practised in the Eastern church; but then it was intended to represent the elevation of Christ upon the cross, and was made immediately before the communion; and there is no mention of this ceremony in the Western church before the eleventh century. But then it immediately followed the consecration, though no adoration is said to have been intended by this ceremony till the thirteenth century, when it was expressly appointed in the Constitutions of Honorius III. and Gregory IX.; the latter of whom, in 1227, ordered the ringing of a bell, to warn the people to fall down on their knees and adore the consecrated host.[2] This, however, seems to have been done before by Guy Paré, the Pope's legate, in Germany; who, when he was at Cologne, in 1201, ordered, that when the host was elevated in the celebration of the mass,

the people should prostrate themselves in the church at the sound of a bell.[3]

The ceremony of carrying the host in procession to communicate the sick seems to have been first used in this country. For, at the end of the twelfth century, Hubert, archbishop of Canterbury, and legate of Pope Celestine, held a synod at York, in which, among other things, he commanded that when any sick persons were to receive the communion, the priest himself should carry the host, clothed with his proper habits, and with lights borne before it, suitable to so great a sacrament.[4] We are also informed that, in the beginning of the thirteenth century, Odo, bishop of Paris, in one of his synods, made several Constitutions relating to the sacrament; as, about the manner of carrying it to the sick, of the adoration of the persons who should meet it, of keeping it in the best part of the altar, of locking it up safe; with several precautions in case it should happen that any part of the consecrated elements should fall to the ground, or any fly or spider should fall into the wine.[5]

Considering how solemn a thing the business of *communicating* was made, in consequence of the doctrine of transubstantiation, we do not wonder that it was ordered by the Council of Trent, that, how contrite soever a sinner should feel himself, he should not approach the holy eucharist without having made his *sacramental confession*, nor at the solemnity which the receiving of the communion gave to an oath. This appeared, when Pope Gregory VII. proposed to the emperor Henry, who was charged with many crimes, to exculpate himself, by taking one part of a consecrated host, while he himself should take the other. This proposal staggered the emperor so much, that he desired the affair to be referred to a general council.[6] But

Larroche, p. 581. (*P.*)
[2] Ibid. p. 102. (*P.*)

[3] Histoire des Papes, III. p. 131. (*P.*)
[4] Larroche, p. 483. (*P.*)
[5] Ibid. p. 484. (*P.*)
[6] Fleury, A. D. 1077. (*P.*)

we are more surprised that, upon any occasion whatever, any person should be permitted to *eat* before he received the communion; and yet, application being made to the Pope on the part of the king of France, in 1722, that he might take some nourishment before he received the communion, on the day of his consecration, as it was thought that he would not be able to go through the fatigue of the ceremony without it, the request was granted. It must be presumed, however, that no other than the Pope himself could have given so great a dispensation.[1]

It was owing to the great awfulness of the real masses, and the many ceremonies that were necessary to be observed in the celebration of them, that, for four or five hundred years, what are called *dry masses* (or the ceremonies of the mass without the consecration of the elements) were much used in the Church of Rome. They were more especially used by gentlemen who went a hunting early in the morning, or returned late, or when a new-married couple wanted to receive benediction, &c. St. Louis often used this ceremony on board his vessel, and it served for a consolation to pilgrims, when they had no opportunity of having real masses in their return from the Holy Land. These dry masses were so common at one time, that there was a rubric in the Romish ritual prepared for them. But the Reformation opening men's eyes upon the subject, Eckius confessed that what had been practised so long was, in truth, an impiety and blasphemy against God. The Council of Trent did not, however, correct the abuse; but the bishops since that time have abolished it by degrees, and now it is only used on Good Fridays, and during storms at sea.[2]

We see the farther progress of superstition in the various methods that were devised in order to prevent the waste or abuse of the consecrated elements, which increased after the doctrine of transubstantiation. In the tenth century the priests began to put the bread into the mouths of the communicants, and in the eleventh they began, in some churches, to use little hosts, like *wafers*, made round, white, and very thin; but this was not till after the condemnation of Berenger, and was disliked by many at that time; and the former custom of breaking the bread into little pieces, and also that of giving the bread steeped in the wine, were still used in many places, till near the end of the twelfth century, after which the use of thin wafers became universal.

At length, in order to leave the least room for waste or abuse possible, the custom of communicating the laity with the *bread only* was introduced; and the doctrine of transubstantiation made this practice much easier than it could otherwise have been. For it being now agreed that the consecrated bread was the *whole* body of Christ, it contained the blood of course; and consequently the wine, which was the blood only, became superfluous.

Thomas Aquinas defended the custom of communicating with the bread only, but he says that it was not observed in all churches; and the laity, in many places, in order to prevent the spilling of the wine, or, as they called it, the blood of Christ (against which they were always most particularly cautioned) sucked it through quills, or silver pipes, which were fastened to their chalices for that purpose. But at length, and especially from the custom of giving the bread steeped in the wine, came, by degrees, the custom of *communion in one kind only*, without any express authority for the purpose, in almost all the Western churches, till it was established by the Council of Constance, in 1415.[3] But the custom of communicating in both

[1] Hist. des Papes, V. p. 499. (*P.*)
[2] Basnage, II. p. 686. (*P.*)

[3] See *L'Enfant*, "Histoire du Concile," 1714, L. iii. Sect. xxx p 253. By the same decree, the sacrament was to be received, *fasting*, instead of *after supper*, unless in cases of necessity allowed by the church.

kinds was still practised in several places, and the Pope himself is said at one time to have administered the wine to the deacons and ministers of the altar, and to other persons of eminent piety, whom he thought worthy of so great a gift.

The Council of Trent confirmed that of Constance, but left it to the Pope to grant the use of the cup to those whom he should think proper. Accordingly Pius IV. granted the communion in both kinds to those who should demand it, provided they professed to believe as the church did in other respects.[1] The Bohemians also were allowed, with the Pope's consent, to make use of the cup.

The high reverence for the eucharist, which was produced by the doctrine of transubstantiation, made a change in the posture of receiving it. For, till the thirteenth century, all persons had communicated *standing*, but about that time the custom of receiving it *kneeling* came into use, and this is continued ever since in the Church of Rome, and from that in the Church of England. Frequent communion also was now no more to be expected; and, indeed, so early as the tenth century, Ratherius, bishop of Verona, was obliged to order his priests to warn believers to come four times a year to the communion;[2] and now the Catholics are not required to communicate more than once a year, and this is generally at Easter.

There are various other superstitious practices respecting the eucharist, in the Church of Rome, the origin of which it is not easy to trace. There are six several sorts of *vestments* belonging to the officiating priest, and eight or nine to the bishop, and there is not one of them but has some mysterious signification, and a corresponding separate consecration; not to mention the dif-

ferent *colours* of them, and the different occasions on which they are used; and they are all so necessary, that the smallest variation in the ritual makes the masses be deemed imperfect.

As I observed before, that two masses must not be celebrated on the same altar in the course of one day, and even a priest cannot officiate at any altar when a bishop has done it before him, they are now multiplied exceedingly. The masses also are reckoned defective, unless the altar be covered with three cloths, consecrated by the bishop, the last of which must be longer than the other; and it must, after all, be covered with a *stuff* of some particular colour, according to the festival on which it is used. But the altar must be stripped of all its ornaments on Good Friday, for reasons which may be seen in *Basnage* (I. p. 48), together with many other superstitious observances relating to the eucharist, which I do not think it worth while to recite.

In the eleventh century there arose violent debates between the Greek and Latin Churches on account of the former using *unleavened bread* in the celebration of the eucharist. Such, however, it is very evident, must have been the bread that our Saviour himself made use of in the institution, as there was no leaven to be had during the whole season of Passover; and at length the Latin Church conformed to this custom.

Considering the many gross abuses which prevailed with respect to the Lord's supper, after the time of Paschasius, it is no wonder that we meet with some persons who laid it aside altogether. This was the case with the *Paulicians* in the ninth century, who considered both baptism and the Lord's supper as something figurative and parabolical.[3] This was also the case with some persons in France, in the beginning of the eleventh century, and they were condemned at the synods of Orleans, and again at Arras,

[1] Histoire des Papes, IV. p. 679. (P.)
[2] Larroche, p. 137. (P.) In the Greek Church "the laics are obliged to receive the blessed sacrament four times a year." Smith's *Account*, p. 157.

[3] Mosheim, II. p. 176-178. (P.) Cent. ix. Pt. il. Ch. v. Sect. vi.

in 1025.[1] Also, in the twelfth century, one Tanchelin[2] persuaded the people of Antwerp, and other persons in Flanders, that receiving the Lord's supper was not necessary to salvation. But, indeed, this he might do, without wishing them to omit the celebration of it altogether.

As little can we wonder that unbelievers should take advantage of such a doctrine as this, to treat the Christian religion with contempt. Averroes, the great freethinker of his age, said that Judaism was the religion of children, and Mahometanism that of hogs; but he knew no sect so foolish and absurd as that of the Christians, who adored what they ate.[3]

SECTION IV.

OF THE RECOVERY OF THE GENUINE CHRISTIAN DOCTRINE CONCERNING THE LORD'S SUPPER.

As the corruption of this doctrine took place very early in the Christian church, and proceeded farther than any other, so it was with great difficulty rectified; and, indeed, it is in general but very imperfectly done to this day, especially in the established reformed churches. The minds of the reformers, in general, were impressed with an idea of something peculiarly mysterious and awful in the nature of the eucharist, as well as with a firm persuasion concerning the divinity of Christ.

Wickliffe was late in settling his notion about the Lord's supper; so

that, in different parts of his writings, he contradicts himself on this subject.[4] John Huss believed the doctrine of transubstantiation and the real presence; but in answer to a person who had said that a priest, after his consecration, was the *Father of God*, and the *creator of God's body*, he wrote a treatise to prove that Jesus Christ is the author of the transubstantiation, and the priest only the minister of it.[5]

It is remarkable, that with respect to most of the reformers from Popery, in the sixteenth century, the article of the eucharist was the last in which they gained any clear light, the doctrine of transubstantiation being that which they parted with, with peculiar reluctance, and in all public disputations their popish adversaries had more advantage with respect to this than to any other subject. They advanced to the conferences with the utmost boldness when this was to be the subject of their disputation, having the prejudices of their audience, and, in a great measure those that were their adversaries too, on their side.

Though Luther rejected transubstantiation, he nevertheless retained the doctrine of the *real presence* of the body of Christ in the eucharist; believing that even the body of Christ might be omnipresent, as well as his divinity; and in the Lutheran *Form of Concord*, which they made the terms of communion with them, this article was inserted. Luther, in his attempts to explain his doctrine on the subject of the eucharist, (which, to distinguish it from that of the Papists, he called

---

[1] Fleury. (*P.*)

[2] Or Tanquelinus. If the accounts of his enormities are true, he must have been insane. He was assassinated in 1125. See *Nouv. Dict. Hist.* V. p. 497. Mosheim says he was a mystic, but that probably "blasphemies were falsely charged upon him by a vindictive priesthood." *Cent.* xii. Pt. ii. Ch. v. Sect. ix.

[3] Memoires pour la Vie de Petrarch,'III. p. 760. (*P.*) Averroes was a native of *Cordova* in Spain, where he died in 1226. See *Nouv. Dict. Hist.* I. p. 259.

[4] Gilpin's Life of him, p. 65. (*P.*) Brit. Biog. I. pp. 38, 46.

[5] L'Enfant's History of the Council of Constance, I. p. 432. (*P.*) "Un certain prédicateur de Bohème avoit avancé, qu'un prêtre avant sa première messe n'étoit qu'enfant de Dieu, mais qu'après avoir officié il étoit Père de Dieu et Créateur du corps de Dieu. Jean Hus fit un Traité pour réfuter une proposition si étrange, quoiqu'elle ne fût pas nouvelle, et il soutint que c'est J. C. qui est l'Auteur de la *Transubstantiation*, et quele prêtre n'en est que le ministre, en vertu des paroles sacramentales." *Histoire* L. iii. Sect. liii. See also Sect. v. and L. ii. Sect. lxxiii. *Amst.* 1714, pp. 169, 201, 280.

M

consubstantiation,) said, that "as in a red-hot iron, two distinct substances, *iron* and *fire*, are united, so is the body of Christ joined with the bread in the eucharist."[1]   Some Lutherans maintained, "that all the properties of the divine nature, and consequently its omnipresence, were communicated to the human nature of Christ by the hypostatic union" between them.[2] But these were more rigid than Luther himself, and it is supposed that being convinced by the reasons of Melancthon, he would have entertained the opinion of the other reformers on this subject, if death had not prevented him.[3]   Carolstadt, Luther's colleague, maintained "that the bread and wine were no more than external *signs* or *symbols*, designed to excite in the minds of Christians the remembrance of the sufferings and death of the Divine Saviour, and of the benefits which arise from it."[4]

It is remarkable that Zuinglius was much more rational than Luther on this subject. For he, like Carolstadt, considered the bread and wine as no more than signs and symbols of the body and blood of Christ, and that we derive no benefit from the eucharist, except what arises from the recollection of the merits of Christ.[5] He "would not allow to the ministers of the church the power of excluding flagitious offenders from its communion," but left all punishment to the civil magistrate.[6] Upon the whole, Zuinglius seems to have thought as rationally on the subject of the eucharist as Socinus, who also considered it merely as a commemoration of the death of Christ.[7]

Calvin was much less rational. For he supposed that a certain divine virtue or efficacy was communicated by Christ, together with the bread and wine.[8] And he not only excluded vicious persons from communion, but likewise procured their banishment from the city.[9]

We have a remarkable example of the confidence of the Catholics on the subject of the eucharist, in the famous conference of Poissy, in 1561, held in the presence of Charles IX. and Catharine of Medicis, in the court of France, between a number of Popish and Protestant divines, of whom the cardinal of Lorraine was the principal on the side of the Catholics, and Beza on that of the Protestants. The cardinal, in his speech on this subject, says, "We must always oppose these words, *This is my body*, to all argumentation, judgments, and speculation of understanding, or human spirit. They will be fire and thunder to all consciences. . . . Let us believe the Lord, and obey him in all things and places; let us not contradict him, because what he tells us seems absurd, improper, and contrary to our senses and thoughts. Let his word overcome everything, and be unto us, as it is, the most precious thing. That it befits us to do everywhere, but especially in the holy mysteries. Let us not look only to the things we

---

[1] Mosheim, III. p. 331. (*P.*) Cent. xvi. Sect. i. Ch. ii. Sect xxi.   Note [z].
[2] Ibid. IV. p. 75. (*P.*) Cent. xvi. Sect. iii. Pt. ii. Ch. ii. Sect. x.
[3] Basnage, II. p. 331.   (*P.*)
[4] Mosheim, III. p. 331.   (*P.*) Cent. xvi. Sect i. Ch. ii. Sect. xxi.
[5] Ibid. IV. p. 76. (*P.*) *Nil esse in Cœna, quam memoriam Christi.* Cent. xvi. Sect. iii. Pt. ii. Ch. ii. Sect. x.   Note [n].
[6] Ibid. IV. p. 115. (*P.*) Cent. xvi. Sect. iii. Pt. ii. Ch. ii. Sect. xxxiii.
[7] Dr. Maclaine says, in a note to Mosheim, that "the sentiments of Zuingle were the same with those maintained by Bishop Hoadly, in his *Plain*

Account" Vol. III. p. 331. Cent. xvi Sect. i. Ch. ii. Sect. xxi. Note [a]. Yet Zuinglius, according to the writer of Ridley's Life, held the same opinion with that bishop, who "always believed and maintained a real presence by grace to faith, and not a mere figure only." (See *supra*, p. 40, Note [10].) He adds, "there were some English fanatics, such as John Webb, George Roper, and Gregory Paske, who believed that the sacrament was only a bare sign of Christ's body, and nothing more than a remembrance of it." These three *fanatics*, who were burned at Canterbury, at the same time, in Mary's reign, appear to have been better *scripturists* than Ridley, and to have anticipated Hoadly's *Plain Account*. The opposite views of these prelates of the same church discover how little the state can do to secure uniformity, when it quits its proper province and affects to establish religion. See the Life of Bishop Ridley, by Glocester Ridley, 1763, pp. 664, 665, and Clarke's *Martyrologie*, 1652, p. 159.

[8] Mosheim, p. 79.   (*P.*)   Cent. xvi. Sect. iii. Pt. ii. Ch. ii. Sect. xii.
[9] Ibid. p. 115.   (*P.*)   Ibid. xxxiii.

see, but let us observe his word; for his word is infallible, and cannot be false nor deceive us. On the contrary, our senses are easily imposed upon, and deceive us often. Since he said then, *This is my body,* let us not doubt of it, but believe, obey, and look upon him with the eyes of our understanding," &c.[1]

On most other subjects the Popish advocates rather declined the contest, but in this they thought they could triumph. This conference ended as all others in those days did, without giving any satisfaction to either party. The cardinal himself would have consented to an article on this subject sufficiently agreeable to the Lutheran doctrine, viz. That the *substance* of the body and blood of Christ is in the eucharist; but his brethren would not admit of it, thinking it captious and heretical.[2]

It is the doctrine both of the Church of England, and of the Establishment in Scotland, that some peculiar *divine virtue* is communicated with the eucharistical elements, when they are properly received, and therefore more preparation is enjoined for receiving this ordinance, than for attending public worship in general. In the twenty-fifth article of the Church of England it is said, that "sacraments ordained of Christ, be not only badges or tokens of Christian men's professions, but rather they be certain sure witnesses, and effectual signs of grace and God's will towards us, by the which he doth work invisibly in us, and doth not only quicken, but also strengthen and confirm our faith in him."

In the *Assembly's Shorter Catechism,* "a sacrament" is defined to be "an holy ordinance, instituted by Christ; wherein, by sensible signs, Christ and the benefit of the new covenant, are represented, sealed, and applied to believers. The Lord's supper" in particular is said to be "a sacrament, wherein, by giving and receiving bread and wine,

according to Christ's appointment, his death is shewed forth, and the worthy receivers are, not after a corporal and carnal manner, but by faith, made partakers of his body and blood, with all its benefits, to their spiritual nourishment, and growth in grace." Agreeably to these ideas, it is there said that, "it is required of them that would worthily partake of the Lord's supper, that they examine themselves, of their knowledge to discern the Lord's body, of their faith to feed upon him, of their repentance, love and new obedience, lest, coming unworthily, they eat and drink judgment to themselves."

This article of superstition has great hold on the minds of Dissenters in general, the Independents requiring before admission to communion, an account of what they call an *experience* in religion, or the evidence of a man's having had what they deem to be a miraculous *work of grace* upon his soul; so that they can have reason to think that he is one of the *elect,* and that he will not fall away. And on this account many Dissenters have *days of preparation* for receiving the Lord's supper,[3] and they do not consider any person to be properly qualified to administer either this ordinance, or baptism, till he has been regularly ordained, though they have no objection to his preaching all his life, if he pleases, without that ceremony, or to attending upon his ministry in all other respects.

It can also be from nothing but the remains of superstition, that the number of communicants, even among the most liberal of the Dissenters, is very small, seldom exceeding one in ten of the congregation; and very few as yet bring their children to communion. On this subject Mr. Pierce wrote a very valuable tract, which has led many persons to think favourably of the practice, as the only effectual method of securing the attendance of Christians in general, when they are grown up.[4]

---

[1] Laval's History of the Reformation in France, I. p. 536. (P.)
[2] Ibid. p. 588. (P.)

[3] See [Rutt's Priestley] Vol. II. p. 80.
[4] Ibid. p. 337, and Notes, and p. 338.

I would only advise the deferring of communion till the children be of a proper age to be brought to attend other parts of public worship, and till they can be made to join in the celebration with decency, so as to give no offence to others. This being a part of public worship, there cannot, I think, be any reason for making them communicate at an earlier age; and to make them do it at any period before it be properly an act of their own, will equally secure their attendance afterwards, which is the object to be aimed at. It is having had no particular fixed time for *beginning* to communicate, that has been the reason of its being so generally neglected as it has been with us. I flatter myself, however, that in due time, we shall think rationally on this, as well as on other subjects relating to Christianity, and that our practice will correspond with our sentiments.[1]

[1] In the "Address, on the Subject of giving the Lord's Supper to Children," published in 1773, Dr. Priestley, adopting the opinion of Mr. Pierce, declares himself "fully satisfied that *infant-communion*, as well as *infant-baptism*, was the most ancient custom in the Christian church." He admits, however, that there is no reference to such communion, in any writer before Cyprian. To that communion, according to Cyprian, infants, in the strictest sense of the term, were brought to partake, without waiting till they could be supposed "to join in the celebration." (See *supra*, p. 145, Notes.)

I know not of any Christian society who practise *infant-communion*, even with Dr. Priestley's qualifications, nor of any who now advocate his opinion, which seems, however, very just, that *infant-baptism* and *infant-communion* depend for their authority on the same arguments from Christian antiquity. The late Rev. Mr. Newton, an *Independent* Minister of Norwich, with whom I had the pleasure of an acquaintance, held the same opinion of *infant-communion* with Mr. Pierce and Dr. Priestley; but I am not aware that he ever wrote on the subject, or that his opinion was entertained by any individual or society in his religious connection. Mr. N. would, of course, lay no stress on the *Calvinistic* custom of requiring an *experience*.

PART VII.

THE HISTORY OF OPINIONS RELATING TO BAPTISM.

THE INTRODUCTION.

THE rite of *baptism* was perhaps first practised by John, whose commission from God, was to *baptize unto repentance* all who should profess themselves to be his disciples. Our Saviour himself was baptized, and probably all the apostles, who, by his directions, baptized others, even in his lifetime; and in his giving his commission to them, he commanded them to *baptize*, as well as *disciple*, all nations. Accordingly we find, in the book of Acts, that all who were converted to Christianity, Jews as well as Gentiles, were received into the Christian church by baptism; and at that time this rite appears to have been generally, though probably not always performed, by dipping the whole body in the water.

As this rite is usually called the *baptism of repentance*, it was probably intended to represent the purity of heart and life which was required of all who profess themselves to be Christians; and therefore a declaration of faith in Christ, and also of repentance, was always made by those who presented themselves to be baptized, at least, if it was required of them. Nothing more, therefore, seems to have been meant by baptism originally, than a solemn declaration of a man's being a Christian, and of his resolution to live as becomes one; and very far was it from being imagined, that there was any peculiar virtue in the rite itself.

It was considered as laying a man under obligation to a virtuous and holy life, as the profession of Christianity necessarily does, but not as of itself making any person holy.

It is certain that, in very early times, there is no particular mention made of any person being baptized by *sprinkling* only, or a partial application of water to the body; but as, on the other hand, the dipping of the whole body is not expressly prescribed,[1] and the *moral emblem* is the same, viz. that of *cleanness* or *purity*, produced by the use of water, we seem to be at liberty to apply the water either to the whole body, or to part of it, as circumstances shall make it convenient.[2] The Greek word βαπτιζω certainly does not always imply a dipping of the whole body in water. For it is applied to that kind of washing which the Pharisees required before eating. See Luke xi. 38; Mark vii. 4.[3] We read in the same evangelist of the baptism not only of cups, pots and

brazen vessels, but also of couches. Also, as in the Old Testament we often read of *sprinkling* with water, as Num. xix. 13, 18; Ezek. xxxvi. 25; and it is referred to in the New, Heb. ix. 19, where we read, " And Moses sprinkled both the book of the law, and all the people;" I think it most probable, that when great numbers were baptized at the same time, the water was applied in this manner, the practice being sufficiently familiar to Jews.

In the three first centuries, it was not uncommon to baptize persons at the hour of death, and in this case they certainly did not dip the whole body. Epiphanius speaks of a Jewish patriarch being baptized by a Christian, who was introduced in the disguise of a physician, on account of his being unwilling that his relations should know it; and the water was brought by a servant, as if it had been for some other purpose.[4] Whether the story be true or false, it equally shows that the minds of Christians in that age, were not shocked at the idea of baptizing in a manner which must have been nearly as it is now used, and that such was deemed a sufficient baptism. It is said, indeed, by some, that the Eunomians made this change in the rite of baptism; thinking it indecent to plunge persons over-head in water, and especially naked; and that "they therefore only uncovered them to the breast, and then poured water upon their heads."[5] But as the Eunomians were a branch of the Arians, it is not probable that the Catholics, as they were called, would adopt the custom from them. Besides, if the practice of *immersion* had always been thought absolutely necessary to baptism, it is not probable that the Christians of that age would have ever departed from it. As superstition increased, we shall have evidence enough, that they were more ready to *add* than to

---

[1] Doddridge inquires, in Lect. ccii. whether *immersion* " be an essential circumstance in baptism?" and resolves, that, "on the whole, that mode of baptism is evidently favoured by scripture examples, though not required by express precept." Yet, how can we better understand a precept of the scripture than by observing the "scripture examples"? Selden approves "the baptizing of children" as a rite which "succeeds circumcision;" yet, referring to the disuse of *immersion*, he says, " In England, of late years, I ever thought the parson baptized his own fingers rather than the child." Table Talk, *Baptism*.

[2] May not such a liberty be pleaded for several practices among Christians, which my author, in the preceding and following pages, has justly exposed; though they have not wanted very specious excuses of utility or convenience?

[3] See a Note *in loc.* added to the 4th edition of the *Improved Version*. Yet Hammond ("Annot. in Mark vii. 4") says, as quoted by Gale, that " the word signifies the washing of any part, as the hands, here, by way of immersion in water, as that is opposed to affusion, or pouring water upon them ;" and that " the *baptism* of cups, is putting into water, all over, rinsing them." *Reflections on Wall*, 1711, pp. 159, 162. See also Wall's *Defence*, pp. 109–113. Le Clerc's version is, " Ils ne mangent point non plus qu'ils n'aient plongé *leurs mains dans l'eau*." Nouv. Test. 1703. Mr. Wakefield says, " the Greek word βαπτιζω, which occurs not unfrequently in classic authors, universally signifies, as far as my observation has extended, *to dip entirely under water*." Plain and Short Account, p. 10. See a large enumeration of passages from the ancients, by Gale, *Reflections*, pp. 95–129.

[4] *Hær.* xxx. Opera, I. p. 128. (*P.*)
[5] See Jortin's Remarks, 1752, II. p. 282. (*P.*) Ed. 1805, II. p. 128.

diminish, with respect to everything that was of a ceremonial nature.

It has been much debated whether *infants* were considered as proper subjects for baptism in the primitive church.[1] Now, besides, that we are not able to trace the origin of infant baptism, and therefore are necessarily carried back into the age of the apostles for it, a controversy arose pretty early in the Christian church, which would naturally have led some persons to deny the antiquity of the practice, if they could; and considering the state of opinions and practices with respect to things of a similar nature, it is natural to suppose that the primitive Christians would baptize infants as well as adult persons.[2]

With respect to this subject, I cannot think that writers have attended so much as they ought to have done to the power of a master of a family (the *patria potestas*) in the East, and particularly have not considered how far his own character and profession usually affected his wife, his children, and his servants, and indeed everything that belonged to him. When the Ninevites repented, they made even their cattle to fast, and wear sackcloth, as well as themselves; not that they could consider their cattle as having any occasion to repent, but

they did it in order to express, in a stronger manner, their own humiliation and contrition. Jonah iii. 7, 8.

Agreeably to these prevailing ideas, though circumcision was a religious rite, instituted as a symbol of the covenant between God and the descendants of Abraham by Isaac and Jacob, yet, not only was Ishmael circumcised, but also all the slaves of Abraham, who had no interest whatever in the promises made to him. The application of this rite, therefore, to Ishmael, and to the slaves of Abraham, was no more than a necessary appendage to the circumcision of Abraham himself, as master of the family. It was *his own act* only, and therefore the consent of Ishmael or of the slaves cannot be supposed to have been in the least degree necessary. From the same fact we must also conclude that circumcision, as such, could not express any interest that the subjects of it had in the things signified by it; for then Ishmael and the slaves of Abraham would have had an equal interest in them.

There can be no doubt but that when the Jews in future ages made converts to their religion, they obliged every master of a family both to submit to this rite himself, and likewise to see that all his household, or all that depended upon him, did the same. For the same reason, whatever other rite had been enjoined them, and whatever it had expressed, the same people would, no doubt, have applied it in the same indiscriminate manner, to the master of the family, and to all his household. It was natural, therefore, for the apostles, and other Jews, on the institution of baptism, to apply it to infants, as well as to adults, as a token of the profession of Christianity by the master of the family only; and this they would do without considering it as a substitute for circumcision, and succeeding in the place of it, which it is never said to do in the Scriptures, though some have been led by some circumstances of resemblance in the

---

[1] See ... "View of the Chief Arguments for and against Infant Baptism." Doddridge, Lect. cciii.–ccv. Also Bishop Taylor's "Liberty of Prophesying," Sect. xviii. He there quotes the very extraordinary "testimony of a learned Pædo-baptist, *Ludovicus Vives*, who, in his annotations upon St. Austin, *De Civit. Dei*, L. i. C. xxvii. affirms *Neminem nisi adultum antiquitus solere baptizari*," No. xxv. *ad fin.* Ed. 2, p. 321. "Wall's History of Infant Baptism," (Ed. 3, 1720.) Gale's *Reflections* on Wall, 1711, and Wall's *Defence*, 1720, appear to contain all that can now be discovered as to the *mode* and *subject* of apostolic baptism. The reader will find much information respecting the arguments and authorities for the *immersion* of *Adults*, as the only Christian baptism, in *Wisowatius's* Note to the *Racovian Catechism*, in Mr. Rees's translation, pp. 253–257. Mr. Belsham, in his *Plea for Infant Baptism*, has given the argument from tradition all the force of which it is capable.

[2] The author's early and latest opinion upon this subject appears to have been, that "the baptism of children is to be considered as one part of a man's own profession of Christianity." See [Rutt's Priestley] Vol. II. p. 385, and Note.

two rites to imagine that this was the case. According to the general ideas, and the established custom of the Jews and other Asiatics, in similar cases, they would not have thought of adopting any other practice than that of infant baptism, without particular directions.

Accordingly, we find in the Scriptures, that the jailor, on professing his faith in Christ, was baptized, *he and all his,* Acts xvi. 33; and that Lydia was baptized and *all her household,* ver. 15.[1] Now it is certain that to a Jew these phrases would convey the idea of the children, at least, if not of the domestic slaves, having been baptized, as well as the head of the family. A Roman also could not have understood them to imply less than all who were subject to what was called the *patria potestas.*

It also appears to me to be very evident from ecclesiastical history, and the writings of the Christian fathers, that infant baptism was the uniform practice of the primitive Christians, and continued to be so till, along with other superstitious notions, they got the idea of the efficacy of baptism *as such* to wash away sins, and consequently of the peculiar safety of dying presently after they were baptized, before any fresh guilt could be con-

tracted. Now, an argument derived from the uniform practice of the primitive Christians cannot but be allowed to have considerable weight, as an evidence of its having been a practice of the apostolical times, and having the sanction of apostolical authority. It is from the evidence of tradition only, deduced from the uninterrupted practice of the Christian churches, that we now set apart not the seventh but the first day of the week, for the purpose of public worship. There is no express authority for this in the New Testament.

Tertullian, indeed, advises to defer baptism till persons be of age to be Christians, lest it should bring their sponsors into danger; alleging also, that their innocent age had no need to hasten to the remission of sins.[2] But he nowhere insinuates that infant baptism was not even the universal custom of his time, or that it had been an *innovation;* which, in pleading against it, he might naturally have been expected to insist upon. He was only offended at the too great readiness with which all persons were admitted to baptism, when some of them were afterwards a disgrace to their profession. He therefore advises to defer it *in all cases,* and in that of infants also.

If we trace the progress of this affair a little farther, we shall find that when, by the prevalence of the liberal sentiments of Christianity, more account was made of slaves, as being of the same species with their masters, and equally interested with them in the privileges and promises of the gospel, and especially when, in consequence of this, they acquired more civil rights, and were allowed to act for themselves more than they had done, they were considered as having religious interests of their own.[3] Indeed, in the time of the Romans, slaves, being of different nations, were allowed (agreeably to the

---

[1] See [Rutt's Priestley] Vol. II. p. 334. Yet it is thus argued, on the other side. " By *whole families,* in scripture, is meant all persons of reason and age within the family; for it is said of the Ruler at Capernaum, (John iv.) that *he believed and all his house.*" Lib. of Proph. Sect. xviii. No. xxiv. p. 319. "It is certain the word *house* or *household* is often used where none are meant but such as are come to years of understanding. For example, John iv. 53, *Himself believed and his whole house;* Acts xviii. 8, *Crispus ...believed on the Lord with all his house.* Of the three examples of households baptized, it is expressly said of the one (the jailor's), that Paul and Silas ' spake the word of the Lord to him, and to *all that were in his house.*' If all the families in Great Britain were obliged to take an oath of allegiance, any man who should hereafter read our history, would make a very wrong inference if he should, merely from the word *families* or *households,* conclude this oath was administered to children." *Plain Account* of Baptism, in Letters to Bishop Hoadly, 1758, Ed. 2, 1766, pp. 99, 100. See also Wakefield's " Plain and Short Account," p. 24.

[2] *De Baptismo,* Sect. xviii. Opera, p. 231. (*P.*)
[3] See [Rutt's Priestley] Vol. II. p. 334, and Note.

genius of the pagan system) to practise some of their peculiar religious rites; and a great many of the first Christian converts were slaves; their masters, at that time, not finding themselves or their interest affected by it, and therefore not taking any umbrage at it.

It happened, also, that the power of a father over his children was much less in these Northern nations of Europe, than it was in the East, or among the Romans, with whom, likewise, it sensibly declined. On this account, and also because, from the very first promulgation of Christianity, it could not but be manifest, that persons were interested in it, as *individuals*, and not as members of families, or societies, I make no doubt but that, in general, if there were adult children or slaves in a family, at the time that the master professed himself a Christian, they were not baptized without their own consent; but no consideration, that can be supposed to have occurred either to Jews or Romans, could have led them to make the same exception in favour of infants.

Considering how very different are the ideas and customs of these times, and these parts of the world, from those which prevailed among the Jews, when baptism was instituted, the peculiar reasons for applying it to infants have, in a great measure, ceased. But still, as the practice is of apostolical authority,[1] it appears to me that no innovation ought to be made in it by any power whatever; but that we ought rather to preserve those ideas which originally gave a propriety to it, especially when there is nothing unnatural in them. For my own part, I endeavour to adhere to the primitive ideas above mentioned, and therefore I consider the baptizing of my children, not as directly implying that they have any interest in it, or in the things signified by it, but as a part of my own profession of Christianity, and consequently as an obligation which, as

[1] This question must, at least, be regarded as still *sub judice.*

such, I am under, to educate my children, and also to instruct my servants, in the principles of the Christian religion. In this view of the ordinance of baptism, infants are indirectly interested in it, whether they adhere to the professions of Christianity, and thereby secure the blessings of it when they become adults, so as to think and act for themselves, or not.

It is possible that, at this time, and in these parts of the world, we may not see so much reason for any *positive institutions;* but with the Jews, and indeed throughout all the East, nothing is more common than to express sentiments and purposes by appropriated actions. Now, washing with water so naturally expresses purity of heart, and is a thing so agreeable in itself, especially in hot countries, we cannot wonder it should be made choice of to denote the profession of a religion which brings men under the strictest obligations to repent and reform their lives; and particularly that John the Baptist, whose immediate business it was to preach repentance, should be directed to enjoin it.

Whether baptism be of earlier antiquity than John the Baptist, I have not been able to satisfy myself. Maimonides and the earliest Jewish writers speak of solemn baptism as a necessary attendant on circumcision, whenever any new converts were made to their religion, and also as a practice that was immemorial among them. But whether it was tacitly implied in the original institution of circumcision, or whether it had been adopted afterwards, as naturally expressive of the new converts cleansing themselves from the impurities of their former state of Heathenism, it was probably the custom of the Jews in the time of our Saviour.

If this was the case, and the Jews did both circumcise and baptize all that were capable of it, when families were converted to their religion, there was both the less reason for explaining the nature and the use of the rite on the first mention of it, or for describing more particularly than has been done, who were the proper subjects of baptism. And we may rather suppose that our Lord would have expressly restricted the application of it to adult persons, if he had intended that the prevailing custom should be altered. Consequently, when a master of a family was converted to Christianity, he would, of course, be required to baptize all his household, and consider himself as bound to instruct them in the principles of the religion that he professed.

If any controversy was ever calculated to bring a fact of this nature to light, it was that of Pelagius and Austin about original sin, in which the latter maintained, that baptism was necessary to wash it away, the second spiritual birth counteracting the effects of the first carnal birth. Now the utmost that Pelagius appears to have replied on this subject was, that infant baptism was not necessary. But he did not pretend to say that the practice was not then universal, or that it had not always been so. Nay, Austin says that it was agreed between him and his opponent, that infants ought to be baptized, and that they differed only about the reason why they were to be baptized.[1]

We also find no trace of its being thought that the baptism of either the master of a family, or of his household, on their first profession of Christianity, might suffice for their descendants; and though the Jews did not repeat that baptism which accompanied circumcision, yet the circumcision itself was repeated on every male, so that if the Christians in the primitive times had been influenced by any *analogies* between the Jewish religion and their own, they would rather have been led to repeat the rite of baptism with respect to their children, than to discontinue it.

Lastly, I am not able to interpret 1 Cor. vii. 14, " The unbelieving hus-

band is sanctified by the wife, ... else were your children unclean, but now are they holy," more naturally than by supposing that, as by *holy* the Jews meant *devoted to God*, so by *a child being holy*, they meant that it had a right to the ceremonies of their holy religion. As therefore a child born of one Jewish parent had a right to circumcision, so a child born of one Christian parent had a right to baptism. Indeed, I do not see what other rational meaning can be assigned to the *holiness of a child*.[2]

It is remarkable that the Christians in Abyssinia repeat their baptism annually, on the festival of Epiphany.[3]

SECTION I.

OF THE OPINIONS AND PRACTICES OF THE
CHRISTIANS RELATING TO BAPTISM, TILL
THE REFORMATION.

THERE is this difference with respect to the corruptions of the rite of baptism,

[1] *De Verbis Apostoli Sermo*, xiii. Opera, X. p. 318. (*P.*)

[2] After a large exposition of this passage, Mr. Wakefield says, " If baptism made children *holy*, the fears of the Corinthians were needless..because *then*, whoever their parents might be, they would soon become holy through baptism : so that we must not conclude the holiness of such children to be the consequence of baptism, but of something else, and that is, if we may take St. Paul's word for it, the being born of Christian parents." *Plain and Short Account*, pp. 54–64.

Le Clerc says on the passage, " Ces expressions sont tirées de l'usage des Juifs, qui nommoient ceux de leur religion *saints ; c'est-à-dire consacrez* à Dieu ; et les autres *impurs* et *souillez*. Ceux qui étoient nez d'un Juif et d'une Greque, passoient pour Juifs d'extraction, comme si leur père et leur mère avoient été Juifs ; et il en étoit de même de ceux qui étoient d'un père Grec et d'une femme Juive, comme Timothée ; pourvû néanmoins que ces enfans embrassassent la religion Judaïque." *Nouv. Test.* p. 143. See also Gale s *Reflections*, pp. 513, 540.

[3] Geddes's *Church History of Ethiopia*, 1696, p. 33. (*P.*) " They are said to have divers forms of baptism, viz. I baptize thee in the Holy Spirit ; I baptize thee in the water of Jordan ; Let God baptize thee ; Come thou to baptism. They circumcise both males and females, and all are baptized every year, on the feast of *Epiphany*. They hold that men derive their souls, no less than their bodies, from their parents ; and that the children of Christian parents, and especially of a Christian mother, are saved, notwithstanding they die without baptism."

and those of the Lord's supper, that though they both began about the same time, those relating to baptism were perhaps the earlier of the two, and the progress of superstition, in consequence of this corruption, was rather more rapid in the first century of Christianity, it was by no mean so afterwards. For after the time of those who are more properly called *fathers*, we find no material alteration in the rite of baptism itself (though the business of *confirmation* grew out of it) whereas, we have seen that the most material additions were made to the doctrine of the eucharist, so late as the ninth century.

In the age immediately following that of the apostles, we find that *baptism* and *regeneration* were used as synonymous terms; and whereas, originally, the pardon of sin was supposed to be the consequence of that reformation of life which was only *promised* at baptism, it was now imagined that there was something in the *rite itself*, to which that grace was annexed; and in general it seems to have been imagined that this *sanctifying virtue* was in the *water*, and in no other part of the ordinance as administered by the priest.

Tertullian says, that the Holy Spirit was always given in baptism; and yet he expressly denied that it was bestowed by the laying on of hands. This writer says farther, that the Spirit of God descends upon the water of baptism, like a dove. Cyprian adds, that the adorable Trinity is ineffably in baptism. Paulinus says, that the water conceives and contains God; Chrysostom, that the water ceases to be what it was before, and is not fit for drinking, but is proper for sanctifying. He says that the Christian baptism is superior to that of John, in that his was the *baptism of repentance*, but had not the power of *forgiving sin*.[1] And Austin adds, that it touches the body and purifies the heart.[2]

Christians having now got the idea that baptism washed away sin, a field was opened for much seducing eloquence on the subject, which could not fail to confirm and increase the prevailing superstition. Chrysostom, speaking of baptism, says, "When you are come to the bed of the Holy Spirit, to the portico of grace, to the dreadful and desirable bath, throw yourselves upon the ground, as prisoners before a king."[3]

Superstitious practices, similar to those which followed the corruption of the doctrine of the eucharist, did not fail to accompany this undue reverence for the water of baptism. We find that in the third century the noviciates returned from baptism adorned with crowns, and clothed with white garments, in token of their victory over sin and the world. If they scrupled eating before they received the eucharist, they made a great scruple of washing after baptism. They would not do it till the end of the week; and immediately after baptism they wiped the bodies of the catechumens lest a drop of the sacramental water should fall to the ground. They went to church on the Sunday to put off their white garments, and to receive what was called the *ablution*.

It was even believed that a miracle was wrought on the water that was drawn on the day of Epiphany, because Jesus Christ had been baptized at that time. They carried it with respect, to their houses, after it had been consecrated; it was kept with care, and Chrysostom said that it would keep sweet many years.[4] This water was even given instead of the eucharist, to penitents who were not entirely reconciled to the church; and Austin says, the catechumens among other means are sanctified by it. "The water," he says, "is holy, though it be not the body of Christ. It is more holy than the other aliments, because it is a sacrament." He says, at the same time, that the catechumens are

[1] *Hom.* xxiv. Opera, I. p. 312. (*P.*)
[2] Basnage, *Histoire*, I. p. 138. (*P.*)
[3] Ibid. p. 139. (*P.*)
[4] *Hom.* xxiv. Opera, I. p. 311. (*P.*)

sanctified by the sign of the cross, and by the imposition of hands, which had also been made appendages of baptism at that time.[1] It appears by a passage in Austin, that the African Christians usually called baptism *salvation*, and the eucharist *life*, preferring the former to the latter.

When once it was imagined that a person newly baptized was cleansed from all sin, it is no wonder that many persons deferred this sanctifying rite as long as possible, even till they apprehended that they were at the point of death. We find cases of this kind at the beginning of the third century. Constantine the Great was not baptized till he was at the last gasp, and in this he was followed by his son Constantius; and two of his other sons, Constantine and Constans, were killed before they were baptized.

When baptism was administered to persons near the point of death, the patient must generally have been in bed, and consequently the ceremony could not have been performed by *immersion;* and it appears in the history of Novatian, that this was actually the case. On these occasions, the *unction*, and other ceremonies which had been added to the simple rite of baptism, were omitted; but they were performed afterwards, if the sick person recovered. We even find that, rather than omit baptism entirely, it was usual to baptize persons who were actually dead. Epiphanius, Chrysostom, and Theodoret, observe, that this custom prevailed in some places in their time.[2]

After the age of Justin Martyr, we find many additions made to the rite of baptism. It was then the custom to give the person baptized milk and honey, and to abstain from washing, all the remainder of the day, for which Tertullian says they had no authority from the Scripture, but only from tradition. They also added unc-

tion, and the *imposition of hands;* the unction, probably, referring, in a symbolical manner, to their preparation for a spiritual combat; and in applying the oil the priest touched the head or the forehead in the form of a cross. Tertullian is the first who mentions the *signing with the sign of the cross*, but only as used in private, and not in public worship; and he particularly describes the custom of baptizing, without mentioning it. Indeed, it does not appear to have been used in baptism till the latter end of the fourth or fifth century; but then we find great virtue ascribed to it. Lactantius, who lived in the beginning of the fourth century, says, the devil cannot approach those who have the heavenly mark of the cross upon them, as an impregnable fortress to defend them;[3] but he does not say it was used in baptism.

After the Council of Nice, Christians added to baptism the ceremonies of *exorcism*, and adjurations, to make evil spirits depart from the persons to be baptized. They made several signings with the cross, they used to light candles, they gave salt to the baptized person to taste, and the priest touched his mouth and ears with spittle, and also blew and spit upon his face.[4] At that time also baptized persons were made to wear white garments till the Sunday following, as was mentioned above. They had also various other ceremonies, some of which are now abolished, though others of them remain in the Church of Rome to this day. Blowing in the face, putting salt in the mouth, giving milk and honey, and also kissing the baptized persons, and making them abstain for some time from wine, are now no longer in use. The reason of these ceremonies may be pretty easily conceived. I

---

[1] *De Peccatorum Meritis.* L. iv. C. xxvi. Opera, VII. p. 711. (*P.*)

[2] Busnage, *Histoire*, I. p. 187. (*P.*)

[3] Inst. L. iv. C. xxvii. p. 439. (*P.*) "Quanto terrori sit dæmonibus hoc signum sciet, qui viderit quatenus adjurati per Christum de corporibus, quæ obsederint, fugiant." *De Mirandis per Crucis Virtutem effectis, ac de Dæmonibus.* Op. I. 345.

[4] See *Hist. of Pop.* 1785, I. p. 114.

shall, therefore, only observe, that the *salt* was used as a symbol of purity and wisdom; and that exorcism took its rise from the Platonic notion that evil demons hovered over human souls, seducing them to sin.

In a decree of the Council of Laodicea, held in the year 364, mention is made of *two anointings*, one with simple oil before baptism, and the other with ointment (μυρῳ) after baptism; and it is there expressed that the first unction was for the participation of the Holy Spirit, that the water was a symbol of death, and that the ointment, which was applied with the sign of the cross, was for the seal of the covenant.[1] This latter unction we shall find was afterwards reserved for the bishops, and became the subject of a distinct sacrament in the Church of Rome, called *confirmation*.

Originally the bishop only, or the priests by his permission, administered baptism as, with his leave, they also performed any other of his functions; but it appears from Tertullian that, in his time, laymen had, in some cases, the power of baptizing. This baptism, however, we may be assured, required the confirmation of the bishop, and would not be allowed but in case of necessity, as at the seeming approach of death, &c. At a synod at Elvira, in 306, it was allowed that a layman, provided he had not been married a second time, might baptize catechumens in case of necessity; but it was ordered that, if they survived, they should be brought to the bishop for the imposition of hands. Afterwards, when the bounds of the church were much enlarged, the business of baptizing was left almost entirely to the priests, or the country bishops, and the bishops of great sees only *confirmed* afterwards.

Great doubts were raised in early times about the validity of baptism as administered by heretics. Tertullian, before he became a Montanist, wrote a treatise to prove that here-

[1] Sueur, A. D. 364. (P.)

tics, not having the same God, or the same Christ, with the orthodox, their baptism was not valid. Cyprian called a synod at Carthage, in which it was determined, that no baptism was valid out of the Catholic church, and therefore, that those who had been heretics should be re-baptized. But Stephen, the bishop of Rome, did not approve of this decision, and by degrees his opinion, which continued to be that of the Church of Rome, became everywhere prevalent. Indeed, when so much stress was laid on baptism itself, it would have introduced endless anxiety if much doubt had remained about the power of administering it.

Having given this account of the corruption of the doctrine of baptism, and the principal abuses and superstitions with respect to the practice of it, I shall go over what farther relates to the subject, according to the order of administration.

When Christians, from a fondness for the rites and ceremonies of Paganism, and a desire to engage the respect of their heathen acquaintance for the religion which they had embraced, began to adopt some of the maxims and rites of their old religion, they seem to have been more particularly struck with what related to the *mysteries*, or the more secret rites of the pagan religion, to which only few persons were admitted, and those under a solemn oath of secrecy. In consequence of this disposition, both the positive institutions of Christianity, *baptism* and the *Lord's supper*, were converted into mysteries, Christians affecting great secrecy with respect to the mode of administering them, and no person could then be admitted to attend the whole of the public worship before he was baptized; but all who were classed with the *catechumens* were dismissed before the celebration of the eucharist, which closed the service.

Farther, those who were admitted to the heathen mysteries had certain *signs* or *symbols* delivered to them, by which they might know each other, so that by declaring them they might be admitted into any temple, and to the secret worship and rites of that god whose symbols they had received. In imitation of this, it occurred to the Christians to make a similar use of the *Apostles' Creed,* or that short declaration of faith which it had been usual to require of persons before they were baptized. This creed, therefore, (which does not appear to have been published, and indeed was altered from time to time, as particular heresies arose in the church,) they now began to call a *symbol,* affecting to conceal it from the Pagans, and not revealing it even to the catechumens themselves, except just before they were baptized; and then it was delivered to them as a symbol by which they were to know one another.

Cyprian says, "that *the sacrament of faith,* that is *the creed,* was not to be profaned or divulged," for which he cites two texts of scripture, the one, Proverbs xxiii. 9, "Speak not in the ears of a fool, for he will despise the wisdom of thy words;" and the cther, Matt. vii. 6, "Give not that which is holy unto the dogs, neither cast ye your pearls before swine," &c. Ambrose most pathetically exhorts to the utmost vigilancy, to conceal the Christian mysteries, and in particular to be very "careful not by incautiousness to reveal the secrets of the *Creed,* or the *Lord's Prayer.*"[1] This last appears very extraordinary, as the Lord's Prayer is contained in the gospels, where it might be seen by any person.

In the second century, baptism was performed publicly only twice in the year, viz. on Easter and Whit-Sunday. In the same age, *sponsors* or *godfathers* were introduced to answer for adult persons, "though they were afterwards admitted also in the baptism of infants."[2] This, Mr. Daillé says, was not done till the fourth century.

It should seem, from the Acts of the Apostles, that it was sufficient to the ceremony of baptism to say, *I baptize into the name of Jesus Christ.* But we soon find that the form of words used, Matt. xxviii. 19, was strictly adhered to, at least in the third century, viz. *I baptize thee in the name of the Father, the Son, and the Holy Ghost.* It appears, however, that at the time of Justin Martyr, they did not always confine themselves to these particular words, but sometimes added others by way of explanation. For though these precise words occur in one account of baptism by this writer, in another he speaks of baptism, "Into the name of Jesus Christ, who was crucified by Pontius Pilate, and into the name of the Holy Spirit, who foretold by the holy prophets everything relating to Christ."[3] But perhaps this explanation might be only intended for the use of his readers, and not given by him as a form of words that was used in the administration of baptism itself.

We find very little mention made of baptism, from the time of those who were generally called *fathers,* that is, from the age of Austin to the Reformation. Indeed I have hardly met with anything on the subject worth reciting.

It soon became a maxim, that as baptism was a sacrament that was to be used only *once,* it was exceedingly wrong to *re-baptize* any person; and it is pleasant to observe the precaution that Pope Boniface hit upon to prevent this in dubious cases. In his statutes or instructions he says, "They whose baptism is dubious, ought without scruple to be baptized, with this protestation, *I do not re-baptize thee, but if thou art not baptized, I baptize thee,*" &c. This is the first example that I have found of *conditional baptism.*[4]

From the earliest account of the ordinance, we find that children received the Lord's supper, and that baptism

[1] History of the Apostles' Creed, Ed. 5, p. 20. (*P.*)
[2] Mosheim, I. p. 172. (*P.*) Cont. ii. Pt. ii. Ch. iv. Sect. xiv.
[3] Edit. Thirlby, pp. 89, 91. (*P.*)
[4] Jortin's Remarks, IV. p. 462. (*P.*)

always preceded communion. In a book of divine offices, written, as some think, in the eleventh century, it is ordained that care be taken that young children receive no food after baptism, and that they do not even give them suck without necessity, till after they have participated of the body of Christ.[1]

SECTION II.

THE STATE OF OPINIONS CONCERNING BAPTISM, SINCE THE REFORMATION.

It is remarkable that, though the Waldenses always practised infant baptism,[2] many of the Albigenses, if not all of them, held that baptism ought to be confined to adults.[3] This was the opinion of the Petrobrussians,[4] and also of Berenger.[5]

Wickliffe thought baptism to be necessary to salvation. "The priest," he says, "in baptism administers only the token or sign; but God, who is the priest and bishop of our souls, administers the spiritual grace."[6] And Luther not only retained the rite of baptism, but even the ceremony of *exorcism.* At least, this was retained in the greatest part of the Lutheran churches.[7]

It appeared, however, presently after the Reformation by Luther, that great numbers had been well prepared to follow him, and even to go farther than he did. Very many had been so much scandalized with the abuses of baptism, and the Lord's supper especially, as to reject them, either in whole, or in part. The baptism of infants was very generally thought to be irrational, and therefore it was administered only to adults. Most of those who rejected the doctrine of the divinity of Christ were of this persuasion, as was Socinus himself. Indeed, he and some others thought that the rite of baptism was only to be used when persons were converted to Christianity from some other religion, and was not to be applied to any who were born of Christian parents.[8] It does not appear, however, that those who held this opinion ever formed a separate sect, or that their numbers were considerable;[9] but those who rejected infant baptism were then, and still are, very numerous.

It happened that many of those who held this opinion entertained some very wild notions, especially that of the reign of Christ, or of the saints, upon earth, independent of any secular power; and they made an attempt to set up a monarchy of this kind at Munster in Westphalia, which they seized upon for that

---

[1] Larroche, p. 129. (*P.*) Smith says that in the Greek Church "they give the eucharist...to new-born infants, after they have been christened, in case of imminent danger of death." *Account,* p. 161.

[2] Leger, *Histoire,* p. 65. (*P.*)

[3] They said, according to Limborch, "that the baptism of water, made by the church, was of no avail to children; because they were so far from consenting to it, that they wept." *Hist. of Inquis.* I. p. 44. Mr. Wall says of the Albigenses, that "as France was the first country in Christendom where dipping of children in baptism was left off, so there, first anti-pædobaptism began." *Hist. of Inf. Bap.* Ed. 3, II. p. 220.

[4] Basnage, *Histoire,* I [b]. p. 140. (*P.*) The *Petrobrussians* were named from Peter de *Bruys,* a native of Dauphiny, who was burnt in 1147. *Nouv. Dict. Hist.* I. p. 524. According to Mr. Wall, he held that the Lord's supper "is no more to be administered since Christ's time." *Hist.* II. p. 235.

[5] Fleury, A. D. 1050. (*P.*)

[6] Gilpin's Life of him, p. 64. (*P.*) "He opposed the superstition of three immersions; and, in case of necessity, he thought any one present might baptize." *Brit. Biog.* I. p. 46.

[7] Mosheim, IV. p. 53. (*P.*) Cent. xvi. Sect. iii. Pt. ii. Ch. i. Sect. xliii. Note [1].

[8] "De aquæ baptismo ego ita sentio, cum ecclesiæ in perpetuum præscriptum non fuisse, nec unquam, ut illum acciperent, iis præceptum neque a Christo, neque ab Apostolis fuisse, qui jam ipsi Christo alia quacunque ratione publice nomen dedissent, vel a primis annis in christiana disciplina educati atque instituti essent." *De Ecclesia,* Socini Opera, I. pp. 350, 351. See also *De Baptismo Aquæ Disputatio,* ibid. p. 709, and Toulmin's *Socinus,* pp. 251, 325. Emlyn and Wakefield have adopted the same opinion. See [Rutt's Priestley] Vol. II. p. 335, Note *ad fin.*

[9] There is, probably, an increasing number, at least among Unitarians, who consider *baptism* as having no place among professing Christians, such as have already made the profession for which alone the rite of baptism appears to have been instituted. Of the different opinions on baptism now maintained by Unitarians in Great Britain, Mr. Rees has given a succinct and accurate account, in *Racov. Cat.* p. 257, Note.

purpose, in the year 1534. But an end was soon put to this delusion, and an odium very unjustly remained upon all those who retained nothing but their doctrine concerning baptism. At present, those who are called *Baptists* are as peaceable as any other Christians. In Holland they are called *Mennonites*, from Menno, a very considerable person among them; and these have adopted the pacific principles of the Quakers in England. In this country the Baptists are very numerous. The greatest part of them are called *Particular Baptists*, from their holding the doctrine of particular election; but there are a few societies of them who are called *General Baptists*, from their holding the doctrine of general redemption.

The Church of England retains the baptism of infants, and also the use of the sign of the cross, and of godfathers. It also admits of baptism by women, a practice derived " from the opinion of the indispensable necessity of baptism to salvation. We have that regard to such a common practice," says Bishop Burnet, " as not to annul it, though we condemn it."[1] And indeed it is the language of the public forms of the Church of England, that baptism is necessary to salvation. In the Thirty-nine Articles we find the doctrine of an invisible work of God accompanying baptism, as well as the Lord's supper;[2] and in the Church Catechism it is said, that by baptism a person becomes *a child of God, and an inheritor of the kingdom of heaven.*

The doctrine of the Church of Scotland is of a piece with this. For baptism is said, in their *Confession of Faith,*

(C. xxviii.) to be " a sign and seal of the covenant of grace," of a person's " ingrafting into Christ, of regeneration, of remission of sins," &c. But " the efficacy of baptism " is there said not to be " tied to that moment of time wherein it is administered; yet notwithstanding, by the right use of this ordinance, the grace promised is not only offered, but really exhibited and conferred, by the Holy Ghost, to such, whether of age or infants, as that grace belongeth unto, according to the counsel of God's own will, in his appointed time."

The Dissenters of the Calvinistic persuasion in England may possibly retain the opinion of some spiritual grace accompanying baptism, though I rather think it is not at present held by them. Nothing, however, of it is retained by those who are called *rational Dissenters*. They consider the baptism of adult persons as the mode of taking upon them the Christian profession; and that when it is applied to infants, an obligation is acknowledged by the parents to educate their children in the principles of the Christian religion. Many of them lay so little stress upon it, that I imagine they would make no great difficulty of deferring it to adult age, or indeed of omitting it entirely in Christian families; but they do not think it of importance enough to make any new sect in the Christian church on account of it, or to act otherwise than their ancestors have done before them, in a matter of so great indifference.[3] The Quakers make no use either of this rite, or of the Lord's supper.[4]

---

[1] *Expos.* Art. xxiii. *ad fin.* Ed. 4, p. 238.
[2] " Sacraments.. be certain sure witnesses and effectual signs of grace and God's will towards us, by the which he doth work invisibly in us." Art. xxv.

[3] Such *indifferents*, following the practice of their ancestors without *their* convictions of duty, deserved my author's censure, which no Christian had a better right to inflict.
[4] See Barclay's *Apology*, Prop. xii. xiii.

AN

APPENDIX TO PARTS VI. AND VII.

CONTAINING

THE HISTORY OF THE OTHER SACRAMENTS BESIDES BAPTISM AND THE LORD'S SUPPER.

AFTER it was imagined that there was some *divine virtue* accompanying the administration of baptism and the Lord's supper, and these two rites had obtained the name of *sacraments*, which only priests regularly ordained had the power of administering with effect; other things, by degrees, obtained the same name, some spiritual grace being supposed to accompany them; and this contributed to extend the power and enlarge the province of the priesthood. At length *five* other ceremonies, besides baptism and the Lord's supper, came to be ranked in the same class with them.

Peter Lombard, in the twelfth century, is the first who mentions *seven sacraments*. It is supposed that, from the expression of the *seven spirits of God*, in the book of the Revelation, there came to be a notion of the sevenfold operation of the Spirit. But whether this was the true origin of *seven* sacraments, in preference to any other number, or whether it was used as an argument in support of an opinion already formed, I have not found; nor indeed is the matter of importance enough to make much inquiry about it. Eugenius is the first pope who mentions these seven sacraments, in his *Instructions to the Armenians*, which is published along with the decrees of the Council of Florence; and the whole doctrine concerning them was finally settled by the Council of Trent.[1]

The five additional sacraments are, *confirmation, penance, holy orders, matrimony*, and *extreme unction.* It is, however, with great difficulty that the Papists bring all these things within the description of a *sacrament;* as they say that, in order to constitute one, there must be some *matter*, corresponding to water in baptism, and bread and wine in the Lord's supper (which were a pattern for the rest), and also a *set form of words*, corresponding to *I baptize thee in the name of the Father*, &c. for baptism, and to the words, *This is my body*, for the Lord's supper. The *inward and spiritual grace* was some divine influence which they supposed to follow the due application of this matter of the sacraments, and the proper words accompanying the administration of them.

I shall give a general account of all these different sacraments, though the subjects of some of them will be treated more fully in other places of this work.

From the *second unction*, which was originally an appendage to the rite of baptism, another distinct sacrament was made, and called *confirmation.*

The Church of Rome, in the time of Pope Sylvester, had two unctions of *chrism* (a composition of olive oil and balm, *opobalsamum*), one on the breast, by the priest, and the other on the

novæ legis non fuisse omnia a Jesu Christo, Domino nostro, instituta, aut esse plura vel pauciora quam septem, videlicet, Baptismum, Confirmationem, Eucharistiam, Pœnitentiam, Extremam Unctionem, Ordinem et Matrimonium, aut etiam aliquod horum septem non esse vere et proprie sacramentum; anathema sit." Sess. vii. *De Sacramentis.* Can. i. Con. Trid. *Can. et Decret.* p. 46.

[1] Burnet on the Articles, p. 335. (*P.*) Art. xxv. Ed. 4, p. 246. The following is the decision given at *Trent* in 1547: "Si quis dixerit sacramenta

forehead, by the bishop. But, from the time of Gregory I., the priests had been allowed to anoint on the forehead; and Honoré, of Autun, a writer of the twelfth century, informs us, that after the priest had anointed the head, it was covered with a mitre, which was worn eight days, at the end of which it was taken off, and then the bishop anointed the forehead with the chrism. From this time the Church of Rome, seeing that the unction of the bishop was different from that of the priest, and performed at a different time, made of it a sacrament distinct from baptism, and called it *confirmation*, which can only be administered by the bishop. The first express institution of this sacrament is in the decree of Pope Eugenius, in 1439, in which he says, "the second sacrament is confirmation, the matter of which is chrism blessed by the bishop; ..... and though the priest may give the other unction, the bishop only can confer this."[1]

In administering confirmation in the Church of Rome, the bishop applies the chrism to the forehead, pronouncing these words: "I sign thee with the sign of the cross, and confirm thee with the chrism of salvation, in the name of the Father, the Son, and the Holy Ghost."[2]

In the Church of England the rite of confirmation is preserved, though it is not held to be a sacrament. Also the use of chrism is omitted, but the ceremony can only be performed by the bishop, who puts his hand upon the head of the persons to be confirmed, and prays for the influence of the Holy Spirit upon them, saying, "We have now laid on our hands to certify them, by this sign, of thy favour and gracious goodness."

This is evidently a remainder of the popish sacrament of confirmation. But there is no more authority for this remainder, than for anything that is omitted in the ceremony. Bishop Burnet, and other advocates for the doctrine and discipline of the Church of England, allege in favour of it the conduct of the apostles, who put their hands upon the heads of those who had been converted and baptized, and thereby imparted to them the gift of the Holy Spirit, or a power of working miracles. But, besides that no such power is now pretended to be conferred, this imposition of hands was the province of the apostles only, and not that of a bishop. This custom of reserving the imposition of hands, after baptism, to be performed by the bishop alone, seems to have been begun in the time of Jerome, but he himself did not think that the Holy Spirit was given by the imposition of the hands of the bishop only; and he says, they are not to be lamented, who, being baptized by presbyters or deacons, in little villages and castles, have died before they were visited by bishops. Hilary says that "presbyters confirmed in Egypt, if the bishop was not present." The same also was determined by the Council of Orange.[3]

The origin of *penance*, which is a second additional sacrament now enjoined by the Church of Rome, will be examined in its proper place. It is now considered as a sacrament, in consequence of the *confession* and the *penance* that is enjoined, being together the *matter* of the sacrament; and the words of the priest, *I absolve thee from thy sins, in the name of the Father, and of the Son, and of the Holy Ghost,* is the *form* of it. After this, the *spiritual grace*, or the remission of sins, is held to be conferred. The mention of these things, at this day, is a sufficient exposing of them.

The Church of England retains something of this sacrament also, though without the name of one. For, in the rules of confessing the sick, the priest is directed in certain cases to pronounce an *absolution;* and in the daily prayers of the church, after the

[1] Sueur, A.D. 417. (*P.*)
[2] Burnet on the Articles, p. 336. (*P.*) "Signo te signo crucis, et confirmo te chrismate salutis, in nomine Patris, Filii et Spiritus Sancti." Art. xxv. Ed. 4, p. 247.
[3] Pierce's Vindication, p. 474. (*P.*)

confession, which begins the service, something like absolution is pronounced. In this the compilers of the English liturgy followed the method of the Popish service; and at the time of the Reformation it might serve to make the more ignorant of the people believe that, notwithstanding a change in other respects, the same things *in substance* were to be had in both the communions.[1]

The next sacrament is *holy orders*, the matter of which is the *delivery of the vessels*, used in the celebration of the eucharist, from the bishop to the

priest, giving him a power "to offer sacrifices to God, and to celebrate masses for the living and the dead," adding, as in all the sacraments, *in the name of the Father, and of the Son, and of the Holy Ghost.* This ceremony was not used until after the twelfth century, but then this sacrament of *orders* was held to be a thing distinct from the office of *priesthood* in general, which is said to be conferred by the bishop pronouncing these words, *Receive the Holy Ghost. Whose sins ye remit, they are remitted, and whose sins ye retain, they are retained.* The imposition of hands by the bishops and presbyters is also kept up among the Catholics; but it is not performed, as formerly, during the pronouncing of any prayer, so that it is become a mere dumb show. The prayer which accompanied the ceremony of imposition of hands is, indeed, still used, but not during the imposition.

In consequence of this new sacrament, the Catholics now say, "that a priest has two powers, of *consecrating* and of *absolving;* and that he is ordained to the one by the delivery of the vessels, and to the other by the bishop's laying on of hands, with the words, *Receive the Holy Ghost;* and they make the bishop's and the priest's laying on hands jointly, to be only their declaring, as by a suffrage, that such a person ought to be ordained."[2]

The third sacrament peculiar to the Church of Rome is *matrimony*, the *inward consent of the parties* being supposed to be the *matter* of it, and the *form* is, the priest solemnly declaring them to be man and wife, in the name of the Father, Son, and Holy Ghost. But if the inward consent of the parties be necessary to marriage, as a sacrament, there must be great uncertainty in it. One considerable inconvenience that resulted from making marriage a sacrament was, that the bond was held to be indissoluble. In consequence of this, a sentence of

---

[1] Such was the representation made, on the part of Edward VI., in 1549, to the *Devonshire* rebels: "As for the service in the English tongue, it perchance seems to you a new service; and yet indeed it is no other but the old, the self-same words in English," &c. Fox's *Acts and Mon.* II. p. 1189, in Delaune's Plea, 1720, Pt. i. p. 47.

The following passage from "The Life of Archbishop Whitgift," will serve to show how *the highest style* of Protestant and Papal establishments have been found to assimilate:—"At his first journey into Kent (July, 1580), he rode to Dover, being attended with a hundred of his own servants, at least, in livery, whereof there were forty gentlemen in chains of gold. The train of clergy and gentlemen in the country, and their followers, was above five hundred horse. At his entrance into the town, there happily landed an intelligencer from Rome, of good parts and account, who wondered to see an archbishop, or clergyman, in England, so reverenced and attended: but seeing him upon the next sabbath-day after, in the cathedral church of Canterbury, attended upon by his gentlemen and servants (as is aforesaid), also by the dean, prebendaries and preachers, in their surplices and scarlet hoods, and heard the solemn music, with the voices and organs, cornets and sackbuts, he was overtaken with admiration, and told an English gentleman of very good quality (Sir Edward Hobby), who then accompanied him, that 'they were led in great blindness at Rome by our own nation, who made the people there believe, that there was not in England either archbishop or bishop, or cathedral, or any church or ecclesiastical government; but that all was pulled down to the ground, and that the people heard their ministers in woods and fields, amongst trees and brute beasts: but, for his own part, he protested, that (unless it were in the Pope's chapel) he never saw a more solemn sight, or heard a more heavenly sound.' 'Well,' said the English gentleman, 'I am glad of this your so lucky and first sight; ere long you will be of another mind, and, I hope, work miracles when you return to Rome, in making those that are led in this blindness to see and understand the truth.' "– "The Life of John Whitgift, Archbishop of Canterbury. Written by Sir George Paule, Comptroller of his Grace's Household," 1699, pp. 105, 106.

[2] Burnet on the Articles, p. 354, &c. *P.*) Art. xxv. Ed. 4, p. 261.

divorce in the ecclesiastical court, is only what is called with us, *a divorce a mensa et thoro*, but does not empower the parties to marry again, which is a kind of divorce unknown in any age or country before. The innocent person, however, was allowed to marry again by the popes Gregory and Zachary, and even "in a synod held at Rome in the tenth century. . . . This doctrine of the absolute indissolubleness of marriage, even for adultery, was never finally settled in any council before that of Trent."[1]

The last additional sacrament of the Church of Rome is *extreme unction*,[2] so called from its being used only on the near approach of death. The form of this sacrament, they say, is the application of olive oil, blessed by the bishop, to all the five senses, using these words, "By this sacred unction may God grant thee his mercy, in whatsoever thou hast offended, by sight, hearing, smelling, tasting, and touching;"[3] the priest applying the oil to each of the senses, as he pronounces the name of it.

The first mention that is made of this ceremony is by Pope Innocent. Sacred oil, indeed, was held in great veneration so early as the fourth century, and esteemed as an universal remedy; for which purpose it was either prepared and dispensed by priests and monks, or was taken from the lamps which were kept burning before the relics of the martyrs. But "in none of the lives of the saints before the ninth century, is there any mention made of their having extreme unction, though their deaths are sometimes very particularly related, and their receiving the eucharist is often mentioned." But "from the seventh century, on to the twelfth, they began to

use an anointing of the sick, . . . and a peculiar office was made for it; but the prayers that were used in it show plainly that it was all intended only in order to their recovery, and so . . . it is still used in the Greek Church;"[4] and "no doubt they support the credit of this with many reports, of which some might be true, of persons that had been recovered upon using it."[5]

"But because that failed so often, that the credit of this rite might suffer much in the esteem of the world, they began, in the tenth century, to say that it did good to the *soul*, even when the body was not healed by it, and they applied it to the several parts of the body," after having originally applied it "to the diseased parts" only. In this manner was the rite performed "in the eleventh century. In the twelfth those prayers that had been formerly made for the souls of the sick, though only as a part of the office (the pardon of sin being considered as preparatory to their recovery) came to be considered as the main and most essential part of it. Then the schoolmen brought it into shape, and so it was decreed to be a sacrament by Pope

[4] "The office requires, that they be no less than seven, and assigns to every one of them their particular employment at that time. But this number is not rigidly exacted, and three oftentimes serve. They only anoint the forehead, ears and hands of sick persons. Several prayers are used at the time of unction, and this particularly among the rest: 'O Holy Father, physician of soul and body, who hast sent thy only begotten Son, our Lord Jesus Christ, to cure all diseases, and to redeem from death; heal thy servant of his infirmity both of body and soul, and quicken him by the grace of thy Christ, for the intercession of our Lady the Mother of God, the ever Virgin Mary,' &c., and here they recite the names of several saints...'for Thou, O Christ, our God, art the fountain of all healing; and we give the glory of it to thee and to the Father, and to the Holy Spirit, now and for ever.' After this they give the sick person the holy sacrament, as the last *viaticum*. The houses of the sick persons are also anointed with the same oil, the figure of a cross being made with it upon the walls and posts: at which ceremony the priest sings the 91st Psalm. This oil is not only used upon persons lying *in extremis*: for the people, believing that there is great virtue in it to heal the distempers of the body, in case of any sickness or indisposition, that does not bring in danger of death, use it almost in the nature of a remedy or medicine." Smith's *Account*, pp. 193-195.

[5] Burnet, Art. xxv. Ed. 4. pp. 268, 269.

[1] Furnet on the Articles, p.360. (*P.*) Art. xxv. Ed. 4, p. 265.

[2] See *Doctrina de Sacramento extremæ unctionis.* Sess. iv. Con. Trid. pp. 98-107.

[3] "Per hanc sacram unctionem, et suam piissimam misericordiam indulgeat tibi Deus quicquid peccasti per visum, auditum, olfactum, gustum et tactum." *Rituale Rom. Con. Trid.* Sess. xiv. Burnet, Exp. Art. xxv. Ed. 4, p. 267.

Eugenius, and finally established at Trent."[1]

Notwithstanding the novelty and apparent absurdity of these five additional sacraments, Wickliffe acknowledged all the seven; defining a sacrament to be a *visible token of something invisible.* He even saw nothing unscriptural in extreme unction.[2]

It is much to be wished, that as these five additional sacraments are now universally abandoned in all the reformed churches, Christians would rectify their notions concerning the remaining two, and not consider them, as they did in the times of popish darkness, to be *outward and visible signs of inward and spiritual grace.* For that will always encourage the laying an improper stress upon them, to the undervaluing of that good disposition of mind, and those good works, which alone can recommend us to the favour of God, and to which only his especial grace and favour is annexed.

[1] Burnet on the Articles, p. 365. (*P.*) Art. xxv. Ed. 4, p. 269.
[2] Gilpin's Life of him, p. 66. (*P.*) He "only blamed the exorbitant fees which the avarice of the priests of those times exacted for the performance of it." *Brit. Biog.* I. pp. 46, 47.

PART VIII.

A HISTORY OF THE CHANGES THAT HAVE BEEN MADE IN THE METHOD OF CONDUCTING PUBLIC WORSHIP.

THE INTRODUCTION.

THE subject of this part of my work is no very important article in the history of the Corruptions of Christianity, because mere *forms* are but of little consequence in religion, except when they are put in the place of something more substantial; and indeed too much of this will be found to have been the case in this business. It will, however, be a matter of curiosity to many persons, to see what changes have been made from time to time in the forms of Christian worship; and therefore I did not omit to note such particulars concerning it, as happened to fall in my way, but without giving myself much trouble to look for them. It will seem that, in general, the same spirit dictated these variations that led to other things of more importance to the essentials of religion. I shall begin with a few observations on the buildings in which Christian assemblies were held, their appurtenances, &c.

SECTION I.

OF CHURCHES, AND SOME THINGS BELONGING TO THEM.

AT first, Christians could have no places to assemble in but large rooms in private houses; and when they began to erect buildings for the purpose, it is most probable they were such as the Jews made use of for their synagogues; their manner of conducting public worship, as well as their regulations for the government of churches, being copied from the Jews; and, as far as appears, nothing more simple or more proper could have been adopted for that purpose.

Of the buildings themselves we know but little. The names that were originally given to these places of assembly, were the same as those of the Jewish synagogues, viz. Ευκηρια or Προσευχαι, that is, *houses of prayer;* but afterwards they were called Κυριακα, and in Latin *Dominica,* whence came the German word *Thom* (*Dom*), and the Flemish and English words *Church* and *Kirk*. These buildings were not called *temples* till the time of Constantine. But about that time, in imitation of the Pagans, they called the magnificent buildings which were then erected for the purpose of public worship by that name. And these being generally made to enclose the tombs of martyrs, these tombs were called *altars,* on account of their bearing some resemblance to the altars of the heathen temples. And from this came the custom, at the end of the fourth century, of putting bones and other relics of martyrs in all those places which were used for the celebration of the Lord's supper, instead of the *wooden tables,* which were at first used for that purpose.[1]

When Constantine ordered the Christian churches to be rebuilt, it was done with great pomp; and before they were used for the purpose of public worship, some ceremony of *consecration* began to be used. But at first nothing more was done for that purpose, besides singing of psalms, preaching and receiving the Lord's supper, that is, nothing more, in fact, than going through the usual forms of public worship, but probably with greater solemnity and devotion, followed by feasting and other marks of festivity; and it soon became the custom to repeat this festivity on the same day annually.

In 538, it appears, that the dedications of churches were sometimes made by sprinkling of holy water. For in that year Pope Vigilius says that this ceremony was not necessary; it being sufficient for the consecration of churches to celebrate the eucharist, and deposit relics in them. But in 601, Pope Gregory expressly ordered

that holy water should be added. In 816, a synod was held at Canterbury, in which, besides these things, it was ordered, that the images of the saints, whose names the churches bore, should be painted upon the wall. From the year 1150 they added the signature of the cross, and other figures, on the pavement and walls; and afterwards they traced on the pavement the Greek and Latin alphabet, in the form of a cross; and lastly, they added the litany of the Virgin Mary and other saints.[2]

That some ceremony, or some peculiar solemnity, should be used on the first making use of any building destined for the purpose of public worship, is natural, and certainly not improper, provided nothing more be implied in it, besides solemnly setting it apart for that particular and valuable purpose; and we find that solemn consecrations were made of the temple of Jerusalem, and of everything belonging to the Jewish religion. But the ceremonies above mentioned show that some peculiar virtue was ascribed to them, and that it was supposed they imparted a character of peculiar sanctity to the building itself. And that the *bells* in them (which served no other purpose originally, besides that of calling the people together,) should have any form of consecration in churches, is a little extraordinary. This, however, was done with much solemnity by John XIII. in 968.

There having been cast at that time a larger bell than had ever been made before, for the church of Lateran, at Rome, this pope sprinkled it with holy water, " blessed it, and consecrated it to God with holy ceremonies," from which is come the custom of consecrating all bells used in churches, and which the common people call *baptizing* them. Upon this occasion they pray that when the bell shall sound they may be delivered from the ambushes of their enemies, from apparitions, tempests, thunder, wounds, and every evil spirit. During the service,

[1] Sueur, A. D. 211. (*P.*)

[2] Ibid. A. D. 335. (*P.*)

which is a very long one, they make many aspersions of holy water, and several unctions on the bells, both within and without; and at each unction they pray that the bell may be "sanctified and consecrated, in the name of the Father, of the Son, and of the Holy Spirit, to the honour of Emanuel, and under the patronage of such or such a saint."[1]

The idea of this ceremony, as almost of every other that was used by Christians, was adopted from the Pagan ritual, in which there was a solemn consecration of every instrument used in their worship. And indeed there were consecrations for the same purpose of everything that was made use of in the worship of the Jews. But nothing in the heathen ritual can equal the absurdity of this consecration of bells. For besides what is observed before, in order to make this ceremony a more proper *baptism*, (a name that was first most probably given to it by the vulgar, from the sprinkling of the bell with holy water,) godfathers and godmothers were appointed on this occasion, to answer questions instead of the bell; and they pray that God would give the bell his holy spirit, that it may be sanctified for the purposes above mentioned, and especially for driving away witches and evil spirits, and preventing tempests in the air, which were supposed to be caused by those spirits. The bell had also a name given to it, as in baptism.[2] I shall proceed to mention other things which superstition has introduced into Christian churches, and especially such as were borrowed from the Pagan worship.

In Popish churches the first thing

that we are struck with is a vessel of what is called *holy water*, into which those who enter dip their finger, and then mark their foreheads with the sign of the cross. This holy water, there can be no doubt, came from the *lustral water* of the Pagans, as indeed learned Catholics allow. This water was also placed at the entrance of the heathen temples, and those who entered were sprinkled with it. The first express mention made of holy water among Christians, is an epistle of Vigilius, bishop of Rome, written in 538, in speaking of the consecration of churches, as was mentioned above; though some have thought that to have been holy water which Synesius mentions, as placed at the entrance of the churches, for the purpose of washing their hands before prayer.[3] Middleton farther observes, that the composition of this holy water is the same with that of the Heathens, viz. "a mixture of salt with common water; and the form of the *sprinkling-brush*, called by the ancients *aspersorium* or *aspergillum*, is much the same with what the *priests* now make use of."[4]

A fondness for the *sign of the cross* was one of the first superstitions of Christians. It was probably first used by way of distinguishing themselves from the Heathens, or to show the Heathens that they were not ashamed of that with which they were most reproached, viz. the crucifixion of their Master. From this constant use of it they began to imagine that there was some peculiar virtue in the thing itself. They also imagined it to be alluded to in many passages of the Old Testament, and various rites of the Jewish religion, and they were also pleased to find the traces of it everywhere else. Hence came the custom of marking themselves with it, which is said to have been first done by the Valentinians, and then by the Montanists, of whom was Tertullian, who makes great boast

[1] Sueur, A. D. 968. (*P.*)
[2] Mosheim, II. p. 350. (*P.*) [?] "So real a baptism they make of it, that they have *godfathers* and *godmothers*, forsooth, which hold the rope of the bell in their hands, who give the bell a name, and are to answer on the bell's behalf, to such questions as the bishop or suffragans shall demand of it." See *Caldarinus in Tract. de Interdict.* I. par. No. 79, and *Albericus de Rosatis*, in *Dictionar.* in the word *Campana.* Hist. of Popery, 1735, II. pp. 22, 23.
[3] Sueur, A. D. 457. (*P.*)
[4] Letter from Rome, p. 133. (*P.*) Works, III. p. 72.

of it. But it does not appear to have been used in the public offices of religion in the three first centuries, or that crosses, made of wood or metal, were ever used till it was imagined that Helena, the mother of Constantine, had discovered the true cross in 326.[1]

Burning *wax lights* in the day-time was used in many heathen ceremonies, for which they are ridiculed by Lactantius. "The Heathens," says he, "light up candles to God, as if he lived in the dark; and do not they deserve to pass for madmen, who offer lamps to the author and giver of light?" But not long after this, these very wax lights were introduced into Christian worship.[2]

Another thing that was noted by the early Christians, as peculiar to the Pagans, was *incense*. But so early as the third century, we find this also made use of in Christian churches. And Middleton says, that "we find not only the incense sellers, but the incense itself, and the *thuribulum*, taken into the service of the Christian altars, and mentioned by St. *Ambrose* and St. *Chrysostom*, as of common use, both in the Eastern and Western empire."[3] But both wax lights and incense were first introduced into the Eastern churches, and from them were adopted in the West.

[1] Larroche, p. 538. (*P.*) Hist. of Popery, I. pp. 31, 32. M. Repos. III. p. 483.
[2] "En l'Eglise Romaine, on allume des lampes et des cierges devant les images; et quand les Dévots se trouvent en quelque peril ils vouënt une chandelle à un tel Saint, si par son moien ils en peuvent échapper; témoin cet Irlandois dont parle l'ogge Florentin, (*in Facetiis*,) qui étant sur mer durant la tempeste voua à la Vierge Marie une chandelle de la grosseur du mast du navire, mais quelcun lui aiant dit, Qu'il promettoit plus qu'il ne pourroit effectuer, l'Irlandois lui répondit tout bas, Ne t'én mets pas en peine, si je puis échapper, la bonne Vierge se contentera bien d'une bougie d'un liard." *Les Conformites des Cérémonies*, p. 195. Erasmus, *Colloq. Naufrag.* tells such a story of a Zealander.
[3] Middleton's Letter, *Postscript*, p. 237. (*P.*) Middleton introduces this account with the remark, that these ceremonies occurred "after the establishment of Christianity, when the *church*, as St. Jerome says, 'declined as much in its virtue as it increased in its power.'" Works, III. p. 126.

Lastly, *processions*, which are conducted with great solemnity by the Papists, were also copied from the heathen worship. Among the Romans they were instituted by Numa, and both in the Pagan and Popish processions the chief magistrates often assisted.[4]

SECTION II.

OF CEREMONIES IN GENERAL, AND OTHER THINGS RELATING TO PUBLIC WORSHIP.

HAVING made the preceding observations on the *places* in which the public worship of Christians was performed, and some other things and circumstances belonging to them, I proceed to give an account of what was transacted within the place; but first I shall make a few general remarks on modes and forms in Christian worship.

We may take it for granted, that originally Christians had no proper *ceremonies* in their worship. But after the sign of the cross, wax lights, and incense were introduced, the *ceremonial* of Christian worship came to be as complex as that of the Pagan worship had been. So much progress had been made in these things in the time of Austin, that he complained of it, saying that the church was so full of ceremonial observances, that the condition of the Jews under the law was much more supportable. But the church, he says, amidst much straw and tares bears many things.[5] But so much were

[4] Ibid. p. 189. (*P.*) Works. III. pp. 99, 100. "La procession du sacrament est une des plus solemnelles cérémonies de l'Eglise Romaine et qui se fait toutes les années avec une pompe extraordinaire. Elle a été introduite parmi les Chrétiens à l'imitation du Paganisme, comme Guillaume Du Choul (*De la Religion des Anciens Romains*) l'a reconnu disant, que 'quand les sacrificateurs de la Mère des Dieux faisoient leurs supplications parmi les rues, ils portoient le simulacre de Jupiter; et que par les carrefours étoient dressez des reposoirs pour y mettre son simulacre, ce que l'on fait encore en France,' dit-il, 'à la solemnité de la Fête Dieu.'" *Les Conformitez*, pp. 86, 87.
[5] Epist. cxix. C. xix. Opera, II. p. 577. (*P.*)

ceremonies multiplied before the ninth century, that large treatises were then written to explain them.

There not being in the early ages of the church any power that could enforce uniformity in the methods of worship, it happened unavoidably, that different customs got established in different places. Hence every church of note had its peculiar *ritual*, which was adopted by all the churches that depended upon it; and those of the East differed very considerably from those of the West.

The Western church was loaded with ceremonies chiefly by Gregory the Great, in the sixth century. He had great fertility of invention in this respect, and eloquence to recommend his inventions; but he did not impose them upon others, though perhaps for want of power. Almost every pope in the next century added something new to the ancient rites and institutions; and in the time of Charlemagne, they were propagated through all the Latin churches.

No person urged this business so much as Gregory VII., especially with respect to Spain, where he met with the greatest opposition from the attachment of the people to their ancient Gothic or Mosarabic liturgy. But the Pope carried his point at last, notwithstanding two very remarkable decisions in favour of the Gothic liturgy, at the appointment of the nobles at Castile. They first ordered two champions to fight, one for each of them, when he that was for the Gothic ritual proved to be victorious. They then threw both the missals into the fire, when the Roman was consumed, and the Gothic, they say, was taken out unhurt.[1] Such

was the method of determining most disputes in those days, viz. by an appeal, as they thought, to God, either by the sword, or some kind of *ordeal*, depending upon a divine interposition in the result of it.

At length, however, the Roman ritual was universally used in the Western church. And the English Reformers, instead of framing a new liturgy, had recourse to the offices of the Church of Rome, leaving out what was most offensive.

There can be no doubt but that, originally, all the parts of public worship were performed in the language that was best understood by the assembly; and as the Latin tongue was best understood by the generality of Christians in the West, this, of course, was generally, if not universally used. But after the irruption of the Northern nations, the knowledge of this language was much less general, and in the tenth or eleventh century it was hardly understood at all. But from this time the use of the Latin tongue was continued for other reasons.

In those dark ages the clergy affected to keep the people in ignorance, and in a state of dependence upon themselves, and wished to make them think that the whole business of reconciling men to God was in their hands. The Scriptures were likewise kept from the people, and the whole service was so loaded with ceremonies, that it had the appearance of a *charm*, the whole secret and virtue of which was in the breast of the priest; and to continue the service in an unknown tongue contributed greatly to the impression which they wished to make. The Latin tongue still continues to be used in all the Roman Catholic churches, notwithstanding several attempts have been made to remedy this great and glaring evil.

[1] The Danish Missionaries at *Tranquebar*, in 1706, relate the following circumstances concerning the *Malabar Heathens*: "Some had the confidence to desire us to-day, that we would thrust a book, containing the principles of our religion, into the fire; and they would do the same with another, containing the rites of their worship. If theirs should happen to be consumed by the fire, they would all turn Christians; but if ours should undergo that fate, and theirs remain unhurt, we should then all come over to them, and entertain the same belief and fancies which they did. But in case the fire should destroy both the books, then neither of the contending parties should be in the right. We replied, that we ought not to put the Great God to such trifling trials, contrived by the itch of a vain and wanton curiosity, and no ways grounded on any revelation of God's will." *Propagation of the Gospel in the East*, Pt. i. 1718, Ed. 3, p. 34.

It is not, however, peculiar to the Church of Rome. For it is said that a veneration for antiquity induces the Egyptian Christians to use the Coptic language in their churches. Also the Jacobites and Nestorians use the Syriac language, and the Abyssinians "the old Ethiopic, though all these languages have been long since obsolete, and . . . . unintelligible to the multitude."[1] The Greeks also celebrate the Lord's supper in ancient Greek; but this is sufficiently understood by the common people, the modern Greek not being very different from it.

The *habits* of the clergy could not, originally, have been anything but the usual dress of their respective countries. But it not being thought decent for persons of such grave characters as the clergy to follow new customs and fashions, they retained their old flowing garments, after the Northern nations had introduced the use of short ones. But besides this, the habits of the Pagan priests, which had always been different from those of other persons, at the time of their officiating, were probably imitated by the Christian clergy, though I cannot say that I have met with any particular account of it.

We find, however, that the clergy were distinguished by their habits, while they were officiating, in the time of Sylvester, when mention is made of *dalmatics* for the deacons, and of a certain cloth with which their left hand was to be covered. The fourth canon of the Council of Carthage prescribed the use of the *cope* in reading the gospel, and at the time of the oblation only. And Gregory the Great invented new-fashioned habits, like those described in the ceremonial law of the Jews.[2]

[1] Mosheim, II. p. 343. (*P.*) Cent. xi. Pt. ii. Ch. iv. Sect. ii.
[2] Larroche, p. 539. History of Ancient Ceremonies, p. 82. (*P.*)

SECTION III.

OF THE PROPER PARTS OF PUBLIC WORSHIP.

ORIGINALLY Christians met to read the Scriptures, to explain them, or to preach, to sing psalms, to pray, and to administer the Lord's supper. The *creed* was made use of only at baptism, when it was taught to all the catechumens, who were probably made to recite it after the person who administered the ordinance. Afterwards, when articles of faith were more attended to, and it behoved all the bishops to take care to prevent the growth of heresy, creeds began to be recited by the whole assembly. That this was the true reason of the present practice, is evident from its being the *Nicene Creed*, and not that of *the Apostles*, as it is called, that was first used for this purpose. It was also first introduced by Timothy, bishop of Constantinople, who did it in order to make Macedonius, who rejected that creed, more odious to the people. This was in the reign of the emperor Anastasius, who died in 521. About this time this creed was also repeated in the church of Antioch every time the Lord's supper was administered.

Before this time it had been the custom to repeat the creed only the day preceding Good Friday, when catechizing was more solemnly performed, in order to the celebration of baptism on the Easter Sunday following. The repetition of it on that day was first appointed by the Council of Laodicea. But the constant reading of the creed did not take place in the West till about 590, when it was ordered by the Council of Toledo, in imitation of the Eastern churches. At this time it was the Nicene Creed only that was made use of, and for some time it seemed to eclipse that of the Apostles; but afterwards this latter creed recovered its credit.[3]

[3] History of the Apostles' Creed, p. 44, &c. (*P.*)

It will be just worth while to mention a few particulars concerning the *posture* of the priest and people, during the celebration of the particular parts of public worship.

The usual posture of praying had been standing or kneeling, or, to express great self - abasement and humility, prostration ; but a canon had been made (for what reason I have not inquired) to forbid the practice of kneeling on Sundays from Easter to Whitsuntide, which gave rise to the term *stations*. This, however, was not approved by the Church of Rome.[1] When the Scriptures were read, it is probable that the people sat; but in time it became a custom for the people to stand while the *gospel* was reading. And it is said that Anastasius, bishop of Rome, who died in 402, ordered the priests to stand up, and incline their heads a little, while they read the gospel.[2]

All the Heathens contrived their temples so that they should pray with their faces towards the *East*. This was introduced into Christian worship about the time of Jerome, though it was not then generally approved of. Pope Leo the Great condemned this custom, because it was much used by the Manicheans.[3] By degrees, however, the custom of looking towards the East, during the repetition of the creed, because universal, and likewise the *bowing at the name of Jesus*, in the repetition of it. This practice was countenanced by the literal interpretation of Phil. ii. 10: *At the name of Jesus every knee shall bow*. This, however, was thought to be so very idle a superstition, that it was almost universally laid aside at the Reformation. But it is generally practised in the Church of England; and Bishop Laud severely punished those who did not conform to this ceremony in his time.

Singing seems always to have been a part of the public worship of Christians, and followed the reading of the Scriptures. They sung either the psalms of David, or hymns of their own composing. But the former, Mosheim says, were only received among Christian hymns in the fourth century. The singing of these psalms or hymns was also very common with them in their own houses, in the course of the week. But the method of singing by *antiphony* or *anthem*, that is, one part of the congregation, as the clergy, singing one verse, and the rest, or the people, singing another, is said to have been introduced about the middle of the fourth century, into the church of Antioch, by Flavianus and Diodorus, and into the church of Constantinople by Chrysostom.[4]

This method of singing was introduced into the Church of Rome by Celestine, in 418. Afterwards, Gregory the Great composed an *antiphoniary* for the whole year, with versicles, or responses for every day of it. He then appointed the college or choir of singing men, to chant the office.[5] In the fifth century it was the custom in some places to keep up the exercises of singing both day and night, different sets of persons continually relieving each other.[6]

Musical instruments were not introduced into churches till the thirteenth or fourteenth century. Thomas Aquinas says, "the church does not use musical instruments to praise God, lest she should seem to judaize."[7] But in 1312, Marinus Sanutus introduced organs into churches;[8] and they have been much used ever since, though there have always been persons in all establishments, as well as in particular sects, who preferred a more simple mode of worship ; and even, admitting that music might assist in exciting

---

1 History of Ancient Ceremonies, p. 17. (*P.*)
2 Sucur, A. D. 402. (*P.*)
3 Ibid. A. D. 443. (*P.*)

4 Ibid. A. D. 398. Pierce's Vindication, p. 390. (*P.*)
5 History of Ancient Ceremonies, p. 81. (*P.*)
6 Mosheim, I. p. 397. (*P.*) Cent. v. Pt. ii. Ch. iv. Sect. ii.
7 Pierce's Vindication, pp. 385, 295. (*P.*)
8 Jortin's Remarks, V. p. 409. (*P.*)

devotional feelings, did not choose that, in general, they should depend upon that mechanical assistance.

In the primitive churches preaching was nothing more than the exposition of the Scriptures, a portion of which was always read in the course of the service. Origen is said to have been the first who did this in a more copious and diffusive manner, explaining the Scripture in an allegorical way; and by this means introduced longer sermons than had been usual.[1]

When heathen philosophers and rhetoricians were converted to Christianity, they introduced their custom of haranguing on particular subjects, and particular occasions, and carefully premeditated or precomposed their sermons; sometimes prefixing to their discourses short texts of scripture, probably that they might not pass too suddenly from the old method of interpreting the sacred writings, and sometimes omitting them. In this style are the sermons of Chrysostom, consisting of such kind of eloquence as the Greeks and Romans were fond of displaying, when they harangued the populace, or pleaded at the bar.

So far did Christian preachers in those times depart from the simplicity of the gospel, and so little were they influenced by the spirit of Christianity, that, in imitation of the Grecian orators, some of them even hired persons to clap their hands, and express their applause by other gestures and vociferations at proper intervals, on signals previously concerted between them and the preacher, or his particular friends.

These set harangues were only occasional, and were by no means delivered every Lord's day, in every Christian church; and in the dark ages, few persons being qualified to preach, sermons became very scarce. At this day the Roman Catholics meet only, in general, to hear prayers, and to celebrate mass. They have no ser-

mons, except in Lent, on certain festivals, and on some other particular occasions. It is more particularly observed, that it was in the ninth century that the bishops and priests ceased to instruct the people by sermons as they had done before.[2]

Charlemagne, finding the clergy absolutely incapable of instructing the people by sermons of their own, or "of explaining, with perspicuity and judgment, the portions of scripture which are distinguished in the ritual by the name of *epistle* and *gospel*, ordered Paulus Diaconus and Alcuin to compile, from the ancient doctors of the church, *homilies*, or discourses upon the epistles and gospels, which a stupid and ignorant set of priests were to commit to memory, and recite to the people. "This gave rise to that famous collection, which went by the title of the *Homiliarium* of Charlemagne, and which, being followed as a model by many productions of the same kind, composed by private persons, ... contributed much to nourish the indolence," says Mosheim, "and to perpetuate the ignorance of a worthless clergy."[3] In this, however, as well as in his other regulations respecting the church, he certainly had the best intentions; and in those times it is probable that nothing better could have been done. A scheme of this kind was adopted in England when the present *book of homilies* was compiled, and appointed to be read in churches.

"Before the Reformation, after the preacher had named and opened his text, he called on the people to go to their prayers, telling them what they were to pray for. 'Ye shall pray,' says he, 'for the king, for the pope, for the holy catholic church,' &c.; after which all the people said their beads in a general silence," and the minister, kneeling down, did the same. They would besides say a *Pater noster*,

---

[1] Mosheim, I. p. 235. (*P.*) Cent. iii. Pt. ii. Ch. iv. Sect. ii.

[2] Sueur, A. D. 853. (*P.*)
[3] Eccl. Hist. II. p. 84. (*P.*) Cent. viii. Pt. ii. Ch. iii. Sect. v.

Ave Maria, Deus misereatur nostri, Domine salvum fac regem, Gloria Patri, &c., "and then the sermon proceeded."[1] The manner in which most of the English clergy pray in the pulpit before sermon is still the same, and is what they call *bidding prayers,* or an exhortation to pray for such and such things. But then no time is allowed for the prayers that are so ordered.

In the primitive church the public prayers followed the sermon, and preceded the celebration of the Lord's supper; and it is evident, from many circumstances, that at first all these prayers were delivered without book, and were such as the bishop, or the priest who officiated, could prepare himself. Justin Martyr says, that the president of the assembly offered prayers and thanksgivings, *as he was able,* (ὅση δυναμις αυτῳ). Origen also says, "We pray according to our abilities;" and Tertullian, "We pray to God without a monitor, because our prayers flow from our own minds." Basil gives an instance of a variation in his prayer, for which he was blamed by some, as being inconsistent with himself.[2]

In time, however, partly in order to avoid diversity of opinions, and in part, also, that the congregation might not be offended by prayers prepared by persons who were not capable of doing it with propriety, it came to be the custom to compose the prayers beforehand, and to submit them to the approbation of the principal persons in the church. This was particularly ordered at the third Council of Carthage.[3]

At the Council of Laodicea, held in 364, the same prayers were ordered to be used morning and evening; but, in general, every bishop ordered what prayers he thought proper, till about the time of Austin, when it was ordered that, to prevent heresy, no prayers

should be used but by common advice. Thus in time a great variety of *liturgies,* or forms of celebrating public worship, were in use in different provinces and different sees. The first mention we find of these liturgies is towards the end of the fourth century.[4]

In early times, though the officiating minister delivered the prayers, the people were not entirely silent; for they made small *interlocutions* or responses, as *Lift up your hearts. We lift them up unto the Lord,* mentioned by Cyprian: *The Lord be with you, and with thy spirit,* in the time of Chrysostom.[5]

The last circumstance that I shall notice, relating to the forms of public worship, is, that in the primitive church, where the service always ended with communion, there was recited *a roll,* in which the names of the more eminent saints of the catholic church, and of the holy bishops, martyrs, or confessors, of every particular church, were registered. This was an honourable remembrance of such as had died in the Christian faith. But when the soundness of any person's faith was questioned, his name was not read till that difficulty was removed. Chrysostom having been expelled from the church of Constantinople, it was a long time before his name was inserted in this roll. This was the custom by which, as I have observed before, provision was made for excommunicating persons even after their death.

SECTION IV.

OF FESTIVALS, ETC. IN THE CHRISTIAN CHURCH.

THE primitive Christians had no festivals besides Sunday, on which they always met for public worship, as may be inferred from Justin Martyr. This

---

[1] Neal's Hist. I. p. 33. (*P.*) Toulmin's Ed. I. p. 44.
[2] Pierce's Vindication, pp. 429, 430. (*P.*)
[3] Sueur, A. D. 397. (*P.*)
[4] Neal's Hist. I. p. 37. (*P.*) 1793, p. 49.
[5] Pierce's Vindication, p. 426. (*P.*)

day Constantine ordered to be observed as a day of rest from labour; but husbandmen were allowed to cultivate the earth on that day.[1] By degrees, however, in imitation of the Jews or Heathens, but chiefly the latter, Christians came to have as many annual festivals as the Heathens themselves. Of the principal of these I shall give a general account.

The first that was observed by Christians was *Easter*, on the time of the Jewish passover, being the anniversary of our Saviour's sufferings, death and resurrection. Originally, however, this was probably a *festival*, and respected the resurrection of our Saviour only; but afterwards they began to keep a *fast*, on the anniversary of the crucifixion; but it was a long time before this fast was extended, as it now is, to the whole season of *Lent*, or forty days before Easter.

The primitive Christians used, indeed, to join fasting to prayer upon extraordinary occasions; but this was always voluntary, and those who entirely omitted it were not censured. The first person who is said to have laid down any express rules for fasting was Montanus, who was remarkable for his rigour in other respects. However, a fast on the anniversary of Christ's crucifixion, or what we call *Good Friday*, is of very great antiquity; but both the time, and the degree of fasting, was originally very various, depending upon each person's particular fancy. Irenæus says, that some persons fasted before Easter one day, some two, and some more; but that the unity of the faith was maintained notwithstanding that variety.

By fasting, the ancients always meant abstaining from meat and drink, from morning till evening; and what Tertullian and others call *stations*, or half fasts, were those days on which they assembled for prayer in the morning, and continued that exercise till three in the afternoon, when they received the Lord's supper. They never

fasted on a Saturday or Sunday, and even thought it a crime to do so, except on the Saturday before Easterday, on which they celebrated the resurrection of Christ, because, during that time, they said, the bridegroom was taken from them.

Because the time that our Saviour lay in the grave was about forty hours, this fast was called *Quarantana* or *Quadragesima*, and by contraction *Quaresme*, and *Caresme* or *Carême*, which is the French term for *Lent*. Another reason for fasting at this particular time was, that many persons were then preparing for baptism, and others for communion, which, as superstition prevailed, was frequented more generally, and attended upon with more solemnity, on that day.

Even the Montanists only fasted two weeks in the year, and in these they excepted Saturdays and Sundays.[2] Lent was first confined to a certain number of days in the fourth century. At this time, however, "abstinence from flesh and wine was by many judged sufficient for the purposes of fasting, and this . . . . opinion prevailed from this time" in the Western church.[3] Soon after the time of Tertullian, Christians began to observe Wednesdays and Fridays for the purpose of fasting; and they kept these fasts all the year, except between Easter and Pentecost, in which time they neither fasted nor kneeled in churches. In 416, Innocent I. ordered that the people should fast on Saturdays; but the Greeks and all the East paid no regard to this ordinance.[4]

At the time of the Council of Nice, the week before Easter was called *Quarantana*, or *Lent;* though some observed more days, and some fewer, at pleasure; but within forty years after this council, Lent was extended to three weeks.[5]

"Durandus . . . . tells us Lent was

[2] Ibid. A. D. 206. (*P.*)
[3] Mosheim, I. p. 324. (*P.*) Cent. iv. Pt. ii. Ch. iv. Sect. vi.
[4] Sueur, A. D. 391. (*P.*)
[5] Ibid. A. D. 325, 364. (*P.*)

[1] Sueur, A. D. 320. (*P.*)

counted to begin on that which is now the first Sunday in Lent, and to end on Easter eve, which time, containing forty-two days, if you take out of them the six Sundays on which it was counted not lawful at any time of the year to fast, then there will remain only thirty-six days; and therefore, that the number of forty days which Christ fasted might be perfected, Pope Gregory (the Great) added to Lent four days of the week before-going, viz. that which we now call *Ash Wednesday*, and the three days following it;"[1] so that our present Lent is a superstitious imitation of our Saviour's fast of forty days.

Before the Council of Nice, there had been a great difference between the Eastern and Western churches about the time of keeping Easter, the Christians in the East following the custom of the Jews, with whom the day on which the paschal Lamb was killed was always the fourteenth of their month Nisan, on whatever day of the week it happened to fall; but with the Latins, Easter-day had always been the Sunday following, being the anniversary of our Saviour's resurrection. At the Council of Nice, the custom of the Latin church was established; and as astronomy was more cultivated in Egypt, it was given in charge to the bishop of Alexandria, to publish to the other churches the proper time of keeping Easter, by what were called *paschal epistles.* For the same purpose afterwards the *golden number* was invented.[2]

Pentecost was a Jewish festival, celebrated fifty days after the passover; and being likewise distinguished in the Christian history by the descent of the Holy Spirit, it was observed next after Easter, and, as far as appears, about the time of Tertullian. We call it *Whitsuntide.* These are the only great festivals that Christians were not at liberty to fix where they

pleased. All the other festivals they fixed at those times of the year which the Pagans used to observe with the greatest solemnity, with a view to facilitate their conversion to Christianity.

The feast of *Christmas,* in commemoration of the nativity of Christ, is mentioned by Chrysostom as unknown at Antioch till within ten years of the time of his writing; and therefore he concluded that it had lately been introduced from Rome.[3] It was thought to be first observed by the followers of Basilides, and from them to have been adopted by the orthodox, in the fourth century, when the festival of *Christ's baptism* was introduced; in consequence of which this feast of the nativity was removed from the sixth of January to the twenty-fifth of December: the former retaining the name of the *Epiphany,* which feast only, and not that of the nativity, is observed in the East.[4]

Festivals in honour of the apostles and martyrs are all of late date, none of them earlier than the time of Constantine, when magnificent temples were built round the tombs of some of their martyrs; and then the festivals were only held at the places where they were supposed to have suffered.

Vigils were the assemblies of the ancient Christians by night, in the time of persecution, when they durst not meet in the day-time. Afterwards they were observed before Easter, but they were kept not as feasts, which was done afterwards, but as *fasts,* as appears from Tertullian.

The feast of *Ascension* was observed about the time of Austin. The feast of *Circumcision* is first mentioned by Maximus Taurinensis, who flourished in 450; and the feast of *Purification* was perhaps instituted in the ninth century.[5] The feast of *Advent* is of no

---

[1] History of Popery, I. p. 186. (*P.*) 1785, I. p. 100.
[2] Hist. of Ancient Ceremonies, p. 44. (*P.*)

[3] Basnage, *Histoire,* I. p. 280. (*P.*)
[4] Pierce's Vindication, pp. 509, 510. (*P.*) See "Christ's Birth mis-timed;...proving that Jesus Christ was not born in December." *Phœnix* 1707, I. p. 114.
[5] Pierce's Vindication, pp. 512, 513. (*P.*)

earlier authority than that of Innocent III., in the thirteenth century; and the *Vigils* of the great festivals are all later than the tenth century.[1]

It was Mamert, bishop of Vienne in Gaul, who, about 463, first instituted the fast of *Rogation*, that is, the prayers that are made three days before the feast of Ascension, that is, the Monday, Tuesday, and Wednesday before Holy Thursday; which was expressly contrary to the order established in the ancient church, forbidding all fasting between Easter and Pentecost. This fast of Rogation was generally received in the West presently after the time of this Mamert.[2] The bishop of Venice added the processions to them, in imitation of the *Lustrationes Ambervales* of the Heathens, which were made round their fields, in order to render them fruitful; and these were attended with much intemperance and disorder, being made, no doubt, in all respects, after the Pagan manner.[3]

Alcinus Avitus, who succeeded Hesychius, the immediate successor of Mamert, in the church of Vienne, describes the occasion of instituting this fast in his homily on the Rogation. He there says that the city of Vienne had suffered much by fire, thunderstorms, earthquakes, extraordinary noises in the night, prodigies, signs in the heavens, wild beasts, and other calamities; that on this the bishop of the city ordered the people to fast three days with prayer and repentance, that, by the example of the Ninevites, they might avert the judgments of God. He says that thereupon the anger of God was appeased, and that in commemoration of it, Mamert ordered this fast to be observed every year. His example was soon fol-

lowed, first by the church of Clermont in Auvergne, then by all their neighbours, and afterwards throughout all Gaul. In 801, Leo III. confirmed this fast, and made it universal.[4]

The fast of *Ember Weeks*, or *Jejunia quatuor temporum*, was probably instituted a little before Leo the Great, in the middle of the fifth century.[5] But others think that it is not quite certain that he speaks of it.[6] Some say that Pope Gelasius having ordered that the ordination of priests and deacons should be on the four weeks of Ember, or ember days, viz. the Wednesday, Friday, and Saturday after the first Sunday in Lent, after Whitsunday, after the fourteenth of September, and the thirteenth of December, and this ceremony being always conducted with fasting and prayer, it came to be a custom to fast at that time.[7]

It was upon the idea of the spiritual benefit that would arise from visiting the church of St. Peter at Rome, and also in imitation of the Jewish jubilee, and the secular games among the Romans, that the popish *jubilee* is founded. This festival, which is celebrated with the utmost pomp and magnificence, was instituted by Boniface VIII., in the year 1300, in consequence, as it is said, of a rumour, the origin of which is not known, which was spread among the inhabitants of Rome, in 1299, that all who within the limits of the following year, should visit the church of St. Peter, would receive the remission of all their sins; and that this privilege would be annexed to the same observance every hundredth year.[8]

[1] Sueur, A. D. 392. (*P.*)
[2] Ibid. (*P.*)
[3] See *Tibullus*, L. ii. El. ii. *Virgil*, Ecl. line 74, 75. " Il y avoit parmi les anciens Romains un jour dedié pour faire ces processions, assavoir le 25 d'Avril, qu'ils nommoient *Rubigalia*, c'està-dire, la fête des nielles, parce qu'ils faisoient des sacrifices et des prières aux Dieux, y afin qu'ils conservassent les bleds de cet accident là. Dans l'Eglise Romaine on fait la même cérémonie le même jour qui est la Fête de S. Marc." *Les Conformitez des Cérémonies*, pp. 95. 96.

[4] Sueur, A. D. 462, 463. (*P.*)
[5] Pierce's Vindication, p. 529. (*P.*)
[6] Sueur, A. D. 392. (*P.*)
[7] Hist. of Ancient Ceremonies, p. 67. (*P.*)
[8] " La plus solennelle Fête des anciens Romains étoit celle des jeux qu'ils appelloient séculiers, qui ne se devoit célébrer q'une fois about d'un siècle....A cela a succedé en l'Eglise Romaine le grand Jubilé qui fut institué par Boniface VIII....On invita tous les Chrétiens de venir à Rome, et afin de les y attirer on promit à ceux qui dans l'année viendroient visiter les Temples des Apôtres, l'entiere rémission de leurs péchez non seulement quant à la coulpe, mais aussi quant à la peine." *Les Conformitez*, pp. 109, 110.

The successors of Boniface added a number of new rites and inventions to this superstitious institution, and finding by experience that it added lustre to the Church of Rome, and increased its revenue, they made its return more frequent. In 1350, Clement VI. ordered that the jubilee should be celebrated every fifty years, on pretence that the Jews did the like, and Paul II., in the fifteenth century, reduced the term to twenty-five years.[1] This year of jubilee is called a *holy year;* but, as the author of the *Histoire des Papes* observes, it should rather be called the year of sacrilege, impiety, debauch and superstition.[2]

Many of these festivals have been retained by the reformers, especially those of Easter, Whitsuntide and Christmas, and, like the Papists, they observe them with more strictness than they do the Sundays.

Our Established Church has by no means thrown off the popish superstition with respect to fasting. The fast days in the Church of England, are all the Fridays in the year except Christmas-day, all the days in Lent,

which, besides Fridays, are thirty-three, six more in the Ember weeks, three Rogation days, and the thirtieth of January. The sum of all the festival days is thirty-one. And if to these we add the ninety-five fast days, fifty-two Sundays, and twenty-nine saints' days, all the days in year appropriated to religious exercises, besides vigils, will be one hundred and seventy-eight; and making allowance for some of them interfering with others, they will be about one hundred and seventy.[3]

In so little esteem, however, are these observances held by the more enlightened members of the established church, that there can be no doubt but that, when any reformation takes place, a great retrenchment will be made in this article.[4]

[3] Pierce's Vindication, p. 508. *(P.)*
[4] The Ecclesiastical Commissioners, in 1689, proposed to the Convocation "a new calendar," in which were "omitted all the *Legendary Saints' Days,* and others not directly referred to in the service book," and "that a rubric be made, declaring the intention of the *Lent Fasts,* to consist only in extraordinary acts of devotion, not in distinction of meats." *Calamy,* Abridgment of *Baxter,* &c. Ed. 2, I. p. 453.
"Our *Calender,* every man of judgment will allow, does greatly need revising and reforming. The observations upon the subject are so well known, that they need not be here repeated." *Free and Cand. Disquis.* 1750, Ed. 2, p. 154.

[1] Hist. of Ancient Ceremonies, p. 67. *(P.)*
[2] Vol. V. p. 409. *(P.)*

PART IX.

THE HISTORY OF CHURCH DISCIPLINE.

THE INTRODUCTION.

The changes which the discipline of the Christian church underwent from the time of the apostles to the Reformation, were as great, and of as much importance in practice, as the changes in any other article relating to Christianity. From being highly favourable to good conduct, the established maxims of it came at length to be a cover for every kind of immorality, to those who

chose to avail themselves of them. On this account I have given a good deal of attention to the subject.

To many persons, I doubt not, this will be as interesting an object as anything in the history of Christianity, and to introduce it in this place will make the easiest connection between the two great divisions of my work, I mean the corruptions of *doctrine,* and the abuses of *power* in the Christian church. It will also serve to show in what manner these departures from the Christian system promoted each other.

SECTION I.

THE HISTORY OF CHURCH DISCIPLINE, IN THE TIME OF THE CHRISTIAN FATHERS.

In the purer ages of the church, the offences which gave public scandal were few; but when they did happen, they were animadverted upon with great rigour. For, as many enormities were laid to the charge of Christians, they were exceedingly solicitous to give no just cause of obloquy. It is, indeed, probable, that some time after the apostolic age, the morals of the Christians in general were more strict than we find, by the writings of the apostles, they were in their own times. Nor is it to be wondered at, when we consider that the whole body of the Gentile Christians, being then newly converted from Heathenism, must have retained many of their former habits, or have easily relapsed into them.

Afterwards, most of the cases of scandal we meet with relate to the behaviour of Christians in the time of persecution, from which many shrunk or fled, in a manner that was exceedingly and justly disapproved by the more severe. Consequently, after a persecution, there was much to do about the re-admission to the privileges of church communion, of those who repented of their weakness; and it was a great part of the business of the councils in the fourth and fifth centuries (which was after the establishment of Christianity) to settle rules concerning the degrees of penance, and the method of receiving penitents into the church. Indeed, besides the cases of those who had shrunk from persecution, the governors of Christian churches at that time must have had many offences of other kinds to animadvert upon; considering that Christianity had then the coun-

tenance of the civil powers, and, therefore, that people of all ranks, and of all characters, would naturally crowd into it. On these accounts they found it necessary to have a very regular system of discipline.

In general, we find that, about the third and fourth centuries, Christians distinguished four orders of penitents. The first stood at the entrance of the church, begging in the most earnest manner the prayers of all that went in. The second were admitted to enter, and to hear the lectures that were given to the catechumens, and the exposition of the Scriptures, but they were dismissed, together with the catechumens, before the celebration of the eucharist. The third lay prostrate in a certain place in the church, covered with sackcloth, and after receiving the benediction of the bishop, and the imposition of hands, were also dismissed before the celebration of the eucharist. The fourth order attended that celebration, but did not partake of it. Penitents having passed through all these orders, were admitted to communion by the imposition of the hands of the bishop, or of a priest, in the presence of the whole congregation.[1]

If any persons relapsed into the same fault for which they had been excommunicated, or excluded from the congregation of the faithful, they were not re-admitted to communion, except in the article of death; but towards the end of the seventh century the ancient discipline began to be relaxed in this respect, and they admitted persons to communion after a second offence. In all times there were some crimes for which no repentance could make atonement, so that persons who had been once guilty of them could never be admitted to the peace and communion of the church. These were murder, adultery, and apostacy. In this manner, at least, were these crimes stigmatized, in many churches.

[1] Sueur, A. D. 213. (P.)

o

But about the third century, Pope Zephyrinus began to relax a little of this discipline, admitting adulterers to communion after some years of penance, in which he was vehemently opposed to Tertullian. However, in the time of Cyprian, the penalties imposed by the bishop, which were always a public appearance for a certain time in the character of *penitents*, were often relaxed, or abridged, at the intreaty of the confessors, or those who had been destined to martyrdom; and this was called *indulgence*, of the abuse of which we shall see enough in a later period. But at this time there was not much to complain of in this business, except the improper interference of these confessors, and the too great influence which they were allowed to have in such cases.

Equally innocent was the business of *confession*, as it was first begun; but we see in the course of this history, that it is no uncommon thing for an innocent beginning to lead to a fatal catastrophe. The apostle Paul exhorts Christians to confess their sins one to another; and our Saviour assures us that we must forgive, as we hope to be forgiven. Upon this was grounded the custom of the primitive churches, to require every person who was excommunicated, to make a public confession of his guilt before he was re-admitted to Christian communion. In some cases, also, a public confession prevented excommunication. It was, likewise, the custom for many conscientious persons to confess their private sins to some of the priests in whom they could put the greatest confidence, and whose advice and prayers they wished to have; and what was at first a voluntary thing, was afterwards, but indeed long afterwards, imposed as a positive duty.

Confession was also much encouraged by another circumstance. Many canons made a difference in the degree and time of penance, between those who had accused themselves, and those against whom their crimes were proved. Many persons, therefore, to prevent the se-

verer penalty, came of their own accord to confess their sins; and this was much encouraged, and the virtue of it magnified by the writers of those times. This confession was, originally, always made in public, but some inconveniences being found to attend this (especially when the crimes affected other persons, or the state) a private confession was appointed instead of it. In this case the bishop either attended himself, or appointed some particular priest, who from this office got the title of *penitentiary priest*, to receive these confessions.

The difficulty of re-admission to the privileges of church communion was, in general, very great, and the penances imposed were exceedingly rigorous, and this, in the end, was one great cause of the total relaxation of all discipline.

Novatian particularly distinguished himself by refusing to admit to communion any who had been guilty of the greater crimes, especially that of apostacy, leaving them to the judgment of God only. This arose from the rigour of Tertullian and the Montanists; and it is observable that the Church of Rome still keeps up this rigorous discipline in cases of *heresy*, the *relapsed* being delivered to the secular arm, without being admitted to penance.

It was ordained by the Council of Nice, that those who apostatized before baptism should not be admitted to the communion of the church till after three years of penance, but if they had been of the *faithful*, the penance was to continue seven years.[1] Basil decided, that for the crime of fornication, a man ought to do penance four years. Others for the same offence imposed a penance of nine years, and for adultery eighteen years.[2]

Hitherto we have seen nothing but rigour; and the relaxation did not begin by lessening the time of penance (except in those cases in which the confessors had improperly interfered),

[1] Sueur, A. D. 325. (*P.*)
[2] Basnage, *Histoire*, I. p. 189. (*P.*)

but first in the manner of making the confession, then in the place of penance, and lastly, in the commutation of it.

After the persecution under the emperor Decius, the orthodox bishops, Socrates says, appointed that the penitents should make their confessions to one particular priest, and that they should make a public confession of such things only as should be thought proper for public hearing. This custom continued in the Eastern church till the year 390, when Nectarius, the bishop of Constantinople, abolished the office of penitentiary priests, on account of a woman having been enticed to commit adultery with a deacon of the church, whilst she stayed to perform the duties of fasting and prayer, which had been enjoined her.[1] From this time all confessions, public and private, seem to have been discontinued in the Greek church; and at this day, it is said, that the Greeks make confession to God only.

In the Western church public confession continued till the fifth century, but at that time those offenders who had been used to make public confession of their crimes, were allowed by Leo the Great to confess them privately to a priest appointed for that purpose. By this means a great restraint upon vice was taken away, and the change was as pleasing to the sinner, as it was advantageous to the priests in several respects. Of this, many persons at that time were sufficiently aware; and we find that in 590, a council held at Toledo, forbade confession to be made privately to a priest, and ordered that it should be made according to the ancient canons.

To confession in private soon succeeded the doing penance in private, which was another great step towards the ruin of the ancient discipline, which required, indeed, to be moderated, but in a different manner. In the fifth century, however, penitents

were suffered to do penance secretly in some monastery, or other private place, in the presence of a few persons, at the discretion of the bishop, or of the confessors, after which absolution also was given in private. This was the only method which they ventured to take with those who would not submit to the established rules of the church. "But in the seventh century, all public penance for secret sins was taken quite away. Theodore, archbishop of Canterbury, is reckoned the first of all the bishops of the Western church" who established this rule.[2]

Had Christians contented themselves with admonishing and finally excommunicating those who were guilty of notorious crimes, and with requiring public confession, with restitution in case of injustice, and left all private offences to every man's own conscience, no inconvenience would have arisen from their discipline. But, by urging too much the importance of confession, and by introducing corporeal austerities, as fasting, &c., as a proper mode of penance, and then changing these for alms, and, in fact, for money, in a future period, they paved the way for the utter ruin of all good discipline, and at length brought it to be much worse than a state of no discipline at all. However, we have yet seen but the first steps in this fatal progress.

———

SECTION II.

OF THE STATE OF CHURCH DISCIPLINE IN THE DARK AGES, AND TILL THE REFORMATION.

WE have seen several symptoms of the change and decay of discipline in the last period; but in this we shall see the total ruin of it, in consequence of the increased operation of the same causes, and the introduction of several new ones.

---

[1] See Burnet, *Art.* xxv. Ed. 4, pp. 253, 254.

[2] Burnet, p. 346. (P.) **Art.** xxv. Ed. 4, p. 254.

o 2

After the introduction of *private confession*, it was complained by a council held at Châlons-sur-Saone, in 813, that persons did not confess their offences fully, but only in part; and, therefore, they ordered, that the priest should make particular *inquiry*, under such heads as were thought to include the principal vices that men were addicted to. At this time, however, confession was not reckoned necessary to salvation, and was not made in order to obtain absolution of the priest, but to inform persons how they ought to conduct themselves with respect to God, in order to obtain pardon of him; and therefore the fathers of this council say that confession to God purges sin, but confession to the priest teaches how sins are purged.[1]

This business of confession to priests, before it was held to be of universal obligation, gave rise to a new kind of casuistry, which consisted in ascertaining the nature of all kinds of crimes, and in proportioning the penalties to each. This improvement is ascribed to Theodore, archbishop of Canterbury, above mentioned, who, in a work entitled *The Penitential*, regulated the whole business of penance, distinguishing the different kinds of crimes, and prescribing forms of consolation, exhortation and absolution, adapted to each particular case. From Britain these regulations were soon introduced into all the western provinces, and the *Penitential of Theodore* became a pattern for other works of the same nature. But in the next century this discipline greatly declined, and gave way to the doctrine of indulgences.[2]

However, what is now properly called *auricular confession* was not fully established, and made of universal obligation, before the thirteenth century, when Innocent III. appointed it by his own authority, in a Lateran Council. This doctrine, as it is now re- ceived in the Church of Rome, requires "not only a general acknowledgment, but a particular enumeration of sins and [of] follies," and is appointed to be made to a proper priest once at least every year, by all persons who are arrived at years of discretion. Before this law of Innocent, "several doctors had considered confession as a duty ... of divine authority," but it "was not publicly received as a doctrine of the church." This law occasioned the introduction of a number of new injunctions and rites.[3]

It being notorious to all persons, that all useful church discipline was lost at the time of the Reformation, it was thought proper at the Council of Trent to do, or at least to seem to do, something in the business; and therefore it was ordered that scandalous offenders should do public penance, according to the ancient canons, and that the bishops should be judges of it.[4] But things had gone on so long in a different train, that it does not appear that anything was done in consequence of it.

Together with this change in the business of confession, other causes were at the same time operating to the corruption of church discipline, but nothing contributed to it more than the stress which was then laid upon many things foreign to real virtue, and which were made to take the place of it. Of this nature were the customary devotions of those days, consisting in the frequent repetition of certain prayers, in bodily austerities, in pilgrimages, in alms to the poor, and donations to the church, &c. These were things that could be *ascertained*, so that it might be known with certainty whether the party had conformed with the penalty or not; whereas a *change of heart and of character* was a thing of a less obvious nature, and indeed not much attended to by

---

[1] Sueur, A. D. 813. (*P.*)

[2] Mosheim, II. p. 26. (*P.*) Cent. vii. Pt. ii. Ch. iii. Sect. v.

[3] Ibid. III. pp. 93, 94. (*P.*) Cent. xiii. Pt. ii. Ch. iii. Sect. ii.

[4] Sess. xxiv. Cap. viii. "Publice peccantes publice pœniteant, ni Episcopo aliter videatur." *S. Con. Trid.* p. 214.

the generality of confessors at that time.

"About the end of the eighth century the *commutation of penance* began, and instead of the ancient severities, *vocal prayers* came to be all that was enjoined. So many *Paters* (or repetitions of the Lord's Prayer) stood for so many days of fasting; and the rich were admitted to buy off their penance under the decenter name of giving alms. The getting many masses to be said, was thought a devotion by which God was so much honoured, that the commuting penance for masses was much practised. Pilgrimages and wars came on afterwards."[1]

The immediate cause of this commutation of penances was the impossibility of performing them, according to the canons of the Church; since, in many cases, it required more time than the term of human life. For instance, a ten years' penance being enjoined for a murder, a man who had committed twenty murders, must have done penance two hundred years; and therefore some other kind of penance was judged absolutely necessary; and the person who was chiefly instrumental in settling the commutations of penance was one Dominic, who communicated them to the celebrated Peter Damiani, whose authority in the age in which he lived was very great.

By them it was determined that a hundred years of penance might be compensated by twenty repetitions of the psalter, accompanied with discipline, that is, the use of the whip on the naked skin. The computation was made in the following manner. Three thousand strokes with the whip were judged to be equivalent to a year of penance, and a thousand blows were to be given in the course of repeating ten psalms. Consequently, all the psalms, which are one hundred and fifty, were equivalent to five years of penance, and therefore twenty psalters to one hundred years. It is amusing enough

at this day, and in a Protestant country, to read that Dominic easily dispatched this task in six days, and thus discharged some offenders for whom he had undertaken to do it. Once, at the beginning of Lent, he desired Damiani to impose upon him a thousand years of penance, and he very nearly finished it before the end of the same Lent. Damiani also imposed upon the archbishop of Milan a penance of a hundred years, which he redeemed by a sum of money, to be paid annually.[2] Though Peter Damiani was the great advocate for this system of penance, he did not deny the novelty of it.[3]

Fleury acknowledges that when the penances were made impossible, on account of the multitude of them, they were obliged to have recourse to compensations and estimations, such as these repetitions of psalms, bowings, scourgings, alms, pilgrimages, &c.,—things, as he observes, that might be performed without conversion. However, in a national council in England, held in 747, penances performed by others were forbidden.[4] This enormity was too great to be admitted even in these ignorant and licentious ages; but it must have gained some considerable ground before it was checked by public authority.

The monks becoming confessors contributed greatly to the ruin of ecclesiastical discipline. They, knowing nothing of the ancient canons, introduced a certain *casuistry* by which many crimes were excused, and abso-

---

[1] Burnet, p. 846. (P.) Art. xxv. Ed. 4, p. 254.

[2] Fleury, A. D. 1059. (P.)

[3] Ibid. [Vol.] XIII. [Paris, 1742.] p. 100. (P.) [A. D. 1062.].

[4] Ibid. p. 43. (P.) [Ed. Vidal. Paris, 1836. Tom. IV. pp. 142-3. Cf. A. D. 745.]. This council was held at *Cliffe*, in Kent. A rich layman, who had been excommunicated, employed several persons to fast, on his account, and these were so numerous, that he computed their austerities as equal to a penance of three hundred years, endured by himself. Against this penitence, by proxy, a *canon* was issued, "lest salvation should become more easy to the rich than to the poor, contrary to the express declaration of Jesus Christ." At the same council, the priests were ordered to teach the people the Apostles' Creed and the Lord's Prayer in English See Rapin, *Histoire*, L. iii. Conciles, Ed. 1724, 4to, I. pp. 266, 267.

lution was made easy in all cases, no persons being ever refused, or put off, after ever so many relapses. This relaxed casuistry is the most prevalent in those countries in which the inquisition is established, where, if a person does not make his confession, and consequently receive his absolution, regularly, he is excommunicated, and at length declared suspected of heresy, and prosecuted according to law.[1]

Another thing that greatly promoted the ruin of discipline, and the encouragement of licentiousness, in the middle ages, was the protection given to criminals, who took refuge in churches, which was a custom borrowed from Paganism; this right of *asylum* being transferred from the heathen temples to Christian churches by the first Christian emperors. In the barbarous times of antiquity, the *rights of hospitality* were held so sacred, that it was even deemed wrong to give up to public justice a criminal who had thrown himself under the protection of any person who was capable of screening him. This privilege was, of course, extended to the temples, which were considered as the houses of their gods; and so sacred was it esteemed, that, in cases of the greatest criminality, all that it was thought lawful to do, was to take off the roof of the temple, and leave the wretch who had taken refuge in it to perish with hunger and the inclemency of the weather.

The abuse of this right of asylum, when it was transferred to Christian churches, was complained of by Chrysostom, who persuaded the emperor to revoke the privileges which had been granted by his predecessors. But they were restored, extended, and established afterwards, especially by Boniface V., in the seventh century,[2] and were the subject of great complaints in many countries, especially in England, where the churches and churchyards were in a manner crowded with debtors and criminals, of all kinds. Complaint being made on this subject in the time of Henry VII., the Pope ordered, that if any person who had taken refuge in an asylum should leave it, and commit a new crime, or repeat his old one, he should be deprived of the privilege.[3] It must be observed that crosses on the public road, and various other things and places, which had the reputation of being *sacred*, had, by degrees, got this privilege of asylum, as well as churches. In later times, any criminal was safe from the pursuit of justice within the precincts of the palace of any cardinal; but Urban V. reformed that abuse.[4]

Among the Jews the privilege of asylum was a wise institution, and came in aid of the principle of justice; as it only protected a person who pleaded that he had killed another inadvertently, so that the relations of the deceased could not hurt him, till a regular inquiry had been made into the fact; but he was delivered up to justice if it appeared that the murder was a wilful one. Besides, this asylum was not granted to the temple in particular, but to certain towns, most conveniently situated for that purpose, in different parts of the country.

Another source of great corruption in discipline was the abuse of pilgrimages. These were undertaken at first out of curiosity, or a natural reverence for any place that had been distinguished by important transactions. They began to be common about the fourth century, and it appears by the writers of that time, that some weak people then valued themselves on having seen such places, and imagined that their prayers would be more favourably heard there than elsewhere. But in later times much more stress was laid upon these things, and in the eighth century pilgrimages began to be enjoined by way of penance, and at length the pilgrimage was often a

---

[1] Fleury's Eighth Discourse, p. 42. (*P.*)
[2] Mosheim, II. p. 28. (*P.*) Cent. vii. **Pt. ii.** Ch. iv. Sect. ii.
[3] Histoire des Papes, IV. p. 273. (*P.*)
[4] Memoires pour la Vie de Petrarch, III. p. 676. (*P.*)

warlike expedition into the holy land, or service in some other of the wars in which the ambition of the popes was interested. By this means all the use even of the pilgrimage itself, as a penance, was wholly lost. For, as Mr. Fleury observes, a penitent marching alone was much more free from temptation to sin than one who went to the wars in company; and some of these penitents even took dogs and horses along with them, that they might take the diversion of hunting in these expeditions.[1]

Solitary pilgrimages were, however, much in fashion, and we find some very rigorous ones submitted to by persons of great eminence in those superstitious times; when it was a maxim that nothing contributed so much to the health of the soul as the mortification of the body. In 997, an emperor of Germany, by the advice of the monks, went barefoot to Mount Garganus, famous for the supposed presence of the archangel Michael, as a penance.

Before the eighth century it had been the custom to confine penitents near the churches, where they had no opportunity of relapsing into their offences; but in this century pilgrimages, and especially distant ones, began to be enjoined under the idea that penitents should lead a *vagabond life*, like Cain. This, however, was soon abused; as, under this pretence, penitents wandered about naked, and loaded with irons, and therefore it was forbidden in the time of Charlemagne. But still it was the custom to impose upon penitents pilgrimages of established reputation, especially those to the holy land, to which there was a constant resort from all parts of Europe. This was the foundation of the *Crusades*.[2]

Of all the consequences of the Crusades, the most important to religion was the discontinuance which they

occasioned of the ancient canonical penance. For a man who was not able to serve in the Crusades was allowed to have the same benefit by contributing to the expenses of those who did. Though the Crusades are over, the canonical penances are not returned.[3]

Fleury also observes, that *plenary indulgences* had their origin with the Crusades; for till then it had never been known that, by any *single work*, the sinner was held to be discharged from all the temporal punishments that might be due from the justice of God. Commutations of penance for pilgrimages to Rome, Compostella, or Jerusalem, had been in use before, and to them, he says, the Crusades added the dangers of war.[4] Besides the wars against the Mahometans, the Crusaders, in the course of their expeditions, had frequent differences with the Greek emperor; and then the preservation of the Roman empire against the schismatical Greeks was held to be as meritorious as fighting against the Turks themselves; and this merit was soon applied to all wars which the popes esteemed to be of importance to religion, especially those against heretics, as the Albigenses in France.[5]

As it was the abuse of indulgences that was the immediate cause of the Reformation by Luther, it may be worth while to go a little back to consider the rise and progress of them. It has been observed in a former period, that all that was meant by *indulgences* in the primitive times, was the relaxation of penance in particular cases, especially at the intercession of the confessors. From this small beginning, the nature of it being at length quite changed, the abuse grew to be so enormous, that it could no longer be supported; and the fall of it occasioned the downfall of a great part of the Papal power.

As an expression of penitence and humiliation, a variety of penances, and some of them of a painful and whim-

---

[1] Fleury's Sixth Discourse, p. 27. (*P.*)
[2] Ibid. [Vol.] XIII. [1742] p. 22. (*P.*) [Ed. Vidal. Tom. IV. pp. 135-6.]

[3] Ibid. p. 29. (*P.*)
[4] Ibid. Sixth Discourse, p. 6. (*P.*)
[5] Ibid. Sixth Discourse, p. 16. (*P.*)

sical nature, had been introduced into the discipline of the church. At first they were voluntary, but afterwards they were imposed, and could not be dispensed with but by the leave of the bishop, who often sold dispensations or indulgences, and thereby raised great sums of money. In the twelfth century the popes, observing what a source of gain this was to the bishops, limited their power, and by degrees drew the whole business of indulgences to Rome. And after remitting the temporal pains and penalties to which sinners had been subjected, they went at length so far as to pretend to abolish the punishment due to wickedness in a future state.

To complete this business, a *book of rates* was published, in which the sums that were to be paid into the apostolical chamber for absolution for particular crimes were precisely stated. This practice entirely set aside the use of the books called *Penitentials*, in which the penances annexed to each crime were registered.

So long as nothing was pretended to be remitted but the temporal penances which it had been usual to enjoin for certain offences, no great alarm was given, and no particular reason was thought necessary for the change; the payment of a sum of money being a *temporal evil*, as well as bearing a number of lashes, or walking bare-foot, &c.; and this commutation was admitted with more ease, as it was pretended, that all the treasure raised by this means was applied to sacred uses, and the benefit of the church. But when the popes pretended to remit the future punishment of sin, and to absolve from the *guilt* of it, some other foundation was necessary; and this they pretended to find in the vast stock of merit which had accrued to the church from the good works of saints and martyrs, besides what were necessary to insure their own salvation. These pretended merits still belonged to the church, and formed a *treasure*, which the popes had the power of dispensing. This doctrine was greatly improved and reduced into a system by Thomas Aquinas. And afterwards, to the merits of the saints and martyrs were added, those of Christ, as increasing the treasure of the church.

Among other things advanced by Cardinal Cajetan in support of the doctrine of indulgences, in his controversy with Luther on the subject, he said, that "one drop of Christ's blood being sufficient to redeem the whole human race, the remaining quanity that was shed in the garden, and upon the cross, was left as a legacy to the church, to be a treasure from whence indulgences were to be drawn, and administered by the Roman pontiffs." [1]

Though in this something may be allowed to the heat of controversy, the doctrine itself had a sanction of a much higher authority. For Leo X., in 1518, decreed, that the popes had the power of remitting both the crime and the punishment of sin, the crime by the sacrament of penance, and the temporal punishment by indulgences, the benefit of which extended to the dead as well as to the living; and that these indulgences are drawn from the superabundance of the merits of Jesus Christ and the saints, of which treasure the Pope is the dispenser. [2]

This Leo X., whose extravagance and expenses had no bounds, had recourse to these indulgences, among other methods of recruiting his exhausted finances; and in the publication of them he promised the forgiveness of all sins, past, present, or to come; and however enormous was their nature. These he sold by wholesale to those who endeavoured to make the most of them; so that passing, like other commodities, from one hand to another, they were even hawked about in the streets by the common pedlars, who used the same artifices to

[1] Mosheim, III. p. 311. (*P.*) Cent. xvi. Sect. i Ch. ii. Sect. ix.
[2] Histoire des Papes, IV. p. 407. (*P.*)

raise the price of these commodities, as of any other in which they dealt.

One Tetzel, a Dominican friar, particularly distinguished himself in pushing the sale of these indulgences. Among other things, in the sermons and speeches which he made on this occasion, he used to say, that, if a man had even lain with the mother of God, he was able, with the Pope's power, to pardon the crime; and he boasted "that he had saved more souls from hell by these indulgences, than St. Peter had converted to Christianity by his preaching."[1] There would be no end of reciting the blasphemous pretensions of the venders of these indulgences, with respect to the enormity of crimes, the number of persons benefited by them, or the time to which they extended. Bishop Burnet had *seen* an indulgence which extended "to ten hundred thousand years." Sometimes indulgences were "affixed to particular churches and altars, to particular times or days, chiefly to the year of jubilee. They are also affixed to such things as may be carried about," with a person, to "*Agnus Dei's*, to medals, to rosaries and scapularies. They are also affixed to some prayers, the devout saying of them being a means to procure great indulgences. The granting these is left to the Pope's discretion."[2]

Such scandalous excesses as these excited the indignation of Luther, who first preached against the abuse of indulgences only, then, in consequence of meeting with opposition, against indulgences themselves, and at length against the papal power which granted them.

Before this time the Council of Constance had, in some measure, restrained the abuse of indulgences, and particularly had made void all those that had been granted during the schism.[3] But

it appears, that, notwithstanding these restraints, the abuses were greater than ever, in the time of Leo X.

The Council of Trent allowed of indulgences in general terms, but forbade the selling of them, and referred the whole to the discretion of the Pope; so that, upon the whole, the abuse was established by this council.[4] But though the Reformation may not have produced any formal decisions in the Church of Rome against the abuse of indulgences, so as to affect the *doctrine* of them, the *practice* has been much moderated; and at present it does not appear that much more stress is laid upon such things by Catholics in general, than by Protestants themselves.

Some remains of the doctrine of indulgences are retained in the Church of England, in which the bishops have a power of dispensing with the marriage of persons more near akin than the law allows; which is, in fact, to excuse what they themselves call the *crime of incest*. But there is something much more unjustifiable in the power of *absolution*, or an authoritative declaration of forgiveness of sin, which is also retained from the Church of Rome. For, after confession, the priest is directed to absolve a sick person in this form of words: "Our Lord Jesus Christ, who has left power to his church to absolve all sinners who truly repent and believe in him, of his great mercy forgive thee thine offences; and by his authority committed to me, I absolve thee from all thy sin, in the name of the Father, and of the Son, and of the Holy Ghost." This is exactly a popish absolution, and is therefore liable to all the objections to which popish absolutions and indulgences are liable.[5] One that is not in priests' orders cannot pronounce this absolution.

Whatever was meant by the power of absolution communicated by Christ to

---

[1] Mosheim, III. p. 304. (*P.*) Cent. xvi. Sect. i. Ch. ii. Sect. iii. Note [o].
[2] Burnet on the Articles, p. 282. (*P.*) Art. xxii. Ed. 4, p. 207.
[3] L'Enfant, I. p. 438. (*P.*) L. vi. Sect. xxiii. Histoire, p. 566.

[4] See Sess. xxv. "Decretum be Indulgentiis." *S. Con. Trid* p. 218.
[5] See Free and Cand. Disquis. pp. 124, 329, 330.

the apostles, there is nothing said in the New Testament of its being committed to the ordinary ministers of the church, so that it must have been confined to the apostles only; and we have no example even of their exercising any such authority as the Church of Rome, or that of England pretends to. It is in vain to apologize for this form of absolution, by saying that the pardon of sin is only promised to the *penitent*, for then what occasion was there for mentioning any power committed to the clergyman with respect to the absolution, unless he be at least supposed to know the heart, and thereby be enabled to judge with certainty whether any person be a true penitent, and a proper object of mercy, or not? If the form has any meaning at all, it must imply that it is in the power of the priest to absolve, or not to absolve, as he shall think proper, which is certainly great presumption and impiety.

In many other respects the discipline of the Church of England is very imperfect, and the wisest members of her communion, as well as those among the Papists, lament the evil without seeing any prospect of a remedy. The business of auricular confession, and also that of private penance, is entirely abolished; but the *bishops' courts* remain, which by mixing things of a civil with those of an ecclesiastical nature, are of great disservice to both. And whereas, by the rules of these courts, public penances are enjoined for certain offences, persons are allowed to commute them for sums of money.

SECTION III.

HAVING traced the general course of church discipline, in all its changes, from the time of the apostles, to the Reformation, it may not be amiss to go over the same ground once more,

with a view to consider the methods that have been from time to time taken, in order to enforce the censures of the church; and in this we shall have occasion to lament, among other things, the most horrid abuse of both ecclesiastical and civil power; while men were continually attempting to do by force what it is not in the power of force to do, viz. to guide the conscience, or even to compel an outward conformity, in large bodies of people, to the same religious profession. Of this interference of the civil power in the business of religion, we shall see the first steps in this period, in which a great deviation was made from the admirable simplicity of the rules laid down by our Saviour.

In order to prevent the progress of vice, and in any case to preserve the reputation of Christian societies, our Lord laid down a most excellent rule, as a general instruction for the conduct of his disciples, viz. first to admonish an offending brother in the most private and prudent manner. If that was not effectual, one or two more were to give their sanction to the reproof; if that failed, the case was to come under the cognizance of the whole congregation; and if the offender proved obstinate and refractory in this last instance, he was to be expelled from the society, in consequence of which the church was discharged from all farther attention to his conduct, and he was considered in the same light as if he had never belonged to it. Such, and so admirably simple, and well adapted to its end, was the system of discipline in the constitution of the Christian church; and for some time it was strictly adhered to, and the effects of it were great and happy. By this means Christians effectually *watched over one another in love, exhorting one another daily,* and not *suffering sin in each other.* Thus, also, by forming regular bodies, they became more firmly united and attached to one another, and their zeal for the common cause was greatly increased.

Besides admonition and reproof, private and public, the primitive Christians had no method of enforcing the observance of Christian duties. If this failed, nothing remained but *excommunication*, or cutting off the vicious or refractory member from any visible relation to them, or connexion with them. And, indeed, considering the valuable advantages resulting to every particular member from the rest of the body, a formal exclusion, and, as it necessarily must have been, an ignominious exclusion, from a Christian society, could not but have been regarded, even without any superstition, as a very awful thing.

It was generally concluded, that the censures of the church, passed in a solemn and unanimous manner, would be ratified at the tribunal of Christ at the last day; so that a person cut off from the communion of the church here, would be excluded from heaven hereafter. And, indeed, if a man's conduct were such as exposed him to this censure of his fellow-christians, of whose kindness and affection he had abundant experience, and when they were under no bias or prejudice in giving their judgment, it is probable that it would be just, and therefore be ratified in heaven; and we may presume that, in the primitive times, this was generally the case; though it must be acknowledged that even a whole church may judge uncharitably and rashly, and in this case their censures certainly will not be ratified at the righteous tribunal of God.

Excommunications became much more dreadful when, in the progress of superstition, the participation of religious rites (and especially that of the Lord's supper) came to be considered as a necessary qualification for the favour of God and the happiness of heaven, an opinion which prevailed in very early times.

Whatever was the *cause*, the *effect* of church censures in those times was very extraordinary. It was customary, as we have seen, for persons under sentence of excommunication to attend at the doors of the church with all the marks of the deepest dejection and contrition, entreating the ministers and people, with tears in their eyes; and earnestly begging their prayers, and restoration to the peace of the Church.

Persons the most distinguished for their wealth and power were indiscriminately subject to these church censures, and had no other method of being restored to communion but by the same humiliation and contrition that was expected from the meanest person in the society. When Philip, the governor of Egypt, would have entered a Christian church, after the commission of some crime, the bishop forbade him till he first made confession of his sin, and passed through the order of penitents, a sentence which, we are told, he willingly submitted to. Even the emperor Theodosius the Great was excommunicated by Ambrose, the bishop of Milan, for a barbarous slaughter of the Thessalonians; and that great prince submitted to a penance of eight months, and was not received into the church till after the most humble confession of his offence, and giving the most undeniable proof of his sincerity.

I must add, that whenever a person was excommunicated in any particular church, it was generally deemed wrong to admit him to communion in any other. Sometimes, however, neighbouring churches, being well acquainted with the cause of excommunication, and not approving of it, received into their communion the persons so stigmatized. And when the regular subordination of one church to another was established, it was customary for the excommunicated person to appeal from the sentence of his particular church to a higher tribunal. Many of these appeals were made to the Church of Rome, from other churches not regularly subordinate to it, which laid the first foundation of the exorbitant power of that church.

When Christians began to debate about *opinions*, and to divide and subdivide themselves on that account, it is to be lamented, but not to be wondered at, that they laid an undue stress on what they deemed to be the *right faith*, and that they should apply church censures in order to prevent the spreading of heretical opinions; without waiting till they could judge by observation what effect such opinions had on the temper and general conduct of men, and indeed without considering that influence at all. The first remarkable abuse of the power of excommunication in this way is by no means such as recommends it, being such as would now be deemed the most frivolous and unjustifiable that can well be imagined. For, on the account of nothing more than a difference of opinion and practice with respect to the time of celebrating Easter, Victor, bishop of Rome, excommunicated at once all the Eastern churches. But this was reckoned a most daring piece of insolence and arrogance, for which he was severely reproved by other bishops; nor, indeed, was any regard paid to the censure. It must be observed that, in consequence of appeals being made from inferior churches to the patriarchal ones, these took upon them to extend their excommunications beyond the limits of their acknowledged jurisdiction, viz. to all who held any obnoxious opinion or practice. Persons thus censured often formed separate churches, and in return excommunicated those who had excommunicated them.

In this state of mutual hostility things often continued a long time, till the influence of an emperor, or some other foreign circumstance, determined the dispute in favour of one of them, which was thenceforth deemed the *orthodox* side of the question, whilst the other was condemned as *heretical*. It is well known that the Arians and Athanasians were in this manner reputed orthodox by turns, as both had the sanction of councils and

emperors in their favour; till, in consequence of mere faction, and the authority of the emperors, the party of Athanasius prevailed at last.

The first instance that we meet with of the use of actual *force*, or rather of a desire to make use of it, by a Christian church, was in the proceedings against Paul, bishop of Samosata; when, at the request of a Christian synod, the heathen emperor Aurelian expelled him from the episcopal house.[1] Indeed, having been deposed from his office, if that had been done by competent authority, namely, that of his own diocese, he could not be said to have any right to the emoluments of it, and therefore his keeping possession of the episcopal house was an act of violence on his side.

But as soon as the empire became what is called Christian, we have examples enough of the interference of civil power in matters of religion; and we soon find instances of the abuse of excommunication, and the addition of civil incapacities annexed to that ecclesiastical censure. In a council held at Ptolemais, in Cyrene, Andronicus the prefect was excommunicated, and it was expressed in the sentence, that no temple of God should be open unto him, that no one should salute him during his life, and that he should not be buried after his death.[2]

The emperor Constantine, besides banishing Arius himself, ordered his writings to be burnt, and forbidding any persons to conceal him, under pain of death, deprived many of those who were declared heretics of the privileges which he had granted to Christians in general, and besides imposing fines upon them, forbade their assemblies, and demolished their places of worship. On the other hand, the emperor Constantius banished the orthodox bishops because they would not condemn Athanasius. Nestorius was banished by Theodosius, in whose reign persecution for the sake of religion

[1] Fleury's Seventh Discourse, p. 7. (*P.*)
[2] Sueur, A. D. 411. (*P.*)

made greater advances than in any other within this period. He certainly imagined he made a right use of the power with which God had entrusted him, by employing it in establishing what he thought to be the orthodox faith, without ever reflecting on the impropriety of such a *means* with respect to such an *end*.

Immediately upon his baptism, which, according to the superstitious notions which influenced many persons of that age, he had deferred till his life was in danger by sickness, he published a decree commanding that, in order that all his subjects should make profession of the same religion which the divine apostle Peter taught the Romans, the doctrine of the Trinity should be embraced by those who would be called *catholics;* that all others, whom he says he judged to be *mad*, should bear the infamous name of *heretics*, and that their assemblies should not be called *churches*, reserving their farther punishment in the first place to the vengeance of heaven, and afterwards to the movements with which God should inspire him.[1] In consequence, I suppose, of one of these *movements*, three years after this edict, he published another, forbidding the Arians to hold their assemblies in cities. He, however, was not the person who was inspired with the glorious thought of sentencing all heretics to be burned alive. This was reserved for a more advanced state of the Christian church.

It was of a son of Theodosius, viz. the Eastern Emperor Honorius, that the authority of persecution to death was obtained, by four bishops sent from Carthage for that purpose in 410; and the edict extended to all who differed ever so little from the catholic faith.[2] But it does not appear that this sanguinary decree was carried into execution.

Notwithstanding all the hardships which the Christians had lately suf-

fered from the Pagans, and the just remonstrances they had made on the subject, no sooner were they in possession of the same power, than they were too ready to make a similar use of it; and instead of showing the world the contrast of a truly Christian spirit, they were eager to retaliate upon their enemies, whom they had now at their mercy. But at first the number of the Pagans was too great to make very violent proceedings at all prudent. As the Christians increased in number, the Pagans were soon laid under great restrictions.

In the year 346, it was decreed that all the heathen temples in cities should be shut up, but that those in the villages should not be meddled with; the Christians having increased more in the cities, and superstition, as might be expected, retaining its hold of the minds of men much longer in the villages, where they had less intercourse with strangers, and consequently less opportunity of receiving information. It was in this state of things that the Heathens began to be distinguished by the name of *Pagans* (*Pagani*), that is, inhabitants of villages. In the year 382, these Pagans were laid under farther restrictions: for though they were allowed to frequent their temples as usual, they were not suffered to make any sacrifices there. At the same time, however, the clandestine assemblies of the Manicheans were absolutely forbidden.

Even the more learned Christians, who might have been expected, by reflections upon the past, to have seen things in a juster light, and to have entertained more liberal sentiments, soon became the advocates for the interference of civil power in matters of religion. Austin, the oracle of the church in his own time, and still more so after his death, confessed that he had formerly been of opinion that heretics should not be harassed by catholics, but rather allured by all kinds of gentle methods; yet afterwards he changed his opinion, having

[1] Sueur, A. D. 380. (*P.*)
[2] Taylor on the *Grand Apostacy*, p. 131. (*P.*)

learned by experience, that the laws made by the emperors against heretics had proved the happy occasion of their conversion.[1] His whole *Epistle to Vincentius*, where we learn this, is well worth reading, as being perhaps the first piece in which the use of force in matters of religion is pleaded for. He certainly meant well by it.

As one great source of information is by means of books, all those whose wish it has been to prevent the spreading of any particular opinion, have generally done everything in their power to suppress the books that recommend it. The Heathens made frequent attempts to compel the Christians to give up their sacred books; but the first example of anything of this kind by Christians (except what is mentioned above concerning the writings of Arius) was exhibited by Theodosius, who in 448 made a law, by which it was ordered, that all the books, the doctrine of which was not conformable to the Councils of Nice and Ephesus, and also to the decisions of Cyril, should be destroyed, and the concealers of them put to death. Afterwards Pope Gelasius, in a council held at Rome in 494, specified the books which the Church of Rome rejected, but without laying any penalty on those who should read them.[2]

So far those who were in possession of power, and who were instigated by bigotry, went in these early times. We shall see a much greater extension of this, as well as of every other method of preventing and extirpating heresy, in the following period.

SECTION IV.

OF THE METHODS OF ENFORCING ECCLE-
SIASTICAL CENSURES, FROM THE TIME
OF AUSTIN TO THE REFORMATION AND
AFTERWARDS, BY THE CATHOLICS.

WE are now launching into what has been properly enough called the *dark* age of this Western part of the world; and we shall not be surprised to find *bigotry* and *violence* keep pace with *ignorance*, and that they should not be lessened but by the increase of knowledge, and but very slowly even then.

As, upon the conversion of the barbarous nations to Christianity, the bishops became some of the most considerable land-owners, in consequence of which they had a right to sit in their parliaments, to hold courts, and even to serve in the wars, there necessarily arose an unnatural mixture of civil and ecclesiastical power, the same person serving in both capacities. Since all public concerns, of a spiritual as well as of a temporal nature, were frequently discussed in these parliaments, or assemblies of the states, regulations of all kinds, ecclesiastical as well as others, were enforced by civil penalties.

By this means *compulsory penances* were introduced in the seventh century, when we find proofs of their being in Spain. There the bishops, finding offenders refusing to submit to penance, complained to their parliament, and requested their princes to interpose their temporal power. The punishments that were enjoined in this manner, were prohibitions to eat flesh, to wear linen, to mount a horse, &c.[3] It would have been happy if civil power had proceeded no farther than this in matters of religion, and had extended to no other cases.

In this period the sentence of excommunication became a much more dreadful thing than it had been before, and a proportionably greater solemnity was added to the forms of it. The most solemn part of the new ceremonial was the extinction of lamps or candles, by throwing them on the ground, with a solemn imprecation, that the person against whom the excommunication was pronounced, might in like manner be extinguished or destroyed by the judgment of God. And

[1] Opera, II. p. 174. (*P.*)
[2] Fleury's Seventh Discourse, p. 24. (*P.*)

[3] Ibid. XIII. p. 44. (*P.*) [Ed. Vidal. Tom. IV. p. 143.]

because the people were summoned to attend this ceremony by the sound of a bell, and the curses accompanying the excommunication were recited out of a book, while the person who pronounced them stood on some balcony or stage, from which he would throw down his lights, we have the phrase of *cursing by bell, book and candle.*[1] The first example of excommunication by throwing down lighted lamps was at Rheims, about the year 900, when the bishops excommunicated some murderers in this manner.[2]

When heresies sprang up in the church, and there were many other offenders who were out of the reach of church power, it came to be the custom to pronounce these curses against them on certain days of the year, and we find Thursday before Easter made choice of for this purpose. Thus we read that John XXII., according to the custom of the Church of Rome, on the Thursday before Easter, published a bull, by which he excommunicated the poor of Lyons (or the Albigenses), the Arnoldists and all heretics in general, the Corsairs, the falsifiers of apostolical bulls, and all who usurped the city of Rome or the patrimony of St. Peter.[3]

At length, sentences of general excommunication becoming frequent, (every decretal, though the subject of it was ever so trifling, denouncing this sentence against all who should disobey it,) and consequently whole classes of men, and sometimes whole communities, falling under those censures, they came to be despised and lost their effect.[4]

Leonardo Aretino, who wrote before the Reformation, observes, in his History of Florence, that when the citizens had been used to the papal censures, they did not much regard the interdicts they were laid under; especially as they observed that they were not decreed for any good reason, but depended on the will of those who had most influence with the popes. And in the year 1377, when the city was laid under an interdict, public orders were given to the clergy to pay no regard to it.[5]

When the passions of ecclesiastics were much interested, they were not content with mere church censures; but, having the sanction of the civil power, they annexed the most dreadful civil penalties to their excommunications. These were easily introduced after the Roman empire became Christian; and in many of the imperial constitutions made after that event, we find various civil disqualifications, some of which were mentioned in the former period, added to the censures of the church. But the whole system of this mixed ecclesiastical and civil polity received fresh and stronger sanctions upon the conversion of the Germans, Goths, Celts, and other Northern nations. These people had been used to excommunication in their own Pagan religions; and the consequence of it had always been, the most dreadful civil penalties and disabilities. Among the Gauls, excommunicated persons had been looked upon as wicked and scandalous wretches; all people avoided their company, they were not allowed the benefits of the courts of justice, nor were they admitted to any post of honour or profit in the community.

Of this prejudice of the people the Christian priests willingly took advantage, as by this means they could overawe those who despised mere church censures. Civil penalties for offences against the church were increased by degrees, till heresy came to be considered as a crime of so heinous a nature, that *burning alive* was decreed to be, of all others, the most proper punishment of it. We do not, indeed, wonder to find that, of all crimes, the church, which had so much at stake, should be most alarmed at

[1] See these forms, *Hist. of Popery,* 1785, II. pp. 388, 389
[2] Jortin's Remarks, IV. p. 518. (*P.*)
[3] Hist. des Papes, IV. p. 12. (*P.*)
[4] Fleury's Tenth Discourse, p. 65. (*P.*)

[5] B. iv. pp. 77, 172. (*P.*)

that of *heresy*, and therefore should apply what might be thought to be the most effectual remedy, and the most likely to terrify those who should be exposed to it.

It is, however, curious enough to observe that, as there could be no pretence for ecclesiastics, *as such*, having recourse to civil penalties, or, according to the usual phrase, making use of the *temporal sword;* whenever it was thought necessary that any criminal against the church should be punished with death, they were solemnly delivered over to the civil power. In the Council of Lateran, in 1179, which was before any heretics were punished with death, it is said that, "though the church rejects bloody executions, it may nevertheless be aided by the laws of Christian princes, and that the fear of corporeal punishments often makes persons have recourse to spiritual remedies."[1] And to this day the court of Inquisition not only solemnly delivers over to the civil power all those who are destined to suffer death, but even formally recommends them to mercy,[2] where it is certainly not the wish of those who express this concern for them, that they should find any.[3]

Among other methods of trying whether a person was a heretic, we find, in these dark ages, one of the ordeals of the Northern nations, and the same that till of late years was thought to be the proper test of witchcraft in this country.[4] For, in the persecution of the Albigenses, in order to know whether a person was a heretic, those who suspected him threw him into water, on the supposition that, if he was a heretic, the devil within him being lighter than the water, would prevent his sinking.[5] But, as I have observed before, the punishment that was thought to be the most proper for heresy, was burning alive; and indeed this was the first capital punishment that was decreed for it. There was not, however, any proper capital punishment for heresy till the year 1215, when it was appointed, by the fourth Council of Lateran, that all heretics should be delivered over to the civil magistrates to be burned.

Why this peculiarly dreadful punishment, of all others, should have been thought the most proper for heresy, it is not easy to say. Possibly the crime was thought to be so dreadful and contagious, that it was determined, as far as possible, to destroy and annihilate even the body of the heretic, lest it should taint the earth, the sea, or the air.[6] The Church of

---

[1] Histoire des Papes, III. p. 90. (*P.*)

[2] "Relinquimus.... Curiæ seculari, eandem affectuose rogantes, prout suadent canonicæ sanctiones, ut illis vitam et membra illibata conservet." *Holy Inquisition*, London, 1681, p. 161.

[3] "We, the Inquisitors of heretical pravity, having called on the name of the Lord Jesus Christ, and of his glorious mother the Virgin Mary, and sitting on our tribunal, and judging, with the holy gospels lying before us, by this our sentence put in writing, define, pronounce, declare, and sentence thee, to be a 'convicted, confessing, affirmative and professed heretic, and to be delivered, and left by us as such, to the secular arm ; and we by this our sentence do cast thee out of the ecclesiastical court, as a convicted, confessing, affirmative and professed heretic, and we do leave and deliver thee to the secular arm, and to the power of the secular court ; but at the same time do most earnestly beseech that court so to moderate its sentence, as not to touch thy blood, or to put thy life in any danger.' Is there in all history an instance of so gross and confident mockery of God and the world?"—Geddes's *Inquisition in Portugal*, 1730, Ed. 3, pp. 408, 409. See also Limborch, *Hist. Inquis.* C. xl. II. pp. 288–292.

[4] This *Ordeal* "about the middle ages" was applied to "persons accused or suspected" of *any* crime. After the appointment of various adjurations, prayers and benedictions, it is added, "When the water has been thus exorcised, let those who are to go into it put off their clothes, and kiss the gospel and the cross, and let holy water be sprinkled over them. All that are present ought to be fasting ; and so let them be thrown into the water. If they sink, they shall be reputed innocent; but if they swim on the surface, they shall be adjudged guilty." *Of Ordeal.* "History of Remarkable Tryals," 1715, pp. 8-16.

Verstegan, in 1605, describing the *Cold-water Ordeal*, adds, "This kind of trial is used for such as are accused to be witches, who being cast into the water, with a cord fastened unto them, are said, if they be witches indeed, to float upon the same, and in no wise to be able to sink into it." *Restitution of decayed Intelligence*, pp. 52, 53.

[5] Basnage. Histoire des Eglises Réformées, I (b). p. 229. (*P.*)

[6] I have met with a passage in a bull of Pope John XXIII. against the Wickliffites, quoted by L'Enfant in his *History of the Council of Pisa*, II. p. 98, which sufficiently explains whence the

Rome, having once employed this horrid engine, found it so well adapted to the rest of her system, and so necessary to enforce a regard to decrees not recommended by reason or argument, that she had frequent recourse to it; and though this was the greatest of all abuses of ecclesiastical authority, it was retained, along with other corruptions of Christianity, by most of the first reformers.

The burning of heretics was not, however, the first kind of persecution which the Church of Rome employed to subdue her enemies; and recourse was not had to this, till other methods, and even several of a very violent kind, had been tried without effect. The first object that roused the sanguinary disposition of the court of Rome, was the heresies, as they were called, of the Waldenses, and of the Albigenses, the former of whom inhabited some of the mountainous parts of the Alps, and the latter the southern provinces of France.

These people were dreadfully persecuted by Innocent III., who first prohibited all manner of intercourse or communication with them, confiscated their goods, disinherited their children, destroyed their houses, denied them the rite of sepulture, and gave their accusers one-third of their effects. But in 1198 he erected the court of *Inquisition*, the object of which was the utter extirpation of them, in which Dominic was the chief actor.[1] Afterwards he published crusades against them, promising all who would engage in that war the same indulgences that had been granted to those who engaged

in the expeditions for the recovery of the Holy Land.[2] In consequence of this, great multitudes of them were destroyed with all manner of cruelties.

This war, or rather massacre, continued near forty years, and a million of men are supposed to have lost their lives in it. And of these, it is said, there were three hundred thousand of the Crusaders themselves.[3] However, the consequence of this persecution was the same with that of most others; the reprobated opinion being farther disseminated by this means. Particularly, the kings of England, and the earls of Toulouse (who had been the heads of the Albigenses), being related, many of them came over into England, where great numbers embraced their opinions. They were afterwards imbibed by Wickliffe, and from him they passed into Bohemia.

Perhaps the most horrible and perfidious of any single act of barbarity, committed by the Papists, was the massacre of the Protestants in Paris, on the eve of St. Bartholomew, in 1572; when the Huguenots (as the Protestants in France are called) were lulled asleep by all the forms of pacification, and an attempt was made to rise upon them, and destroy them all in one night. In Paris, and some other towns, it took effect, and great numbers were massacred when they were altogether unapprehensive of danger. Had this happened in a popular tumult, it would have been more excusable; but it was not only a most deliberate act of perfidy, concerted long before the time of execution, but the king himself, Charles IX., bore a part in it, firing upon his own subjects from his window; and Pope Gregory XIII. gave solemn thanks to God for this massacre in the church of St. Louis, whither he himself went in procession.[4]

---

idea of *burning* heretics, rather than putting them to any other kind of death, was borrowed. He says, " We ordain that they be publicly burned, in execution of the sentence of our Saviour, John xv. 6: *If any man abide not in me, he is cast forth as a branch, and is withered; and men gather them, and cast them into the fire, and they are burned.*" (*P.*) Note at the end of the edition 1782.

[1] "The true origin of the Inquisition, by delegation from the Pope, as it is now managed, was about 1216, when *Innocent III.* appointed St. Dominic to be the first inquisitor, to suppress the growing heresie of the Albigenses." *Holy Inquis.* p. 51. See also Limborch, C. x. I. p. 60.

[2] "Catholici, qui crucis assumpto charactere ad Hæreticorum exterminium se accinxerint, illa gaudeant indulgentia, illoque sancto privilegio sint muniti, quæ accedentibus in Sanctæ Terræ subsidium conceduntur." *Holy Inquis.* pp. 54, 55.

[3] Histoire des Papes, III. p. 16. (*P.*)

[4] "Certain it is that the massacres of St. Bar-

P

The guns of St. Angelo were also fired, and bonfires were made in the streets of Rome upon the occasion.[1]

The court of Rome has even employed the same bloody methods to extirpate heresies that arose among the Catholics themselves, those who maintained them adhering to the Popish system in general. This was the case with respect to some Franciscans in the fourteenth century, who maintained, that neither Christ nor the apostles had any personal property. This most innocent opinion was most vehemently opposed by the Dominicans; and John XXII., in 1324, pronounced it to be "a pestilential, erroneous, damnable and blasphemous doctrine, subversive of the Catholic faith; and declared all such as adhered to it, obstinate heretics and rebels against the church. In consequence of this merciless decree, great numbers" of those poor Franciscans "were apprehended by the Dominican inquisitors, ... and committed to the flames."[2]

It would be unjust, however, to suppose that all the members of the *Catholic Church*, as it is called, have been equally bent on the extirpation of heretics by these violent methods. At all times there have been advocates for moderation among very zealous Papists. Thomas Aquinas, who for many centuries was esteemed the bulwark of the Popish cause, maintained, that religion ought not to be extended by force; alleging that no person can believe as he would, and that the will should not be

forced.[5] There were also those who remonstrated very strongly against all the persecutions of the Protestants by the Papists, especially those of Philip II. of Spain, as well as those of Louis XIV. of France. And there is reason to believe that the minds of the Catholics in general are now so much enlightened, partly by reflection, but chiefly by experience, that they would no more act the same things over again, than the Protestants would, who, as will be seen in the next Section, were guilty of almost as great excesses, in proportion to the extent of their power.

As we are naturally more interested in our own history, I shall mention a few more particulars concerning the progress of persecution in this country. There were no penal statutes against heresy, enacted by the authority of an English Parliament, before the fifth year of Richard II., in 1382; when it was appointed, that heretics should be kept in prison "till they justified themselves according to law, and the reason of holy church." The commitment was to be the rule for the chancellor, after the bishop had presented the name of the offender.[4]

Afterwards Henry IV., in order to gain the good will of the clergy, procured an act, in the second year of his reign, 1400, by which convicted heretics might be imprisoned and confined at the discretion of the diocesan or of his commissary, and those who refused to abjure, or who relapsed, were to be burnt to death in some conspicuous place before the people. By this law all heretics were left to the mercy of the bishops in the spiritual courts, who might imprison them or put them to death, without presentment or trial by a jury, as was the practice in all other criminal cases.

tholomew's day, are painted at Rome, in the royal hall of the Vatican, with these words under the picture, *Pontifex Colignii necem probat.*" See the account of the massacre in "An Essay upon the Civil Wars of France, by M. de *Voltaire*, author of the Henriade," Ed. 2, 1728, pp. 12–17. This Essay was written by Voltaire in English, while resident in this country. See Mon. Repos. X. p. 88.

In "Histoire du Parlement de Paris," par M. l'Abbé Big..., but which has been attributed to Voltaire, the author says, "Les détails de ces massacres que je dois omettre ici seront présens à tous les esprits jusqu'à la dernière postérité." *Histoire*, Amst. 1769, p. 180.

[1] Histoire des Papes, V p. 25. (*P.*)
[2] Mosheim, III. pp. 177, 178. (*P.*) Cent. xiv. Pt. ii. Ch. ii. Sect. xxix.

[3] Fleury's Sixth Discourse, p. 32. (*P.*)
[4] Rapin represents as the more probable opinion upon this subject, that the Commons refused to pass the act, but that the bishops were empowered solely by the king. "Les Communes réfusèrent de donner leur consentement au *bill* qui leur fut présenté sur ce sujet, et que ce ne fut que du Roi seulement, que les Evêques obtinrent cette permission." *Histoire*, L. x. III. p. 286.

The reign of his son Henry V., whose interest it was to keep things quiet at home, by obliging the clergy, while he was carrying on his wars abroad, was very unfavourable to free inquiry. In the beginning of his reign, 1414, an act was made against the Lollards or Wickliffites,[1] by which it was decreed that they should forfeit all their lands and goods to the king. In this reign, however, it was that the writ *de hæretico comburendo* was issued from the chancery; by which it seems that the heretics were taken again into the king's protection. But this does not appear to have been necessary, or at least to have been practised, for no such writs are to be found upon the rolls before the reign of Henry VIII. "By virtue of these statutes, the clergy ... exercised numberless cruelties upon the people, there being 'some hundreds of examples,' of persons imprisoned, and probably put to death by them."[2]

The prohibition of books was an evil that was greatly increased after the Reformation, though it began before. There were rigorous edicts against the writings of Wickliffe and John Huss. But Leo X. renewed them in condemning the propositions of Luther, and all the books that bore his name. He made a decree that no book should be published in Rome, or in any other city or diocese, before it had been approved by an officer appointed for that purpose; and he was the first who made any decree of this nature.[3] The popes that succeeded him, forbade, under pain of excommunication, the reading of all the books of heretics; and in order to distinguish them, Philip II. ordered the Spanish Inquisition to print a catalogue of them, which Paul IV. also did at Rome; at the same time ordering them to be burnt.[4] In 1597, Clement VIII. published another catalogue of books prohibited, and among them was

Junius's translation of the Old Testament, and Beza's of the New, though the former might, at the discretion of the bishop, be granted to learned men.

SECTION V.

OF PERSECUTION BY PROTESTANTS.

I HAVE already observed, that this sanguinary method of propagating and establishing religion was adopted, together with other popish maxims, by the Reformers; and, alas, the history of all reformed countries bears too strong evidence of it.

In the wars of Bohemia, both the Protestants and Papists "agreed ... that it was innocent and lawful to ... extirpate with fire and sword, the enemies of the *true religion*." The Protestants acknowledged "that *heretics* were worthy of capital punishment, but they denied obstinately that John Huss was a heretic." Ziska, the general of the Hussites, fell upon the sect of the Beghards in 1421, and "put some to the sword, and condemned the rest to the flames, which dreadful punishment they sustained with the most cheerful fortitude."[5]

Luther had no idea of the impropriety of civil penalties to enforce the true religion. He only objected to the putting heretics to death, but approved of their being confined, as madmen. "He persuaded the electors of Saxony not to tolerate ... the followers of Zuinglius," merely because he did not believe the real presence of Christ in the eucharist; and "the Lutheran lawyers ... condemned to death Peter Pestelius for being a Zuinglian." They also put to death several Anabaptists.[6] It was not till towards the end of the seventeenth century that "the Lutheran churches adopted that leading maxim of the Arminians," that no good subject was justly punishable

---

[1] See Rapin, *Histoire*, L. xi. III. p. 483.
[2] Neal's History of the Puritans, I. p. 5. (*P.*) Toulmin's Ed. 1793, I. p. 7.
[3] Histoire des Papes, IV. p. 389. (*P.*)
[4] Basnage, II. pp. 465, 466. Histoire des Papes, IV. p. 634. (*P.*)

[5] Mosheim, III. pp. 261, 274. (*P.*) Cent. xv. Pt. ii. Ch. iii. Sect. iv. Ch. v. Sect. ii.
[6] Chandler's "History of Persecution," 1736, pp. 310, 311. (*P.*)

"by the magistrate for his erroneous opinions." [1]

Mosheim also says, that Zuinglius is "said to have attributed to the civil magistrate such an extensive power in ecclesiastical affairs, as is quite inconsistent with the essence and genius of religion." [2] He condemned an Anabaptist to be drowned, with this cruel insult, Qui iterum mergit mergatur; *He that dips a second time, let him be dipped.* [3]

Calvin went upon the same plan, persecuting many worthy persons, and even procuring Servetus to be burned alive for writing against the doctrine of the Trinity. He also wrote a treatise in order to prove the lawfulness of putting heretics to death; and in one of his letters he says, " Since the Papists, in order to vindicate their own superstitions, crully shed innocent blood, it is a shame that Christian magistrates should have no courage at all in the defence of certain truth." Even Melancthon, though esteemed to be of a mild and moderate temper, approved of the death of Servetus. [4]

After the Reformation in England, the laws against heretics were not relaxed, but the proceedings were appointed to be regular, as in other criminal cases. Thus it was enacted in 1534, "that heretics should be proceeded against upon presentments" by a jury, or on the oath of "two witnesses at least." [5]

When the new liturgy was confirmed by act of parliament in the reign of Edward VI., in 1548, it was ordered that "such of the clergy as refused" to conform to it, "should, upon the first conviction, suffer six months' imprisonment, and forfeit a year's profits of his benefice; for the second offence forfeit all his church preferments, and suffer a year's imprisonment; and for the third offence imprisonment for life. Such as wrote or printed against the book were to be fined ten pounds for the first offence, twenty pounds for the second, and to forfeit all their goods; and be imprisoned for life, for the third." [6]

Cranmer, whilst he was a Lutheran, consented to the burning of John Lambert and Ann Askew, for those very doctrines for which he himself suffered afterwards; and when he was a sacramentarian, he was the cause of the death of Joan Bocher, an Arian, importuning the young king Edward VI. to sign the death-warrant; and he is said to have done it with great reluctance, saying, with tears in his eyes, that if he did wrong, it was in submission to his authority (Cranmer's), and that he should answer to God for it. [7]

Many were the severities under which the Puritans laboured in the reign of Queen Elizabeth, and the princes of the Stuart family; and the Presbyterians were but too ready to act with a high hand in their turn, in the short time that they were in power; but they were soon repaid with interest, on the Restoration. At the Revolution they obtained pretty good terms, but still all those who could not subscribe the doctrinal articles of the Church of England remained subject to the same penalties as before, and a new and severe law was made against the Anti-trinitarians. This law, which subjects the offender to confiscation of goods and imprisonment for life, if he persists in acting contrary to the law, still remains in force, [8] though many

<hr/>

[1] Mosheim, IV. p. 440. (*P.*) Cent. xvii. Sect. ii Pt. ii. Ch. i. Sect xvi.
[2] Ibid. III. p. 320. (*P.*) Cent. xvi. Sect. i. Ch. ii. Sect. xii.
[3] Chandler's "History of Persecution," p. 328. (*P.*)
[4] Ibid. pp. 321, 323. (*P.*)
[5] Neal's Hist. I. p. 10. (*P.*) Ed. 1793, p. 14.

[6] Ibid. p. 39. (*P.*) Ibid. p. 51.
[7] See Burnet's *Reform.* 12mo. Ed. 6, II. p. 81. M. Repos. VII. p. 363, &c.
[8] Now repealed, with the exceptions in the Toleration Act. [It is interesting to remark the progress of the principle of religious equality in the United Kingdom since the time when Rutt added the preceding note. First came the Catholic Emancipation Act; then, the Dissenters' Chapel Bill. Next, after a considerable interval, a measure, carried by Mr. James Heywood, laid the foundation of religious equality at the two great national Universities. Since then, Church Rates have been abolished; and the Irish Church Bill of 1869 has introduced perfect religious equality into one portion of the United Kingdom. That

other hardships under which Dissenters formerly laboured have lately been removed.

The persecution of the Remonstrants by the Calvinistic party in Holland, was as rancorous in the mode of carrying it on, as any of the Popish persecutions, though the penalties did not extend beyond banishment.

All the Protestant churches have been too ready to impose their own faith upon others, and to bind all their posterity to believe as they did. But the most remarkable public act of this kind occurs in the history of the Protestant church in France. At a synod held in 1612, it was decreed, that they who take holy orders should take this oath: "I, whose name is here underwritten, do receive and approve the confession of faith of the reformed churches in this kingdom, and also promise to persevere in it until death, and to believe and teach agreeably thereunto."[1] In another decree, passed in 1620, they adopt the decrees of the Synod of Dort, promising to persevere in that faith all their lives, and to defend it to the utmost of their power.[2] Is it to be regretted that a church, the principles of which were so narrow and intolerant, should, in the course of Divine Providence, be suppressed? It is to be hoped that when it shall seem fit to the same wise Providence to revive the Protestant interest in that country, it will be more liberal, and more deserving of the name of a *reformed Christian* church.

There is too great a mixture of civil penalties in the ordinary discipline of the Church of England to this day. According to her canons, every person who maintains anything contrary to the doctrine or rites of the church, or

to the authority by which they are enforced, is declared to be *ipso facto* excommunicated. Many other offences which are properly civil, are deemed to be of a spiritual nature, and are punished by excommunication; which is two-fold, the greater and the less. The latter only excludes a man from the sacrament, and communion in the divine offices; but the greater excommunication cuts a man off from all commerce with Christians in temporal affairs; so that, if the orders of the church were universally and strictly observed, the poor wretch must necessarily perish; since no person in the nation might sell him food, raiment, or any convenience whatever.

SECTION VI.

THE HISTORY OF MISTAKES CONCERNING MORAL VIRTUE.

NOT only did the Christian church adopt very wrong and pernicious maxims of church discipline, but Christians have also adopted very false and hurtful notions concerning *moral virtue* itself, which is the end of all discipline; and it may be useful to take a general view of these corruptions, as well as of others.

According to the genuine doctrine of reason and revelation, nothing is of any avail to recommend a man to the favour of God, and to insure his future happiness, besides good dispositions of mind, and a habit and conduct of life agreeable to them. This is the religion of nature, and likewise that of the Old and New Testaments. But the religion of the heathen world, and that of many of the Jews, in the time of our Saviour, was of a quite different stamp. The Heathens, having none but low notions of their gods, had no idea of recommending themselves to their favour, but by the punctual observance of certain rites, ceremonies and modes of worship, which at best had no relation to moral

---

Great Britain will not have many years to wait before obtaining the same degree of religious liberty already accorded to Ireland, is sufficiently apparent, not only from the general tendency of public opinion, but from the course of the recent debate (May 9, 1871) on Mr. Miall's motion for the Disestablishment of State Churches in England and Scotland. J. D.]

[1] Quick's Synodicon, I. p. 348. (*P.*)
[2] Ibid. II. p. 88. (*P.*)

virtue, and often consisted in the most horrid and shameful violation of the plainest natural duties.

The pharisaical Jews, also, overlooking the excellent nature of the moral precepts of their law, and the perfect character of the great Being whom they were taught to worship, and directed to resemble, attached themselves wholly to ritual observances. Upon these, and on their relation to their ancestor Abraham, they chiefly depended for insuring to themselves the favour of God, to the utter exclusion of all the Gentile world, whatever might be their characters in a moral respect.

Our Lord and his apostles took every opportunity of opposing this fundamental corruption of genuine religion, and recalled men's attention to their hearts and lives. And one would have thought that, by the abolition of all the peculiar rites of the Jewish law, and appointing none in their place, (besides baptism and the Lord's supper, which are exceedingly simple, and have obvious moral uses,) an effectual bar would have been put in the way of the old superstitions. But human nature being the same, and men's dislike to moral virtue operating as before, and making them ready to adopt superstitious observances as a compensation for it, *pretences* and *modes* were not long wanting; and at length proper moral virtue was as effectually excluded in the Christian religion, as ever it had been in corrupt Judaism or Heathenism itself; and as great stress was laid upon things that bore no relation to moral virtue, but were, in fact, inconsistent with it, and subversive of it, as had ever been done by the most superstitious and misinformed of mankind.

Did not both the most authentic history, and even the present state of religion in the Church of Rome, furnish sufficient vouchers of this, it would not, in the present enlightened age, be even credible, that such practices as I shall be obliged to mention, could ever have been used by Christians, as

methods of recommending themselves to God.

We find that in early times an undue stress was laid upon the ordinances of *baptism* and the *Lord's supper*, as if these rites themselves, when duly administered (to which their being administered by a person regularly ordained for the purpose was considered as necessary) imparted some *spiritual grace.* Thus baptism was supposed to wash away all past sins, and the act of communion to impart some other secret virtue, by which a title to the blessings of the gospel was secured to the communicant. On this account, many persons who professed themselves to be Christians, deferred baptism till late in life, or even to the hour of death, that they might leave the world with the greater certainty of all their sins being forgiven, and before any new guilt could be contracted.

Those of the early fathers who ascribed the least to the rite of baptism, supposed that by it was done away whatever inconvenience mankind had been subjected to in consequence of the fall of Adam ; so that they made a great difference between the case of those children who died baptized, and those who died unbaptized; and the virtue that was ascribed to the Lord's supper was the foundation of all the superstitions respecting that ordinance, of which an account has already been given.

When moral virtue had been once ascribed to any corporeal action, instituted by divine appointment, Christians were led by degrees to imagine that a similar virtue might be communicated by other actions or signs, not of divine appointment, but bearing some relation to religion. This superstitious use was first made of the *sign of the cross*, which, as has been observed, was used originally with great innocence, perhaps as a private mark of distinction between the Christians and Heathens, in the time of persecution ; or, in peaceable times, to show the Heathens that they were not ashamed of that very circumstance with which they reproached them the most, viz. the crucifixion of their Master.

We first hear of this ceremony among the Montanists; and Tertullian, who became a Montanist, makes great boast of it. In the beginning of any business, says he, going out, coming in, dressing, washing, eating, lighting candles, going to bed, sitting down, or whatever we do, we sign our forehead with the sign of the cross.[1]

In the third century we find the sign of the cross in still more general use, it being thought to be a defence against enchantments and evil spirits; and no Christian undertook anything of moment without it. The use of this sign was brought more into fashion by the emperor Constantine, who, it is said, made use of it as his imperial banner, or standard. And so high did this sign of the cross rise in estimation, in later ages, that the Papists maintain that the cross, and even the sign of the cross, is to be adored with the worship which they call *Latria*, or that of the highest kind.[2]

After the sign of the cross, a sanctifying virtue was ascribed to *holy water*, or salt and water, such as the Heathens had used in their purifications, consecrated by a bishop. An extraordinary power was also ascribed to lights burning in the day-time, to the use of incense, to the relics of the saints, and to their images; and as the superstitious veneration for the real eucharist produced a *mock* one, probably occasioned another superstition, something similar to it, viz. the making of little waxen images of a lamb, which were either invented or much improved by Pope Urban VI. The Pope alone has the power of consecrating them, and that in the first year only of his popedom, and in every seventh year afterwards. In the service on this occasion, which may be

seen in the *History of Popery*, these *Agnus Dei's*, as they are called, are said to be *blessed* and *sanctified*, so as "by honouring and worshipping them, we thy servants may have our crimes washed off, the spots of our sins wiped away, pardons may be procured, graces bestowed, that at last, with thy saints and elect, we may merit to receive eternal life."[3]

Still greater virtue was ascribed to pilgrimages to visit particular churches and places, which were reputed holy, on account of their having been the resort of holy persons, of the theatre of holy actions, &c., and a similar virtue has been ascribed to the attendance on particular ceremonies. In 1071, the Pope promised indulgence for all sin confessed by those who should assist at the dedication of a church at mount Cassin, or who should come to the new church during the octave; which, Fleury says, brought an astonishing concourse of people, so that not only the monastery and the town, but even the neighbouring country was filled with them. Sixtus IV., in 1476, granted indulgences, by an express and particular act, to those who should devoutly celebrate an annual festival in honour of the immaculate conception of the Virgin Mary.[4] This superstitious use of pilgrimages was likewise the foundation of all the *jubilees* which have been celebrated at Rome, of which an account has been given among the *festivals* that have been introduced into the Christian church.

All the popish sacraments are likewise certain ceremonies, to the use of which the members of the catholic church ascribe a supernatural and sanctifying effect upon the mind; and they suppose them to have that weight and influence with the Divine Being, which nothing but real virtue or good dispositions of mind can ever have.

If things quite foreign to virtue have nevertheless been put in the place of it,

---

[1] *De Corona*, C. iv. Opera, p. 102. (*P.*)
[2] Mosheim, I. p. 238. (*P.*) Cent. iii. Pt. ii. Ch. iv. *fin.*

[3] *Hist.* III. p. 531. (*P.*) 1736, II. pp. 109-111.
[4] Mosheim, III. p. 271. (*P.*) Cent. xv. Pt. ii. Ch. iv. Sect. ii.

we shall not wonder that actions of real value in themselves, and which, when proceeding from a right disposition of mind, are real virtues, should have been much magnified, and that the actions themselves should have been imagined to be meritorious, even independently of the proper state of mind.

Thus, since giving to the needy, or being liberal for any useful purpose, is generally a test of virtue, it is no wonder that, in all ages, it has, by many persons, been substituted in the place of it. And, notwithstanding the strong cautions on this head in the New Testament, especially the apostle Paul's saying that he might *give all his goods to feed the poor,* and yet be destitute of *charity,* or brotherly love, this spurious kind of virtue was never made more account of, than in the corrupt ages of the Christian church, when an open traffic, as it were, was kept up between earth and heaven; there being nothing of a spiritual nature that they did not imagine might be bought with money.

In the eighth century, Mosheim says, a notion prevailed, that future punishment might be prevented by donations to religious uses;[1] and therefore few wills were made in which something was not bequeathed to the church.[2] For, of all pious uses, in the disposal of wealth, the *church* (which as it was then always understood, meant the *clergy* or the *monks*) was universally deemed a better object than the poor. Hence that amazing accumulation of wealth, which nearly threatened the utter extinction of all merely civil property.

Obvious as we now think the nature of virtue to be, and fully satisfied as we are, that the nature and excellency of it consists in its tendency to make men happy, in the possession of their own minds, and in all their relations; so grossly has its nature been mistaken, that not only have things entirely foreign to it been substituted in its place, as those above mentioned, but even things that have no other effect than to give pain and make men miserable. This most absurd and spurious kind of virtue began very early in the Christian church; and in process of time the austerities to which Christians voluntarily subjected themselves, in order to make their peace with God, and secure their future happiness, almost exceed belief.

It has been observed before, that the first corruptions of Christianity were derived from Heathenism, and especially from the principles of the oriental philosophy; and there are similar austerities at this very day among the Hindoos. Their notion that the soul is a distinct substance from the body, and that the latter is only a prison and clog to the former, naturally leads them to extenuate and mortify the body, in order to exalt and purify the soul.[3] Hence came the idea of the great use and value of fasting, of abstinence from marriage, and of voluntary pain and torture; till at length it became a maxim, that the man who could contrive to make himself the most miserable here, secures to himself the greatest share of happiness hereafter. As the principle which led to all this system came from the East, we are not surprised to find the first traces of it in those sects of Christian heretics who borrowed their leading sentiments more immediately from the principles of the oriental philosophy.

The Gnostics, considering matter and material bodies as the source of all evil, were no friends to marriage, because it was a means of multiplying corporeal beings: and upon the principle they also objected to "the doctrine of the resurrection of the body, and its future re-union with the im-

---

[1] Vol. II. p. 60. (*P.*) Cent. viii. Pt. ii. Ch. ii. Sect. iii.

[2] One of the regulations of *Code Napoléon* was wisely designed to counteract this tendency. After forbidding medical attendants to profit by testamentary grants from a patient on his deathbed, beyond a fair remuneration, for their attendance, the prohibition is thus extended to the clergy : ·'Les mêmes règles seront observées à l'égard du ministre du culte.'' *Code Napoléon,* L. iii. Ch. ii. *Donations et Testament,* 909. Paris, 1808, p. 226.

[3] See [Rutt's Priestley] Vol. III. pp. 391-398.

mortal spirit."[1] Marcion also, adopting the principles of the oriental philosophy, prohibited marriage, "the use of wine, flesh, and of all the external comforts of life," in order to mortify the body, and call off the mind from the allurements of sense. Of the same nature was the doctrine of Bardesanes, Tatian, and many others.[2]

Some of the heathen philosophers in the Western world had been used, from the same principle, to exercise "strange severities upon themselves and upon their disciples, from the days of Pythagoras down to the time of Lucian, who introduces the philosopher Nigrinus as condemning such practices, and observing that they had occasioned the death of several persons."[3] "The Greek philosophers had a particular dress, and affected to appear rough, mean and dirty.... The Christian monks imitated the old philosophers in their garb and appearance," and they were also often censured for the same "pride and contentious spirit."[4]

To vindicate the doctrine of corporeal austerity, it was pretended, in the second century, that Christ established a double rule of Christianity and virtue, the one more sublime than the other, for those who wished to attain to greater perfection. These thought that it was incumbent on them to extenuate and humble the body, by fasting, watching and labour, and to refrain from "wine, flesh, matrimony and commerce."[5]

Great stress was also laid, both by the Eastern and Western philosophers, on *contemplation*, to which *solitude* was favourable. By thus excluding themselves from the world, and meditating intensely on sublime subjects, they thought they could raise the soul above all external objects, and advance

its preparation for a better and more spiritual state hereafter. Many Christians, therefore, and especially those who had been addicted to the Platonic philosophy, before their conversion, were exceedingly fond of these exercises. And this notion, though more liberal than the former, which led them to torment and mortify the body, naturally led them to be very inattentive to it, seeking the cultivation of the *mind*, and the knowledge of truth, in a fancied abstraction from all sensible objects. In this state of contemplation, joined to solitude and abstinence, it is no wonder that they were open to many illusions; fancying themselves to be inspired in the same manner as the heathen prophets and prophetesses had fancied themselves to be, and as madmen are still generally imagined to be in the East. These pretensions to inspiration were most common among the Montanists, who were also most remarkable for their austerities.

In the third century, in which the doctrine of Plato prevailed much, we find that marriage, though permitted to all priests, as well as other persons, was thought to be unfit for those who aspired after great degrees of sanctity and purity; it being supposed to subject them to the power of evil demons, and on this account many people wished to have their clergy unmarried.[6] Origen, who was much addicted to Platonism, gave in to the mystic theology, and recommended the peculiar practices of the heathen mystics, founded on the notion that silence, tranquillity and solitude, accompanied with acts of mortification, which exhaust the body, were the means of exalting the soul.

The perversions of the sense of scripture, by which these unnatural practices were supported, are astonishing. Jerome, writing against marriage, calls those who are in that state *vessels of dishonour;* and to them he applies

---

[1] Mosheim, I. p. 109. (*P.*) Cent. i. Pt. ii. Ch. v. Sect. v.
[2] Ibid. pp. 178, 180. (*P.*) Cent. ii. Pt. ii. Ch. v. Sect. vii. -ix.
[3] Jortin's Remarks, III. p. 23. (*P.*) Ed. 1805, II. p. 168.
[4] Ibid. pp. 25, 26. (*P.*) Pp. 169, 170.
[5] Mosheim, I. p. 157. (*P.*) Cent. ii. Pt. ii. Ch. iii. Sect. xii.

[6] Ibid. I. p. 218. (*P.*) Cent. iii. Pt. ii. Ch. ii. Sect. vi. From *Porphyrius,* L. iv. p. 417.

the saying of Paul, *They that are in the flesh cannot please God.*

The laws also of Christian emperors soon began to favour these maxims. Constantine revoked all the laws that made celibacy infamous among the ancient Romans, and made it to be considered as honourable.[1]

I must now proceed to mention various other austerities, which poor deluded mortals, whom I am ashamed to call Christians, inflicted upon themselves, vainly imagining to merit heaven by them, for themselves and others. In this I shall, in general, observe the order of time in which I find an account of them in ecclesiastical history; observing that the facts I mention are but a small specimen of the kind, but they may serve to give us an idea of the general sentiments and spirit that prevailed in the dark ages of the church.

Some of the Mystics of the fifth century "not only lived among the wild beasts," but also after their manner. "They ran naked through the lonely deserts with a furious aspect." They fed on " grass and wild herbs, avoided the sight and conversation of men, remained motionless in certain places for several years, exposed to the rigour and inclemency of the seasons; and towards the conclusion of their lives, shut themselves up in narrow and miserable huts; and all this was considered as true piety, the only acceptable method of worshipping the Deity and rendering him propitious;" and by this means they attracted the highest veneration of the deluded multitude. One "Simeon, a Syrian, ...in order to climb as near heaven as he could, passed thirty-seven years of his wretched life upon five pillars, of six, twelve, twenty-two, thirty-six, and forty cubits high." Others followed his example, being " called *Stylites* by the Greeks, and *Sancti Columnares*, or *Pillar Saints*, by the Latins; " and, of all the instances of superstitious

frenzy, none were held in higher veneration than this, and the practice continued in the East till the twelfth century.[2]

Among the popish pilgrims there is a species called *Palmers*, from a bough of palm which they carry with them. These have no home, or place of residence, but travel and beg their bread till they obtain what they call the *palm*, or a complete victory over their sins by death.[3]

Many of the rules to which the monastic orders are subject are extremely rigorous. Stephen, a nobleman of Auvergne, who instituted the order of *Grande-montagne*, with the permission of Gregory VII., forbade his monks, "even the sick and infirm," "the use of flesh," and imposed upon them "the solemn observance of a profound and uninterrupted silence."[4]

The hermits of Luceola in Umbria were not allowed anything of fat in the preparation of their vegetables. They ate only raw herbs, except on Sundays and Thursdays. On other days they ate nothing but bread and water, and were continually employed in prayer or labour. They kept a strict silence all the week, and on Sundays only spake to one another between vespers and complines; and in their cells they had no covering for their feet or legs.

The persons the most distinguished in ecclesiastical history for their bodily austerities and religious exercises, were Dominic, who was one of these hermits, and Peter Damiani, who was his spiritual guide, both of whom were mentioned above. This Dominic for many years had next to his skin an iron coat of mail, which he never put off but for the sake of flagellation. He seldom passed a day without chanting two psalters, at the same time whipping himself with both his hands;

[1] Sueur, A. D. 320. *(P.)*

[2] Mosheim, I. pp. 390, 391. *(P.)* Cent. v. Pt. ii. Ch. iii. Sect. xi. xii.
[3] History of Popery, I. p. 212. *(P.)* Ed. 1735, I. p. 113.
[4] Mosheim, II. p. 308. *(P.)* Cent. xi. Pt. ii. Ch. ii. Sect. xxvi.

and yet this was his time of greatest relaxation. For in Lent, and while he was performing penance for other persons, he would repeat at least three psalters a day, whipping himself at the same time. He would often repeat two psalters without any interval between them, without even sitting down, or ceasing for one moment to whip himself.

Peter Damiani asking him one day if he could kneel with his coat of mail, he said, "When I am well I make a hundred genuflections every fifteenth psalm, which is a thousand in the whole psalter;" and one time he told his master that he had gone through the psalter eight times in one day and night; and at another time, trying his utmost, he repeated it twelve times, and as far as the psalm which begins with *Beati Quorum* of the thirteenth. And in repeating the psalter he did not stop at the hundred and fifty psalms, but added to them the canticles, the hymns, the creed of St. Athanasius, and the litanies, which are to be found at the end of the old psalters. His fasting and his coat of mail made his skin as black as a negro, and besides this he wore four iron rings, two on his thighs and two on his legs, to which he afterwards added four others; and besides this iron shirt, he had another under him to sleep upon. Notwithstanding these severities, he died very old on the fourteenth of October, 1062, which day is dedicated to his honour in the calendar of the Church of Rome.[1] The austerities of Peter Damiani were similar to these, and an account of them may be seen in the same historian.[2]

In the thirteenth century there arose in Italy a sect that was called the Flagellantes, or *Whippers*, and it was propagated from thence over all the countries of Europe. They ran about in promiscuous multitudes, "of both sexes and of all ranks and ages," both

in public places and in deserts, "with whips in their hands, lashing their naked bodies with the most astonishing severity," shrieking dreadfully, and looking up to heaven "with an air of distraction, ferocity and horror; and all this with a view to obtain the divine mercy for themselves and others." For they maintained "that flagellation was of equal virtue with baptism, and the other sacraments;" and "that the forgiveness of all sins was to be obtained by it from God, without the merits of Jesus Christ." These people "attracted the esteem and veneration not only of the populace, but also of their rulers," but being afterwards joined "by a turbulent and furious rabble," they fell into discredit.[3]

The Jansenists carried their austerities so far, that they called those persons who put an end to their own lives by their "excessive abstinence or labour, the *sacred victims of repentance*," and said that they had "been *consumed* by the *fire* of divine love." By these sufferings they thought to "appease the anger of the Deity, and not only contribute to their own felicity, but draw down abundant blessings upon their friends and upon the church.....The famous Abbé de Paris...put himself to a most painful death," depriving himself of almost all the blessings of life, "in order to satisfy," as he thought, "the justice of an incensed God."[4]

So famous was the devout nunnery of *Port Royal in the Fields*, "that multitudes of pious persons were ambitious to dwell in its neighbourhood," and to imitate the manners of those nuns; and this in so late a period as the seventeenth century. "The end which these penitents had in view was, by silence, hunger, thirst, prayer, bodily labour, watchings, sorrow, and other voluntary acts of self-denial, to efface the guilt and remove

[1] Fleury, XIII. p. 99. (*P.*) [A.D. 1062.] See "St. Dominique l'*Encuirassé*." Nouv. Dict. Hist. II. p 463.
[2] Fleury, p. 205, &c. (*P.*) [A. D. 1071-2.]

[3] Mosheim, III. pp. 94, 95, 206. (*P.*) Cent. xiii. Pt. ii. Ch. iii. Sect. iii.; Cent. xiv. Pt. ii. Ch. v. Sect. vii.
[4] Ibid. IV. p. 382 (*P.*) Cent. xvii. Sect. ii. Pt. i. Ch. i. Sect. xlvi.

the pollution the soul had derived from natural corruptions or evil habits." Many persons, "illustrious both by their birth and stations," chose this mode of life.[1]

Dr. Middleton mentions a practice still kept up at Rome, which is equally shocking on account of its cruelty and absurdity. "In one of these *processions*, made lately to St. Peter's, in the time of Lent, I saw," says he, "that ridiculous penance of the *Flagellantes*, or self-whippers, who march with whips in their hands, and lash themselves as they go along, on the bare back, till it is all covered with blood; in the same manner as the fanatical priests of *Bellona*, or the *Syrian goddess*, as well as the votaries of *Isis*, used to slash and cut themselves of old;....which mad piece of discipline we find frequently mentioned, and as oft ridiculed, by the ancient writers."

"But," says he, "they have another exercise of the same kind, and in the same season of Lent, which, under the notion of penance, is still a more absurd mockery of all religion : when on a certain day, appointed annually for this discipline, men of all conditions assemble themselves towards the evening in one of the churches of the city, where whips, or lashes made of cords, are provided, and distributed to every person present; and after they are all served, and a short office of devotion performed, the candles being put out, upon the warning of a little bell, the whole company begin presently to strip, and try the force of these whips on their own backs, for the space of near an hour; during all which time the church becomes, as it were, the proper image of hell, where nothing is heard but the noise of lashes and chains, mixed with the groans of these self-tormentors; till, satiated with their exercise, they are content to put on their clothes, and the candles being lighted again upon the tinkling of a

second bell, they all appear in their proper dress."[2]

Besides the idea of tormenting the body for the good of the soul, the Platonists especially, as I have observed above, had a notion of exalting the soul by *contemplation*, fancying that the mind contained within itself the elements of all knowledge, and that they were best drawn forth by looking within; and also that communion with God was best kept up by an abstraction of the mind from all corporeal things. These notions chiefly gave rise to what is generally called *mysticism*, with which the minds of the early monks were much tinctured, and which, more or less, affected most of those who had recourse to bodily austerities. But others, without taking any particular pains to torment the body, gave themselves almost wholly to contemplation.

This turn of mind, giving great scope for the flights of fancy, produced very different effects on different persons, and in some it operated as an antidote to the vulgar superstition of the Church of Rome, in which hardly anything was attended to for many ages besides mere *bodily exercises*. For though the ideas of the Mystics were very confused, they had a notion of the necessity of aiming at something of *inward purity*, distinct from all ritual observances. Nay, these notions led some of them (seeing the abuse that had been made of positive rites) to renounce them all together, even those of divine appointment, as baptism and the Lord supper.

Mosheim says that, "if any sparks of real piety subsisted" during the reign of papal superstition, it was "among the Mystics," who, "renouncing the subtilty of the schools, the vain contentions of the learned, with all the acts and ceremonies of external worship, exhorted their followers to aim at nothing but internal sanctity of heart and communion with God, the centre and source

[1] Mosheim, pp. 384, 385. (*P.*) Loc. cit. Sect. xlvii.

[2] Letter from Rome, p. 190, &c. (*P.*) Works, III. pp. 100 101.

of holiness and perfection. Hence the Mystics were loved and respected by many persons who had a serious sense of religion;" but, he adds, they joined much superstition with their reveries.[1]

On some persons these notions had a very unfavourable effect. In the thirteenth century there was formed a society called "the Brethren and Sisters of the free spirit, ... called by the Germans and Flemish, Beghards and Beguttes, ... a name usually given to those who made an extraordinary profession of piety and devotion..... In France they were known by the appellation of Beghins and Beghines..... They ran from place to place, clothed in the most singular and fantastic apparel, and begged their bread with wild shouts and clamours, rejecting with horror every kind of industry and labour, as an obstacle to divine contemplation." They maintained "that every man, by the power of contemplation, and by calling off his mind from sensible and terrestrial objects, might be united to the Deity in an ineffable manner," so as to become "a part of the godhead, ... in the same sense and manner that Christ was," and thereby become "freed from the obligation of all laws human and divine." In consequence of this, "they treated with contempt the ordinances of the gospel ... as of no sort of use to the *perfect man.*" Some of these poor wretches were burnt in the Inquisition, and endured various other persecutions.[2]

We even find some who carried their notion of the abstraction of the mind from the body to such a degree, that they fancied that when the mind had attained to a certain pitch of perfection by means of contemplation, no act in which the body only was concerned could affect it; so that they might indulge themselves in any sensual pleasure without contracting the least defilement of soul. The consequences of this opinion could not but be exceedingly pernicious.

Some of the spiritual brethren in Flanders (and who, as Mosheim says, were patronized by several of the reformed churches) maintained, that the Deity was the sole operating cause in the mind of man, and the immediate author of all human actions; and consequently that the distinction of good and evil was groundless, that religion consisted in the union of the soul with God, attained by contemplation and elevation of mind, and that when this was gained, all indulgence of the appetites and passions was perfectly innocent.[3] "Margaret Poretta, who made such a shining figure" amongst the Beghards, and who "was burnt at Paris" in 1310, wrote "an elaborate treatise," to prove "that the soul, when absorbed in the love of God, is free from the restraint of every law, and may freely gratify all its natural appetites without contracting any guilt."[4]

These licentious maxims were ascribed by the Jesuits, but probably without reason, to the Quietists in general, a sect which arose in 1686, and gave great disturbance to the court of Rome. The Inquisition put many of these sectaries in prison, and, among others, Molinos, who was one of the chief of them, and they put him to the torture in order to discover his accomplices. Letters were also written to all the bishops of Italy to exhort them not to suffer Quietism to take root in their dioceses. But, notwithstanding this, the sect made such progress in a short time, by the external marks of mortification, devotion, contemplation, abstraction of mind, and a pretended intimate union with God, that many persons of condition adopted their sentiments; and even some cardinals were infected by them. On this the Popes and the Jesuits exerted themselves so much, that in a general congregation

---

[1] Mosheim, III. pp. 301, 302. (*P.*) Cent. xv. Sect. i. Ch. i. Sect. xix.
[2] Ibid. pp. 122-124. (*P.*) Cent. xiii. Pt. ii. Ch. v. Sect. ix. x. Four friars were burnt as *Beguins* in 1318. See *Limborch,* C. xix. I. p. 105.

[3] Ibid. III. p. 27. (*P.*) Cent. xiii. Pt. ii. Ch. v. Sect. xi.
[4] Ibid. III. p. 202. (*P.*) Cent. xiv. Pt. ii. Ch. v. Sect. iv.

of the Inquisition, Molinos was condemned to perpetual imprisonment, and to renounce his opinions.[1]

This sect made great progress in Italy in 1696, and increased notwithstanding all the opposition which was made to it. The pious Fenelon, archbishop of Cambray, gave in to this visionary system, and his humility and excellent disposition appeared, together with his weakness of mind, and bigoted attachment to the Church of Rome, in his readiness to recant, and condemn his own writings when they were censured by the Pope.[2]

Madame Bourignon was a woman who distinguished herself much by an attachment to the same system. She maintained "that the Christian religion neither consists in knowledge nor in practice, but in a certain internal feeling and divine impulse, that arises immediately from communion with the Deity."[3]

Something similar to the principles of the Quietists are those of the Quakers in England; who, though they are far from substituting anything in the place of virtue, yet expect supernatural illumination and assistance, to enlighten the mind and to form it to virtue. They maintain, that there is concealed in the minds of all men, a certain portion of the same light or wisdom that exists in the Supreme Being, which is drawn forth by self-converse and contemplation. This divine light they usually call the *internal word*, or *Christ within*. But many of the modern Quakers make this hidden principle to be nothing more than that of natural conscience, or reason; though in this they certainly depart from the genuine prin-

ciples of their ancestors, on which their sect was founded. The primitive Quakers (even as the more rigid among them at present do) certainly pretended to speak and act by the same kind of inspiration by which the apostles themselves acted, and therefore they made no greater account of the apostolic writings, or of the Scriptures in general, than of their own suggestions.[4]

As the last effort of human ingenuity and depravity, I shall give a short account of the sophistical casuistry of the Jesuits; a religious order which arose after the Reformation, and which was for some time esteemed to be the great bulwark of the papal power, but is now, in consequence of their becoming suspected by the civil powers, happily abolished.[5]

They employed all the force of their subtle distinctions to sap the foundations of morality, in order to accommodate themselves to princes, and great men, who generally chose their confessors from their body; and in process of time they opened a door to all sorts of licentiousness. Among other things, they represented it as a matter of indifference what motives determined the actions of men; and taught that there is no sin in transgressing a divine law that is not fully known to a person, or the true meaning of which is not perfectly understood by him, or that is not even present to his mind at the time of action. They also maintained "that an opinion or precept may be followed with a good conscience, when it is inculcated by four, or three, or two, nay, even by one doctor of any considerable reputation, even though it be contrary to the judgment of him that follows it, and even of him that recommends it." This they call the doctrine of *probability.*

They also held what they call the

---

[1] Histoire des Papes. V. p. 381. (*P.*) See "A Letter writ from Rome, ... concerning the Quietists." Sect. iv. Suppt. to *Burnet's Letters,* 1688, pp. 1–93.

[2] "Si le Pape condamne mon livre, je serai, s'il plait à Dieu, le prémier à le condamner, et à faire un mandement pour en défendre la lecture." Letter from Paris to the Duke of Beauvilliers, 1697. Life of Fenelon, 1723, p. 97. *Examen.,* &c. 1747, p. 112.

[3] Mosheim, V. p. 65. (*P.*) Cent. xvii. Sect. ii. Pt. ii. Ch. vii. Sect. iv.

[4] See *Barclay,* Prop. ii. iii. on *Immediate Revelation* and the Scriptures.

[5] There has been, lately, a feeble attempt to restore this Order.

doctrine of *philosophical sin*, according to which "an action, or course of actions, that is repugnant to the dictates of reason," might not be " offensive to the Deity." They held that wicked actions might "be innocently performed," if persons could, in their own mind, connect " a good end " with them, or as they expressed it, be "*capable of directing their intention aright.*" Thus, a man who kills his neighbour in a duel would be acquitted by them, if, at the time, he " turn his thoughts from the principle of vengeance to the more decent principle of honour." Agreeably to this, they even held that an oath might be taken with " mental additions and tacit reservations." This, however, does not agree with their being charged with paying no attention to the motives with which actions are performed; but it agrees very well with their maintaining that the sacraments produced their effect by their own virtue, and immediate operation, or what they called *opus operatum*. But it cannot be supposed that all these maxims were held with perfect uniformity by them all.[1]

The folly and wickedness of these maxims were admirably exposed by the famous Pascal, in his *Provincial Letters*, which, for their excellent composition and good sense, were read with the utmost avidity, and the highest approbation, through all Europe; in consequence of which their doctrines were universally exploded, and held in the greatest abhorrence by all men. Indeed the extreme odiousness of them contributed not a little to the downfall of the order.

It is a dangerous maxim, not of the Jesuits only, but of the divines of the Church of Rome in general, to distinguish between *contrition* and *attrition;* allowing great merit even to the latter, though it consist of any kind of sorrow on the account of sin, even for the loss

or disgrace that it brings upon a man, " without a resolution to sin no more. Such a sorrow as this is, they teach, does make the sacrament (of *penance*) effectual. This was settled by the Council of Trent," though the Protestants thought that it struck "at the root of all religion and virtue."[2]

But the most flagrant instance of immorality with which the Church of Rome is charged, is the holding that no faith is to be kept with heretics; and upon this principle the Council of Constance acted, when the safe conduct which the emperor Sigismund had given to John Huss, the Bohemian reformer, was declared to be invalid, as given to an heretic, on which he was arrested and condemned to the flames. From this time it was the opinion of many in the Church of Rome, that no promise made to an heretic is binding.

Pope Eugenius authorized Uladislaus, king of Hungary, to break a solemn treaty with Amurath, emperor of the Turks, which ended as it might be wished that such horrible prevarication might always end. The Turk carried a copy of the treaty into the field of battle, and displaying it in the beginning of the engagement, pronounced aloud, " Behold, O Jesus, these are the covenants which thy Christians, swearing by thy name, made with me. Now, therefore, if thou art a God, revenge these injuries to me, and to thyself, upon their perfidious heads." The consequence was, that the Turks being exceedingly exasperated, and the Christians dispirited, the latter were put to flight; and both the king, and the cardinal, who had urged him to break the peace, and who was along with him, were killed upon the spot.

I have not found any public or general declaration on the subject of keeping no faith with heretics, but that of Clement IX., who, in his *Acts*, printed at Rome, in 1724, expressly

---

[1] Mosheim, III. pp. 467, 468. IV. p. 355, &c. (P.) Cent. xvi. Sect. iii. Pt. i. Ch. i. Sect. xxxv. Note [a]. Cent. xvii. Sect. ii. Pt. i. Ch. i. Sect. xxxv.

[2] Burnet, p. 348. (P.) Art. xxv. Ed. 4, p. 256. Con. Trid, Sess. xiv. Ch. iv. p. 89.

declares that all promises or stipulations made in favour of Protestants, are entirely null and void, whenever they are prejudicial to the Catholic faith, the salvation of souls, or to any rights of the church; even though such engagements have been often ratified and confirmed by oath.

I have no doubt, however, but that the Catholics of this day would reject this doctrine with as much abhorrence as Protestants themselves:[1] and, indeed, if it had not been a general opinion with them, that oaths and subscriptions prescribed by Protestants were binding, no reason can be given why they should not have taken the oaths which have been employed in this country to prevent them from enjoying the advantages of other subjects; and yet, in all the time since the government of this country has been Protestant, no such instance has been produced. The Catholics have universally submitted to their exclusion from all places of honour and profit, the payment of double taxes, &c. &c. without ever endeavouring to relieve themselves by a declaration or oath, which the Protestants say they would

not consider as binding, and for the violation of which they might, it is said, be at least sure of obtaining an absolution at Rome.[2] But even there, it is very probable, that no such absolution would now be given.

It is to be hoped, that in many other respects, Catholics do not lay the stress they have been formerly taught to do on things foreign to real virtue, that is, to good dispositions of mind, and a good conduct in life; as it is to be lamented, that many Protestants are far from being free from all superstition in these respects. But now that the minds of men seem to be so well opened to the admission of religious truth in general, errors so fundamental as these which relate to *morality* will hardly remain long without redress. It will be happy if the reformation of Christians in doctrine and discipline be followed by a suitable reformation in practice.

[1] See the References [Rutt's Priestley], Vol. II. p. 52. Note.

[2] " If there be any Protestant of common understanding and candour, who may still suspect that a *snake lurks in the grass*, I would ask him this plain question: If the English Catholics imagined that the Pope could dispense with their oaths, why have they so long persevered in refusing to take the oaths of *Supremacy*, and the *Test*, and so re-enter, all at once, into their British birth-rights? This consideration, alone, one might think, should stop the mouth of captiousness itself." Geddes's *Apol.* pp. 134, 135.

PART X.

THE HISTORY OF MINISTERS IN THE CHRISTIAN CHURCH, AND ESPECIALLY OF BISHOPS.

THE INTRODUCTION.

THE Christian church was served originally (exclusive of the apostles and other temporary officers) by *Elders* and *Deacons* only, the former being appointed for spiritual matters, and the latter for civil affairs. They were all chosen by the people, and were

ordained to their office by prayer, which, when it was made on the behalf of any particular person, was in early times always accompanied with the imposition of hands. For the sake of order in conducting any business that concerned the whole society, one of the elders was made *president* or *moderator* in their assemblies, but without any more power than that of having a single vote with the rest of his brethren. From this simple constitution, it is certainly astonishing to consider how these *servants of the church* came in time to be the *lords of it*, and of the world; and it is curious to observe the various steps by which this change was made.

SECTION I.

THE HISTORY OF CHRISTIAN MINISTERS TILL THE FALL OF THE WESTERN EMPIRE.

THE first change in the constitution of the primitive churches was making the most distinguished of the elders to be *constant president*, or moderator, in their assemblies, and appropriating to him the title of (ἐπισκοπος), or *bishop*, which had before been common to all the presbyters or elders, but without giving him any peculiar power or authority.

Since the first Christian converts were almost wholly from the common ranks of life, there could be no great difference in their qualifications for any office, except what natural good sense, or age and experience, might give to some more than to others. In this state of things, it is evident, that none of them could have been educated with a view to any employment of this kind. But it was soon found expedient, and especially on account of the controversies which they had with Jews and Heathens, as well as among themselves, that their public instructors, and especially these bishops, should be men of some learning; and accordingly schools were erected, in very early times, in which young men were instructed in such branches of knowledge, as were found to be most useful to them in the discharge of their ministerial duties. Ancient writers say, that the apostle John established a school, or academy of this kind, at Ephesus. However, that which was afterwards established at Alexandria, in Egypt, called the *Catechetic School*, formed upon the plan of those of the Greek philosophers, was particularly famous.

A better education and superior fitness for the more conspicuous duties of Christian societies, in expounding the Scriptures, giving various instruction, public prayer, &c. would naturally create a greater difference than had been known before between Christian ministers and the people, and for the same reason between the bishops and the elders; and power and influence never fail to accompany superior qualifications. But it was several centuries before the common people ceased to have votes in everything that related to the whole society.

The first great change in the constitution of the Christian church was the exaltation of the presbyters into the rank of bishops in churches; which was, in fact, an annihilation of that important order of men, and threw the government of a church into the hands of one person.

The manner in which this change took place was gradual and easy. Whenever the number of converts in any place became too great for them to assemble with convenience in one building, they erected other places of public worship; but considering these not as new and distinct churches, but as branches of the old one, in order to preserve the connexion with the mother church, they did not ordain a new bishop, but had all the ministerial duty done either by some of the former presbyters, or by new ones ordained for that purpose.

In this train things went on, till at length the mother church, or some of the dependent churches, sending out more colonies, and to greater distances, the bishop of the mother church (being the only person in the district who bore that name) came to be a *diocesan bishop*, whose elders and deacons presided in all the separate and dependent

Q

churches. Very few elders also remained in the mother church, because none were now ordained to that office, except such as lived by the ministry. The Church of Rome must have been in this state at the beginning of the fourth century, when Marullus divided it (that is, all the Christians in Rome) into twenty-five parishes, appointing one priest for each of them, to instruct the people, and to administer the sacraments. It was the custom for the bishop to send a part of the consecrated bread, after the administration of the eucharist, to each of these dependent churches.[1]

Sometimes, however, when new churches were erected in places at a distance from any capital town, they were governed by new-made bishops, presbyters and deacons, like the original churches. Beausobre says, that he believes one cannot find an instance so early as the middle of the third century of a church governed by a single presbyter.[2] These country bishops, called *choroepiscopi*, made but a poor figure in comparison with the opulence and splendour of the city bishops. But before they were generally abolished, which was in the fourth century, their rank and power were very much diminished. In a council held at Antioch, in 341, these country bishops were forbidden to ordain priests or deacons, and had only the power of appointing persons to inferior offices in the church. By degrees the country bishops were entirely abolished (though not in all places till so late as the tenth century), when *rural deans* and *arch-priests* were instituted in their place.[3] After this the system of diocesan episcopacy was fully established. There were bishops in capital towns only, and all the churches within their districts were governed by presbyters, or deacons under them.

As the distinction between bishops and presbyters has been the subject of much controversy between the advocates for the Church of England and the Dissenters, I shall produce a few more authorities to prove that originally they were the same order of men.

At first the oldest of the presbyters succeeded of course to the place of president among them. But this ceased to be the case even in the age of the apostles, when the president was chosen by the plurality of votes, and then the title of *bishop*, which before had been common to all the presbyters, was appropriated to him. This, says Sueur, was in the time of Hyginus.[4]

In the age of Cyprian, when distinctions were made among the bishops themselves, and when he himself was the metropolitan of the whole province, and one who was a strenuous advocate for the power and dignity of the clergy, it appears that even this metropolitan bishop had no more authority than to assemble the clergy of his province, to preside in their councils, and to admonish his brethren. There was no act of a spiritual nature that was peculiar to himself; and, in his absence from the church, during his persecution, every part of his office was discharged by his presbyters.

Chrysostom says, that when the apostle Paul gives orders to Titus to ordain elders in every city, " he means bishops. For," says he, " he would not have the whole island (of Crete) committed to one man, but that every one should have and mind his own proper cure; for so the labour would be easier to him, and the people to be governed would have more care taken of them; since their teacher would not run about to govern many churches, but would attend to the ruling one only, and so keep it in good order."[5] Theophylact also interprets the passage in the same manner, saying, " that every city should have its own pastor," and that by *presbyters* in this place the apostle

---

[1] Sueur, A. D. 307, 313. (*P.*)
[2] Hist. of Manicheism, I. p. 113. (*P.*)
[3] Sueur, A. D. 341, 439. (*P.*)

[4] Ibid. A. D. 142. (*P.*)
[5] *In Titum*, L. v. Op. X. p. 1700. (*P.*) Pierce's *Vindication*, p. 375.

"means *bishops*."[1] Occumenius and Theodoret likewise say, "that the apostle would not commit" the charge of "so large an island to one man,"[2] and yet it is not so large as some of our dioceses.

Jerome, on the Epistle to Titus, says, that among the ancients, priests and bishops were the same; but that by degrees the care of a church was given to one person, in order to prevent dissension. This he proves at large from many passages in the New Testament. Let the bishops know, says he, that they are above the priests more by custom than by the appointment of Christ.[3] The same learned father also says that, at the beginning, churches were governed by the common council of presbyters, like an aristocracy; but afterwards the superintendency was given to one of the presbyters, who was then called the bishop, and who governed the church, but still with the council of the presbyters.[4]

At first bishops were appointed by the whole congregation, consisting of *clergy* and *laity*, as they were afterwards called, nor did any church apply to the neighbouring bishops to assist at the ordination. Irenæus was ordained by priests only, and such was the general custom of the church of Alexandria till the beginning of the fourth century.[5] Cyprian also says, that it belonged to the people chiefly to choose worthy pastors, and to refuse the unworthy.

Afterwards, when a new bishop was chosen in any church, it came to be the custom to invite the neighbouring bishops to attend, and assist on the occasion; and while this was voluntary on both sides, there was a decency and propriety in it; as it showed the readiness of the neighbouring bishops to receive the new one as a friend and brother. But this innocent custom had

bad consequences, as the attendance of the neighbouring bishops on the occasion, from being *customary*, came to be considered as *necessary*; and as a considerable number had usually attended, it came to be a rule, that it could not be done without the concurrence of *three*, one of whom laid his hand on the head of the new bishop, when he was recommended to the blessing of God by prayer. In the third century this was always done by the metropolitan bishop; at least it was never done without his consent or order. The second Council of Nice ordered that bishops should be chosen by other bishops. But in the West the people preserved their right of choosing their bishops till after the reign of Charlemagne and his son; and it was not taken from them till the Council of Avignon, in 1050.[6]

The usual ceremony in appointing a bishop was the *imposition of hands*, which, as I have observed, was originally nothing more than a gesture which was always made use of when prayer was made for any particular person. What is imposition of hands, says Austin, but the prayer that is made over the person?[7] Accordingly we find that this ceremony was not always thought necessary. For, instead of imposing hands on the bishops of Alexandria, they only placed them on their chair, a custom which continued many centuries.[8]

Though bishops were originally no other than presbyters, the manner of their ordination being the same, and the presbyters discharging every part of the office of bishop; no sooner was the distinction between them established, than the bishops began to appropriate certain functions to themselves. It appears by the act of the third Council of Carthage, that whereas before, priests had the power of assigning the time of public penance,

[1] Pierce's *Vindication*, p. 375. (*P.*)
[2] Ibid. p. 343. (*P.*)
[3] Opera, VI. p. 193. (*P.*)
[4] Anecdotes, pp. 24, 54. (*P.*)
[5] Basnage, *Histoire*, II. p. 25. (*P.*)

[6] Ibid. p. 24. (*P.*)
[7] *De Baptismo, contra Donatistas*, L. iii. C. xvi. Opera, VII. p. 410. (*P.*)
[8] Basnage, II. p. 29. (*P.*)

and of giving absolution, as also of consecrating virgins, and of making the chrism (or that mixture of oil and balm with which one of the unctions at baptism was made) without the advice of the bishop, all these things were forbidden by these canons, and given to the bishops.[1] But the principal thing by which the bishops were distinguished afterwards was the power of *confirming* the baptized, when that chrism was applied.

After the reign of Adrian, when Jerusalem was utterly destroyed, and the Jews dispersed, an opinion began to prevail among Christians, that their ministers succeeded to the characters, rights and privileges of the Jewish priesthood; and this was another source of honour and profit to the clergy. Upon this the presbyters assumed the style and rank of priests, bishops that of high priests, and deacons that of Levites.[2]

The principal occasion of the great distinction that was made between the clergy and the people, between the bishops and the presbyters, and also among the bishops themselves, was their assembling in synods, to deliberate about affairs of common concern, a custom which began about the middle of the second century; for it cannot be traced any higher. By this means the power of the clergy was considerably augmented, and the privileges of the people diminished. For though at first these bishops, assembled in convocation, acknowledged themselves to be no more than the deputies of the people, they soon dropped that style and made decrees by their own authority, and at length claimed a power of prescribing both in matters of faith and of discipline.

For the more orderly holding of these assemblies, some one bishop in a large district was employed by common consent to summon them, and to preside in them; and this being

generally the bishop of the metropolis, or the city in which the civil governor resided, he was called the Metropolitan or Archbishop. The term archbishop was first used by Athanasius, afterwards by Epiphanius, and from the year 430 it was common in the church.[3]

When the clergy of several provinces assembled, they appointed officers with a more extensive jurisdiction, and called them *patriarchs*, or *primates*. This last term was not used before the time of Leo I. That of *patriarch* was first used by the Montanists, and in time came to be applied to the five principal sees of Rome, Constantinople, Alexandria, Antioch and Jerusalem.[4] "The patriarchs were distinguished by considerable and extensive rights and privileges. They alone consecrated the bishops" of their respective provinces. "They assembled yearly in council the clergy of their respective districts," and all important controversies were referred to their decision, especially where the bishops were concerned; and "they appointed vicars, or deputies," to act for them "in the remoter provinces." Several places, however, in the fifth century, maintained their independence of these patriarchs, and both the emperors and the general councils were obstacles in the way of their ambition.[5]

Many of these abuses were promoted by the constitutions of Constantine, who was the first person that assembled a general council, to which all the bishops of the Christian world were invited. Having made a new division of the empire for civil purposes, he adapted the external government of the church to it. When this division was completed, those who make the correspondence between the civil and ecclesiastical governments the most exact, say that the *bishops* corresponded to those magistrates who

---

[1] Sueur, A.D. 397. (*P.*)
[2] Mosheim, I. p. 146. (*P.*) Cent. ii. Pt. ii. Ch. ii. Sect. iv.

[3] Sueur, A.D. 281. (*P.*)
[4] Ibid. (*P.*)
[5] Mosheim, I. pp. 371, 372. (*P.*) Cent. v. Pt. ii. Ch. ii. Sect. ii.

presided over single cities; the *metropolitan*, or *archbishop*, to the proconsuls or presidents of provinces, comprehending several cities; the *primates* to the emperors' vicars, or lieutenants, each of whom governed in one of the thirteen great dioceses, into which the whole empire was divided; and the *patriarchs* to the prefecti prætorii, each of whom had several dioceses under them. But it is not probable that this subdivision was ever exactly observed. However, the government of the church answered much more exactly to the government of the state in the East than in the West; and in the western parts of Africa there was little or no correspondence between them.[1]

In consequence of this arrangement, a bishop in a metropolitan city acquired the power of ordaining and deposing the bishops of the cities dependent upon his metropolis, and also of terminating their differences and providing for their wants in general. But this power was not absolute, since the metropolitan could do nothing without the consent of the bishops of the province. There were also some bishops who had only the title of metropolitan, without any power annexed to it.[2]

As the metropolitans followed the rank of their metropolis, so the patriarchs, or *exarchs*, as they were sometimes called, followed the condition of the capital cities of their diocese. Thus, as Antioch was the capital city of the East, containing fifteen provinces, the bishop of that city exercised a jurisdiction over all the metropolitans, having a power of assembling the councils of the dioceses, &c. Constantinople being made the seat of the empire, the bishop of it, not content with the title of metropolitan, or even of exarch, was first honoured with that of *Patriarch*, as more expressive of dignity and pre-eminence; and thence he took occasion to give a greater extent to his patriarchate, so as to encroach upon the province of the patriarch of Rome.[3]

As the higher clergy rose above the inferior, so these were not wanting to themselves, but magnified their respective offices in proportion. In the fourth century, those presbyters and deacons who filled the first stations of those orders, obtained the name of arch-presbyters and arch-deacons, and also obtained more power than the rest of their brethren.[4] It was a considerable time, however, before the offices of priests and deacons came to be confounded as they now are in many respects. But when there was peculiar profit or honour in any of the functions of deacons or archdeacons, they were occasionally bestowed upon the priests who retained the name of the lower office. An instance of this we have not only in the present office of *archdeacon* in the Church of England, but in the *deans and chapters* of cathedral churches.

In consequence of all these changes, there did not remain, at the conclusion of the fourth century, so much as a shadow of the ancient constitution of the Christian church; the privileges of the presbyters and people having been usurped by the bishops, who did not fail to assume the state and dignity suited to their new distinctions. Indeed, long before this time, and even before the empire became Christian, a spirit of pride and ambition, that very spirit against which our Saviour so frequently and earnestly cautioned his disciples, had got fast hold of many of the Christian bishops. We find in the writings of Cyprian, that in his time many bishops assumed great state, with splendid ensigns of power, as a princely throne, surrounded with officers, &c. The presbyters and deacons also imitated them in some measure; and this last order, being above the offices to which they were originally appointed. had them done by inferior

---

[1] Anecdotes, p. 75. (*P.*)
[2] Ibid. p. 63. (*P.*)
[3] Ibid. pp. 65, 73. (*P.*)
[4] Mosheim, I. p. 290. (*P.*) Cent. iv. Pt. Ch. ii. Sect. viii.

officers created on purpose, as door-keepers, readers, grave-diggers, &c.

The pride of the bishops was so great in the fourth century, and they set themselves so much higher than the priests, that *Ærius*, a *Semi-Arian*, and a great reformer, thought it necessary to urge, among "his principal tenets, that bishops were not distinguished from presbyters by any divine right; but that, according to the institution of the New Testament, their offices and authority were absolutely the same." His doctrine in general, by which he endeavoured to bring the discipline of the church to its pristine state, excited much disturbance in several provinces of Asia Minor.[1]

The wealth and power of the bishops of the greater sees were soon very considerable, so as to make them resemble princes. Pretextatus, designated consul, being pressed to embrace Christianity, said, according to Marcellinus, "Make me bishop of Rome, and I will become a Christian." And yet the propriety of the clergy in general having no independent fortunes, as well as their not enriching their families out of the revenues of the church, was very evident in those times. Constantine prohibited by an edict any rich man to enter into the church. Jerome was of opinion that none of the clergy should have any property of their own; and Austin admitted none into his church who did not first dispose of all their goods. He did not, however, think this absolutely necessary, but only for their greater perfection.[2]

Sometimes the revenues of a church were not sufficient for the maintenance of the clergy; and in that case it was not thought improper that they should contribute to their own maintenance by their labour. In some cases this was expressly enjoined. Thus the fourth Council of Carthage, held in 398, ordered the clergy and monks to gain their livelihood by some trade, provided it did not divert them from the duties of their office.[3]

It was very early thought to be of great importance that the clergy should have no secular care that would engage much of their thoughts and attention. The apostolical canons, which, though spurious, were written in the fourth century, order that bishops should not meddle with the administration of public affairs; and that if they did, they should be deposed. The same orders were given by the Councils of Chalcedon, Carthage, Mentz, &c. Nay, it appears by the letters of Cyprian, that a clergyman could not even be a guardian or trustee to a child. With this view Constantine exempted the clergy from all public and civil employments. But for the sake of gain, the clergy of those times were too ready to undertake any office or employment whatever. Chrysostom laments that ecclesiastics, abandoning the care of souls, became stewards, and farmers of taxes, employments unbecoming their holy ministry. Bishops, he said, should have nothing but food and raiment, that they may not have their desires drawn after worldly things.[4]

But at the same time that Constantine and other emperors released the clergy from all obligation to duties of a civil nature, they gave them secular business in another way, viz. by enforcing the rules of church discipline, and by giving the bishops the cognizance of all ecclesiastical affairs and ecclesiastical persons, such as had before been brought to the secular judges,[5] and Justinian greatly enlarged this kind of authority.[6] The clergy having thus tasted of civil power, soon got a fondness for it, which required to be restrained. So early as the middle of the fifth century, it was complained that the bishops wished to extend their jurisdiction; and in 452, Valentinian III. made a law, declaring that a bishop

---

[1] Mosheim, I. p. 314. (*P.*) Cent. iv. Pt. ii. Ch. iii. Sect. xxi.
[2] Simon on Church Revenues, p. 24. (*P.*)

[3] Sueur, A. D. 398. (*P.*)
[4] In 1 Tim. v. 17. Op. X. p. 1605. (*P.*)
[5] Sueur, A. D. 856. (*P.*)
[6] Anecdotes, p. 125. (*P.*)

had no power to judge even the clergy, but with their own consent.[1]

In this age, and indeed much later, it was far from being thought improper that the *general regulation* of ecclesiastical matters should be in the hands of the supreme civil power. Constantine made many laws in ecclesiastical matters, as concerning the age, the qualification and duties of the clergy; and Justinian added many more. Appeals were made to the emperors against the injustice of the synods. They received them, and appointed such bishops to hear and try the causes, as happened to be about the court. The emperors called several councils, they even sat in them, and confirmed their decrees. This was the constant practice of the Roman emperors, both in the East and in the West; and when the empire was divided into many lesser sovereignties, those petty princes continued to act the same part.

Though the regulations established by the clergy were numerous in the time of Constantine, they contained nothing that could justly excite the jealousy of the emperors; because it was then universally agreed, that the emperors ought to regulate the ecclesiastical discipline. One book of the Theodosian code is wholly employed on regulations respecting the persons and goods of ecclesiastics.[2]

A kind of ecclesiastical power was also allowed to many rich laymen, as, in many cases, they had the appointment of the bishops; at least they could not be appointed without their consent. This right of *patronage* was introduced in the fourth century, to encourage the opulent to erect a number of churches; which they were the more induced to do, by having the power of appointing the ministers who were to officiate in them. And it was an old heathen opinion, "that nations and provinces were happy, and free from danger in proportion to the number of fanes and temples" they contained[3]

As it was deemed inconsistent with the clerical character to have any secular concerns, so in this age, this idea, together with that of the greater purity of the unmarried state, made it to be thought not quite proper for the clergy to have wives and families, lest their thoughts should be distracted by the cares of this life; though marriage was not absolutely prohibited to the priests. This rigour was introduced by the Montanists. These condemned all second marriages, and this opinion of theirs generally prevailed among Christians afterwards; and not only did they refuse to admit to the priesthood those who had been married twice, but even those who were married at all.

So much were the minds of Christians in general impressed with these sentiments, at the time that the empire became Christian, that it was proposed at the Council of Nice, that the bishops, priests and deacons should cease to cohabit with the wives which they had married while they were laymen. But at the instance of Paphnutius, a venerable old confessor, this did not pass into a decree; and therefore these fathers contented themselves with ordering, that priests who were not already married should abstain from it. But even before this, viz. at a synod held at Elvira, in Spain, in the year 306, celibacy was absolutely enjoined to priests, deacons and subdeacons.[4] However, notwithstanding these regulations, and every provision that was made afterwards to secure the celibacy of the clergy, supported by the general opinion of Christians, the marriage of priests was not uncommon in many parts of the Christian world, quite down to the Reformation.

When learning became less common among the laity in the Western parts of the world, even the clergy

---

[1] Fleury's Seventh Discourse, p. 9. (*P.*)
[2] Anecdotes, p. 99. (*P.*)

[3] Mosheim, I. pp. 320, 321. (*P.*) **Cent. iv. Pt. ii.** Ch. iv. Sect. ii.
[4] Sueur, A. D. 306. (*P.*)

were often found to be very ignorant; though it was remarkable that there was more literature at this time in Britain, which had then suffered less by the invasion of barbarous nations, than in other parts of the empire. When Constantine had appointed a council at Constantinople, Agathon, bishop of Rome, made an apology for the two bishops whom he sent thither, as his legates, on account of their want of learning; saying that, to have had a theologian, he must have sent to England.[1] Even in the East, several bishops, at the Councils of Ephesus and Chalcedon, could not write, so that other persons signed the decrees for them.[2]

It was in part to provide for the better instruction of the clergy, and in part also as an imitation of the monastic life, which rose in its credit as the clergy sunk in the public esteem, that first Eusebius, bishop of Verceil, and after him Austin, formed in his house a society of ecclesiastics, who lived in common, having him, the bishop, for their father and master; and in time this institution gave rise to the *canons* and *prebends* of cathedral churches.[3]

SECTION II.

THE HISTORY OF THE CLERGY FROM THE FALL OF THE ROMAN EMPIRE IN THE WEST, TO THE REFORMATION.

IN the former period we have seen a very considerable departure from the proper character of presbyters or bishops, in those who bore that title in the Christian church. But in this we shall see a much greater departure, and through the increasing ignorance and superstition in the laity, we shall find such a degree of *power* assumed by the clergy, as was nearly terminating in the entire subjection of everything to their will. But in the meantime the different orders of those who sustained a religious character were a check upon each other.

In the first place I shall repeat what was observed with another view in a former part of this work, viz. that a considerable change took place in the idea of the powers supposed to be given to priests by their ordination, and consequently in the form of ordination. Originally nothing was necessary to the conferring of holy orders but *prayer*, and the *imposition of hands*. But in the tenth and eleventh centuries, after the introduction of the doctrine of transubstantiation, a new form was observed, viz. the delivery to the priest of the vessels in which the eucharist was celebrated, with a form of words, expressing the communication of a power of *offering sacrifices to God*, and of *celebrating masses*. Also a new benediction was added, which respected the new doctrine of penance and absolution. For the bishop, in laying on his hands, says, *Receive ye the Holy Ghost. Whose sins ye remit, they are remitted, and whose sins ye retain, they are retained.* According to the system now received in the Church of Rome, the priests have two distinct powers, viz. that of *consecrating* and that of *absolving*. They are ordained to the former by the delivery of the vessels, and to the latter by the bishop alone laying on his hands, and saying, *Receive ye the Holy Ghost, &c.* And it is said that "the bishop and priests laying on hands *jointly*," which from ancient custom is still retained among them, and which was the only proper ceremony of ordination, is nothing more than "their declaring, as by a suffrage, that such a person ought to be ordained."[4]

[1] Sueur, A. D. 680. (*P.*)
[2] Jortin's Remarks, IV. p. 277. (*P.*) "Some of these prelates," says Fleury, "subscribed by the hand of a presbyter ; one because he had a lame wrist ; another because he was sick ; others, I suppose, because they had bones and joints in all their fingers." *Jortin*, Ed. 1805, III. p. 120.
[3] Sueur, A. D. 395. (*P.*)

[4] Burnet on the Articles, p. 355. (*P.*) Art. **xxv** Ed. 4, p. 261.

In the former period we saw that the bishops began to reserve to themselves the power of confirming after baptism. This was fully asserted in this period. When the Bulgarians were converted to Christianity, which was in the ninth century, and their priests had both baptized and confirmed the new converts, " Pope Nicholas sent bishops among them, with orders to confirm even those who had already been confirmed by the priests." [1] However, when the doctrine of transubstantiation was established, it was not possible that the bishops, with respect to their spiritual power, should stand higher than the priests; for what power can be superior to that of making a God? And yet we find that the schoolmen endeavoured to make the episcopate to be a higher degree and extension of the priesthood.

In this period the priests assumed several new badges, or signs of their character, and these were generally borrowed from the heathen ritual. Thus the *shaven head* and *surplices* were borrowed from the Egyptian priests; and the *crosier*, or *pastoral staff*, was the *lituus* of the Roman augurs. [2]

Now also we find what seems to be a quite new order in the church, but in fact it was only an extension of power in the orders that existed before, without any addition to the spiritual character. This is the rank of *cardinal* in the Church of Rome. These cardinals, though they were not heard of in former times, now have the rank of princes in the church, with the sole power of choosing the Pope. It is about the end of the sixth century, and especially in the letters of Pope Gregory, that we first meet with the term *cardinal priests* and *cardinal deacons*, but they were then in many other churches besides that of Rome. [3]

As the term *cardinal* signifies *chief*, or the *principal*, the cardinal priests in the Church of Rome are supposed by some to have been those priests whom Marullus, mentioned above, set over the twenty-five parishes into which he divided the Church of Rome, with priests and deacons under them, so that being next in rank to the Pope, they rose in power and wealth as he did. But till the eleventh century these cardinal priests held no considerable rank, and they were not admitted into their councils till the year 964. Or, though they might assist at them, and likewise at the nomination of the popes, as part of the body of the clergy, they were always named after the bishop; but from this time it became the interest of the popes to advance their dignity. Still, however, there remain traces of their former rank. For the popes never call themselves cardinals, but bishops. They also call bishops their *brothers*, but the cardinals their *beloved children.*

It was only in the year 1059, that the cardinals appear to be necessarily joined with the clergy in the election of a pope, but about a hundred years after this they obtained of Alexander III. that they should have the sole nomination; and since that time they have been continually gaining new privileges and dignities. They are now considered as " the Pope's great council," and " no oath of fidelity" is required of them. " Innocent IV., anno 1244, ordained that cardinals should, when they rode abroad, always wear a red hat, to show that they would venture their heads and expose their blood for the interest of the church; and ... Paul II., about the year 1471, ordered them to wear robes of scarlet.... Whereas all others, be they emperors or kings, must be glad to kiss the Pope's foot, cardinals are admitted to kiss his hands and mouth." If a cardinal accidentally meets a criminal going to execution he has a power of saving his life; and it is said that " No cardinal can be condemned for any crime, unless he be first convicted by *seventy-two* witnesses, if he

---

[1] Burnet on the Articles, p. 338. (P.) 'Art. **xxv.** Ed. 4, p. 248.
[2] Hist. of Popery, III. pp. 340, 355. (P.) Ed. 1735, II. pp. 17, 25. See also *Livy*, L. i. C. xxviii. " On voit aux marbres et medailles antiques la forme de ce *lituus*, ou baton recourbé, toutes semblables à la crosse episcopale." *Les Conformitez*, p. 35.
[3] Anecdotes, p. 222. (P.)

is a cardinal-bishop, *sixty-two* if a presbyter, and *twenty-seven* if he be a deacon.[1]

In very early times we find a number of inferior offices in the churches, with names suited to their business, as *readers*, *sub-deacons*, &c. None of these, however, were considered as distinct orders of clergy, but the last is enumerated as such by Pope Eugenius.

Another order of clergy took its rise in these dark ages, and was suggested by the great corruption both of the clergy and the monks in the seventh century; when many of the clergy belonging to great cathedrals formed themselves into regular communities, and were called *canonici* or *canons*, from observing certain *canons* or *rules*, which were given them by Chrodogang, bishop of Mentz, towards the middle of the seventh century, in imitation of what had before been done by Eusebius of Verceil, and Austin above mentioned. The rule of Chrodogang was observed by all the canons, as that of Benedict by all the monks.[2]

A regulation was made respecting this subject in 1059, when, at a council in Rome, it was ordered that those priests who kept no concubines should eat and sleep together, near the church to which they belonged, and have in common whatever revenues they had from the church, studying, and living an apostolical life. This, says Fleury, was the origin of the *canons regular*. A similar order was made by Nicholas II. in 1063.

The bishops were generally at the head of these societies of clergy, and they were considered as his standing council, and during the vacancy had the jurisdiction of the diocese. But afterwards abbots, deans and provosts, &c., were preferred to that distinction, and several of them procured exemptions from any subjection to the bishop. Our English *deans and chapters* are entirely independent of the bishop,

and had their exemption **from** the bishop's authority secured to them by a proviso in the statute of the twenty-fifth of Henry VIII.[3] With us those canons who have no duty whatever are called *prebends*.

Originally, bishops were always chosen by the people,[4] though they would be naturally much influenced in their choice by the recommendation of their presbyters. But afterwards these presbyters set aside the vote of the people altogether; and when these *chapters* were formed, it grew into a custom in England, that the priests who constituted them, being always at hand, and easy to be assembled on the decease of a bishop, should choose him themselves, without consulting the rest of the priests. They still have the same power nominally, but their choice of a bishop is always directed by the king.

When the bishops, in consequence of their becoming landholders, came to be of great weight in the state, it could not be a matter of indifference to the prince who should be bishops. He would naturally, therefore, interest himself in the elections. Accordingly, we soon find that the bishops of Rome, though they were chosen by the people, could not be confirmed in their office without the approbation of the emperor; and this right in the prince continued undisputed for many centuries. The great authority that Charlemagne exercised respected chiefly the election of bishops, of which he made himself master, with the knowledge and consent of the popes. He did not choose them himself, but he retained the right of approving, which he signified by delivering to them the pastoral staff and ring which was called the *investiture*, after which they were consecrated by the neighbouring bishops. Thus began the *rights of investiture*, which was a source of so much contention afterwards.[5]

[1] Hist of Popery, III. p. 53. (*P.*) Ed. 1735, I. p. 368.
[2] Fleury's Eighth Discourse, p. 9. (*P.*)
[3] *Burnet.* Pierce's *Vindication*, pp. 381, 384. (*P.*)
[4] See [Rutt's Priestley] Vol. II. p. 339. Note†.
[5] Anecdotes, p. 335. (*P.*)

In the eighth general council, in 869, the emperor and all secular princes were forbidden to meddle with the election of any patriarch, metropolitan, or bishop whatever. And at the Council of Bonaventure, in 1087, it was decreed, that if any emperor, king, or other secular person, should presume to give the investiture of a bishopric, or any other ecclesiastical dignity, he should be excommunicated.[1] But by this time the popes had not only emancipated themselves from the power of the emperor, but had arrogated to themselves all power in matters temporal as well as spiritual; and on the subject of investiture, as well as many others, the emperors of Germany, after a struggle of many years, were obliged to yield. In France, however, the nomination of the bishops was always, in fact, in the hands of the prince.

When the bishops were little more than secular persons, it is no wonder, how contrary soever it was to all the notions of the ancients, that bishoprics should be considered as other estates, and in some cases be given, or descend, to minors. In 925 the Pope approved of the appointment of an infant to be bishop of Rheims, another person having the administration of it; an example soon followed by princes, and an evil much complained of by Baronius. In 1478, Sixtus IV. obliged the king of Arragon, by giving the bishopric of Saragossa to a child of six years of age; a pernicious example, and unheard of till then, says the author of *Histoire des Papes.*[1] In this however this writer was mistaken.

This example, pernicious as it is here said to have been, has been followed, in one instance, by Protestants. For the bishopric of Osnaburg, having, like other German bishoprics, become a principality, it was agreed, after the Reformation, that it should be held alternately by Papists and Protestants. At present it is held by the second son of the king of England, who was ap-

pointed to it when he was quite an infant.

In the eighth century, not only were private possessions made over to ecclesiastics and to monasteries, but royal domains, such as used to be held by princes; by which means they came into the possession of whole provinces, cities, castles, and fortresses, with all the rights and prerogatives of sovereignty; and thus churchmen became dukes, counts, and marquises, and even commanded armies. The prince thought that churchmen would be more faithful to him than secular persons, and expected that they would have more influence over their other vassals, and keep them better in subjection.[3] This aggrandisement of the German bishops took place chiefly upon the death of Charles le Gros, when many of the great subjects of the empire made themselves independent.[4]

By these steps the greater clergy came to be entirely secular men, and to have as much to do in civil business of all kinds, as any other members of the community. Thus in England it was far from exciting any wonder, in the days of popish darkness (whatever would have been thought of it in the time of the apostles), to see bishops and mitred abbots called to the great council of the nation, along with the barons; because, though churchmen, they actually were barons. The parliaments of France also, about the middle of the eighth century, were constituted in the same manner, the bishops attending along with the other grandees.

This great absurdity in politics, as well as in religion, remains as a blot in the English constitution to this day, the bishops being admitted to have a seat in the House of Lords, and this evil is the greater in a constitution which pretends to freedom. For certainly these bishops, receiving their preferment from the court, and having farther expectations from it, will, in general, be

---

[1] *Histoire des Papes,* II. p. 601. (*P.*)
[2] IV. p. 254. (*P.*)

[3] Mosheim, II. pp. 61, 62. (*P.*) Cent. viii. Pt. ii. Ch. ii Sect. iv. v.
[4] Sueur, A. D. 889. (*P.*)

in the interest of the court, and consequently enemies to the rights of the people.[1] Useful as this order of men is to the court, the time has been, when the presence of the bishops in the great council of the nation gave umbrage not only to the temporal lords, but to the sovereign. Queen Elizabeth more than once expressed her dislike of the close attendance of the bishops at court and in parliament, and she even threatened to send them into the country, to mind their proper business.

It is not possible that anything should be more foreign to the office of a bishop than to serve in the wars; and yet even this gross abuse naturally arose from clergymen being in possession of the great fiefs which were held by military service. And the habits of those who were made bishops in those times were such, as to make them not wish to be exempted from that obligation. In the seventh century, says Fleury, barbarians, being admitted into the clergy, introduced their habits of hunting and fighting; and from that time the bishops possessing large estates were under obligation to furnish men for the defence of it. Charlemagne excused the bishops from serving in person, but required them to send their vassals.[2] But before his time some bishops distinguished themselves in the wars in Italy, and so early as the year 575.[3]

The impropriety of this practice was, however, soon perceived, and afterwards express laws were made to prevent bishops from appearing in the field in person. Mezerai says, that, at the beginning of the tenth century, bishops

and abbots, notwithstanding the prohibition of councils, still bore arms, and went to the wars; and the custom continued far into the third race of the French kings.[4]

The utter incompetency of the bishops for the duties of their office, and the turn of the age in general, contributed to give them the same fondness for war that other persons of rank in the state had. And when they could not act contrary to the letter of the law, they sometimes had recourse to methods of evading it, which are ridiculous enough. In the thirteenth century, says Jortin, " it was an axiom, that the church abhors the shedding of blood. Therefore bishops and archbishops used to go to battle, armed with clubs; and made no scruple to knock down an enemy, and to beat and bruise him to death, though they held it unlawful to run him through with a sword."[5]

At length the laws got the better of this custom, and the clerical character being deemed an indelible one, in consequence of the spiritual powers supposed to have been imparted by the sacrament of *orders*, it was ordained, in a council of Rouen, in 1174, that clergymen who had been deposed should not, however, bear arms, as if they were laymen.[6]

Originally, bishops were not only carefully excluded from all business of a secular nature, but in the exercise of their spiritual power, they were much restrained by the civil magistrates, even after they became Christians. Justinian, who had a great zeal for the church, forbade the bishops to excommunicate any person before the cause of it had been proved in form; and this was so far from giving offence, that Pope John II. thanked the emperor for his zeal in these respects.[7]

But in this period we find the bishops not only exercising their spiritual power without the least control, but en-

---

[1] Lord Falkland said of the English bishops in 1641, that "they, whose ancestors, in the darkest times excommunicated the breakers of *Magna Charta*, did now, by themselves and their adherents, both write, preach, plot and act against it." *Speeches and Passages of this great and happy Parliament*, 1641, p. 191. During the present reign, the *minority*, against any measure of the court, among *twenty-six* Lords Spiritual, has seldom exceeded *two*.

[2] Fleury, XIII. p. 28. (*P.*) [Vidal, Tom. IV. pp. 137-8.]

[3] Sueur. (*P.*)

[4] Ibid. A. D. 989. (*P.*)

[5] Remarks, V. p. 388. (*P.*) Ed. 1805, III. p. 382.

[6] Fleury. (*P.*) [See A. D. 1190.]

[7] Anecdotes, p. 171. (*P.*)

croaching greatly on the civil power, and controlling princes themselves in the exercise of their proper authority. To this, many circumstances contributed, but nothing more than the admission of the great clergy to seats in the assemblies of the state. The ignorance of the laity also gave great power to the clergy. As these were the only people who could read or write, they were universally secretaries, stewards, treasurers, &c. Hence the word *clerk*, which originally signified a *clergyman* (clericus) came to denote an officer in the law.[1]

Owing to these causes and to the negligence of the princes, who were much weakened by their divisions in the ninth century, the bishops were almost masters of the kingdoms of France and Germany, disposing of everything at their pleasure. Though Arnoul, archbishop of Rheims, was a traitor, and deserving of the greatest punishment, two kings of France, Hugh and Robert, did not pretend to have him judged except by the clergy, in consequence of which he ran no risk with respect to his *life*, and could only have been deposed; and by means of the popes he was confirmed in his see, and continued in it to his death.[2]

The crusades contributed much to the advancement of the clergy; the crusaders leaving their estates to their management, and sometimes selling them, in order to equip themselves for those distant expeditions.[3]

The ceremony of *consecration*, which was introduced in the middle of the eighth century, afforded the priests a pretence to intermeddle with the rights of princes. For in putting on the crown they seemed to *give* the kingdom on the part of God;[4] and this ceremony was soon deemed so necessary by the superstitious people, that no coronation was deemed valid without it, in consequence of which the priests had a

real negative on the claims of kings, and in case of a contest the party favoured by the clergy was sure to prevail.

Also the consequence of the excommunications of those times, which was a cutting off of all intercourse between the excommunicated persons and the rest of the world, affected the prince as well as the people. For the man who was not deemed worthy to transact any civil business, was certainly unfit to be a king. After the death of Louis V. Charles of Lorraine was the presumptive heir to the crown of France; but the clergy, who were then the most powerful order in the state, having excommunicated him, he was reckoned disqualified to wear the crown.

But the first remarkable attempt upon the rights of royalty by priests, was the deposition of Vamba, king of the Visigoths, in Spain, at the twelfth Council of Toledo, in 681. On the pretence of his being a *penitent*, he had been clothed with the monastic habit, though it was unknown to himself, his disorder having made him insensible. For the two characters of *monk* and *king* were deemed to be incompatible. The second example was that of Louis le Débonaire, who had likewise been in a state of penitence, after which the bishops who imposed the penance, pretended that he could not resume the royal dignity.[5] The opinion that bishops had a power of deposing kings made such progress in the eighth and ninth centuries, that the kings themselves acquiesced in it.[6]

The primary cause of the temporal power of the clergy was the *wealth* which they acquired by the liberality of the laity; which, in those superstitious times, knew no bounds. Donations for pious uses were so profuse, as to threaten the utter extinction of all merely civil property; so that no effectual check could be put to it, but by laymen assuming ecclesiastical titles, and by degrees resuming their

[1] Fleury's Seventh Discourse, pp. 12, 19. (*P.*)
[2] Sueur, A. D. 991. (*P.*)
[3] Histoire des Papes, II. p. 527. (*P.*)
[4] Fleury, XIII. p. 50, (*P.*) [Vidal, Tom. IV. p 138.]
[5] Ibid. (*P.*)
[6] Ibid. Seventh Discourse, p. 12. (*P.*)

property, in the character of lay-im-propriations, which has been a subject of great complaint to the clergy. This was certainly an abuse and an irregularity; but one evil is often made use of, in the course of Divine Providence, to correct another.

The notion that temporal and spiritual goods had such an affinity, that the one might be procured by means of the other, could not fail to operate in favour of the wealth, and consequently of the temporal power, of the clergy. These were the venders of a valuable commodity, and the rich laity were the purchasers. And were not many ancient writings and charters, &c., still extant, we should not believe how nearly the grant of money and lands to the church, for the good of men's souls, approached to the form of a bargain and sale in other cases. The grants by which estates, &c., were made to the church, were often express stipulations for the good of their own souls, and those of others.

Thus, when Ethelwolf tythed [1] the kingdom of England, he said, "It was for the good of his own soul, and those of his ancestors." An act of King Stephen says, "I, Stephen, by the grace of God, king, being desirous of sharing with those who barter earthly things for heavenly felicity, and moved thereto by the love of God, and for the good of my own soul, and of my father and mother, and the souls of all my relations, and my royal ancestors; to wit, of King William my grandfather, King Henry my uncle, &c., do, by the advice of my barons, give to God and the holy church of St. Peter, and the monks thereof, the tythes of all lands, &c." [2]

Wealth and power generally go hand in hand, and the one will never fail to introduce the other. With the clergy it was their spiritual power that was the cause of their wealth, and their wealth contributed to create their temporal power. But before the clergy

assumed any proper power over the laity, they exempted themselves from their jurisdiction, which they began to do very early, and with the consent of the Christian emperors, who did not wish to see persons of an order which they so much respected brought into the ordinary civil courts. It was therefore only in extreme cases that any of the clergy were brought before them. Athalaric, the Gothic king of Italy, approved of this custom. [3]

Moreover, as the Christian emperors had a respect for the clergy, and a confidence in them, they chose to extend the effects of church censures; whereby it was in the power of the clergy to prevent or punish many offences of a civil nature, so that in time all the bishops had courts of their own; and when the popes got power, it was necessary that the power of the bishops should rise in some proportion to it. Boniface VIII. made a decree by which the bishops might at all times have their auditories, and consequently put the accused in prison. But this was not much regarded, nor had the ecclesiastics a prison before the pontificate of Eugenius I. [4]

By degrees the dignity of the priests rose so much higher than that of the temporal powers, that it was deemed a thing absolutely intolerable, that a clergyman should be subject to any temporal tribunal; and as the canon law did not punish with *death*, the clergy enjoyed almost an absolute impunity for the commission of any crime whatever. And in those dark and ignorant ages, the disposition of the clergy to violence, and crimes of every kind, was little, if at all, less than that of the laity. It appears in the reign of Henry II. of England, that more than a hundred murders had been committed by clergymen, whom the civil powers could not bring to justice. [5] As to the higher ranks of the clergy, it was hardly possible that they should

---

[1] See Milton, *Hist. of England*, B. **v. p.** 228 Rapin, L. iv. I. p. 290.
[2] Fleury, p. 39. (*P.*)

[3] Anecdotes, p. 188. (*P.*)
[4] Ibid. p. 119. (*P.*)
[5] Hist. of Popery, III. p. 130. (*P.*) Ed. 1735, I. p. 391. See *Rapin*, L. vii. II. p. 187.

be punished for any crime, on account of their right of appeal to Rome, and the certainty of their finding protection there, especially if they had any difference with their sovereign. Besides, in those times no clergyman could be punished capitally without previous *degradation*, and a priest could not be degraded but by eight bishops, to assemble whom was a great expense.

In that reign of superstition, the clergy could be in no want of plausible *pretences* to interpose in civil affairs. Among others, they pretended to have jurisdiction in all cases of *sin*, in consequence of which, says Fleury, the bishops made themselves judges in all law-suits, and even in all wars among sovereigns, and in fact made themselves to be the only sovereigns in the world.[1] In a council of Narbonne, in 1054, persons who refused to pay their debts were excommunicated.[2] Had church censures extended to no other cases than these, the abuse would not have been much complained of.

The case in which the clergy interfered the most was in things relating to *marriage*. For as incest is a sin, they made themselves judges of the degrees of relationship within which it was lawful to contract marriage. And as dispensations for marriage within those degrees was very gainful, it was their interest to extend those degrees, that dispensations might be more frequently wanted.

Before the time of Justin II. ecclesiastical canons began to encroach upon the province of the secular power in this respect, forbidding the marriage of cousins, and of the children of cousins, and introducing a different method of counting the degrees of relationship, which is not more ancient than Pope Gregory or Zachary. According to Fleury, the difference between the canon and the civil law on this subject arose about the year 1065, when two degrees in civil law were made one by the canon law, the former

counting upwards to the common ancestor, and then down again to the persons whose degree of relationship was to be determined. Whereas the custom was now to begin with the common ancestors, and count to the more remote of the two parties. Brothers, therefore, who, according to the civil law, were in the second degree of relationship, according to the canon law were in the first; and cousins-german, which were in the fourth degree, were by the canons brought to the second, &c.[3]

Besides this advantageous method of counting the degrees, the clergy likewise added to the number of degrees within which it was not lawful to contract marriage. Mezerai says, that about the end of the tenth century, the degrees of relationship within which marriage was prohibited were extended to seven, which very much embarrassed sovereign princes, who were generally related to one another within those degrees.

Another method of extending the degrees of relationship was, by considering the relations of one party as those of the other. In 557, a council at Paris forbade the marriage of a wife's sister; many persons having then done it, after the example of King Clotaire, who had married the sister of his deceased wife.[4] Relation by adoption was also made to have the same effect as that by nature. In 734, the Pope not only advised to dissolve the marriage of a man with a woman whose child he had before adopted, but to punish him with death.[5] And what will be thought perhaps more extraordinary, the spiritual relationship, as it was called, or that of godfather or godmother, was made to have the same effect as a natural relation of the same name.[6]

The number of lawful marriages were also reduced. Second marriages were soon reckoned improper, and with respect to the clergy, absolutely unlawful,

---

[1] Seventh Discourse, p. 20. (*P.*
[2] Fleury A. D. 1054. (*P.*)
[3] Ibid. XIII. p. 147. (*P.*) [A. D. 1065.]
[4] Sueur. (*P.*)
[5] Ibid. (*P.*)
[6] Ibid. A. D. 995. (*P.*)

it being soon imagined to be forbidden by Paul, who says, *a bishop must be the husband of one wife.* Epiphanius mentions a person who being a widower married a second wife, that he might not be made a priest. Jerome says, we do not desire, but we allow of second marriages.[1] In 901, the patriarch of Constantinople refused to marry the emperor Leo, a fourth time, alleging a law which he himself had made, that no person should marry more than twice. After much altercation on the subject, it was agreed, in 902, that third marriages should be lawful, but not fourth.[2]

It was thought proper in very early times, that a new-married couple should have the benediction of the bishop or a priest. Thus, in the fourth Council of Carthage, in 398, it was ordered that the bride and bridegroom should be presented to a priest for his benediction, and that, out of respect to it, they should abstain from commerce the first night.[3] This custom of giving the benediction prepared the way for the clergy being considered as the only persons before whom marriage could be legally contracted, and the laity were effectually excluded when matrimony was made one of the seven sacraments. Marriage also came under the cognizance of the clergy by means of the *oath* which the parties took to be faithful to each other. For Fleury says, the clergy included within their jurisdiction everything in which oaths were concerned, as well as where the causes had any connexion with things spiritual. Thus on account of the sacrament of marriage, they took cognizance of marriage portions, cases of dowry, of adultery, of legitimacy, and also of wills; because it was supposed that the church ought not to be without some pious legacy.[4]

The clergy also claimed entire jurisdiction in cases of *heresy* and *schism*, and in matters where the civil law had

not interfered, as in respect to usury and concubinage. And because the crime of heresy drew after it the loss of estates, and of all civil rights, even with respect to the sovereign, the clergy could always accuse of this crime any person whom they meant to destroy; and if the prince would not submit to their sentence, he was accused of not believing the *power of the keys,* and accused of heresy.[5]

The ordinary jurisdiction of the bishops was much restrained by the *Pope's legates,* especially from the eleventh century; and the bishops, thus restrained, endeavoured to extend their jurisdiction at the expense of the lay-judges, by three methods, viz. the quality of the persons, the nature of the causes, and the multiplication of the judges. Boniface VIII. ordained that laymen should have no power over ecclesiastical persons or goods, and the bishops made as many clergy as they pleased, by which means they drew great numbers from the temporal jurisdiction, an abuse which was carried to an enormous extent. Because widows and orphans had been protected by the bishops in early ages, they now undertook all their causes, even those of the widows of kings, and those of kings themselves in their minority. They also took cognizance in all cases in which *lepers* were concerned. Lastly, the bishops multiplied judges, and thereby extended their jurisdiction, establishing their officials in various places besides the episcopal city. The archdeacons and chapters also did the same, and all these had their delegates, sub-delegates, and other commissaries.[6] However, in all great causes, the authority of the bishops was much lessened by the number of appeals to the court of Rome; and afterwards the *Inquisition* also encroached upon the jurisdiction of the bishops, as well as on that of the ordinary judges.[7]

---

[1] Le Clerc's Hist. Eccl. A. D. 158. (*P*)
[2] Sueur. (*P.*)
[3] Ibid. (*P.*)
[4] Fleury's Seventh Discourse, p. 17. (*P.*)

[5] Ibid. p. 17. (*P.*)
[6] Ibid. p. 18. (*P.*)
[7] Ibid. p. 23. (*P.*)

A circumstance which contributed not a little to make the clergy intent upon extending their authority in the state, and to make them formidable in it, was their not being allowed to marry. In consequence of this, great numbers of them became less attached to their respective countries, and made the hierarchy alone their great object. This point, however, was not established without much opposition. A council held at Constantinople under Justinian II. gave the priests leave to marry, though the popes had enjoined the contrary. Many priests had wives even in the West about the year 1000; but, in 1074, Gregory VII. decreed in council, not only that priests "should abstain from marriage," but that they who had wives should either dismiss them, or quit their office. But even this law was often disregarded.[1]

That the true motive to this, in later ages, was not a regard to purity, is evident, from its being no objection to priests to keep many concubines, even publicly. John Cremensis, who came to England to hold a synod for the purpose of prohibiting the marriage of priests, was the very night after the council found in bed with a common prostitute.[2] Father Simon says, that the priests being prohibited from marriage, made no scruple of keeping concubines.[3] It was in 970 that a synod was held at Canterbury, in which it was decreed that the clergy in England should either part with their wives or their livings; a law which Dunstan enforced with great rigour. The priests, however, were much averse to this law, and therefore it was found necessary to hold another synod on this subject at Calne, four years afterwards, in which it was finally decided.[4]

With the high rank and the wealth which the clergy acquired, it is not to be wondered that they should not improve in virtue, heavenly-mindedness, and a careful attention to the duties of their office. Complaints of their arrogance, avarice and voluptuousness, are without end; and yet, vicious as the clergy in general were, they were reverenced almost to adoration by the ignorant vulgar of those ages. This arose, in a great measure, from the sentiments and customs of the Northern nations before their conversion to Christianity; which in those days consisted in nothing more than their being taught to say by rote some general principles of the Christian religion, being baptized, and changing the objects of their superstitious customs. For these were suffered to continue the same as before, only, instead of being acts of homage to their heathen deities, they were now taught to consider them as directed to the popish saints.

Now these people having been before their conversion absolutely enslaved by their priests, having never been used to undertake anything, even in civil or military affairs, without their counsel; when they became Christians, they transferred the same superstitious deference to their Christian priests, who, we may be sure, did nothing to check it.[5] In the dark ages, the profligacy of the clergy perhaps exceeded that of the laity, as the sacredness of their character gave them a kind of impunity. One Fabricius complains of the luxury of the clergy in his time, towards the end of the tenth century, in the following terms:—They no longer saluted one another with the title of *brother*, but that of *master;* they would not learn anything belonging to their ministry, but committed the whole to their

[1] Mosheim, II. p. 284. (*P.*) Cent. xi. Pt. ii. Ch. ii. Sect xii.

[2] History of Popery, III. p. 45. (*P.*) It is creditable to a priest of the same church, "John Brompton, Abbot of *Journal in Richmondshire,* who lived in the reign of Edward III.," that he thus acknowledges and censures the fact: "Res asperrima negari non potuit, celari non decuit; et sic qui summo honore ubique habebatur, ingloriosus et Dei judicio confusus cum summo dedecore in sua repedavit. Hoc si cuiquam displiceat, taceat, ne Johannem sequi videatur." *Hist. of Popery*, 1735, I. pp. 363, 364.

[3] On Church Revenues, p. 78. (*P.*)

[4] At this council the king and nobles were present with the prelates and abbots. See *Rapin,* L. iv. I. p. 367.

[5] Mosheim, II. p. 59. (*P.*) Cent. viii. Pt. ii. Ch. ii. Sect. ii.

R

vicars. Their study was to have horses, cooks, maîtres d'hôtel, concubines, buffoons and mountebanks; and they applied to the emperor for leave to hunt all sorts of wild beasts.[1]

Nothing, perhaps, can show the pride of the clergy in a stronger light, than the decrees of the eighth general council, held at Constantinople, in 869, in which it was ordered that bishops should not go before princes, that they should not alight from their mules or horses, but that they should be considered as of equal rank with princes and emperors; that if any bishop should live in a low manner, according to the ancient and rustic custom, he should be deposed for a year; and that if the prince was the cause of it, that prince should be excommunicated for two years. In the same council it was decreed that bishops only should be present at councils, and not secular princes; for that they ought not to be even spectators of such things as sometimes happen to priests.[2] All writers agree in giving the most shocking picture of the depravity of all ranks of men in the tenth century.[3]

When the occupation of churchmen and temporal lords differed so very little, it is natural to expect that there would be no great difference in their accomplishments. In the ninth century the ignorance of the clergy was so great, that few of them could either write or read. But one reason of this was, that many noblemen and others, wanting sufficient talents to appear to advantage in the field, retired into the church, the great endowments of which were temptations to them. The estates of the church were also often openly invaded, and the ignorant spoilers got possession of the benefices.[4]

Britain, being removed from the seat of the greatest rapine and profligacy, had a greater proportion of learned clergy than the rest of Europe, in the greatest part of the dark ages; and Ireland had perhaps a greater proportion than Britain, as they had suffered still less by the ravages of the barbarians.

The very corrupt state of the clergy made the monks, and their monasteries, of great value to the Christian world. With them almost all the learning and piety of those ages had an asylum, till the approach of better times.[5]

In the Church of England there is a three-fold order of ministers, viz. bishops, priests, and deacons. The deacons may baptize and preach, but not administer the Lord's supper; the priests may administer the Lord's supper, and pronounce absolution; and only the bishops confirm baptized persons, ordain ministers, and govern the church. The bishop's diocese is considered as the lowest kind of a church, and the presbyters are considered as his delegates or curates. But the first English reformers considered bishops and priests as of the same order, and therefore did not require that those who had been ordained by priests should be ordained again by a bishop. Wickliffe, who began the reformation in England, admitted no more than two degrees in the ministerial office, viz., deacons and presbyters or bishops. These two, says he, were known in Paul's time, and others are the invention of impious pride.

There is also another deviation from the primitive state of things in the Church of England, as the people have not in general the choice of their minister,[6] and the bishops are all nominated by the court. For though

---

[1] Sueur, A. D. 989. (*P.*)
[2] Ibid. A. D. 869. (*P.*)
[3] Among others, see Sueur, A. D. 909. (*P.*)
[4] Mosheim, II. p. 119. (*P.*) Cent. ix. Pt. ii. Ch. ii. Sect. ii.

[5] "Where, indeed, could the precious remains of classical learning, and the divine monuments of ancient taste, have been safely lodged, amidst the ravages of that age of ferocity and rapine... except in sanctuaries like these?...There Homer and Aristotle were obliged to shroud their heads from the rage of Gothic ignorance; and there the sacred records of divine truth were preserved like treasure, hid in the earth in troublesome times, safe but unenjoyed." *On Monastic Institutions. Miscel. Pieces*, by J. and A. L. Aikin, 1775, Ed. 2, pp. 91, 92.

[6] In some parishes, the inhabitants have, alternately, a choice; the chancellor nominating to the intermediate vacancy.

the dean and chapter have the nominal choice, the king sends them an express order to choose such as he shall direct.[1] In the reign of Edward IV. this absurd

[1] "The Queen [Anne] grants a license to the *dean* and *chapter*, under the great seal, to elect the person whom, by her letters missive, she hath appointed ; and they are to choose no other." *Rights of the Clergy,* 1709, p. 90. See [Rutt's Priestley] Vol. II. p. 339, Note†. To which add the following testimonies : "This order of admitting none to any ecclesiastical function, but by election of all the faithful, in a general assembly, was inviolably observed, and so continued for about two hundred years." Father *Paul,* on *Eccles. Benef.* Ch. iii. Ed. 3, p. 6. "That the people had votes in the choice of bishops all must grant ; and it can be only *ignorance* and *folly* that pleads the contrary." *Lowth* on Church-power. *Towgood,* Let. ii. Ed. 5, p. 96.

custom was set aside, and the king himself immediately appointed the bishops; but the old custom was renewed in the reign of Queen Elizabeth.

Almost all the inferior ministers are chosen by the bishops, the chancellor, or some lay patrons. When a new rector is to be placed in a parish, the patron of the living recommends whom he pleases to the bishop, and the bishop has no power to refuse. The rights of patronage to livings are openly bought and sold; and it is not reckoned simony to buy the next right of presentation, provided the living be not void at the time.

PART XI.

THE HISTORY OF THE PAPAL POWER.

THE INTRODUCTION.

WHEN we consider that, originally, the bishops of Rome were nothing more than any other bishops, that is, the ministers or pastors of a society of Christians, without any power, even within their own church, besides that of exhortation and admonition, it is truly astonishing that the *popes,* who are no other than the successors of those bishops, should have obtained the rank and authority that they have done; and it is hardly possible to conceive how the one should have arisen from the other. There is not, indeed, in the whole history of human affairs, another example of so great a change in the condition of any order of men whatever, civil or ecclesiastical.

From being in the lowest state of persecution, in common with other Christians, and having nothing to do with things of a temporal nature, they came to be the greatest of all persecutors themselves, and rose to a greater height of temporal power (and a power established on the voluntary subjection of the mind) than almost any sovereign, the most despotic by law or constitution, ever attained. And from being mere subjects, they came to be not only princes, but the most imperious lords of their former masters ; and their ecclesiastical power was still more absolute and extensive than their civil power. I shall endeavour to point out the several steps by which this great change was made.

The ground of the papal pretensions to power, in later ages, was the popes being the successors of the apostle Peter, to whom was delivered by Christ *the keys of the kingdom of heaven.* But whatever was meant by that expression, Peter himself assumed no pre-eminence over the rest of the apostles. Paul opposed him to his face, and says that he himself was not inferior to the *very chiefest apostles.*

Also, though it be probable that Peter was at Rome, and suffered martyrdom there, it is not probable that he was ever the proper bishop of Rome, or of any particular place; the apostles having a general jurisdiction over the church at large, appointing and directing the conduct of all the bishops; an office to which they appointed no successors at all.

The title of *pope* (papa), which signifies *father*, was not originally peculiar to the bishop of Rome, but in early times was commonly applied to other bishops, especially in the greater sees. Thus Cornelius, bishop of Rome, called Cyprian the pope of Carthage; and it was not till about the beginning of the seventh century, that the bishops of Rome appropriated that title to themselves.

One of the most extraordinary circumstances relating to the papal power is, that, though the foundations on which it rested were entirely changed, and those pretences on which the greatest stress was laid, had not been heard of, or hinted at, for many centuries; yet being continually urged, in dark ages, they came at length to be universally acknowledged, and acquiesced in, even by those princes whose interest it was to oppose them. And in time the business transacted at the court of Rome was so great and peculiar, that nothing was more sensibly felt than the want of unity in it, during the great schism in the papacy.[1] All Europe was in the deepest affliction on the occasion; and instead of rejoicing in the division of this enormous controlling power, it was the great object of princes and people to unite the church under its one proper head. Had the sun been divided, and its light been in danger of being extinguished, the Christian world would hardly have been more alarmed than it was; so necessary was the subjection of all Christians *to one supreme*

head *of the church*, at that time, deemed to be. The rise and progress of such an amazing power, from so very low a beginning, is indeed a great object, and well deserves to be considered with attention.

SECTION I.

OF THE STATE OF THE PAPAL POWER
TILL THE TIME OF CHARLEMAGNE.

THE first cause of the increase of power to the popes was the same that enlarged the power of the bishops of all the great cities of the empire; in consequence of which they had the power of calling, and presiding in, the assemblies of bishops within the provinces to which the civil jurisdiction of their respective cities extended: and, by degrees, as has been observed before, they had the power of ordaining the bishops in their provinces, and a negative on the choice of the people.

The bishops of the most important sees were at length distinguished by the title of *patriarchs*, who had all equal power, and differed only with respect to rank and precedency; and in general the bishop of Rome was considered as the first in rank, out of respect to the city in which he presided. After the see of Rome, the preference was given to the other great sees, in the following order, viz. those of Constantinople, Alexandria, Antioch, and Jerusalem. The churches of Africa do not appear to have been subject to any of these patriarchs; and Cyprian, who was bishop of Carthage, in the third century, had the same power that the bishops of Rome had, viz. to assemble the bishops of his province, to preside in their councils, and to admonish his brethren.[2]

The proper authority of the bishop of Rome, though he was the only per-

---

[1] On the death of Gregory XI., in 1378, when there were rival popes, one at Rome, and the other at Avignon.

[2] Mosheim, I. p. 215. (P.) Cent. iii. Pt. ii. Ch. ii. Sect. ii.

son in Italy distinguished by the title of *metropolitan*, did not extend over the whole of Italy, but only the southern parts of it, or those provinces which were called *suburbican*, because they were subject to the *imperial vicar*, who resided at Rome, while all the northern parts were subject to the *vicar of Italy*, as he was called, in temporal matters; and to the archbishop of Milan in spirituals; the vicar of Italy residing in Milan.[1]

But though the power of the bishops of Rome had no legal extension beyond that of other patriarchs, they had much more authority and influence than other bishops, on account of the dignity of their city, which was the capital of the Roman empire, and likewise on account of the great wealth and large revenues of that see. Moreover, as it had been the custom to appeal to Rome in all great civil cases, so if the bishops of Rome were only equal to other bishops of the great patriarchal sees, (and in early times they were probably superior to them in knowledge and character,) it would be natural, when differences of opinion arose, for each party to wish to have the sanction of the see of Rome. On these accounts appeals were more frequently made to Rome than to any other place; and this voluntary deference was afterwards *expected*, and then *insisted upon*, Christians in general having been by habit disposed to yield to its authority.

The Arian controversy afforded the bishops of Rome several opportunities of extending their power. Athanasius himself engaged the protection of Pope Julius; and it was chiefly by the influence of the see of Rome that the Trinitarian doctrine came to be established. But before this time, Victor, bishop of Rome, interposed his authority, but without effect, in the controversy about the time of keeping Easter, proceeding so far as to excommunicate all the Eastern churches, because they did not conform to the custom of the Western

church in this respect. But no regard was paid to his decision, though afterwards the Council of Nice determined the question as he had done.

On this, and on other occasions, the papal pretensions did not pass unnoticed, or without opposition. Some stand, though an ineffectual one, was always made to every encroachment; and the early popes themselves, who began to usurp a little, and to convert that into a matter of *right* which had originally been mere *courtesy*, would have been shocked at the idea of a small part of what was done by their successors. A number of *decretal epistles* have, indeed, been alleged as proofs that the earliest popes always held and exercised a sovereign power in the church. But these were manifestly forged, as the Papists themselves now acknowledge; and many facts in the early history of the church, and of the papacy, prove, incontestably, that the bishops of Rome had no more real power than other metropolitan bishops.

In the sixth Council of Carthage (426) it was concluded by the bishops who composed it, that they would not give way to the encroachments of the bishops of Rome on their rights and liberties, and they gave immediate notice to Pope Celestine, to forbear sending his officers among them, "lest he should seem to introduce the vain insolence of the world into the church of Christ." Various other councils also made decrees to the same purpose. But when the patriarchs of Alexandria and Antioch were oppressed by that of Constantinople, they had recourse to the Church of Rome; and by their example inferior bishops appealed thither also, when they were oppressed by the bishops of Alexandria and Antioch.[2] By this means the bishops of Rome acquired a considerable degree of influence even in the East.

After the prevalence of the Mahometan powers in Asia and Africa, as there remained only two rival metro-

[1] Anecdotes, p. 78. (*P.*)

[2] Mosheim, I. p. 374. (*P.*) Cent. v. Pt. ii. Ch. ii. Sect. vi.

politans, viz. those of Rome and Constantinople, they were continually at variance; and at first the bishops of Constantinople, where the emperor resided, had the advantage. These had extended their jurisdiction so much before the reign of Justin, that it comprehended Illyricum, Epirus, Macedonia, and Achaia. Afterwards it extended to Sicily, and many places in the southern parts of Italy, and they contended with the bishops of Rome for the superintendence of Bulgaria and other countries.[1]

The three other Eastern patriarchates having been either abolished or much reduced, the bishops of Constantinople took occasion from it to carry their pretensions to an authority so much higher than before, that John, who was chosen patriarch of Constantinople in 585, assumed the title of *œcumenical* or *universal bishop*. This title was severely condemned by Gregory the Great, who was then bishop of Rome, as tending to diminish the authority of other bishops. He even called it *blasphemy*, and a name invented by the devil; adding, that whoever called himself, or wished to be called, *universal bishop*, was the forerunner of Antichrist.[2] Nay, upon this occasion, by way of contrast, he took the title of Servus Servorum Dei, or *Servant of the Servants of God*, and he was the first pope who used that style in his letters.[3]

But not more than eighteen years after the death of this Gregory, viz. in 606, Boniface III. obtained of the emperor Phocas, that the bishops of Rome alone should, from that time, have this very title of *universal bishop*. The circumstance which made the assumption of this title the more odious, besides its having been rejected with so much indignation by the predecessors of Boniface, was its being granted by one who had risen to the empire by the murder of the preceding emperor Mauritius, his wife, and all his chil-

dren; and who in this manner courted the friendship of the bishop of Rome, whose power in the western part of the empire was then very considerable. For the popes acquired a great accession of power, and had much more influence in all civil affairs, in consequence of the removal of the seat of empire from Rome to Constantinople. But they were of much more consequence after the Lombards settled in Italy. For by taking part sometimes with them, and sometimes with the emperor, they made themselves formidable to both, and by this means their usurpations passed without censure.

That the authority of the sees both of Constantinople and of Rome arose from the dignity of the cities, is evident from this circumstance, viz. that before the year 381, the see of Constantinople had depended upon that of Heraclea, which had been the former metropolis of the province; but from that time the council ordained, according to the wishes of Theodosius, that the bishops of Constantinople should hold the principal dignity after that of the bishops of Rome.[4] But afterwards, viz. in a council held at Constantinople, under Justinian II., it was ordained that the patriarchs of Constantinople should be equal to those of Rome.

It was in the reign of Valentinian III. that, by the influence of Leo, the popes gained the greatest accession of power in the West, within the period of which I am now treating. Before this time the popes had no proper authority beyond the suburbican provinces.[5] But this emperor extended their authority to all the bounds of his empire, even into Gaul, and ordered that whatever should be done in that country without the authority of the Pope, should have no force.[6] The bishops assembled at Rome in 378, approved of this augmentation of the power of the popes.[7]

[1] Anecdotes, p. 158. (P.)
[2] Sueur, A. D. 595. (P.)
[3] Anecdotes, p. 206. (P.)
[4] Sueur, A.D. 381. (P.)
[5] Anecdotes, p. 81. (P.)
[6] Basnage, I. pp. 243–4. (P.)
[7] Mosheim, I. p. 287. (P.) Cent. iv. Pt. ii. Ch. ii. Sect. vi. Note [n].

An opportunity soon offered of making use of this power. For in the year 440, Chelidonius, being deposed in Gaul, appealed to the Pope, who received him into communion, and by the authority of Valentinian reinstated him. This was the first encroachment that was made by the popes on the liberties of the Gallican church.[1] It was not, however, till a long time after this, that any direct application was made to the popes for preferment in France. Auxanius, bishop of Arles, was the first bishop in France who, in the year 543, sent to ask for the *pallium*, or the archiepiscopal cloak, from Rome. His predecessor had it without asking for; and in this case the Pope answered, that he must first have the consent of the king of France.[2]

After the reign of Valentinian III., the bishops of Rome, finding their powers enlarged, and that they had the superintendence of all the churches of the West, sent their vicars regularly into the provinces, whenever there was the least pretence for it, and thus watched every opportunity of extending their jurisdiction. The first vicars which they established were those of Illyricum and of Thessaly. And the Pope was the more readily acknowledged to be patriarch of all the West by the Greeks, as well as by the Latins, as the former wished to have the bishop of Constantinople to be considered as patriarch of all the East.[3]

In 517, Pope Hormisdas appointed bishops of Gaul, Spain, and Portugal, his vicars in the respective countries. They were glad to be so honoured, as it gave them a rank above their brethren; and by this means the popes greatly extended their authority in those countries.[4] But before this time, viz. in 453, "the popes began to keep spies and informers at Constantinople. St. Leo recommends to the emperor

Marcian, one Julian, whom he declares to be his *legate*, established by him to solicit at the emperor's court all things relating to the faith and peace of the church, against the heretics of the age. This is the beginning of the Pope's legates residing at Constantinople, who were afterwards called *Apocrisiarii.*"[5]

The popes were also very attentive to send legates into nations newly converted, and thereby subjected them to their patriarchate. Thus the Bulgarians being converted, the Pope immediately sent an archbishop thither, which was the beginning of the contest between the patriarchs of Rome and those of Constantinople.[6]

After the fall of the Western empire, the popes found themselves in a peculiarly favourable situation for the increase of their power, the emperor being then at a distance, and therefore obliged to take some pains to keep on good terms with them, in order to keep up his interest in the country. Thus Justinian paid the Pope many compliments, and called the see of Rome the chief of all the churches, hoping by this means to drive the Goths out of Italy.[7]

Also the people of Rome, and of the neighbouring districts, disliking both the Greeks and the northern invaders, and having no other head, looked up to the popes for protection, and at length took an oath of allegiance to Gregory II. But they considered him as their chief, not as their master, meaning to form a republic, governed by its own laws.[4]

As the popes extended their power, they began to provide a broader basis for it. Leo was the first who claimed jurisdiction over other churches, as successor to St. Peter; and when it was decreed at the Council of Chalcedon, that the see of Constantinople should be second to that of Rome with respect

[1] Basnage, I. p. 243. (*P.*)
[2] Sueur, A.D. 543. (*P.*)
[3] Anecdotes, p. 144. (*P.*)
[4] Sueur. (*P.*)

[5] Jortin's Remarks, IV. pp. 297, 298. (*P.*) Ed. 1805, III. p. 125.
[6] Anecdotes, p. 145. (*P.*)
[7] Sueur, A.D. 534. (*P.*)
[8] Anecdotes, pp. 240, 246. (*P.*)

to rank, assigning as a reason for it the pre-eminence of the city, this pope was much dissatisfied, because his pre-eminence was not founded on something more stable than the dignity of the city, and wished to have it rest on the authority of St. Peter, as the founder of the see.[1] From this time we find this foundation for the authority of the see of Rome urged with the greatest confidence; and what is most extraordinary, it seems never to have been disputed. In a synod held at Rome, in 494, Gelasius said that the Church of Rome ought to be preferred to all others, not on account of the decrees of councils, but for the words of our Saviour Jesus Christ, when he said, "Thou art Peter, and upon this rock will I build my church."[2] But there has been much dispute about this decree, and the meaning of it.

It was sometime, however, before the popes thought of claiming absolute *infallibility*, as the successors of an infallible apostle. The first pope who seems to have made this claim was Agatho, who, "in an epistle to the sixth general council, holden at Constantinople, in 680, said, "that the chair of Rome .... never erred, nor can err in any point;" and that "all the constitutions of the .... Roman church are to be received as if they had been delivered by the divine voice of St. Peter."[3] But before this time there had not been wanting persons who flattered the pride of the popes by very extravagant encomiums. Thus, in the fifth century, Ennodius, a flatterer of Pope Symmachus, maintained that the Roman pontiff was "constituted judge in the place of God, which he filled as the vicegerent of the Most High."[4]

With this increase of real power and consequence, we may naturally expect additional higher *titles*, and more *splendour ;* and in this the popes were by no means deficient; and as they approached to the rank of sovereign princes, they omitted none of the usual forms or symbols of royalty. But in this period, as they had not attained to the power, so they did not assume all the pomp that they afterwards appeared in.

As the Christians affected the ceremonies of the heathen worship, the popes were ready enough to avail themselves of it, when it might add to their personal dignity. Accordingly, as the office of *Pontifex Maximus* had been of great dignity in Rome, and had generally been assumed by the emperors; from the end of the fourth century, the bishops of Rome were often called *Pontiffs*, and their office the *Pontificate.* They were also sometimes called *sovereign prelates*, or *sovereign priests.*[5] But the title of *bishops of bishops* was not given to the Pope seriously in the five first centuries.

The ceremony, by which respect is generally shown to the Pope, is *kissing his foot*, which was also done to the Pontifex Maximus of heathen Rome, and was demanded by Domitian, Dioclesian, and some others of the emperors,[6] who were likewise chief pontiffs. The civility was first shown to Pope Constantine 1. by the emperor Justinian II., at Nicomedia. He did it out of voluntary respect, but it was afterwards claimed "as .... due to them of right from the greatest crowned heads."[7]

The custom of carrying the Pope on men's shoulders after his election, which seems to have been borrowed from the customs of some of the Northern nations, in the choice of their chiefs or princes, was first used by Stephen II. He also had all his *bulls*, or *edicts*, sealed with lead.[8] Like other sovereigns, the popes, even in this period,

[1] Sueur, A. D. 451. (*P.*)
[2] Ibid. (*P.*)
[3] Hist. of Popery, II. p. 5. (*P.*) Ed. 1735, I. pp. 135, 136.
[4] Mosheim, I. p. 443. (*P.*) Cent. vi. Pt. ii. Ch. ii. Sect. ii.

[5] Sueur, A. D. 214. (*P.*) *Les Conformites*, Ch. ii. p. 12.
[6] *Caligula* and *Heliogabalus.* See *Les Conform.* Ch. ii p. 27, Whitelocke's Ess. p. 181.
[7] Hist. of Popery, II. p. 10. (*P.*) 1735, I. p. 138.
[8] Sueur, A. D. 752. (*P.*)

made use of the plural number in speaking of themselves. This is said to have been begun by Boniface III. about the year 606; who, in approving the choice of a bishop, used the words *Volumus et jubemus, we will and command.*[1] Afterwards the popes proceeded to assume other titles and forms, not only of royalty, but even of *divinity;* which having been first assumed by the princes of the East, were from them adopted by the Roman emperors, and from them by the popes.[2]

So early as the fourth century, the bishops of Rome surpassed all their brethren in riches and splendour, which exceedingly dazzled the common people; and so great a prize being contended for, there were often great tumults in Rome on the election of a pope, attended sometimes with murder, and violence of all kinds. Many were killed on both sides, in 368, during the contest between Damasus and Ursicinus.

Notwithstanding the power assumed by the popes, and though in many things they acted independently of the emperor, and even opposed him, they were still his *subjects,* and upon some occasions he treated them as such. The election of the bishop of Rome was not deemed valid without the consent of the emperor, and Justinian deposed two popes. But when the seat of empire was removed to Constantinople. little account was made of the consent of the emperor; though the popes kept up a formal submission to the emperors of the East against the Lombard princes till the time of Leo Isauricus.[3] And though Constantine Pogonatus released the popes from their usual payments for their confirmation, he expressly retained the right of confirmation.[4]

The Gothic kings of Italy also considered the popes as their subjects. And it appeared in the dispute between Symmachus and Laurentius, in 501,

when Theodoric was king of Italy, that the popes then acknowledged the authority of the kings, though they were heretics; that they requested of them permission to hold national councils, and that they appealed to them when they were charged with crimes, and submitted to their judgment. Athalaric, to prevent such mischiefs as had been occasioned by former schisms at Rome, made a rigorous edict, prescribing the manner in which the election of bishops and metropolitans should hereafter be made. This edict was drawn up by Cassiodorus, and nobody considered this as any attack upon the authority of the church.[5]

The temporal princes, under whom the popes lived, sent for them, as well as other bishops, and employed them in embassies, whenever they thought proper to make use of them. Pope John I. was sent by Theodoric to Constantinople, to obtain of the emperor Justinian I. the revocation of an edict, which ordained that the churches of the Arians should be put into the hands of the Catholics.[6]

When the empire of the Lombards was entirely put an end to in Italy, the nomination of the popes, at least the right of confirming them, was still in the hands of the temporal princes. Adrian, with his whole synod, acknowledged this power in Charlemagne, and Gregory VII. was himself confirmed in the papacy by that very emperor whom he afterwards deposed. Symmachus had the effrontery to maintain to the emperor Anastasius, that the dignity of the Pope was superior to that of the emperor, as much as the administration of the things of heaven is above that of the things of the earth, and that even a common priest was superior to him. But he was far from alleging this as a reason why the popes should not be subject to the emperor in things of a temporal nature.

---

[1] Sueur. (*P.*)
[2] A particular account of them may be seen in Sueur, A. D. 549. (*P.*)
[3] Anecdotes, p. 209. (*P.*)
[4] Walsh's Hist. of the Popes, p. 97. (*P.*)

[5] Anecdotes, p. 165. (*P.*)
[6] Ibid. p. 187. (*P.*)

One of the prerogatives to which the popes now pretend, is the power of summoning general councils, and of presiding in them. But all the general councils within the first five centuries were summoned by the emperors. Leo I. joined with many other bishops in requesting the emperor Theodosius to summon a council in Italy, but he refused, because he had before appointed one in Ephesus. Nor did the popes, or their legates, preside in general councils in early times; but various other bishops presided in them; and in the first general council, viz. that of Nice, Constantine himself was the principal moderator or director. Speaking to the bishops upon that occasion, he said, "Ye are bishops of things within the church, but I am a bishop as to externals."

SECTION II.

THE first thing that I shall notice in this period, is the changes that were made from time to time with respect to the election of the popes, and the confirmation of them in their office. It is certain that for many centuries the popes could not be consecrated till their election had been approved of by the emperors; and in general a sum of money had been given at the same time, till it was remitted, as I have observed, by Constantine Pogonatus. The same right of confirming the popes was exercised by the Goths, by Charlemagne, and his successors the emperors of Germany. But, in 847, Leo IV. was chosen pope without the consent of the emperor, the Romans being then pressed by the Saracens, and finding a necessity of having a head. However, they deferred the consecration from April to June, waiting for the consent

of the emperor, and they made an apology for it afterwards.

At length Charles the Bald, having obtained the imperial dignity by the good offices of the popes, discharged them "from the obligation of waiting for the consent of the emperors" to their election. "And thus .... from the time of Eugenius III., who was raised to the pontificate, A.D. 884, the election of the bishops of Rome was carried on without the least regard to law, order, or even decency, and was generally attended with civil tumults and dissensions, until the reign of Otho the Great, who put a stop to those disorderly proceedings," and prohibited "the election of any pontiff without the previous knowledge and consent of the emperor;" and this order was enforced to the conclusion of the ninth century. Gregory VII., however, taking advantage of the divisions of the empire, emancipated the see of Rome from this mark of its subjection to the empire.[1]

In early times, the bishops of Rome, like those of other cities, were chosen by the people, as well as the clergy. The first considerable innovation that was made in this respect at Rome, was at a council held in 1059, under Nicholas II.; when it was ordered that, upon the decease of a pope, the cardinal bishops should first consider of a proper person to succeed; that they should then consult with their cardinal clergy, and then, that the rest of the clergy, and also the people, should give their consent.[2] But Alexander III., in the middle of the twelfth century, established the sole right of election in the college of cardinals.

After this time the term *cardinal* was confined to the seven bishops within the territory and city of Rome, who had been used to consecrate the Roman pontiff, and to the presbyters of the twenty-eight Roman parishes,

[1] Mosheim, II. pp. 120, 121, 207, 208, 280. (*P.*) Cent. ix. Pt. ii. Ch. ii. Sect. iii. Cent. x. Pt. ii. Ch. ii. Sect. viii. Cent. xi. Pt. ii. Ch. ii. Sect. x.
[2] Fleury. (*P.*)

or principal churches. To appease the tumults that were made by others of the clergy, who were by this regulation excluded from the privilege of voting, this Alexander III. conferred the dignity of cardinals upon several more of the superior clergy ; and to pacify the inferior clergy, he, or some of his successors, for it is uncertain, made the chief of them *cardinal deacons,* giving them also votes in the election. Lucius III. was the first pope that was chosen "by the college of *cardinals,* alone." [1]

I shall just add to this article, that the almost universal custom of the popes' changing their names upon their election, began with *Bocco di Porco,* in 844, who changed his name to Sergius II., his original name, signifying *Hog's snout,* being thought unsuitable to his dignity.

It is not easy to say whether the spiritual or the temporal power of the popes was the more extravagant, but the temporal power preceded the spiritual, and no doubt laid the foundation for it, though other pretences were alleged. But there is no great difficulty in making merely ostensible pretences to be received, when there is sufficient power to enforce them ; and it was presently after the commencement of this period that the popes acquired that amazing accession of property and power, which placed them on a level with other princes of Europe.

The first large accession was made from the spoils of the Lombards in Italy, with whom Stephen II. had quarrelled, and against whom he undertook a journey to France, to solicit the aid of Pepin, king of France, who promised that if he should drive out the Lombards, he would give the popes the exarchate of Ravenna and the Pentapolis. From their acquisition of the latter, which was made in 774,

the popes ceased to date their letters by the reigns of the emperors.[2] This acquisition was evidently made by such policy as is employed by secular princes to increase their dominions. But Stephen, like other artful princes, was not at a loss for some colour of right, for he pretended that this territory belonged to him, as being the spoil of an heretical prince. For the Lombards, as well as the Goths, were Arians.

When Charlemagne afterwards put an entire end to the empire of the Lombards in Italy, the whole of the exarchate, the capital of which was Ravenna, was given to the popes. He was probably induced to make this large grant of land to the Church of Rome by a pretence, which was about this time made, that Constantine the Great had made a similar grant of territory to the same church ; though it is now universally agreed that this donation of Constantine was a forgery. Notwithstanding these large grants, both Pepin and Charlemagne reserved to themselves the sovereignty of all the lands in Italy. But this was afterwards surrendered to the popes by Lothair I.[3]

The last acquisition the popes made was that of the sovereignty of Rome, the inhabitants of which had always acknowledged the emperor as their sovereign. But, in 1198, the prefect of Rome received his office from the Pope, and not from the emperor.[4] From this time the popes have been as properly independent as any sovereign princes in Europe.

From the ninth to the thirteenth century, "the wealth and revenues of the pontiffs had not received any considerable augmentation; but at this time they were vastly increased under Innocent III. and Nicholas III., partly by the events of war, and partly by the munificence of kings and emperors. Innocent was no sooner seated in the

[1] Mosheim, II. p. 271. [Cent. xi. Pt. ii. Ch. ii. Sect. vi.] The particular rules that are now observed in the election of a pope were settled in 1178, and may be seen in the *Histoire des Papes,* III. p. 88. *(P.)*

[2] Anecdotes, pp. 255, 267. *(P.)*
[3] Ibid. pp. 320, 338. *(P.)*
[4] Histoire des Papes, III. p. 120. *(P.)*

papal chair, than he reduced under his jurisdiction the prefect of Rome," as mentioned above; "he also seized upon Ancona, Spoletto, Assisi, and several cities and fortresses which had, according to him, been unjustly alienated from the patrimony of St. Peter. .... Nicholas IV. followed his example .... and in 1278," he refused "to crown the emperor Rodolphus I. before he had acknowledged and confirmed, by a solemn treaty, all the pretensions of the Roman see;" and immediately upon that he seized "several cities and territories in Italy, that had formerly been annexed to the imperial crown, particularly Romagna and Bologna. It was .... under these two pontiffs that the see of Rome arrived .... at" its highest "degree of grandeur and opulence." [1]

Like other politic princes, the popes gained these advantages chiefly in consequence of divisions in the families of the temporal powers. The divisions between the kings of France of the second race were more particularly the means of advancing the power of the popes to its greatest height. Those who were condemned in France had recourse to the holy see, and always found protection there. In like manner, the popes availed themselves of the contest between the emperors Lewis and Charles, about the middle of the fourteenth century; in consequence of which the imperial power was quite lost in Italy, the popes seizing upon some of the towns, and others setting up for themselves.

The Crusades contributed very much to complete the power of the popes, as temporal princes, and brought business enough of a civil nature upon their hands. For, they had not only many dispensations to grant to those who could not go to those wars, but they made themselves judges of all the differences among those princes that went thither. [2]

But the ambition of the popes was far from being satisfied with the acquisition of an independent sovereignty. They soon began to extend their claims to other territories, and even to the empire itself. For having been accustomed to crown the emperors, they took advantage from that circumstance, together with that of the divisions in the empire, to arrogate to themselves the power of deciding who should be the emperor; and one or other of the candidates was but too ready to yield to the demands of the Pope, in order to secure his interest. In these circumstances John VIII. proclaimed Charles the Bald emperor in 876, in an assembly of the Italian princes at Pavia; and in the same manner were his two successors chosen. From this nomination of Charles the Bald, Sigonius says, that the *empire* has been a fief of the holy see. [1]

After this, viz. in the eleventh century, the popes assumed the character of lords of the universe, and arbiters of kingdoms and empires. "Before Leo IX. no pope" claimed "this unbounded authority" of transferring "territories and provinces from their lawful possessors." But this pontiff granted "to the Normans, who had settled in Italy, the lands and territories which they had already usurped," or which they should be able to conquer from the Greeks or Saracens. [4]

Gregory VII. followed the new maxims, and carried them farther, openly pretending that, as Pope, he had a right to depose sovereigns who rebelled against the church. This he founded principally upon the power of excommunication. An excommunicated person, he said, must, according to the rules of the apostles, be avoided by everybody. A prince, therefore, who is excommunicated, must be abandoned by all the world, even by his own subjects. This pope never made any formal decision of this kind,

---

[1] Mosheim, III. pp. 32, 33. (*P.*) Cent. xiii. Pt. ii. Ch. ii. Sect. v.
[2] Fleury's Sixth Discourse, p. 20. (*P.*)

[3] Sueur, A. D. p. 875. (*P.*)
[4] Mosheim, II. p. 260. (*P.*) Cent. xi. Pt. ii. Ch. ii. Sect. ii.

nor had he the countenance of any council, but he acted upon the maxim.

On the other hand, the defenders of the princes took it so much for granted, that an excommunicated person was subject to all the above-mentioned inconveniences, that they contented themselves with saying, that a prince ought not to be excommunicated; which, says Fleury, was giving the popes a great advantage in the argument. This pope likewise urged that, since the clergy have a right to decide concerning things spiritual, they have, *a fortiori*, a right to decide concerning things temporal. The least exorcist, he said, is above an emperor, since he commands demons; royalty is the work of the devil, being the effect of human pride; whereas the priesthood is the work of God.[1]

Some of the pretensions of this great pontiff were so very absurd, that one would think they must have refuted themselves by the events. In his difference with the emperor of Germany, he says, "We bind him by an apostolical authority, not only with respect to the soul, but to the body. We take from him all prosperity in this life, and victory from his arms."[2]

Later popes continued the same arrogant claims, and the necessity of the times too often induced princes to submit to them, though they had sometimes the spirit to resist. In 1225, Honorius III. applied to the popes the words of Jeremiah i. 10: "I have ... set thee over the nations, and over the kingdoms, to root out, and to pull down, and to destroy," &c.[3] In the fourteenth century, Boniface VIII., in a quarrel with Philip the Fair, king of France, "asserted that Jesus Christ had granted a two-fold power to his church, ... the *spiritual* and *temporal sword;* that he had subjected the whole human race to the authority of the Roman pontiff, and that whoever dared to disbelieve it were to be deemed heretics, and stood

excluded from all possibility of salvation." The king being still refractory, the Pope excommunicated him, but he "appealed to a general council," and sent a party of men to bring the Pope by force before him. In consequence of this he was apprehended at Anagni, but the inhabitants rescued him. He died, however, presently afterwards, of rage and anguish. His successor, Benedict XI., of his own accord, withdrew the excommunication; but by this time the papal power had begun to decline.[4]

When we consider the effects of excommunication in those dark ages, and the acknowledged power of the popes to direct that dreadful weapon, and also to suspend the exercise of all ecclesiastical functions, than which nothing could impress the minds of men in those times with more terror and consternation (as they imagined their everlasting happiness depended on those functions), we cannot wonder either at the arrogance, or the success of the popes. Robert, king of France, not complying with the Pope's decree respecting the dissolution of his marriage, the Pope, for the first time, laid the whole kingdom under this interdict, forbidding all divine service, the use of the sacraments to the living, and of burial to the dead. The people, terrified by this order, yielded such implicit obedience, that even the king's own domestics abandoned him, except two or three, and these threw to the dogs everything that came from his table. No person even dared to eat out of any vessel which he had touched. The king being reduced to this dismal state, was forced to yield, and cancel his marriage.[5]

The degree to which the popes sometimes carried their rage was truly dreadful. John XXIII. not only excommunicated Ladislas, king of Bohemia, but published a crusade against him; inviting all Christian princes to make war upon him, and seize his dominions. His bull upon this occasion contained

[1] Fleury, XIII. p. 48. (*P.*) [Vidal, Tom. IV. p. 145.]
[2] Ibid. A. D. 1078. (*P.*)
[3] Histoire des Papes, III. p. 164. (*P.*)
[4] Mosheim, III. pp. 150–152. (*P.*) Cent. xiv. Pt. ii. Ch. ii. Sect. ii. iii.
[5] Sueur, A. D. 998. (*P.*)

an order to all patriarchs, bishops, archbishops, and prelates, to publish every Sunday and festival-day, by the sound of a bell, and with candles lighted, and then extinguished by throwing them upon the ground, that King Ladislas was "excommunicated, perjured, a schismatic, a blasphemer, a heretic, a relapse, a favourer of heretics, a traitor, and an enemy of the Pope and of the church." He also excommunicated all his adherents and favourers, till by a return to their duty they should receive absolution; and ordered that whosoever should undertake to bury Ladislas, or any of his partisans, should be excommunicated, and not be absolved but by digging up the body with their own hands, and carrying it out of the place of Christian burial; and that the places on which they should lie should be profane for ever.[1]

So fully was this temporal power of the popes established, that they alone were thought to have the right of disposing of kingdoms; and they were as regularly applied to for that purpose, as the temporal courts for titles of nobility, &c. In 1179, Alexander III. "conferred the title of *king*, with the ensigns of royalty, upon Alphonso, duke of Portugal, who, under the pontificate of Lucius II., had rendered his province tributary to the Roman see."[2] Innocent III. gave a king to the Armenians in Asia, and in 1204 he made Primislas, duke of Bohemia, king of that country, and Peter II. king of Arragon. The title of king of Ireland was also a grant of the Pope to our King Henry II.; and when the Portuguese and the Spaniards were pursuing their discoveries and conquests, the one to the East, and the other to the West, the popes drew the line that was to regulate all their future claims to dominion.[3] These acts of universal

despotism were beheld with astonishment, but with silent and passive obedience, by all the temporal powers of Europe.

It was in the eleventh century that the power of the popes may be said to have been at its height. "Then they received the pompous titles of masters of the world, and .... universal fathers. They presided also everywhere in the councils by their legates." They decided "in all controversies .... concerning religion, or church discipline; and maintained the pretended rights of the church against usurpations of kings and princes." But this was not done without opposition both from the bishops, and from the temporal powers.[4]

In order to preserve this amazing power, it was necessary to keep the clergy as dependent as possible upon themselves, and as little attached to their temporal sovereigns. Gregory VII. never forbade the clergy to take an oath of allegiance to their respective sovereigns; but this was done by Urban II., who made an order for that purpose at the Council of Clermont. To complete the temporal character of the popes, I shall in the last place observe, that it was common in the twelfth century to see them at the head of armies.

The insolence with which the popes have acted in the height of their power is hardly credible. Gregory VII. obliged the emperor Henry IV., whom he had excommunicated, and who applied for absolution, to wait three days before he would admit him; though both the emperor, the empress, and their child waited barefoot, in the depth of winter. On the fourth day he was admitted, and as a token of his repentance, he resigned his crown into the hands of the Pope, and confessed himself unworthy of the empire, if ever he should oppose his will for the

---

[1] Histoire des Papes, IV. p. 151. (*P.*)

[2] Mosheim, II. p. 403. (*P.*) Cent. xii. Pt. ii. Ch. ii. Sect. xiii.

[3] "King Henry obtained, at the hands of the Pope, (Martin V.) the perpetual donation to the crown of Portugal, of whatsoever should be discovered from Cape Bajadore to the East Indies,

inclusively: together with an indulgence, in full, for all those devout souls whose bodies should chance to be dropped in the undertaking." Harris, *Voyages*, 1705, I. p. 3.

[4] Mosheim, II. p. 259. (*P.*) Cent. xi. Pt. ii. Ch. ii. Sect. ii.

future; and he was not absolved without very mortifying conditions. [1]

Adrian IV. insulted the emperor Barbarossa, about the middle of the twelfth century, for holding him the left stirrup instead of the right, and at length the emperor was compelled to hold the other stirrup. The next Pope, Alexander III., trod upon the neck of the same emperor, using at the same time this expression of the psalmist, " Thou shalt tread upon the lion and adder; the young lion and the dragon shalt thou trample under feet." Psa. xci. 13.

When Henry VI., the next emperor, was crowned by Celestine III., he kneeled before him as he sat in his pontifical chair, and was obliged to take the crown from his feet ; and when the Pope had kicked it off again, to show his power to depose him, the cardinals were, at length, permitted to crown the emperor once more. This was done to show that the imperial crown depended entirely upon the Pope. [2]

Our own country has not been less disgraced by papal insolence. One of the bravest of our haughty Norman princes, Henry II., could not satisfy the Pope with respect to the murder of the factious and turbulent prelate Thomas à Becket, (of which, however, he was not guilty,) till he walked barefoot to his tomb, and was whipped by the monks at Canterbury. King John was excommunicated, deposed, and made to receive his crown again, at the hands of the Pope's legate, and to acknowledge himself a vassal of the see of Rome.

In order to evade the tyranny of the popes, it was customary, when the times would bear it, not to dispute their power directly, but to prevent the publication of their bulls. Thus when Paul V. laid the state of Venice under an interdict, they banished those of the clergy who complied with the order, and at length the popes were glad to get Henry IV. of France to make their peace with the Venetians, who threatened to break off from their communion.

The temporal power of the popes, as I have observed before, was more ancient than the notion of their *infallibility.* This was not known in the times of Pepin or Charlemagne; and though councils were not then deemed infallible, the authority of the Pope was held to be subordinate to that. That councils are infallible was not pretended till the popes had been deemed to be so; the councils attributing to themselves what they had taken from the popes. [4]

With respect to spiritual power in general, the popes derived much advantage from the ideas of the Northern nations in their state of Paganism. For they considered the bishop of Rome in the same light in which they had before done their *arch-druid,* and transferred to him that boundless reverence with which they had been used to regard the other. Hence the force of the papal excommunications, which, as under the druids, deprived a person of all the common rights of humanity. [5]

However, besides the constant opposition of the Greek church, the overbearing authority of the see of Rome was not always submitted to, even in the West. It was particularly opposed by the church of Milan, which in the former period had been a metropolitan church, with a jurisdiction independent of that of Rome. In 848, Angilbert, archbishop of Milan, separated entirely from the Church of Rome, and continued so nearly two hundred years. At length, however, the popes got the better of this, as of every other opposition.

It is in the ninth century that we find the first seeds of the doctrine of the Pope's infallibility. Then, at least, the popes began to talk in a higher strain than usual on this subject;

---

[1] Fleury, A. D. 1077. (*P.*)
[2] Histoire des Papes, III. p. 112 (*P.*)
[3] Mosheim, IV. pp 319, 320. (*P.*) Cent. xvii. Sect. ii. Pt. i. Ch. i. Sect. xix.
[4] Basnage, *Histoire,* II. p. 597. (*P.*)
[5] Mosheim, II. p. 63. (*P.*) Cent. viii. Pt. ii. Ch. ii. Sect. vi.

maintaining that they could not be judged by any person, and that their decrees, respecting manners, faith, or discipline, ought to be preferred even to those of the councils themselves, if possible.[1] The argument on which this claim was rested was the declaration of our Saviour to Peter, that he would give to him the keys of the kingdom of heaven; and because he likewise said that he had prayed for him, that his faith should not fail, it was concluded that all the successors of Peter at Rome would always maintain the right faith. Weak as this argument is, it was universally acquiesced in, in those dark ages; and the popes acted upon it as upon a maxim that could not be disputed. When the bishop of Constantinople was deposed in 861, the Pope who had been written to on the occasion, but not by way of appeal, said in answer, "If they ought to be heard who sit in the chair of Moses, how much more they who sit in the chair of St. Peter!" and he maintained that no bishop of Constantinople ought to be deposed without the consent of the Pope.[2]

The authority of the popes having gained ground, in the manner that has been described above, the opinion of their infallibility began to appear undisguised and undisputed, about the middle of the eleventh century; Leo IX. declaring that the councils, and all the fathers, had considered the Church of Rome as the sovereign mistress, to which the judgment of all other churches belonged, and which could be judged by none; and that all difficult questions ought to be decided by the successors of St. Peter, because that church had never erred from the faith, and would not, to the end. This is the first Pope who held this language with such firmness. Gregory VII., who succeeded him, with more solemnity decreed in a council, that the Church of Rome never had erred, and never will err, according to the testimony of the Scriptures, on the ground above mentioned. Bernard and Thomas Aquinas gave this doctrine the great weight of their authority, and they were followed by all the schoolmen.[3]

Afterwards, however, several of the popes themselves, when they had any particular point to gain, and when the decrees of former popes were quoted against them, made no difficulty of departing from this doctrine. Thus John XXII., in his quarrel with the *Fratricelli*, who represented to him that three of his predecessors had been of their opinion, answered, that "what had been ill-determined by one Pope and one council, might be corrected by another, better informed concerning the truth." But, except in these occasional deviations, the popes asserted their infallibility, and it was generally acquiesced in till the time of the great schism (1378); when almost all the Christian world, seeing the popes sacrifice everything to their own ambition, dropped the high opinion which they had before entertained of them. Nor was it possible to put an end to the schism, without setting up a council above the popes.

During the time that the doctrine of the Pope's infallibility was generally received, the popes frequently spoke as if their decrees had been dictated by immediate inspiration. Thus Pope John VIII. says, that he had found that such a thing was the council of God, because that of a long time it had been revealed, by celestial inspiration, to his predecessor Nicholas.[4]

Such firm hold had the notion of the infallibility of the popes on the minds of men, that some of the greatest men in the Christian world, and even since the Reformation, were not able to shake it off. Father Paul, the great advocate of the state of Venice against the usurpation of the popes, admitted that they

---

[1] Basnage, II. p. 546. (*P.*)
[2] Sueur, A. D. 861. (*P.*)

[3] On "the opinion of those .... who lodge infallibility in the bishop of Rome," see Geddes, *Mod. Apol.* 1800, pp. 58–62.
[4] Sueur, A. D. 875. (*P.*)

ought to be obeyed in all matters of doctrine, and what related to the administration of the sacraments[1]. It is possible, however, that he might make this concession by way of argument, while he was disputing against their power in things of a temporal nature. But this was not the case with the famous Fenelon, archbishop of Cambray, who, when his book was condemned by the Pope, " declared publicly his entire acquiescence in the sentence." He even read it himself "in the pulpit at Cambray," and exhorted the people " to respect and obey" it.[2]

Originally, as I have frequently obseved, all bishops, and the popes themselves, were chosen by the people. Afterwards the metropolitans interfered, and then the princes reserved to themselves the right of approbation, and thus all abbots and bishops were chosen till the time of Henry III. of Germany.[3] But afterwards the popes claimed the right of nomination to all the greater livings; having made the first attempts of this kind in France, where they took advantage of the weakness of that monarchy. They then began to give out, that the bishops of Rome were appointed by Jesus Christ to be the supreme legislators of the universal church, and that all other bishops derived their authority from them. Opposition was made to these claims, but it was ineffectual; and from the time of Lewis the Meek, European princes in general suffered themselves to be divested of all authority in religious matters.

To gain this point, many memorials, and acts of former times, were forged in this age, and especially " the famous *decretal epistles*," said to have been written by the primitive bishops of Rome. They are generally fathered upon " Isidore, bishop of Seville," who lived in the sixth century.[4]

The popes made so artful a use of the weakness of the French monarchy, that a council held at Rheims, in 991, in which the authority of the Pope had been disputed, is called *the last sighs of the liberties of the Gallic Church*, the bishops of France after this allowing the popes a right to depose them. All the world, says M. de Marca, was obliged to submit to this new opinion, and France was at length forced to yield at the beginning of the third race of their kings. The popes laid all their bishops who had assisted at this council under an interdict, and would not take it off till everything was restored as before the council.[5]

But it was in the eleventh century that the great dispute arose between the popes and the emperors of Germany, about the right of *Investiture.* This consisted, originally, in the prince, or chief, putting a clergyman into the possession of any estate or fief, and was done by the delivery of a bough, or in such other manner as that in which laymen had been usually invested by the same persons. But because, upon the death of any incumbent, the priests used to deliver the *ring* and the *crosier* of the deceased bishop (by which the election of a new bishop had been used to be irrevocably confirmed) to some person of their own choosing, before the vacancy was notified to the prince, an order was given that those ensigns of spiritual power should be transmitted to the prince immediately upon the death of any bishop, and then he delivered them to whom he pleased; after which the same ensigns were again solemnly delivered by the metropolitan bishop. After much contention, and much war and bloodshed upon the occasion, it was compromised, by the Pope's consenting that the emperor should invest by the delivery of a sceptre, and not of a ring or crosier, which were ensigns of a spiritual authority.[6] The principal actor in this great scene

[1] Basnage, II. p. 549. (*P.*)
[2] Mosheim, IV. p. 393. (*P.*) Cent. xvii. Sect. ii. Pt. i. Ch. i. Sect. ii. See p. 222, *supra.*
[3] Simon on Church Revenues, p. 61. (*P.*)
[4] Mosheim, II. p. 126. (*P.*) Cent. ix. Pt. ii. Ch. ii. Sect. viii.

[5] Sueur, A. D. 991. (*P.*)
[6] Mosheim, II. pp. 289-291. (*P.*) Cent. xi. Pt. ii. Ch. ii. Sect. xiv.

was Gregory VII., who, in a council at the Lateran, decided that if any bishop received investiture from a layman, both he and the layman should be excommunicated.

In 1199 the popes pretended to have a right over all benefices, and that all translations from one see to another were the especial privilege of the see of Rome.[1] This right, however, was not fully asserted before it was done by Innocent III. in the thirteenth century, who assumed to himself, as pope, the power of disposing of all offices in the church, whether higher or lower, and of creating bishops, abbots, and canons at pleasure. And though the popes had formerly been strenuous advocates for the free choice of bishops, against the encroachments of the emperors, this pope, and many of his successors, overturned all those laws of election, reserving to themselves the revenues of the richest benefices, conferring vacant places upon their clients and creatures, and often deposing bishops who had been duly elected, and substituting others with a high hand in their room. The bishops, however, opposed these encroachments, but generally to little purpose.

Lewis IX. of France " secured the rights of the Gallican Church " in this respect " by that famous edict, known... by the name of the *Pragmatic Sanction*." This, however, did not make the popes renounce their pretensions, and their legates acted with all the insolence and tyranny of their masters in the countries into which they were sent; insomuch that Alexander IV. made, " in 1256, a severe law against the avarice and frauds of these corrupt ministers, which, however, they easily evaded by their friends and their credit at the court of Rome." At last Leo X. engaged Francis I. " to abrogate the *Pragmatic Sanction*, ... and to substitute in its place another body of laws, more advantageous to the papacy," called " the *Concordat*:" but this was " re-

ceived with the utmost indignation and reluctance." [2]

Another part of the spiritual power claimed by the popes is that of granting dispensations to do what would otherwise be unlawful; and from merely relaxing the severity of discipline, or remitting the penances that had been enjoined for sin (which, in time, made it to be imagined that they had the power of forgiving sin itself *after the commission*), they easily passed to the idea of their having a power to forgive it, and, which was the same thing, of their making it to be no sin, *before the commission*.

It was the wants and the avarice of the popes that first led them to grant these indulgences. The popes, when they were settled at Avignon, not being able to draw so much as they had used to do from Italy, had recourse to new methods of getting wealth. They not only sold indulgences more frequently than formerly, but disposed publicly of scandalous licences of all sorts, at an excessive price. John XXII. was particularly active in promoting this abominable traffic. He enlarged the taxes and rules of the apostolical chamber, and made them more profitable, though he was not the inventor of them.

The height to which the popes, and their advocates, carried their pretensions in this way is indeed astonishing. Innocent III., about 1198, decreed that out of the plentitude of the papal power, the pope could " of right, dispense beyond right;" and according to other decrees the popes claimed the power of dispensing even against the apostles, and the apostolical canons. Gratian, the famous canon lawyer, asserted that all men are to be judged by the Pope, but the Pope himself by no man. And " Cardinal *Zabar*, speaking of the popes, affirms that they might do all things that they will, even things

---

[1] Histoire des Papes, III. p. 126. (*P.*)

[2] Mosheim, III. pp. 31, 32, 289, 290. (*P.*) Cent. xiii. Pt. ii ;Ch. ii. Sect. iii. iv. and Cent. xvi. Sect. i. Ch. i. Sect. vii.

unlawful, and so could do more than God himself." [1]

There are too many instances in history of the popes reducing these pretensions into practice, by actually granting dispensations to do things morally evil, especially to release persons from the obligation of oaths. In 1042, Casimir, king of Poland, having retired to a monastery, deputies were sent to the Pope, and he absolved him from his vows, and permitted him to resume the government of his kingdom.[2] Celestine II. having required Henry, king of England, to re-establish Dunstan in the archbishopric of York, and he saying that he had swore he never would do it as long as he lived, the Pope answered, "I am Pope; if you will do what I require, I will absolve you of that oath." The king, however, declined it.[3] Henry II. of England, having sworn to fulfil his father's will, obtained an absolution from the Pope, and thereupon deprived his brother of his estates, and reduced him to a pension. At the Council of Constance, John XXIII. drew from many cardinals what he wanted to know of them, by releasing them from the oath of secrecy which they had taken.[4] The popes have always granted dispensations to marry within the prohibited degrees of consanguinity. Martin V. is said to have given leave to a man to marry his own sister.

Another power in spiritual matters, which has been claimed by the popes, is that of *canonization*, or the declaring what persons should be deemed *saints*, and the objects of worship. In the Council at the Lateran, in 1179, under Alexander III., "canonization was ranked among the greater and more important causes, the cognizance of which belonged to the pontiff alone." [5]

Another prerogative claimed and long exercised by the popes, and yet most clearly against all ancient custom, was that of calling and presiding in all councils; whereas originally, as I have observed, it was the business of the metropolitan of each district, and afterwards they were called by the temporal princes, first the emperor of Constantinople, and then other princes in their several states. In Germany it had always been the custom for the metropolitans to preside in their councils; but in the year 1047 the Pope claimed a right of sending his legates to preside in them.[6] And, in time, this claim, though the novelty of it was easily proved, came to be universally acquiesced in, and nothing but the factions of the popes themselves could ever have led the world to think or act otherwise. But after the great schism in the popedom, in which there were a long time two popes, and sometimes three, there was an absolute necessity of calling a council, and giving it a power of censuring, degrading, and making popes.

A new power now being established in the world, viz. that of the popes and the bishops, a power governed by maxims unknown to the world before, a new *system of laws* was of course introduced by it. This obtained the name of *canon law*, consisting originally of the decrees of general councils and synods, and then of the constitutions of popes, and decisions made by the court of Rome. In time these laws were collected, and reduced to a system, and became the object of study and practice to a new set of lawyers, as the Roman civil law had been before.

The first collection of ecclesiastical canons was published towards the end of the fourth century, by Stephen of Ephesus, and it was received with universal applause. The Church of Rome made use of this collection till that of Dionysius Exiguus appeared, in the sixth century. These canons

---

[1] History of Popery, I. p. 10. (*P.*) "Quod omnia possint, quicquid liberet, etiam illicita, et sit plus quam Deus." *De Schism. but. Germ. script.* p. 708. Hist. of Popery, 1735, I. p. 6.
[2] Fleury. (*P.*)
[3] Histoire des Papes, II. p. 609. (*P.*)
[4] Ibid. IV. p. 40. (*P.*)
[5] Mosheim, II. p. 403. (*P.*) Cent. xii. Pt. ii. Ch. ii. Sect. xiii.

[6] Fleury. (*P.*)

had no sanctions of a temporal nature, and therefore the councils generally applied to the emperors who had assembled them, to compel the observance of their decrees.[1]

In the seventh century the collection of canons by Isidore of Seville was published, composed of the councils held in Greece, Africa, France, and Spain, and also of the decretal letters of the popes, to the time of Zacharias, who died in 752.[2] This being a dark and ignorant age, all the letters of the popes for the first four centuries were forged, and yet the forgery was for many centuries undiscovered. These decretal letters had no other object than to extend the power of the popes, and the dignity of the bishops.[3] The difficulty of judging bishops, Fleury says, was increased by these decretals; the power of judging them being thereby given to the popes, so that appeals to Rome became very frequent.[4]

Gratian, who made a collection of canons in the twelfth century, went beyond the forged decretals in two important articles, viz. the authority of the popes, and the immunities of the clergy. For he maintained that the popes are not bound by the canons, and that the clergy cannot be tried by the laity in any cases. The constitutions of the popes, after this compilation of Gratian, turned upon the maxims contained in it; and yet, as the power of the popes increased, they kicked away the scaffold by which they had been assisted in climbing to this height of power. For Father Simon says that the decrees of Gratian are not valued at Rome, nor the books of decretals, but so far as they suit their purpose, the great principle of the court of Rome being, that the pope is above all law, which was indeed the great object of Gratian.[5]

In this country the bishops were allowed to have a separate jurisdiction, according to the canon law, after the Norman conquest, and this continued till it was abridged under Henry VIII.[6] Indeed the canon law has never been directly abolished in England, and though a correction was proposed to be made of it, the scheme was never carried into execution. But it was provided, in 1534, " that till such correction of the canons was made, all those which were then received should remain in force, except such as were contrary to the laws and customs of the realm, or were to the damage or hurt of the king's prerogative."[7] And it is perhaps better that the canon law should remain subject to this restraint than that any new system of the same kind should be enacted without any control. These remains, however, of the canon law have been gradually going into disuse, and the whole practice of the *spiritual courts,* in which it is continued, is now held in universal abhorrence and contempt.

The pride and exterior marks of splendour assumed by the popes have sufficiently corresponded to the power which they acquired; and the flatteries which they have received from their partizans have sometimes been in the highest degree abominable and blasphemous.

While the imperial power continued, no mark of respect was paid to the popes that was not paid to other bishops, archbishops, or patriarchs. But after they obtained sovereign power,

[1] Anecdotes, pp. 105, 107. (*P.*)
[2] Ibid. p. 293. (*P.*)
[3] Sueur, A. D. 838. (*P.*)
[4] Seventh Discourse, p. 13. (*P.*)
[5] On Church Revenues, p. 88. (*P.*)

[6] History of Popery, III. p. 70. (*P.*) "This composition [the canon law] thus made beyond the seas, Austin, the monk, slily wafts it over (though in itself a kind of *contraband* commodity) into England, where it remained many years, but in a weak, rickety constitution, till, at last, well suckled by several haughty prelates, as Thomas Becket and others, it grew rampant and unruly. And though often the civil authority gave it *daisy-roots* to hinder its growth; as the statutes of *provisors,* of *mortmain,* of *præmunire,* &c., yet nothing could effectually repress the *monster,* till our English *Hercules,* King Henry VIII., gave it a mortal wound." *Hist. of Popery,* Ed. 1735, I. p. 377.
[7] Neal's History, I. p. 11. (*P.*) Toulmin's Ed. I. p. 15.

they obtained likewise the same titles, and the same marks of reverence and respect, which had been claimed by other princes; and several of these ought to have been appropriated to divinity. The title of *holiness* was often given by one bishop to another, but it was appropriated to the bishop of Rome about the year 1000.[1] The ceremony of the *adoration* of the Pope, after his election, was borrowed from Paganism.[2] This was always done to the Roman Pontifex Maximus, and it is done by the cardinals to the Pope, seated upon the altar for that purpose. The customs of kissing the feet, and being carried on men's shoulders, were also borrowed from the Romans or the Northern nations. "Dioclesian ordained, by a public edict, that all sorts of persons should prostrate themselves before him, and *kiss his feet;*" and for this purpose he had a "*pantofle,* or slipper, enriched with gold, pearls, and precious stones."[3] It was Gregory VII. who ordered in council that even princes should kiss the feet of the Pope only.[4] But Valentine is said to have been the first pope whose feet were kissed after consecration by the cardinals and other persons present, in 827.

The popes, to show their superiority to other sovereigns, have assumed a *triple crown.* At first they wore only a bonnet, a little higher than usual, very much like the Phrygian mitres, which were used by the priests of Cybele; but Clovis, king of France,

having sent to the church of St. John of the Lateran a crown of gold, with which he had been presented by Anastasius, the emperor of Constantinople, Pope Hormisdas put it on his tiara. Afterwards Boniface VIII., in his quarrels with Philip the Fair, to show that things temporal ought to be subject to things spiritual, as a mark of this double authority, used two crowns instead of one, and to them John XXII. added a third, but with what particular view is not said.[5]

The style that has sometimes been assumed by the popes, and made use of in addresses to some of them, without their declining it, is truly blasphemous. Martin IV., 1621, "having excommunicated the people of Sicily, would not be persuaded to absolve them till, by their ambassadors, prostrate on the earth," they entreated it, saying, "*O lamb of God, that takest away the sins of the world, grant us thy peace.*"[6] The fathers of the Council of the Lateran said to Pope Leo X., "We respect your divine majesty; you are the husband of the church, the prince of the apostles, the prince and king of all the universe." They entreated also that he would not let them lose the salvation, and the life, which he had given them, adding, "Thou art the pastor, and the physician, thou art a God;" and declared that he had *all power in heaven and in earth.*[7] The canonists often gave the popes the title of *Dominus Deus noster,* which, indeed, had been assumed by Domitian. "Paul V. ... caused his picture to be put in the first page of divers books dedicated unto him, with this inscription, *Paulo V., Vice-Deo;*" and "Sixtus IV. suffered to be inscribed on a triumphal arch erected to him, anno 1484,

'*Oraclo vocis mundi moderaris habenas. Et merito in terris diceris esse Deus.*'"[8]

---

[1] Sueur, A. D. 366. (*P.*)

[2] See *Les Conformitez*, Ch. ii. p. 28, and "Essays ecclesiastical and civil, by the late learned Sir *Bulstrode Whitlocke*," 1706, p. 181. Yet, according to Sir Thomas Smith, a king or queen of England is as profoundly worshipped as a pope. "No man speaketh to the prince, nor serveth at the table, but in *adoration* and kneeling. All persons of the realme be bare-headed before him; insomuch that in the chamber of presence, where the cloath of Estate is set, no man dare walke, yea, though the prince be not there, no man dare tarry there, but bare-headed." *The Commonwealth of England,* B. ii. Ch. iv. *fin.* 1633, pp. 103, 104. See this passage applied to another subject, M. Repos. VI. p. 226.

[3] Hist. of Popery, III. p. 340, &c. (*P.*) Ed. 1736, II. p. 17.

[4] Sueur, A. D. 711. (*P.*)

[5] Histoire des Papes, III. p. 425. (*P.*)

[6] Hist. of Popery, III. p. 441. (*P.*) "Agnus Dei, qui tollis peccata mundi, dona nobis pacem." *Hist.* 1736, II. p. 66.

[7] Basnage, II. p. 556. (*P.*)

[8] History of Popery, I. p. 94. (*P.*) 1735, I. p. 51.

A circumstance which shows the spirit of the papacy in a particularly strong light, is, that Gregory VII., the most ambitious of all the popes, and who contributed more than any other to increase the power and pride of the popedom, was canonized, and a particular office, or form of prayer, was composed to his honour. This was introduced by Alexander VII., and was read in the churches of Rome and other parts of Europe; and whatever in his life ought to make his memory odious, is recited in this office as an heroic action. It was also authorized by Benedict XIII. But all Europe were offended at it.[1]

There is no giving one character of a set of men so numerous and so various as the popes have been, but, in general, since they have become sovereign princes, they have had all the follies and vices of other sovereign princes, and have spent their revenues in the same manner; more especially (as their power was short, and the office not hereditary) in enriching their families and dependents. At one period they were, for many successions, monsters of wickedness; using every art, and making no scruple even of murder, to gain their ends. A man more abandoned to vice, of the most atrocious kinds, than Alexander VI. was perhaps never known; and Leo X., the great patron of learning, was exceedingly debauched, and probably an atheist.[2]

It must be acknowledged, however, that many of the popes have been men who would have adorned any station in life; being, in the worst times, patterns of virtue, and actuated by the best intentions in the world. But they never had power to reform their own courts, or to accomplish the other reformations they projected.

However, time, and the diminution of their power, has at length done a great deal towards it; and as the bishops of Rome sink to the level of other bishops in the Christian church, they will probably acquire the virtues of their primitive ancestors; but then they will be no longer what we now call *popes.*

It may excite our gratitude for the blessings of the Reformation, to look back upon the state of this country while it was subject to the papal power. The popes seem to have held this country in a state of greater dependence than any other in Europe. To this the obligations that William the Conqueror and others of our princes were under to them, contributed not a little. All the rights and privileges of the English clergy were, in fact, in the hands of the Pope, who taxed them at his pleasure, and who had the absolute nomination to all the richest benefices in the country. These were in general filled with foreigners, especially Italians, who never so much as saw their dioceses, or the country, but had their revenues remitted to them abroad; by which means the country was drained of immense sums. The popes also disposed even of the reversions of the most lucrative places; so that neither the king, nor any other person in England, had anything to dispose of in the church.

This was ill brooked by several of our Norman princes and lords; but no redress was found for this evil till the reign of that spirited prince Edward III., who passed an act called the statute of *provisors,* by which all presentations to livings within the kingdom were taken from the Pope, and appointed to be in the king, or his subjects. But still the popes had considerable power, as in the trials of titles to advowsons, and appeals to the court of Rome. And though, by the seventh of Richard II., the power of nomination to benefices without the king's license was taken from the popes, they still claimed the benefit

[1] Histoire des Papes, II. p. 491, V. p. 597. *(P.)*
[2] " *Raphael Urbin,* the famous painter, ... being taxed by the then Pope for laying too much colour on the faces of Peter and Paul, ... replied, he did it on purpose to represent them blushing in heaven, to see what successors they had got on earth." *Hist. of Popery,* 1735, I. p. 9.

of confirmation, of the translation of bishops, and of excommunication.[1]

The interference of the papal power received another check in the reign of Richard II. For, whereas, before that time the archbishops of Canterbury and York might, "by virtue of bulls from Rome, assemble the clergy of their several provinces, at what time and place they thought fit, without leave obtained from the crown, and all the canons and constitutions concluded upon in those synods were binding without any farther ratification from the king;" an act passed in the sixteenth year of this reign, " called *præ-munire*, by which it was enacted, that if any did purchase translations to benefices, processes, sentences of excommunication, bulls, or any other instruments, from the court of Rome, against the king or his crown, or whoever brought them into England, or did receive or execute them, they were declared to be out of the king's protection, and should forfeit their goods and chattels to the king, and should be attached by their bodies, if they may be found."

From this time no convocation of the clergy could be called without the king's writ, and they could consult on such matters only as he should think proper to lay before them; but still their canons were binding without the king's assent, till the act of supremacy under Henry VIII. This prince assumed the sole right to the nomination and confirmation of bishops; and to the great mortification of the clergy, he also took to himself the first-fruits of all the benefices.[2]

[1] Neal's History, I. p. 2. (P.)

[2] Ibid. II. pp. 2, 10, &c. (P.) 1793, p. 15.

APPENDIX I.

TO

PARTS X. AND XI.

THE HISTORY OF COUNCILS.

To the preceding history of the clergy in general, and of the bishops and popes in particular, it may not be amiss to add a separate account of the *councils* or assemblies of the bishops and clergy, which make a great figure in the history of the Christian church. These assumed a most undue authority, and have been one of the principal supports of the greatest corruptions of Christian doctrine and discipline.

We find in the book of Acts, that when matters of considerable consequence occurred, all the apostles, or as many of them as conveniently could, assembled, to consult about it, and their decrees were universally received in the Christian church. It does not appear, however, that what they resolved on these occasions was directed by any immediate inspiration, for that would have superseded all reasoning and debates upon the subject, and consequently all difference of opinion. Whereas they appear to have debated among themselves, on some of these occasions, with a considerable degree of warmth. And though they conclude their advice to the Gentile Christians about the observance of the Jewish ceremonies, with saying that *it seemed good to the Holy Ghost and to us,* they probably only meant, that they were fully persuaded that the regulations which they prescribed were proper in themselves, and therefore agreeable to the mind and will of God; being conscious to themselves that they were under no improper bias. If they had been conscious of any particular illumination at that time, they would probably have mentioned it. Such, however, was the respect in which the apostles were held, that even their advices had the force of decrees, and in general were implicitly conformed to.

When the apostles were dead, it was natural for the bishops of particular churches to assemble on similar occasions; and though they could not have the authority of the apostles, that office becoming extinct with those who were first appointed to it; yet, as there was no higher authority in the church, had they contented themselves with merely giving *advice,* and confined their decisions to matters of discipline, they would hardly have been disputed. But it has been pretended that *general councils,* consisting of bishops assembled from all parts of the Christian world, succeed to all the power of the apostles, and have even absolute authority in matters of faith. But an assembly of ever so many bishops, being only an assembly of fallible men, can have no just claim to infallibility; nor indeed was this a thing that was pretended to in early times. Our Lord did, indeed, promise, that when two or three of his disciples were gathered together in his name, he would be in the midst of them; but this promise, whatever might be meant by it, was not made to bishops in particular, and might be claimed by two or three individuals, as well as by two or three hundred.

Besides, those general councils, the decrees of which have been urged as of the greatest authority, were in fact assemblies of factious men; in whose proceedings there was not even the appearance of their being influenced by the love of truth. For they determined just as the emperors, or the popes, who summoned them, were pleased to direct. Accordingly, there are, as might be expected, many instances of the decrees of some councils being contrary to those of others; which could not have been the case, if they had been all guided by the spirit of truth.

Though Arianism was condemned by the Council of Nice, it was established at the Council of Ariminum, which was as much a general council as the other, and also in the Councils of Seleucia and Sirmium. There is also a remarkable instance of the decrees of councils, in which the popes themselves have presided, contradicting one another, as those of Chalcedon and Constantinople, in 554. For the former absolved and justified Theodorit of Cyr, and Ibas of Edessa, and received them into their body, as orthodox bishops; whereas, the Council of Constantinople, which is styled the fifth general council, and was approved by the Pope, condemned them as damnable heretics.[1]

The Council of Constantinople also decreed, that images were not to be endured in Christian churches, whereas the second Council of Nice not only allowed them to be erected, but even to be worshipped. In later times, the Lateran Council of Julius II. was called for no other purpose but to rescind the decrees of the Council of Pisa; and whereas the Council of Basil had decreed, that a council of bishops is above the popes, the Lateran Council under Pope Leo, decreed that a pope is above a council.

Besides, there never has been in fact any such thing as a general council. Even the four first, which are the most boasted of, had no bishops from several whole provinces in the Christian world. And the Council of Trent, the authority of which the Papists make so much account of, was perhaps the

[1] Sucur, A. D. 554. *(P.)*

least respectable of all the councils. The chief intention of the crowned heads, who promoted this council, was to reform the abuses in the court of Rome. But the Pope himself, by his legates, presiding in it, pronounced the Protestants, who appealed to it, heretics before they were condemned by that council, and none were allowed to vote in it but such as had taken an oath to the Pope and the Church of Rome. There were hardly fifty bishops present in it, none being sent from several countries. Some that were there were only titular bishops, created by the Pope for that purpose; and some had Grecian titles, to make an appearance of the Greek church consenting to it. It is also well known that nothing was decided in the council without the previous consent of the court of Rome, and the decrees concluded with an express salvo of all the authority of the apostolical see.

In fact, the Papists themselves have found a variety of methods of evading the force of general councils, whenever it has been convenient for them so to do; as if their decisions depended upon a matter of fact, concerning which they were never pretended to be infallible; also, if their proceedings were not in all respects regular, and if their decrees were not universally received, as well as if they had not been approved by the popes. If we may judge concerning councils by the things that have been decreed in them, we shall be far from being prejudiced in their favour; their sanction having been pleaded for things the most repugnant to reason and the plainest sense of Scripture, as has been sufficiently manifested in the course of this work.

Councils were most frequent in the times of the Christian emperors at Constantinople, and of the Christian princes of Europe, from the fall of the Roman empire till towards the end of the eighth century. But the publication of the forged decretals of Isidore at that period made a great change with respect to councils, the jurisdic-

tion of bishops, and appeals. For, councils became less frequent when they could not be held without the Pope's leave; and the interruption of provincial councils was a great wound, says Fleury, to ecclesiastical jurisdiction.[1]

The first who seems to have maintained the infallibility of councils is Barlaam, who exhorts one of his friends to return to the communion of the Church of Rome, because a council at Lyons, being lawfully assembled, and having condemned the errors of the Greeks, he must then be considered as a heretic, cut off from the church, if he did not submit to it. But Occam, who lived at the same time, viz. in the fourteenth century, speaks of it as the opinion of some doctors only, while others say this infallibility was a privilege of the college of cardinals, and others, of the Pope himself. It was a question, however, that did not begin to be agitated till that time, and it was then disputed very calmly. It was more openly debated during the differences between the popes and the councils; when the councils setting themselves up above the popes, determined that themselves, and not the popes, were appointed by God to judge in the last resort concerning articles of faith. The Council of Constance made no decision on this subject, but that of Basil did; saying that it was blasphemy to doubt that the Holy Spirit dictated their resolutions, decrees and canons; while the Pope and his Council at Florence, declared the contrary, and it is not yet determined which of these was a lawful council.[2]

The most eminent of the Catholic writers themselves have maintained different opinions on this subject, and have been much influenced by the circumstances in which they wrote. But this was most remarkably the case with Æneas Sylvius, who had with great boldness maintained the authority of the Council of Basil against Euge-

[1] Seventh Discourse, p. 13. (*P.*)
[2] Basnage, *Histoire*, II. p. 518. (*P.*)

nius IV.; but being made Pope (by the name of Pius II.) " he published a solemn retractation of all that he had written" upon that subject; declaring, "without shame or hesitation, that as Æneas Sylvius he was a damnable heretic, but as Pius II. he was an orthodox pontiff."[1] At present the opinion of the infallibility of the Pope being generally given up by the Catholics, they suppose the seat of infallibility (for it is an incontrovertible maxim with them that there must be such a seat) to be in the councils.[2]

The Protestants themselves had originally no dispute about the authority of truly general councils. Luther appealed to a general council regularly assembled, and engaged to abide by its decision.[3] Calvin maintained in express terms, that the universal church is infallible, and that God must annul his solemn promises if it be otherwise.[4]

At present, however, it is not, I believe, the opinion of any Protestant, that any assembly of men is infallible. But it is thought by some to be lawful and convenient to call such an assembly of divines, to determine what should be the articles of faith in particular established churches, or such as should have the countenance of particular states. The synod of Dort, in Holland, made decrees concerning articles of faith, and proceeded in as rigorous a manner against those who did not conform to them, as any popish synod or council could have done.[5] The time is not yet come, though we may hope that it is approaching, when the absurdity of all interference of *power*, civil or ecclesiastical, in matters of religion, shall be generally understood and acknowledged.

[1] Mosheim, III. p. 247. (*P.*) Cent. xv. Pt. ii. Ch. ii. Sect. xvi.

[2] [It is hardly necessary to point out the fact, so sad and yet so hopeful, that, since the meeting of the recent Œcumenical Council of Rome (1869-70), every faithful Catholic is bound to hold the very opposite opinion to that stated in the text.]

[3] Ibid. III. p. 321. (*P.*) Cent. xvi. Sect. i. Ch. ii. Sect. xiv.

[4] Basnage, II. p. 499. (*P.*)

[5] The French Protestant church also exacted of every minister the following oath:—"I do swear and protest, before God and this holy assembly, that I do receive, approve and embrace all the doctrines taught and decided by the Synod of Dort, as perfectly agreeing with the word of God and confessions of our churches. I swear and promise to persevere in the profession of this doctrine during my whole life, and to defend it with the utmost of my power; and, that I will never, neither by preaching, nor teaching in the schools, nor by writing, depart from it." *Oath* prescribed by a *National Synod* of the reformed churches in France, held at *Aix*, 1620. *Quick's* Synod. pp. 38, 39. See " The Case of Mr Martin Tomkins," 1719, pp. 70, 71. *Nots* Also, p. 213, *supra.*

APPENDIX II.

TO

PARTS X. AND XI.

OF THE AUTHORITY OF THE SECULAR POWERS, OR THE CIVIL MAGISTRATE, IN MATTERS OF RELIGION.

WE have seen the daring attempts to introduce an arbitrary authority, so as to decide concerning articles of faith, as well as concerning matters of discipline, made first by the popes, who were nothing more, originally, than bishops of the single Church of Rome, and afterwards, by councils, or a number of bishops and other ecclesiastical persons. This usurpation led the way to another, not indeed so excessive in the extent to which it has been carried, but much more absurd in its nature. The former usurpations were of the *clergy*, who might be supposed to have studied, and therefore to have understood, the Christian system; but the latter is by mere *laymen*, who cannot be supposed to have given much attention to the subject of religion, and consequently must be very ill-prepared to decide authoritatively concerning its doctrines or rites. Of this nature is the ecclesiastical authority which, upon the Reformation, was transferred from the popes to the secular powers of the different states of Europe, and more especially that which was assumed by the kings and parliaments of England.

The Roman emperors, when they became Christians, did, indeed, interfere in the business of religion; but it was either to confirm the election of bishops, (which was soon perceived to be of considerable importance to them in civil matters,) or to convoke synods, or general assemblies; when, as they apprehended, the peace of the state was in danger of being disturbed by heresies and factions in the church. But though they sometimes signed the decrees of the synods, it was never supposed that their vote was necessary to the validity of them; and though they regulated the revenues, and other things of an external nature respecting the church, they never presumed to pronounce either by their own single authority, or that of the senate in conjunction with them, what was truth or what was falsehood, what ceremonies ought to be admitted, and what ought to be rejected, as has been done by the civil governors of Europe since the Reformation.

Constantine, who was himself president, or moderator, in the Council of Nice, speaking to the bishops on that occasion, said, as was mentioned before, "Ye are bishops of things within the church, but I am bishop as to externals." And long afterwards, when the civil and ecclesiastical powers were much more intermixed, Charlemagne, in a letter to the churches of Spain, says, concerning the council which he had held at Frankfort, "I have taken place among the bishops, both as an auditor and arbitrator. We have seen,

and by the grace of God we have decreed, that which ought firmly to be believed."[1] But though this great prince says, *We have decreed,* it is not probable that he himself had so much as a proper vote in the resolutions. If he had, he would hardly have called himself an *auditor,* or an *arbitrator,* though this seems to imply his having more power than that of giving a vote. Though it is not questioned that the emperors generally carried their points with the bishops, and got them to make what decrees they pleased, it was by their interest with them, and influence over them, and not by a proper authority. And during the prevalence of the papal power, the state was so far from encroaching upon the church, that ecclesiastics usurped upon the secular power, so as even to make and depose kings.

A series of facts, relating to the ecclesiastical history of England, will abundantly confirm what I have here advanced concerning the usurpation of the rights of Christ and of God, by the civil magistracy of this kingdom.

When Henry VIII. shook off his dependence upon the Pope, in 1531, he was far from abolishing their usurped and anti-christian power. He only transferred it from the Pope to himself, claiming the title of *sole and supreme head of the Church of England.* The absurdity of acknowledging a layman as supreme head of an ecclesiastical body, was a thing so new and strange, that the clergy would not admit it at first without this clause, *As far as it is agreeable to the laws of Christ.* But after a year or two, viz. in 1533, *the act of supremacy,* as it was called, passed the parliament, and the convocation also, without that clause.

By this celebrated act the whole power of reforming heresies and errors, in doctrine and worship, was transferred from the Pope to the king, without any regard to the rights of synods,

---

[1] Milot's Hist. of France, p. 62. (P.)

or councils of clergy; and without giving any liberty to those who could not comply with the public standard. This act expresses that "the king,... his heirs and successors,...kings of this realm, shall have full power and authority to visit, repress, redress, reform, order, correct, restrain and amend, all errors, heresies, abuses, contempts and enormities whatsoever they be."[1] It was also ordered in this reign, that "all appeals which before had been made to Rome," were "to be made to his majesty's chancery, to be ended and determined as the manner now is, by delegates."[2]

This king, indeed, in his letter to the convocation at York, assured them that he claimed nothing more by the *supremacy* than what Christian princes in primitive times assumed to themselves in their own dominions. But the contrary of this may easily be demonstrated. For, by an act passed in the thirty-first year of this reign, it was enacted, that whatsoever his majesty should enjoin in matters of religion, should be obeyed by all his subjects. Such language as this was never held by any of the Christian emperors.

The words of Mr. Hooker, who is generally allowed to be one of the ablest advocates of the Church of England, are very express to this purpose. He says, "If the whole ecclesiastical state stand in need of being visited and reformed; or when any part of the church is infested with errors, schisms, heresies, &c., whatsoever spiritual powers the legates had from the see of Rome, and exercised in right of the Pope, for remedying of evils, without violating the laws of God or nature; as much, in every degree, have our laws fully granted to the king for ever, whether he thinks fit to do it by ecclesiastical synods, or otherwise, according to law."[3]

Henry VIII., Edward VI., Queen Mary, Queen Elizabeth, and Charles I., all published instructions or injunctions, concerning matters of faith, without the consent of the clergy in convocation assembled, and enforced them upon the clergy, under the penalty of premunire. So jealous was Queen Elizabeth of this branch of her prerogative, that she would not suffer the parliament to pass any bill for the amendment or alteration of any of the ceremonies of the church; it being, as she said, an invasion of her prerogative. By one clause in the act of uniformity the queen was "empowered, with the advice of her commissioners or metropolitan, to ordain and publish *farther* ceremonies and rites;....and had it not been for this clause of a reserve of power to make what alterations her majesty thought fit, she told archbishop Parker, that she would not have passed the act."[4]

It is not easy to reconcile these claims of Henry VIII. and Queen Elizabeth with that article of the Church of England (XX.) which asserts that the "Church hath .... authority in controversies of faith," if by *Church* be meant the clergy. For the English clergy, as a body, were so far from having any hand in the business of reformation, that they opposed it as far as ever lay in their power. Besides, if it be granted that this absolute power is in the church, the Reformation itself was unlawful, and all that Henry VIII. and our other princes have done in this business is, by their own confession, unjustifiable.

After the act of supremacy, there could be no absolute necessity for our kings to consult even the parliament upon this subject. Henry, however, generally chose to do it, in order to give the stronger sanction to his own decisions. Thus the famous law of the *six articles*, commonly called the *bloody statute*, and which was entitled *An Act for abolishing Diversity of Opinions in certain Articles concerning the Christian Religion*, was an act of parliament, passed

[1] Neal's History, I. p. 8. (*P.*) 1793, p. 11.
[2] Ibid. p. 88. (*P.*) 1793, p. 124.
[3] Ibid. p. 86. (*P.*) 1793, p. 122.
[4] Ibid. p. 93. (*P.*) 1793, p. 130.

in the year 1538.[1] In this act was a ratification of several of the most important doctrines or articles of popery, and it continued in force to the end of this king's reign. In a very short time five hundred persons were imprisoned in consequence of it, among whom was the famous bishop Latimer.

This king seems even to have claimed an *infallibility*, equal to that which had been arrogated by the popes, and to have acted in all respects as if he had the consciences and the faith of all his people at his absolute disposal. For in the thirty-second year of his reign, it was enacted "that all decrees and ordinances, which shall be made and ordained by the archbishops, bishops, and doctors, and shall be published with the king's advice and confirmation, by his letters patent, in and upon the matters of Christian faith, and lawful rites and ceremonies, shall be, in every point thereof, believed, obeyed, and performed, to all intents and purposes, upon the pains therein comprised, provided nothing be ordained contrary to the laws of the realm."[2] And afterwards, when the articles of the Church of England were first compiled, which was under Edward VI., in 1551, they were drawn up by Cranmer and others, and received the sanction of the royal authority in council only, without being brought to parliament or convocations, though the title expresses as much.[3]

In the first year of Queen Elizabeth the parliament alone established the queen's supremacy and the Common Prayer, in spite of great opposition by the bishops in the House of Lords; and the convocation then sitting was so far from having any hand in those acts of reformation, that the members of it presented to the parliament several propositions in favour of the tenets of Popery, directly contrary to the proceedings of parliament.[4]

In the life of Mr. Whiston we have a remarkable instance of the very little consequence which the *Church* of England, as it is generally understood, is of in deciding religious controversies. For when a convocation had sat upon his writings concerning the doctrine of the Trinity, and pronounced them to be heretical and dangerous, Queen Anne interposed, and not choosing to ratify their sentence, all the proceedings came to nothing. Thus, as was observed on the occasion, the voice of a *woman*, which the apostle Paul does not allow to be even heard in the church, had more weight than that of all the *churchmen* in a body.[5] Can

England. Of this princess, whose decision that church seems to regard as final, the Protestantism is as equivocal as her personal virtue. According to her annalist *Camden*, Elizabeth appeared during the reign of Mary to *sail* by a *trade-wind*. He thus describes her policy : "Quum tamen illa, ut navigium ingruente tempestate, sese moderans, ad Romanæ religionis normam sacra audiret, et sæpius confiteretur, imo Cardinale Polo asperius interpellante, se Romano-Catholicam præ terrore mortis profiteretur." *Hist.* I. p. 21.

In her *first* year (1558) Elizabeth permitted "the epistles, gospels, and ten commandments to be read to the people, in the English tongue, howbeit without any exposition : also the Lord's Prayer, the Apostles' Creed and the Litany, she suffered to be used in the vulgar tongue. But in all other things they were to use the Romish rites and ceremonies, till a perfect form of religion should be concluded on by the authority of parliament. In the meantime she performed the obsequies of her sister Queen Mary, with solemn and sumptuous preparations, in the church of Westminster."

In the *second* year of Elizabeth (1559) "were enacted and established ... the Liturgy, and Administration of the Sacraments, which was in use under Edward VI., some few things being changed, and a penalty inflicted upon the depravers thereof, or such as should use any other whatsoever. Of going to church upon Sundays and holidays, a mulct of twelve pence for every day's absence, being imposed upon those that should absent themselves, and the same bestowed upon the poor." Thus was "the Protestant religion now established by authority of Parliament," (with the dissent of nine out of fourteen bishops and two nobles,) nor did the Queen "ever suffer the least innovation therein." See Camden's *History*, 1675, Ed. 3, pp. 9, 17, 19, 27, 31.

[5] Burnet, speaking of "the censure that was passed on Whiston's book," says, "all further proceedings against him were stopped, since the Queen did not confirm the step that we had made." It would be unjust to Burnet's memory to omit what immediately follows :—"This was not unacceptable to some of us, and to myself in particular. I was gone into my diocese when

[1] Neal's Hist. 1793, I. p. 27.
[2] Ibid. 1793, I. pp. 33, 34.
[3] Ibid. p. 50. (*P.*) 1793, p. 68.
[4] It was in the *second* year of Elizabeth, that a Protestant religion was settled for the *Church of*

these things be agreeable to the constitution of the gospel? Both the clergy and the queen were interfering in a business in which they had no right to meddle; and it is sometimes pleasant to see one usurper checking the violence of another.

It is remarkable that this clause in the *articles*, by which it is ordained that the *church*, and not the *king* (who, however, is acknowledged to be the supreme head of the church) should have authority in controversies of faith, was not in the first articles compiled by Cranmer, and which were forty-two in number, but was introduced into them when they were revised and new-modelled, in the reign of Queen Elizabeth. But nobody can tell why or wherefore that clause came to be inserted, it being manifestly inconsistent with other acts of the legislature, and with the conduct of our princes according to those acts.[1]

To these remarks I shall add, that several of the most important acts of spiritual jurisdiction, relating to the revenues and discipline of the Church of England, are performed by laymen. For the chancellors, officials and surrogates, who pass censures and excommunicate, frequently are, and by express law always may be, laymen; and the bishops have no power to control the proceedings of the courts which go by their name.

The House of Commons, which took up arms against Charles I., assumed the same authority in matters of religion that had been usurped by the preceding kings. And the Presbyterians, of which sect they chiefly consisted, would have enacted some persecuting and sanguinary laws, if they

had not been restrained by Oliver Cromwell, at the head of the Independents.[2] These being the smaller number, would certainly have been suppressed by any act of uniformity; and it is not improbable that, in consequence of being in this situation, they might sooner than any other sect in this country hit upon the true Christian principle of religious liberty, which entirely excludes the civil magistrate from interfering with it. At the Restoration, the same church establishment, with the same powers in the king and in the parliament, was resumed; and everything reverted into the same channel, or nearly the same, in which they had been in the reign of Queen Elizabeth.

It is something remarkable, that this glaring impropriety, of merely civil magistrates deciding concerning articles of Christian faith, which must necessarily be undertaken by all civil governors who presume to make any establishment of Christianity (that is, of what they take to be Christianity) in any country, should not strike more than it generally does; and that on this ground only all civil establish-

---

[1] Neal's Hist. I. p. 50. (P.) 1793, p. 69 See "An Historical and Critical Essay on the Thirty-nine Articles," by Anthony Collins, 1724, *passim*.

that censure was passed; and I have ever thought that the true interest of the Christian religion was best consulted, when nice disputing about mysteries was laid aside and forgotten." *Burnet,* O. T. *An.* 1712, Fol. II. 803. See also Whiston's Mem. Ed. 2, pp. 156, 188, 189. Towgood's *Letters,* No. 1, 1779, p. 27.

[2] See p. 46, *supra.* The *Protectorate* commenced with the following provisions against the persecution of any professing Christians, except *papists* and *prelates:*—

"XXXV. That the Christian religion, contained in the Scriptures, be held forth and recommended as the publique profession of these nations. . . . .

"XXXVI. That to the publique profession held forth, none shall be compelled by penalties or otherwise, but that endeavours be used to win them by sound doctrine, and the example of a good conversation.

"XXXVII. That such as profess faith in God by Jesus Christ (though differing in judgment from the doctrine, worship or discipline publiquely held forth), shall not be restrained from, but shall be protected in, the profession of the faith and exercise of their religion; so that they abuse not this liberty, to the civil injury of others, and to the actual disturbance of the publique peace on their parts. Provided this liberty be not extended to Popery or Prelacy, nor to such as, under the profession of Christ, hold forth and practise licentiousness." *The Government of the Commonwealth,* &c. "As it was publickly declared at Westminster, the 16th day of December, 1653.—Published by his Highness the Lord Protector's special commandment." M DC LIII. pp. 42, 43.

ments of Christianity should not be exploded, since all Christians profess to acknowledge no Father besides God, and no Master besides Christ, and to stand fast in the liberty with which he has made us free. If there be any meaning in this, it must be that no human authority should be permitted to make that necessary to Christian communion which Christ has not made necessary, but left undetermined, and consequently indifferent. There are instances, however, of this absurdity having been noticed in several periods of our history, besides that which I have mentioned, when the claim of Henry VIII. to be the supreme head of the church was first started.

When the act of *Uniformity* was passed, in the beginning of the reign of Elizabeth, in 1559, "Heath, archbishop of York, made an elegant speech against it;" observing that it "ought to have had the consent of the clergy in convocation, before it passed into a law. 'Not only the orthodox but even the Arian emperors,' says he, 'ordered that points of faith should be examined in councils; and *Gallio*, by the light of nature, knew that a civil judge ought not to meddle with matters of religion.' But he was over-ruled, the act of supremacy, which passed the house the very next day, having vested this power in the crown."[1]

When that law was made, in the reign of William and Mary, which makes it blasphemy, punishable with confiscation of goods and imprisonment for life, if persisted in, to deny the doctrine of the Trinity, Lord Feversham, who had no objection to the doctrine which was to be guarded by that law, expressed his dislike of the civil magistrate interfering to guard it, in very strong terms. He said that he acknowledged the houses of parliament might lay upon the subject what taxes they pleased, and might even make a king; but he did not like the idea of a *parliamentary*

religion and a *parliamentary God*.[2] Such, however, in fact, is the established religion of this country. It is such a religion as the king, lords, and commons of this realm have thought proper to make for themselves, and to impose upon the people; who certainly ought to judge for themselves, in a matter which so nearly concerns them as individuals, and of which they are as competent judges as their superiors. Such an usurped authority as this ought to be opposed, especially when it is considered that the power by which this mode of religion is enforced, is precisely the same with that of the popes; having been transferred from them to our princes.

Exclusive of everything contained in the religion of the Church of England, it is chiefly the *authority* by which it is enjoined that Dissenters object to in it. Things in their own nature ever so indifferent, are no longer so, when the authority by which they are enforced is improper and boundless. It is upon the same just maxim that we always profess to act in things of a civil nature. A tax of a penny is what no man would value, of itself; but it would be a justifiable cause of a civil war, if our kings only, without the concurrence of parliament, should presume to enforce that tax: because a tax that begins with a penny might end in a pound, or extend to a man's whole property. In like manner, a power that alters a single article of faith, or imposes one rite, might change the whole system. It was, therefore, so far from being the mark of a *weak* mind, that it was an evidence of great, just, and enlarged views, in the Puritans, to resist, as they did, the *imposition* of things in their own nature indifferent. To have submitted, would have been to ac-

[1] Strype, *Ann. Ref.* I. p. 73. *Ap.* No. 6. D'Ew's Journal, p. 29, in Neal's *Hist.* Ed. 1793, p. 130.

[2] See this expression, assigned to the Earl of Peterborough (Rutt's Priestley), Vol. II. p. xvii. *note**. The Earl added, "that if the House were for such an one, he would go to *Rome* and endeavour to be chosen *cardinal;* for he had rather sit in the *Conclave*, than with their lordships, upon those terms." *Tindal's Hist.* IV. p. 647, in Towgood's *Letters*, III. Sect. xiii.

knowledge another supreme power in the church besides that of Christ.

This is the true and solid ground of a dissent from the Church of England. It is declaring (and it is the only proper and effectual mode of declaring) that we will acknowledge no *human authority* in matters of religion; but that we will judge for ourselves in a business which so nearly concerns us, and not suffer others to judge for us; and that, in the worship of God, and what respects our happiness in a future world, we will only obey him whose power extends to that world, that is, *God*, and not *man*.

It is, moreover, evidently agreeable to the maxims of the gospel, that every Christian make an *open declaration*, both by his words and by his conduct, of what he believes concerning it. This is most expressly declared to be obligatory upon us with respect to Christianity in general. And for the same reason, it ought to be extended to every important distinction in the profession of Christianity, and especially what relates to the *seat of power*, or authority in the church of Christ. Our Lord hath said, *Whosoever shall be ashamed of me, and of my words, of him shall the Son of Man be ashamed, when he cometh in his own glory, and the glory of his Father.*

Had Christianity been a system of speculative opinions only, and had not required a conformity in our practice, and such as is *visible to the world*, every degree of persecution might be avoided. But this we know was not the case in the primitive times. All true Christians then thought themselves obliged not to make the least concealment of their opinions, whatever they might suffer in consequence of their profession. In like manner, every Protestant ought to be a declared Protestant, and not deny his principles by communicating with the idolatrous Church of Rome. And for the very same reason, every man who thinks that the Church of England usurps an undue authority over the con-

sciences of men, similar to that of the Church of Rome, ought to be a *declared Dissenter*, and separate from the established church, whatever ridicule or persecution of any kind he may expose himself to on that account.

If the primitive Christians, or the first reformers from Popery, could have been contented with keeping their opinions to themselves, while they conformed to the religion of their country, they might have avoided all the inconveniences to which the public profession of their principles exposed them; and in this they would have followed the example of all the heathen philosophers, whose maxim it was, to *think with the wise and act with the vulgar*, and who ridicule the Christians for not doing the same. For all the philosophers held the popular superstitions in the same contempt with the Christians themselves. But no true Christian or Protestant will venture to sacrifice so much to his worldly ease and safety. And were not many of the present members of the Church of England either grossly ignorant of the nature of religion, inattentive to what belongs to it, or governed by the heathenish maxim above mentioned, they would not dare to countenance by their concurrence, what they may easily know to be gross corruptions of Christianity, and especially an usurpation of the rights of God and of Christ.

There is another state in Europe, in which the prince assumes an ecclesiastical power independent of the Pope. For the kings of Sicily pretend to be by birth *legates a latere* to the holy see, and to have a power of absolving, punishing, and excommunicating all persons, even cardinals themselves, who reside in their kingdom. They also preside in provincial councils, and act in all respects independently of the court of Rome. Their style is, *beatisimo et santisimo padre*, and they attribute to themselves in Sicily the same power that the popes have with respect to the rest of the church. The Sicilians claim this right from a bull of Urban II., granted in 1097 to Roger, the Norman king of Sicily, and to his successors. But the advocates for the court of Rome say that this bull was forged, during the long time that the island had no communication with the holy see: for it continued ninety years under an interdict, beginning in 1282. Hence, however, have arisen violent disputes between the kings of Sicily and the popes. But to this day the kings of Sicily exercise that jurisdiction, and are in fact popes within their own territories. On this account F. Simon says there are three popes in Christendom, viz. at Rome, in Sicily, and in England; the two last, however, deriving their power from the first, the kings of Sicily by voluntary concession, and the kings of England by force.[1]

[1] Simon on Church Revenues, pp. 116, 121. Mosheim, II. p. 231. (*P.*) Cent. xi. Pt. i. Ch. i. Sect. iii.

"Henry's reformation altered the *form* of Popery, but did not remove the grand *principle* of it, human authority in matters of religion; the act of supremacy lodged the same power in the crown, that had been vested in the Pope. In virtue of this power the king exercised ecclesiastical legislation and jurisdiction, appointed by commission articles of religious doctrine and practice for the nation, and supported them by penal sanctions.

"The reformers in the reign of Edward VI. retained the doctrine of royal supremacy; they availed themselves of his minority and youth, put out two service-books, intended a third, and might have put out a thousand on the same principles; they sacrificed the rights of all the nation to a fancied prerogative of a boy.

"Queen Elizabeth's reigning passion was love of despotism; her means of attaining it were full of duplicity, treachery and cruelty: she made religion an engine of government, and framed the English episcopal corporation so as to serve her arbitrary plan of governing. She obtained an absolute supremacy; her bishops acted under it; she imposed articles, ceremonies, oaths, penalties, &c." R. Robinson's "Plan of Lectures on the Principles of Nonconformity," 1781, pp. 5, 6.

Camden having quoted the conciliatory letter from Pius IV. to Elizabeth, dated 15 May, 1560, adds: "The report goeth, that the Pope gave his faith, ' that he would disannul the sentence against her mother's marriage, as unjust, confirm the English liturgy by his authority, and grant the use of the sacraments to the English, under both kinds, so as she would join herself to the Romish Church, and acknowledge the primacy of the chair of Rome; yea, and that certain thousand crowns were promised to those that should procure the same.' Elizabeth, though little solicitous about the *Protestant* faith, was too fond of her *supremacy* to become a *Papist.* Her annalist adds, that she "still persisted, like herself, *semper eadem.*" See Camden, Hist. p. 47. Also *supra*, p. 269, Note [4].

APPENDIX III.

TO

PARTS X. AND XI.

OF THE AUTHORITY OF TRADITION, AND OF THE SCRIPTURES, ETC.

WE have seen the pretensions of the popes, of councils, and also of civil magistrates, to decide controversies of faith. It may not be improper, in the conclusion of this subject, to consider two other authorities, viz. those of tradition and of the Scriptures. As the Jewish and Christian religions are of divine origin, it behoves us to examine, as carefully as we can, the channels by which these divine communications have been conveyed to us; and these can be no other than oral tradition or writing; and of these the latter is certainly preferable, whenever it can be had, provided we have sufficient evidence that we have the genuine writings of the inspired prophets themselves.

T

But in many cases, even tradition ought not to be slighted.

Those Christians who were not converted by the apostles themselves, and who lived before the publication of any of the canonical books of the New Testament, could not have had any other foundation for their faith. We ourselves admit these books to be canonical on no other foundation; and by calling them *canonical*, we mean no more than that they are the genuine productions of those persons whose names they bear, or of the times to which they are usually ascribed; and therefore they are of themselves of no authority, but as the most indisputable evidence of what it was that Christ and the apostles did teach and practise as from God; and it cannot be made to appear that the same thing may not be sufficiently proved by other means. We observe the first, and not the seventh day of the week, as a day of rest, contrary to the known custom of the Jews, which we believe to have been of divine appointment, upon no other authority than that of tradition; it being supposed to have been the invariable custom of the church from the time of the apostles, and it being impossible to account for the origin of the present custom, and of its being observed without the least variation in churches that differ in almost everything else, but upon that supposition. For we do not find in the New Testament any express order of Christ, or of the apostles, that such a change should be made.[1]

When, therefore, we speak of tradition as an improper foundation for faith or practice, we must mean only pretended, or ill-founded traditions; such as were alleged by several of those who were called heretics in very early times, or by the Church of Rome at present. But, in this case, we object to the opinions and practices, not merely because we find no trace of them in the Scriptures, but because we

¹ See, on the observance of *Sunday* [Rutt's Priestley], Vol. II. pp. 322-324, and *Notes*.

find no sufficient authority for them at all.

Some of the ancient heretics are said, by Austin and others, to have availed themselves of this source of credit; laying great stress on our Lord's saying to his disciples, that he had many things to say to them which they were not able to bear at the time that he was with them, and pretending that the apostles themselves, besides preaching to all persons indiscriminately, made a reserve of some things to be taught more privately, and only to a few. But there does not appear to have been any sufficient foundation for that pretence; all their teaching having been public, and nothing concealed from any persons who were desirous of being instructed. Much less was there any reason to think that the particular things which they wished to support by this pretence were among the things revealed to those few. Besides, our Lord himself seems to have precluded every pretence of this kind, by telling his apostles, that whatever they had heard of him in private, they should proclaim in public. Matt. x. 27.

The Church of Rome has adopted a variety of customs, and founded many claims, upon this authority of tradition. But in what was called the *Catholic church*, no recourse was had to tradition, before the second Council of Nice, in 787, in which the worship of images was established; when many things had generally been assented to, and practised before that time, which had no foundation in the Scriptures, or in the reason of things. This council, therefore, expressly anathematized all those who did not receive ecclesiastical traditions, written or unwritten. But the things which the members of this council alleged as proper to be received on such authority are exceedingly foolish and absurd.

The authority of the books of the New Testament, supposing them to be genuine, is the very same with that of the apostles themselves. But in very early times, this does not appear to have been so great as it came to be afterwards. Though it was never doubted that Paul was an inspired apostle, and received the knowledge he had of the gospel from Jesus Christ himself, yet we find by his own writings, that there were violent factions against him all his life, and that his opinions were by no means implicitly received. He himself is far from insisting that everything he asserted was to be received without examination. On the contrary, the various arguments he produces in support of his assertions, without alleging any other authority for them, shows that his conclusions were drawn from the premises which he alleged, and which he submitted to the examination of his readers. He must, therefore, have supposed that they would think themselves at liberty to judge for themselves; and that, as he submitted his reasoning to their examination, they would decide for or against him, according as his arguments should appear to them conclusive or inconclusive.

When this apostle does not reason at all, but merely declares that he had his information from Christ, we receive it on the credit of a man whom we suppose to have been neither imposed upon himself, nor to have had any interest in imposing upon others; and likewise of his being a person whose authority in general was supported by his power of working miracles. Of this kind is the account which he gives us of the resurrection of the dead, and the change that will pass upon the living subsequent to it; and also his account of the institution of the Lord's supper, &c.

Nor was this the case of Paul only, who was peculiarly obnoxious to the Jews, on account of his zeal in preaching the gospel to the Gentiles. For Peter himself, who is called *the apostle of the circumcision*, and was considered as the very *chief of the apostles,* was not more respected, whenever he said or did anything that was thought to be improper. This appeared very clearly in the case of Cornelius, and in the altercation that Paul had with him at Antioch.

On the former of these occasions, when the conduct of Peter was arraigned, he vindicated himself, not by asserting that what he did was by the express direction from heaven, (though he was led to what he did by express revelations made both to himself, and also to Cornelius,) but by a simple narrative of facts, from which they might themselves judge, that what he had done was not without sufficient authority. And even when all the apostles were met, to consider of what was to be done with respect to the supposed obligation of the Gentile converts to observe the Jewish ceremonies, they seem not to have had any immediate inspiration. For they reasoned and deliberated upon the subject; which seems to imply that there was for some time a difference of opinion among them, though they afterwards concurred in giving the advice that they did, and in which they concluded that they had the concurrence of the Holy Spirit.

But even this *decree,* as it is now generally called, which had the authority, as we may say, of the whole college of apostles, does not seem to have been relished by all Christians; as we may infer from the enmity which the Jewish converts in general bore to Paul, and from the Nazarenes or Jewish Christians, never making use of his writings. For though they were not written in a language which they understood, it would not have been more difficult to procure a translation of them, than of the gospel of Matthew, which was also probably written in Greek.

Indeed, what is universally acknowledged to have been the state of the Jewish Christians could not have been true, if they had had the same ideas that were afterwards entertained, of the constant inspiration of the apostles and evangelists. A great part of them rejected the account of our Lord's miraculous conception, and though they made use of the gospel of Matthew in

Hebrew, they omitted the two first chapters, in which it is asserted; not, as far as appears, questioning their being written by Matthew, but not thinking the contents of them sufficiently well-founded; and yet they did not, on account of this difference of opinion, cease to communicate with one another. Nor does Justin Martyr, who mentions their opinion long afterwards, pass any censure upon them on account of it. He only says that he cannot think as they did; and what is more remarkable, he does not mention the authority of Matthew and Luke, as what was decisive against them. These Jewish Christians would certainly have treated the gospel of Luke in the same manner as they did that of Matthew, if they had been acquainted with it, and had thought proper to make use of it at all.

When the Jewish church was first formed, and indeed so late as the publication of the gospel, many of the disciples would think themselves as good judges of the history of Christ, as the evangelists themselves. They did not want those books for their own use, and would judge concerning the contents of them, as they would concerning other books which implied an appeal to living witnesses. That the books were generally received, and not immediately rejected by those to whom they were addressed, is a proof that the history which they contained is in the main authentic, but by no means proves that every minute circumstance in them is true. Indeed, the evangelists, varying from one another in many particulars, (which may be seen in the *Observations* prefixed to my Harmony of the Gospels,)[1] proves that they wrote partly from their recollection, which may be imperfect in things of little consequence, and partly from the best information which they could collect from other persons.

Like other credible historians, all the evangelists agree in the main things,

but they differ exceedingly in the order of their narrative, and with respect to incidents of little consequence; and to contend for anything more than this is in effect to injure their credibility. If the agreement among them had been as exact as some pretend, it would have been natural for the enemies of Christianity to have said, that they must have been written by combination, and therefore that the history has not the concurrent testimony of independent witnesses; and if the exactness contended for cannot be proved, the authority of the whole must be given up.

Besides, what would have been the use of appointing twelve apostles, or witnesses of the life and resurrection of Christ, if their testimony was not naturally sufficient to establish the credibility of the facts; and what would have signified even the original inspiration, unless all error in transcribing, and translating, &c., had been prevented, by the same miraculous interposition, in all ages, and in all nations afterwards? Having written more largely on this subject in my Institutes of Natural and Revealed Religion,[2] and also in the *Preface* to my Harmony of the Gospels, to those works I beg leave to refer any readers with respect to this subject. I would also refer them to what I have written under the signature of *Paulinus*, in the *Theological Repository*, in which I think I have shown, that the apostle Paul often reasons inconclusively, and, therefore, that he wrote as any other person, of his turn of mind and thinking, and in his situation, would have written, without any particular inspiration. Facts, such as I think I have there alleged, are stubborn things, and all hypotheses must be accommodated to them.

Not only the *Nazarenes*, but Christians of other denominations also, rejected several of the books of our New Testament, and without denying the authenticity of them, (for with this they are not, in general, charged,) but be-

---

[1] Sect. xi.-xvi., also the *Essays* in Theol. Repos. Vol. II.

[2] See [Rutt's Priestley] Vol. II. pp. 123-130, 208-211.

cause they did not approve of their contents. Thus the *Gnostics* in general made but little use of the canonical books, and pleaded the authority of tradition, and the *Elcesaites*, in the time of the emperor Philip,[1] are said to have rejected all the epistles of Paul, though the authenticity of them was never questioned.

When the apostles were dead, the authority of their writings would naturally rise, and appeals would be made to them when controversies arose in the church. And this natural and universal deference to the opinion of the apostles produced, I doubt not, at length, the opinion of their infallibility. Their authority was also justly opposed to the many idle traditions that were pretended to by some of the early heretics, and to the spurious gospels that were written after the *four* had acquired credit. Till that time there could be no inducement to write others; and notwithstanding the reception that some of the forged gospels met with in certain places, they never operated to the discredit of the four genuine ones (and indeed they were only written as supplemental to them), it appears that they were easily distinguished from the genuine gospels, and did not retain any credit long. And what we are able to collect of them at this day is enough to satisfy us, that they were not rejected without sufficient reason.

The Jews, in forming their canon of sacred books, seem in general to have made it a rule to comprise within their code all books written by prophets; and therefore though they had other books, which they valued, and might think very useful in the conduct of life, they never read them in their synagogues. These books were afterwards called apocryphal, consisting of pieces of very different character, partly historical and partly moral.

These apocryphal books were not much used by Christians, till they were found to favour some superstitious opinions and practices, the rise of which I have already traced, and especially the worship of saints. For at the Council of Laodicea, in 364, the Hebrew canon was adopted. But in the third Council of Carthage, in 397, the apocryphal books were admitted, as canonical and divine, and were therefore allowed to be read in public, especially Ecclesiasticus, Wisdom, Tobit, Judith, and the two books of Maccabees. The Popes Innocent, Gelasius, and Hormisdas confirmed the decrees of this council.[2]

The church having afterwards adopted the version of Jerome, which followed the Hebrew canon, the apocryphal books began to lose the authority which they had acquired; and it was never fully re-established till the Council of Florence, in 1442; and it was then done principally to give credit to the doctrine of purgatory. It was for a similar reason that the Council of Trent made a decree to the same purpose.[3] Also, though before the second Council of Nice the Scriptures alone were considered as the standard of faith, it was then decreed, for the first time, that they who despised traditions should be excommunicated.[4]

Notwithstanding the apparently little foundation which many of the popish doctrines have in the Scriptures, it was very late before any measures were taken to prevent the common people from using them. Indeed, in the dark ages, there was no occasion for any such precaution, few persons, even among the great and the best educated, being able to read at all. The Sclavonians, who were converted

---

[1] 247. According to Epiphanius, "they received neither the writings of the prophets nor apostles." *Lardner*, IX. p. 513.

[2] Sueur, A. D. 397. Basnage, II. p. 460. (*P.*)
[3] Basnage, II. pp. 463, 465. (*P.*) "Synodus ... statuit et declarat, ut hæc ipsa vetus et vulgata editio ... in publicis lectionibus, disputationibus, prædicationibus, et expositionibus pro authentica habeatur, et ut nemo illam rejicere quovis prætextu audeat vel præsumat." *Decretum de editione et usu sacrorum librorum.* Sess. iv. 1546. *Con. Trid. Can. et Decret.* p. 8. On Jerome's *Vulgate*, see Geddes's *Prospectus*, 1786, pp. 44–51, and Middleton's Works, II. p. 324.
[4] Basnage, II. p. 488. (*P.*)

to Christianity at the end of the ninth century, petitioned to have the service in their own language, and it was granted to them. Pope John VIII., to whom the request was made, thanked God that the Sclavonian character had been invented, because God would be praised in that language. He ordered, however, that the gospels should be read in Latin, but that afterwards they should be interpreted to the people, that they might understand them, as was done, he says, in some churches.[1]

But afterwards, Wratislas, king of Bohemia, applying to Gregory VII. for leave to celebrate divine service in the same Sclavonian tongue, it was absolutely refused. For, said this pope, after considering of it, "it appeared that God chose that the Scripture should be obscure in some places, lest if it was clear to all the world, it should be despised, and also lead people into errors, being ill-understood by their ignorance." This, says Fleury, was the beginning of such prohibitions.[2]

The practice of the Church of Rome at present is very various. In Portugal, Spain, Italy, and in general in all those countries in which the Inquisition is established, the reading of the Scriptures is forbidden. France was divided on this subject, the Jansenists allowing it, and the Jesuits refusing it. For the Council of Trent having declared the Vulgate version of the Bible to be authentic, the Jesuits maintained that this was meant to be a prohibition of any other version[3]

After the Council of Trent, this evil was much increased. For the bishops assembled at Bologna, by order of Julius III. advised that the reading of the Scriptures should be permitted as little as possible, because the power of the popes had always been the greatest when they were least read; alleging that it was the Scriptures which had raised the dreadful tempest with which the church was almost sunk, and that no person ought to be permitted to know more of them than is contained in the mass. His successor profited by this advice, and put the Bible into the catalogue of *prohibited books*.[4]

The cardinal Cusa, in order to justify the condemnation of Wickliffe, in the Council of Constance, said that the Scriptures must be explained according to the present doctrine of the church; and that when the institutions of the church change, the explication of the Scripture should change also; and the Council of Trent has decided that traditions ought to be received with the same respect as the Scriptures, because they have the same authority.[5]

So much were the Roman Catholics chagrined at the advantage which Luther, and the other Reformers, derived from the Scriptures, that, on some occasions, they spoke of them with so much indignation and disrespect, as is inconsistent with the belief of their authority, and of Christianity itself. Prieras, master of the sacred palace, writing against Luther, advances these two propositions, viz. that the Scriptures derive all their authority from the church and the Pope, and that indulgences, being established by the church and by the Pope, have a greater authority than the Scriptures. "How do we know," say some of these writers, "that the books which bear the name of Moses are his, since we have not the originals, and if we had them, there is no person who knows the hand-writing of Moses? Besides, how do we know that all that Moses has said is true? Were the evangelists witnesses of all that they write? And if they were, might they not be defective in memory, or even impose upon us? Every man is capable of deceiving, and being deceived."[6]

All the popes, however, have not

---

[1] Basnage, II. pp. 470, 471. (*P.*)
[2] A. D. 1089. (*P.*)
[3] Basnage, II. p. 468. (*P.*) On *Catholic Versions*, see *Geddes*, pp. 101–113.

[4] Ibid. II. p. 475.   (*P.*)   See *supra*, p. 2, *fin.*
[5] Ibid. p. 480. (*P.*)
[6] Ibid. p. 455, &c. (*P.*)

shown the same dread of the Scriptures. For Sixtus V. caused an Italian translation of the Bible to be published, though the zealous Catholics were much offended at it, [1]

So much were the minds of all men oppressed with a reverence for antiquity, and the traditions of the church, at the time of the Reformation, that the Protestants were not a little embarrassed by it in their controversy with the Catholics; many of the errors and abuses of Popery being discovered in the earliest Christian writers, after the apostolical age. But at present all Protestants seem to entertain a just opinion of such authority, and to think with Chillingworth, that *the Bible alone is the religion of Protestants.* We may, however, be very much embarrassed by entertaining even this opinion in its greatest rigour, as I have shown in the introduction to this Appendix.

[1] Histoire des Papes, V. p. 80. (*P.*)

PART XII.

THE HISTORY OF THE MONASTIC LIFE.

THE INTRODUCTION.

BESIDES those ministers of the Christian church whose titles we meet with in the New Testament, but whose powers and prerogatives have been prodigiously increased from that time to the present, we find that, excepting the *popes* alone, no less conspicuous a figure was made by other orders of men, of whom there is not so much as the least mention in the books of Scripture, or the writings of the apostolical age; I mean the *monks*, and *religious orders* of a similar constitution, which have more or less of a religious character.

The set of opinions which laid the foundation for the whole business of monkery, came originally from the East, and had been adopted by some of the Greek philosophers, especially Plato, viz. that the soul of man is a spiritual substance, and that its powers are clogged, and its virtues impeded, by its connexion with the body. Hence they inferred that the greatest perfection of mind is attained by the extenuation and mortification of its corporeal incumbrance. This notion operating with the indolent and melancholy turn of many persons in the southern hot climates of Asia, and especially of Egypt, led them to affect an austere solitary life, as destitute as possible of everything that might pamper the body, or that is adapted to gratify those appetites and passions which were supposed to have their seat in the flesh. Hence arose the notion of the greater purity and excellency of celibacy, as well as a fondness for a retired and unsocial life, which has driven so many persons in all ages, from the society of their brethren, to live either in absolute solitude, or with persons of the same gloomy turn with themselves. It is the same principle that made Essenes among the Jews, monks among Christians, dervishes among Mahometans, and fakirs among Hindoos.

How apt Christians were to be struck with the example of the Heathens in this respect, we see in *Jerome*, who "takes notice that 'Paganism had many observances which, to the re-proach even of Christians, implied a great strictness of manners and disci-pline. Juno,' says he, 'has her priest-esses, devoted to one husband, Vesta her perpetual virgins, and other idols their priests also, under vows of chas-tity.'[1]

The persecution of Christians by the Heathen emperors, and consequently the more imminent hazard that at-tended living in cities, especially with the incumbrance of families, was another circumstance that contributed to drive many of the primitive Chris-tians into deserts and unfrequented places. The irruptions of the Northern nations into the Roman empire had an effect of the same kind, making all cities less safe and comfortable. More-over, when the great persecutions were over, and consequently the boasted *crown of martyrdom* could not be ob-tained in a regular way, many persons inflicted upon themselves a kind of voluntary martyrdom, in abandoning the world and all the enjoyments of life. "Gregory Nazianzen, celebrating the absurd austerities and mortifica-tions of the monks of *Naziansum*, tells us that some of them, through an ex-cess of zeal, killed themselves, to be released from the wicked world."[2] It is possible, however, that they might not directly kill themselves, or intend to do it, but only died in consequence of depriving themselves of the usual comforts of life. It was these austeri-ties, joined with such imaginary *reve-lations*, and intimate communications with heaven, as have usually accom-panied them, that was the great recom-mendation of Montanism. The Mon-tanists, Tertullian says, had the same rule of faith, but more fasting and less marrying, than others.[3]

These notions and these circum-stances concurring, particular texts of Scripture were easily found that seemed to countenance austerities in general, and celibacy in paticular; as that saying of our Saviour, Matt. xix. 12 : "There are some .... which have made themselves eunuchs for the king-dom of heaven's sake. He that is able to receive it, let him receive it;" and Paul's saying, 1 Cor. vii. 38 : "He that giveth in marriage doeth well, but he that giveth not in marriage doeth better." Both these passages, however, probably relate to the times of persecution, in which it is either absolutely necessary to abandon the satisfaction of family relations and do-mestic society, or at least in which it is most convenient to be free from every attachment of that kind; that when men were persecuted in one city, they might, with more ease, and less distress of mind, flee to another.

But on every other occasion mar-riage is spoken of in the most honour-able terms in the Scriptures, and is, indeed, necessary for the propagation of the human species. Besides, Paul makes it a mark of that man of sin, or *antichristian power*, which was to arise in the latter times, that it was to forbid to marry, as well as to make use of "meats, which God hath created to be received with thanksgiving." 1 Tim. iv. 3. In fact, these two circumstances greatly contribute to point out the Church of Rome as the principal seat of that antichristian corruption, of which so much is said, and against which we are so earnestly cautioned, in the books of the New Testament.

Besides, men's passions are far from being improved by the long con-tinuance of this miserable and soli-tary state. Instead of approaching by this means, as they vainly pre-tended, to the life of angels, they rather sink themselves to the condition of brutes, and some of the most worth-less or savage kinds. Also, living without labour themselves, (as in time the monks came to do,) and upon the

[1] Middleton's Letter, p. 238. (*P.*) "Quid nos oportet facere, in quorum condemnationem habet, et Juno Univiras, et Vesta Virgines, et alia Idola continentes." Hieron, T. iv. Par. i. p. 314. It. Par. ii. pp. 154 & 744. Middleton, Works, III. p. 127.
[2] Jortin's Remarks, III. p. 22. (*P.*) Ed. 1805, II. p. 168.
[3] De Jejuniis, C. i. Op. p. 544. (*P.*)

labour of others, and without adding to the number or strength of the community, they certainly defeat the great purposes of their creation, as social beings; and are not only a dead weight upon the community, but, in many cases, a real evil and nuisance, in those states in which they are established.[1]

SECTION I.

OF THE MONASTIC LIFE, TILL THE FALL OF THE WESTERN EMPIRE.

THERE is always something uncertain and fabulous in the antiquities of all societies, and it is so in those of the monks. The monks themselves acknowledge the first of their order to have been one *Paul*, an Egyptian, who in the seventh persecution, or about the year 260, retired into a private cave, where he is said to have lived many years, unseen by any person, till one Anthony found him just before his death, put him into his grave, and followed his example.

This Anthony, finding many others disposed to adopt the same mode of life, reduced them into some kind of order; and the regulations which he made for the monks of Egypt were soon introduced into Palestine and Syria by his disciple Hilarion, into Mesopotamia by Aones and Eugenius, and into Armenia by Eustachius Bishop of Sebastia. "From the East this gloomy institution passed into the West;" Basil carrying it into Greece,

and Ambrose into Italy. "St. Martin, the celebrated bishop of Tours, erected the first monasteries in Gaul, and... his funeral is said to have been attended by no less than two thousand monks." But the Western monks never attained the severity of the Eastern.[2]

The number of these monks in very early times was so great, as almost to exceed belief. Fleury says, that in Egypt alone they were computed, at the end of the fourth century, to exceed seventy thousand.[3] With this increasing number many disorders were necessarily introduced among them. At the end of the fourth century the monks were observed to be very insolent and licentious; and having power with the people, they would sometimes even force criminals from the hands of justice, as they were going to execution.[4] In the time of Austin many real or pretended monks went strolling about, as hawkers and pedlars, selling bones and relics of martyrs.

The increase of monks was much favoured by the laws of Christian princes, and the encouragement of the popes, as well as by the strong recommendation of the most distinguished writers of those times. "Justinian made a law that a son should not be disinherited for entering into a state of monkery against his father's will;" and Jovian appointed "that whosoever courted a nun, and enticed her to marriage, should be put to death." But this law, being thought too severe, was afterwards mitigated.[5] Syricius, Bishop of Rome, ordered that monks and virgins who married after their consecration to God should be banished from their monasteries, and confined in private cells; that by their continual tears they might efface their crime, and become worthy of communion before they died. The same pope ordered that bishops and priests who were

---

[1] "Esteeming it to be evangelical poverty, to feed upon the labours of other men, in beggary and idleness; these are they who, clad in mean and vile habits,...profess themselves to wear these emblems of poverty and contempt for the sake of Christ and religion; yet swelling inwardly with ambition, and giving to the chiefs of their orders the most arrogant titles....I will not deny, but there are some pious and devout men among them, but the generality of them... deform and deface religion." *Agrippa de Incertitudine*, &c. 1530. "Vanity of Arts and Sciences," Ch. lxii. *On Monks, fin.* 1634, p. 186.

[2] Mosheim, I. pp. 306–308. (*P.*) Cent. iv. Pt. ii. Ch. iii. Sect. xiii. xiv.
[3] Eighth Discourse, p. 8. (*P.*)
[4] Sueur, A. D. 399. (*P.*)
[5] Jortin's Remarks, IV. pp. 27, 38. (*P.*) Ed. 1805, III. pp. 12, 16.

married, and had any commerce with their wives, should be degraded from their office.[1]

The language in which the writers of those times recommended a monkish life was sometimes shocking and blasphemous, especially that of Jerome, who was the greatest advocate for it in his time. Writing to Eustochium the nun, he calls her *his lady*, because she was the *spouse of Christ*; and he reminds her mother, that she had the honour to be *God's mother-in-law*.[2]

Many women were ambitious of distinguishing themselves by some of the peculiarities of the monkish life in these early times, devoting themselves, as they imagined, to God, and living in virginity, but at first without forming themselves into regular communities. Jerome prevailed upon many women in Rome to embrace this kind of life; but they continued in their own houses, from which they even made visits; and it appears by an epitaph which he wrote for Marcella, that before her there was no woman of condition in Rome who lived in this manner, the common people of that city considering it as disreputable, on account of the novelty of the thing.[3] These early nuns were only distinguished by wearing a veil, that was given them by the bishop of the place. It was not till the year 567 that Queen Radigonda founded the first monastery for women, in France, which was confirmed by the Council of Tours.[4]

No perfect uniformity can be expected in the customs and modes of living among men, and least of all, men whose imaginations were so eccentric as those of the monks. Accordingly we find almost endless distinctions among them, some choosing to live in one manner, and some in another. And in later times when they formed themselves into regular societies, and

laid themselves under an absolute engagement to live according to certain rules, we find above a hundred kinds of them, who assumed different names, generally from their respective founders. But these divisions and sub-divisions were the offspring of late ages.

The most early distinction among them was only that of those who lived quite single and independent, and those who lived in companies. The latter were called *Cœnobites* in Greek, in Latin *Monks*, (though that term originally denoted an absolutely solitary life,) and sometimes *Friars* from *fratres, freres, brethren*, on account of their living together as brothers, in one family. These had a president called *abbot*, or *father*, and the place where they lived was called a *monastery*.

On the other hand, those who lived single were often called *eremites* or *hermits*, and commonly frequented caves and deserts. And some make a farther distinction of these into *Anachorites*, whose manner of life was still more savage, living without tents or clothing, and only upon roots, or other spontaneous productions of the earth. In Egypt some were called *Sarabaites*. These led a wandering life, and maintained themselves chiefly by selling relics, and very often by various kinds of fraud.[5]

In early times it was not uncommon for persons to pass from one of these modes of life to the other; and in later ages it was found to be very advantageous to the revenues of the society, for the monks to become hermits for a time, retiring from the monastery with the leave of the abbot. These being much revered by the people, often got rich by their alms, and then deposited their treasures in their monasteries.[6]

Persons who live in Protestant countries, or indeed in Roman Catholic countries at present, can form no idea of the high respect and reverence with

[1] Sueur, A. D. 385. (P.)
[2] *Ad Eustochium*, Ep. xxii. Op. I. pp. 140, 144. (P.)
[3] Sueur, A. D. 382. (P.)
[4] Ibid. A. D. 567. (P.)

[5] Mosheim, I. p. 309. (P.) Cent. iv. Pt. ii. Ch. iii. Sect. xv.
[6] Simon on Church Revenues, p. 54. (P.)

which monks were treated in early times. They were universally considered as being of a higher rank and order than the rest of mankind, and even superior to the priests; and wherever they went, or could be found, the people crowded to them, loading them with alms, and begging an interest in their prayers. In this light, however, they were regarded in general. For some persons may be found who thought sensibly in every age, and consequently looked with contempt upon this spurious kind of religion, and affectation of extraordinary sanctity.

In the fourth century, when all Christian countries swarmed with monks, we find one who, though he chose that mode of life, was sensible of the superstitious notions that were very prevalent with respect to it, and strenuously remonstrated against them. This was Jovinian, who, towards the conclusion of that century, taught, first at Rome, and afterwards at Milan, that all who lived according to the gospel, have an equal title to the rewards of heaven; and, consequently, that they who passed their days in unsocial celibacy, and severe mortifications, were in no respect more acceptable in the sight of God than those who lived virtuously in the state of marriage. But these sensible opinions were condemned, first by the Church of Rome, and afterwards by Ambrose, Bishop of Milan, in a council held in the year 390. The emperor Honorius seconded the proceedings of the council, and banished Jovinian as a heretic. The famous Jerome, also, wrote in a very abusive manner against the treatise of Jovinian, in which he maintained the above mentioned-opinions.

SECTION II.

THE HISTORY OF THE MONKS AFTER THE FALL OF THE WESTERN EMPIRE.

Having given the preceding account of the origin and nature of the monkish establishments, I proceed, in launching out into the dark ages, to point out the steps by which these monks attained that amazing power and influence which they acquired in the later ages, and to note other remarkable facts in their history, showing both the good and the evil that arose from their institution.

The primitive monks, courting solitude, were equally abstracted from the affairs of the world and those of the church; and yet, by degrees, a very considerable part of the business in both departments came to be done by them. The principal circumstance that favoured their advancement, and made their introduction into public life in a manner necessary, was the great ignorance of the *secular* clergy. For by this term the common clergy began to be distinguished, on account of their living more after the manner of the world; while the monks, on account of their living according to an exact *rule*, got the name of *regulars*, and *religious*. The monks spending a great part of their time in contemplation, many of them were induced to give some attention to letters, and soon attained a manifest superiority over the clergy in that respect; and the Christian Church was never without great occasion for learned men.

Several heresies, in particular, springing up in the church, and some learned monks very ably opposing them, it was found convenient to draw them from their solitude, and to settle them in the suburbs of cities, and sometimes in the cities themselves, that they might be useful to the people. In consequence of this, many of them, applying to study, got into holy orders. This was much complained of for some time; but being found useful to the bishops themselves, both in spiritual and temporal affairs, those bishops who were fond of a numerous clergy, and wanted fit men to carry on their schemes, gave them considerable offices; not imagining that they were encouraging a set of men who would afterwards supplant them in their dignities and revenues.[1]

Originally the monks, being subject to the bishops, could do nothing without their consent. They could not even choose their own abbot. But the election of an abbot being sometimes appointed by their *institutions* to be made by the monks of the community, they first obtained from the bishops the power of choosing their abbot, according to the tenor of their constitutions. Afterwards they sometimes got from the bishops exemptions from episcopal jurisdiction. But when the popes got the power of granting such exemptions, they commonly gave, or sold, to the monks as many of them as they pleased, so that their power grew with that of the popes.[2]

In the seventh century, pope Zacharias granted to the monastery of Mount Cassin an exemption from all episcopal jurisdiction, so that it was subject to the Pope only. Similar exemptions had been obtained in the preceding century, but they were very rare. In time they came to be universal, and were even extended to the chapters of regular cathedrals. In return for those privileges, the monks were distinguished by a boundless devotion to the see of Rome. These abuses were checked, but not effectually, by the Councils of Constance and Trent.[3]

The first introduction of monks into holy orders, was by the permission which they obtained to have priests of their own body, for the purpose of officiating in their monasteries, to which there could be no great objection; it being for the convenience of the secular priests themselves, as well as of the monastery; and especially as, with respect to qualification for the office, they were superior to the priests themselves. The first privilege they obtained of this kind was from Boniface III.; but their

ecclesiastical power was completed, and made equal to that of the other clergy, by Boniface IV. in 606. They could then preach, baptize, hear confessions, absolve, and do everything that any priest could do. Upon this the monks began to be, in a great measure, independent of the bishops, refusing to submit to their orders, on the pretence that they were contrary to their rules of discipline, and always appealing to the popes, who were sure to decide in their favour.

The monks, besides theology, studied likewise the canon and civil laws, and also medicine; studies which they began through charity, but which they continued for interest. They were therefore forbidden by Innocent II., in 1131, to study either civil law or medicine. But in the beginning of the following century they were allowed to be advocates for the regulars. These things, says Fleury, brought them too much into the world.[4]

The clergy were soon aware of the encroachments of the monks, both upon their spiritual power and upon their revenues. But the tide of popularity was so strongly in their favour, that all attempts to withstand it were in vain. At the Council of Chalcedon it was ordered that the monks should be wholly under the jurisdiction of the bishops, and meddle with no affairs, civil or ecclesiastical, without their permission. But this, and all other regulations for the same purpose, availed nothing, both the popes and rich laity favouring the monks. When Gregory VII. made a law to compel laymen to restore whatever had been in the possession of the church, such restitutions were generally made either to the cathedral churches, where the clergy conformed to a regular monastic life, or to the monasteries, and seldom to those parish churches to which the estates had originally belonged.[5]

In later times the endowments of

1 Simon on Church Revenues, p. 35. (*P.*)
2 Ibid. p. 65. (*P.*)
3 Anecdotes, pp. 208, 303. (*P.*)

4 Eighth Discourse, p. 17. (*P.*)
5 Simon on Church Revenues, p. 67. (*P.*)

monasteries were equal, if not superior, to those of the churches; and the influence of the monks with the popes and the temporal princes being generally superior to that of the clergy, they used, in many places, to claim the *tithes* and other church dues. When churches depended upon monasteries, they appointed monks to officiate in them, and appropriated the tithes to the use of the monastery. Also bishops were often gained by the monks to suffer them to put vicars or curates into churches, which they pretended to depend upon monsteries;[1] and in other respects, also, they encroached upon the rights of the clergy.

The monks having taken advantage of the ignorance of the secular priests, and having got the government of many churches committed to them, it was not easy to turn them out and re-establish the secular clergy in their places; and on this account there happened the greatest contests between the canons and the monks, especially in England, where the monks had deprived the canons of their canonships, and even obliged the secular priests to turn monks, if they would enjoy their benefices. All the archbishops of Canterbury had been monks from the time of that Austin whom Gregory sent into England, to the reign of Henry I. But, at length, all the bishops in England declared, that they would have no monk for primate; and by degrees they began to take the government of the church into their own hands.[2]

In the ninth century many monks were taken from the monasteries, and even placed at the head of armies; and monks and abbots frequently discharged the functions of ambassadors and ministers of state. For, upon the very same account that the clergy in general were better qualified for these offices than laymen, viz. in point of learning and address, the regular clergy had the advantage of the secular.

The monks, and especially the mendicant orders, assumed so much, and got so much power, both spiritual and temporal, into their hands, some time before the Reformation, that all the bishops, clergy, and universities in Europe, were engaged in a violent opposition to them. And it was in this quarrel that the famous Wickliffe first distinguished himself, in 1360; and from thence he proceeded to attack the pontifical power itself.

Before the sixth century there was no distinction of orders among monks, but a monk in one place was received as a monk in any other. But afterwards they subdivided themselves into societies, altogether distinct from one another; and so far were they from considering all monks as friends and brothers, that they often entertained the most violent enmity against each other; especially those who formed themselves on the same general plan, and afterwards divided from them on some trifling difference in customs or habits.

This distinction of orders began with Benedict of *Nursia*, who in 529 instituted a new order of monks, which presently made most rapid progress in the West; being particularly favoured by the Church of Rome, to the interest of which it was greatly devoted. In the ninth century this order had swallowed up all the other denominations of monks.[3]

Notwithstanding the extreme profligacy of the manners of many of these monks, their number and reputation would hardly be credible, but that the most authentic history bears testimony to it. What the number of them was in Egypt, at a very early period, has been mentioned already. Presently afterwards, viz. in the fifth century, the monks are said to have been so numerous, that large armies might have been raised out of them, without any sensible diminution of their body. And yet this was not

---

[1] Simon on Church Revenues, p. 67. (*P.*)
[2] Ibid. p. 74. (*P.*)

[3] Mosheim, I. pp. 446–449. (*P.*) Cent. vi. Pt. ii. Ch. ii. Sect. v.–vii.

to be compared to their numbers in later ages; and almost every century produced new species of them, and no age abounded more with them than that which immediately preceded the Reformation.[1]

In the seventh century the heads of rich families were fond of devoting their children to this mode of life; and those who had lived profligate lives generally made this their last refuge, and then left their estates to the monasteries. This was deemed sufficient to cancel all sorts of crimes, and therefore the embracing of this way of life was sometimes termed a *second baptism*.

In the eighth and ninth centuries, counts, dukes, and even kings, abandoned their honours, and shut themselves up in monasteries, under the notion of devoting themselves entirely to God. Several examples of this fanatical extravagance were exhibited in Italy, France, Germany, Spain, and England. And others, repenting that they had not done this in time, put on the monastic habit on the approach of death, and chose to be buried in it, that they might be considered as of the fraternity, and consequently have the benefit of the prayers of that order.

This most abject superstition continued to the fifteenth century. For even then we find "many made it an essential part of their last wills, that their carcases, after death, should be wrapped in old ragged Dominican or Franciscan habits, and interred among the Mendicants.[2]

It is said, that in all the centuries of Christianity together, there were not so many foundations of monasteries, both for men and women, or so rich and famous, as those of the seventh and eighth centuries, especially in France.[3] And when monasteries were so much increased, we are not surprised

to find complaints of the want of good discipline among them, Accordingly, in the the ninth century, the morals of the monks were so bad, that some reformation was absolutely necessary; and this was attempted by Benedict, abbot of *Aniane*, at the instance of Lewis the Meek. He first reformed the monasteries of *Aquitaine*, and then those of all France, reducing "all the monks, without exception, to the rule of the famous Benedict, abbot of Mount Cassin." This discipline continued in force a certain time, but the effect of it was extinct in less than a century. The same emperor also favoured "the order of Canons," and "distributed them through all the provinces of his empire." He "instituted also an order of *Canonesses*, which," Mosheim says, "was the first female convent known in the Christian world."[4]

In the tenth century the monkish discipline, which had been greatly decayed, was again revived in some measure by the authority of Odo, bishop of Clugny, whose rules were adopted by all the western kingdoms in Christendom. Thus we find successive periods of reformation in the discipline of monasteries. But no sooner were the new and more austere kinds of monks established, and got rich, than they became as dissolute as their predecessors, which called for another revolution in their affairs; and these successive periods of rigour and of dissoluteness continued quite down to the Reformation.

One of the first great causes of this relaxation of discipline in the monasteries, was the invasion of the Normans, whose ravages fell chiefly upon the monasteries. For upon this, the monks being dispersed, and assembling where and how they could, the observance of their rules was impossible, and many irregularities were introduced. Something of the same kind was the consequence of the great

---

[1] Mosheim, III. pp. 446, 447. (*P*.) Cent. **xvi.** Sect. iii. Pt. i. Ch. i. Sect. xviii.
[2] Ibid. III. p. 164. (*P*.) Cent. **xiv.** Pt. ii. Ch. ii. Sect. xvii.
[3] Sueur, A. D. 720. (*P*.)

[4] Mosheim, II. pp. 129, 130. (*P*.) Cent. **ix.** Pt. ii. Ch. ii. Sect. xi. xii.

plague in Europe, in 1348, when many of the monks died, and the remainder dispersed; and having lived for some time without any regard to their rules, they could not without difficulty be brought to them again.

A more general cause of the relaxation of discipline among all the orders of the monks, as Bernard observed, was their exemption from episcopal jurisdiction.[1]

Another cause of the relaxation of their discipline, was the multiplication of prayers and singing of psalms; for they had added many to those prescribed by Benedict. This, says Fleury, left them no time for labour, of which Benedict had ordered seven hours every day. This contempt of bodily labour was introduced by the northern nations, who were addicted to hunting and war, but despised agriculture and the arts.[2] Mental prayer, he adds, has been much boasted of by the monks for the last five hundred years. It is, says he, an idle and equivocal exercise, and produced at length the error of the Beghards and Beguines, which was condemned at the Councils of Vienna.[3] The original monks, he says, were a very different kind of men, and their discipline much more proper to produce a real mortification to the world, and to suppress inordinate affections. Theirs was a life of contemplation and labour, by which they chiefly supported themselves. The ancient monks had no hair cloths, or chains, and there was no mention of discipline or flagellation among them.[4]

Bodily labour, this writer observes, was likewise excluded by the introduction of lay-brothers into monasteries, and this was another means of the corruption of their manners, the monks being the masters, and the lay-brothers being considered as slaves, and an order of persons much below them, and subservient to them. John Gualbert was the first who instituted lay-brothers, in his monastery of Valombrose founded about 1040. To those lay-brothers were prescribed a certain number of *pater nosters*, at each of their canonical hours; and that they might acquit themselves of this duty without any omission or mistake, they carried grains of corn, or strings, whence came the use of *chaplets*. The same distinction, he says, was afterwards carried into nunneries, though there was no pretence for it.[5]

The monastic orders being almost all wealthy and dissolute in the thirteenth century, the *mendicant* or *begging friars*, who absolutely disclaimed all property, were then established by Innocent III. and patronized by succeeding pontiffs. These increased so amazingly, that they became a burthen both to the people and to the church itself; and at length they were the occasion of much greater disorders than those which they were introduced to redress.

There is a remarkable resemblance, as Middleton observes, between these mendicant friars, and the mendicant priests among the Pagans. "The lazy mendicant priests among the Heathens," he says, "who used to travel from house to house with sacks on their backs, and, from an opinion of their sanctity, raise large contributions of money, &c. for the support of their *fraternity*," were "the very pictures of the begging friars, who are always about the street in the same habit, and on the same errand, and never fail to carry home with them a good sack full of provisions for the use of their convent."[6]

Notwithstanding these disorders, it must be acknowledged that the mendicant friars were instituted with the very best intention, and that they had

[1] Fleury's Eighth Discourse, p. 37. (*P.*)
[2] Ibid. p. 13. (*P.*)
[3] Ibid. pp. 44, 45. (*P.*)
[4] Ibid. p. 6. (*P.*)

[5] Ibid. p. 15. (*P.*)
[6] Middleton's Letter, p. 220. (*P.*) Works, III. pp. 116, 117. "De ces moines d'entre les Payens, les uns étoient rentez, ... les autres étoient mandians comme les religieux de la grande mère des dieux, qui 'allans par les carrefours et par les rues,' comme dit S. Augustin, 'exigeoient du peuple ce dequoi ils vivoient honteusement.'" *Les Conform.* p. 41.

for a considerable time a very good effect. St. Francis, the founder of this order, thought his institute, by which he forbade his monks the use of gold, silver, or any kind of property, the pure gospel; and it was of use, as Fleury observes, in a very corrupt age, to recall the idea of charity and simple Christianity, and to supply the defect of ordinary pastors, the greater part of whom were then ignorant or negligent, and many corrupt and scandalous.[1]

The monks of the ancient religious orders fell into great contempt after the introduction of the Mendicants, who filled the chairs in schools and churches, and by their labours supplied the negligence and incapacity of the priests and other pastors. But this contempt excited the emulation of the other orders, and made them apply to matters of literature.[2]

Afterwards, the mendicant friars, on the pretence of *charity*, meddled with all affairs, public and private. They undertook the execution of wills, and they even accepted of deputations to negociate peace between cities and princes. The popes frequently employed them, as persons entirely devoted to them, and who travelled at a small expense; and sometimes they made use of them in raising money. But what diverted them the most from their proper profession was the business of the *Inquisition*. By undertaking to manage this court, they were transformed into magistrates, with guards and treasures at their disposal, and became terrible to every body.[3]

During three centuries the two fraternities of Mendicants, the Dominicans and the Franciscans, governed, with an almost universal and absolute sway, both church and state, and maintained the prerogative of the Roman pontiff, against kings, bishops and heretics, with incredible ardour and success. They were in those times

what the Jesuits were afterwards, the life and soul of the whole hierarchy. Among other prerogatives, the popes empowered them to preach, to hear confessions, and to pronounce absolutions, without any licence from the bishops, and even without consulting them. The Franciscans had the chief management of the sale of indulgences, and the Dominicans directed the Inquisition.

The amazing credit of religious orders in general, and the reputation of their founders, made many persons ambitious of distinguishing themselves in the same way; and though the Council of Lateran, in 1215, forbade the introduction of any more *new religions*, as they were called, the decree, as Fleury says, was ill observed : for more were established in the two centuries following, than in all the preceding.[4]

Besides the monks and regulars, there is another sort of religious persons who, according to their institution, bear the name of St. John of Jerusalem, from whom are descended the knights of Malta; and similar to them were the knights Templars, and the knights of the Teutonic order. These orders had their origin in the time of the crusades, and their first object was to take care of the sick and wounded, and afterwards to defend them. But they distinguished themselves so much in their military capacity, that the order was soon filled with men of a military turn, and at length they were most depended upon for any military service. Thus, from their undertaking the defence of their hospital, they undertook the defence of the Holy Land, and by degrees that of other Christian countries against all Mahometan powers. The knights of St. John were established in 1090, and being driven from the Holy Land, they retired to Cyprus, then to Rhodes, and they are now settled at Malta.

The knights Templars were established in 1118, taking their name from

---

[1] Fleury's Eighth Discourse, p. 21. (*P.*)
[2] Ibid. p. 32. (*P.*)
[3] Ibid. p. 27. (*P.*)

[4] Ibid. p. 20. (*P.*)

their first house, which stood near the temple in Jerusalem. This order grew very rich and powerful, but withal so exceedingly vicious, and it is said atheistical, that, becoming obnoxious in France, Italy and Spain, the Pope was compelled to abolish the order in 1312.

Other orders of knighthood, which had something of religion in their institution, were formed in several parts of Europe, whence arose what are called *Commanderies*, which were originally the office of taking care of the revenues belonging to the military orders, in distant places. The members of some of these orders may marry, and yet enjoy, under the title of *Commanders*, the church lands that are appropriated to their order. Philip II. of Spain was, in this sense, the greatest prelate in the church, next to the Pope; because he was the great master of the three military orders of Spain, and enjoyed a good part of the tithe of the church within his territories. The king of Spain, F. Simon says, may always be the richest beneficiary in his kingdom; and by appropriating to his own use the revenues of his commanderies alone, may have enough to live like a king.[1]

It may not be improper to add, in this place, that after the destruction of Jerusalem, many of the Latins remained still in Syria, and retreating into the recesses of mount Libanus, lived in a savage manner, and by degrees lost all sense both of religion and humanity.[2]

The last order of a religious kind, of which I think it of any consequence to give an account, is that of the *Jesuits*, which was instituted by Ignatius Loyola, and confirmed by the Pope, with a view to heal the wounds which the Church of Rome had received by the Reformation, and to supply the place of the monks, and especially that of the mendicants, who were then sunk into contempt. The Jesuits held a

middle rank between the monks and the secular clergy, and approached pretty nearly to the regular canons. They all took an oath, by which they bound themselves to go, without deliberation or delay, wherever the Pope should think fit to send them. The secrets of this society were not known to all the Jesuits, nor even to all those who were called *professed members*, and were distinguished from those who were called *scholars*, but only to a few of the oldest of them, and those who were approved by long experience. The court and church of Rome derived more assistance from this single order, than from all their other emissaries and ministers, by their application to learning, engaging in controversy, and preaching in distant countries, but more especially by their consummate skill in civil transactions, and getting to themselves almost the whole business of the *Confessors* to crowned heads, and persons of-eminence in the state; a business which had before been engrossed by the Dominicans.

The moral maxims of this society were so dangerous, and so obnoxious to the temporal princes, (added to the temptation of the wealth of which they were possessed,) that being charged with many intrigues and crimes of state, they were banished, and had their effects confiscated, first in Portugal, then in Spain, and afterwards in France; and at length the Pope was obliged to abolish the whole order.[3]

[1] On Church Revenues, p. 234. (*P.*)
[2] Mosheim. (*P.*) [Vol. III. p. 12. Cent. xiii. Pt. i. Ch. ii. Sect. i. The Druses, their descendants, still inhabit this region.]

[3] See "An Account of the Destruction of the Jesuits in France, by M. D'Alembert," 1766. The following character of the *order*, and remarkable anticipation of their fall, is in a sermon by *Browne*, Archbishop of Dublin, preached in 1551:—"There are a new fraternity of late sprung up, who call themselves *Jesuits*, which will deceive many, who are much after the Scribes and Pharisees' manner amongst the *Jews*. They shall strive to abolish the truth, and shall come very near to do it; for these sorts will turn themselves into several forms; with the Heathen, an Heathenist; with Atheists, an Atheist; with the Jews, a Jew; and with the Reformers, a Reformade, purposely to know your intentions, your minds, your hearts, and your inclinations; and thereby bring you at last to be like the fool, that *said in his heart, there was no God.*

"These shall spread over the whole world,

U

I shall conclude this article with some particulars that lead us to think unfavourably, and others that may incline us to think more favourably, of monks in general.

The religious orders in general have been the great support of the papal power, and of all the superstitions of the Church of Rome, in all ages. The worship of saints, and the superstitious veneration for relics, were chiefly promoted by their assiduity, in proclaiming their virtues everywhere, and publishing accounts of miracles wrought by them, and of revelations in their favour. They were also the great venders of indulgences, the founders of the Inquisition, and the great instrument of the Papal persecutions. The licentiousness of the monks was become proverbial so early as the fifth century, and they are said, in those times, to have excited tumults and seditions in various places.

In some periods the monks,-having an unlimited licence to buy and sell, exercised their permission with so little scruple, that it encouraged many great men to usurp the estates of their neighbours, being sure to find purchasers among the monks. F. Simon relates an instance in the abbey of *Mire* in Switzerland, in which the monk, who compiled the acts of the monastery, gives a list of things which were acquired by unjust means, without the least hint of any obligation to make restitution.[1]

Nothing could exceed the insolence

and arrogance of the Dominicans and Franciscans. They even declared "publicly, that they had a divine impulse and commission to illustrate and maintain the religion of Jesus .... that the true method of obtaining salvation was revealed to them alone;" and they boasted of "their familiar connexions with the Supreme Being, the Virgin Mary, and the saints in glory." By these means they gained such an ascendancy over the common people, that these would trust no others "but the Mendicants with the care of their souls."[2]

St. Francis imprinted upon himself five wounds, similar to those of our Saviour, which his followers asserted were given him by Christ himself; and in this they were encouraged by the mandates of the popes, and by several bulls enjoining the belief of it. They even approved and recommended an impious treatise entitled, "The Book of the Conformities of St. Francis with Jesus Christ," composed in 1383, by a Franciscan of Pisa, in which this saint is put on a level with Christ.[3]

The Carmelites imposed upon the credulous, by asserting that the Virgin Mary appeared to the general of their order, and gave him a solemn promise, that the souls of all those who left the world with the Carmelite cloak or scapulary upon their shoulders, should be infallibly preserved from eternal damnation; and this impudent fiction found patrons and defenders among the pontiffs. Even the late Pope Benedict XIV., who is generally esteemed the most candid and sensible of all the popes, is an advocate for this gross imposition.[4]

It must, however, be acknowledged, that notwithstanding the great mischief that has been done to the Christian world by the religious orders, they have,

shall be admitted into the council of princes, and they never the wiser; charming of them, yea, making your princes reveal their hearts, and the secrets therein unto them, and yet they not perceive it: which will happen from falling from the law of God, by neglect of fulfilling of the law of God, and by winking at their sins. Yet in the end God, to justify his law, shall suddenly cut off this society, even by the hands of those who have most succoured them, and made use of them; so that at the end they shall become odious to all nations: they shall be worse than Jews, having no resting-place upon the earth, and then shall a Jew have more favour than a Jesuit." *Phenix*, 1707, I. p. 136. On this *Order*, see *An Essay*, by C. Villers, 1805, pp. 96, *Note*, and 271.

[1] On Church Revenues, p. 56. (*P.*)

[2] Mosheim, III. p. 61. (*P.*) Cent. xiii. Pt. ii. Ch. ii. Sect. xxix.
[3] Ibid. p. 169. (*P.*) Cent. xiv. Pt. ii. Ch. ii. Sect. xxi.
[4] Ibid. p. 61. (*P.*) Cent. xiii. Pt. ii. Ch. ii. Sect. xxix. Note [g].

both directly and indirectly, been the occasion of some good; and though they were the chief support of the papal power, they nevertheless contributed something to the diminution of it, and to the Reformation.

Such places as monasteries originally were, though they were abused by many, must have been a very desirable retreat to many others, in times of war and confusion. And the opportunity of leisure and meditation, with a total exclusion from the world, must have been of great use to those who had been too much immersed in the bustle and the vices of it. For notwithstanding the irregularities with which monks in general were perhaps justly charged, there must have been, in all ages, great numbers who conscientiously conformed to the rules of them.

There is no period, perhaps, in which the state of Christianity, and of Europe in general, wore a more unfavourable aspect than in the fourteenth century, during the residence of the popes at Avignon; and yet Petrarch, who lived in that age, and who makes heavy and repeated complaints of the vices of it, and especially of the extreme profligacy of the court of Rome, appears to have had a good opinion of the state of many of the monasteries; and his own brother, who had been rather dissolute in his youth, retired to one of them in the very flower of his age, and became truly exemplary for his piety, humanity and other virtues, which were especially conspicuous during the great plague. Indeed, the general credit of the order in all ages cannot be accounted for on any other supposition, than that, as things then stood, they were, upon the whole, really useful.

Another capital advantage which the Christian world always derived from the monks, and which we enjoy to this day, is the use they were of to literature in general, both on account of the monasteries being the principal repositories of books, and the monks the copiers of them, and because, almost

from their first institution, the monks had a greater share of knowledge than the secular clergy. In the seventh century, the little learning there was in Europe was, in a manner, confined to the monasteries, many of the monks being obliged by their rules to devote certain hours every day to study, when the schools which had been committed to the care of the bishops were gone to ruin.[1]

A very respectable religious fraternity was founded in the fourteenth century, confirmed by the Council of Constance, called *the brethren and clerks of common life*.[2] The schools erected by this fraternity acquired great reputation. From them issued Erasmus of Rotterdam, and other eminent persons.[3]

The cause of literature has also been much indebted to the Jesuits, and more lately to the Benedictines; the members of both these orders having produced many works of great erudition and labour, and having employed the revenues of their societies to defray the expense of printing them.

As a proof of the monastic orders having contributed something to the Reformation, it may be sufficient to adduce the following facts. The Dominicans and Franciscans soon quarrelled about pre-eminence, and they differed exceedingly amongst themselves; and these differences among the mendicant orders, as well as the division of the popedom, and the mutual excommunication of the popes and antipopes, "gave several mortal blows to the authority of the Church of Rome, and excited in the minds of the people

[1] Mosheim, II. p. 12. (*P.*) Cent. vii. Pt. ii. Ch. i. Sect. i. ad *init*. See the reference, *supra*, p. 242, and Villers's *Essay*, p. 51.

[2] "Les frères de la vie commune, où des personnes distinguées par leur savoir, et par leur piété, vivoient en commun de ce qu'elles mettoient ensemble pour ne pas vivre dans la fainéantise. On attribue cet établissement à *Gerard Groot, ou, le Grand*, de Deventer, Docteur de Paris, et Chanoine d'Utrecht." *Hist. du Concil. Const. An.* 1418, II. p. 601.

[3] Mosheim, III. p. 254. (*P.*) Cent. xv. Pt. ii. Ch. ii. Sect. xxii.

[most] ardent desires of a reformation in the church." [1]

The *Fratricelli*, or *Fratres Minores*, were monks who, in the same thirteenth century, "separated themselves from the grand community of St. Francis," with a view to observe his rule more strictly. "They went about clothed with sordid garments, or rather with loathsome rags," declaiming in all places "against the corruption of the Church of Rome, and the vices of the pontiffs and bishops." These were persecuted with the utmost virulence by the other Franciscans, who were countenanced by the popes, and they continued in this violent state of war with the Church of Rome till the Reformation, multitudes of them perishing in the flames of the Inquisition. [2] These rebellious Franciscans, therefore, deserve an eminent rank among those who prepared the way for the Reformation, exciting in the minds of the people a just aversion to the Church of Rome in its then very corrupt state. [3]

The original difference of these monks with the Pope was perhaps the most trifling and absurd that can well be imagined, viz. the property of the things that were consumed by them, as bread and other provisions; they maintaining that they had not the *property*, but only the *use* of them. This dispute was at first confined to the monks themselves, but at length the popes interposed, and John XXII. declaring that obedience is the principal virtue of monks, and preferable to poverty, they asserted the contrary, maintaining that they ought not to obey their superiors when they commanded anything contrary to perfec-

tion. John condemning these refractory monks, they declared him a heretic by his own authority. They even went so far as to call him *Antichrist*, and to appeal from his constitution to a future council. At length the revolt went so far, that the monks, supported by the emperor Lewis of Bavaria, pronounced sentence of deposition against the Pope, and set up another in his place. [4]

Since the fifteenth century, in the beginning of which the discipline of the monks was exceedingly relaxed, various reformations have been made, which, Mr. Fleury says, has raised the credit of most of the orders. [5] But notwithstanding these reforms, and though nothing is now objected to them with respect to the observance of their rules, they are found to be of so little use in the present state of society, that it seems to be the determination of most of the Catholic powers to abolish them by degrees; as appears by the regulations that have been made respecting the time of admission, making it so late in life, that very few will not be so far engaged in other pursuits, as to have no inducement to become monks or nuns; and the authority of parents, who often found it convenient to dispose of their younger children in this way, is now generally set aside. In consequence of this, and other causes, which have been operating more silently ever since the Reformation, the religious houses are in general but thinly inhabited. Some of their revenues have already been diverted to other uses, and such is the aspect of things at present, and the wants of the several potentates of Europe, that it is justly to be apprehended, that all the rest will soon share the same fate.

---

[1] Mosheim, III. p. 62. (*P.*) Cent. xiii. Pt. ii. Ch. ii. Sect. xxx.

[2] By "a bloody decree, beginning 'Gloriosam Ecclesiam.'" Limborch, *Hist.* I. p. 104.

[3] Mosheim, III. p. 76. (*P.*) Cent. xiii. Pt. ii. Ch. ii. Sect. xxxix.

[4] Fleury's Eighth Discourse, p. 30. Mosheim, III. p. 74. (*P.*) Cent. xiii. Pt. ii. Ch. ii. Sect. xxxix. *Note.*

[5] Eighth Discourse, p. 47. (*P.*)

PART XIII.

THE HISTORY OF CHURCH REVENUES.

THE INTRODUCTION.

In the preceding parts of this work we have taken a view of the changes which, in the course of time, have taken place with respect to the rank and character of *Christian ministers;* by what steps it came to pass, that, from having no authority whatever, besides what their greater virtue or ability gave them, and especially from having no dominion over the faith of their fellow-christians, the authority of the bishops, with respect to articles of faith, as well as matters of discipline and worship, came to be absolute and despotic; and how, from living in a state of the most submissive subjection to all the temporal powers of the world, and keeping as far as possible from interfering in all civil affairs, they came to be temporal princes and sovereigns themselves, and to control all the temporal princes of Europe, even in the exercise of their civil power. In this part I shall exhibit a similar view of the changes which have taken place with respect to the *revenues of the church;* and shall show by what steps ministers of the gospel, from living on the alms of Christian societies, together with the poor that belonged to them, came to have independent and even princely incomes, and to engross to themselves a very considerable part of the wealth and even of the landed property of Europe.

SECTION I.

THE HISTORY OF CHURCH REVENUES, TILL THE FALL OF THE WESTERN EMPIRE.

In the constitution of the primitive church, the apostles followed the cus-tom of the Jewish synagogues, the members of which contributed every week what they could spare, and entrusted it with those who distributed alms. Like the Jews, also, the Christians sent alms to distant places, and gave to those who came from a distance with proper recommendations. They were so liberal upon these occasions, that Lucian says, that, to become rich in a short time, a man had nothing to do but to pretend to be a Christian. In those times both alms and stipends were often called *honoraries.* Thus when Paul bid Timothy *honour widows that are widows indeed,* he means rewarding them for discharging particular offices, which in those days widows held in churches. So also the phrase *worthy of double honour,* signifies worthy of a double or a larger reward.

The church had no other revenues besides these voluntary alms till the time of Constantine. Indeed, before that time, the Christian churches were considered as unlawful assemblies, and therefore could no more acquire property, than the Jewish synagogues, or other communities not authorized by the state; though in the reign of Marcus Aurelius, the senate permitting any person to give whatever he pleased to communities *already formed,* the church began, in the third century, by toleration or connivance, to possess estates. But under Constantine, Christian churches were considered as respectable societies, and from that time they began to grow rich. In 321 this emperor made an edict, addressed to the people of Rome, by which he gave all persons the liberty of leaving by will to the churches, and especially that of Rome, whatever they pleased. He also ordained that what had been taken from the churches in the persecution of Dioclesian should be restored to them, and that the estates of the martyrs who had no heirs should be given to the churches.[1]

By this means, in time, all churches had what was called their *patrimony*, and that of Rome in the sixth century had a very great one, not only in Italy, but in other countries; and to inspire a greater respect for these patrimonies, they were denominated by the saints that were most respected in each particular church. Thus the territories belonging to the Church of Rome were called the patrimony of St. Peter. But these patrimonies were, like other estates, subject to the laws of the countries in which they were.[2]

Though the bishops and priests had originally no property of their own, but lived upon the stock of the church, Cyprian complains that some of them, in his time, not content with a subsistence in common, began to live in separate houses of their own, and to have each their allowance paid in money, daily, monthly, or for a longer time, and this was soon tolerated. And, whereas part of the church stock had always been given to the poor, the clergy began to encroach upon this part, and to appropriate it almost wholly to themselves. That part also which used to be employed in the repairs of churches, &c. was intercepted in the same manner.

All the civil affairs of Christian societies were at first managed by deacons, but the disposal of money, as well as of everything else, was in the power of the presbyters, by whose general directions the deacons acted; and the bishops having encroached upon the presbyters in other things, did not neglect to avail themselves of their authority with respect to the temporalities of the church. And so great was the confidence which the primitive Christians reposed in their bishops, (and with reason, no doubt, at first,) that they alone were allowed to superintend the distribution of the common church stock to the inferior clergy, as well as to the poor, according to the merits or occasions of each individual. But, in consequence, probably, of some abuse of this discretionary power, we find afterwards, that not the bishop alone, but the whole body of the presbyters made that distribution. Still, however, it cannot but be supposed that, the bishops having superior influence, more would be in their power in this respect, than in that of the presbyters; and these, being subject to the bishops in other things, would not choose to disoblige them in this.

We do find, however, that when churches grew very rich, the bishops often embezzled the estates belonging to them. This evil grew to so great a height, that at the Council of Gangres, in Paphlagonia, held in 324, they were allowed to give some of the church stock to their relations, if they were poor, but were prohibited selling the estates belonging to their churches, and were ordered to give an account of their administration of these temporalities. And that the goods which properly belonged to the bishops might not be confounded with those that belonged to the church, every bishop, upon his election, was ordered to give an account of his possessions, that he might bequeath them, and nothing else, by will. But still the bishops abusing the power that was left them, *stewards* were afterwards appointed to take care of the temporalities of the church, and the bishops were confined to the cure of souls. These stewards, however, being at first chosen by the bishops, the same abuses were resumed; and therefore, at the Council of Chalcedon, in 451, the stewards were appointed to be chosen by the body of the clergy.[3]

These offices of stewards became so considerable in the church of Constan-

[1] Anecdotes, pp. 129, 131. **(P.)**
[2] Ibid. p. 231. **(P.)**

[3] Simon on Church Revenues, pp. 18, 20. **(P.)**

tinople, that the emperors themselves took the nomination of them, till Isaac Comnenus gave it to the patriarch. The power of the steward was not so great in the Western churches, but abuses in them being very flagrant, a custom was at length adopted, of dividing the church revenues into four parts, of which one was for the bishop, another for the rest of the clergy, the third for the poor, and the fourth for repairs, or probably a kind of *church stock*, to defray any contingent expenses.

This distribution of the church stock was the cause of great animosities and contentions between the bishops and the inferior clergy, in which the popes were often obliged to interpose with their advice and authority; and Father Simon ascribes to it most of the disorders which arose in the Western church; the Eastern, where that partition was never made, being free from them. For while no division was made, the idea of the property being in the whole society continued, and consequently the clergy were considered as the servants and beneficiaries of the society at large. But that partition made them absolute masters of their respective shares, and gave them independent property; and riches and independence have never been favourable to virtue with the bulk of mankind, or the bulk of any order of men whatever.

But those corruptions of the clergy which arose from the riches of the church began to be peculiarly conspicuous, when, after the time of Constantine, the church came to be possessed of fixed and large revenues. Jerome says, that the church had indeed become more rich and powerful under the Christian emperors, but less virtuous; and Chrysostom says that the bishops forsook their employments to sell their corn and wine, and to look after their glebes and farms, besides spending much time in law-suits. Austin was very sensible of this, and often refused

[1] Simon on Church Revenues, pp. 20, 21. (P.

inheritances left to his church, giving them to the lawful heir, and he would never make any purchases for the use of his church.[2] Jerome says that the priests of his time spared no tricks or artifices to get the estates of private persons; and he mentions many low and sordid offices, to which priests and monks stooped, in order to get the favour and the estates of old men and women, who had no children.[3]

The disorders of the clergy must have been very great in the time of Jerome, since the emperors were then obliged to make many laws to restrain them. In 370, Valentinian made a law to put a stop to the avarice of the clergy, forbidding priests and monks to receive anything, either by gift or will, from widows, virgins, or any women. Twenty years after, he made another law, to forbid deaconesses to give or bequeath their effects to the clergy, or the monks, or to make the churches their heirs; but Theodosius revoked that edict.[4] We may form some idea of the riches of the Church of Rome towards the middle of the third century, from this circumstance, that in that time, according to Eusebius, it maintained one thousand five hundred persons, widows, orphans, and poor; and it had then forty-six priests, besides the bishop and other officers.[5]

SECTION II.

THE HISTORY OF CHURCH REVENUES AFTER THE FALL OF THE WESTERN EMPIRE.

Upon the invasion of the Roman empire by the Norman nations, both the ecclesiastical laws and revenues underwent a great alteration, and upon the whole very favourable to the church, as a political system, though for some

[2] Ibid. p. 17. (P.)
[3] Ibid. pp. 27, 28. (P.)
[4] Anecdotes, p. 183, &c. (P.)
[5] Hist. L. vi. C. xliii. p. 212. (P.

time, and in some cases, it was unfavourable to the clergy. For these savage conquerors made little distinction between the goods of the church and other property, but distributed both as they thought proper, even to laymen; and children often succeeded to their fathers in church livings, as well as in other estates. Also many estates belonging to churches were transferred to monasteries.

About this time, however, began the custom of granting estates to ecclesiastical persons in the same manner, and upon the same terms, as they had been granted to laymen, viz. for the lives of particular bishops or abbots, as we find about the year 500, under Pope Symmachus, but afterwards to the churches and monasteries in general; the ecclesiastics swearing fealty and allegiance for them, and rendering the same services that the lay lords rendered for their estates. Hence the term *benefice* came to be applied to church livings. For that term was originally applied to estates granted to laymen upon condition of military service.

In no part of the world were the clergy so great gainers by this system as in Germany, where whole principalities were given to churches and monasteries; whereby bishops became, in all respects, independent sovereign princes, as they are at this day. This was chiefly the effect of the liberality of the emperors of the name of Otho. Churchmen, both bishops and abbots, being at this time principally employed in all the great affairs of state, it was not difficult for them to obtain whatever they desired of princes.

In those times of confusion, when property in land, and everything else, was very precarious, many persons chose to make over the property of their estates to churches and monasteries, obtaining from them a lease for several lives. The property being in the church, it was held more sacred, especially after the entire settlement of the Northern nations in the western part of the Roman empire, and when the rage of conquest was over. In these circumstances a lease for a few lives, on an easy rent, was of more value to individuals than the absolute property.

The possession of benefices was attended, however, with one incumbrance, from which the church did not very soon free itself. According to the ancient feudal laws, when a tenant died, the lord enjoyed the revenues till his successor was invested, and had sworn fealty; and it was natural that this law should affect churchmen as well as laymen. This, however, interfered with the ancient custom of the church. For, during the vacancy of a bishopric, the profits were usually managed by the clergy and archdeacons, for the use of the future bishop. But after the general collation of benefices, the princes first demanded the revenues of those estates which they had granted to the church, and afterwards of all church livings without distinction; and this was called *regale*. This right of regale was not settled in France in the third race of their kings,[1] and was probably first established upon the agreement between Pope Calixtus and the Emperor Henry.[2]

Lewis the Young is the first king of France who mentions the right of regale, in the year 1161. And we find in the History of England, that this right of regale was established in this kingdom at the same time that it was in France, and that it occasioned many troubles here.[3]

By degrees, however, the estates which had been long in the possession of the clergy began to be considered as so much theirs, and the temper of the times was so favourable to the claims of the church, that it was thought wrong for laymen to meddle with any part of it; and many princes were induced to relinquish the right of regale. The emperor Frederic II. remitted this right to the church, as if it had been

[1] Simon on Church Revenues, p. 94. (*P.*)
[2] Ibid. p. 97. (*P.*)
[3] Ibid. p. 98. (*P.*)

an usurpation; and several councils prohibited princes and other laymen from invading the goods and revenues of churchmen after their death.[1]

Afterwards, however, when the popes usurped the nomination to ecclesiastical benefices, they thought proper to claim what had been the *regale*, or the value of one year's income, (for to that it had been reduced, as a medium of what had been due to the lord during a vacancy,) and then this perquisite was called *annates*. This claim is said to have been first made by pope Urban VI.,[2] and was paid "not only in England but throughout the western parts of Christendom."[3] In this country the *annates* were transferred to the crown in the reign of Henry VIII., and so they continue to this day, except that small livings were released from this burthen in the reign of queen Anne.

On account of the benefit accruing to the popes from these *annates*, they encouraged resignations and the changing of livings among the clergy. For upon every event of this nature this tax to themselves became due. Originally resignations were made absolutely, into the hands of those who had a right to dispose of the benefice; and when it appeared that there was no lawful reason for the resignation, it was not admitted. But afterwards resignations were made *in favorem*, or upon condition that the benefice should go to some person in whose favour it was made, and with whom a contract had been made for that purpose. This custom is so new, that no mention is made of it in the canon law, the *Decretals*, or the *Sext*. The new canonists called the contract a simoniacal one, and therefore there is a necessity for the Pope to grant a dispensation for it, he being above all canon and positive law. Nothing derogated more from the right of ordinaries and patrons than these resignations *in favorem;* for by this means they who possessed benefices disposed of them as of their own inheritance. By this means they even descended in families.[4]

Another deduction from the value of livings the clergy suffered by the popes claiming the tenth of their value, which was done about the same time that annates were demanded. This they did upon the pretence that the high-priest among the Jews had a tenth of the tythes which were paid to the other priests.[5] Another pretence for making this exaction arose from the crusades. The contributions of those who did not serve in person being casual, the popes imposed a tax upon all ecclesiastical revenues, and the first of the kind was on the occasion of the loss of Jerusalem. Afterwards the popes pretended to a right of disposing of all ecclesiastical goods, and sometimes demanded a twentieth, and even a tenth of their revenues, for other purposes besides the crusades. They also made them over to the kings, who by this means shared with the popes in the plunder of the people.[6] This tenth the popes obtained occasionally in England, from the time of Edward I., when the demand was first made. In the twenty-sixth of Henry VIII. an act was made to annex these tenths to the crown for ever; but they were given to the poor clergy towards an augmentation of their maintenance by queen Anne, and at the same time all small livings were discharged from paying them.

The holy wars in the eleventh century were the cause of great accessions of wealth to the church. Most of the knights made their wills before their departure, and never failed to leave a

---

[1] Simon on Church Revenues, p. 100. (*P.*)
[2] "Of this godly gentleman's invention, as some authors report, were the payments to the Pope called *annates*, ... which . . . . are no other than *prinitiæ*, the first-fruits or profits of every spiritual living for one year, to be paid by the parson that is invested in it, at his first entrance thereupon." *Hist. of Popery*, 1736, II. p. 177.
[3] Hist. of Popery, IV. p. 37. (*P.*) 1736, II. p. 178.

[4] Simon on Church Revenues, p. 239. (*P.*)
[5] "The Pope, as *pastor pastorum*, claimed *decimas decimarum*, — by example of the Jewish High-Priest." Hist. of Popery, 1736, II. p. 178.
[6] Fleury's Sixth Discourse, p. 19. (*P.*)

considerable share of their possessions to the church; and they built churches and monasteries with ample endowments at their return, by way of thanksgiving for their preservation; so that whether they returned or not, the church generally received some permanent advantage from the expedition.

One of the most valuable acquisitions to the revenues of the church, but from the nature of it the most impolitic in various respects, and the most burthensome to the state, is that of *tythes*. It is a great discouragement to the improvement of land, that a tenth part of the clear produce, without any deduction for the advanced expense of raising that produce, should go from the cultivator of the land to any other person whatever. It would be far better to lay an equivalent tax upon all estates, cultivated or not cultivated. For then it would operate as a motive to industry; whereas the present mode of taxation is a discouragement to it. Besides, this method of paying the minister is a continual source of dispute between the clergy and the parishioners, which is of a most pernicious nature; making the people consider as enemies those whom they ought to respect as their best friends, and in whom they ought to repose the greatest confidence.

The original reason for the payment of tythes was the most groundless imaginable, as it arose from considering Christian ministers as an order of men who succeeded to the rights of the *priests* under the Jewish law. This idea was observed to prevail very much about the time of the utter desolation of Judea under Adrian. But it was a long time before there was any idea of claiming those tythes as a right. Even the Jews acknowledge that no tythes were paid by themselves after the destruction of the temple. But about the fifth century laws being made by the emperor, by which the tenth part of the mines and quarries were paid to themselves, and the lords of the soil; there arose a custom, as some say, of paying tythes to the church, which in

time became general; till from the force of example, the omission of it was deemed reproachful, and the clergy began to claim them as due to themselves by the law of Moses.

For some centuries, however, it was usual to give tythes to the poor, and for other charitable purposes. Thus, at a council of Maçon, in 586, it was ordered that a tenth part of the fruits of the earth should be brought into sacred places, to be employed for the relief of the poor, and the redemption of captives.[1] By degrees, however, the clergy excluded the poor, and appropriated the tythes to themselves. And about the year 600, tythes, from being established as a custom, became in some instances *legal rights;* because many estates were bequeathed with an obligation to pay tythes to particular churches. When these tythes were left to distant churches, the priests of the parish in which the estate lay used to complain; and at length, in the reign of King John, the Pope made a law, ordering that all tythes should be paid to the parish priest, and after some time they were levied by law in all parishes without exception. At the Reformation, though those who took the lead in it were sincerely disposed to abolish tythes, they found themselves obliged to continue, and to secure them by act of parliament, in order to conciliate the minds of the popish clergy. Thus this most intolerable evil continues to this day, whereas in other Protestant countries, and especially in Holland, the civil magistrates have adopted a wiser plan, by allowing their ministers a fixed stipend, paid out of the public funds.

The progress of superstition in the dark ages supplied many resources for the augmentation of the wealth of the clergy. In those times "the world was made to believe that by the virtue of so many masses," the recitation of which might be purchased with money, and especially with permanent endowments to churches and monasteries, "souls

1 Sueur. (P.)

were redeemed out of purgatory; and scenes of visions and apparitions, sometimes of the tormented, and sometimes of the delivered souls, were published in all places. Which had so wonderful an effect, that in two or three centuries endowments increased to so vast a degree, that if the scandals of the clergy on the one hand, and the statutes of *mortmain* on the other, had not restrained the profuseness that the world was wrought up to, upon this account, it is not easy to imagine how far this might have gone, perhaps to an entire subjecting of the temporality to the spirituality."[1] And it was carefully inculcated by the priests, that rights acquired to the church belonged to God, and therefore could not be taken away without sacrilege.

It was the fate of this country to suffer more from papal usurpations than almost any other part of Christendom. One tax to the Church of Rome was peculiar to this country, which was *Peter pence*,[2] or a tax of a penny a year for every house in which there were eighty pennyworth of goods. This was "first granted, in the year 725, by Ina, king of the West Saxons, for the establishment and support of an English college at Rome." It was "afterwards extended, in the year 794, by Offa, over all Mercia and East Anglia;" and in the days of Athelwolf, though the popes appropriated the profits of this tax to themselves, it was extended over all England. "It was confirmed by the laws of Canute, Edward the Confessor, William the Conqueror," and of several succeeding princes, though it was long considered as a *free alms* on the part of the nation, and was often refused to be paid, especially by Edward III. However, it

"was never totally abolished till the reign of Henry VIII."[3]

So far did the popish exactions in this country, on one account or other, go, that, in the reign of Henry III., the popes received from England more than the king's revenue, or one hundred and twenty thousand pounds. In 1366, the lord chancellor assured the parliament, that the taxes paid to the Pope were five times as much as the king's revenue; and at length the church is said to have got possession of one third of all the landed property in England.[4]

Notwithstanding the ample revenues of many churches, numbers of the clergy contrived to make large additions to them, by appropriating to themselves the emoluments of several church livings; though they could not reside, and do duty at them all, and nothing could be more contrary to the natural reason of things, or the original constitution of the Christian church. Indeed, the maxim that, where no duty is done, no reward is due, was so obvious, that this was one of the last abuses that crept into the church. But it grew, under various pretences, to a most enormous height; though several attempts were made, at different times, to lessen the evil.

About the year 500, when what we now call *benefices*, came into use, it became customary to ordain without any title, or designation to a particular cure; and many persons got themselves ordained priests, for secular purposes. Also many prelates wanted to increase their authority by attaching to themselves a number of dependents, and many of the people wanted spiritual privileges, in order to exempt them from the jurisdiction of princes. Even bishops (though this was done with more caution) were ordained without any diocese, except in infidel countries, which they never visited; and

---

[1] Burnet, Exposition, p. 280. (P.) Art. xxii. Ed. 4, p. 206.
[2] "*Denarii sancti Petri*" .... in the Saxon .... tongue *Romefeoh;* the fee (or rent) of Rome .... to be paid yearly on Lammas-day, celebrated .... as a festival by the title of *Sancti Petri vincula*, Peter's bonds." *Hist. of Popery*, 1735, I. pp. 168, 169. See also *Romescot*, Rapin, *Hist.* L. iii. I. p. 182.

[3] Mosheim, II. p. 278. (P.) Cent. xi. Pt. ii. Ch. ii. Sect. x. *Note* (e). See also Rapin's *Hist.* An. 794, L. iii. I. pp. 182, 183.
[4] Hist. of Popery, III. pp. 60, 570, V. p. 266. (P.) 1736, II. pp. 53, 130, 397, 413.

these acted as substitutes for those bishops who were too lazy, or too much employed in secular affairs, to do duty themselves. This corruption had arisen to a most enormous height before the Council of Trent.

The consequence of titular ordination was *non-residence*, and where curates were employed the principal could follow his other business. Accordingly the bishops in France, and even the parish priests, substituting some poor priests in their room, passed much of their time at court. And if a bishop could hold one living without residing upon it, it was plain that he might hold two or more, and get them supplied in the same manner.

Titular ordinations, however, which first introduced *non-residence*, were not the only cause of *pluralities*, which are said to have had their origin about the sixth century. Among benefices bestowed upon the churches, some, as prebends, &c., had no *cure of souls* annexed to them. These were judged capable of being held by priests who had other livings with cure of souls. Also parishes which were not able to maintain a minister were allowed to be served by another minister in the neighbourhood, but a dispensation from the Pope was necessary for this purpose. By this means, however, the greatest scandal in pluralities was practised. This abuse gave very great offence, but dispensations of this kind were so necessary to support the dignity of cardinals, that they were made perpetual in the court of Rome. The cardinal of Lorrain, who held some of the best benefices in France, and some in Scotland too, was particularly vehement in his declamation against pluralities in general, at the Council of Trent, without imagining that his own were liable to any objection.

The first account of any flagrant abuse of pluralities occurs in the year 936, when Manasseh, bishop of Arles, obtained of his relation, Hugh, king of Italy, several other bishoprics, so that in all he had four or five at the same time. Baronius says, that this was a new and great evil, which began to stain the church of God, and by which it has been wonderfully afflicted.[1]

A person is said to hold a church *in commendam,* when he is empowered to have the care and the profits of it till the appointment of another incumbent. This practice was of great antiquity, in order to prevent churches receiving any detriment during a vacancy. But on this pretence livings were afterwards granted for a certain time, which was made longer and longer, or till an event which it was known could not take place, and at length for life. This was done by the plenary power of the Pope. In this manner Clement VII. brought pluralities to perfection, by making his nephew, the Cardinal de Medicis, *commendatory universal;* granting him all the vacant benefices in the world, whether secular or regular, dignities, parsonages, simple, or with cure of souls, for six months, and appointing him usufructuary from the first day of his possession. In England, in which every abuse and imposition in ecclesiastical matters were carried to their greatest extent, the richest and best benefices were engrossed by the Pope, and given in commendam to Italians, who never visited the country, but employed questors to collect their revenues.

Other methods of making pluralities, and disposing of church revenues, were contrived by the court of Rome, such as *provisions* and *exemptions,* which are hardly worth describing, and selling the reversions of livings, called *expectatives,* as well as livings actually vacant.

The first attempt that we meet with to check these evils, of pluralities and non-residence, was made by Charlemagne, who made several regulations for that purpose; but they were soon neglected. Several popes also, as John XXII. and Clement V., pretended to reform the same abuses, but without

---

[1] Sueur, A. D. 936. (*P.*)

any real effect; and by the evasion of them even illiterate persons and children, who were never intended to take orders, might enjoy benefices. [1]

The Council of Trent pretended to remedy the evil of pluralities, but they made it worse by admitting of *pensions*, as an equivalent for the change of benefices and other purposes. For these came to be granted by the court of Rome without any consideration, and even to children. They were also more convenient, and made church preferment a more easy traffic in many respects. For instance, resignations were not deemed valid, unless the person who resigned lived twenty days afterwards; whereas a *pension* might be transferred at the point of death. Besides it might be turned into ready money, whereas a benefice could not without simony. [2]

[1] Pennington on Pluralities, p. 58. (*P.*)
[2] F. Paul on Ecclesiastical Benefices, 1736, Ed. 3, pp. 223, 224. (*P.*)

It is to be lamented that these abuses were not corrected at the reformation of the Church of England. On the contrary, it is apprehended that many of them are increased since that period, so as to exceed what is generally to be found of that nature in some Roman Catholic countries. In consequence of this, though the funds for the maintenance of the clergy are sufficiently ample, the inequality in the distribution of them is shameful, and they bear no proportion to the services or merit of those who receive them. This is an evil that calls loudly for redress, and strikes many persons who give no attention to articles of faith, or of discipline in other respects. Probably, however, this evil will be tolerated, till the whole system be reformed, or destroyed. But without the serious reformation of this and other crying abuses, the utter destruction of the present hierarchy must, in the natural course of things, be expected.

THE GENERAL CONCLUSION.

PART I.

CONTAINING

CONSIDERATIONS ADDRESSED TO UNBELIEVERS, AND ESPECIALLY TO MR. GIBBON.

To consider the system (if it may be called a *system*) of Christianity *à priori*, one would think it very little liable to corruption, or abuse. The great outline of it is, that the Universal Parent of mankind commissioned Jesus Christ to invite men to the practice of virtue, by the assurance of his mercy to the penitent, and of his purpose to raise to immortal life and happiness all the virtuous and the good, but to inflict an adequate punishment on the wicked. In proof of this he wrought many miracles, and after a public execution he rose again from the dead. He also directed that proselytes to his religion should be admitted by *baptism*, and that his disciples should eat bread and drink wine in commemoration of his death.

Here is nothing that any person could imagine would lead to much subtle speculation, at least such as could excite much animosity. The doctrine itself is so plain, that one would think the learned and the unlearned were upon a level with respect to it. And a person unacquainted with the state of things at the time of its promulgation would look in vain for any probable source of the monstrous corruptions and abuses which crept into the system afterwards. Our Lord, however, and his apostles, foretold, that there would be a great departure from the truth, and that something would arise in the church altogether unlike the doctrine which they taught, and even subversive of it.

In reality, however, the causes of the succeeding corruptions did then exist; and accordingly, without anything more than their natural operation, all the abuses rose to their full height; and what is more wonderful still, by the operation of natural causes also, without any miraculous interposition of Providence, we see the abuses gradually corrected, and Christianity recovering its primitive beauty and glory.

The causes of the corruptions were almost wholly contained in the established opinions of the heathen world, and especially the philosophical part of it; so that when those Heathens embraced Christianity, they mixed their former tenets and prejudices with it. Also, both Jews and Heathens were so much scandalized at the idea of being the disciples of a man who had been crucified as a common malefactor, that Christians in general were sufficiently disposed to adopt any opinion that would most effectually wipe away this reproach.

The opinion of the mental faculties of man belonging to a substance distinct from his body, or brain, and of this invisible spiritual part, or *soul*, being capable of subsisting before and after its union to the body, which had taken the deepest root in all the schools of philosophy, was wonderfully calculated to answer this purpose. For by this means Christians were enabled to give to the soul of Christ what rank they pleased in the heavenly regions

before his incarnation. On this principle went the Gnostics, deriving their doctrine from the received oriental philophy. Afterwards the philosophizing Christians went upon another principle, personifying the wisdom or λόγος of God the Father. But this was mere Platonism, and therefore cannot be said to have been unnatural in their circumstances, though at length they came, in the natural progress of things, to believe that Christ was, in power and glory, equal to God the Father himself.

From the same opinion of the soul distinct from the body came the practice of praying, first *for* the dead, and then *to* them, with a long train of other absurd opinions and superstitious practices.

The abuses of the *positive institutions* of Christianity, monstrous as they were, naturally arose from the opinion of the purifying and sanctifying virtue of rites and ceremonies, which was the very basis of all the worship of the Heathens: and they were also similar to the abuses of the Jewish religion. We likewise see the rudiments of all the *monkish austerities* in the opinions and practices of the Heathens, who thought to purify and exalt the soul by macerating and mortifying the body.

As to the abuses in the *government of the church*, they are as easily accounted for as abuses in civil government; worldly-minded men being always ready to lay hold of every opportunity of increasing their power; and in the dark ages too many circumstances concurred to give the Christian clergy peculiar advantages over the laity in this respect.

Upon the whole, I flatter myself that, to an attentive reader of this work, it will appear, that the corruption of Christianity, in every article of faith or practice, was the natural consequence of the circumstances in which it was promulgated; and also that its recovery from these corruptions is the natural consequence of different circumstances. *Let unbelievers, if they can, account as well for the first rise and establishment of Christianity itself.* This is a problem which historians and philosophers (bound to believe that no effect is produced without an adequate cause) will find to be of more difficult solution the more closely it is attended to.

The circumstances that Mr. Gibbon enumerates as the immediate *causes* of the spread of Christianity were themselves *effects*, and necessarily required such causes as, I imagine, he would be unwilling to allow. The revolution produced by Christianity in the opinions and conduct of men, as he himself describes it, was truly astonishing; and this, he cannot deny, was produced without the concurrence, nay, notwithstanding the opposition, of all the civil powers of the world; and what is perhaps more, it was opposed by all the learning, genius, and wit of the age too. For Christianity was assailed as much by ridicule and reproach as it was by open persecution; and, be the spread of it what Mr. Gibbon pleases, he cannot deny that it kept uniformly gaining ground, taking in all descriptions of men without distinction, before it had any foreign aid; and what then remained of the old religions was not sufficient to occasion any sensible obstruction to the full establishment of it. The Jewish religion alone was an exception; and this circumstance, together with the rise of Christianity among the Jews, are facts that deserve Mr. Gibbon's particular attention.

Of all mankind, the Jews were the most unlikely to set up any religion, so different from their own; and as unlikely was it that other nations, and especially the polite and learned among them, should receive a religion from Jews, and those some of the most ignorant of that despised nation.

Let Mr. Gibbon recollect his own idea of the Jews, which seems to be much the same with that of Voltaire, and think whether it be at all probable, that they should have originally invented a religion so essentially different from any other in the world, as that which is described in the books of Moses; that the whole nation should then have adopted without objection, what they were afterwards so prone to abandon for the rites of any of their neighbours; or, that when, by severe discipline, they had acquired the attachment to it which they are afterwards known to have done, and which continues to this day, it be probable they would have invented or have adopted another, which they conceived to be so different from, and subversive of their own. If they had been so fertile of invention, it might have been expected that they would have struck out some other since the time of Christ, a period of near two thousand years.

On this subject Mr. Gibbon says, that "in contradiction to every known principle of the human mind, that singular people seems to have yielded a stronger and more ready assent to the traditions of their remote ancestors, than to the evidence of their own senses."[1] A singular people, indeed, if this was the case; for then they must not have been *men*, but beings in the shape of men only, though internally constituted in some very different manner. But what facts in history may not be represented as probable or improbable, on such loose suppositions as these? Such liberties as these I shall neither take nor grant. Jews are *men*, and men are beings, whose affections and actions are subject to as strict rules as those of the animate or inanimate parts of nature. Their conduct, therefore, must be accounted for on such principles as always have influenced the conduct of men, and such as we observe still to influence men.

I wish Mr. Gibbon would consider whether he does not, in the passage above quoted, use the word *tradition* in an improper manner. By tradition we generally mean something for which we have not the evidence of histories written at the time of the events. We never talk of the tra-

---

[1] History, Ch. xv. I. p. 559. (*P.*)

dition of the wars of Julius Cæsar, or of his death in the senate house, nor even of the tradition of the conquests of Alexander the Great; because there were histories of those events written at the time, or so near to the time, as to be fully within the memory of those who were witnesses of them.

Now Moses, and the other writers of the Old Testament, were as much present at the time of the transactions they relate, as the historians of Julius Cæsar or Alexander. An incautious reader (and there are too many such) would be apt to imagine from Mr. Gibbon's manner of expressing himself, that the Jews did not even pretend to have *written histories* of the same age with the origin of their religion, but that it was in the same predicament with what he calls "the elegant mythology of Greece and Rome;" whereas the fact is, that every tittle of it was committed to writing at the time. It is generally in such an *indirect* manner as this, and not by a fair and candid representation of facts, that unbelievers endeavour to discredit the system of revelation.

Let Mr. Gibbon, as an historian, compare the rise and progress of Mahometanism with that of Judaism or of Christianity, and attend to the difference. Besides the influence of the *sword*, which Christianity certainly had not, Mahometanism stood on the basis of the Jewish and Christian revelations. If these had not been firmly believed in the time of Mahomet, what credit would his religion have gained? In these circumstances, he must have invented some other system, which would have required *visible miracles* of its own, which he might have found some difficulty in passing upon his followers; though they were in circumstances far more easy to be imposed upon than the Jews or the Heathens, in the time of our Saviour. This was an age of light and of suspicion; the other, if any, of darkness and credulity. That Christianity *grew up in silence and obscurity,*

as Mr. Gibbon says,[1] is the very reverse of the truth. He could not himself imagine circumstances in which the principal facts on which Christianity is founded should be subject to a more rigid scrutiny. *These things*, as Paul said to king Agrippa, *were not done in a corner.* Acts xxvi. 26.

It appears to me that, admitting all the miraculous events which the evangelical history asserts, it was not probable that Christianity should have been received with less difficulty than it was; but without that assistance, absolutely impossible for it to have been received at all.

Mr. Gibbon represents the discredit into which the old religions were fallen, as having made way for the new one. "So urgent," says he, "on the vulgar is the necessity of believing, that the fall of any system of mythology will most probably be succeeded by the introduction of some other mode of superstition."[2]

But are not the vulgar, *men*, as well as the learned, their understandings being naturally as good and as various, and certainly subject to the same laws; and *necessity of believing* or *proneness to belief*, is not greater in the one than in the other; but the expression is loose and inaccurate, and calculated to impose on superficial readers. Besides, if any set of men had this property of *proneness to believe*, they must, to be all of a piece, have a proportionable unwillingness to quit their belief, at least without very sufficient evidence; and yet those *vulgar* of all nations are supposed by Mr. Gibbon to have abandoned the belief of their own mythology, some time before Christianity came, to supply the vacancy. Such *vulgar* as those I should think entitled to the more respectable appellation of *free-thinkers*, which with many is synonymous to *philosophers*. And, in fact, it was not with the vulgar, but with the philosophers, that the religions of Greece and Rome were fallen

[1] History, Ch. xv. I. p. 535. (P
[2] Ibid. p. 602. (P.)

into discredit. We ought, therefore, to judge of their case by that of the philosophical part of the world at present.

With many of *them* Christianity is now rejected; but do they, on that account, seem disposed to adopt any other mode of religion, or any other system of mythology in its place? And would not such men as Mr. Hume or Helvetius among the dead, and Mr. Gibbon himself among the living, examine with scrupulous exactness the pretensions of any system of divine revelation, especially before he would regulate his life by it, and go to the stake for it? And yet philosophers of antiquity, men of as good understanding as Mr. Gibbon, and who, no doubt, loved life, and the pleasures and advantages of it, as much as he does, embraced Christianity, and died for it.

But besides the *urgency of this necessity of believing,* another cause of the rapid spread of Christianity was, that it held out to mankind something worth believing. " When the promise of eternal happiness," he says, "was proposed to mankind, on condition of adopting the faith, and observing the precepts of the gospel, it is no wonder that so advantageous an offer should have been accepted by great numbers of every religion, of every rank, and of every province in the Roman empire." [1]

Now it is certainly no discredit to Christianity, that the views it exhibits of a future state appeared more rational and more inviting, than the accounts of *Tartarus* and the *Elysian shades.* But besides appearing more *inviting,* they must also have appeared more *credible,* from the general external evidence of the truth of Christianity. And here also Mr. Gibbon seems to have been inattentive to the principles of human nature.

In general, the more *extraordinary* any event appears to be, the more evidence we require of it. It is this consideration that makes more definite evidence necessary for a miracle, than for an ordinary fact; though it is acknowledged that the *desirableness* of any particular event, by interesting our *wishes,* will tend to make us admit it on somewhat less evidence. The great advantages, therefore, proposed to men from any scheme, especially one in which they were to run some risk, and in which they were to make great sacrifices, would not dispose them to receive it without evidence. *It is too good news to be true,* is a remark perpetually made by the very *vulgar* of whom Mr. Gibbon is speaking. When the disciples of our Lord saw him for the first time after his resurrection, it is said (Luke xxiv. 41), that *they believed not through joy;* and when, before this, they were told by three or four women of character, and for whom they had the highest respect, that they had themselves seen him alive, and had a message from him to them, *Their words seemed to them as idle tales, and they believed them not.* Ibid. ver. 11. This was perfectly natural; and such circumstances as these are strong internal evidence of the historian's describing real facts, and real feelings of the human heart corresponding to those facts.

Besides, how can any man, to use Mr. Gibbon's own language, *adopt the faith* of the gospel, whatever promises might be made to him for so doing, unless its tenets appeared to him to be *reasonable?* What would Mr. Gibbon take to believe the doctrine of the Trinity, or what would he sacrifice in this life for the most magnificent promise in a future one, made by a person whose ability to make good that promise he at all suspected? Plato's doctrine of the *immortality of the soul* was sufficiently flattering; but whom was it ever known to influence, like the Christian doctrine of a *resurrection?* The plain reason was, that the latter was proposed with sufficient *evidence,* whereas the former was altogether destitute of it.

[1] History, Ch. xv. I. p. 561. (*P*)

X

It is amusing enough to observe how very differently Mr. Gibbon represents the state of the heathen world with respect to Christianity, when he would insinuate an apology for the persecution of the Christians. "It might be expected," he says, "that they would unite with indignation against any sect or people, which should separate itself from the communion of mankind, and, claiming the exclusive possession of divine knowledge, should disdain every form of worship except its own, as impious and idolatrous."[1]

Mr. Gibbon, I suppose, never asked himself whether it was natural for the same kind of people to be so very differently affected towards the same thing. But, unfortunately, his purpose required that, to account for the ready reception of Christianity upon insufficient evidence, some of those Heathens must be furnished with an *urgent necessity of believing* any new religion that was proposed to them, especially one that promised such great and glorious things as Christianity did; while, on the other hand, to account also for the very ill reception that the preachers of Christianity met with, (which he cannot deny,) others of them must be furnished with a disposition to hate and detest those who pretended to so much.

I do not know anything that can help Mr. Gibbon in this case better than the known principles of his favourite *mythology*. As the present race of mankind are derived from the stones which Deucalion and Pyrrha threw over their heads, (when perhaps they were in too much haste to re-people the vacant world,) they might not be sufficiently attentive to the nature of those materials of the future race of mortals, but take stones of different degrees of hardness. In consequence of this, some of them may have been of a softer disposition, and more easy of belief than others. Being, therefore, so differently constituted, the descendants of some of them might

be instinctive believers, and others instinctive persecutors of those believers. They would then be, of course, as hostile to each other as those men who sprung out of the earth, from the sowing of the serpent's teeth, in the elegant mythology of Greece, as the story is most elegantly related by Ovid.[2]

Besides these considerations, Mr. Gibbon mentions the *zeal* of the primitive Christians, and the strictness of their *discipline*, as causes of the spread of the new religion. But he should have told us whence came that zeal, and that strictness of discipline. If no sufficient *cause* of it had appeared, their zeal would have exposed them to contempt; and their discipline would have discouraged, rather than have invited proselytes.

Any person may hold himself excused from investigating the causes that gave birth to the opinions of *individuals* of mankind, on account of the difficulty and uncertainty of such an investigation. The same may, in some degree, be said of particular classes of men. But Christianity recommended itself to every description of men then existing, and influenced them not for a short time only, which might be accounted for from temporary and local circumstances, but *permanently*; so as to leave no reasonable doubt, but that it would have gone on to establish itself in the world, and to extirpate idolatry, if the civil powers had continued to oppose its progress three thousand, as they did three hundred years; and what is more, notwithstanding the gross corruptions and abuses which soon crept into it.

A fact of this kind requires to be

---

[1] History, Ch. xv. I. p. 622.

[2] I have heard of a young gentleman of a sceptical and jocular turn, taking off his hat to a statue of Jupiter, (who makes the most respectable figure in this system of mythology,) and saying, "If ever you come into power again, please to remember that I showed you respect when nobody else did." Mr. Gibbon, I hope, has no serious views in complimenting the religion of Greece and Rome, meaning to pay his court to the *powers that may be*, as others do to those that *are*. (*P.*)

accounted for from the most obvious principles of human nature, principles common to all men, and all classes of men; and therefore none but the plainest and most cogent *causes of assent*, deserve to be attended to. This assent to the truth of Christianity could only be produced by such evidence as always will, and always ought to determine the assent of the human mind.

It is acknowledged that, to be a Christian, a man must believe some facts that are of an extraordinary nature, such as we have no opportunity of observing at present. But those facts were so circumstanced, that persons who cannot be denied to have had the best opportunity of examining the evidence of them, and who, if they had not been true, had no motive to pay any regard to them, could not refuse their assent to them; that is, it was such evidence as we ourselves must have been determined by, if we had been in their place; and therefore, if not fully equivalent to the evidence of our own senses at present, is, at least, all the evidence that, at at this distance of time, we *can* have in the case. It goes upon the principle that human nature was the same thing then that it is now; and certainly in all other respects it appears to be so.

That miracles are things in themselves *possible*, must be allowed, so long as it is evident that there is in nature a power equal to the working of them. And certainly the *power, principle*, or *being*, by whatever name it be denominated, which produced the universe, and established the laws of it, is fully equal to any occasional departures from them. The *object* and *use* of those miracles on which the Christian religion is founded, is also maintained to be consonant to the object and use of the general system of nature, viz. the production of happiness. We have nothing, therefore, to do but to examine, by the known rules of estimating the value of *testi-*

mony, whether there be reason to think that such miracles have been wrought, or whether the evidence of Christianity, or of the Christian history, does not stand upon as good ground as that of any other history whatever.

Now, though I am far from holding myself out as the champion of Christianity, against all the world, I own I shall have no objection to discuss this subject with Mr. Gibbon, as an historian and a philosopher. We are only two individuals, and no other persons can be bound by the result of our discussion. But those who have given less attention to the subject than we have done, may be instructed by it, and be assisted in forming their own judgment, according to the evidence that shall be laid before them. At least, it may be a means of drawing some degree of attention to a subject which cannot be denied to be, in the highest degree, interesting.

Indeed, if any man can say that it is not an interesting question, whether his existence terminate at death, or is to be resumed at a future period, and then to continue for ever, he must be of a low and abject mind. To a rational being, capable of contemplating the wonders of nature, and of investigating the laws of it, and to a being of a social disposition, his existence, and the continuance of his rational faculties, must be an object of unspeakable value to him; and consequently he must ardently wish that Christianity (which alone *brings life and immortality to light*) may be true. For to a philosopher, who forms his judgment by what he actually observes, the doctrine of a *soul* capable of subsisting and acting when the body is in the grave, will never give any satisfaction. To every person, therefore, who is capable of enjoying his existence, the Christian doctrine of a *resurrection* opens a glorious and transporting prospect.

Voluntarily to shut one's eyes on such a prospect, and really to wish to see no more of the wonders of nature, and of the progress of being, and especially of the human race, towards perfection, but to hide one's head in everlasting obscurity, must be to have a disposition as grovelling, base, and abject, as that of the lowest of the brute creation. A man of the least elevation of mind, and of a cultivated and improved understanding, must, surely, lament such a catastrophe.

The fear might be, that every truly sensible and virtuous man would be too strongly biassed in favour of Christianity, and (if Mr. Gibbon's observation above mentioned be true) give his assent long before he had waited to weigh the evidence as he ought to do. I do not, however, wish Mr. Gibbon to show this disposition. On the contrary, I wish him to examine everything with the greatest rigour, and I will not contend with him for trifles. With respect to some points which he has laboured, though I am satisfied his representations are partial and unfair, I have no objection to concede almost all that he contends for, because, though he has taken very liberally, he has left me enough.

When the circumstances of the Jews and Heathens, at the time of the promulgation of Christianity, shall be sufficiently considered, (but to which it is evident Mr. Gibbon has given but a slight attention,) the reception that this new religion met with among them, and the total subversion of the several systems of Paganism by it, will be found to be a more extraordinary thing, on the supposition of the gospel history not being true, more contrary to the present course of nature, and consequently more improbable, than the history of Christ and the apostles, as contained in the New Testament, which makes the whole of the subsequent history perfectly easy and natural. In short, the question is, whether Mr. Gibbon, or myself, believe in more numerous, more extraordinary, or more useless miracles. On this fair, unexceptionable ground I am willing to meet him.

I also shall not contend with him for quite so much as his late antagonists, members of the Church of England, must include in the system of Christianity. But by abandoning their outworks, I may perhaps be better able to make an effectual defence.

My religion does not suppose, with Bishop Hurd, "that the offices in which the Godhead was employed are either degrading, or such as imply an immoderate and inconceivable condescension."[1] I shall not urge Mr. Gibbon to admit, (as "the great things of which Christ spake,") "that a divine person, divine in the highest sense of the word, should descend from heaven and ... suffer death,"[2] or that "the *divine nature* condescended to leave the mansions of glory, was made man, dwelled among us, and died for us."[3]

I shall not pretend, with the same learned bishop, that "a third divine person ministered ... in giving" this second divine person "the power to cast out devils," and "in raising him from the dead."[4] Neither shall I urge him with "a purpose ... to save and sanctify" mankind "by such means as" he himself can think "fanciful and delusive,"[5] or maintain that Christ, "in virtue of his all-atoning death," did "open the gates of eternal life to the whole race of mortal man,"[6] which the bishop enumerates among "the great things of which Christ spake," and "the amazing topics with which he filled his discourses."[7]

[1] See Bishop Hurd's Sermons, III. p. 34. (*P.*) Strictly speaking, this representation is not the *supposal* of Bishop H., but what he attributes, p. 32, to "the pride of reason;" though it may be more justly charged to the absurdity of *systematic* theology.

[2] Ibid. p. 63. (*P.*)

[3] That the *divine nature* of Christ should *die*, is, surely, more than Dr. Hurd's Christian creed obliges him to assert, unless he may think that without this, his doctrine of *atonement* could not be completed. (*P.*) Dr. Priestley has not given his authority for the passage here *noticed;* nor can I find the *words* in Bishop Hurd's Sermons, though the substance of them frequently occurs.

[4] Bishop Hurd's Sermons, II. p. 337. (*P.*)

[5] Ibid. III. p. 33. (*P.*)

[6] Ibid. p. 63. (*P.*)

[7] Ibid. pp. 63, 64. (*P.*) A common reader might peruse our Lord's discourses many times

I am sensible that it would be in vain to urge any external historical evidence of a revelation, of which such doctrines as these should make a part. They are things that no miracles can prove. As soon should I propose to him the belief of Mahomet's journey to the third heavens, and all his conversations with God while a pitcher of water was falling, or the doctrine of transubstantiation, neither of which are more absurd, and both of them are much more innocent.

I am sorry, however, to have occasion to admonish Mr. Gibbon, that he should have distinguished better than he has done between Christianity itself and the corruptions of it. A serious Christian, strongly attached to some particular tenets, may be excused if, in reading ecclesiastical history, he should not make the proper distinctions; but this allowance cannot be made for so cool and philosophical a spectator as Mr. Gibbon.

He should not have taken it for granted, that the doctrine of three persons in one God, or the doctrine of *atonement* for the sins of all mankind, by the death of one man, were any parts of the Christian system; when, if he had read the New Testament for himself, he must have seen the doctrine of the proper *unity of God*, and also

before he found any such *topics* as these, with which they are here said to be *filled*. But I the less wonder at this when I find this writer attempting to prove at large, that by *washing the disciples' feet*, our Lord meant to teach the great doctrine of *atonement by his blood* and wondering (I. p. 188, note), that Grotius and other commentators should not see it in the same light. *Sermons*, I. pp. 177, &c.

But I own I am surprised that he should maintain, III. p. 67, that Christ "spake by virtue of his own essential right, from himself, and in his own name," as well as "by the special appointment of God the Father," when he himself, in the most unequivocal language, repeatedly asserts the contrary; as John v. 30 : "I can of mine own self do nothing." vii. 16 : "My doctrine is not mine, but his that sent me." xiv. 10 : "The words that I speak unto you, I speak not of myself, but the Father that dwelleth in me, he doeth the works." It must be strong bias in favour of a system that can make a person overlook such texts as these. But even the greatest and best of men have been misled in the same way. (*P.*)

that of his *free mercy* to the penitent, in almost every page of it. As he does speak of the *corruptions of Christianity*, he should have examined farther, both as an historian and as a man. For as an individual, he is as much interested in the inquiry as any other person; and no inquiry whatever is so interesting to any man as this is.

As to what Mr. Gibbon, with a sneer of triumph, says, of Plato having "360 years before Christ" "ventured to explore the mysterious nature of the Deity," and of "the theology of Plato" having been "confirmed by the celestial pen of the last and most sublime of the evangelists,"[1] ninety-seven years after that era; like all his other sarcasms against Christianity, it is founded on ignorance. But he is more excusable in this than in other cases, as too many Christians have been chargeable with the same; confounding the *Logos* of Plato with that of John, and making of it a second person in the Trinity, than which no two things can be more different, as has been clearly explained by my excellent and judicious friend Mr. Lindsey, especially in his *Catechist*, in the preface to which he has very properly animadverted upon this passage of Mr. Gibbon.[2]

Mr. Gibbon has much to learn concerning the gospel before he can be properly qualified to write against it. Hitherto he seems to have been acquainted with nothing but the corrupt establishments of what is very improperly called Christianity; whereas it is incumbent upon him to read and study the New Testament for himself. There he will find nothing like Platonism, but doctrines in every respect the reverse of that system of philosophy, which weak and undistinguishing Christians afterwards incorporated with it.

Had Mr. Gibbon lived in France, Spain or Italy, he might, with the same reason, have ranked the doctrine of transubstantiation, and the worship

[1] History, Ch. xxi. II. pp. 237, 240. (*P.*)
[2] See Pref. Ed. 1818, pp. xix.-xxiv.

of saints and angels, among the essentials of Christianity, as the doctrines of the Trinity and of atonement.

The friends of genuine, and I will add of rational Christianity, have not, however, on the whole, much reason to regret that their enemies have not made these distinctions; since, by this means, we have been taught to make them ourselves; so that Christianity is perhaps as much indebted to its enemies, as to its friends, for this important service. In their indiscriminate attacks, whatever has been found to be untenable has been gradually abandoned, and I hope the attack will be continued till nothing of the wretched outworks be left; and then, I doubt not, a safe and impregnable fortress will be found in the centre, a fortress built upon a rock, against which *the gates of death will not prevail.*

When the present crisis is over, (and I think we may see that the period is not far distant,) that by means of the objections of unbelievers, and the attention which, in consequence of it, will be given to the subject, by believers, Christianity shall be restored to its primitive purity, the cool and truly sensible part of mankind will, in this very circumstance, perceive an argument for its truth; and thus even the corruptions of Christianity will have answered a very valuable purpose; as having been the means of supplying such an evidence of its truth, as could not have been derived from any other circumstance. Let any other religion be named that ever was so much corrupted, and that recovered itself from such corruption, and continued to be professed with unquestionable zeal by men of reflection and understanding, and I shall look upon it with respect, and not reject it without a very particular examination. The revival of a zeal for the religion of Greece and Rome under Julian, is not to be compared with the attachment to Christianity by inquisitive and learned men in the present age. Let literature and science flourish but one century in

Asia, and what would be the state of Mahometanism, the religion of the Hindoos, or that of the Tartars, subject to the Grand Lama? I should rejoice to hear of such a challenge as I give Mr. Gibbon, being sent from a Mahometan Mufti to the Christian world.[1]

Should what I call pure Christianity, (the most essential articles of which I consider to be the proper *unity of God*, and the proper *humanity of Christ*,) continue to spread as it now does, and as, from the operation of the same causes, I have no doubt but that, in spite of all opposition, it will do, and literature revive among the Jews and Mahometans, (who, it is remarkable, were never learned and inquisitive, but in an age in which all the Christianity they could see must have struck them with horror, as a sytem of abominable and gross idolatry, to which their own systems are totally repugnant): learning and inquiry, I say, once more revive among the Jews and Mahometans, at the same time that a great part of the Christian world should be free from that idolatry which has given them such just offence, they would be much more favourably impressed with the idea of Christianity than they were in former times.

It, also, can hardly be supposed, but that the general conversion of the Jews, after a state of such long and violent opposition, (which will in all future time exclude the idea of their having acted in concert with the Christians,) will be followed by the conversion of all the thinking part of the world. And if, before or after this time, the Jews should return to their own country, the whole will be such a manifest fulfilment of the prophecies of Scripture, as will leave no reasonable colour for infidelity.

[1] This passage was sarcastically noticed by *Mr. Gibbon,* in the *Correspondence,* which Dr. Priestley published in 1794, at the end of his *Discourses.* It is also among the Letters in Mr. Gibbon's Miscellaneous Works. See on the temper discovered by the Historian, Mon. Repos. X. p. 8, Note.

In the prospect of this great and glorious event I rejoice; and I wish to contribute a little towards hastening its approach, both by unfolding the history of Christianity, with all the corruptions of it, and submitting to the most rigid examination whatever I think to be really a part of it. To this, all the friends of genuine Christianity will cheerfully say, AMEN.

PART II. OF THE GENERAL CONCLUSION;

CONTAINING

CONSIDERATIONS ADDRESSED TO THE ADVOCATES FOR THE PRESENT CIVIL ESTABLISHMENTS OF CHRISTIANITY, AND ESPECIALLY BISHOP HURD.

AFTER relating, with so much freedom, the rise, progress, and present state, of what I deem to be *Corruptions of Christianity*, and especially in the established systems of it, all of which I consider as *antichristian*, being both exceedingly corrupt in their *principles*, and supported by a *power* totally foreign to that of the kingdom of Christ; I cannot help expressing my earnest wishes, that something may be done by those who have influence, to remove these evils, or at least to palliate them. And I cannot help considering those prelates who really have influence in these matters, as highly criminal, in this enlightened age, if they are not apprised of the abuses, and if they do not use their endeavours to rectify them.

It will not be imagined that I have the least prospect of being benefited myself by any alteration that can take place in the ecclesiastical system of my own country. All I wish, as a Christian, from the powers of this world, is, that they would not intermeddle at all in the business of religion, and that they would give no countenance whatever to any mode of it, my own, or that of others, but shew so much confidence in the principles of what they themselves deem to be true religion, as to think it able to guard itself.

But though I have nothing to ask for myself, much may, and ought to be done for those who do not look quite so far as I do. Many excellent men among the clergy of the Church of England are exceedingly distressed with the obligation to subscribe what they cannot believe, and to recite what they utterly condemn; and yet their circumstances are such, as too strongly tempt them to make the best of their situation, rather than absolutely starve; and many others are continually prevented from entering the church by the same state of things in it. Even the guilt of those men who are induced to comply, to the disquiet of their consciences, will lie, in a great measure, at the door of those who could relieve them, if they were in earnest to do it.

Those who have any principle themselves must feel something for those who find themselves obliged by a principle of conscience absolutely to abandon their preferment in the church. Many and painful must have been their struggles, before they could bring themselves to execute a resolution, which is viewed with wonder and regret by many of their best friends, and with indifference or contempt by the world at large. But they have respect to *other spectators*, at present invisible, but whose approbation will hereafter be of more value than all things else; and while they are conscious that what they *forsake* in this world is *for the sake of Christ, and the gospel,* Matt. xix. 29, they cannot be unhappy even now. Few of these cases, it is probable, come to the hearing of those whom no such scruples disturb.[1] But while such is the state of things in this country, and the cry for reformation grows louder every day, "Woe to them that are *thus* at ease in *our* Zion." Amos vi. 1.

If I could for a moment wish myself in the situation of those prelates who have influence in the present state of things in this country, (but, indeed, I am far from considering their situation as an enviable one, thinking my own, as a Dissenting minister, despicable as I am sensible it must appear to them, to be in reality more useful, more honourable, and more happy,) it would be to acquire that immortal renown which it is in their power to secure by promoting such a Reformation. But the same situation would probably lead me to see things in the same light in which they see them; and being easy myself, I might feel as little as they do for those who were ill at ease under me.

It is, I am sensible, extremely difficult to put one's self exactly in the place of another person, and therefore it is equally difficult to make proper allowance for the sentiments and conduct of other persons. But if it be a *situation* that necessarily leads any set of men to judge and act wrong, it should be a reason with those who see the influence of that situation, to remove the cause of offence. This work we may assure ourselves, will be done; and if those in whose power it now is, be not the proper instruments for it, others will be found, in God's own time, both in Roman Catholic countries, and in this.

The work of reformation is advancing apace in several Roman Catholic countries,[2] and this will make it doubly reproachful to us, at least, not to *keep* the lead we have hitherto plumed ourselves upon taking, in what relates to *religious liberty*, and to which we must be sensible that we owe much of the honour, and even the flourishing state of our country.

One of the worst symptoms of the present time is, that men of the greatest eminence in the church, and of the most unquestionable ability, appear to be either wholly indifferent to the subject, or instead of promoting a farther reformation, employ all their ingenuity to make men acquiesce in the present system; when all they can urge is so palpably weak, that it is barely possible they should be in earnest; not indeed in their wishes to keep things as they are, but in thinking their arguments have that weight in themselves which they wish them to have with others. To see such men as Bishop Hurd in this class of writers, a class so little respectable, when he is qualified to class with Tillotson, Hoadley and Clarke, equally excites one's pity and indignation.

This truly able writer has all the appearance of being really serious, in alleging that the Reformers of the church of England were as well qualified to judge concerning the system of Christianity as we now are. "They had only," he says, "to copy, or rather to inspect . . . . the *Sacred Scriptures*, which lay open to them as they do to us;"[3] as if it required nothing more than *eyes*, capable of distinguishing the *words* of Scripture, to enter into their real *meaning*. But had not the Papists, the Lutherans, the Calvinists, the Anabaptists, and the Socinians, of the same age, *eyes*, as well as the Reformers of the Church of England? And, I may add, were they not men of as good understanding?

But he adds, "The *Sacred Scriptures* . . . . being taken by them . . . . for their sole rule of faith, what should hinder them, when they *read* those Scriptures, from seeing as distinctly as we do at this day?"[1] I answer, the same thing, whatever it is, that makes men interpret the Scriptures so differently from the truth, at this day. Was that an age exempt from *prejudice;* or were the Reformers in England the only persons so privileged? All the classes of Reformers above enumerated appealed to the Scriptures alike.

However, it is far from being true that the English Reformers, whatever they might *pretend*, were determined by the authority of Scripture only. It is evident to most persons, though it may not be so to Bishop Hurd, that they were much influenced by the doctrines of the second, the third, and even later centuries. What else could have led them to adopt the Nicene, and especially the Athanasian Creed? This was going far beyond the canon of the Scriptures. Or should the English Reformers have seriously proposed to themselves to make the Scriptures their only rule, how was it possible for them, educated as they were, in the complicated system of Popery, to read them with unprejudiced eyes?

But "the Reformation," he says, "was not carried on with us in a precipitate, tumultuary manner, as it was, for the most part, on the Continent. On the other hand, it advanced, under the eye of the magistrate, by slow degrees; nay, it was more than once checked and kept back by him. Hence it came to pass, that there was time allowed for taking the full benefit of all discoveries made abroad;" and "for studying the chief points of controversy with care. . . . . In short, ... between the first contentions in Germany on the account of religion, and the final establishment of it in the Church of England under Elizabeth, there was a space of near half a century."[2]

It is obvious to remark, that the very same encomium might have been bestowed upon the Church of England, if it had been fixed in any of the different periods, in which it was *fixed* (and which is here called being *checked* and *kept back*) by one prince, or advanced by another, as well as where it was *checked* and *kept back* (for this, Bishop Hurd cannot deny to have been the case) by Queen Elizabeth. It would also have been equally applicable to any different establishment that should have been made after the Reformation had been moving on a *complete half century*, as well as *nearly one*, or if it had gone on afterwards (still under the controlling eye of the magistrate) to this day. For why should not our present civil governors be as good judges in matters of religion as any persons in the same situations could have been two hundred years ago? Just so much more time has elapsed since "the first contentions in Germany on the account of religion," and consequently more time would have been allowed for taking the full benefit of all the discoveries that have been made both at home and abroad, &c. And it cannot be doubted but that if a new establishment should be made at this day, it would be, in many respects, considerably different from the present.

On the other hand, had all our sovereigns after Queen Mary been Papists, and the Reformation never been resumed, a present bishop of Worcester might have said that the experiment had been tried, and had not answered, and that what had been established by the wisdom of ages, in all the countries of Europe, it could not be safe to alter. Besides, what can a Christian, jealous for the purity of his religion, expect from the *controlling eye of the magistrate*, but such a modification of it, or something bearing its name, as should be thought to be most subservient to his own interest? It does not require the understanding of Bishop Hurd to see the full force of this reply; but it may require a mind less fascinated by prejudice in favour of long-established forms.

[1] Sermons, I. pp. 235, 236. (*P.*)
[2] Ibid. pp. 239, 240. (*P.*)

In one respect this learned prelate acknowledges that the English Reformers were not sufficiently enlightened, and that was with respect to the doctrine of *toleration*. But he says, "no peculiar charge of ignorance can be brought against the Reformers for misapprehending a subject not only difficult in itself, but perplexed with endless prejudices."[1] But surely Bishop Hurd himself will not say, that the doctrine of *toleration* is more difficult in itself, or more perplexed with prejudices, than the doctrine of the *Trinity.*

In another case, also, if he be at all ingenuous, he must acknowledge that the English Reformers did not see quite so clearly as he himself now does. He says, "the Christian system has .... been reviled by such as have seen or would only see it through the false medium of Popish, or Calvinistical ideas."[2] Calvinism, therefore, according to him, is not true Christianity. But let any competent judge of the subject read the *Thirty-nine Articles* of the Church of England, and say whether they have not a strong tinge of Calvinism.[3]

It is not merely from such a general expression as that above quoted, that I conclude Bishop Hurd is no friend of Calvinism. He directly contradicts the fundamental article of that system when he says, that "a divine person, &c., in virtue of his all-atoning death," has opened "the gates of eternal life to the whole race of mortal man."[4]

According to the plainest sense of the articles of the Church of England,

the gates of eternal life are not opened to the *whole race of mortal man ;* but only to those who "by the everlasting purpose of God, ... before the foundations of the world were laid," being "chosen in Christ out of mankind," are "decreed by his counsel, secret to us," and are delivered "from curse and damnation."[5] It must be a strange *latitude of interpretation,* (for which his Lordship is an advocate,) that can reconcile these two contrary positions; and yet in the preface to these articles it is said, "that they were agreed upon for avoiding diversity of opinions, and establishing consent touching true religion." Let Mr. Madan,[6] Dr. Hurd, and the excellent bishop of Carlisle, together with some unbelievers among the clergy, all subscribers to the same articles, confer together, and tell us what this *consent touching true religion* is.

What reformation can we expect in any important doctrinal articles of religion, when Bishop Hurd expresses himself so strongly, as we have seen, in favour of the *divinity of Christ, in the highest sense of the word ?* By which he must mean that he is fully equal, in power and glory, to the Father, whom Christ himself styles *his Father and our Father, his God and our God.* It was a long time, as I have shown, before any Christians, after they contended that Christ was God, had any idea of his being so, except in some qualified sense. I will venture to say that no person before, or at the Council of Nice, would have used such language as this of Bishop Hurd.

With respect to the doctrine of *atonement,* which I think I have proved to be quite a modern thing, and hardly to have been known before the Reformation, Bishop Hurd says, "The Scriptures are unintelligible, and language itself has no meaning, if *the blood of the Lamb slain* had not a true, direct and proper efficacy (considered in the literal sense of *blood*),

---

[1] Sermons, I. pp. 240, 241. (*P.*)

[2] Ibid. p. 37. (*P.*)

[3] Hence the first Lord Chatham is said to have described the Church of England as possessing "a Calvinistic Creed, a Popish Liturgy, and an Arminian Clergy." Burnet, who was too honest to deny what it ill-suited him to admit, says on Art. xvii. that "it is very probable that those who penned it, meant that the Decree was absolute." Yet "since they have not said it," he provides a convenient *sense* for the *Remonstrants,* though he confesses, that "the *Calvinists* have less occasion for scruple, since the article does seem more plainly to favour them." *Expos.* Ed. 4, p. 165. See also *The Confessional,* Ed. 3, pp. 331-333.

[4] Sermons, III. p. 63. (*P.*)

[5] Art. xvii. (*P.*)

[6] A *rector* in Birmingham, who gave occasion to the *Familiar Letters.* 1790.

in freeing us from the *guilt* of sin, or, in other words, from the *punishment* of it.[1]

It is impossible, however, not to observe, that the Papists use the same language in defence of the doctrine of *transubstantiation*, appealing also to the literal sense of more texts of Scripture than one. Besides, how is it possible that the *blood* of any man (and the *divinity* of Christ certainly had no *blood*), considered in a *literal sense*, should cleanse from sin? Surely there must be something figurative in such language as this; and why should the figurative sense end just where Bishop Hurd would fix it, rather than where Socinus would choose?

Nay, it should seem that, according to Bishop Hurd, our salvation depends upon the *belief* of this novel doctrine of atonement. For I can see no other natural interpretation of what he says: "They must place their entire hope and confidence in the *blood* of the covenant, who would share in the blessings of it."[2] If this is to be understood according to the literal sense of the words, all the heathen world are excluded from salvation, as well as Socinians.

To me it appears extraordinary, that a man of Bishop Hurd's good sense should not be more staggered than he appears to have been, at the very manner in which he himself describes the doctrines of the *divinity of Christ*, and of *atonement for sin by his death*, every sentence, and every clause of a sentence, being calculated to excite astonishment; but I shall only transcribe a part of it. After describing the gradual unfolding of the scheme under the Jewish dispensation, he says,—

"At length Jesus Christ came into the world, to fulfil and to declare the whole will of God on this interesting subject; and from him, and from those commissioned by him, we learn what the wisest men, and even *angels had* desired to look into, and could at most discern but imperfectly, through the types and shadows of the patriarchal and Mosaic dispensations. The great mystery, now unveiled, was briefly this, that God . . . . would only confer this mighty privilege at the instance, as it were, and for the sake, of a transcendently divine person, his only-begotten Son, the second person in the glorious Trinity, as we now style him; that this divine person . . . . should descend from heaven, should become incarnate, ... should even pour out his blood unto death, and by that blood should wash away the stain of guilt. . . . In this awfully stupendous manner (at which reason stands aghast, and faith herself is half confounded) was the grace of God to man at length manifested."[3]

The natural effect of such a pause of astonishment as this, should be a close examination, whether a thing that even supernatural evidence can barely make credible, did ever take place; for in all cases, the more extraordinary any *thing*, any *event*, or any *proposition* is, the more evidence it requires. And when we consider the true meaning of the figurative language of Scripture, it will be found to assert nothing on this subject at which even reason can stand aghast.

Our author himself, after enumerating the strongest figurative expressions of the Scriptures on this subject, as those in which the terms *redemption*, *ransom*, *propitiation*, *sacrifice*, &c., occur, closes the whole with this observation: "Now let men use what art they will in torturing such expressions as these, they will hardly prevent our seeing what the plain doctrine of Scripture is, [viz.] That it pleased God to give us eternal life only *in his Son*, and in his Son *only* as suffering and dying for us."[4] All this I readily admit, believing as firmly as Bishop Hurd can do, that it was expedient and necessary that such a person as Jesus Christ

[1] Sermons, I. p. 193. (*P.*)
[2] Ibid. I. p. 194. (*P.*)
[3] Ibid. II. pp. 285–287. (*P.*)
[4] Ibid. II. pp. 288, 289. (*P.*)

should preach as he did, and that he should die and rise again, or the end of the gospel, in forming men to a happy immortality, could not have been gained. This is certainly the doctrine of the New Testament, but then it is far from being the doctrine of *atonement;* which I think I have shown to be a very different thing from that which was taught by Christ and the apostles, and indeed to have been unknown for several centuries after Christ.

It is no wonder that this writer should say, that "no Christian is bound to make this solicitous inquiry into the doctrinal .... part of the gospel; and that very "possibly his conduct is then most acceptable, when he looks no farther than to the authority of the gospel, agreeably to that well-known decision of our Lord himself, *Blessed is he who hath not seen, and yet hath believed.*"[1] For certainly such tenets as those above cited can never be believed on any other terms. Faith in them must be implicit, and without inquiry. It is rather extraordinary, however, that this writer did not perceive that the saying which he quotes of our Saviour relates only to a *matter of fact,* of which it was not possible that more than a very few persons could be eye-witnesses; whereas the things that he is contending for are *doctrines,* of which all persons at this day are competent judges, provided they make use of their reason, and examine the Scriptures for themselves. But even the looking no farther than to the *authority of the gospel* for articles of faith, may make a very *solicitous inquiry* absolutely necessary, considering how much, and how long, some articles of faith have been misrepresented.

In fact, if the learned prelate could fancy himself out of the fetters of his church's creed, he might find the very articles which he so zealously contends for among the "quibbles and .... metaphysics which" (with a strain of pleasantry not usual to him, and indeed

rather uncommon in a sermon) he says the Pagan philosophers, when they "pressed into the church, in their haste, forgot to leave behind them."[2]

But however these doctrines came in, to repeat the bishop's own words, "the presumptuous positions of particular men, or churches, are forwardly taken for the genuine doctrines of Christianity; and these positions being not unfrequently either wholly unintelligible, or even contrary to the plainest reason, the charge of nonsense, or of falsehood, is thus dexterously transferred on the gospel itself."[3] This very just and well-expressed observation I cannot help thinking to be peculiarly applicable to several articles of the creed of Bishop Hurd himself, as I think must be sufficiently evident from the preceding history.

This writer, not content with what he himself had advanced against all improvements, or alterations, in the church in which he presides, quotes with the highest approbation what Mr. Burgh, in his reply to Mr. Lindsey, says against the idea of a *progressive religion,* viz. that "All that" *the Bible* "contains was as perspicuous to those who first perused it, after the rejection of the papal yoke, as it can be to us now, or as it can be to our posterity in the fiftieth generation."[4]

This is evidently a mis-stating of the case; because it is not a *progressive religion,* but a *progressive reformation* of a corrupted religion, that is pleaded for. And as it cannot be denied that the corruption of Christianity was a gradual and progressive thing, can it be so very unnatural to expect that the restoration of it to its primitive purity should be gradual and progressive also? If the Reformation was not progressive, why does not this bishop prefer the state of it under John Huss and Jerome of Prague to that of Luther and Cranmer? He may say that they had not then completely *rejected the papal yoke.*

[1] Sermons, III. p. 52. (*P.*)
[2] Ibid. III. p. 205. (*P.*)
[3] Ibid. p. 209. (*P.*)
[4] Ibid. I. [Note] p. 244. (*P.*)

But if by papal yoke he meant all the corruptions of Christianity contained in the system of Popery, and which had been enforced by the authority of the see of Rome, I say, that neither Luther nor Cranmer rejected the papal yoke, because their reformations were partial.

Besides, if we make the sentiments of the divines of that particular age, which Mr. Burgh and Bishop Hurd may call the proper *æra of the Reformation*, to be our standard, why should we adopt those of Luther or Cranmer in preference to those of Socinus, or even those of the Anabaptists of Munster, who were all of the same age? I know of no reason but that the opinions of Luther and Cranmer had the sanction of the *civil powers*, which those of Socinus, and others of the same age, and who were equally well qualified to judge for themselves, had not.

It is nothing but the *alliance* of the kingdom of Christ with the kingdoms of this world (an alliance which our Lord himself expressly disclaimed) that supports the grossest corruptions of Christianity; and perhaps we must wait for the fall of the civil powers before this most unnatural alliance be broken. Calamitous, no doubt, will that time be. But what convulsion in the political world ought to be a subject of lamentation, if it be attended with so desirable an event? May the *kingdom of God*, and of Christ (that which I conceive to be intended in the Lord's Prayer), truly and fully *come*, though all the kingdoms of the world be removed, in order to make way for it!

APPENDIX TO THE GENERAL CONCLUSION;

CONTAINING

A SUMMARY VIEW OF THE EVIDENCE FOR THE PRIMITIVE CHRISTIANS HOLDING THE DOCTRINE OF THE SIMPLE HUMANITY OF CHRIST.

As the doctrine held by the primitive church, and especially by the Jewish Christians, is of particular consequence, it may give satisfaction to some of my readers, to see the evidence for their holding the simple humanity of Christ stated in a more concise and distinct manner than it is done in the body of this work. I shall, therefore, attempt it in this place, and take the opportunity of introducing a few more circumstances relating to it.

1. It is acknowledged by early writers of the orthodox persuasion, that two kinds of heresy existed in the times of the apostles, viz. that of those who held that Christ was *simply a man*, and the other that he was *man only in appearance*. Now the apostle John animadverts with the greatest severity upon the latter; and can it be thought probable that he should pass over the former without censure, if he had thought it to be an error?

2. Athanasius is so far from denying this, that he endeavours to account for Christ being spoken of as a man only, in several parts of the New Testament, and especially in the book of Acts, from the apostles not being willing to offend the Jews (meaning the Jewish Christians) of those times, and that they might bring them to the belief of the divinity of Christ by degrees. He adds, that the Jews being in this error (which he states as their believing Christ to be ψιλος ανθρωπος) drew the Gentiles into it also.

3. It is acknowledged by Eusebius

and others, that the ancient Unitarians themselves, constantly asserted that their doctrine was the universal opinion of the Christian church till the time of Victor.

4. Hegesippus, the first Christian historian, himself a Jew, enumerating the heresies of his time, mentions several of the Gnostic kind, but not that of Christ being a mere man. He moreover says, that, in travelling to Rome, where he arrived in the time of Anicetus, he found all the churches that he visited held the faith which had been taught by Christ and the apostles.

5. Justin Martyr, who maintains the pre-existence of Christ, is so far from calling the contrary opinion a *heresy*, that what he says on the subject is evidently an apology for his own. As Hegesippus was contemporary with Justin, he must have heard at least of the doctrine of the simple humanity of Christ; but he might not have heard much about the opinion of Justin, which was different from that of the Gnostics, though the pre-existence of Christ was a part of both.

6. Irenæus, who wrote after Justin, only calls the opinion of those who held that Christ was the son of Joseph as well as of Mary, a heresy. He says nothing of those who, believing him to be a mere man, allowed that he had no human father.

7. Those whom Epiphanius calls *Alogi,* among the Gentiles, held that Christ was merely a man ; and as they had no peculiar appellation before his time, and had no separate assemblies, it is evident they could not have been distinguished as heretics in early times.

8. The first who held, and discussed, the doctrine of the divinity of Christ, acknowledged that their opinion was exceedingly unpopular with the *unlearned* Christians, and that these latter were pious persons, who dreaded the doctrine of the Trinity, as thinking that it infringed upon that of the supremacy of God the Father.

9. The divinity of Christ was first advanced and urged by those who had been heathen philosophers, and especially those who were admirers of the doctrine of Plato, who held the opinion of a *second God.* Austin says, that he considered Christ as no other than a most excellent man, and had no suspicion of the *word of God* being incarnate in him, or how "the catholic faith differed from the error of Photinus," (the last of the proper Unitarians whose name is come down to us,) till he read the books of Plato; and that he was afterwards confirmed in his opinion by reading the Scriptures.[1] Constantine, in his oration to the fathers of the Council of Nice, speaks with commendation of Plato, as having taught the doctrine of "a second God, derived from the supreme God, and subservient to his will.[2]

10. There is a pretty easy gradation in the progress of the doctrine of the divinity of Christ; as he was first thought to be a God in some qualified sense of the word, a distinguished emanation from the supreme mind, and then the *logos* or wisdom of God personified; and it was not till near four hundred years after Christ that he was thought to be properly *equal to the Father.* Whereas, on the other hand, it is now pretended, that the apostles taught the doctrine of the proper divinity of Christ; and yet it cannot be denied that, in the very times of the apostles, the Jewish church, and many of the Gentiles, held the opinion of his being a *mere man.* Here the transition is quite sudden, without any gradation at all. This must naturally have given the greatest alarm, such as is now given to those who are called *orthodox* by the present Socinians; and yet nothing of this kind can be perceived. Besides, it was certainly more probable that the Christians of those times, urged as they were with the meanness of their Master, should incline to *add to* rather than *take from*, his natural rank and dignity.

[1] Confessiones, L. vii. C. 19, &c. (*P.*)
[2] C. ix. p. 684. (*P.*)

CONSIDERATIONS

IN EVIDENCE THAT

THE APOSTOLIC AND PRIMITIVE CHURCH

WAS UNITARIAN.

[These Considerations are derived from the letters of Dr. Priestley, addressed to Bishop Horsley, the Bench of Bishops, and others, and from his work called "An History of the Early Opinions concerning Jesus Christ." The above volumes are out of print and very scarce. The matter here presented is an abridgement, but, we may add, it is additional to what was promised to the subscribers to this Volume.]

THE UNITY OF GOD: THE FATHER THE ONLY TRUE GOD.

THE most express declarations concerning the unity of God, and the importance of the belief of it, are frequent in the Old Testament. The first commandment is, Exod. xx. 3: "Thou shalt have no other gods before me." This is repeated in the most emphatical manner, Deut. vi. 4: "Hear, O Israel, the Lord our God is one Lord." . .

In the New Testament we find the same doctrine concerning God that we do in the Old. To the Scribe who enquired which was the first and greatest commandment, our Saviour answered, Mark xii. 29: "The first of all the commandments is, 'Hear, O Israel, the Lord our God is one Lord.' And the Scribe said unto him, ver. 32: "Well, Master, thou hast said the truth ; for there is one God, and there is none other but he." . . . . .

Why is this ONE GOD in the New Testament always called the *Father*, and even *the God and Father of our Lord Jesus Christ?* And why are we nowhere told that this one God is the *Trinity,* consisting of *the Father, the Son, and the Holy Ghost ?* . . . .

There are many, very many, passages of Scripture which inculcate the doctrine of the divine unity in the clearest and strongest manner. Let one such passage be produced in favour of the Trinity. And why should we believe things so mysterious without the clearest and most express evidence ? . . .

Had there been any distinctions of persons in the divine nature, such as the doctrine of the Trinity supposes, it is at least so like an infringement of the fundamental doctrine of the Jewish religion, that it certainly required to be explained, and the obvious inference from it to be guarded against. . . . . .

I will venture to say, that for one text in which you can pretend to find anything harsh or difficult to me, I will engage to produce ten that shall create more difficulty to you. How strangely must you torture the plainest language, and in which there is not a shadow of figure, to interpret to your purpose, 1 Tim. ii. 3: "There is one God, and one mediator between God and man, the man Christ Jesus ; 1 Cor. viii. 6: " To us there is but one God, the Father, of whom are all things. and we in him, and one Lord Jesus Christ, by whom are all things, and we by him ;" or that expression of our Saviour himself, John xvii. 2: "That they might know thee, the only true God, and Jesus Christ whom thou hast sent." Never upbraid us Unitarians with torturing the Scriptures, while you have these and a hundred other plain texts to bend to your Athanasian hypothesis, besides many *general arguments*, from reason and the Scriptures, of more real force than any particular texts, to answer. . . . . .

You cannot say that this is a matter of no great consequence in Christianity. It affects the most fundamental principles of all religion, the first and the greatest of all the commandments, which says, " Thou shalt have no other God besides me ;" and such is the nature of this great doctrine of the Unity of God, that there never was a departure from it which did not draw after it very alarming practical consequences. . . .

THE JEWS IN ALL AGES WERE BELIEVERS IN THE DIVINE UNITY.

THE Jews always interpreted their Scriptures as teaching that God is simply ONE. . . . .

" The Jews," says Eusebius, " were not taught the doctrine of the Trinity, on account of their infant state." *Basil* gives the same account. . . . . .

" The doctrine of the Trinity," says the *Rabbi Isaac*, "as held by learned Christians, rests on the slightest evidence, and is contrary to the doctrine of the prophets, the law, and right reason, and even the writings of the New Testament. For the divine law gives its sanction to the Unity of God, and removes all plurality from him." . . . . .

Some writers of yesterday have maintained that the Jews always believed in a Trinity, and that they expected that their *Messiah* would be the Second Person in that Trinity; but the Christian fathers, who say just the contrary, were as much interested as any men could be, in finding that doctrine among the Jews, and they were nearer the source of information. . . . . .

Basnage, who studied the history and opinions of the Jews more carefully, perhaps, than any other modern writer, and who has written largely on this very subject, though a Trinitarian himself, has exploded all the pretences of *Cudworth* and others, to find the doctrine of the Trinity, either among the ancient or the modern Jews. " The Christians and the Jews," he says, " separate at the second step in religion. For after having adored together one God,

absolutely perfect, they find immediately after, the abyss of the Trinity, which entirely separates them. . . . . .

RELIGIOUS WORSHIP.

Jesus Christ, says, " The true worshippers shall worship the Father." . . . . .

Our Saviour directs his disciples to pray to the same great Being, whom only we ought to serve. . . . . .

Accordingly, the practice of praying to the Father only, was long universal in the Christian church, the short addresses to Christ, as those in the Litany, " Lord have mercy upon us, Christ have mercy upon us," being comparatively of late date. . . . . .

Origen speaks of no Christian praying to any other than the God who is over all. " If we know," says he, "what prayer is, we must not pray to any created being, not to Christ himself, but only to God, the Father of all, to whom our Saviour himself prayed." . . . . " In this we are all agreed, and are not divided about the method of prayer ; but should we not be divided, if some prayed to the Father, and some to the Son ?" . . . . .

When I was myself a Trinitarian, I remember praying conscientiously to all three persons without distinction, only beginning with the Father ; and what I myself did in the serious simplicity of my heart, when young, would, I doubt not, have been done by all Christians from the beginning, if their minds had been impressed as mine was, with the firm persuasion that all the three persons were fully equal in power, wisdom, goodness, omnipresence, and all divine attributes. . .

In the Clementine liturgy, the oldest that is extant, contained in the *Apostolical Constitutions*, which were probably composed about the fourth century, there is no trace of any such thing as prayers to Christ. . . .

Idolatry, which began with the worship of Jesus Christ, soon proceeded to that of the Virgin Mary, and terminated in as many objects of worship as the heathens ever adored, and sufficiently similar to them. . . . . .

With idolatry, which is paying divine worship to that which is not God, you cannot charge me, because the being that I worship is also the object of worship with you ; and the far greater part of your public devotions are addressed to no other. But the charge will fall with all its weight upon you, if the Father only be God, and you worship two other persons besides him. . . .

You cannot but acknowledge that the proper object of prayer is God the Father, whom you call the first person in the Trinity. Indeed, you cannot find in the Scriptures any *precept* that will authorize us to address ourselves to any other person, nor any proper *example* of it... Our Saviour himself always prayed to his Father, and with as much humility and resignation as the most dependent being in the universe could possibly do`; always addressing him as his *father*, or the *author of his being;* and he directs his disciples to pray to the same great being, *whom only*, he says, *we ought to serve.* . . .

To conclude, from the single case of Stephen, that all Christians are authorized to pray to Christ, is like concluding that all matter has a tendency to go upwards, because a needle will do so when a magnet is held over it. When you shall be in the same circumstances with Stephen, having your mind strongly impressed with a vision of Christ sitting at the right hand of God, you may then, perhaps, be authorized to address yourself to him as he did ; but the whole tenor of the Scriptures proves that, otherwise, you have no authority at all for any such practice. . . . . .

THE TRINITY.

DIVINES are content to build so strange and inexplicable a doctrine as that of the Trinity upon mere inferences from casual expressions, and cannot pretend to one clear, express, and unequivocal lesson on the subject. . . . . .

I wish you would reflect a little on the subject, and then inform us what there is in the doctrine of the Trinity, *in itself considered*, that can recommend it as a part of a system of religious truth. For there is neither any fact in *nature*, nor any one purpose of *morals*, which are the object and end of all religion, that requires it. . . . .

If the doctrine of the Trinity be true, it is, no doubt, in the highest degree important and interesting. Since, therefore, the evangelists give no certain and distinct account of it, and say nothing of its importance, it may be safely inferred that it was unknown to them. . . . . .

Why was not the doctrine of the *Trinity* taught as explicitly, and in as definite a manner, in the New Testament at least, as the doctrine of the divine *Unity* is taught in both the Old and New Testaments, if it be

a truth? And why is the doctrine of the *Unity* always delivered in so unguarded a manner, and without any exception made in favour of the Trinity, to prevent any mistake with respect to it, as is always now done in our orthodox catechisms, creeds, and discourses on the subject? . . . . . .

The doctrine of Transubstantiation implies a *physical impossibility*, whereas that of the Trinity, as unfolded in the Athanasian Creed, implies a *mathematical* one ; and to this only we usually give the name of *contradiction*. . . . . .

Now I ask, Wherein does the Athanasian doctrine of the Trinity differ from a contradiction ? It asserts, in effect, that nothing is wanting to either the Father, the Son, or the Spirit, to constitute each of them truly and properly God ; each being equal in eternity and all divine perfections ; and yet that these three are not *three Gods*, but only *one God*. They are, therefore, both *one* and *many* in the same respect, viz., in each being *perfect God*. This is certainly as much a contradiction as to say that Peter, James, and John, having each of them everything that is requisite to constitute a complete man, are yet, all together, not *three men*, but only *one man*. For the ideas annexed to the words *God* or *man* cannot make any difference in the nature of the two propositions. . . . . .

Why, then, should you be so desirous of retaining such a doctrine as this of the Trinity, which you must acknowledge has an uncouth appearance, has always confounded the best reason of mankind, and drives us to the undesirable doctrine of *inexplicable mysteries?* Try, then, whether you cannot hit upon some method or other of reconciling a few particular texts, not only with common sense, but also with the general and the obvious tenor of the Scriptures themselves. In the meantime, this doctrine of the Trinity wears so disagreeable an aspect, that I think every reasonable man must say, with the excellent Archbishop Tillotson, with respect to the Athanasian Creed, "I wish we were well rid of it." This is not setting up reason against the Scriptures, but reconciling reason with the Scriptures, and the Scriptures with themselves. . . . . .

I therefore think it of the greatest consequence to Christianity, that this doctrine of the Trinity, which I consider as one of its most radical corruptions, should be renounced in the most open and unequivocal manner by all those whose minds are so far enlightened as to be convinced that it is a corruption and an innovation in the Christian doctrine, the reverse of what it was in its primitive purity; and that they should exert themselves to enlighten the minds of others. . . . . .

THE ATHANASIAN CREED.

This creed of Athanasius is no act of any council. You neither know who composed it, when it made its first appearance, or how it came into the public offices of the church.

Bishop Taylor says, "If it were considered concerning Athanasius's Creed, how many people understand it not, how contrary to natural reason it seems, how little the Scripture says of those curiosities of explication—it had not been amiss if the final judgment had been left to Jesus Christ." . .

Many, no doubt, *do* subscribe to this creed in this light and careless manner; which shows the dreadful effect of the *habit of subscribing*. It leads to the utter perversion of the plainest meaning of words, and opens a door to every kind of insincerity. By your lordship's own confession, you yourself no more believe what you have subscribed with respect to this creed, than you do the Koran. . . . . .

If your lordship defends these damnatory clauses on the principle of *meaning nothing at all by them,* you vindicate the common cursing and swearing that we every day hear in our streets. If the phrase *perish everlastingly* does not mean perish everlastingly, your lordship should have informed us what it does mean. It is certainly no *blessing*, but a *curse* of some kind or other. . . . . .

We think it our duty to *cry aloud, and not spare,* when we see such abominations in the public worship of Almighty God as are to be found in all the civil establishments of Christianity in the world; corruptions borrowed from heathen polytheism, and which in their nature and effects are very similar to it. . . . . .

CHRIST PROPERLY AND ONLY A MAN.

Christ was a man, naturally possessed of no other powers than other men have, but a distinguished messenger of God, and the chief instrument in his hands for the good of men; this was the original faith of the Christian church, consisting both of Jews and Gentiles. . . . . .

It must strike every person who gives the least attention to the phraseology of the New Testament, that the terms Christ and God, are perpetually used in contradistinction to each other, as much as God and man . . .

Christ himself always prayed to this one God, as his God and Father. He always spoke of himself as receiving his doctrine and his power from him, and again and again disclaimed having any power of his own, John v. 19: "Then answered Jesus and said unto them, Verily, verily, I say unto you, the Son can do nothing of himself." Ch. xiv. 10: "The words that I speak unto you, I speak not of myself, but the Father that dwelleth in me." . . . . . .

He calls his disciples his brethren, John xx. 17: "Go to my brethren, and say unto them, I ascend unto my Father and your Father, and to my God and your God." Can any person read this, and say that the Unitarians wrest the Scriptures, and are not guided by the plain sense of them? . . . . .

God promised to Abraham, Gen. xii. 3., that in his seed all the families of the earth should be blessed. This, if it relate to the Messiah at all, can give us no other idea than that one of his seed or posterity should be the means of conferring great blessings on mankind. . . . . .

What else will be suggested by the description which Moses is supposed to give of the Messiah, Deut. xviii. 18: "I will raise them up a prophet, from among their brethren, like unto thee, and will put my words in his mouth, and he shall speak unto them all that I shall command him"? . . .

Here is nothing like a second person in the Trinity, a person equal to the Father, but a mere prophet, delivering, in the name of God, whatever he is ordered so to do. . .

Had the apostle Paul considered Christ as being anything more than a man, with respect to his nature, he would never have urged, with the least propriety or effect, that "Since by man came death, by man came also the resurrection of the dead." For it might have been unanswerably replied, This is, not the case; for, indeed, by man comes death, but not by man, but by God, or by God the creator of man, under God, comes the resurrection of the dead. . . . . .

The disciples certainly saw and conversed with him at first on the supposition of his being a man as much as themselves. Of this there can be no doubt. Their surprise, therefore, upon being informed that he was not a man, but really God, or even the maker of the world under God, would be just as great as ours would now be on discovering that any of our acquaintance, or at least a very good man and a prophet, was in reality God, or the maker of the world. Let us consider, then, how we should feel, how we should behave towards such a person, and how we should speak of him afterwards. No one, I am confident, would ever call that being a *man*, after he was convinced that he was *God*. . . . . .

I would further recommend it to your consideration, how the apostles could continue to call Christ *a man*, as they always do, both in the book of Acts and in their Epistles, after they had discovered him to be God. After this it must have been highly degrading, unnatural, and improper, notwithstanding his appearance in human form.

THE DEITY OF CHRIST.

Is not one self-existent, almighty, infinitely wise, and perfectly good being fully equal to the production of all things, and also to the support and government of the worlds which he has made? A second person in the godhead cannot be really wanted for this purpose, as far as we can conceive. . . . . .

You speak of the *impiety* of the Unitarians. Before you repeat any expressions of this kind, I beg you would pause a little, and consider how such language might be retorted upon yourself. If it be impiety to reduce a God to the state of a man, is it not equally impious to raise any man to a state of equality with God,—that God who has declared that he will not give his glory to another, who has no equal, and who in this respect styles himself a jealous God? . . . .

As Christ expressly says, that he did not know the day of judgment, he certainly either was, or pretended to be, ignorant of something which, at least in his divine nature, he must have known. Here, then, is a question worthy of an *Apollo* to answer; and it may be amusing to observe what different solutions have been given of this difficulty. . . . . .

There is also another consideration which I would recommend to you who maintain that Christ was either God, or the maker of the world under God. It is this. The manner in which our Lord speaks of himself, and of the power by which he worked miracles, is inconsistent, according to the common construction of language, with the idea of his being possessed of any proper power of his own, more than other men had.

If Christ was the maker of the world, and if in the creation he exerted no power but what properly belonged to himself, and what was as much *his own* as the power of speaking or walking belongs to man—though depending ultimately upon that supreme power in which we all live, and move, and have our being—he could not with any propriety, and without knowing that he must be misunderstood, have said that *of himself he could do nothing*, that the *words which he spake were not his own*, and that *the Father within him did the works*. . . . .

It would also be a shocking abuse of language, and would warrant any kind of deception and imposition, if Christ could be supposed to say *that his Father was greater than he*, and at the same time secretly mean only *his human nature*, whereas his divine nature was at the same time fully equal to that of the Father. Upon the same principle a man might say that Christ never suffered, that he never died, or rose again from the dead, meaning his divine nature only, and not his human. Indeed, there is no use in language, nor any guard against deception, if such liberties as these are to be allowed.

SON OF GOD NOT GOD THE SON.

With respect to calling Jesus the Son of God, this phrase was, in the mouth of a Jew, synonymous to the *Messiah*. . . . . .

If the mere appellation *Son of God* implies *equality with God*, Adam must have been a God, for he is called the Son of God, Luke iii. 38. Solomon also must have been God; and so must all Christians, for they are called *Sons of God*, 1 John iii. 2. John i. 12. Rom. viii. 14. Phil. ii. 15.

OPINIONS WHICH PREPARED THE WAY FOR THE DEITY OF CHRIST.

The great obstacle to the reception of Christianity, especially with persons distinguished for their learning, or their rank in life, was the meanness of the person and condition of Christ, and especially the circumstance of his having been crucified as a common malefactor. . . . . .

Not content with alleging that though their Master died the death of a malefactor he had not lived the life of one; that his death had answered the greatest purposes in the plan of Divine Providence . . . . the more learned among them availed themselves of the philosophy of their age, and said that the Christ was a person of much higher rank than he appeared to be, even much higher than that of any other man, a great super-angelic-spirit sent down from heaven . . . for it was the opinion of many that angels in the shape of men had appeared, and were only temporary forms of flesh and blood.

If any new opinions be introduced into a society, they are more likely to have introduced them who held opinions similar to them before they joined that society. . . . .

The divinity of Christ was first advanced and urged by those who had been heathen philosophers, and especially those who were admirers of the doctrine of Plato, who held the opinion of a second God. . . . .

It happened that the philosophy which was most in vogue in that age was Platonism, the principles of which have been seen to be more conformable to those of revealed religion in general than those of any other system that was taught in the Grecian schools, as it contained the doctrines of the unity of God, the reality of providence, and the immortality of the soul. . . . .

Platonism unhappily making a difference between the Supreme Being himself and his *mind* or *ideas*, and giving an obscure notion of its being by means of a divine efflux that all truth is perceived by the mind, as common objects are seen by the beams of the sun, they imagined that a ray of this wisdom, or the great second divine principle in their system, might illuminate Jesus Christ, and even had permanently attached itself to him. . . . .

Some of those Greek philosophers having embraced Christianity, and being, as was natural, desirous of making converts of others, therefore wished to recommend it to them, by exhibiting it in such a light as they imagined would make it appear to the most advantage and ; in order to do this, they endeavoured to make it seem to be as little different from the philosophy to which they had been addicted as possible. . .

When Christians had found *two natures* in Christ, a *divine* as well as a *human* nature, they would easily answer this reproach of the heathens. "Who was it," says Arnobius, " that was seen hanging on the cross ? The man whom he put on, and whom he carried with him. The death you speak of was that of the man he had assumed—that of the burthen, not of the bearer." This was an answer that we do not find to have occurred to the apostles. . . . .

There is a pretty easy gradation in the progress of the doctrine of the divinity of Christ ; as he was first thought to be a God in some qualified sense of the word, a distinguished emanation from the Supreme Mind ; and then the *logos*, or the *wisdom of God* personified ; and this *logos* was first thought to be only occasionally detached from the Deity, and then drawn into his essence again, before it was imagined that it had a permanent personality, distinct from that of the source from which it sprung. And it was not till the fourth century that this *logos*, or Christ, was thought to be properly equal to the Father. . . . .

THE FATHER GREATER THAN THE SON.

[We here adduce only a tithe of the evidence found by Dr. Priestley in the writings of the Christian Fathers before the Council of Nice, 325, that they regarded the Son as subordinate to the Father.]

THE great object of the orthodox in the second century, was to make a God of Christ, but a far *inferior* God, and also a God *of* or *out of* God the Father, lest he should be thought to be *another God*, and independent of the Father. On the other hand, the great object of the orthodoxy of a later period, was to exalt the Son to a perfect equality with the Father. . . . .

Bishop Bull acknowledges that *Justin Martyr, Tertullian*, and *Novatian* thought that the Father could not be confined to place, but the Son might. . . . . .

Justin Martyr, who insists so much on the pre-existence and divinity of Christ, speaking of the *logos*, says, "Than whom we know no prince more kingly, and more righteous, after the God who generated him." Speaking of the God in heaven and the God upon earth, who conversed with Abraham, he says, "The former is the Lord of that Lord who was upon earth as his Father and God, the cause of his existence, and of his being powerful, and Lord and God." . . . . .

Irenæus evidently supposed, that the time of the day of judgment was altogether unknown to the Son, and he advises us to acquiesce in our ignorance of many things, after his example. . . . No better reason can be given, but that we may learn of our Lord himself, that the Father is above all ; for he said, "The Father is greater than I." . . . .

Clement Alexandrinus calls the *logos* "the image of God, the legitimate son of his mind ; a light, the copy of the light, and man the image of the *logos.*" He calls the Father the only true God. . . He speaks of Christ as subservient to his Father's will, and only called God by way of figure. . . .

The early fathers, before the Council of *Nice,* say that the Son was generated *in time,* that there was a time when God was without a Son, and that this generation took place immediately before the creation, in order to the Son's being instrumental in it. . .

Tertullian expressly says, that " God was not always a father or a judge; since he could not be a Father before he had a Son, nor a judge before there was sin ; and there was a time when both sin and the Son, which made God to be a judge and a father, were not." . . . . .

Tertullian considers "The monarchy of God as not infringed by being committed to the Son, especially as it is not infringed by being committed to innumerable angels, who are said to be subservient to the commands of God." "How," says he, "do I destroy the monarchy, who suppose the Son derived from the substance of the Father, and does nothing without the Father's will ; he being a servant to his Father ?" He says that Paul is speaking of the Father only, when he speaks of him whom no man has seen, or can see, and as the king eternal, immortal, and invisible, the only God. "According to the economy of the gospel, the Father chose that the Son should be on earth and himself in heaven ; wherefore, the Son himself, looking upwards, prayed to the Father, and teaches us to pray, saying, Our Father, who art in heaven." . . . . .

Origen says, that " God is the αρχη (the origin) to Christ, as Christ is the αρχη to those things which were made in the image of God." "Both the Father and the Son," he says, "are fountains : the Father, of divinity ; the Son, of logos." "The Father only is the good, and the Saviour, as he is the image of the invisible God, so he is the image of his goodness." "The logos did whatever the Father ordered." "The Saviour and the Holy Spirit," he says, "are more excelled by the Father, than he and the Holy Spirit excel other things." . . . . .

Novatian, whose orthodoxy, with respect to the doctrine of the Trinity, was never questioned, says, "The Father only is the only

good God." "The rule of truth teaches us to believe, after the Father, in the Son of God, Christ Jesus, our Lord God, but the Son of God, of that God who is one and alone the maker of all things." "Though he was in the form of God, he did not attempt the robbery of being equal with God. For, though he knew he was God of God the Father, he never compared himself with God the Father ; remembering that he was of the Father, and that he had what the Father gave him." . . . . .

Arnobius says, that "the Omnipotent, and only God, sent Christ." And again, "Christ, a God, spake by the order of the principal God." . . . . .

"God," says *Lactantius,* "the framer and ordainer of all things, before he undertook the construction of this world, generated an incorruptible spirit, which he called his Son." . . . . .

"The Son patiently obeys the will of the Father, and does nothing but what the Father wills or orders." "He approved his fidelity to God ; for he taught that there is one God, and that he only ought to be worshipped ; nor did he ever say he was God. For he would not have preserved his allegiance, if, being sent to take away a multiplicity of gods, and to preach *one God,* he had brought in another, besides that one." . . . . .

The same language was held by *Eusebius,* who wrote about the time of the Council of *Nice.* "Christ," he says, "the only begotten Son of God, and the first-born of every creature, teaches us to call his Father the only true God, and commands us to worship him only." "There is one God, and the only-begotten comes out of him." "Christ being neither the supreme God, nor an angel, is of a middle nature between them ; and being neither the supreme God, nor a man, but the mediator, is in the middle between them, the only-begotten Son of God." . . . . .

THE REASON WHY THE APOSTLES DID NOT AT FIRST TEACH THE DEITY OF CHRIST.

THE Christian Fathers in general represent the apostles as obliged to use great caution not to offend their first converts with the doctrine of Christ's divinity, and as forbearing to urge that topic till they were first well established in the belief of his being the Messiah. . . . . .

After treating pretty largely of the conduct of the apostles with respect to their insisting on the doctrine of the *Resurrection* of Christ, rather than that of his *Divinity*, immediately after the descent of the Holy Spirit, Athanasius says, "As to the Jews, who had daily heard, and been taught out of the law, *Hear O Israel, the Lord thy God is one Lord, and besides him there is no other;* having seen him (Jesus) nailed to a cross, yea, having killed and buried him themselves,. and not having seen him risen again, if they had heard that this person was God, equal to the Father, would not they have rejected and spurned at it ?' "On this account," he adds,' "they (the apostles) brought them forwards gently, and by slow degrees, and used great art in condescending to their weakness." . . . . .

Now if we look into the book of Acts, we shall clearly see that they had not got beyond the first lesson in the apostolic age ; the great burden of the preaching of the apostles being to persuade the Jews that *Jesus was the Christ.* That he was likewise *God,* they evidently left to their successors ; who, indeed, did it most effectually, though it required a long course of time to do it. . . . .

Theodoret observes, that in the genealogy of Christ given by Matthew, this writer did not add *according to the flesh,* " because the men of that time would not bear it." This writer also says, that the Apostle Paul, in mentioning the subjection of Christ to the Father, in his Epistle to the Corinthians, "spake of him more lowly than was necessary on account of their weakness." . . . . .

Chrysostom says, that "if the Jews were so much offended at having a new law superadded to their former, how much more would they have been offended if Christ had taught his own divinity." He represents the apostle as beginning his epistle to the Hebrews with saying, " that it was *God* who spake by the prophets, and by his Son, and not that *Christ* himself had spoken by them, because their minds were weak, and they were not able to bear the doctrine concerning Christ." He even says that " when he there speaks of Christ as above the angels, he still spoke of his humanity. See," says he, " his great *caution.*" He adds, at Athens Paul calls him (Jesus) simply a *man,* and nothing further, and for a good reason. For if, when they had heard Christ himself speaking of his equality to the Father, they would on that account have often stoned him, and called him a blasphemer ; they would hardly,

therefore, have received this doctrine from fishermen, especially after speaking of him as crucified. And why do I speak of the Jews, when at that time, even the disciples of Christ himself were often disturbed, and scandalized at him, when they heard sublime doctrines; on which account he said, I have many things to say to you, but ye are not yet able to bear them. . . . . .

I cannot help observing how extremely improbable is this account of the conduct of the apostles given by Athanasius, Chrysostom, and other orthodox fathers of the church, considering what we know of the character and the instructions of the apostles. They were plain men, and little qualified to act the cautious part ascribed to them. And their instructions certainly were to teach all that they knew, even what their master communicated to them in the greatest privacy. Whereas, they must have suffered numbers to die in the ignorance of the most important truth in the gospel, lest, by divulging it too soon, the conversion of others should have been prevented. The case evidently was, that these fathers did not know how to account for the great prevalence of the Unitarian doctrine among the Gentiles as well as the Jews in the early ages of Christianity, but upon such a hypothesis as this [that the apostles did not at first teach the deity of Christ]. . . . . .

In how unworthy a manner, and how unsuitably to their real character and conduct, these fathers represent the apostles as acting. They were all plain men, far from being qualified or disposed to act so cunning a part as is here ascribed to them. . . . . .

EARLY OPINIONS ABOUT THE HOLY GHOST.

It is remarkable, that, notwithstanding the doctrine concerning the person of Christ had been the great subject of controversy ever since the promulgation of Christianity, there is no mention made of any difference of opinion concerning the *Holy Spirit,* that attracted any notice, till after the commencement of the Arian controversy, and even till after the Council of Nice. . . . . .

Justin Martyr, to whom we are indebted for the first rudiments of the doctrine of the divinity of Christ, says but little concerning the Holy Spirit ; and from that little it is not easy to conclude what his real opinion was. But it is probable that he considered the Spirit as a created being, since he represents him as inferior to Christ. . . . .

Irenæus seems to have considered the Holy Spirit as a divine influence, and no proper person. "By the name of Christ," he says, "we are given to understand one who anoints, one who is anointed, and the unction with which he is anointed. It is the Father who anoints, but the Son is anointed in the Spirit." . . . .

Valentinus thought the Holy Spirit to be of the same rank with the angels. . . . . .

Origen considered it as doubtful whether, since all things are made by Christ, the Holy Spirit was not made by him. And after discussing the question a little, he says, "We who maintain three hypostases, the Father, Son, and Spirit, and believe that the Father only is unbegotten, think it more agreeable to piety and truth, to maintain that the Holy Spirit is superior to all things that were made by Christ." . . . .

Tertullian seems to have thought that the Holy Spirit was derived from Christ, in the same manner as Christ was derived from God. . . . .

Novatian, who had as much orthodoxy with respect to the Trinity as any person of his age, certainly did not believe in the divinity of the Holy Spirit, whom he represents as inferior to the Son, whom also he makes greatly inferior to the Father. "Christ," says he, "is greater than the Paraclete; for he would not receive of Christ if he was not less than he." . . . .

Athenagoras considered the Holy Spirit as an efflux from the Deity, flowing out and drawn into him again at pleasure, as a beam from the sun. . . . . .

Eusebius, who appears to have been as orthodox as other writers of his age with respect to the Son, (if his writings may be allowed to testify for him,) and who certainly was not bold in heresy, scrupled not to consider the Spirit as made by the Son. "The Holy Spirit," says he, "is neither God nor the Son, because he did not derive his birth from the Father, like the Son, but in one of the things that was made by the Son; because all things were made by him, and without him was nothing made." . . . .

Even *Hilary*, who wrote so largely concerning the divinity of the Son, seems not to have had the same persuasion concerning that of the Holy Spirit; but, in the little that he says on the subject, seems rather to have considered the Spirit as a divine influence. . . . . .

The reasoning of the fathers concerning the divinity of the Holy Spirit lies in a much smaller compass than that concerning the divinity of the Son. One principal reason of this is, that so little mention is made of the Holy Spirit in the Scriptures, and still less that can possibly be construed into an evidence of his being a divine person. This is a circumstance that could not escape notice, and which required to be accounted for by the orthodox. . . . .

Among others, *Epiphanius* has advanced a reason which is curious enough. It goes upon the idea of the Holy Spirit being that person of the three which immediately dictated the Scriptures. He says, that "the Holy Spirit says little concerning himself, that he might not commend himself, the Scriptures being written to give us examples." . . . .

It was *Athanasius*, the great advocate for the divinity of Christ, and his consubstantiality with the Father, who also exerted himself strenuously and effectually in behalf of that of the Holy Spirit, whose divinity was denied by *Macedonius*. He informs us, that he was in the deserts of Egypt when he heard of that heresy, and that he wrote from thence to prevent the spread of it. He had so much influence in Egypt, that a Synod was immediately called there, which he attended, and where the Holy Spirit was for the first time decreed to be consubstantial with the Father and the Son. . . . .

Not long after this, the divinity of the Holy Spirit was more solemnly determined at a council held in Constantinople, and from that time it was deemed equally heretical to deny the divinity of the Spirit as that of the Son.

THE FIRST APOSTLES STRICTLY UNITARIAN.

WHEN the apostles first attached themselves to Jesus, it is evident they only considered him as being such a Messiah as the rest of the Jews expected, viz. a man, and a king. When Nathaniel was introduced to him it was evidently in that light, John i. 45. "Philip findeth Nathaniel, and saith unto him, We have found him of whom Moses in the law, and the prophets, did write, Jesus of Nazareth, the son of Joseph." . . . .

At the time that Herod heard Jesus, it was conjectured by some that he was Elias, by others that he was a prophet, and by some that he was John risen from the dead; but none of them imagined that he was either the most high God himself, or the maker of the world under God. It was not so much as supposed by any person that Jesus performed his mighty works by any proper power of *his own.* . . . . .

If he was known to be a God at all before his death, it could only have been revealed to his disciples, perhaps the apostles, or only his chief confidents among them, Peter, James, and John, suppose on the mount of transfiguration, though nothing is said concerning it in the history of that transaction. Certainly what they saw in the garden of Gethsemane could not have led them to suspect any such thing. But if it had ever been known to Peter, can we suppose he could have denied him as he did ? . . . . .

If the doctrine of the deity of Christ had been actually preached by the apostles, and the Jewish converts in general, had adopted it, it could not but have been well known to the unbelieving Jews; and would they, who were at that time, and have been ever since, so exceedingly zealous with respect to the doctrine of the divine unity, not have taken the alarm, and have urged this objection to Christianity, as teaching the belief in more Gods than one, in the apostolic age ? . . . .

As soon as ever the Jews had any pretence for it, we find them sufficiently quick and vehement in urging this their great objection to Christianity. To answer the charge of holding *two* or *three Gods,* is a very considerable article in the writings of several of the ancient Christian fathers. Why then do we find nothing of this kind in the age of the apostles ? The only answer is, that there was no occasion for it, the doctrine of the divinity of Christ not having been started. Athanasius strongly expresses this objection, as made by both Jews and Gentiles, to the incarnation of the Son of God, though as a thing that was gloried in by Christians. "The Jews," says he, "reproach us for it ; the Gentiles laugh at it ; but we adore it. . .

Paul tells the elders of| the church of Ephesus (Acts xx. 27) that "he had not failed to declare unto them the whole counsel of God." We may be confident, therefore, that, if he had any such doctrine (the deity of Christ) to divulge, he must have taught it in the three years that he spent in that city. But if we attend Paul thither, where we

have a very particular account of all the proceedings against him, we shall find no trace of anything of the kind. All their complaints against him fell far short of this. . . . . .

Considering the known prejudices, and the inveteracy of the Jews, no reasonable man need desire any clearer proof than this, that neither Paul, nor any of the apostles, had ever taught the doctrine of the divinity of Christ. . . . . .

If we consider the charge that was advanced against Peter and John at the first promulgation of the gospel, we shall find it amounts to nothing but their being disturbers of the people, by preaching in the name of Jesus. What was the accusation against Stephen, but his speaking blasphemous words against the temple and the law ? . . .

The apostles, to the latest period of their writings, speak the' same language ; representing the Father as the only true God, and Christ as a man, the servant of God, who raised him from the dead, and gave him all the power of which he is possessed, as a reward of his obedience. Peter says, Acts ii. 22, 24, "Ye men of Israel, hear these words : Jesus of Nazareth, a man approved of God among you, by miracles, and wonders, and signs, which God did by him, &c., whom God hath raised up." Paul also says, 1 Tim. ii. 5, "There is one God, and one Mediator between God and men, the man Christ Jesus." Heb. ii. 9, 10: "We see Jesus, who was made a little lower than the angels," *i.e.,* who was a man, "for the suffering of death, crowned with glory and honour," &c. . . . . .

Speaking of those who believed Christ to be a mere man, *Facundus* says, "The apostles themselves were once imperfect in the faith, but never heretics. For while they believed too little concerning Christ, they received power to cast out unclean spirits, and to cure diseases, when our Lord sent them, and gave them a commission. If, therefore, the apostles, in the very time of their ignorance, were not heretics, how can any one call these so who died such ?" . . .

The Apostles' Creed affords a strong argument for the antiquity and purity of the ancient Unitarian doctrine. This argument was urged by Photinus (A.D. 346, a Unitarian), who, according to *Ruffinus,* pleaded that the "Apostles' Creed, literally understood, was in his favour." *Marcellus* (A.D. 330, a Unitarian) in his epistle, quotes the whole of the Apostles' Creed, and assents to it. . . . . .

THE PRIMITIVE CHURCH UNITA-
RIAN.

IT is owned by *Eusebius* and others, that the ancient Unitarians themselves constantly asserted that their doctrine was the prevailing opinion of the Christian church till the time of Victor. The Trinitarians denied this. . . . . .

That there were as proper Unitarians in the very age of the apostles as any who are so termed at this day (myself by no means excepted), and differing as much from what is now called the orthodox faith, I will venture to say was never questioned ; and that these ancient Unitarians were not then expelled from Christian societies as heretics, is, I believe, as generally allowed. . . . . .

Facundus says that "Martha and Mary would never have said to Christ *if thou hadst been there*, had they thought him to be God omnipresent." He adds, "neither would Philip have said to him *Show us the Father*, if he had entertained any such idea of him." . . . . .

As one argument that the primitive church of Jerusalem was properly Unitarian, maintaining the simple humanity of Christ, I observe, that "Athanasius himself was so far from denying it, that he endeavoured to account for it by saying that all the Jews were so firmly persuaded that their Messiah was to be nothing more than a man like themselves, that the apostles were obliged to use great caution in divulging the doctrine of the proper divinity of Christ." . . . . .

Theodoret, commenting on 1 Cor. viii. 6, "To us there is but one God the Father,— and one Lord Jesus Christ," says, "Here Paul calls the one, *God*, and the other, *Lord*, lest he should give those just freed from heathenism, and had learned the truth, a pretence for returning to their heathenism and idolatry. In his exposition of 1 Cor. xv. 28, in which the apostle says, that the Son was subject to the Father, says, "The divine apostle, fearing the evil that might arise from the Grecian mythology, added these things, speaking in low terms for their advantage." And the plain inference from this is, that the orthodox fathers must necessarily have supposed, that the Christian church in general was at first Unitarian, and that it continued to be so a considerable time. . . . . .

"Hegesippus" (a Jewish Christian), Eusebius says, "wrote the history of the preaching of the apostles in five books. Conversing with many bishops in his journey to Rome, he found the same doctrine with them all." . . . . .

That Hegesippus (A.D. 170), though a Unitarian himself, should speak as he does of the state of opinions in the several churches which he visited, as then retaining *the true faith*, is, I think, very natural. The only heresy that disturbed the apostle *John*, and therefore other Jewish Christians in general, was that of the *Gnostics*. . .

THE GOSPEL OF JOHN AND THE
GNOSTICS.

[The Gnostics were a sect of Christians who, among other things, believed that Jesus Christ was a man, only in appearance, and it was against this sect John's writings were directed, not the Unitarians.]

IRENÆUS, speaking of the Corinthians and Nicolaitans, says, that "John meant to refute them, and show that there is only one omnipotent God, who made all things by his word, visible and invisible, in the introduction to his gospel." "No heretics," he says, "hold that the word was made flesh." Again, he says, "John alludes to the Gnostics both in his gospel and in his epistle, and describes them by the name of Antichrist, and those who were not in communion with Christians. . . . . .

Tertullian, indeed, maintained that, by those who denied that *Christ was come in the flesh*, John meant the Gnostics, and that by those who denied that *Jesus was the son of God*, he meant the Ebionites [Unitarians who did not believe in the miraculous conception]. He had no idea that the former expression only could include both. But as the Gnostics maintained that *Jesus* and *the Christ* were different persons, the latter having come from heaven, and being the son of God, whereas Jesus was the son of man only, the expression of *Jesus being the son of God* is as directly opposed to the doctrine of the Gnostics as that of *Christ coming in the flesh*. . . . . .

It is remarkable, however, and really curious, that before the Unitarians were considered as heretics, we find a very different account of the reasons that induced John to write both his epistles and his gospel; Ignatius says it was solely with a view to the Gnostics, and so does Irenæus, again and again. This, therefore, was the more ancient opinion on the subject ; and, I doubt not, the true one. And it was not till long after this (Tertullian, I believe, is the first in whom it occurs) that it was imagined that the apostle had any view to the Unitarians in any of his writings. This is a circumstance that well deserves to be attended to. . . . . .

Is it not extraordinary that, if this apostle conceived the indignation that you suppose him to have entertained against the Unitarians, he should give no intimation of it except in this one ambiguous expression? You own that he marks the Gnostics clearly enough, and expresses the strongest aversion to them. How came he then to spare the Unitarians, who have been so odious since? You must own that, in the course of his gospel, he inserts many expressions which, when literally interpreted, militate strongly against the doctrine of the divinity of Christ; as when, according to him, our Saviour says, "The Father is greater than I; I can do nothing of myself; I live by the Father; the Father within me he doth the works. The Father is the only true God," &c. If the apostle knew that there were in his time those who believed that Christ was a mere man, while he himself believed him to be God, is it not extraordinary that he should give them such an advantage from the language of our Saviour in his own gospel; and that he should have taken no care to qualify or explain it? Persons who are aware of a dangerous opinion, and wish to guard others against it, do not write as he does. . . . . .

JEWISH CHRISTIANS; EBIONITES AND NAZARENES.

THE Nazarenes, as well as the Ebionites, the genuine descendants of the old Jewish Christians, and who cannot be proved to have departed from the faith of their ancestors, were all believers in the simple humanity of Christ; and certainly the presumption is, that they learned this doctrine from the apostles. For who else were their teachers? . . . . .

It is plain there was a very great agreement between these two ancient sects; and though they went under different names, yet they seem only to have differed in this, that the Ebionites had made some addition to the old Nazarene system. For Origen expressly tells us, "They were called Ebionites, who from among the Jews own Jesus to be the Christ." . . . . .

That the Ebionites comprised all the Jewish Christians in the time of Origen, is evident from the passage, "When you consider what belief they, of the Jewish race, who believe in Jesus, entertain of their redeemer, some thinking that he took his being from Mary and Joseph, some indeed from Mary only and the divine Spirit, but still without any belief of his divinity you will understand." . . . . .

The peculiar opinions of the *Ebionites* and the *Nazarenes* are represented by the most respectable authorities as the very same; only some have thought that the Nazarenes believed the miraculous conception, and the Ebionites not. But this has no authority whatever among the ancients. . . . . .

Theodoret, who, living in *Syria*, had a great opportunity of being acquainted with the *Nazarenes*, describes them as follows: —"The Nazarenes are Jews who honour Christ as a righteous man. . . . . .

Justin particularly mentions his having no objection to hold communion with those Jewish Christians who observed the law of Moses, provided they did not impose it upon others. Now, who could those be but Jewish Unitarians? for, agreeable to the evidence of all antiquity, all the Jewish Christians were such. . . . . .

Tertullian is the first Christian writer who expressly calls the Ebionites *heretics*. Irenæus, in his large treatise concerning heresy, expresses great dislike of their doctrine, always representing them as believing that Jesus was the son of Joseph; but he never confounds them with the heretics.

UNITARIANS NOT AT FIRST RE-GARDED AS HERETICS.

HAVING proved that the great body of Christians in early times were Unitarians, it follows that they could not have been considered as *heretics*, or persons out of communion with the Catholic church. . . . .

Justin Martyr treats the ancient Unitarians in a way as evidently showing that in his time his own doctrine stood in need of an *apology*. There are two passages in this writer in which he speaks of *heretics* with great indignation, as "not Christians, but as persons whose tenets were absurd, impious, and blasphemous, with whom Christians held no communion;" but in both the passages he evidently had a view to the *Gnostics only*. . . . . .

Hegesippus, the first Christian historian, enumerating the heresies of his time, mentions several of the Gnostic kind, but not that of Christ being a mere man. He, moreover, says, that in travelling to Rome, where he arrived in the time of *Anicetus*, he found all the churches that he visited held the faith which had been taught by Christ and the apostles, which, in his opinion, was probably that of Christ being, not God, but man only. . . . . .

Ignatius also frequently mentions *heresy* and *heretics*, and, like John and Polycarp, with great indignation; but it is evident to every person who is at all acquainted with the history, learning, and language of those times, and of the subsequent ones, that he had no persons in his eye but the Gnostics only. . . . . .

No man took more pains to inculcate the doctrine of the *logos* than Origen, and he thought meanly of those Christians who did not adopt it, considering them as of an inferior rank; but I believe he never classes them with *heretics*. . . . . .

Clemens Alexandrinus makes frequent mention of heretics, and expresses as much abhorrence of them as Justin Martyr does; but it is evident that, in all the places in which he speaks of them, his idea of heresy was confined to Gnosticism. He considers it as an answer to *all heretics* to prove that "there is one God, the almighty Lord, who was preached by the law and the prophets, and also in the blessed gospel." He also speaks of heresy as "borrowed from a barbarous philosophy;" and says of heretics, that "though they say there is one God, and sing hymns to Christ, it was not according to truth; for that they introduced another God, and such a Christ as the prophets had not foretold." He never includes the Gentile Unitarians among heretics. . . .

But there is an evident reason why the Ebionites were pretty soon considered as heretics, and a reason which did not affect the Unitarians among the Gentiles. For the Jewish Christians, on account of their using a different language, held *separate assemblies* from those who used the Greek tongue; and besides, Jerome expressly says they were deemed heretics ONLY *on the account of their attachment to the institutions of Moses.* . .

THE UNITARIANS WERE THE GREAT BODY OF THE CHRISTIAN CHURCH UP TO THE FOURTH CENTURY.

WHEN this investigation shall be completely finished, it will, probably, be matter of surprise to many, that it was not sooner discovered that the Unitarians *must have been*, and certainly *were*, the great body of common Christians till after the Council of Nice. . . . . .

The common or unlearned people in any country, who do not speculate much, retain longest any opinions with which their minds have been much impressed; and therefore we always look for the oldest opinions in any country, or any class of men, among the common people, and not among the learned. . . . . .

There can be no doubt, therefore, but that the doctrine of the Trinity was a long time very unpopular with the common people among Christians; and this is a fact that cannot be satisfactorily accounted for, but on the supposition that the doctrine of the simple humanity of Christ was that which had been handed down to them by tradition from the apostles. . . . . .

Justin Martyr, A.D. 140, is generally supposed to have been the first platonising Christian, and it would appear his doctrine was not popular from the phrase, "neither do I agree with the majority of Christians, who may have objected to my opinion," which is nearly the most literal rendering of the passage, (though I would not be understood to lay much stress on that circumstance,) will naturally be construed to mean that the majority actually *did* make the objection, or that Justin suspected they *might* make it. . . . . .

Nothing can well be more evident than that Tertullian represents the great body of unlearned Christians in his time as Unitarians, and even holding the doctrine of the Trinity in great abhorrence. "The simple, the ignorant, and unlearned, who are always the greater part of the body of Christians, since the rule of faith," meaning, probably, the Apostles' Creed, "transfers the worship of many gods to the one true God, not understanding that the unity of God is to be maintained but with the œconomy, dread this œconomy; imagining that this number and disposition of a Trinity is a division of the Unity. They, therefore, will have it that we are worshippers of two, and even of three Gods, but that they are the worshippers of one God only. We, they say, hold the monarchy. Even the Latins have learned to bawl out for the monarchy, and the Greeks themselves will not understand the œconomy." It is hardly possible in any words to describe the state of things

more clearly than *Tertullian* here does. It
is the language of strong feeling and complaint, the clearest of all proofs that he did
not misstate things on that side, as it would
have been for the purpose of his argument
to have represented the Unitarians as being
inconsiderable on account of their numbers,
as well as despicable on account of their
want of learning. . . . . .

It is evident to me that in the time of
Origen, viz. the beginning of the third
century, the doctrine of the divinity of
Christ was so far from being generally received, except by the bishops and the more
learned of the clergy, that it was considered
as a sublime doctrine, proper indeed for
persons who had made advances in divine
knowledge, but not adapted to the vulgar,
who were content with the plain doctrine of
Jesus Christ, he says, "the multitudes (*i.e.*
the great mass or body) of believers are instructed in the shadow of the logos, and not
in the true logos of God, which is in the
open heaven. Wherefore the gospel must
be taught both corporeally and spiritually ;
and, when it is necessary, we must preach
the corporeal gospel, saying to the carnal
that we know nothing but Jesus Christ and
him crucified. But when persons are found
confirmed in the spirit, bringing forth fruits
in it, and in love with heavenly wisdom, we
must impart to them the *logos* returning
from his bodily state, in that he was in the
beginning with God."—*Origen.* . . . . .

Origen well describes the different classes
of Unitarians of his time in the following
passage : " Hence may be solved the doubts
which disturb many who allege a principle
of piety, and a fear of making two Gods,
and by this means fall into false and impious opinions ; either denying that the
identity of the Son differs from that of the
Father, saying, that the Son is God only in
name ; or denying the divinity of the Son,
while they allow his identity, and that he
is a different person from the Father," &c.
The first that he describes were the philosophical Unitarians, who allowed the divinity
of the Son, but said it was the same with
that of the Father ; whereas the latter
(probably the common people) denied the
divinity of the Son altogether. It is evident from this passage, that the Unitarians,
in the time of *Origen*, were numerous ; for
he calls them *many*, which he would not
have done unnecessarily. The argument by
which he solves their doubts has been mentioned before, viz. that the Father is God

with the article prefixed, and the Son *without*
it. . . . .

Athanasius also acknowledged that the
Unitarian doctrine was very prevalent among
the lower class of people in his time. He
calls them *οἱ πολλοι, the many,* and describes
them as persons of low understanding. "It
grieves," he says, "those who stand up for
the holy faith that *the multitude,* and especially persons of low understanding, should
be infected with those blasphemies. Things
that are sublime and difficult are not to be
apprehended, except by faith ; and ignorant
people must fall, if they cannot be persuaded to rest in faith, and avoid curious
questions." . . . . .

Gregory Nazienzen, who was contemporary with *Basil,* complains of the small
number of the orthodox, saying, "They
were the smallest of the tribes of Israel."
He represents the common people as excusable for their errors, and safe, from not
being disposed to scrutinize into things. . .

I think we may learn from *Facundus,* who
wrote so late as the reign of Justinian, that
in his time many of the common people were
well known to consider Christ as a *mere man,*
and yet were not disturbed on that account.
As the passage in his writings from which I
infer this is a pretty remarkable one, I shall
cite it at full length. Speaking of the condemnation of Theodorus, in whose favour he
is writing, he says, that "in condemning
him they condemned all those who thought
as he did, even though they afterwards
changed their opinion....What will they do
with Martha, and then with Mary, the sisters of Lazarus, who were particularly attached to our Lord while he was upon earth?
And yet both of them, first Martha and
then Mary, are said to speak to him thus :
"Lord, if thou hadst been here, my brother
had not died ;" who, though they thought
that he was the Son of God who was to
come into the world, yet would they not
have said *if thou hadst been here,* if they
had believed him to be God omnipresent.
They therefore only thought as Theodorus is
said to have done, and were excommunicated along with him ; and how many of
this kind do we know, by the writings of
the apostles and evangelists, there were at
that time, and how many even now are
there still in the common herd of the faithful, who, by only partaking in the holy
mysteries, and by a simple observance of
the commandments, we see pleasing God ;
when even the apostles themselves, the first

teachers, only thought as those whom we see to be included in this condemnation of Theodorus." . . . . .

Unitarians, however, were far from being all of the common people, and unlearned. There were several considerable writers among them. "*Beryllus* of Bostra," *Nicephorus* says, "left elegant writings behind him." *Marcellus* and *Photinus* distinguished themselves as writers, and *Gregory Nazianzen* says that the heretics boasted of the number of their books. Unhappily there are none of them now extant.

OPPOSITION TO THE DOCTRINE OF THE DEITY OF CHRIST AND THE TRINITY IN THE EARLY CHURCH.

Tertullian testified that the greater part of the body of Christians complained that their teachers were worshippers of two, and even of three Gods. . . . . .

Tertullian appears, however, not a little embarrassed with the question, how the Father can be called the one God, if the Son, though connected with him, can, in any proper sense, even where the Father is not mentioned, be called *God;* but he seems to satisfy himself with saying, that as the proper style of the Father before he had a Son was that of the one God, he could not lose it in consequence of having a Son, especially as that Son derives his divinity from his inseparable connection with the Father. "Without injuring the rights of the Son, the Father," he says, "may be called the only God." . . . . .

With a view to the *Unitarians*, who were the majority of the common Christians in the time of Tertullian, as he particularly acknowledges, he is obliged to use a good deal of management, and though he contends for the propriety of calling the Son God, as a branch from God the Father, yet so great was the superiority of the Father to the Son, that he says he does not choose to call the Son God, when the Father had been mentioned immediately before. . . . . .

Origen says, "It is probable that some will be *offended* with our saying, that the Father being called the only true God, there are other gods besides him partaking of his divinity." *Novatian* speaks of the Unitarians as "*scandalized*" at the doctrine of the divinity of Christ." And the state of things was not different about the time of

the Council of Nice. *Eusebius,* in his controversy with Marcellus, says, "If they are afraid of making two Gods."—"Some, for *fear* of introducing a second God, make the Father and the Son the same."—"But you are dreadfully afraid lest you should be obliged to acknowledge two hypostases of the Father and Son." . . . .

Alluding to the *Unitarians,* with whom, it is plain, Origen wished to stand on good terms, says, "We may by this means solve the doubts which terrify many men, who pretend to great piety, and who are afraid of making two Gods." . . . . .

Photius very truly observes that, "to recite all the answers which the fathers have given to the question, why, when the Father, Son, and Spirit are each of them separately God, we should not say that there are three Gods? would make a book, instead of an epistle." . . . . .

Cyril of Jerusalem complains of heretics, both Arians and Unitarians, as in the bosom of the church. "Now," says he, "there is an apostacy; for men have departed from the right faith, some confounding the Son with the Father," meaning the Sabellians, "others daring to say that Christ was created out of nothing," meaning the Arians. "Formerly heretics were open, but now the church is full of concealed heretics." . . . . .

"We are torn in pieces," *Basil* says, "on the one side by the Anomeans, and on the other by Sabellius." "Is not the mystery of godliness everywhere laughed at; the bishops continuing without people and without clergy, having nothing but an empty name, able to do nothing for the advancement of the gospel of peace and salvation? Are there not discords concerning God, and blaspheming from the old impiety of vain Sabellius?" "You know," says he, "my dear brethren, that the doctrine of Marcellus overturns all our hopes, not acknowledging the Son in his proper personality." . . . . .

"When I was lately praying before the people," says *Basil,* "and sometimes concluding with the doxology to the Father, with the Son, and Holy Spirit, and sometimes through the Son in the Holy Spirit, some who were present said, that I used phrases which were not only new, but contradictory." He says that "he was accused of novelty, and as an inventor of new phrases, and that they spared no kind of reproach, because he made the Son equal to the Father, and did not separate the Holy Spirit from the Son." . . . . .

The authority of the church was also had recourse to, as an argument to enforce the reception of what could not be proved or explained. "Some tenets in the church," says *Basil,* "we receive as preserved in writing, but some are of apostolic tradition, handed down as *mysteries,* both of which have the same force with respect to piety, and no one will question them, who is at all acquainted with the laws of the church." . . . . .

Austin pleaded for implicit faith by the authority of the prophet *Isaiah.* "It was, therefore," he says, "rationally said by the prophet (chap. vi.), Unless ye believe, ye will not understand; where he doubtless distinguishes these two things, and advises that we first believe that we may be able to understand what we believe; so it seems reasonable that faith should precede reason." . . . . .

Nor were the Heathens less backward than the Christians to upbraid the orthodox fathers with their own *Polythcism,* while they pretended to reclaim them from theirs. The Heathens, according to Chrysostom, would say to them, "Who is this Father, who is this Son, or this Holy Spirit? Do not you make three Gods, while you accuse us of Polytheism?" . . . . .

PRINCIPLES AND ARGUMENTS OF THE ANCIENT UNITARIANS.

THE great stronghold of Unitarians was the Scriptures, and the plain literal sense of them. "They bawl out," says Basil, "with their proofs from Scripture, and make no account of the unwritten traditions of the fathers." And Photinus, in his dispute with Basil, said that "he could prove his doctrine by a hundred passages of Scripture." The orthodox in general complained of the advantage which the Unitarians had in appealing to the literal sense of the Scripture. "If," says Gregory Nyssen, "a man rests in the bare letter, so far he Judaizes in opinion, and has not learned that a Christian is not the disciple of the letter, but of the spirit; for the letter killeth, but the spirit giveth life." . . . . .

The two decisive texts in proof of the unity of God, and the proper humanity of Christ, in these epistles are the following: Eph. iv. 5, 6, "One Lord, one faith, one baptism, one God and Father of all, who is above all, and through all, and in you all;" which was urged, as Eusebius informs us, by Marcellus; and 1 Tim. ii. 5, "There is one God, and one Mediator between God and man, the man Christ Jesus," which was pleaded by the same. This was also alleged by Photinus. . . . . .

Epiphanius says that Theodorus argued from Acts ii. 22, where Peter calls Christ "a man approved of God." And indeed it was acknowledged by the orthodox, that, in all the period to which the history of Luke extends, the apostles did not openly preach such offensive doctrines as those of the pre-existence and divinity of Christ. . . . . .

We learn from Epiphanius that Theodotus urged Luke i. 35: "The spirit of the Lord shall come upon thee;" arguing that he did not enter into her, as the orthodox supposed. And John viii. 40, "Ye seek to kill me, a MAN who told you the truth." Austin says that the Sabellians urged John vii. 16, "My doctrine is not mine." Basil's enemies quoted against him John vi. 57, "I live by the Father." . . . . .

When the Unitarians were urged with the Father and the Son being said to be *one,* they said that they were one by consent and harmony, and proved it from Christ's saying that his disciples might be one with them, as they two were one. . . . . .

That the ancient Unitarians had much recourse to reasoning, and that they often disputed with great acuteness and subtilty, so as to puzzle their opponents, may be inferred from what is said of them by Eusebius, viz. that "they neglected the Scriptures, and reasoned in syllogisms." [They used both reason and Scripture.] . . . . .

UNITARIANS HAD NO SEPARATE ASSEMBLIES.

[THE ANCIENT UNITARIANS were known by the names of Ebionites, Nazarenes, Paulians, Arians, Monarchists, &c. &c.]

THE Unitarians were originally nothing less than the whole body of Christians, and that the Trinitarians were the innovators; appearing at first modest and candid, as was natural while they were a small minority, but bold and imperious when they became the majority. . . . . .

There was no creed used in the Christian church, besides that which was commonly called *the Apostle's,* before the Council of

Nice; and even after that there was no other generally used at baptism. This creed, as has been seen, contains no article that could exclude Unitarians; and there was nothing in the public services that was calculated to exclude them. . . . . .

Accordingly, we find that all the Unitarians continued in communion with the Catholic church till the time of *Theodotus,* about the year 200, when it is possible that, upon his excommunication, some of his more zealous followers might form themselves into separate societies. . . . . .

We have no certain account of any separate societies of Unitarians till the excommunication of *Paulus Samosatensis,* about the year 250, when, after him, they were called Paulians, or Paulianists. Others also, about the same time, or rather after that time, formed separate societies in Africa, on the excommunication of *Sabellius,* being, after him, called Sabellians. . . . . .

"Sabellianism," which was precisely the same thing with Unitarianism in former times, Dr. Lardner says (Credibility, vol. iv. p. 606), "must have been very agreeable to the apprehensions of many people. Eusebius speaks of its increasing very much in Egypt, when Dionysius of Alexandria opposed it. According to Athanasius, the occasion of Dionysius writing upon that head was, that *some of the bishops of Africa followed the doctrine of Sabellius, and they prevailed to such a degree, that the Son of God was scarce any longer preached in the churches.* It is also remarkable that the first treatise that was ever written against the Unitarian doctrine was that of Tertullian against Praxeas, with whom he was particularly provoked, on account of the active part he had taken against Montanus, in getting him excommunicated and expelled from the church of Rome. This, says Le Sueur, was the cause of the bitterness with which Tertullian wrote against him. Now there were treatises against the Gnostics in a much earlier period. Why, then, were none written against the Unitarians, since pure Unitarianism was certainly as old as Gnosticism; and if it had been deemed a *heresy* at all, it would certainly have been thought to be of the most alarming nature, as it is considered at present? . . . . .

REDEMPTION OF MANKIND.

WHATEVER may be meant by the *redemption of the world,* is not the Being who made it equal to that also? If his creatures offend him, and by repentance and reformation become the proper objects of his forgiveness, is it not more natural to suppose that he has *within himself* a power of forgiving them, and of restoring them to his favour, without the strange expedient of another person, fully equal to himself, condescending to animate a human body, and dying for us? We never think of any similar expedient in order to forgive, with the greatest propriety and effect, offences committed by our children against ourselves. . . . . .

Whatever you suppose to be the use of a *third person,* in the Trinity, is not the influence of the first person sufficient for that also? The descent of the Holy Spirit upon the apostles was to enable them to work miracles. But when our Saviour was on earth, the Father within him, and acting by him, did the same thing. You also cannot deny that, exclusive of some particular texts, the general tenor of Scripture does not suppose such a Trinity as you contend for. Is it not the general tenor of the Old and New Testaments, that the supreme God himself, and not any other person acting under him, was the proper maker of the world; and that he himself, and not any other being, supports and governs it? Is not the same great Being, the God and Father of us all, and even the *God and Father of our Lord Jesus Christ,* represented as forgiving the sins of his penitent offspring *freely,* and exhorting us to forgive as we ourselves hope to be forgiven? And are we to require any ransom, recompense, or atonement of a penitent brother? . . . . .

If there be any religious truth of practical importance, next to that of a future state of rewards and punishments, it is that which leads us to consider all adorable and amiable attributes as centring in one undivided being, whom we can look up to as our maker, preserver, and benefactor, the author of all good; who has within himself mercy for the penitent, not requiring to be made placable by the sufferings of another, but by the repentance of the sinner only, and whose constant presence with us is sufficient for all the purposes of providential care respecting the mind or body; so that we have not to look to one divine person for one thing, and to another for something else. . . . . .

This, you know, has been not only the tendency, but also the actual consequence of the belief of the doctrine of the Trinity, at least with the vulgar. With them mercy is the exclusive attribute of the Son, and a constant invigorating influence the sole province of the Spirit; and nothing but power, and that not of a benevolent and engaging nature, but something unknown and terrific only, is left to the Father. . . . . . .

THE CAUSE OF SCHISM.

We Unitarians should never exclude you from joining in our devotions, because we should not use any language that you could not adopt; but your Trinitarian forms absolutely exclude us. If there be any sin in *schism*, it lies wholly at your door; because it is you who force us to separate ourselves, when, without any violation of your consciences, you might admit us to join with you. . . . . .

What, then, is there unreasonable in our demands, when you might grant them in their utmost extent without the least injury to yourselves? Thus the *unity of the church*, and the *extinction of all sects*, which is your own favourite object, depend entirely upon yourselves. . . . . .

How glorious would it be to the heads of any Christian establishment to require nothing of the members of it besides the profession of our *common Christianity*, and to leave all particular opinions to every man's own conscience! Every cause of unpleasing contention would then be removed, and one of the most popular objections to Christianity would be removed with it, viz. the want of harmony among Christians. We should then meet as brethren, and the disciples of one common master; and with respect to all our differences, having no object but *truth*, they would be discussed without animosity. No opinion having then anything in its favour besides its own proper evidence, all prejudice would much sooner give way; and truth, which we all profess to aim at, would be much sooner attained, and become universal. . . . . .

But the honour of producing so great and glorious a revolution is, I believe, too great for any powers, civil or ecclesiastical, that will be able to effect it. It is a scheme worthy of God only, and which in due time will be brought about by his good providence, contrary to the wishes of all the ruling powers of the world, or of those who direct their councils. In the meantime we Unitarians shall not fail to do everything in our power to exhibit these enlarged views of things; confident that in this we are the instruments in the hands of providence; that our principles, being frequently exposed to view, will in time recommend themselves to all who are truly liberal and unprejudiced; and that all bigotry, like the darkness which it resembles, will at length give way before the light of truth. . . . . .

With this glorious prospect before us, we willingly bear all the obloquy and every temporal inconvenience to which the open profession of our faith can expose us, and are infinitely happier in being opposed and frowned upon by the powers of the world, than you are in opposing us, with every advantage that the world can give you. . . . .

Woodfall and Kinder, Printers, Milford Lane, Strand, London, W.C.